NIXON'S SECRETS

NIXON'S SECRETS

ROGER STONE
With Mike Colapietro

SKYHORSE PUBLISHING

Skyhorse Publishing books may be purchased in bulk at special discounts for sales promotion, corporate gifts, fund-raising, or educational purposes. Special editions can also be created to specifications. For details, contact the Special Sales Department, Skyhorse Publishing, 307 West 36th Street, 11th Floor, New York, NY 10018 or info@skyhorsepublishing.com.

Skyhorse® and Skyhorse Publishing® are registered trademarks of Skyhorse Publishing, Inc.®, a Delaware corporation.

Visit our website at www.skyhorsepublishing.com.

10 9 8 7 6 5 4 3 2 1

Library of Congress Cataloging-in-Publication Data is available on file.

Print ISBN: 978-1-62914-603-4

Printed in the United States of America

To my beloved wife,
Nydia, who supports me when I am right and when
I am wrong, and my beloved dogs, Milhous, Taft,
Dewey, Pee Wee, Buster, and Oscar. All noble dogs.

CONTENTS

ACKNOWLEDGMENTS		1
INTRODUCTION	Nixon's the One!	5
CHAPTER ONE	The Man	15
CHAPTER TWO	"Your Good Dog"	33
CHAPTER THREE	Murray and the Mob	51
CHAPTER FOUR	The Great Train Robbery	77
CHAPTER FIVE	Ike and Dick	101
CHAPTER SIX	Stolen	115
CHAPTER SEVEN	"California Needs a Decisive Leader"	175
CHAPTER EIGHT	The Wilderness Years	201
CHAPTER NINE	The Bright Young Men	233
CHAPTER TEN	The Big Enchilada and Rise of the Merchandisers	259
CHAPTER ELEVEN	The Comeback	291
CHAPTER TWELVE	Plastic and Steel	349
CHAPTER THIRTEEN	A New Beginning	375
CHAPTER FOURTEEN	The Break-ins	407
CHAPTER FIFTEEN	Gemstone	455
CHAPTER SIXTEEN	Nixon and the Bushes	493
CHAPTER SEVENTEEN	Woodstein	515
CHAPTER EIGHTEEN	"Pardon Me"	529
CHAPTER NINETEEN	Fighting For His Legacy	567
APPENDICES		595
BIBLIOGRAPHY		663

ACKNOWLEDGMENTS

Anyone writing a book about Richard Nixon is blessed with an abundance of sources. The most durable figure in American politics in the twentieth century, Nixon has been the subject of fascination and public debate for six and a half decades. The literature runs the gamut from devastating psychological profiles such as Fawn M. Brodie's *Richard Nixon: The Shaping of His Character* and Arthur Woodstone's *Nixon's Head*, which can find no redeemable qualities in Nixon, and Lord Conrad Black's *Richard M. Nixon: A Life in Full*, which can find no fault in the man.

In order to grasp the full scope of Nixon and to carefully balance both his attributes and his faults, one must delve deeply into the literature on our thirty-seventh president. William Safire's *Before the Fall* is required reading for anyone who wants to understand Nixon, as is Raymond K. Price's *With Nixon*. The three-volume biography of Nixon by historian Stephen Ambrose presents a fine and balanced portrait of Nixon and his times. The fact that Ambrose wrote an excellent multivolume biography of Dwight Eisenhower gave Ambrose additional insight into the complicated relationship between Ike and Dick. *The New York Times* reporter Tom Wicker's *One of Us* has the same balance and perspective.

I am particularly indebted to Nixon law partner Leonard Garment for his iconoclastic view of Nixon as reflected in *Crazy Rhythm* and *In Search of Deep Throat: The Greatest Political Mystery of Our Time*.

Jules Witcover is perhaps the best reporter on the 1968 campaign with his much overlooked *The Year the Dream Died*, his *The Resurrection of Richard Nixon*, and his more recent *Very Strange Bedfellows:The Short and Unhappy Marriage of Richard Nixon and Spiro Agnew*. Witcover's shrewd insights and eye for color make him one of the best political reporters of our time.

Generally speaking, the books by Theodore White on US presidential elections are close to worthless. White, an affable man, was mesmerized by the stylish and dashing John Kennedy. White in his seminal *The Making of the President, 1960* would weave a narrative in which Kennedy is a star and Nixon is a black-hatted villain. White bought into JFK's expensively promoted image of style, grace, and intellectualism. Kennedy's young and carefully dressed wife and his beautiful young children were part of the mystique. White wondered why the Nixon entourage would treat him coolly when he joined the Nixon campaign tour wearing a Kennedy button. Fortunately three authors have written retrospectives on the 1960 campaign, which put the photo-finish election in better perspective. First among these is David Pietrusza's *1960—LBJ vs. JFK vs. Nixon: The Epic Campaign That Forged Three Presidencies*. Also invaluable for a more balanced assessment of that race is Professor Edmund F. Kallina Jr.'s *Kennedy v. Nixon: The Presidential Election of 1960,* although the good professor underestimates the important role of organized crime in stealing votes for Kennedy. *The Kennedy Brothers* by former Arizona Secretary of State Richard D. Mahoney is the definitive account of the efforts of the Chicago mob to intimidate voters in that city as well as the mob's earlier role in the West Virginia primary. Also required reading for a better understanding of the 1960 election is W. J. Rorabaugh's *The Real Making of the President.*

Because of the circumstances of his death and the effects on him by his brother's assassination, public awareness of Robert F. Kennedy is more vague today. Because of Robert Kennedy's tactics in the 1960 election, he is an extraordinary factor in the Nixon narrative. I relied upon the aforementioned *The Kennedy Brothers* by Richard D. Mahoney as well as Jeffrey K. Smith's *Bad Blood: Lyndon B. Johnson, Robert F. Kennedy, and the Tumultuous 1960s* and Jeff Shesol's *Mutual Contempt: Lyndon Johnson, Robert Kennedy and the Feud that Defined a Decade.* Robert Kennedy was among the most ruthless political operators of the 1960s, a fact you won't find in Arthur Schlesinger's *Robert Kennedy and His Times.*

Pulitzer Prize–winning reporter J. Anthony Lukas, in his stunning book *Nightmare: The Underside of the Nixon Years*, bores in on several areas of Watergate and the Nixon administration where knowledge is scant, includingthe role of Robert Bennett and his CIA front the Mullen Company in the break-in, the 1969–71 wire tapping on Nixon's aides, the Howard Hughes–Nixon relationship, the Saturday night massacre, and the connection between the Watergate break-in and a high-end house of prostitution operating out of the Columbia Plaza Apartments only blocks from the Watergate.

Although most Nixon loyalists heap abuse on investigative journalist Anthony Summers book *The Arrogance of Power: The Secret World of Richard Nixon*, I found it both fascinating and readable. Don Fulsom's *Nixon's Dark Secrets* has an agenda but is also valuable. The reporting of Dan E. Moldea is invaluable, particularly regarding Nixon's long and complicated relationship with Teamster leader James "Jimmy" Hoffa.

I am, however, particularly indebted to four ground-breaking journalists who have had the courage and tenacity to examine the accepted Watergate narrative and poke substantial holes in it. *Secret Agenda* by Jim Hougan is the important first cut at permeating the many falsehoods the public accepts about Watergate.

In their book *Silent Coup*, Leonard Colodny and Robert Gettlin advanced the narrative first uncovered by Hougan. Working with Tom Shachtman, Colodny's *Forty Years War* outlined in graphic detail the foreign policy hard-liners attempts to undo Nixon's policy of détente. Fox News White House Correspondent James Rosen's biography of Nixon Attorney General John N. Mitchell, *The Strong Man*, fifteen years in the writing, is a vital corrective for many of the myths of Watergate. A must-read is also veteran journalist Phil Stanford's *White House Call Girl*, which breaks important new ground in the Watergate narrative.

The public can more accurately understand what really transpired in Watergate through the writing and scholarship of former

White House lawyer Geoff Shepard, who has exhaustively examined the words and actions of former White House Counsel John Dean and has written a devastating critique of Dean's most recent book, *The Nixon Defense*. This analysis is included in this volume as Appendix 5.

Beyond these authors as well as many others, I am indebted to Craig Shirley, Michael Caputo, former *Reader's Digest* Washington Editor Bill Schulz, Jeffrey S. Bell, Douglas Caddy, Ed Cox, Scott and Sonia Kaiser, John Taylor, Andrew Cettina, Travis Irvine, Sharon Kaplan, Dianne Thorne, Robert Morrow, William Maloney, and Roger Ailes. I am indebted to our publisher Tony Lyons of Skyhorse Publishing, a man of uncommon courage, my editors Steve Price and Krishan Trotman, and of course, my coauthor Mike Colapietro, who labored without complaint to make our deadlines.

Roger Stone

Miami Beach, Florida

NIXON'S THE ONE!

> "A man is not finished when he is defeated. He is finished when he quits."
>
> —Richard Nixon[1]

I stood in the rain at Nixon's funeral. I was given a color-coded badge that assigned me to sit with the immediate family and friends. Forty-two thousand people filed past his casket.[2] The line had at one point been as long as three miles.[3] As the shiny black hearse sped away, preceded by California Highway Patrol motorcycles, thousands more people thronged the streets in the rain to catch a glimpse of the casket containing one of the most powerful politicians of the twentieth century. I reflected on the Nixon I knew—or rather, the Nixon he wanted me to know, the Nixon he chose to show me: "The Man in the Arena," as he would call it.

Nixon himself defined his career as the ultimate political warrior with a quote from a speech that Theodore Roosevelt gave on April 23, 1910, at the Sorbonne in Paris:

> "It is not the critic who counts; not the man who points out how the strong man stumbles, or where the doer of deeds could have done them better. The credit belongs to the man who is actually in the arena, whose face is marred by dust and sweat and blood; who strives valiantly; who errs, and comes short again and again;

because there is not effort without error and shortcoming; but who does actually strive to do the deeds; who knows the great enthusiasms, the great devotions; who spends himself in a worthy cause, who at the best knows in the end the triumphs of high achievement and who at the worst, if he fails, at least fails while daring greatly, so that his place shall never be with those cold and timid souls who know neither victory or defeat."[4]

Like the great politicians of his day, John and Robert Kennedy, and Lyndon Johnson, Richard Nixon had both a dark side and a light side. He achieved great things and sometimes used hardball tactics. He was a man of ideas married to an innate political pragmatism, coupled with the instincts of a survivor. He could be magnanimous as well as venal. This book seeks to illuminate both the light and dark sides of our thirty-seventh president.

As a veteran of eight national presidential campaigns, who cut his teeth with Nixon before going to work for perhaps the greatest president in my lifetime, Ronald Reagan, I have been the recipient of an enormous amount of political intelligence. I know how the game is played. This book will tell you what I think happened in Richard Nixon's ultimate downfall and the method in which he got a pardon for crimes he may have committed in the scandal known as Watergate. I will make a compelling case that it was not White House Counsel John Dean who brought Nixon to ruin. Dean acts in his self-interest, and he is but the weasel of our narrative. Although Dean would significantly weaken Nixon, it was General Alexander M. Haig who greased the skids for Nixon through a series of purposeful blunders in Nixon's handling of the legal, public, and political problem triggered by the Watergate break-in.

Before we can understand the rise and fall of Richard Nixon, we must first examine this complex and sometimes confusing man.

Few have had the opportunity to work for and befriend their boyhood hero as I have. I was drawn to Richard Nixon not because of his philosophy; he had none. It was his resilience and his indestructibility that attracted me. "Flexibility is the first principle of politics," he would say.[5] Nixon's Lazarus-like rise from the political dead is a story of determination, perseverance, political cunning, timing, skill, and above all, discipline. This combined with a commitment to the drudgery and hard work of retail politics. Nixon's physical and intellectual energy is often underestimated.

I am uniquely qualified to tell this tale. I am an admitted Nixon friend. He fascinates me still. He was the most durable public figure in the twentieth century. The idea of anyone having almost a fifty-year run in American politics is incredible. Nixon, like LBJ, JFK, and Eisenhower, was a giant. At Nixon's funeral, Bob Dole would correctly call the 1950s to the 1980s "the era of Nixon."

While I myself had many policy disagreements with Nixon, it was his sheer resilience and persistence and his will to compete and win that I admired. No matter how many electoral or political setbacks he suffered Nixon persevered in his drive for the presidency. I myself had a tattoo of Richard Nixon inked on my back. It is the image of a floating head about the size of a grapefruit equidistant between my shoulder blades. I wear it as a reminder that no matter what life's setbacks and disappointments are, one must always get up from the mat and fight again.

I was the Connecticut Chairman of Youth for Nixon during his 1968 campaign. I parlayed this august post into becoming a gofer for Nixon's law partner, and later attorney general, John Mitchell, at the Miami Beach convention. I later worked in Nixon's White House press shop as a volunteer cutting clippings for Mort Alin, an assistant to Nixon's aide Patrick J. Buchanan. At age nineteen, other than those who worked in Young Voters for the President, I was the youngest staffer at the *Committee to Reelect the President* (CRP). I reported to Herbert L. "Bart" Porter, who would later serve thirty days in jail for lying to the grand jury in the Watergate scandal. Porter, in turn, reported to CRP Campaign Director Jeb Stuart Magruder. I myself was called before the grand jury in the Watergate matter.

I had a friendly disagreement with Nixon in 1977 when he attempted to convince me to work in the presidential campaign of former Democrat and Texas Governor John Connally. Connally's camp had put forward an offer, transmitted by Connally Press Secretary Jim Brady and approved by Connally's right-hand man Julian Read. It was a lot of money. Nixon overestimated the strength and potential of Connally and greatly underestimated Reagan. Nixon thought Ron was too old. I made the case for Reagan over dinner at Nixon's manse in Saddle River, New Jersey. "After his near loss in '76, it's clear Reagan is better positioned for the race than anyone else," I told Nixon. Connally would famously spend $11 million and win one delegate.

I saw Nixon up close. He was brilliant, devious, insightful, obtuse, determined, and sometimes less than truthful. Above all, he was disciplined. It was his persistence that inspired me. He never gave up fighting, first for the presidency and then for the legacy of that presidency. This book will, however, also examine the underbelly of Nixon's politics, his tactics, subterfuges, his diversions, and financial ties to organized crime that he shared with John F. Kennedy and Lyndon Baines Johnson. We will focus on his long-term relationship with the CIA and the fateful events that brought him to Dallas on November 22, 1963, the very day Nixon's moribund political career had been renewed.

Nixon's Secrets is not a sanitized version of his political life, nor is it an attempt to rehabilitate his reputation. Don't expect a whitewash of Nixon's sins because "no man is a hero to his valet." On balance, I conclude that Nixon's greatness and his vision for a global political realignment to achieve world peace must be viewed as well as his numerous mistakes.

Rather I will show that Nixon engaged in politics the way politics were in the 1950s and 1960s. Johnson, Nixon, and Kennedy all had relations with organized crime. All three took campaign contributions that were illegal. All three engaged in break-ins to secure political intelligence. All three ordered the bugging of their opponents prior to election. Kennedy would make an unholy alliance with the Mob. Johnson would order the murder of as many as seventeen men to cover up his trail of corruption. He stole votes and participated in electoral fraud.

Nixon's Secrets may prove that he was not the man you think he was. He was an excellent poker player, ringing up enough winnings while running a "friendly game" in the navy to bankroll his initial congressional campaign. He liked a drink or two, as we shall see. As the procurement officer for his naval battalion, his greatest talent was in acquiring alcohol at a makeshift hamburger stand, where he gave both hooch and grub away. He was immensely popular with his men.

Nixon, Kennedy, and Johnson would all stray from the marital bed, although the sexual appetites of JFK and his running mate were more voracious than Nixon's. In fact, Nixon had a long-term discreet liaison with a courtesan in Hong Kong. She would move to Whittier, California, his hometown, after his election as president and visit him in the White House on at least three occasions. Nixon had sent her a bottle of Chanel No. 5 perfume and a note inviting her to visit him in the United States after their first encounter in Asia. The liaison was not Nixon's only sexual indiscretion. Jackie Kennedy would tell playwright Tennessee Williams that Nixon made a pass at her in Washington one weekend when Nixon and Kennedy were both in the House and JFK was away campaigning.

Nixon's advance man John Ehrlichman would remember an inebriated Nixon making clumsy passes at girls in his suite when Nixon invited friends to celebrate his successful 1964 introduction of the nominee Barry Goldwater to the Republican ticket.[6]

I seek to put Nixon in the context of his times. It's a warts-and-all story of a bare-knuckled brand of politics that Nixon and every other contender in 1960 played. David Pietrusza's book *1960: LBJ vs. JFK vs. Nixon* gives a great account of Nixon and his contemporaries Kennedy and Johnson at that time. Crucial to Nixon's comeback were the tumultuous events of the 1960s, which created the vacuum he would fill. As Oliver Stone so pointedly said in his movie *Nixon*, the death of John and Robert Kennedy, the murder of Dr. Martin Luther King, the raging war in Vietnam, and the unrest on US campuses and in America's urban centers, a white backlash, and the lack of "law and order" created a dynamic that made the return of Richard Nixon to power possible.

Although I worked on the campaign in 1968, I only shook Nixon's hand once that year at a "Party Unity" luncheon at the National Republican Women's Club in New York City. New York Governor Nelson Rockefeller, who had little use for Nixon, attended and embraced Nixon for the wire photographers. I would not shake Nixon's hand again until 1972 when he toured the Committee to Reelect the President headquarters in Washington where I worked.

It was not until 1977 that I got to know our thirty-seventh president on more intimate terms. When I was elected National Chairman of the Young Republican National Federation, the former president asked me to come west. He invited me to visit him in exile in San Clemente. Although scheduled for a thirty-minute meeting, we ended up talking presidential politics for four and half hours. It was the first time that I sharply and outwardly disagreed with his assertion that former Texas Governor John Connally, who had served in the Nixon cabinet as treasury secretary, would be a strong candidate for president. I made an effective case for Reagan as the 1980 nominee. Nixon was amused.

Before long I was talking to the former president by telephone every Saturday morning. His hunger for political gossip was insatiable. He would begin every conversation by saying, "So, what is the state of play?" I began doing odd political chores such as passing messages or memos to members of Congress, evaluating speaking invitations and checking out Republican prospects in various states and districts.

Charles McWhorter, who had first worked in Nixon's vice presidential office, had an encyclopedic knowledge of Republican politics and a network of relationships across the GOP. After Nixon became president, McWhorter, who favored large and garish turquoise jewelry with his business suits, would become a "lobbyist" with AT&T while on permanent loan for Nixon. "You know Charlie McWhorter?" Nixon asked me. "Charlie's retiring, and I need someone to review invitations, check out certain political situations, and convey messages to party leaders and others. John Taylor [Nixon's chief of staff] is a good man, but he's not political," Nixon said. "Would you lend us a hand?" "Of course," I said. "I'd be delighted."

Throughout the 1960s, considering himself ready to be president, Nixon had little interest in the ideas of others. He worked a room like the political pro he was, memorizing names and details of the families of those he needed support from so he could make polite inquiries and mask his acute discomfort with small talk. Voracious in his appetite for gossip, he collected information on the sexual misconduct of his political allies and enemies alike, and his private conversation was laced with ethnic slurs and profanity. Nixon was perpetually in the process of self examination.

By the 1970s Nixon was interested in meeting a new generation of journalists who had not covered Watergate. I arranged a series of private off-the-record dinners that included the *New York Times's* Howell Raines and Gerry Boyd, the *Chicago Tribune*'s Steve Neal, David Hoffman of *The Washington Post*, Susan Page of *Newsday*, Paul West of the *Dallas Times Herald*, Michael Kramer of *New York Magazine*, and Sidney Blumenthal, then of the *New Republic*, and others. Nixon would mesmerize the young reporters with his vast knowledge of international geopolitics. The dinners focused on international issues and foreign policy, and no questions from the reporters were barred. The old man would raid his wine cellar for the best vintages for his guests from the fifth estate. There was no discussion of Watergate at these intimate dinners; instead Nixon held forth on the state of Sino-Soviet and American relations and entertained questions.

Richard Nixon was proud of his martini-making skills. He called them "silver bullets." After two martinis Nixon would be drunk. He had a low tolerance for alcohol. A drunken Nixon was a loquacious Nixon.

Here is Nixon's recipe, which he told me was given to him by Winston Churchill:

> Obtain a bottle of large-sized olives.
> Drain the juice.
> Fill the olive bottle with Vermouth.
> Refrigerate the bottle until cold.
> Put three fingers of gin or vodka over ice in a silver martini shaker.
> Shake vigorously until shards of ice permeate the alcohol.
> Pour in a chilled martini glass. Drop in one olive from the jar.

Nixon was a loner with a tendency to "retreat deeper into a mystic shell." Although his low tolerance for alcohol has been noted, Nixon would drink heavily, which seemed to lighten his lost moods. A Nixon aide said that the vice president let down his cold guard of "grimness and glacial determination" when he was drinking with friends. "We order extra dry Gibson's with Nixon darkly muttering; 'it was a great mistake.' Then a second round. Then RN, having relaxed enthusiastically, briskly demanded a third. His inhibitions and fears apparently gone. Then a sound California Inglenook white pinot, oysters and baked Pompano." "Venturing out in Nixon's vice presidential limousine, the vice president would cruise to a tavern called Martins in Georgetown where he would first coif great drafts of beer followed by scotch. Nixon would put down two scotches fast followed by corned beef and cabbage."[7]

Any definitive profile of Nixon must include his greatness and his flaws. I have sifted out the "party line," the so-called official version of events, to talk about Nixon the man and the deep-seated resentment and ambition that drove him for fifty-six years, including six years in the "wilderness," when his prospects looked bleak at best. We will look at his meticulous preparation, his early understanding of mass media and the need for both "message and image manipulation," as well as the opponents he slashed, rivals he pummeled, and corners he cut to seize his dream of the White House. In short, we will examine the underside of Richard Milhous Nixon.

NOTES

1. Nick Thimmesch, "Nixon: A Man Is Not Finished When He Is Defeated." *Sarasota Herald-Tribune*, December 11, 1978.
2. Anthony Summers, *The Arrogance of Power*, x.
3. Ibid.
4. Suzanne Clark, *Cold Warriors: Manliness on Trial in the Rhetoric of the West*, p. 59.
5. Otis L. Graham, *Toward a Planned Society: From Roosevelt to Nixon*, p. 1892.
6. John Ehrlichman, *Witness to Power: The Nixon Years*, p. 34.
7. *Anthony Summers, The Arrogance of Power*, p. 144.

CHAPTER ONE

THE MAN

C rucial to Nixon's comeback were the tumultuous events of the 1960s, which created the vacuum he would fill. Nixon created a dynamic that made the return of Richard Nixon to power possible. To his credit, Nixon was well prepared when this vacuum occurred. A meticulous brooder, given to enormous self-analysis, Nixon had carefully promoted his public image and had used his stature as a former vice president and foreign policy expert to stay in the public eye. At the same time, he clearly saw the need for a "New Nixon," better press relations, and an entirely different manner of communicated to American voters.

Above all, Nixon was extraordinarily disciplined, while at the same time stiff, formal, and seemingly uncomfortable in his own skin. His appetite for hard work was extraordinary. He paid careful attention to what he ate, opting for a healthy diet long before that became popular. He had a solemn rule of eating only half of whatever was on his plate. He exercised religiously and essentially kept the same weight from the time he was forty-five years old until his death. His chief of staff H. R. "Bob" Haldeman would call Nixon's discipline "unnatural." Although he hated campaigning, he did it with gusto and focus, carefully honing his words and messages and fencing with the press. From 1952 until 1969, he traveled literally millions of miles on the road on behalf of Republican causes and candidates. Nixon would spend more than 250 days a year on the road carefully tending the party gardens and garnering IOUs.

While he famously listened to *Victory at Sea* and Richard Rodgers, Nixon would also have classical music piped in to his New York study and later the White House, which he would listen to while reading. He smoked a pipe. He had an extensive knowledge of wine and an excellent cellar. He wore reading glasses but was virtually never photographed in them. This of course does not fit the common perception of him as a middle-class boob of pedestrian tastes, a man JFK said "had no class."

Also, while many thought Nixon had "ice water in his veins," he could show what one aide would call "a subliminal sentimental streak." Nixon aide James Bassett remembered meeting Nixon for lunch on the Upper East Side. Nixon was carrying a wrapped package. "It's a doll," he said.

"For Julie and Tricia?" Bassett asked.

Nixon frowned. "No, it is actually for a little crippled kid I read about in the paper this morning. She is in a charity hospital. It said she wanted a doll. So I am going to drop this off after we are finished." Bassett noted that it would be a good story for the press. "If you leak this to the newspaper," he said, "I will cut your balls off."[1]

*   *   *

Ironically, it was Nixon's deep secrets that would plant the seeds of his downfall and provide the leverage to avoid federal prosecution and jail. The terrible secrets of Richard Nixon not only guaranteed his tumble from supreme power, but also would assure his own survival and lay the groundwork for his final public rehabilitation, which reached its zenith at the time of his death.

Twenty years after his death, the public remains fascinated with Richard Milhous Nixon. His mawkish and uncomfortable mannerisms and political persistence generated the pop culture persona of the most durable American political leader of the last third of the century. Nixon's extreme features, heavy jowls, and stiff manner made him a magnet for caricature and satire at the hands of the counterculture. Headshops featured black-light posters of Nixon and Agnew depicted as Hells Angels bikers. Nixon bongs and pipes were readily available. One outfit in San Francisco even produced Tricky Dick rolling papers. Impressionists David Frey, Rich Little, and Randy Credico would imitate the thirty-seventh president. His dark eyebrows, five-o'clock shadow, and V for victory sign were all parts of a public persona of Nixon reflected in the brutal cartoons of the *Washington Post*'s Herblock. "Here he comes," a party chieftain said in one iconic cartoon as Herblock drew Nixon climbing out of a manhole from the sewer.

Yet, Nixon had what all truly successful politicians had: the gift of charisma. As a young man his black-Irish coloring and intense eyes made him handsome despite his oversized head and ski-jump nose that would later serve cartoonists so well. As Nixon matured, his features changed. As his hairline receded, the Nixonian widows peak became more pronounced. His face was darkly lined and jowly. Somehow these changes made Nixon more, not less, compelling. Even as Nixon's face aged, his smile remained sunny and dazzling, particularly in contrast to his otherwise stern manner. His staff and peers found his presence utterly commanding.

Nixon was a man of contradictions, both great and flawed, both good and bad. He had the loftiest of ideals, but sometimes used the shabbiest of methods. He was a loner, a striver. He could be transparent or opaque in his motives. He could be amazingly blunt or quite equally duplicitous. He could be both perceptive and naive. When he asked me why a former high-level Eisenhower administration official who had often escorted Rose Mary Woods had never married her and I told him the gentleman was gay, he was shocked.

In his book, Don Fulsom, who claims that Nixon was gay and that he and Bebe Rebozo were lovers, is wide of the mark. The charge is false. I saw Nixon's reaction when I told him one of his aides who wore flamboyant jewelry was gay. He was stunned.

In fact, Nixon could be quite naive. In the late 1950s, the US State Department made jazz great Louis Armstrong a "goodwill ambassador" and underwrote a series of concert tours in Europe and Asia. On his return from the first two tours, based on Satchmo's ambassadorial status, Armstrong and his entourage were waived through customs without a search. Yet, upon a later return, upon landing at Idlewild Airport in New York in 1958, he was directed to the customs lines. Custom agents had been tipped off that contraband was being imported into the country. Armstrong joined a long line of travelers lined up for inspections. Unfortunately, the jazz trumpeter was carrying three pounds of marijuana in his suitcase. Once Armstrong realized he was about to be busted and would bring shame on the country he was traveling on behalf of, he began sweating profusely.

Just then the doors swung open and Vice President Richard Nixon, in step with his security detail, swept in the room followed by a gaggle of reporters and photographers. Nixon, seeing an opportunity for a wire photo with Armstrong, went up to the jazz man and said, "Satchmo, what are you doing here?"

"Well, Pops [Armstrong called everyone Pops], I just came back from my goodwill ambassador's tour of Asia, and they told me I had to stand in this line for customs."

Nixon grabbed both of Satchmo's suitcases and said, "Ambassadors don't have to go through customs, and the vice president of the United States will gladly carry your bags for you." Whereupon Nixon "muled" three pounds of pot through United States Customs without ever knowing it.

When Nixon was told what happened by Charles McWhorter, who served as a traveling aide to Nixon (who heard the tale from one of the jazz musicians traveling with Satchmo), a startled Nixon exclaimed, "Louie smokes marijuana?"[2]

Nixon had a passion for secrecy and compartmentalizing his dealings. He could play twenty different hands of political poker with none of the other players aware that there were other games going on or who was playing or being played.

No one knew everything about Nixon. His own campaign manager and advisor, Attorney General John Mitchell did not know that Nixon, as vice president, had approved a CIA alliance with organized crime to assassinate Fidel Castro until 1971, three years after Nixon was elected president. This alliance, known as Operation 40, would morph into the Kennedy assassination. Nixon was familiar with many of the CIA operatives involved. The assassination stemmed from the CIA's deep hatred of John Kennedy in the wake of the Bay of Pigs fiasco.

Nixon was a shrewd judge of his adversaries and ever-shifting allies.

He was in awe of Jack Kennedy but said LBJ was an "animal,"[3] Gerald Ford was a "dumb-shit,"[4] Ambassador Joseph P. Kennedy, who helped fund Nixon's election to the US Senate, a "crook," called Bobby Kennedy a "little SOB,"[5] and said Teddy Kennedy was the "best politician in the family,"[6] all the while searching for dirt to use to end Teddy's career. He said Nancy Reagan was "a bitch"[7] and that Ronald Reagan "made it look easy." [8] Nixon was a shrewd judge of his adversaries and ever-shifting allies.

Particularly, his appetite for work both physical and intellectual was prodigious, but both were less than his love of intrigue, intelligence, and gossip. His appetite for political intelligence was voracious. We spoke every Saturday morning on the telephone at 10:30 a.m. He would invariably start the conversation by saying, "Is this a good time?" as if anyone would turn down an hour's conversation with one of the most intriguing and reviled men in the world. I carried memos to the White House and an endless stream of verbal messages to senators, governors, and congressmen. Having served as a House member, he was always interested in the rising stars of the House. "Who are the nut-cutters?" he would ask. "Tell them Nixon says...," he would instruct. He wanted the dope on everybody, "who's screwing whom" and who had talent. He was never impressed, but would become a steadfast supporter and back-channel advisor once the Gipper got to the White House. First Lady Nancy Reagan was careful to listen on the bedroom extension to the extensive phone conversations between her husband and Nixon. It was Nixon who would persuade Reagan to appoint General Alexander Haig as secretary of state.

"Richard Nixon's comeback . . . is a story of determination, perseverance, and political brilliance almost unseen in US politics," said former Nixon speechwriter Pat Buchanan. "Nixon not only survived and recovered, but went out to revive, unite, and led to victory a Republican party which in 1965 and 1966 had been outnumbered two-to-one in both Houses of Congress. His 1968 victory, which began a string of five Republican triumphs in six straight presidential elections, was little short of miraculous."[9] Nixon's presence on five national tickets would be surpassed only by Franklin Roosevelt, and only because he ran unsuccessfully for vice president in 1920.

Although late to see the GOP's lurch to the right under Goldwater and the power shift in the party from the eastern establishment the Sunbelt conservatives, once he comprehended it, Nixon would court and nail down the right as a prelude to his comeback bid.

No review of Nixon's life can be complete without an understanding of his tortured relationship with the medium of television. Skillful use of television would save Nixon's skin in the effective Checkers speech of 1952, destroy his chances after the disastrous first debate with JFK in 1960, and lead many to give him up for dead after the televised meltdown of 1962. His mastery and control of the medium would both pave the way for 1968 comeback as well as provide the televised backdrop for his fall in Watergate in 1974. "The American people don't believe anything's real until they see it on television," Nixon would tell me.[10]

His discomfort in his own skin, physical gracelessness, carica-turist's dream features, and a propensity to sweat and appear shifty on TV made his mastery of the medium all the more compelling. In doing so he would change how the game of presidential politics was played, this change most recently evident in the presidential campaigns of Mitt Romney and Barack Obama in 2012.

Nixon was an introvert in an extrovert's business. Painfully shy, private, and reserved, alcohol would prove a social lubricant. It was only after a few cocktails that his tongue would loosen and he would become loquacious. It was then that I would learn some of Nixon's darkest secrets.

* * *

Late one night while working with speechwriter William Safire, Nixon pondered his greatest character trait. Safire recalled that "Nixon tried to encapsulate his more recent predecessors in a single word or phrase: 'Truman—a fighter. Eisenhower—a good man. Kennedy—charisma. Johnson—work. Me—what?' I did not have a good answer that night in 1970; I do now. Nixon—an inspiring resilience."[11]

One thing was for sure, by 1962, according to virtually every pundit, Nixon was done in politics. These men and women did not count on Nixon's resilience. "I, Richard Nixon, do solemnly swear that I will faithfully execute the office of president of the United States and will to the best of my ability preserve, protect, and defend the Constitution of the United States," said Nixon on January 22, 1969. Only six years after his California self-immolation, Richard Milhous Nixon finally grabbed the elusive prize that had narrowly evaded his grasp in 1960 and appeared hopelessly out of reach after 1962. He staged the greatest comeback in American political history.

Nixon's razor-thin loss to JFK scalded him and sent him into a deep depression. Getting worked over by the efficient Kennedy machine with their hardball tactics and Madison Avenue imagery,

Nixon self-managed a defensive, unfocused campaign, driving him to the brink of collapse with fatigue. More importantly he let Kennedy dominate the dialogue and with it, the outcome. Lost in history, though, is the fact that JFK was stalled in the polls in the closing weeks and Nixon's superhuman effort was closing the gap. The late movement in the polls was in favor of Nixon. He triumphed in the last three of the four debates. Contrary to the conventional history, the TV audience grew in the last of the four debates and virtually matched that of the first.[12] It was considered Nixon's best debate. Nixon closed fast but not fast enough . . . or did he? As we shall discover, voter irregularities in Illinois and Texas probably cheated Nixon out of his come-from-behind victory. In addition, a case can be made that Nixon actually won the popular vote while losing the Electoral College.

"They say RN is paranoid," Nixon's veteran advance man Nick Ruwe told me. "You'd be paranoid too if the presidency had been stolen from you."

Nixon would drive himself to nervous exhaustion in his effort to catch and pass Kennedy. Kennedy paced himself while his wealthy father paid for an outstanding professional staff and media campaign. "We're going to sell Jack like soap flakes," the elder Kennedy promised. Nixon vowed a defeat due to imagery in lieu of hard issues would never happen again. He, too, could run a mass media campaign using television. He too would pace himself.

From Nixon's defeat in the 1962 race for governor of California and his valedictory outburst at the press that you "won't have Nixon to kick around anymore" to his inauguration as president in 1969 in a period of only six years, it is Nixon's savvy reading and manipulation of events that make this account all the more interesting.

An extraordinary set of circumstances opened the door for Nixon's stunning comeback. The assassination of John F. Kennedy, the murder of Dr. Martin Luther King, the assassination of Robert F. Kennedy, the escalated and seemingly hopeless war in Vietnam and the unrest caused on America's campuses coupled with a newly militant demand for civil rights and the resulting resentments of a white middle class all provided a confluence of events that gave Dick Nixon another shot.

It is only in recent years that a more balanced portrait of John F. Kennedy has come into focus. So successful was Kennedy's embodiment of the spirit of a younger generation of Americans in the early 1960s, and so adept was JFK at the use of Madison Avenue "image making," fueled with his father's money, that only today do we realize JFK was a philandering husband whose voracious sexual appetite was likely heightened by his taking of methamphetamine injections allegedly to address the pain in his back.

Just as history demands a balanced portrait of JFK, the good and the bad, so should history demand a balanced portrait of Richard Nixon. His achievements for a safer, more peaceful world, a cleaner environment, and greater social justice cannot be discarded, for unlike JFK, more bad is known about him than good. My goal in *Nixon's Secrets* is not to provide an apologia for the thirty-seventh president, nor to rehabilitate him. Rather, my aim is to provide a balanced portrait based on the historical record and the many opportunities I had to learn more than the "official version of events." It is also my aim to connect the dots between the CIA's Operation 40 (a Nixon-led, anti-Castro operation), the Bay of Pigs, the Kennedy assassination, Nixon's downfall, and the exact circumstances of the pardon, which ultimately allowed Nixon to stage his greatest comeback. Nixon's fervent anti-Communism, his arm's-length relationship with organized crime, his tortured relationship with the CIA, and his personal ambition would be the threads that sewed these events together.

Nixon was a single-minded individual. His only passion outside of the political arena was professional sports. He was as fervent and as knowledgeable about baseball as he was government and politics. Gonzo Journalist Hunter S. Thompson, whose hatred for Nixon ran so deep it led Thompson to label him an "American monster," connected with the presidential candidate over a mutual love of professional football while on the '68 campaign.

Thompson got an audience with Nixon only on the condition that they could discuss football and nothing else. Nixon's travel aide Nick Ruwe arranged a car ride with Nixon upon his arrival in New Hampshire on a private jet, and Thompson almost ignited the plane in jet fuel with a careless cigarette clenched in a holder, which would have killed Nixon, Thompson, and Ruwe on the spot.

"We had a fine time. I enjoyed it—which put me a bit off balance, because I figured Nixon didn't know any more about football than he did about ending the war in Vietnam. He had made a lot of allusion to football on the stump, but it had never occurred to me that he actually *knew* anything more about football than he knew about the Grateful Dead.

But I was wrong. Whatever else might be said about Nixon— and there is still no doubt in my mind that he could pass for Human—he is a goddamn stone fanatic on every fact of pro football. At one point in our conversation, when I was feeling a bit pressed for leverage, I mentioned a down & out pass—in the waning moments of a Super Bowl mismatch between Green Bay and Oakland—to an obscure, second-string Oakland receiver named Bill Miller that had stuck in my mind because of its pinpoint style and precision.

He hesitated for a moment, lost in thought, then he whacked me on the thigh and laughed: "That's right, by God! The Miami boy!"[13]

Beyond sports, Nixon had no interests; neither food, movies, plays, nor the reading of fiction interested him. He spent his time thinking, brooding, and plotting. When he wasn't doing these things, he was reading or writing about the only thing he understood—strategy.

The extent to which politics consumed Richard Nixon was extraordinary. Despite the fact that he would, for the first time in his life, make big money as a lawyer after moving East in the wake of his 1962 gubernatorial defeat, he would quickly grow bored.

Nixon's ambition was born of resentment. He was a westerner, an outsider whose taste and sensibility reflected the American middle class. He didn't go to Harvard or Yale, but matriculated instead at Whittier College and would shoehorn his way into the Duke University School of Law. Nixon had, as JFK would sniff, "no class."

Author Russ Baker had been particularly perceptive in his view of Nixon's deep resentment of the nation's privileged and moneyed elites. It galled Nixon that without independent wealth he was forced to grovel for campaign contributions that would fuel his drive for the presidency. He remembered well that the *New York Herald-Tribune*, the very voice of the Wall Street/corporate wing of the party would first embrace his vice presidential candidacy and then be first to urge that he be thrown over the side when questions about his integrity surfaced in the so-called "fund crisis" of 1952. Nixon would utilize a cocker spaniel to thwart those who would dump him.

In fact Nixon would channel his resentment of the financial and cultural elite into the "politics of resentment." Nixon practiced the politics of "us" vs. "them." Nixon would use his bristling resentment and hatred of those who felt entitled to forge a middle-class constituency that would weld small-town Republicans with white Southern Democrats and big-city Northern Catholics to take back the White House for the GOP after a twelve-year drought during which many in the mainstream media speculated that the Republican Party was finished and would go the way of the Whigs.

"What starts the process, really, are laughs and slights and snubs when you are a kid," he told former aide Ken Clawson. "But if you are reasonably intelligent enough and your anger is deep enough and strong enough, you learn that you can change those attitudes by excellence, personal gut performance while those who have everything are sitting on their fat butts."[14]

Like FDR, Nixon's politics were about cobbling together a new and enduring electoral base for the GOP by uniting Republicans, a distinct minority out of power for many years with Southern whites leery of civil rights and Northern ethnic Catholic Democrats. So durable was this coalition that it would almost reelect Gerald Ford in 1976, only two years after Nixon's resignation, and go on to elect Ronald Reagan to two terms and George H. W. Bush to one.

Nixon understood that politics was about addition. You had to galvanize those who shared your values, resentments, and anger to reach a governing majority by winning an election. Unlike many of the party's right, politics was about *winning*.

But Nixon also understood the human psychology that makes it easier to get people to vote against something than for something. Politics is also about division. It's us against them: the elites, the government, the privileged, the Ivy Leaguers, liberals on the US Supreme Court, those to the manor born who inherit. Nixon rallied the strivers, the small-business men who were getting screwed by the big corporations, the little people who paid their taxes, served in the military, belonged to the Rotary, and didn't burn their draft cards. It was the politics of resentment.

Nixon viewed all his opponents as elites. His first major opponent, Jerry Voorhis, was a millionaire banker's son, Helen Gahagan Douglas was a famous actress and friend of Eleanor Roosevelt, and Alger Hiss, whose downfall Nixon would cause, was Ivy League. John F. Kennedy, wealthy and debonair as Nixon would never be, was seen as another child of privilege, "a rich kid whose father bought it for him," Nixon would tell me.

Nixon hated the Eastern elite even more so because he had to rely on them financially. Although carefully styled as a small-time boy from the city of Whittier, his political career was not only first financed by the oil, agricultural, and defense industries in Southern California, but Eastern interests funneled money to Nixon as well. There was significant Eastern funding for Nixon's 1946 campaign against veteran New Deal Congressman Jerry Voorhis.

It is notable that Nixon fled Southern California immediately after his 1962 debacle in the governor's race. He returned to New York, indeed to Wall Street, the bosom of the very moneyed and elitist crowd he claims to detest. Pharmaceutical king Elmer Bobst swung profitable legal business to the firm of Nixon, Mudge, Rose, Guthrie, and Alexander where Nixon was a "law partner." As we shall see, Pepsico's Don Kendall would give the firm legal business that would bring Richard Nixon to Dallas on November 21 and 22, 1963. It is notable that none in Nixon's circle of close, deep-pocketed financial supporters and intimates had Ivy League degrees or social connections.

While Nixon could always count on his friends Charles "Bebe" Rebozo, *Reader's Digest* owner Hobart Lewis, Aerosol valve inventor Robert Abplanalp, coal and railroad heiress Helen Clay Frick, Pepsico's Don Kendall, and Chicago insurance executive W. Clement Stone, he had to go to Wall Street and the big boys in New York for the real money again in 1968. As vice president, Nixon had to grovel for the money to face JFK. In 1962, with his star in eclipse, he struggled to raise money in his failed gubernatorial comeback bid.

It was the Eastern boys who got him on the ticket with Dwight Eisenhower in 1952. The selection of Nixon was engineered by New York Governor Thomas E. Dewey, two-time presidential loser in 1944 and 1948 with the vigorous backing of Senator Prescott Bush of Connecticut, Senator Henry Cabot Lodge and his brother, Connecticut Governor John Davis Lodge, and Wall Street lawyers Allen and John Foster Dulles as well as Eisenhower campaign manager and later attorney general Herbert Brownell. These men picked Nixon not because of their high regard for his intellect, but because they thought he brought the ticket both age and geographical balance. The anti-Communist credentials earned in his successful pursuit of Communist spy Alger Hiss made Nixon a favorite with the conservative wing of the party, and it was thought that he would appeal to the disgruntled supporters of Senator Robert A. Taft, from whom Ike had snatched the presidential nomination. The Eastern establishment was old money, history, and connections. Nixon was thought of as a pawn, not a prize, and they would attempt to sacrifice him without thought to the contrary.

Nixon was never *of* the establishment, although he would enjoy the support of the Dulles brothers, Henry Luce, Herbert Brownell, John McCloy, Tom Dewey, and the Whitneys, Bushes, Walter Thayer and other pillars of the Eastern establishment. Nixon also deeply remembered that these were precisely the folks who had urged Eisenhower to force him to resign from the ticket in 1952 when a scandal involving an alleged "secret fund" put together by a group of businessmen was claimed to support Nixon's lifestyle. Minutes after Nixon gave him this bad news, Nixon launched his televised Checkers speech that would save his career. Nixon never forgot that the Eastern snobs had rallied to cut his throat. He would court them, he would take their money, but he would always hate them.

What historians like Rick Perlstein fail to grasp is not only that Nixon resented and envied the glamorous Kennedys, with their privileged lifestyle and well-funded political ascendency, Nixon also resented those in his own tribe like Nelson Rockefeller, to whom he would always be beholden. Ironically, Nixon would move into a Park Avenue apartment building Rockefeller owned and lived in. Rocky would be Nixon's neighbor and landlord. Nixon's new law firm would handle real estate transactions for the Rockefeller owned bank Chase Manhattan.[15]

Nixon, who had seen his father, Frank Nixon, a dirt-poor roustabout, literally work himself to death, resented the country club elite with their fancy educations and their trust funds. Nixon's father would be fierce and loud in his political opinions and fast with his fists. The resentment developed in Nixon from watching his father's struggle would only intensify when, after law school graduation, every white-shoe New York law firm he applied to rejected him. His application to become an FBI agent would also be rejected.

That brings us to the issue of Nixon's ideology; he was without one. He was most definitely an internationalist and favored an aggressive foreign policy that was held in disdain by the isolationist GOP old guard. His successful nailing of Communist spy and New Deal darling Alger Hiss brought him national name identification, a large and fervent national base, and popularity among grassroots conservative Republicans. In fact, Nixon was a centrist who still believed the center of gravity within the Republican Party was in the center/left as late as 1960. Nixon's concessions to New York Governor Nelson Rockefeller on the platform (referred to as the Munich of the Republican Party by Senator Barry Goldwater)[16] and Nixon's unfortunate selection of liberal Republican Henry Cabot Lodge in 1960 and his capitulation to Rockefeller on the party platform both proved this point.

Although Nixon would be late in understanding his party's 1964 shift to the right, the scene of the Goldwater-dominated 1964 convention lustily booing Nelson Rockefeller would graphically show Nixon that the center ground had shifted from beneath him. Nixon would launch a stop-Goldwater effort and deliver stinging criticism of the Arizona Senator long after Goldwater had the nomination wrapped up. The former vice president would then pivot to become Goldwater's biggest supporter only days later and would shrewdly campaign in more states for the ticket in '64 than Goldwater himself. Nixon was schooled on "sounding" conservative. By 1968, he had learned how to manipulate the *symbols* of conservatism, attacking a runaway federal government, stirring violence in the inner cities, and white resentment of what they perceived as munificent government benefits of African Americans. When the GOP shifted right, Nixon's *imagery* would shift right while his pragmatism remained the same. When it came to his domestic record philosopher Noam Chomsky would tell the *Huffington Post* in 2013, "Nixon was our last liberal president."[17]

There are several leitmotifs that pervade the Nixon life story. His deep resentment of the speed by which the Eastern establishment that was so quick to dump him in 1952 from the ticket, left him wary of their future support and sensitive to their private derision. His narrow defeat by John Kennedy in which he believed he had been cheated out of, left him with what aide John Ehrlichman called a "Kennedy obsession." And his entanglement with a secret loan from mysterious industrialist Howard Hughes would plague his 1960 and 1962 campaigns and play a crucial role in Watergate.

This book is also about Nixon's long and tortuous relationship with the American right. Fervent anti-Communism and the stalwart support of party conservatives undergirded Nixon's early rise. The support of party conservatives was instrumental in his comeback. The themes of conservative values were crucial in galvanizing his governing majority, but as we shall see it was the very foreign policy hard-line anti-Communists who would come to distrust Nixon and then actively undermine his détente policies to defuse tension with the Soviets and the Chinese. In the end, a cabal of the joint chiefs of staff and the CIA spied on Nixon and utilized the president's struggle with the Watergate scandal to remove him.

Also central to any analysis are the rules of engagement for politics in the decade in which Nixon lived. "Everyone does it," was the excuse rejected by the American people in the wake of the Watergate fiasco. As we will show, that is certainly true, as all of Nixon's contemporaries would utilize the same hardball tactics and shady campaign financing that Nixon himself would excel at. Nixon's belief that his campaign had been bugged in 1960, 1962, and 1968 left his entourage with the idea that the Democrats could be bugged in 1972, because "everybody bugs everybody," as Nixon put it. The story of Richard Nixon is one of the highest highs and the lowest lows.

While I don't think Nixon gave approval or ordered the break-in at Watergate, he created an atmosphere where surrounded by yes-men and advance men, there was no one to say no. By 1968, those Nixon aides willing to argue with him had been relegated to the outer circle, their access was denied, or they were purged. As we shall see, more even-keeled early advisors, such as Robert Finch and Herbert G. Klein, as well as newcomers such as John P. Sears to his early 1968 comeback bid, were moved behind the "Berlin Wall" of H. R. "Bob" Haldeman and John Ehrlichman, setting the stage for Watergate. "Never hire anyone over thirty," Nixon would tell aide Lyn Nofziger." Get young guys who do as they are told."[18]

As we shall see, Nixon surrounded himself with bright young conservative intellectuals for his comeback bid only to discard them for a coterie of ad men, advance men, and PR merchandisers. Nixon would wisely latch on to John P. Sears, Richard Whalen, Pat Buchanan, Alan Greenspan, and Jeffrey Bell. Even "liberals" in this group, like speechwriter Raymond K. Price and Daniel Patrick Moynihan, were men of the moderate center. But after the arrival of the Berlin Wall of straitlaced authoritarian Christian Scientist advance men Haldeman and Ehrlichman, the men of ideas were out and the enablers were in. Those who could say no to Nixon were vanquished or their access was denied. Federal Reserve Chairman Arthur Burns had a scheduled meeting with the president. He got up to leave only to remember he had forgotten to tell the president something. "Your appointment is over, Dr. Burns," Haldeman would bark. When Burns told him what he wanted to tell the president, Haldeman said, "Put it in a memo."[19]

Nixon's trajectory is extraordinary. After a dizzying climb from a lieutenant commander in the navy to a whisker loss of the White House in just fifteen years, Nixon would be cheated out the presidency and would fail at a bid for governor of his home state. Written off for dead, he would shake off the label of "loser " to rise Lazarus-like in the greatest comeback in American history only to be brought low by his terrible secrets. Yet one of those secrets would spare him prison and allow him to stage his last comeback as respected foreign policy statesman, advising President Bill Clinton on how to handle the Russians and the Chinese.

"Only if you have been in the deepest valley, can you ever know how magnificent it is to be on the highest mountain," said Nixon.[20] *"The man in the arena,"* like JFK, deserves a closer look.

NOTES

1. Anthony Summer, *Arrogance of Power*, p. 144.
2. Conversation with Pete Barbuti.
3. *Crossfire*, CNN, November 1982.
4. Interview with John Sears, November 8, 1979.
5. Richard J. Whalen, *Catch the Falling Flag*, p. 156.
6. Ibid. p. 223.
7. Robert Sam Anson, *Exile: The Unquiet Oblivion of Richard Nixon*, p. 144.
8. Conversation with author.
9. Sandy Fitzgerald, "Pat Buchanan Writes Book About His Years With Nixon," Newsmax, Feb. 8, 2014.
10. Roger Stone, "Nixon on Clinton," *New York Times*, April 28, 1994.
11. William Safire, "Sizing up Nixon: an inspiring resilience," *Gadsen Times*, April 26, 1994.
12. "Nixon at 100," Huffington Post, January 9, 2013.
13. Hunter S. *Thompson, Fear and Loathing at Rolling Stone: The Essential Writing of Hunter S. Thompson*, pp. 138–139.
14. John Aloysius Farrell, "The Operatic Life of Richard Nixon," *The Atlantic*, January 9, 2013.
15. Gary Allen, *The Man Behind the Mask*, p. 223.
16. Brian R. Farmer, *American Conservatism: History, Theory and Practice*, p. 279.
17. Christine Conetta, "Noam Chomsky: Richard Nixon Was `Last Liberal President.'" Huffington Post, Feb. 21, 2014, http://buchanan.org/blog/pjb-the-neocons-and-nixons-southern-strategy-512.
18. Lyn Nofziger, Nofziger, p. 123.
19. Richard Reeves, Alone in the White House, p. 71.
20. President Nixon's final remarks at the White House, August 9, 1974.

CHAPTER TWO

"YOUR GOOD DOG"

"I've often wished that Richard and his brothers had not been burdened with the hardships they had to endure as boys; they should have had more fun."[1]

—Hannah Nixon

To understand Nixon it is important to understand the developmental history of the man. Nixon was born to Francis A. Nixon and Hannah (née Milhous) Nixon on January 9, 1913, in Yorba Linda, California. Richard's mother was a Quaker, to which his father converted to after their marriage, and they maintained a conservative household. While the conversion placated the family somewhat, from the beginning the Milhous clan was ambivalent at best at the prospect of Frank's addition to the family.[2] One of Hannah's sisters would later recall writing into her journal, "Hannah is a bad girl"— reflecting on the difficult relationship between the Nixons and the Milhouses.[3] "I don't think they ever let Hannah forget the fact that she married outside of her status," said a family friend.[4]

His father, born in Ohio in 1878, played an important role in Richard's early life. Francis Anthony "Frank" Nixon had only a few months of formal education and for much of his life was something of a drifter.[5] Frank Nixon was also unafraid to voice his opinions on the political issues of his day, from agitating for heating the cabs of the streetcars in which he worked as a motorman and suffered frostbitten feet, to his outspoken advocacy of the virtues of self-improvement, add to this his stalwart and vocal support for President Warren Harding and Frank Nixon was what many would call a "loudmouth."[6] He was fast with his tongue and his fists. Frank Nixon was a Republican (one of his favorite stories was of having met William McKinley in Ohio and McKinley complimenting Nixon's horse after riding it in a parade) and didn't shy away from telling friends and neighbors about how he saw things. He became a small-business man who would fail in a number of ventures, including an orange grove. Nixon himself would lose money on a frozen orange juice scheme that he pursued while practicing law. Frank's angers and frustrations, borne from his own hardships and failures, were exerted onto Richard and his brothers; he was a demanding and abusive taskmaster. Frank at one time caught one of the Nixon boys swimming in the canal that ran by their home. Father Nixon reportedly "beat him so bad his hollering could be heard all up and down the ditch," said a Nixon cousin.[7]

Nixon was devoted to his mother, Hannah, a cold, proper woman who, while fiercely encouraging to her son, never expressed anything approaching affection. "Think how great he might have been if anyone had loved him," Henry Kissinger said after his death. Richard clearly favored his mother, whom she perpetually called "Richard," and he perpetually called "Mother." A letter ten-year-old Richard wrote to his mother was indicative of both his burgeoning self-awareness as an outsider and his subservient devotion to Hannah:

My Dear Master,

The two boys that you left me with are very bad to me. Their dog, Jim, is very old and he will never talk or play with me.
One Saturday the boys went hunting. Jim and myself went with them. While going through the woods one of the boys triped [sic] and fell on me. I lost my temper and bit him. He kiked [sic] me in

the side and we started on. While we were walking I saw a black round thing in a tree. I hit it with my paw. A swarm of black thing [sic] came out of it. I felt a pain all over. I started to run and as both of my eys [sic] were swelled shut I fell into a pond. When I got home I was very sore. I wish you would come home right now.

Your Good Dog
Richard[8]

Campaign aide John Sears recalled Nixon visiting his mother in 1962 after a prolonged period. "With news cameras rolling, Nixon knocked on her front door only to shake her hand when she opened it." *Los Angeles Times* reporter Richard Bergholz described the greeting as "weird." Still, in his farewell to his staff just before his resignation, Nixon would extol the virtues of his mother, saying, "My mother was a saint."

In 1922, the Nixon family ranch in Yorba Linda failed, and the family moved to Whittier, California. Whittier was a small, conservative Quaker town named after the great poet and Quaker John Greenleaf Whittier. In Whittier, Frank Nixon opened a grocery store and gas station. Richard Nixon had four brothers, Harold, Donald, Arthur and Edward, of whom two, the eldest Harold and Arthur would die from tuberculosis. When Arthur died, the first of the two to occur when Richard was thirteen, his mother described Richard's reaction as follows: "I can still see Richard when he came back. He slipped into a big chair and sat staring into space, silent and dry-eyed in the undemonstrative way in which, because of his choked, deep feeling, he was always to face tragedy."[9]

While his mother was generally rather withdrawn, she was also clearly devoted to her family. In the words of a Nixon cousin and author Jessamyn West, "Not a saint in the sense that she had had a great spiritual experience, [but] enormously thoughtful and loving."[10] And Frank Nixon, while by all accounts a loud and opinionated individual, was quite clearly a man doing his best to support his family in difficult times and by the standards of the time nowhere near as severe as some. Given the angel of death that at times it must have seemed to hover over the family, Nixon's upbringing was likely less traumatic than it could have been due to his parents' efforts.

However, Frank and Hannah Nixon did not always act in such a way as to make their lives and the lives of their children easier. While charity is a virtue, Hannah in particular was known for often being overly lenient with offers of credit to those who frequented their store. Once she refused to punish a shoplifter, instead offering her a generous line of credit.[11] She did this on the recommendation of young Richard, who went to school with two of her sons.

Additionally, Frank Nixon was a polarizing figure in the community, particularly for his propensity for engaging patrons of his shop in political "debates. His debates were so great in length and competitiveness that he at times would run patrons from the store.[12] Neither Hannah's generosity with strangers nor Frank's difficult nature was particularly helpful to a family struggling to support themselves. Still, selling a variety of fresh vegetables, patent medicines, and local poultry and pumping gasoline, the small Nixon store thrived for a time.

Hannah, ever the conservative Quaker, made it her duty to ensure her children were raised to be properly God-fearing individuals. In one story of Richard's childhood, when Hannah caught Richard and his older brother Harold eating grapes taken from a neighbor's property, she made them use their hard-earned savings to pay the neighbor, Mrs. Trueblood. Hannah did this despite Mrs. Trueblood's objection that it wasn't necessary. In the words of Yorba Linda native Richard Gardner, "From that day on, nobody can remember the Nixon boys ever did a dishonest thing."[13]

Nixon attended East Whittier Elementary School, where he was president of his eighth-grade class. Even at that young age his intelligence was obvious to his teachers and fellow students alike. Nixon's mother had taught him to read before he began kindergarten, and his memory was prodigious. A neighboring child remembers the teacher bringing Nixon into her third grade class when he was in kindergarten to recite a lengthy poem. The neighbor, Virginia Shaw, is quoted as saying, "It was amazing that a kindergartener could learn that vast amount of poetry . . . I remember all of us were very, very envious."[14] Nixon would be advanced from the first grade directly to the third in response to his academic prowess.

Further evidence of Nixon's intelligence and ambition can be found in a letter he drafted at age eleven, for an application to a job with the *Los Angeles Times*, the paper to which the Nixon family subscribed. "Please consider me for the position of office boy mentioned in the *Times* paper. I am eleven years of age and I am in the Sixth grade of the East Whittier grammar school. I am very willing to work . . . I am willing to come to your office at any time and I will accept any pay offered."[15] While Nixon, the working-class boy from the suburbs, was not offered the job, this provides us with early evidence of the man he would become—driven, hardworking, and confident in his intelligence.

For his first two years of high school, Richard attended Fullerton Union High School, at which he received excellent grades despite needing to ride a bus for an hour each way to school his freshman year (during his sophomore year, he would live with an aunt in Fullerton during the week). At Fullerton, he played football and was an accomplished debater.[16]

For his final two years of high school Richard transferred to Whittier High School. His older brother Harold had been diagnosed with tuberculosis the preceding year, and Richard was put in charge of the vegetable counter at the family grocery store in his brother's stead. As a result of this responsibility, Richard woke at 4 a.m. to drive into Los Angeles to purchase vegetables at the market. After returning with the vegetables, he washed and displayed them at the store, all this before making his way to school. At Whittier, Nixon attempted to join as many clubs and organizations as he possibly could, but that at which he most excelled was debate.

Nixon's debate coach would later be quoted speaking admirably regarding his competency. According to Mrs. Clifford Vincent,

"He was so good that it kind of disturbed me. He had this ability to kind of slide around an argument instead of meeting it head on, and he could take any side of a debate."[17] Naturally, to those who have sought to demonize Nixon since the end of his time in office, this statement is not praise, but rather a criticism. However, this was high praise, particularly the closing phrase that Nixon "could take any side of a debate." As anyone who has had any exposure to competitive debate will tell you, having the mental flexibility to address an issue from all angles and understand all credible arguments is of the utmost importance for success. Perhaps most impressively, despite all these drains on his time, Nixon managed to finish third in his class at Whittier High. Never let it be said that Richard Nixon wasn't a driven man.

While at Whittier High, Nixon had met a fellow student by the name of Ola Florence Welch, with whom he appeared in the school's rendition of Virgil's *Aeneid*.[18] Ola, the daughter of Whittier's deputy chief of police, played the role of Dido (Queen of Carthage and love interest of Aeneas), and their romance developed from their involvement in the play. Their relationship would follow Nixon to college, where it would continue to flourish despite their vast differences in personality and politics. Ola was a staunch Democrat and supporter of Franklin Roosevelt, a thoroughly outgoing person, and a lover of dance.[19] Nixon, like his father, remained a Republican, as distant as he had ever been, and as a byproduct of his Quaker upbringing, or simply a manifestation of his shyness, was a very unenthusiastic dancer.[20] Nixon's activity in amateur theater would hold him in good stead. He would not only meet future wife Thelma Ryan in an amateur theater production, but he would develop an uncanny ability to cry at will. He would use this in future theatrical productions, and it would become handy in his future political career.

While Nixon was accepted to Harvard University with a tuition grant, his brother's continued illness and the cost of Harvard tuition in total caused him to remain at home and attend Whittier College. Whittier, while a rather academically rigorous institution, was very much a product of its Quaker heritage. Students were expected to participate in a mandatory chapel hour daily, and the administration and policies of the college were unabashedly Christian. Nixon's inability to attend Harvard University would be both a badge of honor and a source of resentment—honor for how far he was able to come and resentment at the treatment he received from those who believed themselves his superior as a result of their inheritance. In my opinion, this is what watered the seeds of Nixon's hatred for the Ivy League and those he perceived as privileged or feeling themselves entitled. His hatred of the Kennedys with their Harvard pedigree would never disappear. "No Harvard men," he would bark at Chief of Staff Haldeman during his 1968 presidential transition.

While Whittier did not have fraternities and sororities, their traditional role was played instead by Whittier's literary societies. At the time of Nixon's admission there was only one active men's literary society, a group known as the Franklins. The Franklins were, or at least the Franklins viewed themselves as, occupants of the highest end of the social milieu. They were the children of the prominent and wealthy, who had been groomed for, and taught the ins and outs of, high society.[21] They were, in short, the antithesis of Nixon in terms of background or breeding.

Nixon, despite his love of literature and superior intelligence, was predictably snubbed by the blue-blooded Franklins. Nixon, always sensitive to his humble roots, responded to this injustice by becoming a founding member of a new society, the Orthogonian Society, Orthogonian meaning, "square shooters." This name was a sort of self-deprecating humor from the new group, made up of many football players and others not academically, or socially, qualified for the Franklins. Nixon would later describe the difference between the Franklins and the Orthoginians as such, "[The Franklins] were the haves and we were the have-nots."[22] In a courageous gesture, the Orthogonians even inducted fellow athlete William Brock, a black man, into the society.[23] To Nixon it didn't matter that he was black, only that like Nixon himself, he, too, was an underdog wrongly discriminated against by the Franklins. Brock would repay Nixon's principle later in life when he would defend Nixon against accusations of racism.

That Nixon was able to rally a group comprised primarily of the members of the Whittier football players to his side is not as shocking as it might seem. While Nixon was a rather poor football player, he was a determined player. He was allowed to practice with the team, and then in games decided by a large margin was allowed to play in games, having earned the respect and affection of his fellow players in something of a precursor of his navy years. Still, his coach at Whittier and a lifetime friend, Wallace Newman, has admitted to worrying about Nixon during practices: "When he scrimmaged he was the cannon fodder. I used to get concerned at how we worked him over."[24] Nixon's determination appeared to win himself a number of accolades at Whittier, as a former teammate from his time on the team recalled, "I shall never forget the tremendous roar which went up from the rooting section when Dick got into the lineup for the last few minutes of a few games."[25]

During his time at Whittier College, Nixon successfully built on his prior debate experience to become an extraordinarily accomplished debater.[26] Despite founding the Orthogonians and finding great success both academically, and as a champion debater, Nixon would never forget the slight he received from the Franklins. Indeed, the resentment he harbored toward the Franklins, and those like them, would fuel Nixon for the remainder of his life. Nixon would take a certain amount of revenge on the Franklins his senior year when he orchestrated a successful campaign for the presidency of the student council, defeating a Franklin.[27] Through his collegiate interactions with the Franklins, Nixon had begun to learn a lesson, fully realized in his later navy years, which would have great bearing on his electoral success; Nixon, through his thoroughly unremarkable roots, was attractive to others because of how outwardly average he appeared. Nixon was not, nor could he ever be, a Franklin; the majority of those he interacted with could never be Franklins either. Nixon resented the Franklins of the world for trying to make him feel inferior when Nixon knew fully well he was their intellectual superior he would spend his life trying to prove it to them. After graduating from Whittier in 1934, Nixon received a full scholarship to attend Duke University School of Law, then a new school seeking to make a name for itself. While the school offered a large number of scholarships to first-year students, it reduced the numbers of those offered for second- and third-year students. This incited an intense competition among the student body. Nixon excelled during his time at Duke, despite sharing a room with three other students in a farmhouse a mile from campus without running water and heated only by a small stove.[28] During his second year, Nixon was elected president of the Duke Bar Association and, upon his graduation as third in his class in 1937, inducted into the elite Order of the Coif; the order's membership now extends to forty-five of the top fifty law schools in the country and limits its membership to the top 10 percent of each school's graduating class.[29]

While by almost any measure Nixon's time at Duke was a great success for him, in terms of his personal life it was a more mixed bag. Ola, his relationship with her having survived Whittier College, would not stay faithful to him upon his departure for Duke.[30] While he would never speak out against her as many other men would have in his place, and to her credit she was always kind in her words to those who would ask her about him, he surely was disappointed to find she had left him for a man who was, "more fun."[31]

On the advice of his friend, Dean Horick, Nixon returned to Whittier and took a job at the law firm of Wingert & Bewley. He accepted the position after completing a bar examination course in three months rather than the expected five. However, Wingert & Bowley was not Nixon's first choice. He spent Christmas of his final year in law school interviewing for positions at the top-tier New York City law firms. His lack of pedigree, coupled with Duke's status as a newly created law school, meant he was unable to land one of those coveted positions.[32] Once again, Nixon found himself weakened by his lack of social standing, despite whatever other merit he had.

Wingert & Bewley represented local oil companies, as well as handling wills and some other similar matters.[33] It did not handle criminal matters and handled very little in the way of litigation. However, through Wingert & Bowley's representation of many of Whittier's major commercial ventures, Nixon was exposed to many of the individuals who would help launch his political career in his first bid for public office.

Within a year at Wingert & Bewley, Nixon became a partner and the firm became Wingert, Bewley, and Nixon. As a part of his partnership Nixon opened a new branch of the firm in the town of La Habra. His secretary during his time at Wingert and Bewley notes that the young Mr. Nixon "would sleep on the couch in his office some nights."[34] Despite an exhausting work schedule, he participated in a number of civic programs. Nixon became president of the Whittier 20-30 Club, sat on the Board of Trustees at Whittier College, and took part in amateur theater productions. It was during his time with the amateur theater that Nixon met Thelma Patricia "Pat" Ryan.

Pat Ryan endured a childhood that was even more difficult than that of Nixon. Her father, a failure at everything he tried, drank heavily and eventually died from tuberculosis when Pat was eighteen years old.[35] Her mother having died from liver cancer four years earlier, Pat was left in charge of the family home. She was offered an escape from California by family in Connecticut, and took a job for two years working with her aunt. Her aunt was a nun and head of the X-ray and pharmacy unit at the Sisters of Charity's Seton Hospital.[36]

After her years in New York she seized the opportunity to return to California to attend the University of Southern California with assistance from her brother Tom, with whom she would live after moving to Los Angeles. As one of her many jobs during her time at USC, Pat Ryan worked in the upscale department store Bullock's during Christmas 1935, during which time she found herself developing a distaste for the pretension of the idle rich.[37] This distaste would be reflected equally powerfully in Richard Nixon; an understanding for the value of hard work would be a unifying aspect of their eventual life together.

Nixon fell hopelessly in love with Pat Ryan, only to have her reject him several times before finally agreeing to date him. After two years of dating, Pat agreed to Nixon's proposal, and they were married on June 21, 1940. After a honeymoon in Mexico, the Nixons would begin their life together still in Whittier. Richard and Pat Nixon would have two children, Tricia (born 1946) and Julie (born 1948).

In January 1942, the Nixons moved to Washington, DC, where Nixon had accepted a job at the Office of Price Administration. During his time in Washington, Nixon was assigned to the tire-rationing division, particularly responsible for replying to correspondence. After four months in Washington, Nixon had grown jaded with the functioning of the OPA and the petty bureaucrats governing it. Nixon wrote of the individuals he was forced to work with at the OPA, saying they "were obsessed with their own power . . . and seemed to delight in kicking other people around."[38]

As a result of his dissolution with civilian service, Nixon decided to apply for a commission in the navy. Nixon offered to serve his country despite the fact that, having been born a Quaker, he could have claimed exemption from the draft (in point of fact he was doubly exempt, as his employment with the federal government provided him an exemption as well). He was inducted into the navy in August 1942. It is an interesting aside that later in life Nixon would admit to having spent the years leading up to the war as an avowed isolationist. "In 1939 I thought Neville Chamberlin was the greatest living man and Winston Churchill a madman," he said. "It was not until years later that I realized Neville Chamberlain was a good man, but Winston Churchill was right."[39]

Nixon's years in the navy were enormously important in his development. As with all previous work he had set his mind to, he was enormously successful and was very popular with the troops. In a 1971 interview with reporters, Nixon himself described the importance of his time in the navy stating, "I grew up in the navy, because I had to."[40] Nixon was, for the first time in his life, exposed to a world much more like that to which most of us are used; prior to the navy he lived in Quaker Yorba Linda, worked feverishly at Duke, and in his months working for the federal government was so consumed by work that he had very little exposure to a world such as the navy. For the first time, Nixon was living in a world where swearing was endemic, drinking not only accepted but expected, and in thousands of other ways immensely different from the con- servative Quaker-dominated towns in which he grew up.

At the onset of the war, after completing his initial training and being commissioned a lieutenant (junior grade, or "JG"), Nixon was sent off to Ottumwa, Iowa, to help oversee the construction of an airfield for use in pilot training.[41] After a winter spent in Iowa (per- haps appropriate were the navy planning to send him to the arctic circle, quite a different story when so much of the navy was invested in the South Pacific), Nixon seized the opportunity for deployment overseas and found himself assigned to the South Pacific Combat Air Transport Command on the island of New Caledonia.[42]

During his time on New Caledonia Nixon and his unit were responsible for preparing manifests and flight plans for C-47 cargo planes, Nixon was responsible for supervising the loading and unloading of supplies and the wounded.[43] However, by the end of 1943 New Caledonia had fallen too far behind the advancing allied forces and Nixon and his unit were pushed forward to the Solomon Islands and the Bougainville airfield that had only fallen to American forces two months before his January 1944 arrival. In his unit's first month deployed at Bougainville, they endured

Japanese attacks for almost thirty nights. Despite being very much out of his element, or perhaps because of it, Nixon thrived during his time in the navy. He won multiple commendations and both the respect and admiration of many of the men with whom he served. Nixon was relaxed, at peace, and, in the eyes of the Department of the Navy, wonderfully efficient. While surely no one at Yorba Linda would have predicted it, Nixon and the navy were a match made in heaven. One junior officer with whom Nixon had served went on to describe his time at Bougainville as follows:

"He had no more rank than most of us, he was our age generally speaking, but he commanded a lot of respect from the guys with whom he came in contact. When things got a bit hectic, he never lost his head. No matter how badly things got fouled up, Dick got his part of the operation straightened out, and he did it without a lot of hullaballoo."[44]

During February 1944, Nixon and his unit moved to Green Island in the wake of a US invasion, and it was here where Nixon's legend amongst the men truly took hold. It turns out that the frugal Nixon found another outlet for his talent at managing supply and quite possibly put to use some of the talents he developed working for his father's grocery store. Nixon set up "Nick's Snack Shack," the lone hamburger stand of the South Pacific. Along with slinging free ground rounds to hungry flight crews, Nixon also swapped his stock for Australian beer, whiskey, fruit juice, and coffee that he would distribute equally to other officers regardless of their rank. As a fellow officer Ed McCaffrey described Nixon's skill at obtaining supplies for his operation: "Nick (Nixon) was able to wheedle the supplies for his Snack Shack from other outfits that were better stocked. Some of the stuff was, shall we say, 'liberated'—but Nick would swap anything. Just a small trade would set in motion a series of bigger trades."[45]

Obtaining better-quality food, and even the occasional booze, for the men was only the beginning of Nixon's service to his fellow soldiers. During his time on Green Island Nixon set up an informal school for the soldiers and sailors on the island, where he taught lectures on business law. He explained to them how to set up small-business corporations, how to draw up leases, and more. Nixon was particularly proud of the messages he received from the attendees of these "lessons," informing Nixon of the help they provided to these men in starting their own businesses.

The navy made equals out of Americans from all walks; and this was likely what made Nixon's time there so special for him. For the duration of the war it didn't matter whether he had grown up with money or not; it mattered not whether he was a Franklin or an Orthogonian. Nixon, for the duration of his time in the navy, could just be Nixon: the efficient, considerate, intelligent individual he was. Years later, Nixon's fellow enlisted men would compare him to Mr. Roberts, the beloved fictional naval lieutenant played by Henry Fonda, who time and again put the needs of his men before himself. It was Nixon's unparalleled hard work and discipline that endeared Nixon to his fellow enlisted men. The chip on his shoulder briefly disappeared, and Nixon's demons, perhaps for the only time in his life, were left behind.

In the navy, the conservative Nixon of Quaker upbringing who before becoming a seaman did not drink, smoke, or swear, became a card shark and added a gaming expansion to his burger shack. One of the young men deployed alongside Nixon, a Lieutenant James Stewart, recalled instructing Nixon on the playing of poker, during which time Nixon asked Stewart, "Is there any sure way to win at poker?" Stewart's response to Nixon might have had an oversize impact on Nixon going forward. Stewart's theory on poker was not to stay in a pot unless he was sure he held a winning hand. It would become readily apparent that Nixon's skills of observation, ability to hide his emotions, and first-rate brain made him a more than adequate poker player. Although he claimed that his poker playing enthusiasm was overblown, Nixon admitted that he once forfeited the chance to meet famed American aviator Charles Lindberg because of a card game he had promised to host. Nixon ascribed his decision to "the intense loneliness and boredom of the South Pacific,"[46] but more than a passion or a hobby to while the time away, poker was a character builder and a source of income for the artless Nixon. One man who served with Nixon said that he would play cards for hours upon hours and "a hundred navy officers will tell you that Nix never lost a cent at poker."[47] In fact, in his time in the service Nixon had managed to stockpile over $10,000 in winnings, which he would use to help finance his political aspirations.[48] In perhaps his most famous poker story from his time in the service, he was reportedly able to bluff a lieutenant commander on a $1,500 pot when he was holding but a pair of twos.[49]

When he returned stateside, Nixon's men threw a party on his behalf. In the words of one biographer, during his service in the Pacific, Nixon realized "his ability to understand the working-class perspective, its wants and needs, and its resentments proved invaluable in his subsequent political career."[50] After the Pacific theater Nixon spent several weeks' leave in Whittier, giving speeches to various clubs and church groups regarding his wartime experiences, and by all appearances positioning himself to run a future campaign against five-term Congressman Jeremiah "Jerry" Voorhis.

Now a lieutenant commander, Richard Nixon resigned his navy commission effective New Years Day 1946. In the months leading up to his discharge from the navy, he was consciously writing the Republican Party players in Rep. Voorhis's district, making himself available for the party's nomination against the incumbent. By all accounts, during the preceding campaign, the party nominated a political lightweight against Voorhis. As such, Nixon's timing was impeccable. Republicans needed a credible candidate against Voorhis, and Nixon, champion debater and war veteran, was nothing if not credible. Nixon was soon to meet his mentor Murray Chotiner and would begin his climb to the White House.

From the Nixon family homestead in Yorba Linda to his naval service, Nixon had been dogged in his determination to do something memorable despite his modest roots. In California's twelfth congressional district his determination was realized.

NOTES

1. Leonard Lurie, *The Running of Richard Nixon*, p. 15.
2. Conrad Black, *A Life in Full*, p. 8.
3. Fawn Brodie, *Richard Nixon: The Shaping of His Character*, p. 38.
4. Roger Morris, *Richard Milhous Nixon: The Rise of an American Politican*, p. 56.
5. Conrad Black, *A Life in Full*, p. 7.
6. Ibid. pp. 7–11.
7. Wayne Karol, *Across the Great Divide: Nixon, Clinton, and the War of the Sixties*, p. 22.
8. Leonard Lurie, *The Running of Richard Nixon*, p. 19.
9. Ibid.
10. Fawn Brodie, *Richard Nixon: The Shaping of His Character*, p. 53.
11. Conrad Black, *A Life in Full*, p. 14.
12. Rick Perlstein, *Nixonland*, p. 22.
13. Fawn Brodie, *Richard Nixon: The Shaping of His Character*, p. 33.
14. Ibid. p. 73.
15. Ibid. p. 78.
16. March Butz, *Yorba Linda: Its History*, p. 153.
17. Stephen Ambrose, *Nixon: The Education of a Politician*, p. 46.
18. Conrad Black, *A Life in Full*, p. 23.
19. Ibid. pp. 29–30.
20. Ibid. 30.
21. Rick Perlstein, *Nixonland*, p. 22.
22. Fawn Brodie, *Richard Nixon: The Shaping of His Character*, p. 114.
23. Ibid. p. 115.
24. Ibid. p. 45.
25. Ibid. p. 112.
26. March Butz, *Yorba Linda: Its History*, p. 154.
27. Rick Perlstein, *Nixonland*, p. 23.
28. March Butz, *Yorba Linda: Its History*, p. 154.
29. Ibid.
30. Conrad Black, *A Life in Full*, p. 35.

31. Ibid.
32. Fawn Brodie, *Richard Nixon: The Shaping of His Character*, p. 132.
33. Conrad Black, *A Life in Full*, p. 39.
34. Leonard Lurie, *The Running of Richard Nixon*, p. 33.
35. Conrad Black, *A Life in Full*, p. 41.
36. Ibid. p. 42.
37. Ibid.
38. Ibid. p. 56.
39. Fawn Brodie, *Richard Nixon: The Shaping of His Character*, p. 163.
40. Stephen Ambrose, *Nixon: The Education of a Politician*, p. 105.
41. Ibid. p. 106.
42. Ibid. p. 106–107.
43. Ibid. p. 108.
44. William Costello, *The Facts About Nixon*, p. 31.
45. Stephen Ambrose, *Nixon: The Education of a Politician*, p. 110.
46. Richard Nixon, *The Memoirs of Richard Nixon*, p. 29.
47. William Costello, *The Facts About Nixon*, p. 31.
48. Leonard Lurie, *The Running of Richard Nixon*, p. 41.
49. Conrad Black, *A Life in Full*, p. 61.
50. Edmund Kallina, *Kennedy v. Nixon*, p. 43.

CHAPTER THREE

MURRAY AND THE MOB

"Wherever you find Murray Chotiner, there is a trail of blood behind."
—Capt. Weinberger, Reagan's defense secretary.[1]

A s a nineteen-year-old staffer for President Nixon in 1972, the youngest member of the staff (excluding Young Voters for the President), part of my responsibility was to receive a daily news summary, which Pat Buchanan's shop at the White House compiled by 7 a.m. by scouring the daily newspapers and teletypes to prepare for the president, the vice president, White House Chief of Staff Haldeman, and the White House senior staff. It went first to Jeb Magruder's office (he was a California marketing guy, pulled in through Haldeman to run the Committee to Re-elect the President, which we abbreviated as CRP, but the media would later dub CREEP), and then to the office of Fred LaRue, a lanky and taciturn Mississippi Republican who had been part of the crowd that snatched the nomination for Goldwater and was by 1972 a close confidant of Attorney General John Mitchell. From there, I took it to Robert Mardian, who had been an assistant attorney general under Mitchell and was his eyes and ears at CRP. Later in the campaign, Fred Malek would join my distribution list. He was sent by White House Chief of Staff Bob Haldeman to keep an eye on Jeb

Magruder. I remember that when I delivered to Fred at 7:20 a.m. each morning, he was in his office but always in his stocking feet. I liked him.

The best part of my job was hand delivering a copy of it to the small, dark, secret office of Murray Chotiner, located catty-corner from the White House in a different building from CRP. Murray was not on the directory, and his door didn't even have a number. Chotiner, a portly Jewish attorney originally from Pittsburgh, had moved west with his brother. They prospered as criminal defense attorneys mostly for Mob guys. Murray and his brother had represented over 221 hoodlums in one year. More importantly, Chotiner was the first "political consultant." Murray Chotiner understood how to communicate systems and the need to push simple and understandable, *mostly negative*, messages to the voters. Chotiner would be present for the duration of Nixon's political career; although at many points hidden in the shadows, he was always only a phone call away.

Chotiner's secretary didn't get in until 8 a.m., and I knew if I delivered the news summary at 7:45 a.m., Murray himself would answer the door. After making my third delivery to him in person, Chotiner asked me my name, where I was from, and how the hell I got my job. I told him I was a proud protégé of Connecticut Governor John Lodge and that I loved Richard Nixon. He smiled, and our relationship bloomed.

Murray was paunchy with dark, wavy hair and deep circles under his eyes. He was always wearing an expensive suit and usually a Jack Ruby–type fedora. The best way to describe Murray was rumpled; he had a penchant for silk ties and jeweled stickpins, described by the *New York Times* as a man who "buys good clothes, but manages to wear them in such a way that he looks more like an accountant or an instructor in a technical school."[2] He was unkempt but expensively dressed with a cigar frequently clenched between his teeth. I can still remember Murray with a salami sandwich in one hand and the racing form in the other. Frequently, his tie was stained with cigar ashes.

It was from Chotiner that Dick Nixon learned the dark arts of politics. Murray was *the* pioneer. His theory was simple: Make every election about the other guy. Identify his weakest point and pound on it relentlessly. Attack morning, noon, and night. Attack, attack, attack, never defend, always pivot and attack. Chotiner drilled this into the green Nixon, and it was, by 1960, ingrained in the future president's blood.

"Attack, attack, attack, never defend," was the Chotiner mantra that I would adopt for Stone's Rules, my own list of axioms regarding the practice of politics and life. Chotiner "didn't mind accepting the fact that politics is shabby most of the time, filled with lies and deceptions," Nixon's future White House counsel Len Garment later said.[3]

Fresh from the war, Nixon, a political neophyte, enlisted Chotiner for his run for congress against five-term incumbent Horace Jeremiah "Jerry" Voorhis. Chotiner was the only paid Nixon staffer on the '46 campaign, netting $500 as a consultant after giving Dick a perfunctory inspection. Chotiner had previously masterminded Earl Warren's run for governor of California and at the time was running William Knowland's senatorial campaign. Chotiner had served as field director for Warren and when given credit for constructing the Nixon image would retort, "The real man I created was Earl Warren." This drove Warren crazy.

Warren despised Chotiner. Although not displeased with his overwhelming victories in *both* major party primaries (California had this strange cross-filing system in which candidates could run, despite their party affiliation, in the other parties primary— a relic from the reform period of progressive Governor Hiram Johnson), which Chotiner had engineered. But Chotiner's aggressiveness and tactics appalled the starchy Warren. Chotiner would ultimately mastermind Nixon's way onto the Eisenhower ticket, which thwarted Warren's own ambition to be president. Even after

Chotiner was briefly made the general counsel of the Office of the Special Representative for Trade Negotiations on the White House staff, Warren would never be in the same room as him. But Chotiner did in fact create him.

Nixon major domo Bob Haldeman disliked Murray because the old man was one of the few who could contact Nixon directly and needed no appointment. Chotiner would handle ornate ballot security efforts for the 1968 race, dubbed "Operation Eagle Eye," designed to ensure that the kind of voter theft that had defeated Nixon in Illinois and Texas in 1960 did not happen again. Beyond that, few knew exactly what Chotiner did, but everyone knew Murray had the president's private phone number and that he and Nixon spoke late at night after "the old man" had a few belts.

In 1956, not long after Nixon's ascension to the vice presidency, Chotiner got jammed up for influence peddling and became a target for Senate Labor Committee Counsel Robert Kennedy. Kennedy was probing organized crime connections in the labor movement and accused Chotiner of influence peddling. Congressional investigator and Kennedy operative Carmine Bellino, a constant foil to Nixon who would later order the bugging of Nixon's hotel room on behalf of Kennedy prior to the 1960 debate, discovered a $5,000 check made out to "M. Chotiner" from a New Jersey uniform manufacturer convicted of defrauding the government.[4] Murray tried to explain away the check and dodge the Senate Subcommittee on Investigations, but Bellino, dogged in his pursuit, found an informant who further contextualized Chotiner's dealings. "The informant," Bellino recalled, "stated that Chotiner had been engaged because of his friendship with Nixon and Deputy Attorney General William Rogers, and he was expected to help in connection with the tax case then being considered for possible prosecution by the Department of Justice . . ."[5] Although Murray would beat the rap, Chotiner's name would be irreversibly damaged, and it required him to operate in the background in the 1958 and 1960 campaigns. Still, Murray would be in Nixon's suite and try to console the angry candidate when Nixon flamed out in the 1962 California governors race. Murray was not present at any of the seminal meetings regarding Nixon's nascent 1968 comeback, but he would always be there, lurking in the shadows.

It is clear that Chotiner had a career-long influence on Nixon. Haldeman hated him because he could always get through to Nixon and couldn't be blocked. The rest of the White House feared him. He had a White House pass and senior mess privileges at the "Casa Blanca" as the Nixon men called it.

During the Nixon-Voorhis run, Chotiner was an effective political operative. Young Nixon excelled at public speaking and debating. Murray took the callow, young Nixon and showed him the bag of tricks. Chotiner had a fourteen-thousand-word word treatise on political operations and tactics he would use to teach to future political operatives in Republican Party training schools that gave insight on the early campaigns of Richard Nixon.

Chotiner's political chops are covered well in *The Facts about Nixon* by William Costello:

> Chotiner was one of the fathers of the new synthetic Madison Avenue-style politics in America. For years Hollywood had shown what could be done with movie stars and crooners by conditioning and manipulating attitudes. The early crudities of press gentry had over the years been refined. Big business had added respectability by pioneering market research, opinion polling, mass advertising and the niceties of product identification. Chotiner's discovery was that, by choosing an acceptable stereotype, a political personality could also be packaged and merchandised without reference to any of the serious issues of life and politics.

To wage a successful campaign, you must begin "one full year ahead," Chotiner prescribed, "because you need that time to deflate your opposition . . . There are many people who say we don't want that kind of campaign in our state. They say we want to conduct a constructive campaign and point out the merits of our own candidate. I say to you in all sincerity that, if you do not deflate the opposition candidate before your own candidate gets started, the odds are that you are going to be doomed to defeat."[6]

The manifesto also gave perspective on the fair use of what his opponents would call "dirty tricks."

"What is the difference between legitimate attack and smear? It is not a smear if you please, if you point out the record of your opponent . . . of course, it is always a smear, naturally, when it is directed to our own candidate."[7]

Murray was a maven for research. "Find out everything you can. Canvass their neighbors. Go through their garbage. Have your opponent followed. Everyone has something. Find it. Sift their voting records—look for damaging votes or votes that can be made to sound damaging. Go to the newspaper morgues and dig up every word the son of a bitch has ever said. Reduce the quotes to index cards. Sort them by subject. Look for inconsistencies and contradictions. Pull their deeds and access their mortgages. Grease the local police and find out what they know. Find something to hit 'em with," Murray told me while gnawing on the end of a cigar. Murray was the early king of "oppo research."

Although single-minded when necessary, Chotiner was a supremely practical pol. His rough tactics were to win votes, not aggravate the opposition, although he understood they would have that effect. Chotiner had nothing but disdain for the sophomoric "dirty tricks" of the 1972 campaign. "It's not about pissing off your opponent, it's about winning votes. A hundred percent of your time should be spent pummeling your opponent to the mat and never letting him up. If your energies and resources aren't used for winning votes, what is the point?"

Chotiner later thought the UCLA and USC frat boys around Nixon—like Haldeman and Ehrlichman and their underlings— lost sight of the ball. "A real candy-ass," said Murray of Magruder. "Those guys are going to get Dick in trouble one day."

Chotiner reserved special disdain for White House counselor Charles "Chuck" Colson, a toughtalking ex-marine who had come to the White House from the staff of Massachusetts Senator Leverett Saltonstall. Colson's strategies about how to woo Catholics, unions, and other key elements of the silent majority appealed to Nixon. While Colson wooed the Teamsters for a 1972 endorsement, Chotiner quietly brokered the deal in which the prison sentence of imprisoned Teamster official Jimmy Hoffa would be commuted and Hoffa would be barred from future union activity to the delight of the mobsters who had taken firm control of the union in Hoffa's absence.

Colson's love of intrigue and dirty tricks appealed to Nixon's dark side. Colson also had access to Nixon, which was granted through Nixon's instructions to Haldeman. "He's a total phony," Chotiner told me. "Half the shit he says in memos he's doing never gets done. He's bullshitting Dick and seeking to expand his empire," the paunchy pol told me. Chotiner particularly hated Colson's tendency to question the loyalty to Nixon of anyone who disagreed with his plans.

* * *

Chotiner maintained many strange relationships. In his biography, Senator Lowell Weicker of Connecticut, who excoriated Nixon on the Senate Watergate Committee, maintained a cordial relationship with Murray. In his biography he recalled an olive branch Chotiner had extended him in a 1970 Senate race:

> Before Dodd announced his candidacy, I was approached by Murray Chotiner, who was best known as a longtime hatchet man for Richard Nixon. Chotiner did not enjoy a savory reputation in Washington, but for one reason or another he had been good to me. When I opposed Nixon on any issue, or from time to time said things as a House member that weren't complimentary, Chotiner always took up my cause in the White House. He was not just a friend but a good friend.

Chotiner came to me and said, "Lowell, if you would like, we will encourage Tom Dodd to get in this race. Do you think you can profit by a three-way race?" The idea was that Dodd would siphon Democratic votes from Duffy.

I said, "Listen, Murray, I don't want you guys laying a finger on this race, I don't want you doing anything. Nothing; I can win on my own. I don't need a three-way race." Chotiner said, "If that's your wish, I'll convey it."[8]

Murray handled the Senate race quite differently than Weicker thought. Chotiner told me in a lecture about the dynamics of a three-way race that he had funneled cash to Tom Dodd, the hard-line anti-Communist Democratic senator from Connecticut who had been censured by the US Senate and was running for his seat as an Independent.

Dodd had been a congressman and one of the Nuremburg prosecutors. He had the profile of a Roman senator with wavy, silver hair. He always wore a watch fob and chain and pocket watch in the breast pocket of his suit. He chewed cigars more than smoked them but his topcoat was still often flecked with ashes. Murray told me that two suitcases of cash were delivered to a lawyer from Connecticut in the lobby of the Mayflower Hotel. Murray bragged that the handoff was made while J. Edgar Hoover was lunching only feet away, eating his daily fruit salad and coffee in the Town & Country lounge with his live-in deputy Clyde Tolson. Murray said the money came up from Miami sent from Charles "Bebe" Rebozo, Miami millionaire and Nixon's best friend, who I later learned kept secret bank accounts for "RN," as all the older Nixon guys who had been around in the '60 and '62 campaigns called him.

Weicker thinks he won on his own. In actuality, he won because Tom Dodd, fueled by money from Murray Chotiner, got 25 percent, draining Democratic votes from dove Democrat Joe Duffey.

Nixon aide Pat Hillings had considerable insight on Chotiner and his role in the birth of the modern American political consultant:

Murray Chotiner was among the first of the political consultants which are now so popular, or unpopular, as the case may be. Recent books have come out attacking political consultants in campaigns and that sort of thing. In those days, most work was done by volunteers. But now political consultants are the dominant theme, along with the media in the campaigns. Murray Chotiner was one of the first. He was a lawyer, a brilliant lawyer, from Beverly Hills. But who was always interested in politics. He did not feel that he had the appeal to run for office himself, although he tried it once and lost. But he became an advisor to various city officials, and was quite successful.

So when the time came to find someone to help Richard Nixon run for the Senate, a lot of his friends in Los Angeles said to bring in Murray Chotiner. So Murray Chotiner was the paid manager of the campaign. But often the pay was pretty small and I still think he made his living primarily as a lawyer, at least at that point. And he was tough. When I say tough, I don't mean dirty or mean. But Murray was a very aggressive, hard driving fellow. And he tried to encourage Nixon to take more aggressive stands on issues and to work harder, at least work harder in attacking the opposition.

He was a mechanic, a nuts and bolts man. He found, for instance, that Nixon was reading letters in the car as he'd be driving, and signing the letters, letters going out to people thanking them for their help. And he took them away from him. He said the only thing he should be doing in that car is thinking of his next speech. And he did all kinds of things like that that were based on detail. But Murray Chotiner became a very effective fellow and was probably the smartest and most experienced political operative in the Nixon campaign at that time.[9]

The initial task before Nixon and Chotiner was not easy. Jerry Voorhis was a tough nut to crack. He was a straight-shooting New Dealer, an idealist, and generally a moderate. Chotiner initially could not locate an effective point of attack. "We don't have enough meat!" Chotiner griped to Nixon early in the campaign.[10] Murray would come up with the plan that worked. Careful never to say that Voorhis was a Communist, Nixon merely asked, "Is Voorhis a Communist?"

Murray came up with the strategy of causing confusion between a pro-Soviet labor lobbying union, the CIO-PAC (Political Action Committee of the Congress of Industrial Organizations) and the NC-PAC (National Citizens Political Action Committee), a liberal organization that, ironically, a then liberal Ronald Reagan belonged to. The NC-PAC had publicly endorsed Voorhis and contributed donations to his campaign. Nixon implied that the incumbent had taken contributions from the Communists. The false claim that Voorhis was tied with the militant communist union was reiterated in pro-Nixon publications, on leaflets, and through telephone lines.

Nixon himself would remember the PAC dupery in his 1978 personal narrative *The Memoirs of Richard Nixon*:

> The PAC had been established as a political arm of organized labor to support Franklin Roosevelt in the 1944 election. A sister organization, the National Citizens Political Action Committee (NCPAC), was set up to permit non-union participation. Until his death, labor leader Sidney Hillman served as chairman of both groups, and many other leaders of CIO-PAC also served on NCPAC. Both groups interviewed candidates and then made funds and campaign workers available to those whom they endorsed. It was estimated that in 1944 the two PAC organizations contributed over $650,000 to political campaigns. Although the leadership of both groups was non-Communist, the organizations were known to be infiltrated with Communists and fellow travelers who, because of their discipline, wielded an influence disproportionate to their numbers. Such influence was viewed as a problem because there was an emerging concern about Soviet postwar intentions and a corresponding apprehension about the communist movement in America.
>
> Voorhis had been endorsed by CIO-PAC in 1944. In 1946, however, CIO-PAC decided to withhold its endorsement—ostensibly because he had not supported some measures in Congress considered important by the union leadership. In the spring of 1946,

the Los Angeles County chapter of the NCPAC circulated a bulletin indicating that it was going to endorse Voorhis regardless of what CIO-PAC did. The May 31, 1946, issue of *Daily People's World*, the West Coast Communist newspaper, ran an article with the headline: "Candidates Endorsed by Big Five." The "Big Five" labor and progressive coalition was made up of CIOPAC, NCPAC, the railroad brotherhoods, the Progressive AFL, and the Hollywood Independent Citizens Committee of the Arts, Sciences, and Professions. The *Daily People's World* article reported that the Big Five had interviewed the candidates and included the list of endorsements for the June 4 primary. The first name on the list was H. Jerry Voorhis. Following his name was this note: "No CIO endorsement." In answer, then, to the charge that he was endorsed by PAC, Voorhis had replied that he was not that year—endorsed by CIO-PAC. To me that was an irrelevancy.

When the question was raised in the South Pasadena debate, I pulled from my pocket a copy of the NCPAC bulletin announcing its endorsement recommendation and walked across the stage to show it to Voorhis. Reading aloud the names of the board members of each organization, many of which were the same, I demonstrated that there was little practical difference between a CIO-PAC endorsement and an NCPAC one.

Voorhis repeated his claim that CIO-PAC and NCPAC were separate organizations, but I could tell from the audience's reaction that I had made my point. A few days later Voorhis himself underscored it by sending a telegram to NCPAC headquarters in New York requesting, "whatever qualified endorsement the Citizens PAC may have given me be withdrawn." Had he repudiated the endorsement before he was backed onto the defensive and forced to act, the issue might never have developed. But since he had not, I thought then, and still think, that the endorsement was a legitimate issue to raise.

After this debate, the PAC became a peripheral but heated issue in the campaign. While Voorhis equivocated, my campaign director, Harrison McCall, came up with the idea of passing out plastic thimbles saying: "Nixon for Congress—Put the Needle in the PAC."[11]

That Murray was the senior partner in the new relationship was clear from the following excerpt from Nixon's memoirs:

> This first "debate" was so successful that many of my support-
> ers urged me to challenge Voorhis to other joint appearances. I
> had some reservations, because each one would require two or
> three days of concentrated preparation, and I did not want to take
> off any more time from campaigning. Murray Chotiner, the bril-
> liant and no-nonsense public relations man who was running Bill
> Knowland's senatorial campaign and advising me part-time on
> mine, went straight to the point. "Dick," he said, "you're running
> behind, and when you're behind, you don't play it safe. You must
> run a high-risk campaign." He paused for a moment until I nod-
> ded my agreement, and then he said, "Good. I've already arranged
> for an announcement challenging Voorhis to more debates."[12]

Chotiner knew that Nixon was a first-class debater and that Voorhis would confidently agree to a series of debates against the unknown Nixon. Chotiner also knew that the debates would be a forum where Nixon had nothing to lose and Voorhis had nothing to gain. From the opening argument, Chotiner's gamble paid off. Nixon had Voorhis on his heels. Nixon, remembered in later years for awkward gesticulation, was, in his school years, a thespian. In his debates against Voorhis, Nixon utilized his acting chops, debating skill, and the charge-first tactics of Chotiner. "Voorhis found himself sinking as he made fruitless attempts to answer his opponent's hydra-headed charges," wrote Nixon biographer Leonard Lurie. "Voorhis was generally ineffective in his answers. On the other hand, the young attorney from Whittier was so vig-orous, so condemning and his past was so vacant, so spotlessly blameless."[13]

Upon arrival to one debate, two months before Election Day, the audience members, half of who were organized by and strategi-cally planted in the auditorium by Chotiner, were given a two-page handout titled "Facts about Jerry Voorhis." The pamphlet tied the congressman to both Socialism and the CIO-PAC.[14] Nixon took to the stage following Voorhis's opening remark, pulled the NCPAC endorsement out of his pocket, and stalked the incumbent congressman across the stage asking him to comment on the allegations. A shocked Voorhis returned to his podium and read the endorsement aloud. He then stated that there was confusion between the two organizations, which elicited a cacophony of deafening boos from the crowd and a vehement denial by Nixon.

Voorhis, back to the ropes, never regained his balance. Voorhis would lose the election by fifteen thousand votes and later write that Nixon was "quite a ruthless opponent '[with] one cardinal and unbreakable rule of conduct' [which was] to win, whatever it [took] to do it."[15]

Nixon would confirm Voorhis's charge of ruthlessness. "Of course," Nixon said, "I know Jerry Voorhis wasn't a Communist . . . I suppose there was scarcely ever a man with higher ideals than Jerry Voorhis, or better motivated . . . but . . . I had to win. That's the thing you don't understand. The important thing is to win."[16]

To those who hate robo calls from politicians, they have Murray Chotiner to thank for the "campaign innovation." Chotiner used the telephone like a weapon. Many prospective voters during the race would be treated to an anonymous caller. "This is a friend of yours," the call began, "but I can't tell you who I am. Did you know that Jerry Voorhis is a communist?"[17] The call would then end abruptly.

To beat Voorhis, Nixon had benefited mightily from the red-baiting tactics of Chotiner. However, there was a darker truth to the victory of '46. Murray and his brother Jack had for years been involved in a general practice law firm that represented clients who were anything but general. A 1956 congressional probe unearthed records that found the Chotiner brothers, in one four-year stretch, had handled at least 221 bookmaking cases.[18] In almost all of these cases the "bookies" represented by the Chotiners got off with a suspended sentence or a slap on the wrist.[19]

The *Los Angeles Times* propagated that the Nixon campaign expenses totaled $370,[20] $130 less than Chotiner was reportedly paid, and $630 less than Nixon's opponent reportedly spent. Cash and services were taken in from many off-the-book donors. With campaign finance reporting laws virtually nonexistent in 1950, these figures were wildly misleading.

We have already established the money from the Eastern establishment that was funneled into the '46 campaign, but there was also a steady flow of underworld cash facilitated by Chotiner, for he was on intimate terms with Los Angeles Mob boss Mickey Cohen. Cohen, an ex-boxer and colorful gangster portrayed by Sean Penn in the movie *Gangster Squad*, a mobster short in both stature and temper, was approached by Murray and asked to provide for the campaign. Cohen was Meyer Lansky's man on the West Coast and ruled the Los Angeles mob with an iron fist. He was a vicious killer who had murdered a bookmaker named Maxie Shaman a year prior.[21]

According to Cohen, "In addition to helping Mr. Nixon financially, I made arrangements to rent a headquarters for Nixon in the Pacific Finance Building at Eighth and Olive Streets in Los Angeles, which was the same building occupied by Attorney Sam Rummel. We posted Nixon signs and literature, and I paid for the headquarters for three to four weeks in that building. During the period that I ran the Nixon Headquarters, I contacted most of the gambling fraternity who started him off with $25,000."[22]

In 1960, Cohen and fellow mobster Camel Humphreys would storm out of a Chicago meeting with other mob chieftains, and JFK's father, Ambassador Joseph Kennedy, tried to put the bite on the mob boys for money and muscle for JFK's campaign. They were invested in Nixon and contributed to him. Both Nixon and Kennedy got mob money in 1960. Kennedy would get the muscle as well, as we shall see. The Mob would not wait long to cash in on favors doled out to Nixon for the 1946 congressional race.

A year after his victory, Nixon would be told that low-level mob functionary Jack Ruby would need employment. Ruby had just moved from Sam Giancana's Chicago territory to Carlos Marcello's New Orleans turf and would collect a paycheck, tucked away on the House Un-American Activities Committee, an investigative committee created to uncover communist ties within the United States. Ruby's hire was also a favor for Lyndon Johnson, at that point a congressman, who did favors for Marcello through bagman Jack Halfen.

* * *

Setting the Mafia element of the '46 campaign aside, Chotiner's tact to destroy Voorhis on his "red" ties *had* worked, and though the trumped-up charges against Voorhis were unfounded, Nixon took the threat of Communist infiltration seriously. Anti-Communism as a creed would serve Nixon well. He won his nationwide anti-Communist credentials by unmasking FDR protégé, State Department employee Alger Hiss as a Soviet spy. In many ways, the Hiss case would forge Nixon's understanding of the mass media of the day and just how quickly one could become "an overnight sensation."

On August 3, 1948, Whittaker Chambers, a pudgy and waxen-looking editor at *Time* magazine, took the stand before the House Un-American Activities Committee (HUAC) and plainly stated that Harvard-educated diplomat Alger Hiss, who was at FDR's right sleeve at Yalta and was a friend of both Secretary of State Dean Acheson and Adali Stevenson, was a Communist while working for the US government. Chambers, who had been a passionate Communist for fourteen years before deserting the party, claimed to have belonged to a sleeper cell of government employees and said that he recognized Hiss, amongst others, as a member of the group.[23] A defiant Hiss denied the charges and requested an opportunity to testify before the committee.

In front of HUAC on August 5, 1948, Hiss was asked by Nixon for the name of the person who had recommended he come to Washington. Hiss rather slyly flipped the script, proposing that Nixon was only asking for a name to further fuel the Red Scare with an innocent American.

"Is it necessary?" Hiss asked Nixon. "There are so many witnesses who use names loosely before your committee?"[24] Hiss would treat Nixon with elitist disdain.

Hiss proceeded to chip away at Nixon's education and background, which fed into Nixon's Eastern resentment. Hiss may have been suspected of Communist leanings, but he was also Ivy League. It was Nixon, Hiss implied, who was the outsider.

"I am a graduate of Harvard Law School," Hiss said defiantly. "And I believe yours is Whittier?"[25]

Hiss was then shown a photograph of Whittaker Chambers, held up by Robert Stripling, HUAC's Chief Investigator. "If this is a picture of Mr. Chambers," Hiss said to the delight of his powerful friends in the room, "he is not particularly unusual looking. He looks like a lot of people. I might even mistake him for the Chairman of this Committee."[26]

The media and committee members in the room rushed to congratulate Hiss at the conclusion of the testimony. "He had won the day completely," Nixon later wrote. "It would not be an exaggeration to say that probably ninety percent of the reporters at the press table and most of the committee members were convinced that a terrible mistake had been made, a case of mistaken identity, and that the Committee owed an apology to Hiss for having allowed Chambers to testify without first checking into the possibility of such a mistake."[27] It would be the beginnings of a decade-long crusade by the liberal media to defend, and later, to exonerate Hiss.

According to Nixon, Hiss put on "a virtuoso performance," but he also thought Hiss was bluffing. Hiss, in Nixon's estimation, was overstating his case and had been a bit too "mouthy,"[28] yet he "had been careful never to state categorically that he did not know Whittaker Chambers."[29] Nixon believed he could prove Hiss and Chambers knew each other.

When Nixon got Chambers back in front of the committee, he elicited many important details from the portly magazine editor that only a man who knew Hiss could provide. The pet names Hiss and his wife used in each other's company, the shelter they brought their dog to, and most importantly, a 1929 Ford car Hiss had donated to the Communist Party. Chambers said from 1936 to 1937 he was constantly in contact with Hiss and sometimes stayed over his house, which Chambers called a "kind of headquarters." Hiss was "the closest friend I ever had in the Communist Party," said Chambers.[30]

"The story checked out in every detail where corroborative evidence was available," said Nixon.[31]

When the committee again questioned Hiss on August 16, his story changed. Backed by new evidence, no longer was the picture of Chambers unrecognizable. Chambers, Hiss now believed, resembled a man he once knew named George Crosley, a man who, in Hiss's words, "was a writer."

"He hoped to sell articles to magazines about the munitions industry," Hiss recalled.[32] Hiss said he *had* lent the man cash, provided him shelter, and bequeathed him his dinged-up Ford. But Hiss said he did not believe that this man Crosley was Whittaker Chambers.[33]

Nixon felt Hiss was back peddling and wanted to strike before he had time to regain balance. "The obvious thing to do then was to confront these two men," Nixon said, "since it was apparent that both men must know each other in view of the testimony we had."[34] The very next day, Hiss and Chambers met before the subcommittee in a suite of the Commodore Hotel in New York City.

Hiss, who had such a difficult time identifying Chambers only two weeks prior, was now faced with a litany of details coloring in the relationship between the two men and, indeed, with Chambers himself. Hiss backed further into his lies. "The ass under the lion's skin is Crosley," Hiss proclaimed, admitting now that he knew Chambers, but only as Crosley and not as a Communist. "I have no further question at all. If he had lost both eyes and taken his nose off, I would be sure."[35] Disgusted, Hiss proclaimed that Chambers should repeat his claims in a public forum, where they would be deemed libelous.

Chambers would take up Hiss's challenge and on August 27 appeared on the radio program *Meet the Press*, declaring that "Alger Hiss was a Communist and may be now."[36] Hiss, perhaps distressed over Chambers' public assertion, went weeks without taking action or making a statement. "Mr. Hiss himself has created a situation in which he is obliged to put up or shut up," declared an article in the *Washington Post*.[37] Hiss eventually would take action, seeking $75,000 in damages in a defamation of character lawsuit. Hiss's lawyers demanded proof to confirm his accusations.

On November 17, Chambers obliged and produced four notes in Hiss's handwriting and sixty-five typewritten copies of State Department documents that had been copied on Hiss's typewriter.

On December 2, pushed for even more evidence, Chambers and two HUAC investigators went to retrieve it. "At about 10 o'clock that night, three men came out of the back door of a white farmhouse on Pipe Creek Farm off Bachman Valley Road near Westminster headed for a small pumpkin patch," journalist Gilbert Sandler wrote in the *Baltimore Sun*. "When they arrived at a particular pumpkin, one of the men, the short and stout one, bent down and removed the lid of the hollowed-out gourd. To the amazement of the other two, he reached in and pulled out several cylinders containing rolls of microfilm."[38]

There were five strips of microfilm, some of which contained photographs of State Department documents, which contained the unique imprint of the Hiss typewriter. As the evidence mounted, Hiss was indicted for perjury.

Chambers asked HUAC investigator Robert Stripling to find the typewriter, and when Hiss arrived for trial in the summer of 1949, the Woodstock machine, serial no. N230099, was set on a table before him. "It had a powerful psychological impact," Hiss said, "...sitting there like a murder weapon."[39] Hiss though denounced the papers and claimed they were forgeries. "Even his most ardent supporters could not swallow such a ridiculous charge," Nixon later said. "A typewriter is, as you know, almost the same as a fingerprint. It is impossible, according to experts in the field, to duplicate exactly the characteristics of one typewriter by manufacturing another."[40]

Hiss was convicted on two counts of perjury and sentenced to five years in prison.

The case made Nixon a political star overnight. American liberals who hated Nixon have argued, particularly after Watergate, that Nixon smeared an innocent man in his climb to the top. "I have often thought that my liberal friends in the Eastern establishment—of which I have been a part—could never forgive him for being right about Alger Hiss," said Nixon speechwriter Ray Price.[41]

We now know however, that KGB files attained after the fall of the Soviet Union proved that Hiss was a spy and that Nixon's instincts were correct. In 1996, translations of decrypted Soviet cables were released, detailing atomic-era spies in America. One of the spies pinpointed in the cables, code named "Ales," was thought by many to be Alger Hiss.[42] Alexander Vassiliev, a former KGB officer and journalist, who for two years labored over declassified Stalin-era KGB files, later confirmed the suspicion.[43]

While the Hiss case and Nixon's role in it would win the animosity of liberal elites and large swathes of the left-leaning media of the day, it would also win him millions of adherents and admirers. This anti-Communist base, when combined with organizational Republicans, sustained Nixon through it all. When he was under fire as Eisenhower's vice presidential running mate in the famous "Secret Funds Scandal," it was the anti-Communist and

Republican base that remained by this side. It was this base that allowed him to be picked as Ike's VP to begin with. It was this base that allowed him to come within an eyelash of being president in 1960 and from which he launched his 1968 comeback. It was the same 30 percent base in the country that stuck with him through Watergate and to whom he pitched his rehabilitation after avoiding prison through a presidential pardon.

Mobster Mickey Cohen came through for Nixon again in 1950 when one of California's US Senate seats opened up with the surprise retirement of Senator Sheridan Downey. Hollywood Congresswoman Helen Gahagan Douglas, the wife of actor Melvyn Douglas and a close friend of Eleanor Roosevelt, and Nixon would emerge as the two contenders. It was a slugfest.

Cohen convened a meeting at the Hollywood Knickerbocker Hotel on North Ivar Avenue, Hollywood, to which he invited more than several hundred associates from the gambling business, some of whom flew in from Las Vegas. Cohen was later to say, "There wasn't a legitimate person in the room." Attending a meeting were representatives of Meyer Lansky, Los Angeles mobster Jack Dragna, and representatives of the Cleveland mob including John Scalish and Jewish mobster Bill Presser, whose son, Jackie Presser, would parley his relationship with Ronald Reagan into the presidency of the International Brotherhood of Teamsters.[44]

Cohen would later write that the goal for the evening was $75,000 for Nixon's coffers from his crime and gambling associates and that he ordered the doors locked when the group came up $20,000 short, refusing to let anyone leave until the financial goal was met.

Nixon had met with Cohen who dominated the Los Angeles mob scene for Lansky while Benjamin "Bugsy" Siegel watched Lansky's business in the growing Las Vegas, as early as 1946 at Goodfellow's Grotto, a fish restaurant in Orange County where the booths were private and politics could be talked frankly.

Cohen made it clear that the orders to help Nixon in 1950 came from "back East," meaning New York boss Frank Costello and Meyer Lansky, both of whom set up the National Mob Syndicate.

On the Democratic side, a glamorous former movie actress who had starred in light opera, on Broadway, and in Hollywood, Congresswoman Helen Gahagan Douglas, the wife of actor Melvyn Douglas, would face off with conservative Democrat Manchester Boddy, the publisher of the *Los Angeles Daily News*, in the Democratic primary. Nixon would exploit the bloody primary in which Boddy insinuated that the left-leaning Mrs. Douglas was sympathetic to the Communists. Chotiner picked up the theme.

Douglas would make an error she would live to regret. She would tie Nixon to Congressman Vito Marcantonio from Harlem, a pro-Communist radical claiming a "Nixon-Marcantonio Axis." On every key vote Nixon stood with party hard-liner Marcantonio against America in its fight to defeat Communism," she said.[45] She printed a flyer with the charge on yellow paper.[46] Mrs. Douglas began the red-baiting in the 1950 campaign.

Chotiner would then compare the voting records of Congresswoman Douglas and Marcantonio, claiming they were kindred souls, but Murray did it on *pink* paper. Marcantonio was a pro-Stalin leftist hard-liner. In truth, Marcantonio disliked the socially pretentious Mrs. Douglas and had gotten drunk with Nixon on more than one occasion when they served together on a House subcommittee. "Tell Nicky [Nixon] to get on this thing because it is a good idea," Marcantonio would tell a Nixon associate, giving his approval to review the records.[47]

Chotiner claimed, "Mrs. Douglas has voted with the notorious Communist hard-liner 86 percent of the time. She votes the Moscow line."

"She's pink right down to her underwear," Nixon would say on the stump.

Nixon and Chotiner had carefully studied the 1948 campaign of Miami's playboy congressman "Gorgeous George" Smathers of

Florida. A handsome conservative, Smathers had attacked Florida's incumbent liberal Senator Claude Pepper, who was a public friend of Joe Stalin as "Red Pepper" in a slashing campaign that toppled the incumbent. Chotiner would amend this appellation to "The Pink Lady" in California.

In the final days of the campaign Chotiner would launch a telephone drive promising anyone who answered the phone with the words "Vote for Nixon."

> PRIZES GALORE!!! Electric Clocks, Silex coffeemakers with heating units—General Electric automatic toasters—silver salt and pepper shakers, sugar and creamer sets, candy and butter dishes, etc., etc. WIN WITH NIXON!

Nixon's reputation as a dirty campaigner would grow from the hardball tactics he and Chotiner employed in Senate race in 1950. Forgotten now is that Douglas's attacks on Nixon were equally vituperative and far more *personal*. She frequently called Nixon a "pipsqueak" and "peewee."[48] Of course, most devastatingly of all, she would hang a sobriquet of "Tricky Dick" around his neck. It would stick with him throughout his career. "It's a brutal thing to combat," Nixon would tell his speechwriter Richard Whalen twenty-seven years after the US Senate race.[49] The notion that he was tricky and duplicitous was the greatest obstacle in his 1968 rehabilitation.

In fact, Nixon pulled his punches on Douglas' greatest secret. Congresswoman Douglas spent little time together with her movie actor husband. Her children were parked in private school and summer camps. She was conducting a torrid affair with Congressman Lyndon B. Johnson.

Throughout the late 1940s, it would not be uncommon to see Johnson and Douglas at Washington parties holding hands. The bullheaded Texan did not make a strong attempt to hide his affair with the California congresswoman. "Lyndon would park his car in front of [her] house night after night after night," said a friend of

Johnson. "It was an open scandal in Washington."[50] Nixon, serving in the House with both Johnson and Douglas was well aware of their relationship.

Johnson and Douglas "essentially lived together for a period," said a Johnson intimate.[51]

The affair would carry on into Johnson's presidential years. Johnson's wife, Lady Bird, once overheard a private phone call in the Oval Office in which President Johnson would tell Douglas, "He never knew you like I did," referring to her husband, actor Melvyn Douglas.[52]

"Hell, I knew Johnson was screwing her, but we didn't use it," Nixon would tell me, reminiscing about the 1950 campaign and the punch he had pulled.

Nixon's tactics in 1946 and 1950, under the tutelage of Chotiner when combined with his role as vice president, in which he was required to "carry the partisan load" as "spokesman" for the party, while the wily Eisenhower remained above the fray as a "non-political" president, only contributed to his reputation as a slashing and negative campaigner. Nixon led the attack on Democrats in his backbreaking campaign schedule in 1954–1958. Nixon was also frustrated that while he did Ike's dirty work, Eisenhower was always disturbed by the negative attacks back. "He would tell me to go out there and kick Truman, Stevenson, and the Democrats in the balls and then when I did, he would tell me, 'too hard.'"

As far as Nixon's early campaigns are concerned, there is no evidence that they were any worse than those waged by his opponents. In many cases liberals and Democrats made after-the-fact judgments about them. In fact, Nixon won because both 1946 and '50 were Republican years and both his opponents ran exceedingly poor campaigns, despite their sharp tone.[53]

Nixon would, of course, become the most *polarizing* figure in American politics in the twentieth century. His vilified campaign tactics in the early campaigns: the successful pursuit of Hiss; the sharp language and ghastly debate performance he used to excoriate

Stevenson, Truman, Acheson, and the Democrats "all brought the disdain of the liberal-oriented media, liberals, partisan democrats, and those who would comprise the Nixon haters."

Nixon and Chotiner shrewdly knew that this coin had another side. Nixon was deeply respected and enthusiastically supported by anti-Communists, organizational Republicans, and conservatives and held his own among conservative-leaning Independents. These would comprise a base that would make his political longevity possible. It would make the 1968 comeback possible. Even in the doldrums of Watergate, approximately 30 percent of the American people supported Nixon and opposed his ouster, most of them seeing Watergate as a partisan coup d'état.

"Base is everything. But you can't win with just them." Nixon would tell me over a martini at New York's Metropolitan Club after he addressed a national Republican Senatorial Committee "briefing" for which wealthy people paid $5,000 a seat. "You can stretch your base but never break with them . . . Lock up the conservatives and start looking for moderates and independents. If your base isn't slightly aggravated, you probably aren't reaching left enough. It's all about the arithmetic, ya see. You gotta get to fifty-one. You can't do it without the conservatives and can't do it with just the conservatives. Barry proved that."

While Nixon's ascent from the House to the Senate was meteoric, Chotiner had much bigger things in mind. Immediately after Nixon's election to the Senate, Chotiner began plotting how to get Nixon onto the 1952 ticket for vice president. The mysterious Chotiner would repay Governor Earl Warren's disloyalty.

NOTES

1. Terry McAuliffe, *What A Party!*, p. 59.
2. *New York Times*, "Lone Wolf of Politics," May 4, 1956.
3. Anthony Summers, *The Arrogance of Power*, p. 51.

4. Anthony Summers, *The Arrogance of Power*, p. 51.
5. Ibid.
6. William Costello, *The Facts about Nixon*, pp. 44–45.
7. Ibid.
8. Lowell Weiker, *Maverick*, p. 36.
9. Interview with Patrick Hillings, *American Experience*, PBS.
10. Christopher Matthews, *Kennedy and Nixon*, p. 36.
11. Richard Nixon, *RN: The Memoirs of Richard Nixon*, pp. 38–39.
12. Ibid. p. 39.
13. Leonard Lurie, *The Running of Richard Nixon*, pp. 50–51.
14. Conrad Black, *Richard M. Nixon: A Life in Full*, p. 81.
15 *New York Times*, "Jerry Voorhis '46 Nixon Foe," Sept. 12, 1984.
16. Anthony Summers, *The Arrogance of Power*, p. 45.
17. Stephen Ambrose, *Nixon: The Education of a Politician*, p. 138.
18. Anthony Summers, *The Arrogance of Power*, p. 52.
19. Tere Tereba, *Mickey Cohen: The Life and Crimes of L.A.'s Notorious Mobster*, p. 271.
20. Conrad Black, *Richard M. Nixon: A Life in Full*, p. 86.
21. Paul Lieberman, "The Gangster Squad Cops who Made the Mob Look Soft," Daily Mail Online, January 9, 2013, http://www.dailymail.co.uk/news/article-2259932/The-Gangster-Squad-cops-mob-look-soft-New-film-reveals-story-LA-officers-carried-machine-guns-violin-cases-dangled-enemies-bridges.html.
22. Tere Tereba, *Mickey Cohen: The Life and Crimes of L.A.'s Notorious Mobster*, p. 270.
23. Stephen Ambrose, *Nixon: The Education of a Politician*, p. 169.
24. Conrad Black, *Richard M. Nixon: A Life in Full*, p. 111.
25. Anthony Summers, *The Arrogance of Power*, p. 67.
26. Stephen Ambrose, *Nixon: The Education of a Politician*, p. 171.
27. Richard Nixon, *Six Crises*, p. 9.
28. Ralph de Toledano, *Nixon*, p. 67.
29. Richard Nixon, *Six Crises*, p. 10.
30. Lewis Hartshorn, *Alger Hiss, Whittaker Chambers, and the Case That Ignited McCarthyism*, p. 119.
31. Ralph de Toledano, *Nixon*, p. 68.
32. Stephen Ambrose, *Nixon: The Education of a Politician*, p. 180.
33. Ibid. p. 180.
34. Ralph de Toledano, *Nixon*, p. 69–70.

35. Ibid. p. 182.
36. Ralph de Toledano, *Nixon*, p. 71.
37. Ibid. pp. 71–72.
38. Gilbert Sandler, "Revisiting the Pumpkin Papers," *The Baltimore Sun*, Oct. 25, 1994.
39. Anthony Summers, *The Arrogance of Power*, p. 70.
40. Ibid. p. 71.
41. Deborah Hart Strober and Gerald S. Strober, *The Nixon Presidency: An Oral History of the Era*, p. 48.
42. "Secrets, Lies, and Atomic Spies," Nova Online, http://www.pbs.org/wgbh/nova/venona/dece_hiss.html.
43. Alex Kingsbury, "Declassified Document Reveal KGB Spies in the US," *U.S. News & World Report*, June 17, 2009.
44. Drew Pearson, "Mickey Cohen Talks About Nixon," *The Toledo Blade*, Oct. 31, 1968.
45. Stephen Ambrose, *Nixon: The Education of a Politician*, p. 215.
46. Julie Nixon Eisenhower, *Pat Nixon: The Untold Story*, p. 108.
47. Greg Michell, *Tricky Dick and the Pink Lady*, p. 106.
48. Julie Nixon Eisenhower, *Pat Nixon: The Untold Story*, p. 107.
49. Richard Whalan, *Catch the Falling Flag*, p. 20.
50. David L. Robb, *The Gumshoe and the Shrink*, p. 62.
51. Ingrid Scobie, *Center Stage*, p. 172.
52. Randall Bennett Wood, *LBJ: Architect of American Ambition*, p. 481.
53. Edmund F. Kallina, *Kennedy v. Nixon*, pp. 44–45.

CHAPTER FOUR

THE GREAT TRAIN ROBBERY

"There comes a time in matters like this when you've either got to shit or get off the pot."
—Nixon to General Dwight D. Eisenhower[1]

A hot and humid Chicago summer scene in July served as the setting for the 1952 Republican National Convention, held at the since demolished International Amphitheatre. At the time, the venue was called the Chicago Amphitheater, and the convention was the first ever to be broadcast live via television in the United States.[2] In fact, television had never been this present at a political convention before. All three networks were given their own studio spaces to cover the event with all the known technology of the time. Seven large cameras caught all the action on the convention floor with almost seventy others catching any additional happenings in the halls. Lastly, correspondents were able to show off their new innovations like mobile microphones, which allowed them to mingle with delegates and see the convention's events in real time.[3] Of course, the International Amphitheatre would go on to hold other key national conventions like the Democratic Party's most infamous in 1968. The platform that the GOP decided to run on that year included ending the unpopular war in Korea, curtailing the economic policies implemented by Roosevelt and Truman, reforming the State Department, opposing discrimination, and using the federal government to eliminate lynching. [4]

Vying for the top spot on the ticket was Ohio Senator Robert Taft, the longtime beacon of conservatism within the Republican Party. Taft was a man who had run unsuccessfully for the nomination in 1940 and 1948. The widely conceived notion going into 1952 was that this was Taft's year. Sure enough, the convention essentially became a contest between the internationalist and isolationist foreign policy viewpoints, with Taft admitting that isolationism was dead but also maintaining his stance that the United States shouldn't get involved with the Cold War.[5] Taft was popular with Republicans in the Midwest and parts of the South but was always considered too conservative for the party's top bosses ever to give him the nomination. At sixty-two, this was Bob's last chance. New York Governor Thomas E. Dewey, an ardent internationalist, was the GOP nominee in 1944 and 1948 and was widely disliked by the the mid western conservatives in the party.

Taft's main competition was General Dwight D. Eisenhower, who had decided to run only after begrudgingly being persuaded by the grassroots "Citizens for Eisenhower" movement. In fact, the citizen's group was fronted for Thomas Dewey's wing of the party, which included General Lucius Clay, Dewey's former campaign manager Herbert Brownell, Long Island Republican leader Russell Sprague, Massachusetts Senator Henry Cabot Lodge, Kansas Senator Frank Carlson, and Connecticut Governor John Davis Lodge. Democrats Oveta Culp Hobby and banker Robert Anderson gave the group its bipartisan flavor. Public relations maven Tex McCrary and his actress/model/tennis star wife, former showgirl Jinx Falkenberg, would promote the group through their popular radio show Tex and Jinx. McCrary would stage a Madison Square Garden rally so massive that films of the event were hand carried to Ike in Europe, where the general was mightily impressed by the growing power of the "Citizens for Eisenhower" movement. "It was a moving experience," Eisenhower later wrote, "to witness the obvious unanimity of such a huge crowd—to realize that everyone present was enthusiastically supporting me for the highest office in the land . . . the incident impressed me more than had all the arguments presented by the individuals who had been plaguing me with political questions . . ."[6]

Eisenhower's party affiliation was at this point unknown. President Truman had unsuccessfully attempted to get Eisenhower to run as a Democrat in 1948. Eisenhower was still fresh from his role as a five-star general in World War II and now an influential NATO general. Ike was successfully persuaded to run by the moderate East wing of the party. The moderate or internationalist wing of the party had accepted the global role of the United States in a post-WWII world. They also accepted the permanence of the social welfare programs developed by Roosevelt and the New Deal. What they could not accept was another Democrat president. Dewey and his team knew Ike had the national popularity to beat the Democrats at a time when the Republicans hadn't won a national election since 1928. Ike was viewed as nonpartisan; he was a war hero who appealed to Democrats and Republicans alike. Eisenhower had become an almost mythic figure. Nixon had seen Eisenhower's appeal firsthand. In 1945, he had been one of the four million people who gathered in New York City to view General Eisenhower in his victory parade. "I was about thirty stories up— but I have the picture that there he came, with his arms outstretched and his face up to the sky, and that even from where I was I could feel the impact of his personality," Nixon said. "I could just make him out through the snowstorm of confetti, sitting in the back of his open car, waving and looking up at the cheering thousands like me who filled every window of the towering buildings. His arms were raised high over his head in the gesture that soon became his trademark."[7]

By the fall of 1951, columnists and polltakers alike had decided that the race would be between Ike and Taft. Ike was clearly the choice of the Republican media, with support for the general coming from the *Herald Tribune, Time, Life,* and *Fortune.* The *Tribune* even endorsed Eisenhower for the presidency as early as October 1951 with a glowing review: "At rare intervals in the life of a free people the man and occasion meet," the newspaper's editorial staff wrote. "[Eisenhower] is a Republican by temper and disposition."[8] For Nixon, the writing was on the wall as well—Eisenhower had the popularity to win a national election, and he had the party's financial and media muscle behind him.

The next most prominent candidate in the mix for the vice presidential nomination was Governor Earl Warren of California, though barely a candidate from the beginning. Both he and Nixon ran statewide in California in 1950—with Warren remaining in the governor seat and Nixon becoming a US Senator. Warren was obviously very popular in his home state, with Western delegates, and with independent voters but refused to campaign in the primaries and thus severely limited any chances of his getting the nomination. Nonetheless, he had the full support of the California delegation, including Nixon, who supported Warren in the California primary and served on his delegation. Naturally, Nixon was *invaluable* to anyone hoping to sway the opinion of the California delegation.[9]

Sure enough, that California delegation of seventy votes would prove to be crucial coming into the convention. Eisenhower began his campaign with a victory in the New Hampshire primary, upsetting Taft on a purely write-in driven campaign. But from there, the two candidates essentially split the remaining primary states evenly, with Taft picking up Nebraska, Wisconsin, Illinois, and South Dakota and Ike nabbing the New Jersey, Pennsylvania, Massachusetts, and Oregon primaries. Warren naturally held up his home state of California with all the state party's leadership—including Nixon—supporting him, and by July, the nomination to be expected out of Chicago was just too close to call.

Herbert Brownell, the able Wall Street lawyer who would guide Eisenhower to victory first approached Murray Chotiner to inquire about Nixon's potential as a vice presidential running mate. So that Murray could not say he had an "offer" it was couched as ascertaining Chotiner's arguments for Nixon or Senator William Knowland for the VP spot. The notion of Knowland as vice president was ludicrous, but Chotiner could not tell the press Nixon had been "felt out," a deft touch by Brownell. The die was cast. The Dewey crowd around Ike was playing its hand.

Eisenhower once asked an aide after meeting with Knowland, "How stupid can you get?"[10] Knowland was the scion of the publisher of the *Oakland Tribune*. He was a tall, handsome, gregarious, bluff man who was both affable and not terribly bright. He was on the Neanderthal right of his party. He was so much a "hail fellow well met" man that his colleagues elected him majority leader in the brief period they controlled the Senate in the 1950s. Knowland had greater presidential aspirations and personal wealth than he had brains. In 1958, he announced that he would seek election to the governorship, challenging sitting governor and liberal Republican Goodwin Knight. Knight was no Nixon fan, but the vice president, in the interest of party unity, convinced a reluctant Knight to run for the US Senate seat Knowland was vacating. It was a disaster, leaving Nixon in control of what little Republican apparatus existed in the California Republican Party in the run-up to the 1960 election. It also put a Democratic governor in the governor's mansion when Nixon needed to carry his home state in a close contest with Kennedy. Knowland would later play a key role in convincing a reluctant Ronald Reagan to challenge Nixon at the 1968 convention. Knowland was also a prolific cocksman, and marital infidelities would be frequent. Knowland later left his wife of forty-five years to move in with a twenty-two-year-old and end up shooting himself in the mouth with a revolver in a San Francisco hotel room when he became despondent over severe financial debts to organized crime figures. In other words, Knowland was never really under consideration for vice president in 1960.[11]

It's worthy to note that with Nixon's stealth defection, Knowland stayed loyal to Warren. Knowland supported Warren, his home state governor, despite the fact that they were ideologically miles apart. Warren no doubt saw it as a way to keep peace in the California Republican Party. Knowland was offered a VP slot with Taft if he could sway the delegation to that side, and Eisenhower's campaign had courted his support and may have given him the impression he was being considered for VP. He denied both and didn't get anything from either.

Nixon had to make his own moves so he could personally guarantee the invaluable California vote either to Taft or Eisenhower, which of course would first require him to abandon his pledge to Warren. Political veteran Frank Mankiewicz asserted in his book *Perfectly Clear* that Nixon had been offered and accepted the vice-presidential spot—with Ike's approval—months earlier through Dewey.[12]

Nixon knew the price of the vice presidential nomination was delivery of California's votes in a carefully staged floor fight in which the Eisenhower forces would unseat Taft delegates in three Southern states, seating Eisenhower backers in their stead. The ingenious aspect of this maneuver was that the Taft delegates in the disputed states could not vote on their own fate; they called it the Fair Play Amendment. With these votes deducted from Taft's strengths, the Eisenhower forces easily prevailed, particularly if Nixon could deliver California's seventy delegates for the proposition. When Knowland tried to call for an even split of the state's delegate votes on the so-called Fair Play Amendment, he was only beaten back by Nixon taking the floor and asking the delegation to stand united in the floor fight to seat the Eisenhower delegates. Warren's chances evaporated when the Eisenhower forces won the procedural vote. Nixon was to remain "committed" to Warren while pushing for a credentials challenge that would doom Warren's chances, preventing the governor's name ever being entered for the nomination. Warren would barter his support for Eisenhower in return for a pledge that he would be appointed to the first open Supreme Court seat. After Eisenhower's election, when Chief Justice Fred Vinson died unexpectedly, Eisenhower tried to argue that he had not committed to appoint Warren chief justice. Warren argued that he was promised the *next* opening and went on to be chief justice. Eisenhower would go on to claim the appointment was one of his greatest mistakes.

Nixon told Dewey that he would welcome the vice presidential nomination in the diminutive, but dapper, mustachioed governor's suite in the Roosevelt Hotel. Nixon had been invited by the New York State Republican Committee as their featured speaker. The black-tie dinner was made up of precisely the kind of people Nixon despised: Ivy league, old-money WASPs who controlled Wall Street and the financial sector; socially sophisticated publishers like Henry Luce; titans of industry; the political elite; and the Eastern moneyed of the Republican Party were present. The speech was essentially an audition for Dewey. Nixon hit it out of the park, and the governor invited him upstairs for a chat. It was here that Dewey told him the vice presidency would be his if he submarined Warren.

Warren had rejected entreaties from the Eastern crowd to join the Eisenhower bandwagon. Warren had been Dewey's running mate for vice president in 1948 and Dewey thought he had turned in a nonenergetic performance, even losing California to Truman and Barkley. Warren would not budge, hoping an Eisenhower-Taft stalemate would turn the convention to him as a compromise.

Nixon tackled his goal with gusto. He began to rally the troops. He made it publicly clear about his appointed delegates' preference for Eisenhower, which naturally enraged Warren. As Mankiewicz writes, "If a historian wonders a few generations from now why Earl Warren . . . has never had a good word to say about Richard Nixon, he need look no further . . . than to the weeks prior to the

Republican convention of 1952." Nixon, almost immediately after the California primary, began to jettison his support for Warren and speak publicly on the radio and elsewhere about the opportunity for California's delegates at the national convention in the event of a Taft-Eisenhower deadlock. Ten years later, Warren's son Earl Jr. also lamented that "Mr. Nixon, through backdoor tactics, pulled the rug out—for political gain for himself."[13]

Nixon's intentions became somewhat obvious when Dick mailed his campaign's former precinct chairmen a poll—paid for by his Senate office's funds—asking them that "if" Warren wasn't the nominee, who they thought would be the "strongest" candidate the party could nominate. The Warren campaign naturally regarded this as "virtual treachery," especially when the word came back from Washington that Eisenhower was easily the favorite choice.

To seal the deal, one of Nixon's handpicked delegates was in charge of booking the California delegation's travel to Chicago, complete with assigning rooms on the train. Sure enough, Nixon was able to use this to his advantage—as soon as he and Chotiner joined the delegation on the train in Denver, his room became the focal point of the entire delegation's trip. Delegate after delegate came to visit Nixon to listen to his case about why Eisenhower was a sure thing, and if California pulled for the general, they would be rewarded and Nixon would likely get the vice president spot on the ticket. For years later, Warren would refer to the trip as the Great Train Robbery[14] and thereafter referred to Nixon as "Tricky Dick."

According to reports at the time, Nixon was in constant motion at the convention, milling in the halls and lobbies with everyone he knew, and even mingling with some celebrities he didn't know, such as baseball great Jackie Robinson, a registered Republican. Nixon recalled seeing Robinson play against Oregon during his collegiate career, and this impressed the young ballplayer.[15] Dick was in rare form that week.

Naturally, the highly competitive race and dead seasonal heat also gave the convention a fiery atmosphere. Eisenhower's campaign had accused Taft's of "stealing" votes from Southern delegates in Texas and Georgia by denying Eisenhower delegates spots to the convention through the credentials committee, which was heavily stacked with Taft men. Dewey and Massachusetts Senator Henry Cabot Lodge Jr., both in charge of Ike's campaign, threatened to evict the pro-Taft delegates through a minority report they filed with the committee, in hopes of replacing them with pro-Eisenhower delegates via a proposal they called the Fair Play resolution. At Nixon's urging the California delegation voted 57 to 8 in favor of the Fair Play resolution. Without the Southern delegates, Taft's momentum slowed and the California vote grew absolutely crucial to any nomination.

It may be important to note at this point Eisenhower Convention Manager Herbert Brownell's role in this official selection, or for that matter, his role in developing the Fair Play strategy that really secured Ike the nomination. Brownell had successfully elected Dewey governor of New York in 1942 and managed both of Dewey's campaigns in 1944 and 1948. Brownell had traveled extensively and had broad contacts in the Republican Party in both wings where he was known as a man of his word and a straight dealer. According to his memoirs, *Advising Ike*, Brownell says the "control of the convention" was to be determined by which slate of delegates were actually seated from each state. Thus, Brownell used his past experience as a party chairman to utilize an old rule change tactic that he developed by studying the entire minutes from the 1912 Republican National Convention, when Robert Taft's father, President William Taft, was battling former president (and former friend) Teddy Roosevelt for the party's nomination. From studying the outcomes of the 1912 convention, which subsequently forced Teddy to leave the Republicans and form his own party, Brownell understood what his team had to do. "First, we had to amend the convention rules so that they could not be used, as in 1912, to prevent even the consideration of changes to temporary-delegate roll and discussion of whether contested delegates could vote on contested delegations. Second, we had to present our arguments in carefully prepared briefs . . . We would not repeat Roosevelt's mistakes."[16] In short, Brownell was the man with the plan, and it worked.

Similarly, when it came to the vice presidential choice, Brownell often wondered why Warren didn't seize the initiative and deliver the California delegation's votes to Ike. The only explanation Brownell could offer was the possibility that Knowland, a proud Warren supporter, was going to bring the Taft votes to Warren in the event of an Eisenhower-Taft deadlock, just to spite Dewey and the entire moderate wing. It's possible that Warren just stayed in it in hopes he would receive the nomination himself if everything went his way. At the time, Warren was not counting on the subterfuge of Dick Nixon.

The Eisenhower delegates were seated, and Ike narrowly secured the nomination on the first ballot by barely defeating Taft by ninety-five votes. After the first ballot at the convention, Ike actually went to visit Taft in his hotel suite. Taft was congratulatory on Eisenhower's victory but held resentment on what he felt were untrue charges of "stealing delegates." Taft withheld public support for Ike's campaign for several weeks after the convention until the two again met in New York City, and he only gave his support after Ike agreed to a number of Taft's demands. The requests were largely on domestic issues, as the two essentially agreed on most of those; their differences came primarily on foreign policy.[17]

The divided convention had, as with any political maneuvering, the inevitable bitter emotions that come with political trickery. Senator Everett Dirksen of Illinois, a fervent Taft supporter, accused Dewey on the convention floor of leading Republicans "down the road to defeat." Dirksen, considered one of the greatest orators in the Republican Party, spoke for the party's conservatives who blamed moderate nominees for losing the 1940, 1944, and

1948 elections. The golden-tongued Dirksen would point his finger in Dewey's face as the Illinois delegation was seated hard by the New Yorkers. The diminutive governor would merely glare at his accuser. There were even fistfights between different members of the two camps.

Nixon would dissemble with his own wife and advisors other than Chotiner about his likelihood of being offered the vice presidential nomination. The Nixon family would go through a prolonged discussion of the merits of Nixon accepting the second slot. He would also play coy with the press. When asked by reporters, Nixon would say that the chance of him getting the vice presidential spot was too remote for him even to consider it. Of course while he was saying that, Nixon was already meeting with Herbert Brownell and practically escorting Eisenhower around during his visit to the California delegation. When a *Los Angeles Times* journalist asked him about an Eisenhower-Nixon ticket, Dick said, "It's the first time I ever heard of it, and I expect it will be the last." However, Dick knew better. The final selection of Nixon was ratified Friday afternoon in a smoky room at the Conrad Hilton where Dewey, Cabot Lodge, and Brownell were present.[18]

It is important at this point to draw a distinction between Eisenhower's public perception during his presidency and the reality of Dwight David Eisenhower. Professor Fred Greenstein began a historical reappraisal of Eisenhower in his seminal work *The Hidden Hand Presidency.* Despite the role Eisenhower cultivated with the press as a solid but somewhat bumbling and nonpolitical naïf, Eisenhower was in fact a cunning, devious, and brilliant political strategist. He purposely used tortured syntax and obfuscation with the press to hide his real motives and efforts. Eisenhower would claim that he hadn't been aware that it was his prerogative to choose a vice presidential running mate after winning the nomination. I find this unlikely. In truth, Dewey had the nomination wired as long as Nixon delivered in California, which he did.

Nixon would be sweating in his overheated hotel room with Pat while trying to nap when the phone call from Brownell came through. Eisenhower wanted to meet with him immediately to extend the vice presidential nomination. Brownell called the room and informed Nixon's campaign people that he had been chosen by Ike's closest advisors and, at that same time, Brownell was also informing Eisenhower. "We picked you," Brownell told Nixon. "[Ike asked] if you could come see him right away . . . That is, assuming you want it." Nixon wanted it, and though he was sleep-deprived, sweating, and needed a fresh shave, he quickly went to the general's suite and accepted.[19]

Eisenhower gave Brownell a list of six or seven candidates that he would approve of, and Nixon was one of them. When Ike authorized Brownell to hold a meeting of Eisenhower campaign leaders to chose the second spot on the ticket, "Dewey carried the day when he presented Nixon's name." In fact, Brownell admits he knew of Dewey's "decision to secure a place for Nixon on the ticket" for several months. "Before the meeting was ever convened, I knew that Nixon was the candidate."[20]

Eisenhower would meet privately with his young subordinate. The general made it clear that he intended to stay above the political fray to win the vote of millions of Democrats and independents who revered him as a war hero. Nixon's designated job was to carry the partisan load. Nixon was to take the point in attacking the Democrats, presidential candidate Adlai Stevenson and Senator John Sparkman, the segregationist the Democrats had nominated for vice president. This would be the division of labor that would ultimately cause Nixon to be among the most polarizing and controversial figures in American political life. Eisenhower would use Nixon as his attack dog while the affable general avoided politics. Nixon, for his part, would take on his role with relish, attacking the Truman-Acheson foreign policy calling Truman's state department "the Cowardly College of Communist Corruption" and charging that Truman, Acheson, and Stevenson were "traitors" to the great principles of the Democratic Party. Truman would never forgive Nixon for this slur, claiming the Californian had impugned his patriotism.

The Eisenhower-Nixon campaign used the most sophisticated Madison Avenue techniques pioneering the use of television ads to promote the election of a presidential candidate. The medium of television was young, but the audiences who tuned in for *Texaco Star Theatre Featuring Milton Berle* or *Bishop Fulton J. Sheen's Program Life Is Worth Living* would see the first primitive TV spots using the slogan "I Like Ike." Eisenhower himself proved an uneven campaigner, but improved with time. His superstar status really rendered his performance unimportant. He was Eisenhower.

* * *

On September 14, 1952, Peter Edson, a reporter for the Newspaper Enterprise Association, questioned Nixon about a campaign fund based on a leak from a disgruntled supporter of Governor Warren. "He told me the basic facts and said it was all right to use them," Edson said and added that Nixon was "perfectly willing to have the thing published."[21] Nixon also referred Edson to Smith for further inquiry. The column the journalist wrote on September 18 was, as Nixon described it, "fair and objective."

Leo Katcher of the *New York Post* also interviewed Smith. Katcher's story ran with published the headline, "Secret Rich Men's Trust Fund Keeps Nixon in Style Far Beyond His Salary."[22] The article referred to Nixon's "Scandal Fund,"where he was accused of of taking money from the $18,000 fund raised by a group of his supporters. UPI picked up the story as "Nixon Scandal Fund." The calls for Nixon's resignation ensued from the Democratic National Committee.

Nixon's detractors' accusations of improper use of funds to reimburse himself for campaign, of taking money from the $18,000 fund raised by a group of his supporters, came at this critical time for Nixon in his political career. "This should blow that moralizing, unscrupulous, double-dealing son-of-a-bitch out of the water," said *New York Post* editor Jimmy Wechsler. "I'd love to see Ike's face when he finds out that Tricky Dick, his partner in the fight against Democratic corruption, has been on the take for the last two years."[23] With the accusations of shady funding, Nixon's place on the Republican ticket as Eisenhower's running mate was seriously compromised.

As aforementioned, in 1950, California Congressman Richard Nixon had beaten Representative Helen Gahagan Douglas in the US Senatorial race. Senator Nixon's annual salary was $12,500, (roughly equivalent to $117,600 in 2014). His $75,000 expense account covered the costs of his twelve-member staff, office supplies, telephone and telegram services, and other expenses. Murray Chotiner and campaign chairman Bernie Brennan proposed they create a year-round campaign that would continue during Nixon's six-year term as senator in preparation for a run for reelection in 1956.

Nixon's aides suggested they appeal for funds from his supporters to finance this campaign, to have the means for Nixon to travel, to make speeches, etc. Campaign treasurer Dana Smith suggested "the fund, which he would administer to pay for Nixon's political expenses. Nixon was to remain uninformed of the names of the contributors.

"The fund had been carefully established, limiting contributions to individuals, not corporations, and to a maximum single contribution of $500, so that no one could be accused of buying special favors," said Nixon. "The money was solicited from regular party contributors and it was administered by Smith as trustee. The funds were kept in a Pasadena bank and were subject to regular audits."[24]

The fund had raised $16,000 by October 30, 1951, mostly from contributors in the Los Angeles area. Nixon spent about $12,000 of that total. His Christmas card expenses for 1950 and 1951 totaled over $4,000. The fund only raised $2,200 from November 1951 to July 1952.

When inquisitive reporters on the campaign trail brought up the topic of the trust fund, Nixon dismissed the rumor as smear tactics by Communist hatemongers. In California, at Marysville Depot, when asked about the fund, Nixon said, "the purpose of those smears is to make me, if possible, relent and let up on my attacks on the Communists and the crooks in the present administration. As far as I am concerned, they've got another guess coming: because what I intend to do is to go up and down this land, and the more they smear me the more I'm going to expose the Communists and the crooks and those that defend them until they throw them all out of Washington."[25]

The *Washington Post* and *New York Herald-Tribune* called for Eisenhower to dump Nixon. Campaign manager Murray Chotiner kept this from Nixon, but a reporter informed the candidate of the condemning editorials. Newspapers such as the *Sacramento Bee* and the *Pasadena Star-News* published stories that painted Nixon in the most accusatory fashion as taking money for his personal luxury lifestyle. The *Pasadena Star-News* reported that the Nixon fund requested from one contributor a donation because the Nixon family needed a larger home with maid service—both of which the Nixon's couldn't afford. Over one hundred newspapers had fueled the suspicions of secrecy and wrongdoing, which motivated public protests accusing Nixon of taking "bribe money" and repeating slogans that targeted Pat Nixon, "What are you going to do with the bribe money?" and "No mink coats for Nixon—Just Cold Cash." Murray Chotiner, always the disciplined tactician, had an idea: find a way to circumvent the press. "What we have to do is to get you the biggest possible audience so that you can talk over the heads of the press to the people," said Chotiner.[26] The ploy was a nationally televised, prime-time spot. "This is politics," Chotiner said in an attempt to embolden Nixon. "The prize is the White House."[27]

President Eisenhower was less than supportive of his running mate and, as noted, typical to his style, uncommitted to a strong public opinion on the matter.

The Eisenhower-Nixon ticket would sweep thirty-nine states, winning an Electoral College majority of 442 over 89 and carrying the popular vote by six million. As vice president, Richard Nixon was one rung closer to his ultimate goal: the White House.

"I have come to the conclusion that you are the one who has to decide what to do,"[28] was the only advice the presidential candidate privately offered Nixon. Nixon did receive positive advice from his aides to stay on the ticket. Nixon's mother, Hannah, sent a telegram in support of her son. Some messages to Nixon were discouraging, however. Minnesota Governor Harold Stassen urged Nixon to resign as Eisenhower's running mate, while Murray continued to push the idea to counterattack. "If you get off this ticket because Eisenhower forces you off, or if you do so on your own volition, Eisenhower won't have the chance of a snowball in hell to win in November," Chotiner said. "Your friends and those who supported Taft will never forgive him, and the Democrats will beat him over the head for his lack of judgment in selecting you in the first place. This whole story has been blown up out of all proportion because of the delay and indecision of the amateurs around Eisenhower. Every time you get before an audience, you must win them."[29]

When an appearance on *Meet the Press* was suggested, Chotiner quickly shot down the idea. Nixon, Chotiner believed, must attack the issue alone, without interference from combative news hosts.[30] A half hour of time following *Texaco Star Theatre featuring Milton Berle* was agreed upon.

Nixon and his aides worked on the speech throughout the night up to the morning of September 22. The RNC raised the $75,000 for the thirty-minute TV time slot, and Eisenhower's staff obtained sixty NBC affiliates to broadcast the speech along with CBS and Mutual radio coverage. The Eisenhower-Nixon campaign aides arranged for it to be broadcast from the El Capitan Theatre in Hollywood.

On the flight to Los Angeles, Nixon made notes that included the accusations that had upset Pat Nixon regarding their family's finances. He thought of Franklin D. Roosevelt's Fala speech in which FDR issued a sarcastic response to Republican charges that he had sent a battleship to rescue his dog, Fala. Nixon remembered the dog given as a gift to his children.

On September 23, an hour before Nixon presented his case to the nation, New York Governor Thomas E. Dewey, a member of the Eisenhower inner circle, called Nixon using his code name "Mr. Chapman" and suggested that Nixon publicly rescind the nomination for vice president. "If they want to find out they'd better listen to the broadcast," Nixon shouted at Dewey, "and tell them I know something about politics too."[31] Nixon was not going to resign on national television, but Dewey's message was worrisome. Nixon would recall that Dewey "went on to say that he was sure that, in view of the close relationship between those with whom he had talked and Eisenhower, they would not have asked him to call unless this represented Eisenhower's view as well as their own."[32] "It was Nixon's first experience with that side of Eisenhower," wrote Jeffrey Frank in *Ike and Dick*, "the invisible commander who liked to issue an order and have it carried out as if the order had arisen spontaneously."[33] Nixon knew Eisenhower and his team had deserted him.

"Dick looked like someone had smashed him," said longtime Nixon confidant Pat Hillings.[34] But Nixon's allegorical speech would thwart those in the Eastern establishment around Eisenhower who had decided to dump him.

Richard Nixon delivered the television address that came to be known as the Checkers speech on his own terms. Nixon sat at a desk and began with, "My fellow Americans, I come before you tonight as a candidate for the vice presidency, and as a man whose honesty and integrity have been questioned" and that the best response to smear "is to tell the truth."

Nixon defended himself and appealed to viewers nationwide to contact the Republican National Committee and to ask whether he should stay on the ticket. Nixon stated the fund was wrong if he had profited from it or if it had been a secret fund. He went on to assure the public that not a penny was misspent for his personal use: "Every penny of it was used to pay for political expenses that I did not think should be charged to the taxpayers of the United States." He said the fund was no secret and there were no special favors doled out to contributors. Nixon gave an angry response that struck a note in public consciousness: as far as improper gifts, Nixon said there were no mink coats for anyone in his family, and he was "proud of the fact that Pat Nixon wears a good Republican cloth coat, and she's going to continue to."

Nixon spoke without notes, and his eye contact with the camera was intimate. He came across as a man baring his soul and his meager personal finances. Pat Nixon sat in the shot, a grim smile on her face as she stared directly at her husband in his crucible moment. Now Nixon would take more advice from Chotiner, launching a counterattack on the Democrats. The savvy Chotiner had noticed from the beginning of the fund controversy that Adlai Stevenson had not joined the chorus of those criticizing Nixon. "He was hiding something—otherwise he would have been at your throat like the rest of them," Murray had said.[35] The *Chicago Tribune* had recently reported that Stevenson had his own fund supplied by prominent Illinois businessmen who had supported his political activities. Additionally, it had been revealed that Senator Sparkman had maintained his own wife on the US Senate payroll. Nixon would call for full disclosure by both. Then Nixon, knowing that Eisenhower had taken an unconventional tax break on his substantial income from the publication of his memoir *Crusade in Europe*, called for full financial disclosure from all the candidates. Eisenhower, watching the speech on TV, would reportedly stab the yellow pad he had in his hand, breaking the point of a sharpened pencil when he heard Nixon's call for financial divulgence.

Now, Nixon, recalling Franklin Roosevelt's clever use of his own dog, Fala, to twit Republicans in 1940, would turn the tables on his tormentors. On a warm summer day in 1952, a traveling sales- man named Lou Carrol had shipped a crate to Nixon's daughters, Julie and Tricia. Inside was a black and white cocker spaniel that the Nixon girls named Checkers. Carrol had read a newspaper arti- cle in which Pat Nixon said that the Nixon girls wished for a dog. Fortuitously, Carrol's spaniel Boots had just given birth to a litter, and he thought it would be a nice gesture to gift one to the Nixon clan. "We packed bits of dog food for the train men to feed her along the way," Carrol said. "I had no idea she'd be such a big deal."[36]

Although Checkers would never live in the White House (he died four years before Nixon became president), the treasured family pet would become perhaps Nixon's greatest political asset on his path to 1600 Pennsylvania Avenue. Checkers helped char- acterize Nixon as an American individualist, humble in his roots, modest in his needs, and under attack by the establishment.

Despite these horrid attacks, there was one gift he intended to keep, he said: "One other thing I probably should tell you because if we don't they'll probably be saying this about me too, we did get something—a gift—after the election. A man down in Texas heard Pat on the radio mention the fact that our two youngsters would like to have a dog. And, believe it or not, the day before we left on this campaign trip we got a message from Union Station in Baltimore saying they had a package for us. We went down to get it. You know what it was?

It was a little cocker spaniel dog in a crate that he'd sent all the way from Texas. Black and white spotted. And our little girl— Tricia, the six-year-old—named it Checkers. And you know, the kids, like all kids, love the dog and I just want to say this right now, that regardless of what they say about it, we're gonna keep it."

Nixon thought his speech was a failure. Upon returning to the Ambassador Hotel, Nixon met a mob scene of well-wishers, but there was no immediate response from Ike or his entourage.

Dwight and Mamie Eisenhower watched the speech in Cleveland in the manager's office of Cleveland's Public Auditorium, where Eisenhower was scheduled to speak. There were fifteen thousand Eisenhower supporters who had listened to the Checkers speech over the public address system. Congressman George H. Bender asked the crowd if they were in favor of Nixon. The crowd responded by chanting, "We want Nixon!"

"General, you'll have to throw your speech away," said Eisenhower press secretary James Hagerty. "Those people out there want to hear about Nixon."[37] Eisenhower was noncommittal in his speech. He applauded Nixon but stated that the two would have to meet before he made the final decision on Nixon remaining on the ticket. Eisenhower sent a telegram to Nixon to ask him to meet in Wheeling, West Virginia, the general's next stop. Nixon was sure that it was to ask for his resignation. He dictated a telegram to his secretary, Rose Mary Woods, to go to the RNC announcing his resignation. Chotiner interceded and ripped up the sheet. He felt that Nixon should allow time for the public wave of support to put pressure on Eisenhower. Now Chotiner would duck calls from the traveling party around Eisenhower. "Let the bastards wait for us this time," he would snort.[38]

Chotiner returned the call of RNC Chairman Arthur Summerfield and demanded a promise that Nixon would be confirmed a nominee at Nixon's meeting with Eisenhower or Nixon wouldn't go to Wheeling. Chotiner said, "Dick is not going to be placed in the position of a little boy going somewhere to beg for forgiveness." [39] Nixon recalled the scene in *Six Crises:*

> His [Summerfield's] conversation with Murray Chotiner went something like this:
> "Well, Murray, how are things out there:"
> "Not so good."
> "What in hell do you mean, not so good?"
> "Dick just wrote out a telegram of resignation to the General."

"What! My God, Murray, you tore it up, didn't you?"

"Yes, I tore it up, but I'm not so sure how long it's going to stay torn."

· "Well, Dick is flying to Wheeling to see the General, isn't he?"

"No, we're flying tonight to Missoula."

"What? My God, Murray, you've got to persuade him to come to Wheeling."

"Arthur, we trust you. If you can give us your personal assurance direct from the General that Dick will stay on the ticket with the General's blessing, I think I can persuade him. I know I can't otherwise."[40]

Nixon sent Eisenhower a short acknowledgment of his telegram and suggested they meet in Washington, DC, the following week. Nixon's friend journalist Bert Andrews got hold of Nixon by phone, and Andrews also advised him to go to Wheeling. Nixon, however, flew to Missoula.

The response among an impressive number of the sixty million who had watched it on TV proved the opposite of what Nixon thought. The responses poured in. Of more than four million letters, postcards, phone calls, and telegrams sent to the Republican National Convention headquarters, 75 percent were in favor of Nixon. Checkers even received a year's worth of dog food, collars, and toys. It was Nixon's first lesson in the power of a television image. As his political career unfolded, Nixon would become the prototypical political test subject for the new medium. His highest and lowest moments as a politician would be facilitated by television and scrutinized for years following. In 1952, television was still thought of as a fad to Nixon, but the forum allowed the politician to get his message across unfiltered and emotional. Although today, the speech is often invoked as schmaltzy, shameless hucksterism, in its day it was an innovation both in politics and communication. Nixon had his back to the ropes, but he was still swinging. "His revelations came across as painful, anguishing for everyone watching," Thomas Doherty, a professor of

American studies at Brandeis University said.[41] The speech had saved Nixon's career.

Indeed, Nixon would write in his in his book *Six Crises*, "If it hadn't been for that broadcast, I never would have been around to run for the presidency."[42]

On September 24, Summerfield and Humphreys called Nixon at his hotel in Missoula. He agreed to fly to Wheeling only on Chotiner's terms. They then briefed Eisenhower on the wave of public support, and Eisenhower agreed that Nixon would remain on the ticket. Nixon made speeches in Missoula, stopped in Denver, and arrived in Wheeling late in the afternoon. Meanwhile, Eisenhower announced in his speech in Wheeling that his running mate had been the victim of an "attempted smear."

Eisenhower went to the airport to meet Nixon, and three thousand people who had come to meet the plane cheered the candidates. When Nixon's plane landed, Eisenhower himself would board the Nixon craft to find his running mate. "General, you didn't have to come here," said Nixon.

"Why not?" asked Eisenhower, "You're my boy." Eisenhower's comment was reasserting his status as a general over a junior officer. At City Island Stadium, Eisenhower introduced Nixon to the crowd as a "colleague" who had "vindicated himself" from a "vicious and unprincipled attack" and who "stood higher than ever before."

Nixon's Checkers speech would both save his political career and add to his derision by America's intellectual elite, who saw his performance as corny and trite. While highly successful, the speech would add to Nixon's status as the most polarizing figure in American politics in the 1950s.

NOTES

1. Jonathan Aitken, *Nixon: A Life*, p. 212.
2. "TV Goes to the Conventions," *Popular Mechanics*, June 1952, p. 94.
3. Jeffrey Frank, *Ike and Dick: Portrait of a Strange Political Marriage*, p. 30.

4. "Republican Party Platform of 1952," *Political Party Platforms: Parties Receiving Electoral Votes: 1840–2012*, The American Presidency Project, retrieved 13 October 2012.

5. James Chace, *Acheson: The Secretary of State Who Created the American World*, p. 326.

6. Rumbough, Stanley M. Citizens for Eisenhower, p. 51

7. Jeffrey Frank, *Ike and Dick: Portrait of a Strange Political Marriage*, p. 2.

8. Jeffrey Frank, *Ike and Dick: Portrait of a Strange Political Marriage*, p. 25.

9. Frank Mankiewicz, *Perfectly Clear: Nixon from Whittier to Watergate*, p. 58.

10. Edmund Kallina, *Kennedy v. Nixon*, p. 13.

11. Gayle B. Montgomery and James W. Johnson, *One Step From the White House: The Rise and Fall of Senator William F. Knowland*.

12. Edmund Kallina, *Kennedy v. Nixon*, p. 58.

13. Ibid. p. 31.

14. Christine L. Compston, *Earl Warren: Justice for All*, p. 63.

15. Jeffrey Frank, *Ike and Dick: Portrait of a Strange Political Marriage*, p. 32.

16. Herbert Brownell, *Advising Ike: The Memoirs of Attorney General Herbert Brownell*, p. 110–111.

17. James T. Patterson, *Mr. Republican: A Biography of Robert A. Taft* (HMH).

18. Jeffrey Frank, *Ike and Dick: Portrait of a Strange Political Marriage*, p. 32–33.

19. Ibid. p. 35.

20. Ibid. p. 120.

21. "Peter Edson First to Get Nixon Story," *Sarasota Herald-Tribune*. September 21, 1952.

22. Leonard Lurie, *The Running of Richard Nixon*, p. 123.

23. Leonard Lurie, *The Running of Richard Nixon*, p. 121.

24. Richard Nixon, "The Fund That Treatened to Wreck a Career," *Time*, March 16, 1962.

25. Jeffrey Frank, *Ike and Dick: Portrait of a Strange Political Marriage*, p. 40–41.

26. Leonard Lurie, *The Running of Richard Nixon*, p. 131.

27. Ibid.

28. Associated Press, "'Checkers Speech' defined Nixon's Style," *Sun Journal*, September 23, 1992.

29. Richard Nixon, *Six Crises*, p. 95.

30. Ibid. p. 96.

31. Associated Press, "'Checkers Speech' defined Nixon's Style," *Sun Journal*, September 23, 1992
32. Leonard Lurie, *The Running of Richard Nixon*, p. 135.
33. Jeffrey Frank, *Ike and Dick: Portrait of a Strange Political Marriage*, p. 48.
34. Ibid. 49.
35. Richard Nixon, *Six Crises*, p. 106.
36. Tom McCann, "50 Years Ago, It Was Pup that Saved Nixon," *Chicago Tribune*, Oct. 20, 2002.
37. Ralph de Toledano, *Nixon*, p. 141.
38. Herbert Klein, *Making It Perfectly Clear*, p. 138.
39. Conrad Black, *Richard M. Nixon: A Life in Full*, p. 258.
40. Richard Nixon, *Six Crises*, p. 121.
41. David LaGesse, "The 1952 Checkers Speech: The Dog Carries the Day for Richard Nixon," *U.S. News & World Report*, Jan. 17, 2008.
42. Richard Nixon, *Six Crises*, p. 129.

CHAPTER FIVE

IKE AND DICK

"I love that Mamie [Eisenhower]. She doesn't give a shit for anybody."

—Richard Nixon[1]

In the same way their political partnership was draconically cobbled together in a dark, "smoke-filled room" by high-powered GOP minds, Eisenhower and Nixon's personal relationship often existed the same way. A secretly wise, publicly aloof Eisenhower used Nixon as a hatchet man to handle some of the "messier" tasks of Washington and his administration. Dick had to do some of the GOP's most negative campaigning against the Democrats during the 1952 presidential campaign, and similarly, he was also often given the job of dealing with the Eisenhower administration's "dirty" work throughout his years as vice president. "He [Eisenhower] was a military man and he believed that people who are subordinates were to carry out what the chief wants," Nixon said years later. "It didn't bother me a bit. That was my job. A vice president, a member of the cabinet, a member of Congress is a member of the president's party. He should always consider that he is dispensable and should do what the man wants, to carry out his policy, because otherwise, the man's got to get down in the ring. What happened to Richard Nixon when Eisenhower was president would be bad for me, but wouldn't matter that much to the country. What happened to him would be disastrous."[2]

Despite Nixon's attentiveness to his commander in chief, for the eight years of the Eisenhower administration, there was a rift between the two men. To begin with, there was a gulf of twenty-three years between the former general and his vice president. Eisenhower, despite his humble Kansas roots, enjoyed the company of wealthy men with whom he played bridge and golf. To a man, Ike's "gang" had made real money. Eisenhower viewed them as his peers. Eisenhower would never look on Nixon that way. Though Nixon publicly claimed that Eisenhower's gruff indifference toward him was just part of the job, it took a tremendous toll on the insecure vice president's psyche. Nixon knew that Eisenhower had not supported him during the fund crisis and that approval was only the result of outmaneuvering Ike. For the many tasks Nixon carried out in his capacity as vice president, he was rewarded with a slow loathing from Eisenhower. "He [Nixon] worked for a man, and I know you shouldn't say this kind of thing—but he worked for a man who in my book was just a complete sadist, and who really cut Nixon to pieces," Nixon biographer Ralph de Toledano said. "He would cut him up almost just for the fun of it and I don't think Nixon ever really survived that. I don't think I am talking out of school and I say that when he was Vice President and I saw him quite frequently, he would come back from the White House and as much as he ever showed emotion you'd think he was on the verge of tears."[3]

To his credit, Eisenhower never blocked Nixon's access to information in the administration. Indeed, Nixon would plot with the CIA, the Pentagon, and others to persuade Ike to a harder line in both Cuba and Indochina. Nixon attended and could speak at all cabinet meetings and was present at all National Security Council (NSC) briefings. Nixon received the same national intelligence briefing every morning as the president.

Nixon would use his eight years in the vice presidency to burnish his reputation as a world traveler and foreign policy expert.

Nixon's assigned duty was to travel around the world conducting goodwill missions on behalf of the United States. President Eisenhower believed these trips would help dismiss damaging notions of America. He took a tour of the Far East in 1953 that was considered a success in terms of generating positive feedback for the United States, and Nixon began to appreciate the region's potential for industrial development and economic power—an appreciation that helped him decide to initiate economic relations with the area later on as president. He also visited the cities of Saigon and Hanoi when the region was still referred to as French Indochina, fifteen years before he would be elected as president and have to deal with saving the country from war and destruction, all while pulling out American troops and appeasing a war-weary public without seeming soft on communism.[4] Nixon's speeches "added conviction to the general opinion that American desire to aid in winning this war against communism . . . is sincere and continuing," said the American ambassador in Vietnam.[5] After the 1953 trip, Nixon decided to devote more time to foreign relations. Nixon biographer Irwin Gellman even said that "Eisenhower radically altered the role of his [vice president] by presenting him with critical assignments in both foreign and domestic affairs . . . Because of the collaboration between these two leaders, Nixon deserves the title 'the first modern vice-president.'"[6] Nixon would use these foreign trips to network with both foreign leaders and the leading opposition in many countries. He would carefully cultivate and maintain these relationships by letter and would travel abroad extensively in the early 1960s when, out of office, continuing to maintain the flow of information about geopolitics around the globe.   When   the Democrats took control of Congress in the 1954 midterm elections, Nixon began to question if he wanted to remain in politics after he served his first term as vice president. Pat Nixon had never gotten over the public embarrassment of the Checkers speech and wanted Nixon to retire to make some money and spend more time with his daughters. Life as Ike's thankless prat boy was draining Nixon of energy and wearing on the nerves of the vice president. Nixon did not shy away from this period of dejection in his memoirs:

> As the attacks became more personal, I sometimes wondered where party loyalty left off and masochism began. The girls were reaching an impressionable age, and neither Pat nor I wanted their father to become the perennial bad guy of American politics. During the last week of the 1954 campaign, when I was so tired that I could hardly remember what it felt like to be rested, I decided that this would be my last campaign. I began to think more and more about what Murray Chotiner had said almost two and a half years earlier at the convention in Chicago: I should pretty much be able to write my own ticket after retiring for the vice presidency at age forty-four. By the time I made a nationally televised broadcast on election eve, I had decided not to run again unless exceptional circumstances intervened to change my mind.[7]

Fate had a different plan than political retirement. It was on September 24, 1955, President Eisenhower suffered a severe heart attack, and the level of damage done to the old man's body was deemed to be potentially fatal at first. For six weeks, Eisenhower was unable to perform his duties as president of the United States. As the Twenty-Fifth Amendment to the Constitution had not yet been implemented or even conceived, the vice president did not have the formal authority to act in the absence of the president. Nonetheless, Nixon acted in place of Ike for the entire duration, presiding over cabinet meetings just as he had trained to do, making sure that no one tried to take power. Nixon would conduct cabinet meetings from his usual vice presidential chair rather than move into the seat the president usually occupied. As Ambrose noted, during that time Nixon "made no attempt to seize power."[8]

As a result of his political maturing, Nixon naturally decided to stick out a prospective second term as vice president with Ike, but by December 1955, some of Eisenhower's top aides—perhaps out of jealously for Nixon's political craft—wanted to have Dick replaced.

Hostility toward Nixon "was little more than a whisper during the administration's first two years," wrote *U.S. News & World Report*,[9] but with the presidency only a heartbeat away, the thought of Nixon as commander in chief became real. Ike did nothing to quell the tide that was rising against Nixon. When Eisenhower announced his reelection bid in February 1956, he was faced with one question from reporters, "Would you again want Vice President Nixon as your running mate?"[10] For a while Eisenhower avoided supplying an answer, which only proliferated the rumor that Nixon was a goner. When Ike finally did answer, he stated that indeed, it was the vice president who had not come to an answer regarding his role as vice president, and it would be inappropriate to answer for him. Nixon should be allowed "to chart his own course," Eisenhower said.[11] Privately Eisenhower would urge Nixon to shift to a cabinet, where he could gain "administrative experience." Ike said he could have any slot but state, where the redoubtable John Foster Dulles reigned. Nixon didn't take the bait. Party regulars like GOP Chairman Len Hall pressed Nixon's case with Ike, who ultimately folded, essentially letting Nixon announce that he would be delighted to run again for vice president. Eisenhower would then instruct Press Secretary Jim Hagerty to announce that Ike was delighted by the news. Once again, Eisenhower had left Nixon twisting in the wind and had done nothing to squelch a dump-Nixon movement ginned up by former Governor Harold Stassen, who proposed replacing Nixon with Massachusetts Governor Christian Herter, a liberal Republican who would ultimately replace Dulles at state. Once again, Nixon had survived.

Nixon continued to bare the scars of Eisenhower's mistreatment but had survived once again. In anticipation of Eisenhower's early ambivalence about Nixon seeking another term as vice president, Nixon supporters had quietly staged a write-in effort in the New Hampshire primary. This was a precursor of Nixon's grassroot strength among Republican Party regulars, won through nonstop stumping on behalf of Republican candidates through the 1950s.

Sure enough, Ike and Dick rolled to victory in 1956 once more with another healthy—and even larger—margin of victory over Illinois' former Governor Adlai Stevenson.

By 1957, Nixon resumed his diplomatic travels, this time embarking on a major trip to Africa. As the presiding officer of the Senate, he would play a crucial role in the landmark passage of the Civil Rights Act of 1957. Senate Majority Leader Lyndon Johnson, who had led the Southern block to prevent the passage of any civil rights legislation in the 1950s, decided he would have to pass a civil rights bill to make himself acceptable to Northern liberals within his party in a 1960 presidential bid. At the same time, Johnson would prepare a poison pill amendment that required that violators of the new federal law would be tried before state rather than federal juries. LBJ knew no all-white jury in the South would convict a white man of a transgression against a Negro. The amendment renders the law unenforceable.

Nixon actively lobbied his Republican colleagues against the amendment, although Massachusetts Senator John F. Kennedy would vote for the new amendment, which rendered the new law completely symbolic and totally unenforceable. Still Nixon would rally Republicans for final passage for which civil rights leader Martin Luther King would write him a letter of praise. Nixon would strongly urge Eisenhower to support the bill.[12]

The debate over the bill would lead to the longest one-man filibuster in United States history by a Democratic South Carolina Senator named Strom Thurmond, a man who would later become a Republican and play a key role in the reinvented Richard Nixon's procurement of the GOP nomination for the presidency in 1968.

Through the late 1950s, Ike's health continued to deteriorate, and in November 1957 he suffered a mild stroke, a blockage of a blood vessel leading to the brain. The stroke caused stammering and other speech difficulties. "He tried to tell me something," said Eisenhower's secretary Ann Whitman, "but he couldn't express himself. Something seemed to have happened to him all of a sudden."[13] In New York, key stocks fell seven points when news of the president's illness hit Wall Street.[14] The stroke raised the possibility that the president's mental faculties had been damaged to the point that he could not carry out the duties of the presidency. Once again, Nixon was on the doorstep of the Oval Office.

This time, Nixon's leadership in the wake of Eisenhower's absence was put on public display. He gave a press conference and assured the entire nation that the White House was functioning well while Ike had briefly taken ill. Eisenhower recovered and Dick was anxious to return to his diplomatic and domestic campaign duties, but 1958 would prove to be difficult year on both fronts.

During an April 1958 goodwill tour with Pat to South America, Nixon would be confronted by anti-American mobs, in many cases spurred on by Communist agitators. At first the trip was uneventful. In Uruguay, Nixon made one unplanned stop at a college campus and did an impromptu question-and-answer session with a group of students on US foreign policy. But when the Nixon entourage got to Lima, Peru, they came face-to-face with student demonstrations. Nixon, still in his forties and genuinely wanting to connect with the student body, chose to get out of his car to confront the students and stayed standing in front of them until he was forced back into his car by a barrage of thrown objects. The "communist-led mob stoned him, threw garbage, spat on him and desecrated the American flag."[15] In Caracas, Venezuela, on the same trip, Nixon and his wife were both spit on by an anti-American group of protestors, and their limousine was viciously attacked by a mob of protestors wielding pipes who attacked the vice presidential limousine. As Ambrose wrote, Nixon's conduct during the South America trip "caused even some of his bitterest enemies to give him some grudging respect."[16] His stature grew, and the coolness in which he handled himself brought wide praise at home.

A deep recession would produce the worst election cycle for the Republican Party since the Civil War. While the political party in the White House always tends to lose seats in a midterm election during a second term, the losses in the 1958 midterm races were particularly huge. Because Nixon once again undertook the role of campaigning for the party's candidates across the country, he would suffer much of the blame for GOP defeats. The Democrats took forty-eight seats in the House—maintaining their already very commanding majority—and even nabbed thirteen Republican seats in the Senate, including one in West Virginia that would keep the same Democrat, a man named Robert C. Byrd, in office until his death in 2010, becoming one of the longest-serving Senators in American history. That year also elected Democrats who would gain national attention in the 1970s, like Eugene McCarthy and Edmund Muskie. The Democrats even won two brand new Senate seats from the new state of Alaska. In California, both US Senator William Knowland and Governor Goodwin Knight were defeated after they attempted to switch offices. Knowland wanted the governorship for the basis of a future presidential bid, and Nixon and Knowland had bludgeoned Knight into running for the seat Knowland was vacating. Things were looking bleak for the Republicans in the coming election of 1960.

A public relations coup would, however, boost Nixon before the 1960 election. In July 1959, Ike sent Nixon to the Soviet Union for the special American National Exhibition in Moscow. The event was to be sponsored by the American government, to model a similar Soviet Union exhibit in New York City that same year. The event aimed to showcase both countries' latest "home appliances, fashions, television and hi-fi sets, a model house priced to sell [to] an 'average' family, farm equipment, 1959 automobiles, boats, sporting equipment and a children's playground,"[17] and it was designed in hopes of narrowing the gap between the two countries and improving the political climate. Of course, Nixon also knew that the event would present the perfect opportunity for him to challenge his Soviet counterparts on the merits of capitalism, and with the 1960 election right around the corner, he knew the chance could not be wasted. On July 24, while Nixon was touring the exhibits with Soviet Premier Nikita Khrushchev, the two men stopped at a model of an American kitchen and engaged in an impromptu exchange comparing the countries' two economic styles. This unplanned discussion through their interpreters took place throughout the exhibit, but was referred to at the time as the "Kitchen Debate"—since the most famous exchange between the two leaders took place in that American model kitchen—and the name has fittingly stayed around in history books. Nixon knew the model kitchen was full of laborsaving technologies and highly engineered recreation devices like television, which Nixon made a direct reference to as the exchange was being recorded on videotape and subsequently rebroadcast in both countries many times.

The crux of the Kitchen Debate came when Khrushchev surprised Dick by going into a rather fiery protest over a recent resolution that Congress passed condemning the Soviet Union for its control over Eastern Europe. The resolution called for Americans to pray for the "captive" peoples of Eastern Europe, and the Soviet premier seemed to take this to heart. After this tirade, Khrushchev then dismissed all the American technologies he had seen in the exhibit so far and declared that the peoples of the Soviet Union would have all the same things in a few years' time, and then his people would say to the United States "bye-bye" as they passed by.[18] Khrushchev had a few other good zingers during the debate, mocking the luxury of some of the appliances in the model kitchen by asking if there was an American machine that "put food in the mouth and pushed it down." Nixon kept his composure and admired that the competition between the countries through the exhibit was technological instead of military, and ultimately both of the leaders agreed that their two countries should find areas in which they could work together. The exchange, though, was heated. At one point the cameras caught Nixon jabbing Khrushchev with his finger. Fortunately for Nixon, this was the Associated Press photo that was distributed in newspapers across the United States.

The debate famously concluded with Khrushchev asking for everything he said in the debate to be translated into English and broadcast in the United States Nixon calmly responded, "Certainly it will, and everything I say is to be translated into Russian and broadcast across the Soviet Union. That's a fair bargain." Upon hearing this proposal, Khrushchev extended his hand, and the men vigorously shook. Of course, the Russians would famously only partly translate Nixon's comments and aired the debate on television at a late hour, when most of the country was sleeping.[19]

Time magazine praised Nixon for his performance, saying he "managed in a unique way to personify a national character proud of peaceful accomplishment, sure of its way of life, confident of its power under threat."[20] Nixon gained even more popularity with Americans who were devoutly anti-Communist, and he impressed his competitor in the debate, Premier Khrushchev. According to then-PR man William Safire, who was present at the exchange, "The shrewd Khrushchev came away persuaded that the advocate of capitalism was not just tough-minded but strong-willed."[21] Khrushchev later said he did all he could to cause Nixon's loss to Kennedy.

* * *

Nixon had a pivotal meeting in April 1959 with the highly romanticized, cigar-smoking, fatigue-wearing Cuban liberator, Fidel Castro. Castro had been sworn in as prime minister of Cuba in February after years of guerrilla warfare drove Fulgencio Batista from his ruthless dictatorship of the small island. Castro was in the United States for a fourteen-day stay at the invitation of the American Society of Newspaper Editors. Little was known about Castro's intentions for Cuba at the time, and the meeting gave Nixon a chance to evaluate the mysterious revolutionary.

Though Castro steadfastly denied he had a history of communist involvement, as an undergraduate at the University of Havana, he had been a member of a student organization with communist members.[22] Nixon had his suspicions prior to the encounter.

The two-and-a-half-hour meeting in Nixon's Washington office was private, but it is known that Nixon clearly took the time to learn about Castro, while at the same time lecturing the young rebel about the growing Communist influence in Cuba. "This man has spent the whole time scolding me," Castro later told an aide.[23]

Nixon got a firm impression of Castro, which he conveyed in a memo to President Eisenhower. Castro was "either incredibly naïve about Communism or under Communist discipline," Nixon wrote.[24] The vice president also noted that Castro's antagonistic feeling toward the United States was "virtually incurable." In Nixon's opinion, Castro was dangerous and if left in power would become a large problem only a short distance (ninety miles) off the coast of Florida. Many on the left later criticized Nixon and claimed that if we had embraced Castro after the 1959 meeting and plied him with cash, we could have pulled Fidel from the Soviet orbit. This is false.

In the late eighties, Nixon's son-in-law, New York lawyer and a longtime friend of mine Edward F. Cox, would be granted a rare interview with the aging dictator at the Palace of Justice in Havana. Castro would ramble in a two-hour tirade against the United States, but was otherwise cordial and somewhat friendly. When their time was up, the aged dictator would ask Cox, "So, how did your father-in-law know I was a Communist?"

Nixon's advice to Eisenhower that Castro had to go would sow the seeds of the Bay of Pigs, the Kennedy assassination, and Nixon's ultimate downfall. In late 1959, then director of the CIA Allen Dulles put forth a proposal that stated that "thorough consideration be given to the elimination of Fidel Castro . . . Many informed people believe that the disappearance of Fidel would greatly accelerate the fall of the present government."[25] The proposal led to the Dulles-formed Operation 40, a team of CIA assassins that, along with members of the Mafia, would attempt to assassinate Castro.

Because Castro had expelled all known CIA assets from Cuba, the agency needed the Mafia's contacts in the various hotel casinos in Havana to collect intelligence about Castro's movements.

The CIA may also have thought that the Mob could get an assassin close to El Commandante. The Mob believed this marriage would be helpful in reclaiming their Havana gambling establishments and garner leverage with the US government.

Nixon, who had been assigned as the "desk officer" of Cuban affairs by Eisenhower, pushed the plan to have the CIA recruit the active help of the Mafia in eliminating Castro. Former FBI man and longtime Howard Hughes retainer Robert Maheu would be authorized to reach out to Mob fixer Johnny Rosselli to weld the agency and La Cosa Nostra together in an effort to kill the Cuban leader.

Nixon was clearly hoping that the hit on Castro would take place in the fall before the 1960 election, providing a major foreign policy victory for the Eisenhower-Nixon administration and a boost in Nixon's prospects to prevail in the 1960 election, where it was crucial to Nixon to win the votes of Democrats and independents. The removal of Castro would be "a real trump card," Nixon told his press secretary Herb Klein. "He wanted it to occur in October, before the election," Klein added.[26] Nixon's deep involvement in Operation 40 made him fully aware of the CIA assassination team that included CIA agents E. Howard Hunt, Frank Sturgis, and Bernard "Macho" Barker. Operation 40, with the assistance of Mafia agents failed to eliminate Castro in 1960. These men would reappear at the failed Bay of Pigs operation, an offshoot of Operation 40 that anticipated a full-fledged invasion of Cuba concurrent with another attempt on Castro's life.

Hunt, Sturgis, and Barker were on the ground in Dallas the day of the Kennedy assassination and were subsequently arrested at the Watergate Hotel in 1972. Nixon clearly understood the thread that ran from Operation 40 to the Bay of Pigs, the Kennedy assassination, and the CIA role in Watergate, the caper that would ultimately bring Nixon down.

NOTES

1. Conrad Black, *A Life in Full*, p. 210.
2. *Crossfire*, November, 1982.
3. Leonard Lurie, *The Running of Richard Nixon*, p. 161.
4. Jonathan Aitken, *Nixon: A Life*, pp. 225–227.
5. Jeffrey Frank, *Ike and Dick*, p. 76.
6. Melvin Small, *A Companion to Richard M. Nixon*, pp. 102–120.
7. Richard Nixon, *The Memoirs of Richard Nixon*, p. 163.
8. Stephen Ambrose, *Nixon: The Education of a Politician*, pp. 375–376.
9. Herbert S. Parmet, *Richard Nixon and his America*, p. 259.
10. Leonard Lurie, *The Running of Richard Nixon*, p. 209.
11. Ibid.
12. Conrad Black, *A Life in Full*, pp. 349–352.
13. Leonard Lurie, *The Running of Richard Nixon*, p. 232.
14. "President suffers 'mild stroke,' will need several weeks' rest; Nixon denies he'll take charge," Associated Press, November 27, 1957.
15. *Spokane Daily Chronicle*, May 9, 1958.
16. Stephen Ambrose, *Nixon: The Education of a Politician*, p. 254.
17. "The Russian People Can Take a Peek at U.S. Civilization," *Saturday Evening Post*, August 1, 1959.
18. "Nixon in USSR Opening US Fair, Clashes with Mr. K," *Universal International News*, July 1959.
19. Associated Press, "Soviet TV Shows Tape of Debate," *The New York Times*, July 28, 1959.
20. "Better to See Once," *Time*, August 3, 1959.
21. William Safire, "*The Cold War's Hot Kitchen*," *New York Times*, July 24, 2009.
22. Herbert Matthews, "From the Sierra Maestra to Havana, the Ideals Never Changed," *New York Times*, April 5, 1959.
23. Jim Rasenberger, *The Brilliant Disaster: JFK, Castro, and America's Doomed Invasion of Cuba's Bay of Pigs*, p. 21.
24. Ibid.
25. Anthony Summers, *The Arrogance of Power*, p. 184.
26. Anthony Summers, *The Arrogance of Power*, p. 185.

CHAPTER SIX

STOLEN

"Will God forgive me for stealing Illinois from Nixon?"[1]
—Chicago Mayor Richard Daley, on his deathbed

"Of course they stole the election."[2]
—Richard Nixon

The 1960 election was viewed as a "generational change" election. America would chose between two young veterans of World War II, one who offered the staid continuation of the Eisenhower policies of peace and prosperity, and the other who urged a more activist vision for the future.

Incredibly, three of the four candidates on the two national tickets would eventually become president. (John F. Kennedy, Lyndon B. Johnson, and Richard M. Nixon would all win the White House.) The election took place during one of the most turbulent times in American history. With the nation confronting communist aggression in Cuba and Indochina as well as a standoff with the Russian in East Berlin, the Cold War was near its peak. Voters believed that the election would determine the fate of free world. Both Nixon and Kennedy would run as Cold Warriors.

In spite of their disparate origins, the early careers of Nixon and Kennedy were curiously parallel. Both had been naval officers during

World War II. Both began their political careers in the House in 1947 and had served together as junior members of the House Labor Committee. Both foreign policy hard-liners, they enjoyed a friendly relationship traveling to McKeesport, Pennsylvania, to debate the fine points of the Taft–Hartley labor law. Nixon was the hardscrabble upstart from California and Kennedy the politically connected rich kid from Boston, but both found common ground sharing the Pullman compartment on the Capitol Limited. "We went back by train to Washington from McKeesport," Nixon recalled. "It was a night train because we had to get back for a vote the next day. And so we drew as to who got the upper berth and who got the lower berth, and I won, one of the few times I did against him. I got the lower berth, but it didn't make a lot of difference, because all night long, going back on the train, we talked about our experiences in the past, but particularly about the world and where we were going and that sort of thing. I recall that was the occasion too, as we were going back on that train, we—I told him about me being stationed at Vella LaVella, and found that his PT boat had put in there, and we reminisced about whether we might have possibly met on that occasion. So we each assumed we did."[3]

Nixon was deeply affected by Kennedy's serious illness and hospitalization in 1947 when it appeared that young Kennedy would not survive. The married Kennedy, a notorious ladies man, upon hearing that Nixon would travel to Paris dropped by the ungainly Congressman's office with names and phone numbers Nixon could call for a steamy romp in the City of Lights. Nixon didn't follow up.

Although Nixon had a high regard for Kennedy it appears that JFK did not have the same high regard for his Republican competitor. Nixon smarted from the rejection of his House colleague, and his sense of resentment to the Eastern elite would only grow. Not only did they dislike him, he believed they stole the White House from him. Senator George Smathers, the handsome friend of both Nixon and Kennedy said, "Nixon had a greater admiration for Kennedy than Kennedy had for Nixon . . . Nixon told me several times he admired Jack, and I happen to know the feeling was not particularly mutual. I don't think Jack ever thought too highly of Nixon, either of his ability or of him as a man of great strength of character . . . He felt that Nixon was a total opportunist."[4]

Sometimes JFK could reciprocate Nixon's goodwill. "Nixon is a nice fellow in private, and a very able man," Kennedy said. "I worked with him on the Hill for a long time, but it seems he has a split personality, and he is very bad in public, and nobody likes him."[5] Kennedy's opinion of Nixon would only deteriorate during the hard-fought campaign. JFK speechwriter Richard Goodwin would hear Kennedy say of Nixon, "He's a filthy, lying son of a bitch, and a very dangerous man."[6]

Theodore H. White would both pioneer a new form of journalism and write the official story of the 1960 campaign in *The Making of the President, 1960*. I got to know "Teddy" well in 1979–80, when he wrote his book on the 1980 race. He was infatuated with Kennedy. His narrative focused on Kennedy's image and style, while Nixon was a middle-class afterthought. White, like many Americans, bought into the Kennedy mystique and seemed oblivious to the well-funded Madison Avenue effort to sell America on John F. Kennedy's "style." He was movie-star handsome, with a beautiful wife and adorable children. American's were interested in his family, and his taste in art and music, and among the intellectual class, the Kennedy style dazzled. To a certain extent, John F. Kennedy was a confection, sold to the American people by what Nixon would call "the most ruthless group of political operators," and cutting edge advertising techniques, paid for by the multimillionaire Joseph P. Kennedy. "We're going to sell Jack like soap flakes," Joe Kennedy proclaimed.[7] Nixon speechwriter Richard Whalen would analyze the mesmerizing effect of the Kennedy style on America. "In Kennedy-enchanted America, 'style' was everything," Whalen wrote. "Not style in the familiar sense, as mode, manner, or aspect of something, but style as a supreme value in itself, style for it own splendid sake. The line between image and substance disappeared. A thing well said was a thing accomplished."[8] Indeed, after his death, the mythology of Kennedy weaved around the fictional Camelot allowed for imagination to fill in the rest of his incomplete life and presidency: The end to the Vietnam War, and the Cold War or the passing civil rights. None were accomplished under Kennedy, but the mythology allowed that all were possible.

Because of the circumstances of his death, and the incomplete record of his life and presidency, one can project on Kennedy whatever one wants to see. Add to that fifty years of nostalgia, and an accurate assessment of the Kennedy-Nixon race becomes difficult. JFK did not start as the toast of party liberals or organizational Democrats. The tightly organized and relentless campaign run by his brother Robert Kennedy would take first the Democratic nominating process, and then the nation, by storm.

Nixon was without a doubt a polarizing figure, but had managed to soften his image in 1959 and early 1960, launching the first of the "New Nixons." From the beginning the national polls reflected a skintight race. Professor Edmund Kallina would reflect a more balanced view of Nixon's "negatives":

> On balance, it is fair to say that Nixon's reputation as a dirty campaigner was exaggerated and that Helen Douglas and California Democrats were the first to raise questions about Congressman Vito Marcantonio, who Murry Chotiners, pink flyers would make a household name in the closing days of the 1950 Senate race. The extreme left abhorred Nixon and they constantly drove the narrative of "Tricky Dick," who they saw as manipulative, deceitful, and underhanded. Polls in 1960 showed that this view was largely limited to liberal Democrats and a more balanced perspective of Nixon was held by Republicans, the vast majority of Independents and some conservative Democrats. There is no doubt that the animus on the hard left emanates from Nixon's pursuit of Hiss and his defeat of Mrs. Douglas with a bare-fisted campaign would only intensify this hatred.[9]

The contest was dirtier and more hard-fought than depicted in White's book. In the intervening years, *Kennedy v. Nixon* by Kallina and *The Real Making of the President* by W. J. Rorabaugh provided a more balanced perspective on the photo-finish election. The contest was fought close and tough with Nixon, the more seasoned politician and famed debater, making a series of unforced errors.

No election for president has matched the overall voter turnout, and yet the 1960 election was remarkable in other ways. It was the dirtiest in American history. The mythologizing of John F. Kennedy after his death has obscured his father's and brothers' ruthlessness and commitment to do anything it took to put Kennedy in the White House.

Dirty tricks? Break-ins? Illegal cash? Bugging? Today these tactics are readily identified with the Nixon administration, but could just as easily describe the Kennedy campaign of 1960. Ambassador Joseph P. Kennedy and his campaign manager son Robert would engage in all of them as well as dealings with organized crime to elect John F. Kennedy.

They would employ these tactics first to Senator Hubert Humphrey and then to Richard Nixon. This campaign stratagem, in turn, bred the "everyone does it" attitude of the Nixon men, which allowed the crimes of Watergate to happen twelve years later. The 1960 campaign would include a successful effort by the Kennedy men to bug Nixon's hotel suite on the eve of Nixon's second debate, a surreptitious entry into the office of Nixon's psychiatrist and the bugging of an official at the Republic National Committee as well as a break-in at the accountant's office of industrialist Howard Hughes in search of incriminating evidence against Richard Nixon. Robert Kennedy was a tough and ruthless political operator who used private detectives and illegal wire taps in the campaign for JFK's ascendancy to the White House. RFK's activities included the bugging of an executive in Boston who had evidence that John Kennedy had an affair with a nineteen-year-old college student in the Bay State.[10]

It is Nixon who bears the reputation as a "dirty campaigner," but in the context of the era it was just part of the game. "Well, for Christ's sake, everybody bugs everybody else. We know that," President Nixon said in private conversation in September 1972.[11]

One of the great ironies of the 1960 campaign is that Nixon, who had enjoyed robust health and a phenomenal capacity for physical energy and hard work, would be plagued by a series of maladies throughout the 1960 campaign, while Kennedy, who projected an aura of athletic vitality, but had been plagued throughout his life by serious and even life-threatening health issues, would pace himself in a way that allowed him to physically stand up to the rigors of the campaign.

The question of both candidates' health would play out in more devious and surreptitious ways as the major candidates for president in 1960, Nixon, Kennedy, and Johnson, all maneuvered to get the goods on each other. Although Nixon's 1972 campaign that resulted in the Watergate scandal would become synonymous in the public mind with illegal break-ins, wiretapping, illegal money, and dirty tricks, the 1960 campaign would have these tactics utilized by the Kennedys and Senator Lyndon Johnson. While Kennedy was the picture of hale good health in public, the reality was much more problematic. Kennedy suffered from Addison's disease and required regular injections of cortisone to augment his deadly adrenal insufficiency. When this accurate diagnosis became public, John F. Kennedy would simply lie.

Someone broke into the New York City offices of Dr. Eugene Cohen, an endocrinologist who treated Kennedy. The offices were in shambles with the lock jimmied; filing cabinets rifled and discarded patient files strewn on the floor. On the same day, someone attempted another burglary at the offices of another doctor who was treating Kennedy, Dr. Janet Travell. The perpetrators had not been able to penetrate the lock on her office door. While Dr. Travell was not treating Kennedy for Addison's disease per se (that care fell to Dr. Cohen), she was treating Kennedy for his chronic back pain and was fully aware of his advanced Addison's disease.

After the break-in at both doctors' offices, Kennedy would ask Dr. Travell to contact every hospital where he had ever been treated and secure his records.

In a 2002 *Vanity Fair* article JFK biographer Robert Dallek pinned the break-ins on Nixon, but has never provided proof for his assertion. "It appears that Richard Nixon may have tried at one point to gain access to Kennedy's medical history," Dallek opined. "Although the thieves remain unidentified, it is reasonable to speculate that they were Nixon operatives." Nixon's longtime spokesman and advisor Herb Klein vehemently denied this. "It couldn't have happened," said Klein. "Anything that would have been close to [a break-in] would have been discussed with me, and it wasn't."

Dallek ignored the most obvious perp in the break-ins, Lyndon Baines Johnson, and LBJ would use the information only weeks before the Los Angeles convention. It was Lyndon Johnson, not Richard Nixon, who would lay Kennedy's secret before the American people at the the Los Angeles convention. With Kennedy's medical records secretly in hand, LBJ acolytes Texas Governor John Connally and Vice Chairwoman of the Democratic National Committee India Edwards would hold a convention press conference to publicly announce that Kennedy had Addison's disease and therefore was not healthy enough to be president. Johnson himself would spread the intel through interviews and other publicity, at one point referring to Kennedy as that "little scrawny fellow with rickets."[12] The more probable sponsor for the break-ins at both Kennedy doctors' offices was Senate Majority Leader Lyndon Johnson.

Edwards would quote a "reliable" source when she charged Kennedy with the assertion that he "would not be alive today if it were not for cortisone."[13] This was, of course, true. Following his assassination, it was found that JFK's adrenal glands had wasted away to almost nothing due to the disease.[14] He had been kept alive with cortisone, which gave his face the puffy look notable in his later years.

That the Kennedy forces knew Johnson, not Nixon was behind the illicit seizure of Kennedy's health records was confirmed when Robert Kennedy sought out Johnson at the Los Angeles Democratic Convention. "You Johnson people are running a stinking damned campaign, and you're gonna get yours when the time comes," Bobby fumed.[15]

The belief that Robert Kennedy thought it was LBJ, not Nixon, who broke into the Kennedy doctor's offices is bolstered by the timing of both the break-in and the subsequent attack on JFK. We know that the attack on Kennedy from Johnson's camp followers occurred *before* the Democratic Convention in July.

Kennedy was forced to release a letter from Dr. Travell and Dr. Cohen, who wrote in a largely false statement saying that Jack's "adrenal glands do function." In an action of false bravado the doctors advised Kennedy to bring suit any claim to the contrary, even if they "have had access to old medical records"— a clear reference to the records that Robert Kennedy was worried had been stolen from his brother's doctor's office.

The Kennedys understood the need to immediately refute this health claim lest the Kennedy bandwagon would be halted. Both Kennedys denied the accusations. "I do not have it," Kennedy told Arthur Schlesinger, "and I never had it." A press conference was held shortly after to bolster their claims. More than thirty years later in an oral history, Dr. Travell would come clean about JFK's Addison's disease.

Perhaps the reason Nixon never overtly raised the question of Kennedy's Addison's disease was because he himself had health issues that were less serious than Kennedy's but enough to sink a presidential candidacy in 1960. Nixon had sought the treatment of a psychiatrist throughout the 1950s. The former US president began seeing Dr. Arnold Hutschnecker in 1952 with a litany of maladies that Nixon suspected were psychosomatic, including back pain and insomnia. The Kennedy forces would use a surreptitious entry to gain proof of Nixon's visits to the shrink.

Nixon knew that in 1960 the American people were unlikely to elect a man who was "seeing a shrink." Although the advances in our perceptions about psychiatry and mental health issues have advanced, even in 2014, it is also notable that no man elected president has admitted to psychiatric care.

Kennedy's father had paid a source in Los Angeles who had made Nixon's visits to Dr. Hutschnecker known to the Kennedy's through crooner Frank Sinatra.[16] A private detective who sold the records to Kennedy had learned about Dr. Hutschnecker's treatment of Nixon through Attorney Louis Neustein, who was not only the doctor's lawyer, but also a close friend. The detective managed to get into Nixon's psychotherapist's office under false pretenses in September 1960, where he stole Nixon's medical file, but he also would be arrested three years later for stealing classified state documents.

No matter who was behind the 1960 break-ins at JFK's doctors' offices, Jack Kennedy knew it was an opponent. Jack's powerful and protective father had every reason to prevent Nixon from using stolen medical files against Jack by getting his hands on Richard Nixon's own medical files. After LBJ's attack on Kennedy, Nixon was certainly *aware* of the allegations that Kennedy had Addison's disease. With his own dark secrets to hide, he never raised the issue, unlike LBJ. Before the start of the Democratic Convention, there was one other politician who might have had a reason to want to steal Kennedy's medical records—a politician who wanted the Democratic nomination for himself. Like Nixon, this politician had a long history of doing anything it took to win, and on the eve of the Democratic Convention, would have two of his subordinates call a press conference and tell reporters that Kennedy had Addison's disease.

That politician was Lyndon Baines Johnson, who would later become Jack's running mate in the 1960 election. Like Nixon,

Johnson had the means, motive, and opportunity to stage such a crime.

The tactics that defeated Nixon were more devious than merely the stealing of medical records and votes that Lyndon Johnson specialized in. The Kennedy camp learned that in 1957, Howard Hughes lent Nixon's brother Donald $205,000 to bail out his "Nixon's" drive-in restaurant in Whittier, California. Even though the restaurant featured "Nixonburgers," it went bankrupt less than a year later. Author Mark Feldstein claimed the Hughes funds were diverted to Richard Nixon to purchase a home, but the candidate said he received no portion of the loan and that his mother had posted family property as collateral. "It was all she had," he said. Strangely, the loan had been extended through third parties, apparently to hide its origins, the terms never called for repayment and the property was never seized after the restaurant failed.

Los Angeles accountant Phillip Reiner, who had served as one of the middlemen in the Hughes transaction, tipped off the Kennedys. Reiner, who had been terminated by the accounting firm that handled the Hughes business, saw an opportunity to make money. After the accountant met with Robert Kennedy and received a $100,000 payment, his former office was robbed. The accounting firm filed a burglary report with the Los Angeles Police Department, but the perpetrator was never apprehended.

Supposedly, in return for the Hughes funds Nixon had arranged the approval of giant defense contracts and interceded with Eisenhower's Justice Department on Hughes' behalf regarding antitrust issues. There was no evidence of this then, and none has ever surfaced since, but the revelation of the unusual loan undermined Nixon's campaign just as he was gaining ground.[17]

The Kennedy men sought to plant the loan story in the *St. Louis Post-Dispatch* and *Time* magazine in the final days of the campaign, but neither news outlet would publish the story without documented corroboration. With time running out, the Kennedys turned to sworn Nixon enemies Drew Pearson and his associate

Jack Anderson, whose *Washington Post* syndicated column had been fiercely critical of Nixon during his vice presidential years.

Kennedy lawyer James McInerney contacted Anderson and handed him documents revealing that Hughes had sent $205,000 through intermediaries to the Nixon family. Armed with the purloined documents documenting the loan, Pearson and Anderson broke the controversial story in their syndicated column on October 26, just one week before Election Day. Although their column was generally carried by seven hundred newspapers, it is notable that the majority of them declined to run the last-minute attack. A number of newspapers did carry the story, however, and Nixon believed the revelation of the Hughes loan was a major factor in his narrow loss.

Indeed, the Hughes matter vexed Nixon and hardened his hatred of reporters who raised it. When AP later reported that a reporter had tipped JFK that the Hughes loan story was coming, he would write me:

> Incidentally, the January 14, 1971 memo to Haldeman which was the lead of the AP story was in fact not news. Both Haldeman and Dean had the memo in their books!
>
> If anyone had any doubt that the media was trying to help Kennedy, his note with regard to the Hughes loan story should disabuse them. In all of my campaigns, I can never think of a case where a member of the press—even one friendly to us—leaked a story in advance to us so that we could exploit it.
>
> While I know that you have to disagree, I still believe that the best way for a conservative to handle the media is to treat them with "courteous contempt." As you may recall, I made this point in one of my press conferences. One of the reporters asked if I hated the press. I answered, "No." "Love and hate have one thing in common. You must respect the individual involved." I regret that there are very few members of the fourth estate who deserve respect as objective, fair reporters.[18]

After being blitzed by the Kennedy machine Nixon wrote:

> We were faced in 1960 by an organization that had equal dedication to ours and unlimited money, that was led by the most ruthless group of political operatives ever mobilized for a presidential campaign. Kennedy's organization approached campaign dirty tricks with a roguish relish and carried them off with an insouciance that captivated many politicians overcame the critical faculties of many reporters. . . From this point on I had the wisdom and wariness of someone who had been burned by the power of the Kennedys and their money and by the license they were given by the media. I vowed that I would never again enter an election at a disadvantage by being vulnerable to them—or anyone—on the level of political tactics.[19]

The burglary to acquire loan documents that fueled an attack on Nixon was among many surreptitious and illegal break-ins during the 1960 campaign. A private detective named John Leon claimed McInerney retained him to steal the Hughes-Nixon loan documents. Leon also concluded from a conversation with colleagues the day after the first Nixon-Kennedy debate that Kennedy's men "successfully bugged the Nixon space or tapped his phones prior to the television debate."[20]

In 1973, Leon produced five sworn affidavits from former FBI agents and DC police officers who said they had bugged Nixon's suite at the Ward Park Sheraton where he prepared for his second debate. Several of them also admitted to using electronic eavesdropping devices.

Leon was among the country's earliest experts in the use and development of the lie detector. Leon would identify former CIA officer John Frank, congressional investigator Edward M. Jones, and Joseph Shimon, a former inspector for the Washington Police Department, who all came forward with sworn affidavits claiming that RFK had ordered the bugging of Nixon's room. They all worked for Carmine Bellino, one of Robert Kennedy's retinue of operatives.

Investigator Joseph Shimon told of how he had been approached by Kennedy operative Oliver W. Angelone, a former FBI agent. Angelone said that he was working for Carmine Bellino and needed his help to gain access to the two top floors of the Wardman Park Hotel just before they were occupied by Nixon on the eve of the Nixon-Kennedy television debate.

Edward Murray Jones, then living in the Philippines, said in his affidavit that he had been assigned by Bellino to tail individuals at Washington National Airport and in downtown Washington to the hotel.[21]

Leon said he was retained by Washington attorney James M. McInerney, the same man who brokered the deal for information leading to the break-in at Howard Hughes' accountant's office to steal the Hughes Nixon loan documents.

When JFK seemed to anticipate Nixon's thrusts in the debate, Angeleone told Leon "Jonesy [the team's wire man] had done his job."[22]

They also admitted to electronic eavesdropping at the Republican National Committee. Bellino was fired as an investigator for the Senate Watergate Committee when his involvement in the 1960 allegations became public. Bellino denied having any role at all.

Strangely, Leon died only hours before a scheduled press conference to charge that the Democrats had wiretapped Nixon's campaign suite in 1960 and had used electronic surveillance devices on officials at the Republican National Committee. The weight of the evidence indicated that Robert Kennedy wiretapped the Nixon campaign in 1960 and, as we shall see, would do so again in 1962.

It is understandable, therefore, why Nixon would believe that buggings and black bag break-ins were standard operating procedure in the political realm. He had been wiretapped and had information stolen from this camp. His doctor's office was infiltrated as well as damaged by the break-in at the Hughes accountant's office. Nixon vowed never to be caught unprepared again.

I would later become friendly with Bobby's chief "dirty trickster" Paul Corbin. Corbin was a hard-bitten former Communist and ex–union organizer. Although personally dedicated to Bob Kennedy, Corbin was a man without scruples while at the same time enormously resourceful. "We managed to get a million pieces of anti-literature mailed to Catholic homes in Wisconsin," Corbin would tell me when I joined him for a friendly game of poker at the home of a mutual friend. "We made it look like it came from Humphrey," he said, alluding to Kennedy's opponent in the crucial Wisconsin primary. Corbin also reminisced about a charge that the Kennedys had trumped up against Humphrey in West Virginia. Robert Kennedy convinced Franklin D. Roosevelt Jr., son of the New Dealer, to attack Humphrey as a draft dodger who had fraudulently used an issue to avoid military service. FDR initially resisted the order but due to his difficult financial circumstances would ultimately agree to make the accusation.[23] There was only one problem. It was a lie. Humphrey was furious, and it would ruin Roosevelt's political career. "We got a flyer to every VFW and American Legion Post in the state," chortled Corbin. "Hubert never knew what hit him."

Unlike the Kennedys, who had a fierce battle to win the Democratic nomination, Nixon was never in true danger of being challenged for the 1960 Republican presidential nomination. Nixon would, however, fly unannounced to New York to meet with his rival Governor Nelson Rockefeller, who demanded concessions in the 1960s platform pertaining to both civil rights and defense spending.

In an effort to paper over his rift with Rockefeller, Nixon would agree to some fairly innocuous language changes, which he then imposed on the platform committee chaired by Bell and Howell exec Charles "Chuck" Percy, who would run a losing race for governor of Illinois before being elected to the US Senate. The outcry from the party's conservative wing was immediate. "It's the Munich of the Republic Party," said Senator Barry Goldwater.[24] The maneuver did not endear Nixon to grassroots party conservatives to whom Rockefeller seemed a big-state, big-spending liberal. Ironically, Rockefeller was pushing a platform plank that called for sharp increases in defense spending, which Nixon privately supported, but which was anathema to the budget-conscious Eisenhower.

Nixon's eight-year service to Eisenhower and the need for Eisenhower's help and support were severely limiting. This situation was exacerbated by a highly developed Democratic campaign theme first espoused by Senator Stuart Symington and then adopted by both Lyndon Johnson and John Kennedy that a "missile gap" existed between the United States and the Soviet Union and that the Soviets were pulling ahead in nuclear armament superiority. Eisenhower, with access to real intelligence information, knew the charge was bogus but never effectively refuted it. Nixon was reduced to standing by while Kennedy effectively utilized the fear of a nation to call for a steep increase in America's offensive nuclear capability. "Those who oppose these expenditures are taking a chance on our very survival as a nation," declared Kennedy.[25] Americans would learn after the election that there was no missile gap and that reports of Soviet advances were wildly exaggerated.

From the beginning Nixon faced a more difficult path to the White House in collecting the 270 electoral votes needed to win. Nixon needed to win at least four of the nine states with the largest numbers of electoral votes. Texas was problematic for Nixon because of Lyndon Johnson and his well-oiled Democrat-dominated political machine, which was adept at vote stealing and election fraud. The Texas GOP, still in its infancy, was nonexistent outside of a few suburban areas like Ft. Worth, Dallas, and Houston.

New York looked tough for Nixon because of its heavily Roman Catholic vote, and Nixon knew he could not count on the Rockefeller machine. Nixon also faced uphill climbs in New Jersey, Pennsylvania, and Michigan, where Republican state organizations were weak and Democratic governors held sway. In Illinois, the Republicans were strong, but there was an unpopular Republican governor running for a controversial third term and a weak US Senate candidate. New Jersey was in play. Ohio and California were winnable, but they were not guaranteed. Nixon never solved this Electoral College dilemma and had difficulty in deciding where his resources should be concentrated,[26] on the big Northern industrial states or . . . should he make a play for the Deep South?

Nixon faced a geographic dilemma that did not confront the Democrats. Would he contest the large Northern industrial states where there were existing Republican organizations or would he rolle the dice on making inroads into Dixie where there were plenty of conservative voters but party organization was virtually non-existent? Out of this dilemma was born Nixon's foolhardy pledge to visit all fifty states, theoretically devoting time to every region in the country.

Nixon made this stunning pledge at the Chicago convention. When sidelined with a knee injury that required hospitalization after September 1, 1960, Nixon had a perfect excuse to abandon his fifty-state campaign pledge. While campaigning in Tennessee, Nixon had been surged by an enthusiastic crowd of voters and bumped his knee getting into his limousine. The leg swelled, and Nixon applied ice. In a television interview with Jack Paar, Nixon could be seen flinching when the host put his hand on the vice president's knee. Doctors at Walter Reed hospital diagnosed a virulent infection that required intensive medication and weeks in bed.

To be out of the game for two weeks was Nixon's worst nightmare. Now, his fifty-state campaign pledge was more problematic, as he had too few days to travel to all of the places he would be required to visit. Indeed, the final days would have him leave the lower fifty to visit Alaska, a state in which he held a seventeen point lead. Nixon's advisors begged him to scrap his fifty-state campaign pledge, but with the support of wife Pat, Nixon kept his word. It was a costly mistake. Nixon was forced to visit small states that he had securely locked up prior to his unfortunate debilitation, at the same time trying to concentrate on big states. By contrast, Kennedy campaigned relentlessly in ten target states and rarely touched down in smaller states where the Democratic ticket was out in front.

Nixon's fifty-state pledge locked the exhausted candidate into a grueling physical schedule set further back by his knee injury. JFK also second-guessed his scheduling when his final week's drive took him to New York, where he enjoyed a comfortable lead, instead of California, which was close. JFK's first instinct was correct: Nixon carried California only when the Republican-leaning absentee ballots were counted.[27]

The other strategic dilemma facing Nixon was the question of whether to concentrate on the black vote or the white southern vote. Nixon's civil rights record was impeccable. Dr. Martin Luther King had personally thanked Nixon for rounding up the Republican votes in the Senate for the 1957 Civil Rights Bill. Eisenhower had run well with black voters. Nixon had opposed and worked against the jury trial amendment LBJ had dropped in the 1957 Civil Rights Act as a "poison pill." Kennedy had voted for Johnson's amendment. Nixon was keenly aware that the New Deal Coalition that included segregationists in the South, African Americans in the North, and big city Catholic machines, was beginning to fray. Nixon had to decide between making a play for blacks in New York, Pennsylvania, Michigan, and Illinois or white Democrats in the needed border states of Virginia, Tennessee, Kentucky, and the Carolinas as well as a foray into the Deep South. JFK, whose civil rights record was weak and who had little following among civil rights leaders, moved to make the decision moot. The big-city machines had long mined the "Negro vote" and were adept at getting Kennedy's message out to these voters.

Nixon badly bungled an opportunity that the Kennedy men would seize. When Dr. Martin Luther King was arrested and jailed in Atlanta, some Nixon advisors suggested that Nixon reach out to King's concerned wife or to the judge in the case. Nixon, ever the lawyer, felt these contacts would be inappropriate. Unfazed by ethics, Kennedy, egged on by brother-in-law Sargent Schriver and aide Harris Wofford, would place a greatly publicized call to Coretta King. Robert Kennedy, an attorney himself, first contacted Ernest Vandiver, a hard-line Atlanta segregationist who was nonetheless a Kennedy supporter and the judge in the King case, to have King released. As a result, Dr. King's father, "Big Daddy" King, a Republican who had supported Eisenhower and Nixon in 1956, publicly switched from Nixon to Kennedy saying, "I've got a suitcase of votes, and I'm going to take them to Mr. Kennedy and dump them in his lap.[28] He condemned Eisenhower and Nixon for "not saying a mumbling word." Years later, Dr. King would express disappointment that Nixon had not seized the opportunity. "I always felt that Nixon lost a real opportunity to express . . . support of something much larger than an individual, because this expressed support of the movement for civil rights in a way," said King.[29] Nixon press secretary Herb Klein said that Eisenhower Attorney General William P. Rogers had been pivotal in convincing Nixon to make no gesture toward King.[30] Baseball great Jackie Robinson, who was campaigning for Nixon, beseeched the vice president to do *something*. When Nixon declined, Robinson said, "Nixon doesn't deserve to win."[31] Robinson and Nixon became estranged, with the civil rights trailblazer supporting first Rockefeller, then Humphrey, for president in 1968.

In retrospect, Nixon's 32 percent share of the African American vote in 1960 represents a high-water mark for the Republican Party. The GOP's percentage of the black vote subsequently dwindled, dipping into single digits by 2000.

The Democrats managed to have it both ways. JFK, running with a strong civil rights plank in the platform and the support of big-city Democratic bosses as well as their African American constituents went after black votes in the North, while Lyndon Johnson traveled through the South, quietly reassuring the white courthouse crowds that Kennedy wasn't serious about the "Nigrahs."[32] The strategy worked, although Nixon would peel away the border South, Kennedy would be the last Democrat to carry the Deep South until Jimmy Carter arrived on the scene in 1976. LBJ, a lifelong segregationist who had blocked every civil rights and anti-lynching measure in the US Senate in the 1950s, had credibility with the old boys and helped Kennedy hold together the Roosevelt coalition for one more election.

The religious issue was also largely problematic for Nixon. The Kennedy camp had recognized the strengths of a Catholic candidate as early as 1956 when they had Connecticut Democratic State Chairman John Bailey circulate a cogent memo outlining why putting a Catholic on the ticket with Adlai Stevenson would be a plus. The memo read:

> If [a Catholic candidate] bought into the Democratic fold only those normally Democratic Catholics who voted for Ike, he would probably swing New York, Massachusetts, Rhode Island, Connecticut, Pennsylvania, and Illinois—for 132 electoral votes. If he also wins the votes of Catholics who shifted to the Republicans in 1948 or earlier, he could also swing New Jersey, Minnesota, Michigan, California, Wisconsin, Ohio, Maryland, Montana and maybe eve New Hampshire—for a total of 265 electoral votes.[33]

JFK's 1960 religious strategy counted on shaming voters who might have had vague anti-Catholic feelings, but whom largely appealed to fair play and anti-bigotry. The Democrat's constant repetition of fair play also aroused the sympathy of voters who otherwise might have supported Nixon. Most important, Kennedy's tactic energized Catholic voters—including those who were Republicans or independents—to turn out *for* a coreligionist movement and to unprove any anti-Catholic argument. A post-election analysis concluded that because of increased Catholic support, Kennedy won six states that he otherwise would have lost: Connecticut, New York, New Jersey, Pennsylvania, Illinois, and New Mexico, with a total of 132 electoral votes. Anti-Catholic voting, on the other hand, cost him ten states that, as a Democrat, he otherwise might have won: Tennessee, Florida, Montana, Idaho,

Utah, California, Oregon, Virginia, and Washington, with a total of 110 electoral votes. The Catholic issue yielded Kennedy a net of 22 electoral votes—a substantial part of his winning margin of only 33 (over the 270 required). His net gain may well have been larger, since it is by no means clear that he could have carried California and Florida had he not been Catholic. In any case, Kennedy's religion cost him more *states* but won him more electoral votes. These results confirmed Richard Nixon's preelection expectation, as he described it in *Six Crises* a year after the election. "I believed that Kennedy's religion would help him in states he needed to win."[34]

It was not however the universal view among Democratic Party chieftains early in 1960 that Kennedy's Catholicism was an advantage. Kennedy moved aggressively to galvanize and maximize his vote among Catholic voters; indeed, thousands of Catholic Republicans crossed party lines to vote for him in the Democratic states that allowed crossovers. Nixon understood early that he could not be tied to any anti-Papist or anti-Catholic effort, and to his credit there is no evidence that he attempted to benefit at the ballot box from Kennedy's Catholicism. Protestant Minster Norman Vincent Peale and the Reverend Billy Graham were involved in some national anti-Catholic efforts, but Nixon's ties to these activities were never proven or established. Just as Barack Obama would act as if his African ancestry was an impediment to his election, Kennedy would act as if his religion was something that he would have to "overcome" when in fact it was an asset. When President Harry Truman was asked whether he was disturbed by Kennedy's status as a Roman Catholic and would worry about undue papal influence in US affairs, "Give 'em hell" Harry would reply, "It's not the Pope I am worried about, its the Pop," referring to John Kennedy's ambassador father Joseph P. Kennedy Sr.

In 1960 former Democrat Congressman, Assemblyman, and later Mayor of Los Angeles Sam Yorty would cross party lines with a widely distributed book titled, *Why I Can't Take Kennedy*. It was thinly disguised anti-Catholicism. Yorty would endorse Nixon for governor in 1962. Yorty is among the most colorful and peripatetic men in his political era.

Yorty made an unsuccessful bid for US senator in 1940, losing to Republican incumbent Hiram Johnson. He was then elected to the United States House of Representatives in 1950 and was reelected in 1952 and ran for the US Senate in a 1954 for the two years remaining of the term of Richard M. Nixon. Yorty received 45.5 percent to Senator Thomas H. Kuchel's 53.2 percent. Kuchel, a former attorney general and moderate Republican, was appointed to the seat in 1953 by then Governor Earl Warren when Nixon became vice president. The following year, Yorty ran for mayor of Los Angeles against incumbent Norris Poulson. Yorty won. In 1965, Yorty was reelected over Democratic Congressman James Roosevelt, son of the late President Franklin D. Roosevelt. Roosevelt's campaign cost around $450,000. Yorty ran on his record of cutting city taxes, streamlined city government, and improved garbage pickups. He swamped Roosevelt 57.9 percent of the vote to Roosevelt's 36.5 percent.

Yorty then challenged incumbent Democratic Governor Pat Brown in the 1966 gubernatorial Democratic primary. He won (37.6 percent) to Brown's 1,355,262 ballots (51.9 percent). Right-wing oilman and Reagan backer Henry Salvatori funded Yorty's campaign in a bid to weaken Brown in the fall. Yorty showed up election night at the victory party of Ronald W. Reagan, who had won the Republican nomination. Yorty would win another term as mayor in 1969 over Los Angeles City Councilman and former Police Commissioner Tom Bradley in a bitter, racially tinged campaign. In 1970 Yorty would challenge Assembly Speaker Jesse "Big Daddy" Unruh for governor in the Democratic primary and lose.

On November 15, 1971, Yorty announced that he would seek the Democratic nomination for president in 1972. Yorty had received strong support from influential New Hampshire publisher William Loeb. He campaign actively distributing a glossy newspaper with his life story and campaign positions. Yorty was in fact a ringer in the race put in to draw blue-collar votes from Senator Ed Muskie and therefore boost Sen. George McGovern.

My path would cross his in 1972. Yorty would continue while I was working at the Committee for the Re-election of the President.

My boss, Bart Porter, had me take a locked suitcase to Los Angeles Mayor Sam Yorty and his campaign manager, Robert Philbrick, in New Hampshire. Yorty, a conservative Democrat, was running a campaign for president in the New Hampshire Democratic primary. He was taken seriously only because he had' garnered the support of the *Manchester Union Leader* and its right-wing editor, William Loeb, who liked to do his political proselytizing in front-page editorials.

The paper had a following among the working class in Manchester and was the largest daily paper in the state. The idea was to siphon Catholic votes from Maine Senator Ed Muskie to boost the prospects of far-left candidate George McGovern.

I knocked on a motel room door to have "Travelin' Sam," as he was known, open the door. He said nothing but took the briefcase and motioned me in, locking the door behind me. He motioned me to a chair. I sat.

I took a key from a sealed envelope given to me by Porter. Philbrick counted the money by pouring it on the bed. It appeared to be in stacks of thousands. "Twenty-five thousand dollars," said Philbrick. Yorty turned on me. "You tell Murray it was fifty and I want the other half. Now get the fuck out." Yorty would poll but 6 percent statewide but siphoned off up to 12 percent in some of the wards of Manchester, hurting Muskie, who was already wounded by his public meltdown over a Nixon dirty trick, the famous Canuck letter smearing Muskie as well as a *Manchester Union Leader* front-page editorial critical of his wife.

Nixon would also long be criticized for not making more effective use of Eisenhower in the campaign. A flip comment Eisenhower made at a news conference had haunted the vice president as he attempted to stress his experience in the advisory role he had played in the Eisenhower administration. Asked at a press conference to name a Nixon idea that he had adopted, Eisenhower responded with, "If you give me a week I might think of one. I don't remember." It was just a slip, at worst facetious, but it led to terrible press for Nixon.[35]

Eisenhower's comment, expressed in a fit of pique when reporters kept pressing him on Nixon's role, severely undercut the "Experience Counts" theme Nixon was campaigning on.

It damaged Nixon's campaign badly as the press corps, enthralled with Kennedy and hostile to Nixon, jumped on it.

Eisenhower himself was hurt and frustrated that Nixon did not ask him to take a more active role in the campaign. Unbeknownst to Eisenhower, his wife, Mamie, and Dr. Howard Snyder had secretly told Nixon that Eisenhower's frail health and weak heart would not tolerate an aggressive campaign schedule. Mamie Eisenhower would appeal directly to Pat Nixon on the matter. "Ike must never know I called you," Mamie said.[36]

After a luncheon meeting in which Nixon declined to ask Ike to increase the limited campaign schedule to which he had agreed, Eisenhower would be privately angry. "Goddammit, he looks like a loser to me," said Eisenhower. "When I had an officer like that in World War II, I relieved him."[37] Nonetheless, Eisenhower did make late-campaign appearances in Philadelphia, New York City, Cleveland, and Pittsburg in the final week. Eisenhower's participation drew large and enthusiastic crowds and greatly aided Nixon's closing drive in. Even with Ike's limited help, Nixon would essentially move to a tie with the better-funded JFK.

Eisenhower was invigorated on the stump and took Kennedy on. He seized full advantage of his limited, late appearances, and his tone took on an impassioned partisan and political color uncharacteristic of the old general. "Now I have heard complaints about the country not moving," Eisenhower said, making a sly and bashing reference to the Kennedy slogan "Let's Get this Country Moving Again." "Of course you can move easily—you can move back to inflation, you can move back to deficit spending, you can move back to the military weakness that allowed the Korean War to occur . . . no trouble at all."[38]

Two days later, Eisenhower attacked Kennedy's qualifications and questioned his judgment. "More money, they say, will be saved by military reorganization . . . Now where did this young genius acquire the knowledge, experience, and wisdom through which he will make vast improvements over the Joint Chiefs of Staff?"[39] Ike came though for Dick, taking on a tough tone that was uncharacteristic but effective.

Nixon shut out his closest aides and advisors, making all decisions regarding the campaign, speech content, press releases, and tour arrangements himself. The campaign was marked with horrible temper outbursts and tantrums. Nixon became more exhausted and haggard as he campaigned at a frantic pace to make up for lost ground. One secret service agent said he "would snap when the campaign became too much." Bob Haldeman recalled a day when Nixon became frustrated over a poor schedule while touring Iowa by car. "Don Hughes, Nixon's military aide, was in a seat directly in front. Suddenly, incredibly, Nixon began to kick the back of Hughes's seat with both feet. And he wouldn't stop . . . The seat and the hapless Hughes jolted forward jaggedly as Nixon vented his range. When the car stopped at a small town in the middle of nowhere, Hughes, white-faced, silently got out the car and started walking straight ahead, down the road and out of town. He wanted to get as far away as he could from the Vice President."[40]

In was in this period that veteran journalist Tom Wicker would note:

It was in 1960, also, that Nixon's dependence on H. R. ["Bob"] Haldeman began to affect his conduct, with other aides as well as toward the public. Haldeman was the perfect defender of Nixon's desire to "do it all" for himself, and to share credit with no one—a desire that led naturally to a growing isolation of the candidate from friends and advisers. Haldeman—ostensibly only the campaign "tour director"—knew how to fend off unwanted advice, and how to make himself an indispensable guardian at the door of the candidate's introversion.

Haldeman's latent instinct for power and how to get it, and Nixon's instinct to prove that he needed no one, melded into a combination with long consequences. In 1960, the immediate effect was to shield Nixon from the kind of political give-and-take that might have steered him away from some of his mistakes and that would have helped create a more cohesive and dedicated staff. Haldeman was not a man to tell the boss he was wrong, and as the campaign went on, he saw to it that few others had the chance to do so.[41]

Nixon's pollster Claude Robinson showed that Nixon consistently ran better alone than with any running mate. Kennedy, however, would reluctantly take on the only vice presidential running mate who made an actual difference in a presidential election in Lyndon Johnson.

As I indicated in my book *The Man Who Killed Kennedy: The Case Against LBJ*, Johnson essentially blackmailed his way onto the ticket with Kennedy after the Massachusetts senator had already asked his Missouri colleague Stuart Symington to take the vice presidential nomination. LBJ appeared at Kennedy's hotel room late at night with speaker Sam Rayburn. Johnson had with him a dossier on Kennedy's sex life, which had been compiled by LBJ ally J. Edgar Hoover. Kennedy got the message, and the offer Kennedy had made to Stuart Symington was withdrawn. Had LBJ not bludgeoned his way onto the ticket, Kennedy would not likely have been elected, particularly in light of voter fraud in Texas, which would tip the Lone Star State to the Kennedy-Johnson ticket by a slim forty-six thouand votes. Fifty thousand Nixon-Lodge votes were thrown out in Dallas County alone under the watchful eyes of Democrat-dominated election officials and the LBJ man who served as county sheriff. LBJ would also use his Senate connections to pressure local Democrats to back the national ticket and work to thwart the independent elector strategy segregationist were using to block Kennedy and Nixon and throw the election into the US House of Representatives.

Nixon would not be so fortunate in his choice of a running mate. His list came down to Lodge, Dr. Walter Judd, a respected conservative from Minnesota, and Thruston B. Morton, an affable senator for the border state of Kentucky. Polls showed in both 1960 and 1968 that Nixon ran best with no running mate. Nixon would tell me, "[D]on't look for someone who can help you; try to find someone who won't hurt you." I recall distinctly when Nixon would call me in the televised wake of George H. W. Bush announcing that he would take Senator Dan Quayle as his running mate. "Has he lost his goddamn mind," he bellowed. Nixon's strong opinions were belied by the fact that in both 1960 and in 1968 he would pick running mates who would not help his electoral prospects and may have actually hurt him. In essence, Nixon made the same mistake *twice.*

Senator Thruston Morton, the fifty-two-year-old Republican national chairman, was a moderate Republican from Kentucky. The border states, including Kentucky, Tennessee, Virginia, and the Carolinas, were crucial to Nixon's strategy. Morton, a Yale graduate who had served in both the House and the Senate, had defeated incumbents for both offices after serving in Eisenhower's State Department. Morton's brother Rogers Morton was a veteran congressman from Maryland who would later serve as the floor manager for Nixon's 1968 convention operation. Both Mortons were Nixon men. Nixon recalled, "[Thruston] Morton wanted the position badly."[42] Morton was known as a heavy drinker on Capitol Hill. *National Review* publisher Bill Rusher called him "Thirsty" Morton.

A staunch anti-Communist congressman from Minnesota, Dr. Walter Judd was born in a small town in Nebraska and was both a medical doctor and Christian missionary. In 1925, Dr. Judd went to South China as a missionary for the Congregational Church. Overcome by malaria, he would return to the United States. He returned to China in 1934 to continue his missionary work only to see Japan's brutal invasion of the Chinese mainland. Returning to the United States in 1938, Dr. Judd spoke out across the country about the growing might of Japan's military. After the attack on Pearl Harbor, Dr. Judd was elected to Congress, where he served for twenty years, mainly as a member of the House Committee on Foreign Affairs. A fiery orator, Judd would overcome a badly scarred face caused by his early use of radiation in his rustic medical practice in China. In spite of Judd's physical deformities, his powerful voice and mastery of the language could stir an audience.

Conservative organizer Marvin Liebman would form a committee to draft Walter Judd for vice president, which was funded by former New Jersey Governor Thomas Edison. Judd was clearly the favorite of grassroots conservatives in the party, many of whom would have preferred Barry Goldwater as the improbable 1960 Republican nominee. Liebman would bring the Judd boomlet to Chicago, where the Minnesota congressman was the favorite of many of the rank-and-file delegates.

Liebman remembered the Chicago boom that was ignited by Judd's convention keynote speech. "Telegrams urging Judd's nomination were pouring in to the Nixon headquarters from all over the country," said Liebman. "By the time the Tuesday night session was over, the entire convention was talking about the possibility of Walter Judd as Nixon's running mate. All the delegate hotels had Judd signs in their lobbies, and many of the delegates were wearing Judd buttons. Our campaign had snowballed in just a few hours."[43]

As he would do in 1968 Nixon went through the motions of consulting party leaders on the choice of a running mate in the hours after his nomination. Thirty-eight Republicans, senators, congressmen, governors, state party chairmen, and party elders, including Governor Tom Dewey, Senator John Bricker, Congressman (later Senator) Everett Dirksen, Governor William Stratton, and President Eisenhower's brother Milton met in Nixon's Sheraton-Blackstone hotel suite in the Windy City. Nixon would tell the group of party leaders that Dr. Walter Judd had taken his name out of consideration for "health reasons." Four years later Kleindienst would see Judd in Phoenix where Judd was addressing a group. "Before the program began, I expressed to Judd my sincere regrets that he had, for health reasons, asked Nixon not to consider him as a running mate."

"I asked him not to do what, for what reason?" he responded with surprise and incredulity.[47] Judd said he had met with Nixon and that Nixon had told him that the choice was down to Judd and former Massachusetts Senator Henry Cabot Lodge. Judd responded that Lodge's brother, former Connecticut brother John Davis Lodge, who served in the House with Judd, had told Judd that the decision was made and that Nixon had asked Cabot Lodge to be his Vice Presidential running mate and that "Cabot was drafting his acceptance speech." Nixon denied that Lodge had been selected and said that his mind was still open. Judd claimed he made complimentary comments about Lodge but insisted that he himself would be a stronger candidate. More importantly, Judd had no memory of eliminating himself for "health reasons."[48]

Kleindienst would recall that the meeting of party elders he attended had seemed "scripted," with former Ohio Senator and Governor John Bricker weighing in for Morton, as did former-Eisenhower Interior Secretary Fred Seaton and Illinois Governor William Stratton. Nixon then turned to former New York Governor Tom Dewey, who had been the Republican nominee for president in 1944 and 1948 and had largely engineered not only Eisenhower's nomination in 1952, but also Nixon's own vice presidential nomination that year. Kleindienst felt that Dewey's advocacy of Lodge "had the distinct characteristics of advance preparation." After Dewey's eloquent statement for Lodge, Nixon declared, "That's it—it has to be Cabot."[49] Kleindienst believed that Nixon had flown to New York on the morning of July 22 to secure the support of Nelson Rockefeller and Dewey and that their quid pro quo was Lodge's nomination.[50]

"Nixon, so often a cold, dispassionate judge of electoral strategies, had flung logic out the window," wrote David Pietrusza in *1960: LBJ vs. JFK vs. Nixon*. Pietrusza makes a compelling argument. "Instead, his choice was dictated both by a deep-seated obsession to curry favor with the party's still influential Rockefeller-Dewey Eastern wing and by deep-seated social insecurity—an idea that by placing the ultra-Brahmin Lodge on his ticket he might compensate for his own filling station–grocery store origins, particularly against the Harvard-Palm Beach Kennedy organization."[51]

Barry Goldwater, whose supporters championed Judd, the most conservative choice for VP, called Nixon's choice of Lodge "a disastrous blunder."[52] Judd, who Nixon had eliminated for "health reasons," would be vigorous and active into his nineties. When Ronald Reagan awarded Judd the Presidential Medal of Freedom in 1981, he would call Judd "an articulate spokesman for all those who cherish liberty and a model for all Americans who aspire to serve mankind as physicians, spiritual leaders and statesmen."[53]

Ironically, Nixon would continue to promulgate the myth that Judd had removed himself from consideration in a 1988 letter to the congressman.

"As I was listening to the convention in New Orleans this week, I thought back to 1960 and the greatest keynote speech I have ever heard at the convention of either party," Nixon wrote to the then ninety-year-old Judd. "You will remember that I talked to you thereafter about the possibility of your going on the ticket. You declined in part because you felt that your experience was exclusively in the legislative branch of the government and in part because of what you thought was your advanced age! And now you are ninety and still going strong. It is no reflection whatever on Cabot, incidentally, that had you gone on the ticket we might have won."[54]

Nixon's choice for a running mate, former Massachusetts Senator Henry Cabot Lodge, was a strategic error. While Lodge was liked by the Eastern Republican establishment and was a favorite of Eisenhower, he had been defeated for his Senate seat in 1952 by Congressman John F. Kennedy. Lodge would antagonize the Taft wing of the party by serving as the campaign manager for Eisenhower and forcing the Convention Rules, or "Fair Play," Amendment that would seat Eisenhower delegates in the South, thus snatching the nomination from the Ohio senator. Lodge would put no large state in play, and while his selection was seen as bolstering the ticket's foreign policy credentials (Lodge had been Ike's UN ambassador), Lodge himself was bright but obtuse, somewhat lazy, and his aloof patrician manner put voters off. Additionally, Lodge had no appeal in the South or the West and did not help Nixon make inroads in the Northeast. When, to Nixon's surprise, Lodge announced without notice that the "Nixon cabinet would have a Negro appointee," a furious Nixon was forced to repudiate him. Lodge was famous for taking midafternoon naps on the campaign trail, and he would don pajamas to do so every afternoon for two hours. "We can't beat the Democrats with a man who campaigns only an hour or two a day," said Arizona Senator Barry Goldwater.[55] He brought nothing to the Nixon ticket.

* * *

After a two-week stay in the hospital to treat his knee injury, Nixon would come roaring back from a substantial deficit in the polls only to be damaged in the first televised debate in which he looked haggard and nervous. Nixon's greatest error was his decision to debate the lesser-known Kennedy on television. Nixon would make the historic mistake of believing that *substance* would prevail over style and appearance. This was another costly mistake.

As a two-term, eight-year vice president who had bested Khrushchev in the Kitchen Debate, Nixon held a substantial stature advantage over the rather junior Kennedy. Kennedy benefited just by being on the stage with Nixon. Nixon had little to gain from the exchange, while Kennedy could only benefit from the massive exposure to voters that a one-on-one debate would bring. Debates on the air were now possible following a change in broadcast law. Kennedy accepted immediately when the networks called for debates after the Democratic convention. JFK knew a debate was "the one way to break through"; he knew his advantage lie in television. Despite the success and the game, changing ability provided him by the Checkers speech, one of the most viewed political speeches in US history, Nixon still derided television as a "novelty," which by 1960 had "worn off."[56] Nixon was wrong.

Nixon's advisers were unanimous in opposing televised debates. Nixon initially agreed with them. "Nixon felt that he had a name, that he was known as a debater, and that he would be better off campaigning on his own, and not bring Jack Kennedy along," Nixon's press secretary, Herb Klein, recalled. "His instructions to me were not to commit to a debate, although I was under tremendous pressure."[57] His running mate Lodge would advise Nixon that a debate could "erase the assassin image"[58]

Then, out of the blue, the sometimes-capricious Nixon changed his tune. He wanted a debate. Press secretary Herb Klein "almost fell over" when he heard of Nixon's acceptance. When Len Hall asked Nixon to explain, he "just looked up at the sky and didn't answer. The rain started coming down . . . he still stood there looking up at the sky."[59]

Nixon was overconfident about the coming exchange with Kennedy and felt he could deal JFK one knockout blow. "Kennedy speaks over people's heads . . . I'll murder Kennedy," Nixon proclaimed.

Nixon's only hesitation, he told an aide, was that "he might clobber that kid Kennedy too tough on the first debate, and thus womp up a 'sympathy factor' for the guy . . ."

"I can take this man," he told aides after watching Kennedy's convention speech on television.[60] He was wrong.

Nixon got to Chicago late, looking tired, haggard, and under-weight from recent hospitalization and famously refused make-up. While JFK wore a smart navy blue suit, Nixon would make the error of wearing a light gray suit, which blended in to the back-drop.[61] Still ill from his hospital stay, one observer said, "His face was as gray as his suit." Nixon's shirt collar hung on him, at least two sizes too big because of his weight loss in the hospital.

Then Nixon bumped his knee on the car door. He winced in pain. He would later tell Speechwriter Richard Whalen, "I was sick as a dog."[62]

During the lighting check, Nixon would hear a CBS producer ask JFK if he wanted makeup. The tanned Kennedy declined only to repair to his dressing room where his private makeup man pre-pared him for broadcast. Hearing this, Nixon also declined makeup, despite the argument of his television advisor Ted Rogers.

However, when John F. Kennedy arrived in Chicago for the first presidential debate, he spent the afternoon not with briefing books and aides but sunbathing on the roof of his Chicago hotel with two buxom young ladies. Kennedy would have a fifteen-minute ses-sion with one of the two prostitutes in his hotel suite to relax him.[63] When Kennedy entered the NBC studio for the debate, journalist Theodore H. White wrote, "He looked like a bronzed god." CBS producer Don Hewitt said, "Kennedy arrived tanned, tall, lean, well-tailored in a dark suit . . . he looked like an Adonis."[64]

Rogers convinced Nixon to use a product called Beard Stick for Nixon's dark jowls. This too would be a mistake, as the makeup would begin to run as Nixon began to sweat under the hot TV lights. JFK remained tanned and confident. Nixon melted.

Having looked pale in his first debate with the bronzed JFK, by 1968 Nixon was using a sun lamp at home before major TV appear-ances. Nixon called it "home cooking" but was careful to avoid sun-burns, using just enough of the lamp's rays to have a healthy glow.

"Fire the make-up man," a supporter told Klein. "Everybody in this part of the country thinks Nixon is sick. Three doctors agreed he looked as if he had just suffered a coronary."[65] Nixon's own mother would call Secretary Rose Mary Woods and ask, "Is Richard ill?"[66]

"My God," exclaimed Chicago Mayor Richard Daley, "they've embalmed him before he even died."[67]

To Pulitzer Prize–winning journalist David Halberstam the only thing that mattered in the debate was "what they looked like. All the insecurities and doubts and inner tensions of Nixon were disclosed in his sweating face by the brutal relentless cameras," Halberstam wrote in his account of the clash.[68] "Those debates changed the conversation entirely," noted Larry Sabato, professor of politics at the University of Virginia. "Television is all about image, not substance."[69]

Watching the debate on television, Nixon's running mate Lodge would be heard to mutter, "That son of a bitch just lost us the election."[70]

Kennedy had another advantage beyond his tan. Kennedy was getting regular shots from Dr. Max Jacobson, also known as Dr. Feelgood. Jacobson was administering methamphetamine shots to Kennedy obstensively so that he could deal with his back pain. *New York Post* reporter Larry Getlen describes the first Nixon-Kennedy clash in the stunning book *Dr. Feelgood* by Richard A. Lertzman and William J. Birnes.

"The night of the first Kennedy-Nixon debate, Kennedy met with Jacobson just a few hours before he took the stage. The senator was 'complaining in a voice barely above a whisper of extreme fatigue and lethargy.' Jacobson plunged a needle directly into Kennedy's throat and pumped methamphetamine into his voice box."

The result was clear within minutes, and an artificially energized Kennedy changed American history that night by upstaging Nixon.[71] When presidential brother Robert Kennedy learned about Jacobson and his injections and the fact that JFK had convinced Jacqueline Kennedy to begin a course of treatments, the attorney general would have the ingredients analyzed by an FBI lab and determined that they were a mix of hormones and methamphetamine. When he confronted the president, JFK would famously say, "I don't care if it's horse piss, it makes me feel good."[72]

Nixon would recover in the last three of the four debates. Many like to point out that people who listened to the first debate on the radio said Nixon won, while those who had watched on TV gave it to JFK. Although Nixon would bounce back in subsequent debates, some historians correctly point out that the audiences for the second and third debate were dwarfed by the first face-off by the two candidates. What historians failed to tell you is that the fourth debate—the one in which many felt Nixon's victory over Kennedy was the most complete—had a larger audience than debates two and three and would come close to matching the audience size of the first debate. Nixon's strong performance would fuel a late surge while Kennedy's poll numbers were flat. Nixon was closing fast, and now, finally outspending the Democrats on television advertising, Nixon drove himself to nervous exhaustion, stumping across the country to make up ground. Now despite the huge Democratic voter registration edge, Eisenhower's comment denigrating his input in the administration, his disastrous fifty-state campaign pledge, his lost time in the hospital, and his flop in the first debate, it was Nixon who was closing the gap. Despite all his missteps, Nixon came back to an essential tie with Kennedy.

There is substantial evidence that Kennedy's expensive Madison Avenue campaign peaked too early. Eisenhower's late campaigning and tough challenge to Kennedy got national coverage. Nixon, having gained back ten pounds with a regimen of milk shakes did an effective coast-to-coast telethon on the Sunday night before the election.

Ironically, Nixon, who was heavily favored, would lose this race when the staunchly anti-Communist Kennedy would run to Nixon's right on foreign policy and defense issues. Constrained by his loyalty to the Eisenhower administration, Nixon could not call for the massive increases in defense spending that Kennedy favored, nor could he reveal the Eisenhower-Nixon plans against Communist Cuba when JFK urged a stronger line against the island gulag under the control of Fidel Castro. Nixon, who had always been a hard-liner, found JFK to be more hard-line than he was.

Nixon was particularly furious when he learned that CIA Director Allen Dulles had briefed Kennedy on the agency's plan for the invasion of Cuba. Kennedy had used the information to out-flank Nixon in the debates, charging that the Republican admin-istration was lax in their efforts to topple Castro when Kennedy, based on the CIA briefing, knew better. In his memoir *The Ends of Power*, Haldeman would say that this betrayal by the agency would only intensify Nixon's distrust of the CIA.[73] Thus, as we shall see, the seeds of Watergate were sown.

Until that time, Nixon was on a winning streak that included winning two elections for the House (in 1948 he was the nominee of both the Republican and Democratic parties, having won both party primaries under California's strange cross-filing system), tri-umphed in the Senate election, and won two terms as vice presi-dent on a ticket with one of the most popular Americans of all time. Nixon had worked hard in Eisenhower's second term to tone down his partisanship and erase his image as a political hit man. He was the early favorite over the callow JFK and was thought to be the most effective debater and campaigner in his party. The Eisenhower cabinet, and particularly the CIA, expected Nixon to be elected.

Nixon's frustration in his narrow loss was in fact magni-fied by the true trajectory of the race; Nixon was closing fast, and the momentum was with him in the closing days of the race. Ironically, this was not the public or private perception of the press or the Kennedy camp. Kennedy's pollster Louis Harris predicted a Kennedy margin of nine points, and the national media of its day was openly predicting a significant Kennedy-Johnson win. The mood among Democrats was euphoric to optimistic while Republicans despaired their candidate was behind. In fact, Nixon's pollster Claude Robinson predicted a close race, and there is evidence that Nixon himself understood the race to be closer than the public perception during some of the darkest days of his grueling come from behind campaign.

From the beginning, Nixon expected a close outcome and planned to outwork his opponent. Unlike the Kennedy effort, whose campaign ran at full speed for as long as it could from the beginning, Nixon planned for his campaign to climax in the final days. Nixon had carefully peaked at exactly the right times in his 1946 House and 1950 Senate races.

In Nixon's view, a campaign had peaks and valleys, with the last few weeks crucial. Nixon traveled nationwide, fulfilling his fifty-state pledge at great cost, but the campaign also husbanded its resources for one last great push in the final weeks. The Kennedy operation burned money at a furious rate from the beginning of the year, with Ambassador Joe Kennedy sparing no expense to put his son in the White House. The Republicans reserved large purchases of television time to dominate the closing days. While Nixon was well financed, he would be massively outspent, and an analysis of polling now showed his late-spending strategy to be sound. Nixon closed in fast on Kennedy in the final days for a photo finish. With the final momentum going to Nixon, both he and his wife would reach Los Angeles on Election Day believing they would win. I believe he did, and there is overwhelming evidence that voter fraud was used to steal the 1960 election.

Did Chicago Mayor Richard J. Daley steal Illinois and thus the 1960 presidential election for John F. Kennedy? Kennedy carried Cook County, which includes Chicago, by 318,736 votes—more than double his national margin of 118,574 votes. Indeed, on his deathbed Daley would cry, "Will God forgive me for stealing Illinois from Richard Nixon?"[74] Mayor Daley himself gave away the game on election eve when he said, "With the Democratic organization and the help of a few close friends," the Democrats would prevail on Election Day. There is sufficient evidence that the "few close friends" mentioned included Chicago crime boss Sam Giancana.

The alliance between organized crime and the John Kennedy campaign for president was not an inevitable one, despite, and to a certain extent because of the Kennedy patriarch's criminal past during Prohibition. Joe Kennedy Sr. had extensive mob connections dating back to Prohibition; he was still viewed with distrust by many in Cosa Nostra for his competition in the booze-running business of Prohibition.

Joe Kennedy's competition was perhaps the least burning concern on the heads of the many crime "families" when Joe Sr. summoned them to a lunch meeting to discuss the campaign on February 29, 1950, at Felix Young's restaurant in Manhattan. The distinction of "enemy-in-chief" at that time went instead to Kennedy's third son, the relentless moralist Robert Kennedy. Bobby, as he was known, had earned the hatred of much of the organized crime community through his never-ending crusade against them during the 1950s.

"I took the reservation," said a hostess at Young's. "And it was as though every gangster chief in the United States was there. I don't remember all the names now, but there was John Roselli, Carlos Marcello from New Orleans, the two brothers from Dallas, the top men from Buffalo, California, and Colorado. They were all top people, not soldiers. I was amazed Joe Kennedy would take the risk."[75]

The meeting started poorly when Kennedy, after insisting that all present leave their bodyguards at the door, arrived fifteen minutes late. While Joe wanted desperately to talk up Jack's campaign, the conversation inevitably turned to Bobby's crusade against the Mob.[76] In response to Joe's request for $500,000 for Jack's campaign, as well as the Mob's support through the primaries and into the general, a lieutenant of Chicago Mob boss Sam "Momo" Giancana asked Joe bluntly why they should aide the brother of a man who had publicly referred to Giancana as a "sissy" in front of the press.[77]

Kennedy's response was that it was Jack running for president, not Bobby, and that his request was, "business not politics."[78] When Joe Kennedy left the meeting shortly thereafter it had been deemed an unmitigated disaster. However, Roselli, friend of Jack through Italian-American crooner Frank Sinatra, emphasized to his friends in the Chicago family that Joe Kennedy had come to them with the request and in doing so had shown a certain element of modesty and deference. This pitch appears to have been more successful, and a week later $500,000 was delivered to Joe Kennedy's Manhattan office.

The ambassador was forced to go to the Chicago mob through a frequent Palm Beach golfing partner, Chicago hood Johnny Roselli. Kennedy also utilized Frank Sinatra to reach out to Chicago mobsters Sam "Momo" Giancana, Joe Accardo, Murray "the Camel" Humphreys Jack Avery, and Jake "greasy-thumb" Gruzik. They in turn enlisted New Orleans mob's kingpin Carlos Marcello and Florida's Santo Trafficante.

Kennedy collected sizable contributions from all but Humphreys, a Republican who said Joe Kennedy was "full of shit" and pointed out how Bobby Kennedy had harassed the mob as counsel to the Senate's McClellan looking into labor racketeering. Humphreys sent $100,000 to Nixon while the midwestern and southwestern families (with some kicked in from the Bonnanos in New York) gave more than a million to Kennedy as well as pledging their army of enforcers to find votes for Jack Kennedy.

Mob activity for Kennedy on Election Day included nonexistent voters voting, registered voters denied the right to vote, and manipulation of the count. Poll watchers for Nixon provided Polaroids of money changing hands for votes outside of polling places. Voters were intimidated and in many cases threatened, and bones were broken. There is no doubt that Sam Giancana and the Chicago outfit had stolen Chicago for JFK.

Giancana would also later be overheard on an FBI wiretap discussing the "donations" the gangsters had made during the vital primary campaign. John Kennedy's lover Judith Carbell alleged years later that Kennedy took outrageous risks to en Giancana's help, covertly meeting with him in person at least twe.

But the Mob played heavily on both sides. In his ound-breaking *Bobby and J. Edgar*, Burton Hersh wrote that Jimmy Hoffa and the Teamsters gave Nixon $1 million dollars while the East Mob chieftains, like Frank Costello and Meyer Lansky, rounded another million for the Nixon cause. Hoffa was actually funneli cash for Mob bosses Carlos Marcello and Santos Trafficante. Hoff ad a particular interest in Nixon's success: the Justice Department as breathing down his neck due to his old nemesis Robert Kenndy. Bobby targeted Hoffa when the young lawyer was counsel to e Senate Labor Racketeering Committee. Kennedy's game was espelly dangerous because his brother Robert was committed to the purit of organized crime and in particular to the downfall of Jimmy Ha, the crooked Teamsters leader. When he continued that pursuit attorney general, the mob chieftains were so furious that some including the House Assassinations Committee—would come to spect the Mafia was among those behind the 1963 assassination.

Both Kennedy and Nixon solicited the he of the Mob. Kennedy's father had made much of his fortune bgangsters during Prohibition, and compelling information indices that he and his politician son used the mob connection as a spping stone to power in 1960. Chicago Mafia boss Sam Giancana ould be overheard on an FBI wiretap discussing the "donation" the gangsters had made during the vital primary campaign. hn Kennedy's lover Judith Campbell alleged years later that Kendy took outrageous risks to enlist Giancana's help, covertly meng with him in person at least twice.

Nixon was also vulnerable. Before the 1960 mpaign started an informant passed documentation to Robert Kenedy indicating that Meyer Lansky's people had footed Nixon's ill on a visit to Cuba. RFK made no use of the information, prolbly because his brother haimself been compromised in Cuba when Lansky fixed him up wiwomen there.

Floridaob boss Santo Trafficante, who was aware of that episode, despd Kennedy and favored Nixon. "Santo," recalled his attorney Frk Ragano, "viewed Nixon as a realistic, conservative politician w was 'not a zealot' and would not be hard on him and his mob frids. The Mafia had little to fear from Nixon."[79]

"We'll ctribute to Nixon, too . . . We'll hedge our bets. Just like we did it in California when Nixon was running for senator . . . You n't know what the hell Jack'll do once he's elected. With Nixon,ou know where you stand," said Giancana before the 1960 eleon, according to his brother Chuck. "Marcello and I," Giancanallegedly added, "are giving the Nixon campaign a million buck[80]

Carlos Mcello, Mafia boss of New Orleans who controlled the mob in Louisna and Texas, also reportedly made a massive contribution to Non in September that year at a meeting in Lafayette, Louisiana. Amformant told the FBI Marcello did so in September, at a meeting iLafayette, Louisiana. "I was right there, listening to the conversatn. Marcello had a suitcase filled with five hundred thousand dolrs cash, which was going to Nixon . . . The other half was comg from the mob boys in New Jersey and Florida." Five hundred ousand dollars, at today's values, would be around $3 million.

Richard Non had always had his own arm's-length relationship with e Mob. Hollywood gangster Mickey Cohen, who was Meyer Lsky's top lieutenant on the West Coast, had funneled money trough Myford Irvine, whose ranch was a big agribusiness in Onge County, into Nixon's 1946 and 1950 campaigns. Nixon campai manager and mob lawyer Murray Chotiner asked Cohen to raiseunds for Nixon's 1950 effort. The Chotiner brothers' law firm d defended a number of Cohen's underlings for illegal bookmalng.

Back in 1946, Cohen convened a meeting at the Hollywood Knickerbocker Hotel on North Ivar Avenue, Hollywood, to which he invited more than several hundred associates from the gambling business, some of whom flew in from Las Vegas. Cohen was later to say, "There wasn't a legitimate person in the room." Cohen would later write that the goal for the evening was $75,000 for Nixon's coffers from his crime and gambling associates and that he ordered the doors locked when the group came up $20,000 short, refusing to let anyone leave until the financial goal was met.[81]

Nixon had met with Cohen, who dominated the Los Angeles mob scene for Lansky while Benjamin "Bugsy" Siegel watched Lansky's business in the growing Las Vegas, as early as 1946 at Goodfellow's Grotto, a fish restaurant in Orange County where the booths were private and politics could be talked about frankly. Cohen made it clear that the orders to help Nixon in 1950 came from "back East," meaning New York boss, Frank Costello, and Meyer Lansky, both of whom set up the National Mob Syndicate.[82]

With the support of the Chicago family secured, the family's attention could turn fully to winning the Democratic nomination. The April 5 Wisconsin primary, which Jack Kennedy won by a disappointing 8 percent over Hubert Humphrey of Minnesota, was a terrible setback for Kennedy's campaign. After the Wisconsin primary, the country's political focus turned to the May 10 Democratic primary in West Virginia—long seen as extraordinarily difficult territory for Kennedy because of its heavily Protestant electorate.[83] Polls taken immediately after the Wisconsin victory showed Kennedy being trounced by at least 20-percent. The Windy City Mob again aided the Kennedy cause.

Even Mob troubadour Frank Sinatra recorded a Kennedy campaign song.

1960's the year for his high hopes
Come on and vote for Kennedy
Vote for Kennedy

Keep America Strong

The original version of the song "High Hopes" was written by lyricist Sammy Cahn for the 1959 Sinatra movie *A Hole in the Head*. The revamped version, written as a Kennedy campaign song, was put on repeat and drummed into the heads of the West Virginia voting public.

W. J. Rorabaugh detailed the Kennedys' prolific spending:

> Humphrey spent no more that than $30,000 in the state. West Virginia television was cheap: Humphrey paid $2,000 and Kennedy paid $34,000. Overall, the Kennedys spent much, much more that Humphrey. Official estimates for the Kennedy campaign ranged from $200,000 to $400,000, but one private estimate ran as high as $4 million, which included the value of unpaid time for all the volunteers. Perhaps a more realistic estimate would be $1.5 to 2.5 million. About $150,000 went to Charleston, which was won narrowly; $100,000 was spent in Huntington, which was lost. About $100,000 went to Logan County, considered to be among the most corrupt. The campaign thus spent $350,000 for just three counties, and the state had fifty-five counties. One Kennedy operative who managed only part of one county recalled years later that he received $60,000 in cash from a courier from Boston. Another minor operative wanted $3,500, asked for "35" and got $35,000. In addition to slating, much of the money was used to make contributions to Protestant churches, especially black churches. Unlike in Wisconsin, Kennedy won the small African American vote in West Virginia. Joe Kennedy and Cardinal Cushing in Boston jointly decided which preachers would get $500 and which $1,000. Cushing gave Joe Kennedy $950,000 cash from the diocese's Sunday collection plates, and in return Kennedy wrote a tax deductible check to the church for $1 million.[84]

West Virginia politics were perhaps the epitome of old-style machine politics at work. Various factions of the Democratic Party

in West Virginia would put out "slate cards" in which the organization demonstrated to its members for whom they should cast their
votes; these were distributed the day before any election. Some ves-
tiges of this system continue to exist in the endorsements various
organizations issue today, however, in the spring of 1960 the system
was functioning at its most effective.[85]

The slate cards were determined not by the general membership
of the union, interest group, club, etc. but rather by the group's leadership. As such, the easiest way for a candidate to win the votes of a
given group, particularly in as remote an area as rural West Virginia,
was to win the endorsement of these party grandees. While theoretically this could be done by an impassioned campaign of issues,
in reality this was often done through bribery, blackmail, and the
promise of patronage following an election. This is illustrated in
the story of Logan County Democratic Boss Raymond Chafin. The
Kennedy clan simply asked Chafin how much he needed to deliver
the votes. "Thirty-five," was Chafin's response, meaning $35,000.[86]
Later in life, Chafin would point out that this bribe only covered his
faction in the county, and his was the smaller of the two major factions of the local Democratic Party. Logan County is only one, and
a smallish one at that, of fifty-five such counties in West Virginia. It
doesn't take a mathematical genius to deduce that if Kennedy was
willing to spend at least $35,000 in Logan County, he was willing to
spend hundreds of thousands, and possibly even over one million,
dollars on the campaign.

When the results rolled in on May 10 the national press was
shocked. Kennedy had defeated Humphrey by a devastating margin
of 61 percent to 39 percent. There are some who say that money cannot solve all problems; however, its effect in West Virginia may have
disabused more than a few of that notion. Money had made, through
the shocking aftermath of the West Virginia primary, Jack Kennedy the
Democratic Party's candidate for president. The Chicago family took
notice. FBI wiretaps would later show that they believed their money
had paved the way for Kennedy's victory. "Your boyfriend wouldn't

be in the White House if it wasn't for me," Giancana said to Judith Campbell, a woman shared carnally by the Chicago mobster and the president.[87]

It is also important to note what it is that made the Chicago mob so much more important and influential than other families. When most of us hear of the Mafia, we think New York City's "Five Families," made famous by Francis Ford Coppola in his film adaptation of the aforementioned novel *The Godfather*. There are, indeed, five families in New York City, which divide the city and influence between themselves as part of an often-fractious relationship. What set Chicago apart was that in 1960, unlike the dysfunctional multipolar world of East Coast mafiosi, the Chicago family ruled with a united front, holding complete and total control over one-third of the city of Chicago, no fewer than four Las Vegas casinos, a close relationship with Chicago Mayor Richard Daley, and control of two congressmen, and the head of the Illinois Department of Revenue was one of their own.[88]

Within their territory the Chicago family was an unparalleled political machine, capable of running up electoral margins of victory greater than 90 percent. This political power was what Joe Kennedy was after when he brought Giancana into the fold with the $500,000 donation. Illinois in 1960 was a key electoral target, comprising the fourth-highest number of electoral votes; and unlike today, Illinois was a state both sides could reasonably foresee winning. As such, the Kennedy camp knew that winning a historic victory in metropolitan Chicago would likely be necessary to carry Illinois, and its twenty-seven electoral votes. Giancana and Mayor Daley were the keys to finding that margin, and both expected a Kennedy victory to be a substantial boon to their own empires.

Still, the vote stealing in Chicago was breathtaking. Few have reported on this with the detail of W. J. Rorabaugh in *The Real Making of the President:*

In 1960 Daley put pressure on the precinct captains and ward bosses to produce fixed vote margins for each precinct and ward for Kennedy. Any member of the organization that failed to produce was likely to lose both his political party post and his city job. Efficient precinct captains identified voters made sure they were registered, and got them to the polls on Election Day. In 1960, Chicago had an impressive 89.3 percent turnout, far above the national average.

Many tricks were used in Chicago. Republicans were removed from the rolls, a fact that they only discovered when they tried to vote. One turned out to be an irate columnist for the *Chicago Tribune*. Persons who had been dead for years often were found to have voted. In Ward 4, Precinct 31, both a dead man and a son who had taken care of the man and then moved away performed their civic duty. Rolls could be padded in other ways. In Ward 5, Precinct 46, registration closed with 636 voters listed. But on Election Day the poll book contained 751 names, the extra 115 names having been added at city hall. Of these fraudulent registrants, 49 voted. Democrats paid cheap boardinghouses one dollar per head for each resident who voted. Managers also got an additional twenty-five dollars to fifty dollars to keep Republicans from entering to talk with the tenants. Bans carried "floaters" from precinct to precinct to cast multiple votes, electioneering sometimes took place inside polling places, and votes were bought just outside the door.

Many precincts had fake Republican election judges. In Ward 4, Precinct 6, the "Republican" judge tried to assist a Republican voter in voting a straight Democratic ticket. The judge had to be physically restrained from casting the ballot for the voter on the machine. Final results were Kennedy 451, Nixon 67. In Ward 6, Precinct 38, the voting machine at 10:15 A.M. showed 121 votes, but only 43 voters had signed in. The final total was Kennedy 408, Nixon 79. In half a dozen precincts, the number of votes counted exceeded the number of registered voters by more than 75.

Chicago Republicans paid for a partial recount. In many of the city's 3,327 voting machine precincts, the numbers that remained visible on the machines disagreed with the official tally sheets. The bigger problem, however, was in the 634 precincts that used paper ballots, where numbers on the tally sheets often bore no relationship to the ballots in the ballot box, when they were recounted at the courthouse in the presence of Republicans. In 1960 vote counting on election night in most jurisdictions in the United States was done in the precincts with counted ballots and completed tallies then taken to the courthouse. Nor was it reassuring that about 60 percent of the ballot boxes either had seals that were missing or broken when they were brought from storage into the counting room.

In many precincts, an inspection of the ballots showed that Republican votes had been erased. In Ward 27, Precinct 20, there were fifteen straight Republican ballots in a row that had been spoiled by an extra X being placed into the Socialist Labor Party column. Although impossible to prove, it was easy to conclude that the marks had been added during the counting. The tally sheets almost always favored Democrats more than did the recount of the actual ballots. Apparently, local precinct officials had simply made up results to provide the margins that Daley had demanded. The press identified 677 election judges in 133 precincts who had stolen votes. The investigation, however, accomplished little. One Chicago politician told the journalist Alistair Cooke, "When a vote is stolen in Chicago, it stays stolen."[89]

Election night 1960 was a stressful time for all involved. The Kennedy campaign, driven by the twin pillars of Joe Kennedy's money, and Bobby Kennedy's unwavering refusal to lose, had retreated to the Kennedy compound in Hyannis Port. Across the country the Nixon camp was established in the Ambassador Hotel in Los Angeles. Both sides had reason for optimism, but confidence was probably too strong a word to describe the mentality of either side.

In 1960, with the Democratic hold on the South still relatively solid (there was a nascent move to send unpledged electors by Southern Democrats unwilling to cast votes for a Catholic liberal, which sent a number of unpledged electors from Mississippi and Alabama who would end up voting for Democratic Senator Harry Byrd), the Democratic camp could expect the election to develop in a somewhat predictable manner. As expected, Republicans were able to jump out to leads in most of the northeast on the backs of suburban and rural voters, only to have democratic votes in eastern cities change the calculus and send Kennedy into the lead.

By 11 p.m., on the backs of large margins of victory in New York City, Philadelphia, and Boston, Kennedy had taken a lead of an estimated one million votes, according to the campaign's internal estimates.[90] The Kennedy campaign was concerned and only became more so as the returns began coming in from the Midwest and Farm Belt. The campaign was underperforming across the entirety of the Midwest, at that time still the cradle of the Republican Party.

Shortly after Ohio was called for the Nixon ticket, Jack Kennedy approached his brother to ask for an update—four key states remained outstanding: California, Illinois, Michigan, and Minnesota. Jack Kennedy looked at his brother upon hearing of the silence out of Illinois and asked him if he had spoken to Daley yet. Bobby immediately called Daley's office and had a brief conversation with the mayor, upon the conclusion of which Bobby relayed to Jack that, "[Daley] said we're going to make it with the help of a few close friends."[91] Those "friends" were Johnny Roselli, Sam Giancana, and the Chicago family.

The victory wasn't going to come easy for Daley and the Chicago gang; the Kennedy campaign was in significant trouble, as their ticket ran significantly below their projections in the rest of the state. The political calculus of Illinois in 1960 was straightforward for both parties. In Chicago, Democrats were going to win, and they were going to win big; everywhere else in the state, the Nixon ticket was going to run away with a victory—in short, if Kennedy was going to win the state's twenty-seven electoral votes turnout would have to be so high in Chicago, and the margin so great, that the rest of the state could not cancel out Chicago. Both sides were well aware of this facet of Illinois politics, and as such the state was notorious for its poor turnaround time in reporting votes; after all, it is easier, to say nothing of drawing less attention, to wait for your opponent to play his hand before rigging your own. It's not impossible to discover votes had been "misplaced" after a precinct was already reported (as indeed, Lyndon Johnson showed on many occasions during his own crooked career) . . . but it does tend to draw attention.

To the memory of Kennedy campaign aide Kenny O'Donnell, Daley called Kennedy headquarters around 3 a.m. to complain about the competition between the Republican and Democratic machines in Illinois: "Every time we announce two hundred more votes for Kennedy in Chicago, they come up out of nowhere downstate with another three hundred votes for Nixon. One of their precincts outside of Peoria, where there are only fifty voters, just announced five hundred votes for Nixon."[92]

While there were certainly voting irregularities on both sides, Daley's complaints are hypocritical almost past the point of humor. The unofficial motto of the Daley political machine was (as was later documented in a book of this title), "We don't want nobody [that] nobody sent." The election of 1960 raised this corruption to an art, and Johnny Roselli, Sam Giancana, and the Chicago mob were at the operation's heart. On Election Day the mob deployed approximately nine hundred of their goons to work the polls by destroying opposing ballots, "helping" voters cast their ballots, and intimidating those whose commitment to the cause was considered insufficiently pure. Bones were broken. Poll watchers for Nixon provided Polaroid photographs of money changing hands for votes outside of polling places. In mob-run territory the Kennedy ticket received over 80 percent of the vote. In the end, the fraud was enough to hand Kennedy the victory with a margin of 8,858 votes out of 4.75 million counted, a margin of 19 percent.[93]

Mayor Daley was known for rigging elections, and vote quotas were handed out to ward bosses and precinct captains. Two recounts of Chicago-area voting proved that the old Democratic machine had likely stolen tens of thousands of votes for the Democratic ticket. Special prosecutor Wexler's April 1961 report found "substantial" miscounts in the 1,367 precincts it examined, which included unqualified voters, misread voting machines, and math mistakes. In one precinct, free lunches were handed out by a ward boss. In another, free hams were raffled to buy eligible voters. In many precincts, boardinghouse bums and vagrants were promised and given shots of whiskey for votes. There is substantial evidence that these fraudulent voters were shuttled from polling place to polling place and were "repeaters." Wexler's inquiry was hampered by the noncooperation of Cook County officials and the Democratic machine, where Wexler was stonewalled. Wexler brought contempt charges against 667 election officials, but a Democratic judge dismissed the cases. Three people were convicted on criminal charges.

Historian Edmund Kallina noted, "Winning Illinois would not have been enough to propel the Republican into the White House; [Kennedy] would have had to carry Texas or a combination of other states to give him the 269 electoral votes needed then to win." That is, of course, the point. The evidence of voter fraud in Texas, where the Kennedy-Johnson ticket carried the state by a scant fifty thousand votes was as widespread and odious as that of the daily machine in Chicago.

Thousands of Texas ballots were thrown out on the technicality that all of those who went to the polls did not scratch out the names of the candidates for the presidency for whom they did not want to vote, as the law required. Republicans—who were not joined by Nixon, who was graceful in defeat, if privately furious, charged this had taken the state's electoral vote away from the vice president. The requirement was applied in some counties and not in others. Lyndon Johnson's vote stealing capabilities marred his first election to the Senate, where ballot boxes disappeared while others were stuffed, requiring a US Supreme Court ruling, by which Johnson stole his US Senate Seat from Conservative Democrat and former Governor "Coke" Stevenson.

I believe that the 1960 election was stolen famously in Mayor Richard Daley's Chicago, but the theft was only completed by vote rigging in Lyndon Johnson's Texas. Johnson's prowess in rigging elections was legendary. Readers of my book *The Man Who Killed Kennedy: The Case Against LBJ* know that Johnson stole his 1948 Senate election with two hundred nonexistent votes in Box 13 in Jim Wells County, where the local Patron was a Johnson crony. Texas Governor Allen Shivers would publicly accuse Johnson of ordering the murder of deputy sheriff Sam Smithwick, who was preparing to testify to a grand jury regarding the voter fraud.

The Johnson machine would outdo themselves in 1960. In Texas that year the state ballot was designed so that rather than circling the candidate's name you preferred, voters were required to cross off the names of all the candidates they were *not* for. Not all counties applied this standard vigorously, but in many large counties controlled by Lyndon Johnson and his cronies, this was used to void the ballots of thousands of voters who had circled the name of Nixon and Lodge. The Kennedy-Johnson ticket would carry Texas over Nixon and Lodge by a scant forty-six thousand votes. Lyndon Johnson's flunkies would invalidate 100,000 votes in Dallas County alone.

Again, we must rely on the meticulous work of W. J. Rorabaugh in his monograph *The Real Making of the President*. Lyndon Johnson and his cronies had perfected voter fraud as an art form:

After the election, the greatest complaints concerned Illinois and Texas. If both states had voted for Nixon, he would have won. Virtually all locally elected officials in Texas were Democrats. So were the precinct judges. Furthermore, Texas law made no provision for challenging a presidential election. In fact, in many places there were more votes cast than registered voters in the jurisdiction. In Fannin County, 4,895 voters cast 6,138 ballots. In Navarro County, Dawson Precinct, 479 registered voters cast 315 votes for Kennedy and 219 for Nixon. In some heavily Democratic jurisdictions, votes for president and vice president were added, giving each side double the number of votes. In Angelina County, Precinct 27, 86 people voted. Kennedy got 147 votes and Nixon got 24. The judge had added 74 votes for Kennedy to 73 votes for Johnson. In Lee County, Precinct 15, 39 people voted but 64 votes were counted for president. By comparing poll books to the vote count, it was clear that 100,000 votes had been counted that simply did not exist, but Republicans were prevented from seeing any actual ballots.

Texas voting law also contained one oddity, which resulted in an ingenious way to manipulate the result. Although thirteen counties containing about half of Texas voters used mechanical voting machines, the rest of the state voted with "negative" paper ballots. In 1957 the law had been changed to require that voters strike out the names of all the candidates they opposed. In 1960 there were four candidates on the Texas presidential ballot. Thus, a voter had to cross out three names to cast a valid vote. In some counties, it was charged, Democratic election officials disallowed votes that had only Kennedy struck out, but they counted votes for Kennedy that had only Nixon struck out. In Wichita Falls, middle-class Eagle Lake gave Nixon 475, Kennedy 357, and had 234 voided, while lower-class Precinct 54, which went to Kennedy by six to one, presented only two voided ballots. A certain amount of variation simply reflected the whim of the officials in each precinct. In rural Wichita County, Precinct 43, 3 percent of ballots were invalidated. In adjacent Precinct 35, an essentially identical rural precinct, 22 percent of ballots were invalidated.

The evidence suggests that Democratic officials purposely used different standards in different kinds of precincts of counties in order to manipulate the overall result. For example, in some precincts that voted heavily for Nixon, 40 percent of the votes were voided, while in Starr County, a poor county on the Mexican border that voted more than 93 percent for Kennedy, only 1.5 percent were thrown out. In Fort Bend County, Precinct 1, Nixon drew 458, Kennedy drew 350, and 182 were disallowed. In Precinct 2, Kennedy received 68 voted, Nixon 1, and none were voided. In one strong Kennedy precinct where a recount in a local election allowed outside observers to see the ballots, about 200 Kennedy votes were seen that should have been voided for striking out only Nixon. Republicans charged that more than 100,000 Republican ballots had been disallowed in Texas, and thousands of Democratic ballots with the same type of error had been added in. Kennedy's margin was 46,000. However, without an official investigation, there was no way to know whether this kind of vote counting fraud provided Kennedy's margin of victory in the Lone Star State.[94]

Texas Republicans were also hurt by a last-minute Johnson dirty trick. In an appearance in Dallas, Johnson and his attractive wife, Lady Bird, were subjected to a small-scale version of some of the unpleasantries that Nixon and his wife had encountered in their tumultuous visit to Latin America. The Johnsons were jostled and heckled as they inched their way through a crowded hotel lobby. There was some spittle aimed at them as they made their way across the street to another hotel. It was one of those things that most Texans don't like to have happened to their own, particularly to a Texan accompanied by his lady. Johnson charged that Republican Congressman Bruce Alger organized the demonstration and that Republican money paid for the preparation of the Johnson-scorning placards that were borne aloft by an unruly crowd in an attempt to downgrade Johnson as the native son. Alger told Senator Barry Goldwater that both were patently false and that Alger was not on the scene. The crowd was likely part of Dallas's bustling right-wing community, but Johnson exploited the situation adroitly. It is interesting to note that Alger was handily reelected.

"LBJ and Lady Bird could have gone through the lobby and got on that elevator in five minutes," said D. B. Hardeman, an aide to House Speaker and Texan Sam Rayburn, "But LBJ took thirty minutes to go through that crown, and it was all being recorded and photographed for television and radio and the newspapers, and he knew and played it for all it was worth."[95]

The shift of Illinois and Texas, where victory was indeed stolen from Richard Nixon, would have elected Nixon president. The selection of Lyndon Johnson would both guarantee Kennedy's election and his murder in Dallas as Johnson, on the verge of federal indictment and prison for corruption engineered the killing of the president in the city where LBJ controlled the investigation. LBJ would helm a plot that yoked a coalition of interests who needed JFK gone including the CIA, the Mob, and big Texas oil. Those interested in this history should read *The Man Who Killed Kennedy — the Case Against LBJ*.

There are those who have argued that as some measure of fraud has been documented on both sides of the campaign, and we must conclude the race as a wash. This is a deliberately misleading reporting of the truth—that the Kennedy-Johnson fraud campaign in 1960, particularly with the aide of organized crime, was of such substantial size as to have stolen the presidency for Kennedy. Theodore White, friend of the Kennedy family and originator of the Camelot mythos through which we have enshrined Kennedy, admitted in his book *Breach of Faith*, regarding the downfall of President Nixon, "Democratic vote-stealing had definitely taken place on a massive scale in Illinois and Texas (where 100,000 big-city votes were simply disqualified); and on a lesser scale elsewhere."[96]

White was not alone in believing the Kennedys stole the election, among those who recognized the truth was FBI Director J. Edgar Hoover. Shortly after sending a brief congratulatory note to President-elect Kennedy, Hoover called Philip Hochstein, editorial director of the Newhouse group of newspapers, and "mounted a tirade accusing the Kennedys of having stolen the election in a number of states [and] would Hochstein join the effort to reverse the election results?"[97] Shortly after President Kennedy took the oath of office, the FBI's special agent in charge in the Chicago office reported back to the Justice Department that it was his belief that the election had been stolen for Kennedy.[98] Unsurprisingly, no action was taken in response to the report.

JFK may even have lost the popular vote. Five states—Georgia, Louisiana, Mississippi, South Carolina, and Alabama—flirted with running unpledged slates of Democratic electors in an effort to throw the election into the House. This was a reaction to the civil rights plank adopted by the Democrats in Los Angeles. Alabama ended up with five electors pledged to Kennedy and six unpledged. Mississippi would run both a Kennedy and an unpledged slate of electors. In those states voters were asked to vote for specific electors rather than casting their votes for Kennedy or Nixon. Political scientists have continued to argue about how votes should be counted and distributed because of the peculiar and arcane nature of the clash in which the diehard segregationists Democrats in the South sought to block JFK from winning the electoral votes in their states by trying to block out the national Democrats and run slates of "unpledged" electors. Fifteen of these renegades would ultimately vote in the Electoral College for Harry F. Byrd Sr. The complexity of this disagreement on how the votes should be cast is addressed in an outstanding monograph by Sean Trende of *Real Clear Politics,* which is reproduced in Appendix 4. At least one reasonable method of counting the vote results in a Nixon victory of approximately sixty thousand votes nationally. This was the methodology initially used by *Congressional Quarterly* in their reporting, only to be amended after Kennedy was declared the popular vote victor by the mass media of the day. The election of 1960 was so close that Nixon *may* have won the popular vote.

In 1960, the records tell us that Sen. John F. Kennedy defeated Vice President Richard Nixon in an incredibly close popular vote, 34,220,984 to 34,108,157, a difference of only 112,827 votes. Unfortunately, this is wrong. In fact, it would be *Kennedy* that would lose to Nixon in a photo finish.

Party conservatives would feel that Nixon had pulled his punches in the race with Kennedy and had wasted time in urban northeastern states like Pennsylvania and New York, instead of spending more time in the Deep South. "If all Republicans had worked as hard as did those in the South, we would have won the election hands down," he said. "If we had taken Texas, South Carolina, North Carolina, and had done better in the rural areas of Alabama and Georgia, we could have had an almost solid South," proclaimed Barry Goldwater.[99] The Arizona Senator could not deduce why black Americans leaned

Democratic, but to Goldwater, it was a problem that could have been avoided by utilizing resources elsewhere. "If you are going hunting for ducks, you go where the ducks are," Goldwater said.[100]

The negative reaction from the conservative wing of the party was rooted in the "Sellout of Fifth Avenue," the secret meeting with Nelson Rockefeller, which Goldwater had alternatively dubbed "the Munich of the Republican Party." The meeting was perceived by many on the right as a double-cross, an act of treason that would not wash off easily after the narrow loss. That Nixon had lost because he had subscribed to "me-too Republicanism" in lieu of a hard-hitting Republican Party platform. The votes were hardly in the ballot box when Goldwater, who had supported Nixon in the days preceding, went on the attack. Nixon had offered conservative voters "an insufficient choice," in the words of Goldwater. "There wasn't enough difference between the two candidates' position," he said. "Had Nixon started banging away at Kennedy's domestic proposals he would have won. Every time Kennedy said something about federal aid, Dick said something about federal aid. But the people felt that if we're going to have a welfare state, let's have a president whose whole experience is in the welfare state field and whose whole philosophy is welfare state, rather than one whose party had worked against the idea."[101]

Senator Styles Bridges of New Hampshire echoed the Goldwater assessment that Nixon had mollified liberals and handled Kennedy with kid gloves. In Bridges's view, Nixon could have won "if he had slugged hard enough against Kennedy in the last three weeks of the campaign."[102]

Though Goldwater was critical of Nixon's strategy, he too thought the election had been stolen out of Republican hands by the depraved and power-hungry Lyndon Johnson. "You can't discount Johnson in this thing," Goldwater said. "With the tactics he used, we don't know whether we lost Texas or not. I don't think we did. I think Texas might have been stolen, frankly. I was through that state too much and too often to believe that they could have switched in the last ten days to the extent that the vote count showed they did."[103]

In the end, it would have taken only twenty-eight thousand Texans and four thousand Illinoisans to shift the electoral vote victory to Nixon. Kennedy ended up with 303 electoral votes to Nixon's 219. The shift of Illinois and Texas would have made the difference. Nixon had come roaring back, and they robbed him. Victory was stolen from Richard Nixon.

Vice President Nixon repeatedly declared himself "convinced that wiretapping had been a key weapon in the Kennedy arsenal during the campaign of 1960." In old age he still talked of how he had been "victimized by all kinds of dirty tricks."Nixon said Robert Kennedy "was the worst. He illegally bugged more people than anyone. He was a bastard."[104]

NOTES

1. Leonard Garment, *Crazy Rhythm*, p. 77.
2. Richard Whalen, *Catch the Falling Flag*, p. 14.
3. "The First Kennedy-Nixon Debate—1947," http://coloradopols. com/diary/14886/the-first-kennedy-nixon-debates-1947.
4. Anthony Summers, *The Arrogance of Power*, p. 202.
5. David Pietrusza, *1960: LBJ vs. JFK vs. Nixon*, p. 49.
6. Kate Milner, "Flashback: 1960 Kennedy Beats Nixon," *BBC News*, Nov. 9, 2000.
7. John Davis, *The Kennedys: Dynasty and Disaster*, p. 151.
8. Richard Whalen, *Catch the Falling Flag*, p. 108.
9. Stone, Roger Stone, "Did JFK Steal the 1960 Election?" *The Stone Zone*, Dec. 7, 2010.
10. Victor Lasky, *It Didn't Start With Watergate*, p. 42.
11. White House Recording, Friday, Sept. 15, 1972.
12. Jeff Shesol, *Mutual Contempt*, p. 34.
13. Jeff Shesol, *Mutual Contempt*, p. 35.
14. Ralph Martin, *Seeds of Destruction*, pp. 196–197.
15. Jeff Shesol, *Mutual Contempt*, p. 40.

16. Anthony Summers, *The Arrogance of Power* (Kindle Locations 13336-13339).
17. Charles Higham, *Howard Hughes: The Secret Life.*
18. Letter from Richard Nixon to Roger Stone.
19. http://millercenter.org/president/nixon/essays/biography/2.
20. Anthony Summers, The Arrogance of Power, p. 212.
21. Webster Griffin Tarpley and Anton Chaitkin, *George Bush: The Unauthorized Biography*, p. 256.
22. Victor Lasky, *It Didn't Start With Watergate*, p. 44.
23. Carl Solberg, *Hubert Humphrey: A Biography*, p. 209.
24. Elizabeth Shermer and Tandy Barry, *Goldwater and the Remaking of the American Political Landscape*, p. 150.
25. Christopher A. Preble, "Who ever believed in the 'missile gap'? John F. Kennedy and the Politics of National Security," *Presidential Studies Quarterly*, Dec. 1, 2003.
26. Edmund Kallina, *Kennedy v. Nixon*, p. 108.
27. Edmund Kallina, *Kennedy v. Nixon*, p. 109.
28. Edmund Kallina, *Kennedy v. Nixon*, p. 155.
29. Jeffrey Frank, "When Martin Luther King Jr. and Richard Nixon were Friends." *The Daily Beast*, Jan. 21, 2013.
30. Herb Klein, *Making It Perfectly Clear*, p. 308.
31. Tom Wicker, *One of Us: Richard Nixon and the American Dream*, p. 242.
32. Ibid. p. 108.
33. Ibid. p. 236.
34. Richard Nixon, *Six Crises*, p. 307.
35. Anthony Summers, *The Arrogance of Power*, pp. 205–206.
36. David Pietrusza, *1960: LBJ vs. JFK vs. Nixon*, p. 386.
37. Anthony Summers, *The Arrogance of Power*, p. 205.
38. Tom Wicker, *One of Us: Richard Nixon and the American Dream*, p. 244.
39. Ibid.
40. Anthony Summers, *The Arrogance of Power*, pp. 204–205.
41. Tom Wicker, *One of Us: Richard Nixon and the American Dream*, p. 245.
42. David Pietrusza, *1960: LBJ vs. JFK vs. Nixon*, p. 226.
43. Marvin Liebman, *Coming Out Conservative*, p. 148.
44. David Pietrusza, *1960: LBJ vs. JFK vs. Nixon*, p. 227.
45. Richard Kleindienst, *Justice*, p. 37.
46. Richard Kleindienst, *Justice*, p. 28.
47. Richard Kleindienst, *Justice*, p. 29.

48. Ibid. p. 27.
49. Ibid. p. 27.
50. David Pietrusza, *1960: LBJ vs. JFK vs. Nixon*, pp. 228–229.
51. David Pietrusza, *1960: LBJ vs. JFK vs. Nixon*, pp. 228–229.
52. "Walter H. Judd, 95, Missionary to China and U.S. Representative," *New York Times*, Feb. 15, 1994.
53. Letter from Richard Nixon to Walter Judd, Aug. 16, 1988.
54. *Time*, March 20, 1964.
55. Christopher Matthews, *Kennedy & Nixon*, p. 144.
56. David Folkenflik, "When Kennedy Overran Nixon," *The Baltimore Sun*, Oct. 1, 2000.
57. Theodore White, *The Making of the President*, 1960, p. 258.
58. Anthony Summers, *The Arrogance of Power*, pp. 204–205.
59. Anthony Summers, *The Arrogance of Power* (Kindle Locations 4944-4954).
60. Ibid. p. 207.
61. Richard Whalen, *Catch the Falling Flag*, p. 14.
62. Anthony Summers, *The Arrogance of Power*, p. 206.
63. Christopher Matthews, *Kennedy & Nixon*, p. 148.
64. David Greenberg, "Rewinding the Kennedy-Nixon Debates," Slate, Sept. 24, 2010.
65. Anthony Summers, *The Arrogance of Power*, p. 208.
66. Ibid.
67. David Halberstam, *The Powers That Be*, p. 477.
68. Monica, Davey, "1960: The First Mass Media Election," *New York Times*, Oct. 6, 2008.
69. Theodore White, *The Making of the President, 1960*, p. 258.
70. Larry Getlen, "The Kennedy Meth," *New York Post*, April 21, 2013.
71. Ibid.
72. H. R. Haldeman, *The Ends of Power*, p. 27.
73. Leonard Garment, *Crazy Rhythm*, p. 77.
74. Ralph Martin, *Seeds of Destruction*, p. 250.
75. Richard D. Mahoney, *The Kennedy Brothers: The Rise and Fall of Jack and Bobby*, p. 48.
76. Ibid. p. 50.
77. Ibid.
78. Frank Ragano, *Mob Lawyer*, p. 135.
79. Chuck Giancana, *Double Cross*, p. 64.

80. Drew Pearson, "Nixon's Early Years Come Under Scrutiny," *The Nevada Daily Mail*, Oct. 31, 1968.
81. Ibid.
82. Richard D. Mahoney, *The Kennedy Brothers: The Rise and Fall of Jack and Bobby*, p. 52.
83. W. J. Rorabaugh, *The Real Making of the President*, p. 54.
84. Richard D. Mahoney, *The Kennedy Brothers: The Rise and Fall of Jack and Bobby*, p. 197.
85. David Pietrusza, *1960: LBJ vs. JFK vs. Nixon*, p. 126.
86. Ronald Goldfarb, *Perfect Villains, Imperfect Heroes*, p. 260.
87. Mahoney, Richard D. *The Kennedy Brothers: The Rise and Fall of Jack and Bobby*, p. 49
88. W. J. Rorabaugh, *The Real Making of the President*, p. 189–190.
89. Richard D. Mahoney, *The Kennedy Brothers: The Rise and Fall of Jack and Bobby*, p. 79.
90. Richard D. Mahoney, *The Kennedy Brothers: The Rise and Fall of Jack and Bobby*, p. 81.
91. Ibid. p. 82.
92. Burton, Hersh, *Bobby and J. Edgar: The Historic Face-Off Between the Kennedys and J. Edgar Hoover That Transformed America*, p. 203.
93. W. J. Rorabaugh, *The Real Making of the President*, p. 187–188.
94. David Pietrusza, *1960: LBJ vs. JFK vs. Nixon*, p. 387.
95. Victor Lasky, *It Didn't Start With Watergate*, p. 48.
96. Burton, Hersh, *Bobby and J. Edgar: The Historic Face-Off Between the Kennedys and J. Edgar Hoover That Transformed America*, p. 203.
97. Ibid.
98. Jack Bell, *Mr. Conservative: Barry Goldwater*, p. 166.
99. Jack Bell, *Mr. Conservative: Barry Goldwater*, p. 165.
100. Ibid. p. 165.
101. Ibid.
102. Ibid. p. 169.
103. Anthony Summers, *The Arrogance of Power*, p. 212.

CHAPTER SEVEN

"CALIFORNIA NEEDS A DECISIVE LEADER"

Knock, knock.
Who's there? ˙
Nixon.
Nixon who?
What, you forgot already?
> —Children's chant overheard on the streets of San
> Francisco, circa December 1962

Nineteen sixty-two would prove to be a year in which Nixon would make damaging miscalculations about the direction of the Republican Party and, in an effort to keep his White House dream alive for the long term, he became a candidate for California governor.

Early polling showed that Nixon, who had narrowly carried the state in 1960, could easily defeat incumbent Pat Brown, whom voters generally saw as an overweight, affable yet bumbling chief executive. Brown made a terrific comeback. Just two years earlier in 1960, after he had given a reprieve from a death sentence to the sensational murderer Caryl Chessman, Brown's popularity was so low that few believed Brown could be reelected. Nixon led by 16 percent in the field poll. Nearly one-third of voters thought that Brown was doing a poor job. Sample voters described him as "weak," "vacillating," and "indecisive."[1] Not only did early polling show Brown losing to Nixon, but also trailing both former Governor Goodwin Knight and San Francisco Mayor George Christopher, both of whom had expressed an interest in running. The ad men around Nixon would seize on this poll finding in their campaign slogan: "Give California a Decisive Leader." Haldeman's marketing background would also show when the Nixon campaign used uniform yellow-and-blue graphics as well as a painted portrait of Nixon on their posters and billboards rather than a photo. "Win with Nixon" was a curious additional campaign slogan, but was presumably meant to spur some bandwagon effect.

It was clear from the beginning that Pat Nixon was opposed to another race for public office. The Nixon's had settled into a palatial home in the Trousdale Estates area outside Los Angeles. Nixon's purchase of a lot for construction of his new home was criticized when it was revealed that he bought the property at a bargain basement price of $35,000 from the developer. The International Teamsters Pension Fund funded the real estate project, but the developer was even more interesting. It was Clint Murchison Jr., whose ranch Nixon would visit on the eve of John F. Kennedy's assassination three years hence. In my book *The Man Who Killed Kennedy*, I make the case that Murchinson, a longtime crony of Lyndon Johnson with deep connections to both military intelligence and organized crime, was one of the funders of the Kennedy assassination.

The ill-fated Nixon bid for governor started seriously in January 1962 with a long afternoon brainstorming session at the beach home of a prominent California Republican Margaret Brock. Nixon's advisors were called to the beautiful residence on Trancas Beach, near Malibu, overlooking the Pacific. There were divergent opinions expressed by Rose Mary Woods, Bob Finch, journalist Earl Mazo, and longtime friends Jack Drown and Ray Arbuthnot. Longtime Nixon financial supporter Elmer Bobst, who had made millions in pharmaceuticals, was opposed to the race, saying Nixon "would risk much but win little."[2] The Malibu discussion on the governorship ended as the sun was sinking into the Pacific. With darkness setting in, Nixon said he would run for governor.

His only hedge was that he wanted to talk with his family on the matter. But in fact he was already discussing the date for a formal announcement and how it would be handled. Pat Nixon would tell her husband, "Let's not run. Let's stay home. Let's be a family."[3]

The night Nixon announced his candidacy in 1961, Pat would tell Bob Finch's wife, Carol, "I'm trapped. Which way can I go? He can't help it. He must always have a crusade."[4] While Pat Nixon would not campaign for her husband as extensively as she had in 1960, even she would undertake a separate tour in the closing weeks of the campaign. Nixon's daughters were supportive, with fifteen-year-old Trisha telling her father, "Daddy, come on. Let's show 'em."[5]

Today it is difficult to determine who was for Nixon's running and who was opposed to it. There were others Nixon consulted extensively, including the late Thomas Dewey, Herbert Brownell, Eisenhower's first attorney general, William Rogers, Nixon's close friend, and two veterans of the Nixon and Eisenhower campaigns, Leonard Hall, Nixon's 1960 manager, and J. Clifford Folger, the 1960 finance chairman. Most were from New York, in touch with major party financial powers, and most urged Nixon to run.

Nixon also received substantial encouragement from outside the state to make the race. Both President Eisenhower and Governor Tom Dewey were among those urging him to run to position himself with a political future. Herbert Brownell Jr. and William P. Rogers, both of whom had served as attorney general for Ike, joined Nixon's 1960 finance chairman Clifford Folger and former Republican National Chairman Leonard W. Hall in urging Nixon to make the race. Former President Herbert Hoover and General Douglas MacArthur opposed the run.

From the beginning it was clear that Nixon had no interest in state issues such as smog, traffic, the state education system, water problems, and the like. Echoing the 1952 campaign, he pledged to "clean up the mess in Sacramento," which voters took as a non-issue in view of the fact that voters did not think there was a mess in Sacramento.[6]

Nixon also had to deal with a badly divided Republican Party. After a disastrous 1958 election in which Senator William Knowland and Governor Goodwin Knight tried to exchange seats, leading the party to ignominious defeat, the party had splintered into right and left wings. The John Birch Society had grown like wildfire in Southern California. Its members practiced a pure brand of anti-Communism that deeply distrusted the bipartisan establishment in the East. Birch Society founder Robert Welch believed Roosevelt was a Communist, Truman was a dupe of the Communists, and Eisenhower was a "conscious agent of the Communist conspiracy." While not all these Birches were this extreme, this appalled Nixon, who was ever sensitive about his relationship with Eisenhower anyway. The Birches had actually elected two of their members to Congress, John Rousselot and Edgar Hiestand. Both were on good personal terms with Nixon. Many Republican candidates for Assembly and State Senate were Birchers. Repudiating the Birch Society meant repudiating many local Republicans, whose support Nixon needed.

Nixon was shocked to learn that AC "Cy" Rubel, former president of the Union Oil Company and a past major union donor, was raising money for Joe Shell. The Los Angeles Young Republicans, once a hotbed of support for Nixon, had been taken over by a conservative faction, as had the Los Angeles County Committee.[7] Both were supporting Shell. While Nixon would defeat Shell in the primary, he would do so only with substantial effort. Nixon would publicly repudiate the Birch Society in his campaign. It would be a costly mistake. Four years later actor Ronald Reagan would finesse the Birch issue on his way to 993,000-vote margin over Pat Brown.[8]

Nixon would be opposed in the Republican primary by fire-brand conservative Assemblyman Joe Shell. Nixon had earlier told Shell he didn't plan to run, so Shell had moved ahead with a candidacy. Former Lieutenant Governor Howard J. "Butch" Powers withdrew from the race, calling Nixon a "discard from the rubble heap of National politics."[9] In the meantime, liberal Republicans were deserting the former vice president. Former Governor Goodwin Knight endorsed Brown. So did Norris Pulson, former Republican mayor of Los Angeles, and Earl Warren Jr., son of the chief justice and former California governor. Interestingly, Democrat actor Ronald Reagan would endorse Nixon, setting the stage to his switch to the Republican Party.

Thirty-six-year-old H. R. "Bob" Haldeman, who had been an advance man in the 1960 campaign, returned to manage Nixon's campaign efforts. Herb Klein, thirty-four, would return to handle the press. Herbert Kalmbach was the Southern California campaign director and would later raise hush money for the Watergate burglars. Alvin Moscow, who had worked with Nixon on his book *Six Crises*, was the campaign writer. Richard "Sandy" Quinn, thirty-seven, was a press assistant. Ronald Ziegler, twenty-two, was a press aide. Maurice Stands was the Finance Chairman, and the dependable Rose Mary Woods served as Nixon's personal secretary. Field men included Dwight Chapin, Bob Finch, veteran advance man Nick Ruwe, and John Ehrlichman. It was quite a comedown for Finch, who had held the title of campaign director in 1960. Gone were the old Nixon hands that would stand up to him. Among this younger crowd, few told Nixon when he was wrong, and all were afraid of his outburst of temper. Tom Wicker of the *New York Times* wrote, "The candidate is his own strategist, campaign manager, speech writer and fundraiser." His campaign aides did as they were ordered. None were really advisors.

Nixon was again dogged by the loan extended to his brother by industrialist and defense contractor Howard Hughes. Word of the loan had become public in the closing days of the 1960 campaign

after Robert Kennedy authorized the break-in at Hughes accountant's office on the basis of a tip Ambassador Joseph P. Kennedy
paid $100,000 to an informant for. The loan was for Nixon's
brother Donald to prop up a fast-food restaurant that featured
Nixonburgers. Evidently, the house specialty was not well received
by the palates of Southern Californians. The restaurant was a bust.
Despite the $205,000 loan, Donald Nixon's restaurant went bank-
rupt. Vice President Nixon said that he received no portion of the
loan and that his mother had posted the property on which she
lived as collateral. "It was all she had," said Nixon. Strangely, the
loan had been extended through third parties, and the Nixon property was never seized after the bankruptcy of the restaurant. The
loan would plague Nixon as an issue, and when he visited San
Francisco's Chinatown, Democrat dirty trickster Dick Tuck managed to string a banner in native Chinese that said, "Nixon, what
about the Hughes loan?" over Nixon's platform. Nixon would
angrily confront Governor Pat Brown during the one debate they
had. Brown repeatedly rejected Nixon's demands for a series of
debates. Brown would merely shrug the attack off, denying that he
himself had raised the loan issue.

Nixon *eminence grise* Murray Chotiner was back. Chotiner
knew Nixon needed to rally party conservatives, so he skillfully
hammered out a compromise resolution that would placate the
Birchers yet disassociate the GOP from Robert Welch for the powerful California Republican Assembly, a large grassroots conservative Republican activist group that would placate the Birchers yet
disassociate the GOP from Robert Welch. "I usually worked nights
at the campaign office when I was there," said scheduling director John Ehrlichman, who had served as an advance man in 1960.
"I could not miss seeing Murray Chotiner coming and going after
hours with unidentified visitors. Haldeman told me about some
aspects of campaigning I had not seen as advance man. During that
California campaign I have heard and saw more dirty politics—on
both sides—than in all of my 1960 national-campaign experience.

The trash from our opponent's wastebasket was regularly collected by a friend of Chotiner's to be sifted through for information. At times I was shown Pat Brown's advance schedule, salvaged by the garbage gleaners."[10]

Chotiner also launched a campaign to fight Communism in California. Bumper stickers saying "Is Brown Pink?" and "If it's Brown, flush it!" popped up. In truth, the left wing of the Democratic Party was not that enamored of old-time Democrat Pat Brown, but they loathed Nixon. The Communist charge seemed dated and ineffective, although it was clearly designed to bring back Birchers and conservatives disenchanted with Nixon.

Nixon had good reason for red-baiting in the 1962 campaign. From his standpoint it was not merely a simple tactic to attack Governor Brown. A 1961 statewide poll showed a high percentage of California voters agreed with a statement that Communists threatened the United States from within. The public responded when Nixon spoke of domestic Communist subversion. His use of the issue probably helped in galvanizing a fractured Republican Party, but it was not useful in winning Independents and Democrats to whom it seemed dated.[11] At the same time, Democrats so outnumbered Republicans in California that a Republican nominee for governor badly needed a united party solidly behind him. Attacking Brown for being soft on communism seemed a good way to woo these lagging Republicans, especially since Nixon had angered them when he publicly repudiated the support of the extreme right-wing John Birch Society.[12]

Nixon and Maurice Stans, his finance chairman, had trouble raising money. Donors back East eager to write checks for Nixon's "sure thing" presidential campaign in 1960 were not particularly affected by the possibility of him being governor. Richard Jones, a man carrying $65,000 in cash for the Nixon campaign, died carrying the valise in an airplane crash.[13] Aerosol valve king Robert Abplanalp and Leonard Firestone helped, but the campaign simply lacked the funds for the same kind of television saturation in the last two weeks that had aided Nixon in the last two weeks of the presidential race.

Nixon was forced to barnstorm as he had in his 1950 Senate campaign because of the lack of television funds. He deeply resented that a man of his stature would be reduced to hustling the back roads of California. When a supporter urged him to go and schmooze a local newspaper editor, he erupted, "I wouldn't give him the sweat off my balls." Word on the street was that Nixon had disdain for the common folk of his home state. "That's what you have to expect from these local yokels, he said when turnout at a Nixon campaign rally was light.

Nixon was also plagued about a restrictive covenant that was found in the deed to the home he had owned in Washington, which "forbids its sale to Negroes." The covenant was quite standard for DC in the 1940s and 1950s. However, in 1960 the Kennedy-Johnson campaign had distributed a flyer throughout the South hitting Nixon membership in the NAACP. Nixon couldn't catch a break.

Also hurting Nixon became the most substantial change in the coverage of the race by the *Los Angeles Times*. Prior, the *Los Angeles Times* had functioned as a Republican organ leading the charge for Nixon on his 1946 and 1950 races. Political Editor Kyle Palmer was dying of cancer and new publisher, Otis Chandler, was committed to more equitable coverage. One *Los Angeles Times* reporter, Richard Bergholz, demonstrated the hostility in the California press core. Early in 1962, on his first political swing through California, Nixon went to the reporter's section of his campaign bus and announced that he would hold a background conference, a standard Washington technique that meant he could not be quoted by name. Bergholz fixed the former presidential candidate with a cold eye. "Nixon," he said, "you're a candidate for governor of California. Out here, candidates say it on the record or not at all."[14] The assertion was, of course, absurd. All California reporters spoke to sources on background and without attribution on a regular basis, even in 1962.

The campaign was dirty on both sides. Nixon and Haldeman were both sued by the Democratic State Party chairman over mailings designed to mislead Democrats. "Remember when that little jerk sued us," he would ask Haldeman years later on a famous White House tape. The extent to which Nixon was running his own campaign was extraordinary. "He wanted to be horse and jockey," said James Bassett.[15] It was revealed in the litigation over Nixon's campaign mailers that Nixon himself approved the copy and layout for the disputed mail pieces. Bob Haldeman admitted this in his deposition in the case. Having worked in several big state gubernatorial campaigns, I can tell you that no candidate is involved at the level of preparing voter mailings.

Brown would get permission from federal authorities to have a lawyer interview imprisoned gangster Mickey Cohen, who was serving time in a California penitentiary. Attorney General Robert Kennedy himself was said to have approved the interview. Cohen, seeking a reduction in his sentence, signed an affidavit outlining mob funding for Nixon's early campaign, including the story about convening a group of gangsters at the Hollywood Knickerbocker Hotel and locking the doors of the meeting room until everyone ponied up. Cohen signed a statement in which he admitted mob funding of Nixon's 1946, 1950, and 1960 campaigns. The Brown camp would spread Cohen's affidavit to reporters.

Brown would also hire a private detective to find dirt on Nixon and get more detail about the Hughes loan. What Brown's camp did not know was that the private dick had just been engaged by the Nixon campaign for defensive operation on behalf of Nixon, which involved periodic sweeps for bugs in Nixon's home in Bel Air and the Nixon headquarters on Wilshire Boulevard. The private detective, an electronics expert, found transmission equipment, including a bug on the phone of campaign manager H. R. Haldeman. Pacific Telephone and Telegraph Vice President John Davies confirmed the line had been illegally tapped. Nixon's security team tracked the buggers, who were monitoring the transmission from an automobile, and followed them to their waiting plane. Having colleagues pick them up at Washington National Airport, they tailed them directly to Bobby Kennedy's home in Hickory Hill in McLane, Virginia.[16]

"We were bugged in '62 running for governor," Nixon would one day claim in a recorded Oval Office conversation. "Goddamndest thing you ever saw!" The wiretap expert confirmed Nixon's claim for investigative journalist Anthony Summers.

In the end both Nixon and Brown would be knocked off the front page and out of the voters' consciousness by the Cuban Missile Crisis. As voters rallied behind their young president, Nixon knew immediately that his campaign would lose oxygen for a strong closing drive. Nixon concluded he would lose. Press Secretary Herb Klein noted Nixon's condition. "Nixon was haggard, with the lack of sleep showing particularly in his eyes. He looked bad. But his spirits did not seem as low as I had anticipated. We talked for some time about the campaign; where it had gone well and where it had gone badly. He was philosophical about it. He felt—with some justification I thought—that he might have won if it had not been for the Cuban Missile Crisis, which had taken attention away from the election at a time when he hoped a late sprint would influence undecided voters and allow him to catch up with, and perhaps pass, Brown."

Nixon also spoke to campaign aide Stephen Hess. "Do you think you're still going to lose?" Hess asked. "Yes," Nixon answered. He had come to that conclusion when the missile crisis broke.

"You may be wrong," Hess said.

"I'm not wrong," replied Nixon, the realist.[17, 18]

While Nixon lost in 1962, Nelson Rockefeller, George Romney, and William Scranton became potential presidential candidates by scoring major victories, winning the governorship of the large states of New York, Michigan, and Pennsylvania, respectively. They, not Nixon, became the threats to the nomination of Barry Goldwater.

Nixon's disdain for the press was total. When he learned that his press assistant Sandy Quinn was working to accommodate the reporters, he said, "He even sends fruit to their hotel room. Being nice doesn't make a damn bit of difference."[19]

Looking at Nixon's press conference statement about TV, it should be noted that a candidate's impressions of television comes more from what he is told about it than from what he actually sees. Campaign schedules permit little time for television viewing.

Still, Nixon understood the rudimentary of television. He liked the medium when he could control it, as he would later do from the Oval Office. He understood the need to speak over the heads of reporters directly to the voters. Just as the Checkers speech had served him well in 1952, his election eve telethon in 1960 drew an enormous audience. The telethons he did in the California race were not as effective, but I believe that is because the Cuban Missile Crisis had dominated all press coverage in the closing days of Nixon's 1962 drive.

The centerpiece of the 1962 Nixon television advertising program was a series of eight telethons, each broadcast on a local regional basis in cities from Salinas to Los Angeles and San Diego. The telethons, produced theatrically by Jack Rourke, averaged about three hours in length and were patterned after the four-hour Nixon national telethon from Detroit that had such a dramatic influence on the voters in the waning hours of the 1960 presidential race. One estimate was that the 1960 telethon had changed up to 4 percent of the vote. Nixon's press secretary remembered the format. "The California telethon formula, which was also adopted by Nelson Rockefeller in his race for governor of New York, basically had the candidate answering questions telephoned in by viewers. Pretty volunteers were seen answering telephones, and the staff screened the questions. The press was allowed to examine some of the questions to see if they thought the screening was fair. Interspersed with the questions were celebrity appearances, which inevitably led to on-the-air endorsements. It was "show biz" with a town hall flavor.

There were two other major Nixon television appearances in the final days of the lagging campaign, one regarding the Cuban Missile Crisis, the other aimed at "campaign smears." Nixon was at a motel in Oakland when he heard of the Cuban Missile Crisis. The news came as a shock. Nixon's prospects already looked doubtful. Now he was certain he would lose.

On his telethon Nixon said he was afraid that President Kennedy might give up some missile sites in Europe near the Communist-bloc nations in exchange for removal of the base in Cuba. Nixon's prediction would be prescient. The American people would learn thirty years after the crisis that Jack and Robert Kennedy agreed to withdraw American missiles from Italy and Turkey, thus changing the balance of power in the European theater. While the American people were not told this, the Pentagon and CIA were well aware of the Kennedy moves, and I believe they were a factor in the plot both participated in to remove Kennedy in Dallas. Nixon, to his credit, urged Californians to support the president against the Soviet Union. Nixon's appeal had little impact.

Kennedy would call Brown to the White House to chair a governor's conference on civil defense in the wake of the Cuban Missile crisis. Kennedy campaigned in California for Brown, as did six of his cabinet members, plus Vice President Johnson. They ignored Nixon's complaints about an "invasion of carpetbaggers." Nixon responded by bringing in Eisenhower, who spoke in his behalf at a $100-a-plate dinner that was broadcast over closed-circuit television. "Everything he has done has increased my respect for him," Eisenhower said of Nixon. "I can personally vouch for his ability, his sense of duty, his sharpness of mind, his wealth in wisdom." Nixon replied, "All the work I've done has been worth it just to hear these words from the greatest living American." But as one of his aides remarked about Eisenhower's warm endorsement, "If he'd only given that speech two years ago, Dick Nixon would be president."[20]

A week before the election, Nixon predicted that his opposition would "launch the most massive campaign of fear and smear in the history of California elections." Nixon's positioning was preemptive. Having been burned by dirty tricks by the Kennedys in the 1960 campaign, Nixon planned his own.

Nixon's forces would launch a last-minute mail piece that Democrats felt crossed the line. The mailing features a questionnaire wherein they pretend to be taking a poll of public attitudes on issues. Questions were worded to lead to a preconceived conclusion. In this case, the questions were written by Leone Baxter, noted California publicist, and were sent out in a mailing to Democrats under a front name of nominal Democratic chairman. It was a thinly disguised pro-Nixon ploy. The purpose was to lead those who answered the questions into a thought process that would make the governor seem soft on Communism on the University of California campus. The Democrats would file a lawsuit. In 1972 a San Francisco judge settled the suit regarding the mailing and had reprimanded Nixon, Chotiner, and the 1962 campaign manager, Bob Haldeman.

One of Nixon's few breaks came in a joint appearance with Brown before the press at a state convention of editors of newspapers subscribing to United Press International. It took place during the morning, not on prime time. Questions for the televised appearance were to come from editors and publishers in the audience.

The most sensitive questions were over the Hughes loan, an issue that first surfaced in the 1960 campaign and was being raised again in 1962. It involved a loan made by the Hughes Tool Company to the candidate's brother, Don Nixon, against a collateral of Whittier family property that was developed as a lease site for a gasoline filling station. Don Nixon needed the money for financing the ill-fated restaurant location. Opponents claimed that the loan was made by Hughes in an effort to seek help with government contracts.

In an effort to avoid Nixon being questioned directly about the Hughes loan, Herb Klein negotiated conditions for the 1962 joint appearance with Brown. One of the conditions imposed was that the debate would be on issues and would include no questions of a personal nature.

About midway in the UPI debate, Tom Braden, later a national columnist and but then a California publisher and a Brown appointee as chairman of the California Board of Education, stood up and asked a question about the Hughes loan. The moderator, Theron Little, publisher of the Salt Lake City *Desert News*, declared the question out of order because of the rules on personal questions.

Nixon looked properly pained but jumped up and said he would like to overrule the moderator and answer the question once and for all. The tactic and the answer won the debate and won the applause of the California publishers and editors. "Nixon said Brown 'retreated like a whipped dog.'" The joint appearance, however, would not affect Brown's impending victory.

Nixon's quest for the governorship would end November 6, 1962. The next day Nixon would engage in an act of self-immolation in his "last press conference."

It is imperative to review Nixon's actions on that depressing election eve. Nixon knew the odds against his winning were tremendous. He needed a miracle to beat Pat Brown. Nixon himself kept notes on his thoughts that day. On a ruled yellow pad, he kept a careful diary of some of his thoughts.

Nixon's notes stated:

"No prediction—however we won't wait as long as in '60, absentee already being counted."

In his election night notes on his yellow pad in 1962, Nixon also observed:

"Maybe won't know result until tomorrow if it stays in this neighborhood."

"Will not make statement until results are known."

"Only God and people know who is winning."

"This race will be 50½ – 49 ½ somebody will win by a noze [he spelled it that way presumably to amuse himself]—only hope my noze is longer."

"Was going to house but called and found family had already eaten," and further noted that he had sent out for dinner: "pineapple milkshake and coffee."

"Last results showed we are 10,000 votes ahead," he wrote. "No trend as yet however."

Then, finally, reality set in as the returns mounted.

"Never," he wrote.

Press Secretary Herb Klein, Bob Finch, and the ever-present Murray Chotiner canvassed party leaders by phone periodically and reported the results to Nixon, who sat alone in his suite. Klein described him as quiet, alone in his thoughts, and "virtually immobile."

Downstairs the press was out of control as press assistants Ron Ziegler and Sandy Quinn tried to mollify them. The newsmen tasted blood. Klein said, "It was almost as if the press sensed a kill and was anxious to get at it. Defeat was a bigger story than victory in this case."

Klein made periodic appearances at the podium at the hotel ballroom but admitted to finding it difficult to show any optimism.

Veteran entertainer Johnny Grant attempted to keep the enthusiasm of the crowd of Nixon supporters up, but the handwriting was on the wall, as reporters demanded an audience with the candidate or at least a statement of concession in time to make various national deadlines. The reporters were howling for a concession by Nixon. At midnight Nixon decided to concede. He was exhausted, stunned, and began drinking bourbon out of a coffee cup supplied in his suite. Nixon dictated a telegram to Governor Pat Brown.

Because some of the Republican areas in Orange and San Diego counties had still not reported and all the press deadlines had passed, Nixon decided that he would release Klein to read the telegram in the morning. Nixon shuffled off to bed depressed and exhausted, and Klein announced to the gaggle of reporters waiting that there would be a press conference at 10 a.m.

The Nixon men would huddle over the returns the following morning. With turnout exceeding 81 percent and with more than 5.5 million votes cast, Brown had been reelected by about 300,000 votes. It was decided that Klein would face the press and read the telegrams of concession to Brown and of appreciation to the campaign workers.

The staff heard that Nixon was stirring around and looking for coffee. Finch, Haldeman, and Klein went into his suite to brief him. He knew by then that he had lost. Campaign scheduler John Ehrlichman recalled the sequence of events. "[A]s soon as he had arrived at the hotel on Election Day Nixon had begun greeting defeat with lubrication but without grace. Haldeman and the others had decided that in view of deteriorating conditions, there would be no Nixon interviews to the big TV cameras that were waiting at the far end of the hall on Nixon's floor. As the evening wore on I gathered that our candidate was good and drunk; Finch, Haldeman, and Klein were apparently having some trouble keeping him away from the telephones in his suite and buttoned up inside his room."[21]

Nixon's first words were, "Herb, don't try to talk me into going down and facing the press. Damn it, I am not going to do it. Screw 'em." Klein agreed with him. The plan was for Nixon to go home to his family while Klein faced the howling press scrum in the ballroom.

The plan was to have Nixon leave during the press conference. Advance man Pete Wilson, later governor and US senator of California, found a back entrance from the hotel where Nixon could be met with a car and then driven home.

Klein went to the ballroom, where he opened the 10 a.m. news conference. He announced that Nixon was exhausted and would not make an appearance that day. Klein read the telegrams to the impatient reporters.

At that point Nixon wandered out of his suite to thank members of the staff individually. It was an emotional scene, with many of the campaign volunteers and staff crying. Nixon was then embraced by an emotional Italian staff television producer, who also broke into sobs.

At that point, Ray Arbuthnot and Jack Drown, two of Nixon's oldest friends, arrived and learned of Nixon's plan for departure. They were indignant. One led off by telling the now emotionally upset Nixon, "You can't let the press chase you out the back door. You ought to face them or at least go out in your own style!"

The shouting reporters in the ballroom could be heard on a television set just off the hallway where Nixon stood with his friends Arbuthnot and Drown. Something in Nixon snapped. As Nixon headed for the elevator and announced he was going down to make a statement to the press.

Haldeman somehow ran down the hotel stairs and got ahead of Nixon and his entourage. He rushed to the side of the platform where Klein was addressing the press. Haldeman waved at Klein frantically, and Klein took that to mean that all was clear, that Nixon had departed for home.[22]

Klein announced that Nixon had left the hotel, but within seconds, scattered applause was heard from the adjacent lobby of the hotel.

Gladwin Hill of the *New York Times* described the scene, "[As] Klein was pursuing a rambling colloquy with the reporters, there was a sudden buffeting of the velvet drapes behind him. Klein turned and his jaw dropped. Nixon, neatly dressed in a blue suit, blue shirt, and blue tie that emphasized his blue-jowled haggardness, stepped out and made his way to the cluster of microphones."[23]

"Now that Mr. Klein has made a statement, now that all the members of the press I know are so delighted that I lost, I would just like to make one myself," Nixon started.

Nixon would unload:

> *I appreciate the press coverage in this campaign. I think each of you covered it the way you saw it. You had to write it in the way according to your belief on how it would go. I don't believe publishers should tell reporters to write one way or another. I want them all to be free. I don't believe the FCC [Federal Communications Commission] or anybody else should silence [word lost in transmission].*
>
> *I have no complaints about the press coverage. I think each of you was writing it as you believed it.*
>
> *I congratulate Governor Brown, as Herb Klein has already indicated, for his victory. He has, I think the greatest honor and the greatest responsibility of, uh, any governor in the United States.*
>
> *And if he has this honor and this responsibility, I think that he will now have certainly a position of tremendous interest for America and as well as for the people of California.*
>
> *I wish him well. I wish him well not only from the personal standpoint, because there were never on my part any personal considerations.*
>
> *I believe Governor Brown has a heart, even though he believes I do not.*
>
> *I believe he is a good American, even though he feels I am not.*
>
> *And therefore, I wish him well because he is the governor of the first state. He won and I want this state to be led with courage. I want it to be led decisively and I want it to be led, certainly, with the assurance that*

the man who lost the campaign never during the course of the campaign raised a personal consideration against his opponent—never allowed any words indicating that his opponent was motivated by lack of heart or lack of patriotism to pass his lips.

I am proud of the fact that I defended my opponent's patriotism.

You gentlemen didn't report it, but I am proud that I did that. I am proud also that I defended the fact that he was a man of good motives, a man that I disagreed with very strongly, but a man of good motives.

I want that—for once, gentlemen, I would appreciate if you would write what I say, in that respect. I think it's very important that you write it—in the lead—in the lead.

Now, I don't mean by that, incidentally, all of you.

One last thing: What are my plans? Well, my plans are to go home. I'm going to get acquainted with my family again. And my plans, incidentally, are, from a political standpoint, of course, to take a holiday. It will be a long holiday. I don't say this with any sadness. I couldn't feel, frankly, more—well, frankly, more proud of my staff for the campaign. We campaigned against great odds. We fought a good fight. And I take the responsibility for any mistakes.

One last thing: People say, what about the past? What about losing in '60 and losing in '64? I remember somebody on my last television program said, "Mr. Nixon, isn't it a comedown, having run for president, and almost made it, to run for governor?" And the answer is I'm proud to have run for governor. Now, I would have like to have won. But, not having won, the main thing was that I battled—battled for the things I believed in.

One last thing. At the outset, I said a couple of things with regards to the press that I noticed some of you looked a little irritated about. And my philosophy with respect to the press has really never gotten through. And I want to get it through.

This cannot be said for any other American political figure today, I guess. Never in my sixteen years of campaigning have I complained to a publisher, to an editor, about the coverage of a reporter. I believe a reporter has got a right to write it as he feels it. I believe if a reporter believes that one man ought to win rather than the other, rather it's on television or radio or the like, he ought to say so. I will say to the reporter sometimes that I think well, look, I wish you'd give my opponent the same going over that you give me.

*The last play. I leave you gentlemen now and you now write it.
You will interpret it. That's your right. But as I leave you I want you to
know—just think how much you're going to be missing.*

*You won't have Nixon to kick around any more, because, gentle-
men, this is my last press conference and it will be one in which I have
welcomed the opportunity to test wits with you. I have always respected
you. I have sometimes disagreed with you.*

*But, unlike some people, I've never canceled a subscription to a
paper and also I never will.*

*I believe in reading what my opponents say and I hope that what I
have said today will at least make television, radio, the press, first recognize the great responsibility they have to report all the news and, second,
recognize that they have a right and a responsibility, if they're against
a candidate, give him the shaft, but also recognize if they give him the
shaft, put one lonely reporter on the campaign who will report what the
candidate says now and then.*

Nixon would conclude by saying, "Thank you, gentlemen, and
good day," and he would depart for the hotel's front entrance
where his car had been moved. Nixon turned to Klein and said,
"Damn it, I know you didn't want me to do that. But I had to say it.
I had to say it."

The press reaction came in many forms—none of it good. Mary
McGrory of the *Washington Star* described it as "exit snarling."[24]

Nixon's campaign aide John Ehrlichman described Nixon as
"hungover, trembling, and red-eyed," but alert and in strong voice.
A number of veteran newsmen who had covered Nixon had the
same impression, although interestingly, none wrote it that way.
Nixon would be described as peevish and irritable, but no one
reported that he had been drinking heavily the night before.[25]
Nixon himself wrote he was angry.

The *Los Angeles Times* was angry about Nixon's rant because the
paper had supported Nixon in every race he had entered. Nixon's
singled out reporter Carl Greenberg for praise in his caustic remarks,
and it was a dig at his colleague Richard Bergholz. Bergholz, also of

the *Los Angeles Times,* was the reporter who bothered Nixon most, and his reporting, more than anyone else, explains the press conference references to Greenberg and the *Times.* Bergholz was relentless in his dislike of Nixon even insisting that California reporters never speak "off the record" or "on background" when Nixon attempted to have a background discussion with the press. "Out here we say it on the record, Nixon, or we don't say it at all." Many of Bergholz's own colleagues found him grating. Reagan Press Secretary Jim Lake told me, "Bergholz was a real prick."[26]

A Nixon staff member overheard a motel switchboard operator placing a call from Bergholz to Brown's press secretary. The report would reverberate through the campaign, eventually making it to Nixon himself. Nixon was convinced that Bergholz was spying on him and reporting to Brown. Considering Bergholz's later antagonism for Governor Ronald Reagan as well as Nixon, I think it is entirely possible. The report infuriated Nixon.

Greenberg was known for both fairness and objectivity. Bergholz always added his own negative personal observations, few of which Nixon hated. He felt this reflected liberal in the state's largest newspaper. Bergholz also pressed relating to the Hughes loan to Nixon's brother, Don. Nixon loathed him.

Publisher James Copley, of the *Copley News Service,* was angry because Nixon had cited only Greenberg as a fair reporter. He felt that his and many other newspapers had covered the campaign thoroughly and fairly. Copley joined most of the other resentful newspaper publishers who had endorsed Nixon in feeling resentful over the candidate's references to television as the medium that had kept the record straight.

Ironically, in 1960 and 1962, Nixon had complained privately over the unfairness of media reporting. Nixon's outburst would reveal his contempt and resentment for the press. By the second year of his presidency he no longer felt great need to disguise his hatred of the press.

Now, it is critical to examine whether the press was unfair to Nixon in 1962. The answer is mixed. Jack McDowell, then of the *Call-Bulletin*, Squire Behrens, dean of the Press Corps and political reporter for the *San Francisco Chronicle*, and Don Thomas of the *Oakland Tribune* certainly were fair. Reading the clippings of that long-ago campaign, I can find no animosity in the reporting of Harry Farrell of the *San Jose Mercury News*, Jim Anderson of *United Press International*, Maurie Lansberg, the Sacramento bureau chief of *Associated Press*, or Syd Kossen of the *San Francisco Examiner.* They showed emotion occasionally, but they were strong, honest newsmen. It would be hard for Nixon to fault the writing of Henry Love of the *San Diego Union* or Ralph Bennett of the *San Diego Evening Tribune*. In truth, Nixon was more aggravated by the reporting of the Eastern press, which, while damaging to Nixon's national image, had little impact of California voters.

On the other side of the coin was Mark Harris of *Life* magazine, who wrote openly of his desire to assassinate Nixon after the campaign. Harris later wrote *Mark the Glove Boy*, a nasty celebration of the political demise of Richard Nixon. But even Harris was forced to note on the dust jacket that the murder of John F. Kennedy gave new life to Richard Nixon even after his 1960 defeat. "President Kennedy's last days approached without premonition," Harris wrote. "The assassin who betrayed us granted, with the same action of his finger, reprieve to Mr. Nixon, whose last days seemed to me so certain the day before yesterday. Now the likelihood appears that we shall be required to judge him once more in the year ahead, as we judged him in the nation in 1960 and in California in 1962."

The early sixties were years of growth for conservatives in the Republican Party. Senator Barry Goldwater had surfaced as a national figure at an emotional moment at the 1960 Republican National Convention when his name was briefly put in nomination for president. Journalist William F. Buckley was slowly redefining the face of American conservatism. These were years when the John Birch Society thrived. The Birch Society was named for the first American serviceman theoretically killed in the Cold War against the Communists in the immediate aftermath of World War II. The society was the vehicle of eccentric Massachusetts candy maker Robert Welch. The hardline conservative activists looked upon Nixon, a moderate conservative, as a liberal who had sold out to Rockefeller in the platform battle of 1960 and had helped undermine Senator Joe McCarthy who, although dead, was still a hero on the far right.

Nixon learned of the full impact of this early in the California primary when he found himself in a bruising battle with a lesser-known conservative legislator, Joe Shell, who refused to back out of the race for the gubernatorial nomination. Shell gained about one-third of the votes in the primary—a large number against a man who had carried California when he sought the presidency— and the primary battle wounds never were healed, although Shell would agree to introduce Nixon at a rally in the closing days.[27]

Had Nixon won the governorship in 1962, inevitably he would have charged into battle with Senator Barry Goldwater, where, win or lose, the bloodletting was much more likely to lead to political death than anything which happened in 1962.

"This man will never be president," Eisenhower said after the 1962 defeat. "The people don't like him." In November 1962 *Time* magazine reported, "Barring a miracle, Nixon's public career has ended." "He was shot down and left for dead," was the way his friend Bryce Harlow expressed it. Only two years earlier Nixon had come this close to becoming president. Now, James "Scotty" Reston would opine in the *New York Times* that Nixon was "unelected and unmourned, an unemployed lawyer." Reston's name would pop up on the so-called Enemies List, which would become public with the Watergate scandal.

President Kennedy rejoiced over the news of Nixon's defeat. Aboard Air Force One en route to Eleanor Roosevelt's funeral, the journalist Mary McGrory watched Kennedy as he sat with Chief Justice Earl Warren, an old Nixon foe. "They had their heads together over the clippings," she recalled, "and were laughing like schoolboys."

"You reduced him to the nuthouse," Kennedy told the victor, Governor Brown, in a phone call taped at the White House.

"You gave me instructions," Brown replied, "and I follow your orders."

"God," said the president, "that last farewell speech of his . . . it shows he belongs on the couch."[28]

"This is a very peculiar fellow ," Brown agreed. " I really think he is psychotic . . . an able man, but he's nuts . . . like a lot of these paranoiacs."

"Nobody," the president had said, "could talk like that and be normal."

Nixon, too, believed his career was over. "It's finished," he told Billy Graham. "After two straight defeats it's not likely I'll ever be nominated for anything again or be given another chance."

Murray Chotiner, who had known him from the beginning, was a lone voice predicting otherwise. "It would be hard for me," he said, "to visualize Nixon's removal from the American scene."[29]

ABC News broadcast the documentary *The Political Obituary of Richard Nixon*, described in this book's introduction. ABC invited comment from a number of Nixon's past adversaries, including convicted perjurer and Communist spy Alger Hiss. ABC newsman Howard K. Smith was the announcer. ABC's switchboard was flooded by outraged Americans. Mail and postcards deluged the network. The program's political obituary left no doubt that the news network considered Nixon politically dead. So, it seems, did nearly everyone else.

NOTES

1. Ethan Rarick, California Rising, p. 230.
2. Herbert Klein, Making It Perfectly Clear, pp. 46–48.
3. Anthony Summers, The Arrogance of Power, p. 225.

4. Will Swift, Pat and Dick, p. 176.
5. Ibid.
6. Gladwin Hill, Dancing Bear: An Inside Look at California Politics, p. 174.
7. Robert D. Novak, The Agency of the G.O.P. 1964, pp. 367–368.
8. Stephen E. Ambrose, Nixon: The Triumph of a Politician, 1962–1972, p. 652.
9. Stephen E. Ambrose, Nixon: The Triumph of a Politician, 1962–1972, p. 659.
10. John Ehrlichman, Witness to Power: The Nixon Years, p. 22.
11. Kenneth Franklin Kurz, Nixon's Enemies, p. 202.
12. Kenneth Franklin Kurz, Nixon's Enemies, p. 203.
13. Gary Allen, The Man Behind the Mask, p. 219.
14. Stephen Ambrose, Nixon: The Education of a Politician, p. 650.
15. Anthony Summers, The Arrogance of Power, p. 205.
16. Victor Lasky, It Didn't Start With Watergate, p. 86.
17. Stephen Ambrose, Nixon: The Education of a Politician, p. 667.
18. Mark Harris, Mark the Glove Boy, from the dust jacket.
19. Herbert Klein, Making It Perfectly Clear, p. 60.
20. Stephen Ambrose, Nixon: The Education of a Politician, p. 600.
21. John Ehrlichman, Witness to Power: The Nixon Years, p. 48.
22. Gladwin Hill, Dancing Bear: An Inside Look at California Politics, p. 164.
23. Ibid.
24. Herbert Klein, Making It Perfectly Clear, pp. 52–64.
25. Kenneth Franklin Kurz, Nixon's Enemies, p. 208.
26. Conversation with James H. Lake.
27. Mark Harris, Mark the Glove Boy, p. 138.
28. Anthony Summers, The Arrogance of Power, p. 237.
29. Anthony Summers, The Arrogance of Power, p. 238.

CHAPTER EIGHT

THE WILDERNESS YEARS

"If ten more wiretaps could have found the conspiracy [to assassinate JFK]—uh, if it was a conspiracy or the individual, then it would have been worth it."

—Richard Nixon

After a devastating loss to Brown, Nixon joined the Wall Street law firm of Mudge, Rose, Guthrie, Alexander, and Mitchell. This necessitated moving the family to New York. While the firm had not actively sought him, Nixon's old pal Elmer Bobst of the Warner Lambert Pharmaceutical Company reportedly brokered the deal. Nixon moved into 810 Fifth Avenue, owned by Nelson Rockefeller, ironically the same apartment where Nixon and Rockefeller had brokered the infamous "Compact of Fifth Avenue" deal back in 1960.

While in law practice Nixon had an income of $200,000 per year, of which more than half went to pay for the apartment in Rocky's building. By 1968, he reported his net worth as $515,830, while assigning a value of only $45,000 to his partnership in his increasingly flourishing law firm. Nixon listed total assets of $858,190 and liabilities of $342,360. For the first time in his life, Nixon was making substantial money. He was also moving up in social circles. Theodore White said, "He himself [Nixon] belonged uptown to the Links Club, the most Establishment of New York's Establishment clubs. Downtown, he belonged to the Recess Club and India House." Nixon also joined three exclusive and expensive golf clubs, including the famous Baltusrol in Springfield, New Jersey. When a scandal broke out accusing the club of "Barring Jews and Negroes" Nixon penned a letter of resignation there. "In view of my nomination by the Republican Party for the Presidency of the United States, I believe it appropriate that I dissociate myself from all organizations and activities not related to the commitment I have accepted for the foregoing nomination." The letter was posted on the Baltusrol bulletin board.[1]

In a strange way, the defeat of Richard Nixon in the race for governor of California in 1962 eventually became a factor that helped him win the Republican nomination for president in 1968.

A victory over incumbent governor Pat Brown in 1962 would have propelled Nixon into an all-out bid for the presidency in 1964, a year when Lyndon Johnson was ultimately unbeatable and Republicans were enamored of Barry Goldwater. As much as he denied it, Nixon ran for governor with the idea that it would keep him alive politically on the national scene and that it would be a stepping stone for another run for the presidency. The governorship did not interest him that much. Local issues did not challenge him. He denied such presidential ambitions, as do most candidates. But fact is fact. He had the presidential bug.

In his book *The Resurrection of Richard Nixon,* Jules Witcover saw it this way:

> Nixon was not seeking a stepping-stone to a 1964 rematch against John F. Kennedy; he was seeking a sanctuary from it. Far from wanting to use the state-hours in Sacramento to launch another Presidential bid in 1964, as Brown successfully charged in the 1962 campaign, Nixon actually had hoped to use it as a four-year hiding place, from which he could avoid making another losing race against Kennedy. Inherent in his decision to run for governor was a Presidential timetable not of 1964, but of 1968, when he

finally did make his second try. Thus, though he lost in California in 1962, the gubernatorial contest in the end served the political purposes intended at the start—to keep Nixon off the national ballot in 1964 and to make him the Republican Party's logical choice in 1968! The circumstances that produced both these results never of course were anticipated. But because Richard Nixon did not win in California in 1962 and did not run for President in 1964, he was able to emerge again in 1968, when his party found itself with a rare opportunity for victory, but facing a leadership vacuum.[2]

* * *

Whenever Nixon welcomed visitors, even in his post-presidential years, he would invariably rifle through his desk drawer to give them a memento. It could be a presidential tie bar, golf ball, or, for ladies, a stickpin.

Nixon would send me a warm, personally inscribed copy of his memoirs and all of his subsequent foreign policy books. In 1989, I visited him at 26 Federal Plaza, the space the federal government supplied the former president for his office. The old man rattled through a drawer at the conclusion of our "chat" and produced a gold medallion from his 1972 inaugural.

"Now you are one of four men who have this," he said. "Clem Stone [W. Clement Stone, millionaire insurance executive], Bob Alplanalp [the millionaire developer of the aerosol spray can], Clint Murchison [the millionaire oilman who would invite Nixon to Dallas on November 21, 1963], and you."

Nixon would famously attend a cocktail party in honor of FBI Director J. Edgar Hoover at the Texas ranch of Clint Murchison Jr. on the eve of Kennedy's assassination. This is not to be confused with a meeting later that night at the Murchison estate that was attended by Vice President Lyndon Johnson. Nixon stopped by for social reasons and left early. We know this because later that evening, Nixon was seen at the rooftop restaurant of the Statler Hilton hotel, where musical comedy star Robert Clary, later of Hogan's Heroes fame, performed.[3] The sighting of Nixon at dinner did not preclude him from attending the earlier cocktail party in honor of FBI Director J. Edgar Hoover. Like Hoover, and Lyndon Johnson, Nixon had enjoyed Murchison's hospitality at Del Charro, a resort he owned outside of San Diego. As we detailed in *The Man Who Killed Kennedy: The Case Against LBJ*, it was not until the late night meeting, well after 11 p.m., attended by LBJ, Murchinson, Hoover, and oil tycoon H. L. Hunt, among others, where the final touches were put on the plan for Kennedy's assassination the very next day. Nixon was not there.

Charlie McWhorter was Nixon's political aide for eight years. "Murchison was one of the few who came through for Nixon in '62. He was having trouble raising money because Rockefeller had turned off the spigots in the East. At that point, Rocky contemplated his own '64 run," the gnome-like, meticulous McWhorter said. "Murchison put in two hundred grand," said the longtime political staffer. "Nick Ruwe went to pick it up in Dallas because it was cash."

"There was no way the old man could refuse an invitation to see Murchison while he was in Dallas," said McWhorter. "Nixon's presence that day though had more to do with Don Kendall."

It requires some examination as to why Nixon was in Dallas that fateful day. The answer to that question lies in Nixon's relationship with Don Kendall, the head of Pepsi-Cola.

Kendall and Nixon had a shared uncertainty about Castro and his Communist intentions in Cuba. The island was the world's leading supplier in sugar, an essential ingredient in Kendall's Pepsi-Cola, and the trade embargo was bad for business.[4] Kendall had an interest in Nixon because Nixon had a scorn for Castro and an elimination of both Castro and the trade embargo would lower the cost of sugar for Kendall's famous cola. Kendall maintained more than a casual interest in foreign policy, and as Russ Baker speculated in *Family of Secrets*, the CIA had more than a casual interest in Pepsi-Cola:

"The agency used bottling plants, including those run by Pepsi, Coca-Cola, and other companies, for both cover and intelligence," wrote Baker. "Moreover, the local bottling franchises tended to be given to crucial figures in each country, with ties to the military and the ruling elites."[5]

Kendall had many ties to the CIA. Kendall would book the Pepsi-Cola bottler's convention at Dallas, Texas's biggest venue, the Market Hall, on November 22, 1963. Ultimately, the move would assist the JFK assassination conspirators. The removal of the Market Hall from the list of potential locations JFK was to speak at in Dallas helped force JFK's motorcade through the Dealey Plaza, where he was assassinated.

JFK's advance man Jerry Bruno had wanted the luncheon at the Women's Building following the motorcade from Love Field. He mapped out the original route. The route for the Women's building would have passed by Dealey Plaza briefly at a high rate of speed, "without taking any turns in or around the Plaza."[6] The HSCA 1979 report on the motorcade stated that the "Secret Service initially preferred the Woman's Building for security reasons, and the Kennedy staff preferred it for political reasons."[7] Texas Governor John Connally argued passionately with JFK's advance man Jerry Bruno for the Dallas Trade Mart to be the luncheon venue. According to Connally, Vice President Lyndon Johnson would not stand for it. The governor's unwavering position on the Trade Mart, the only point of contention in Kennedy's five-city tour of Texas, ignited a quarrel between the Kennedy and Johnson people.

"Dallas was removed and then put back on the planned itinerary several times," wrote JFK's longtime secretary Evelyn Lincoln. "Our own advance man urged that the motorcade not take the route through the underpass and past the Book Depository, but he was overruled."[8]

As a compromise, Kendall booked Market Hall as the luncheon venue. This was essential to the negation of the Woman's Building as an option, making it easier for LBJ and his cronies to detour the motorcade through the winding Dealey Plaza, where the long, midnight blue presidential Lincoln would have to slow to an almost complete stop.

The bottler's convention had been falsely reported as a Pepsi-Cola corporate board meeting due to the presence of movie star Joan Crawford, a Pepsi-Cola board member. Some point to the fact that there are no minutes logged of a corporate board meeting in Dallas to signify that there is something suspicious about Nixon's trip. In fact, it signifies nothing. Nixon and Crawford were both being paid for their celebrity. Nixon, as a lawyer, was billed by the hour.

Nixon's actions while in Dallas, which were wholly unrelated to his business with Kendall and Pepsi-Cola, however, also deserve some examination. It was clear that the embers of political ambition still burned in the former vice president.

I asked McWhorter about the claim of Madeleine Duncan Browne, Johnson's longtime mistress, that Nixon and Johnson had a quiet visit at the Adolphus Hotel on the 21st. "There is a three-hour lapse in his formal schedule in which he left his hotel, the Baker," said McWhorter. "So it was possible. "

Nixon would hit LBJ hard at a press conference on November 21, suggesting what was true: JFK was likely to dump LBJ, who had become a liability because of rumors of massive corruption. Indeed, Charles McWhorter, Nixon's longtime political aide, told me that Nixon was well aware of an impending Drew Pearson column scheduled for November 23, which outlined in graphic terms LBJ's taking of a bribe to deliver a multi-million dollar defense contract to General Dynamics for the TFX project. The air force had already resigned after carrying out Johnson's orders to scuttle the contract, which had be awarded to Boeing. "The old man knew Johnson's days were numbered and that Bobby Kennedy was on his ass," said McWhorter. "That's why he was so confident in his press conference prediction that LBJ was on his way out."

Johnson's longtime mistress Madeleine Brown insisted that on his trip LBJ also met with Nixon privately on the afternoon of November 21 at a suite at the Adolphus Hotel in Dallas. Neither

Johnson nor Nixon ever publicly acknowledged the Adolphus Hotel meeting or what was discussed. In fact, during the conversation, a seed was planted within Nixon that was intentionally designed to mislead him.

To misdirect Nixon, Johnson told him of his concern for the president's safety due to the atmosphere of hate in Dallas. Johnson warned Nixon of the dangerous right-wing cauldron that boiled in the city. Only weeks earlier, US Ambassador to the UN and former presidential candidate Adlai Stevenson had been attacked in the street by an angry mob, which spat on him and knocked him to the ground.

Johnson had tried to use this line before. On November 4, 1960, he and Lady Bird were in Dallas at the Adolphus Hotel to rally support for Kennedy when the two were confronted by a right-wing mob holding signs that read, "LBJ sold out to Yankee Socialist" and "Beat Judas." Johnson alleged that conservative Republican Congressman Bruce Alger organized the riot (a claim Alger later vehemently denied). Using the protestors to his advantage, Johnson turned the event into an extravaganza.

"LBJ and Lady Bird could have gone through the lobby and got on that elevator in five minutes," said D. B. Hardeman, an aide to House Speaker and Texan Sam Rayburn, "but LBJ took thirty minutes to go through that crowd, and it was all being recorded and photographed for television and radio and the newspapers, and he knew and played it for all it was worth. They say he never learned how to use the media effectively, but that day he did."[9]

Johnson would later again cite Alger to intentionally misdirect Nixon. It was Alger, claimed Johnson, who ginned up the "mink coat mob." Johnson first thanked Nixon for a statement that the former vice president had released in Dallas urging courteous treatment of the president. The vice president asked Nixon to contact Congressman Alger, who Johnson said had been whipping up right-wing enmity in Dallas, to suggest Alger tone it down. With this clever deflection, LBJ laid the groundwork for Nixon's subsequent conclusion that a right-wing cabal had killed JFK.

In fact, Johnson sent Nixon on a wild goose chase—Alger attended the Murchison party only hours after Nixon and Johnson had met privately at the Baker Hotel. Although a virulent right-winger, Alger carried water in Washington for the same oil barons who funded LBJ's ambitions.

After his midday conversation with Johnson, Nixon stopped by early at Murchison's right-wing bash and was no doubt peppered with anti-Kennedy sentiment. LBJ arrived at the party long after Nixon had left, and his ploy to amplify right-wing hatred in Dallas had worked. It is not surprising that Nixon dialed Hoover in the hours after Kennedy's death to ask if JFK had been killed by "one of the right-wing nuts." Clearly Nixon was stunned when Hoover told him a left-leaning communist was the sole gunman.

In the aftermath, a clearly confused Nixon told of how he had learned of the assassination. One version had him in New York, taking a cab from the airport following his return from Dallas. "We were waiting for a light to change when a man ran over from the street corner and said that the president had just been shot in Dallas," Nixon told Reader's Digest in 1964. Another version also occurred in the cab ride, but the cab driver "missed a turn somewhere and we were off the highway . . . a woman came out of her house screaming and crying. I rolled down the cab window to ask what the matter was, and when she saw my face, she turned even paler. She told me that John Kennedy had just been shot in Dallas."[10]

A third story had the former vice president returning from his trip to his New York apartment when the building doorman informed him of the assassination. Nixon's confusion as to his whereabouts could be attributed to LBJ's misdirection. Shortly following Kennedy's death, Nixon was "very shaken," said writer Stephen Hess. "He took out the Dallas morning paper, which had a story about the press conference he had had the day before. He had talked about how the people of Dallas should have respect for their political adversaries . . .

208

He was saying to me in effect, 'You see, I didn't have anything to do with creating this.' He was very concerned that Kennedy had been assassinated by a right-winger, and that somehow, Nixon would be accused of unleashing political hatred."[11]

Nixon was genuinely rattled over the loss of the president. The night of the assassination, he sat down to write a letter to Jackie:

Jackie,

In this tragic hour Pat and I want you to know that our thoughts and prayers are with you.

While the hand of fate made Jack and me political opponents I always cherished the fact that we were personal friends from the time we came to the Congress together in 1947. That friendship evidenced itself in many ways including the invitation we received to attend your wedding.

Nothing I could say now could add to the splendid tributes, which have come from throughout the world to him.

But I want you to know that the nation will also be forever grateful for your service as First Lady. You brought to the White House charm, beauty and elegance as the official hostess of America, and the mystique of the young in heart which was uniquely yours made an indelible impression on the American consciousness.

If in the days ahead we could be helpful in any way we shall be honored to be at your command.

Sincerely,
Dick Nixon [12]

Jackie's response was gracious and especially revealing of Nixon's political future:

Dear Mr. Vice President—

I do thank you for your most thoughtful letter—

You two young men—colleagues in Congress—adversaries in 1960—and now look what has happened—Whoever thought such a hideous thing could happen in this country—.

I know how you must feel—so long on the path—so closely missing the greatest prize—and now for you, all the question comes up again—and you must commit all you and your family's hopes and efforts again—Just one thing I would say to you—if it does not work out as you have hoped for so long—please be consoled by what you already have—your life and your family—

We never value life enough when we have it—and I would not have had Jack live his life any other way—though I know his death could have been prevented, and I will never cease to torture myself with that—

But if you do not win—please think of all that you have— With my appreciation—and my regards to your family. I hope your daughters love Chapin School as much as I did—

Sincerely,
Jacqueline Kennedy[13]

Though Nixon could still feel John Kennedy's cold rejection of him, the two men had a very real personal connection. Len Garment wrote, "The two men had been locked in combat just three years earlier; now Nixon, spared Kennedy's fate, was seen as a survivor. Something of the triumphant Kennedy lived on in the defeated Nixon—a collection of memories, a kind of physical closeness, and an unexpected metaphysical reward for being the living member of a historic duo. Kennedy's death made Nixon more of a celebrity. As Kennedy passed into history, Nixon pushed forward."[14] Kennedy's death would enflame the embers that burned within Nixon.

Only two days after writing his letter to Jackie, Nixon would be jolted again when on national television he saw Dallas strip club owner Jack Ruby murder the gunman who allegedly assassinated JFK. "Murray Chotiner brought him in back in '47," Nixon told me. "[He] went by the name of Rubenstein. An informant. Murray said he was one of Lyndon Johnson's boys . . . we put him on the payroll." Some have misconstrued this reference. I don't mean to imply that Ruby was a direct crony of Lyndon Johnson, but rather that Johnson prevailed on Nixon to hire Ruby as a favor to Ruby's ultimate boss, Carlos Marcello. Ruby's ties to Marcello, while actively ignored by the Warren Commission, have now been clearly established. As established in my book *The Man Who Killed Kennedy: The Case Against LBJ,* an unearthed document from the US Justice Department later proved Nixon's appointment of Ruby.

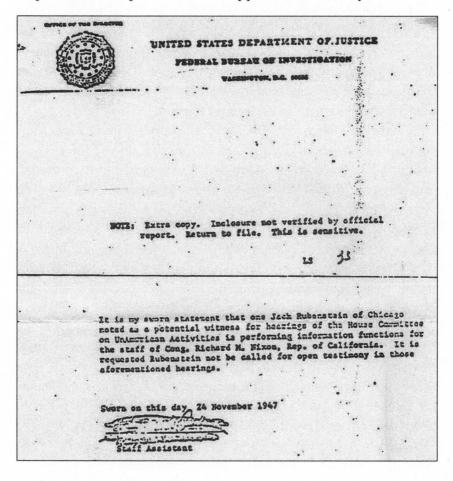

Ruby would later have a key role in the cover-up of the assassination of John F. Kennedy, rubbing out the alleged killer of the president, Lee Harvey Oswald, while in Dallas police custody. Oswald was a CIA asset, a Mafia stooge, a patsy, and finally, a liability. From the moment Nixon saw Oswald shot on national television, he recognized the spark plug who pulled the trigger.

"The old man was as white as a ghost," Nick Ruwe told me. "I asked him if everything was all right."

"I know that guy," Nixon muttered.

Ruby's involvement would make it crystal clear to Nixon that Lyndon Johnson and Carlos Marcello were up to their necks in the Kennedy assassination. Nixon also understood the CIA's unhappiness with Kennedy over both the Bay of Pigs and the Cuban Missile Crisis. In fact, President Nixon would try in vain to secure proof of the CIA's involvement in Kennedy's murder.

There is evidence that Nixon's CIA Cuban hit squad, Operation 40, made an appearance in Dallas during the time of the assassination. Years later, on his deathbed, E. Howard Hunt confessed involvement in the JFK assassination. Hunt said that he was approached to be a "benchwarmer" on the assassination, which was known in certain channels as "The Big Event." Was Hunt in Dallas on November 22, 1963? In 1974, The Rockefeller Commission concluded that Hunt used eleven hours of sick leave from the CIA in the two-week period preceding the assassination. Saint John Hunt, E. Howard's son, remembered his mother informing him on November 22, 1963, that Howard was on a "business trip" to Dallas that day. Later, eyewitness Marita Lorenz testified under oath in a district court case in Florida that she saw Hunt pay off an assassination team in Dallas the night before Kennedy's murder. "One of the things he [E. Howard] liked to say around the house was let's finish the job," said Saint John Hunt. "Let's hit Ted Kennedy."

Operation 40 members and future Watergate burglars Frank Sturgis and Bernard Barker had similar, ridiculous alibis for where they were during the Kennedy Assassination. "I remember, sir, that

I saw the assassination of President Kennedy on television," Sturgis testified to the Church Committee.[15] Barker also testified that he was watching television that afternoon and witnessed "the whole parade, how the whole thing happened."[16]

The two men were lying. The Kennedy assassination was not shown live on television or replayed later that tragic day. The first airing of the assassination would not be shown until 1975, when Geraldo Rivera aired it on his late night program *Good Night America*.

In fact, Barker was in Dallas on November 22 and identified by eyewitnesses in Dealey Plaza. In 1975, when shown a photograph, Deputy Seymour Weitzman identified Barker as the man he ran into behind the fence on the grassy knoll. Barker showed Weitzman Secret Service credentials, and Weitzman regrettably let him go. The man "had dirty fingernails and hands that looked like an auto mechanic's hands." Eyewitness Malcolm Summers also encountered the man with the gun on the knoll, whom he later identified as Bernard Barker.

Three Dallas Police Department officers—Weitzman, D. V. Harkness, and Joe Marshall Smith—said that they also encountered men disguised as Secret Service agents just following the assassination. Officer Smith, directed to the grassy knoll from a woman who heard the shots, ran into someone who flashed him Secret Service credentials. This could only have been a counterfeit agent because all the Secret Service agents with the motorcade proceeded instantly to Parkland Hospital.

If the Operation 40 team was in Dallas and Bernard "Macho" Barker was the man guarding the knoll, it meant that Nixon's authorization for the CIA recruitment of Mob assassins to assist in the assassination of Fidel Castro before the 1960 election had backfired. I believe Nixon fully understood that this plan had gone awry and had morphed into the assassination of JFK. The cast of characters involved in both endeavors (and later, the Watergate break-in) is more than coincidental. *60 Minutes* producer Don Hewitt would recall an anecdote revealed to him by Senator Howard Baker. Baker asked Nixon who really killed Kennedy. "You don't want to know," Nixon tersely replied.

* * *

"History intervened," his colleague Len Garment noted. "John Kennedy's death had the ironic consequence of restoring Richard Nixon to life as a national political figure." Nixon had sensed his opportunity immediately. The very morning after the assassination Nixon would convene a handful of his advisors to assess the impact and regeneration of his political career and trajectory to the White House.[17]

Although he wanted the 1964 nomination, he had neither the organization nor fundraising capability, nor the time to launch a serious bid. He realized his one chance to be the 1964 nominee would be to emerge as a *compromise* candidate after the party's liberal and conservative wings slugged it out. Once again Nixon would count on his acceptability to the broad middle and the grudging support he could get from both wings of the party lest each be saddled with leadership from the hated others. Nixon recognized that Barry Goldwater was accident-prone and probably too extreme to win the general election, while he knew that wide swaths of the Republic faithful couldn't abide Nelson Rockefeller. Central to Nixon's stealth effort would be a concerted effort to remain unseen as favoring either faction so as to become unacceptable to either while at the same time constantly advertising his "availability."

It is also important to note that Nixon would call for victory in Vietnam and criticizing the Johnson administration for not doing enough in Vietnam and not doing what they were doing fast enough. This also probably fueled Nixon's continued standing with both rank-and-file Republican voters and some party professionals. Free of the constraints of servicing the Eisenhower administration, Nixon was blazing his own trail, and his attacks on the issue assured that Nixon was the second choice of many Goldwaterites and certainly better than the loathed Rockefeller.

While early polls showed Nixon with strong residual strength, Nixon knew that many party conservatives were still upset by what they thought was a "me too" campaign against JFK in which Nixon should have laid out a more stark ideological difference.

With Goldwater and Rockefeller attacking each other, a draft movement emerged in New Hampshire for Ambassador Henry Cabot Lodge, Nixon's old 1960 running mate, then serving as US ambassador to Vietnam for President Lyndon Johnson. Nixon, disclaiming any intention to become an active candidate but insisting that he would be "available for any role that the party chose him for" counted on his own write-in the Granite State honchoed by former Governor Wesley Powell.

Lodge (write-in)	33,521
Goldwater	21,775
Rockefeller	19,496
Nixon (write-in)	15,752
Smith	2,812
Stassen	1,285

While Nixon's total was barely respectable, he noted that he had spent no money on the effort, whereas the Lodge forces had been able to finance several statewide mailings with detailed instructions on how to write in the ambassador's name. Paul Grindle, David Goldberg, and Gerald "Gerry" Carman, later GSA Director under Ronald Reagan, ran the Lodge write-in.

All the while Nixon maneuvered the primaries, he played a cagey backstage game urging first Lodge, then Romney, and finally Pennsylvania governor William Scranton to stop Goldwater. Late in the contest he would get Eisenhower, who feared a Goldwater national candidacy to urge Scranton to run. Nixon, by and large, kept his behind-the-scenes maneuvering from the public eye.

Nixon's next opportunity to demonstrate his strength was in the Nebraska primary. Again a write-in effort was required because having his name on the ballot would require a certificate of candidacy that he did not want to sign. Nixon had always run well in Nebraska. Former Eisenhower Secretary of the Interior Fred Seaton was now back in Hastings, Nebraska, as a newspaper publisher. Seaton directed an aggressive write-in effort. It is important to note that write-ins were easier to execute in Nebraska and that Nebraska Republicans had a record of being adept at them.

Nixon himself would visit Omaha for a long-scheduled "non-political" speech before a luncheon of the National Conference of Christians and Jews. Nixon's speech got broad coverage in the Cornhusker State. Seaton unleashed a direct mail blitz to educate Nebraska voters on how to write-in Richard M. Nixon. The results were impressive.

Goldwater	67,369	49%
Nixon (write-in)	42,811	35%
Lodge (write-in)	22,113	16%[18]

In April, an *Associated Press* poll of Republican party chairmen showed that among the party professionals, Nixon was "the most likely nominee," 526 for Nixon to 427 for Goldwater, but when asked to express a personal preference, the vote was 722 for Goldwater and 301 for Nixon.

Nixon's next opportunity would be in the Oregon primary, where his name appeared on the ballot, as all probable candidates were listed and he would be required to sign an affidavit stating that he would not *accept* to have it removed. Rockefeller would mount a major effort in the state while Goldwater would stumble badly.

Rockefeller camped out in the state while Goldwater made himself scarce. A big win by Rockefeller would obscure a strong showing by Nixon despite the fact his 1960 finance chairman, Cliff Folger had trouble raising money for the effort, facing amazing resistance from well-heeled businessmen who used to cough up sizable checks for Dick Nixon. The Lodge operatives led by Maxwell Rabb and Robert Mullin were undermined when Lodge asked that his name be removed from the ballot without signing the required form. Lodge himself was silent and absent. Suddenly running on the slogan "He cared enough to come," Rockefeller won a smashing victory while Nixon kept pace with Goldwater.

Rockefeller	85,000	33%
Lodge	71,000	27%
Goldwater	45,000	18%
Nixon	43,000	17%
Smith	7,000	3%
Scranton	4,000	2%

Nixon immediately recognized that the deadlock he required could only be produced by the results of the looming California primary. The Goldwater forces sent political director Dick Kleindienst to California to take the helm of their campaign in the Golden State. Rockefeller would retain the high-powered political consulting firm of Stuart Spencer and Bill Roberts to run his California effort. Spencer and Roberts would emerge as key players in the election of Ronald Reagan only two years later.

Although he would pour millions in the state, Rockefeller's efforts would be ruined by the birth of his son, Nelson Rockefeller Jr., with his second wife, Margarita "Happy" Fitler Rockefeller. Voters were rudely reminded that Rockefeller had dumped his first wife Mary Todhunter for the younger Mrs. Fitler, who was also married at the time. None of this sat well with Republicans. Goldwater would narrowly win the primary and end any doubts that he would be the Republican nominee.

Nixon realized that Goldwater was piling up delegates in the unheralded caucuses and state conventions. Nixon badly tipped his hand when he attended a Republican governors conference in Cleveland, where he met privately with both Governor George Romney and Governor William Scranton to urge both to enter the lists and "stop Goldwater." After months of trying to cultivate Goldwater, Nixon went public in an attack on the Arizona Senator in a press briefing at the conference.

Nixon fired a frontal attack at the senator's stands on foreign policy, Social Security, the TVA, "right to work" laws, and civil rights.

"Looking to the future of the party," he said, "it would be a tragedy if Senator Goldwater's views as previously stated were not challenged—and repudiated."[19]

Even more surprisingly, Nixon now urged Romney to enter as an active candidate. For five months, Nixon had been maneuvering for a stalemate, after which Nixon would be tapped as the natural compromise candidate. Now he was trying to rush that process in six short weeks. With Rockefeller dead and Scranton apparently uninterested, Romney was the only man to play the role of Nixon's stalking-horse. But Romney declined.

Goldwater was furious at Nixon's remarks and fired back, "I guess he doesn't know my views very well. I got most of them from him." He even added, "Nixon is sounding more like Harold Stassen every day." [20] Stassen, a former governor of Minnesota, ran for president in 1944, 1948, 1952, 1964, 1968, 1976, and 1980.

Nixon would enlist Eisenhower to privately urge Scranton to make the last-ditch "establishment" bid to stop the surging conservative revolution going on in the Republican Party. Neither Ike nor Dick would publicly endorse Scranton, however. Nixon had attacked Goldwater to set the stage for a white knight whom was neither Romney nor Scranton. Nixon was still angling for another shot at the brass ring as the "only man who could unite both the moderate and Goldwater forces."

Despite Goldwater's early stumbles in the primaries, his ultimate victory in California would seal his nomination. Political organizer par excellence F. Clifton White and a cadre of rabid

Goldwater supporters had organized and turned out Goldwater supporters to sweep state conventions and caucuses collecting the masses who would fill the cow palace for Barry. The Taft wing of the party energized by Goldwater, William F. Buckley, and, particularly that year, Ronald Reagan would finally seize control of the National Republican Party, throwing off the chokehold of the Eastern Wall Street crowd.

Nixon flew to London for a two-day business trip. When he got to the airport, aide John Whitaker told him, "It's on the radio that Romney's *not* going to run."

Nixon was shocked. "What do you mean he's not going to run? He told me he was."[21]

While in London, Nixon told the press he would not endorse Scranton, but he welcomed the governor's entry into the race. Goldwater supporters began to grumble about Nixon trying to stop their man, and Goldwater himself complained, "It's just like Nixon to set this up and run off to London."[22]

When he returned to the States, Nixon realized that he had nothing to gain from antagonizing the by-now-certain nominee. He could also see, with Goldwater's defeat guaranteed, a new role as Nixon-party unifier. Nixon spun on a dime to be the doomed Goldwater's biggest backer.

After Goldwater led the party into disastrous defeat, Nixon would be the only man available to act as party unifier, to lead the rehabilitation of the Republicanism, and help himself at the same time.

Now sensing that Goldwater could not win and that liberal Republicans like Rockefeller and his ally Senator Jacob Javits would decline to support Goldwater, Nixon saw opportunity and repositioned himself as Goldwater's biggest booster, declaring Goldwater's views to be in the "mainstream." Nixon made it clear that "I, for one Republican, do not intend to sit it out, take a walk."[23]

Nixon wisely convinced Republican National Chairman Bill Miller, a congressman from upstate New York, to move his scheduled speaking slot at the San Francisco convention to the night *after* the nominations to introduce nominee Barry Goldwater to his cheering supporters. No one could accuse Nixon of trying to stampede the convention if he spoke after the nomination vote. The convention itself was raucous and the GOP bitterly divided. Governor Bill Scranton had decided to make a late effort to wrench the nomination from Goldwater and had launched a vitriolic last-minute attack on the Arizona senator that accused him essentially of being a mentally unstable warmonger. Just the same, under the brilliant organizational structure and management of F. Clifton White, Goldwater had a lock on the delegates.

When Pennsylvania Senator Hugh Scott, a Scranton backer, proposed the convention adopt an anti-extremist plank that denounced the Ku Klux Klan, lumping them with the John Birch Society, Rockefeller mounted the podium to speak for the plank. The convention hall erupted in a cacophony of boos and catcalls, as the grinning Rockefeller seemed to taunt the crowd. Scott's resolution was defeated on a resounding voice vote.

Nixon told the convention that he represented "the ministry of party unity," and in introducing Goldwater he said, "And to those few, if there are some, who say they are going to sit it out or take a walk or even go on a boat ride, I have an answer. In the words of Barry Goldwater in 1960, 'Let's grow up, Republicans, let's go to work—and we shall win in November.'"

Nixon introduced Goldwater, and the crowd went wild. Nixon thought it was one of the finest speeches of his career as he spoke party unity and support for the nominee while blasting LBJ and the Democrats. The convention hall was on fire as Goldwater approached the podium. It was near pandemonium. Then Nixon watched Goldwater commit political suicide. "Anyone who joins us in all sincerity we welcome," Barry said. "Those who do not care for our cause we do not expect to enter our ranks in any case. Extremism in the defense of liberty is no vice. Moderation and the pursuit of justice is not virtue," the squared-jaw Arizonan would bellow. Nixon later wrote he was "almost physically sick" when he heard the nominee. The place exploded as the conservatives exulted over finally capturing the nomination from the Eastern elite. It was then and there that I believe that Nixon recognized how the center of gravity had shifted in the Republic Party and how the conservatives, who had been defeated in 1936, 1940, 1944, 1948, and 1952, had finally taken control of the Republican Party. It was to be a vital lesson for Nixon's own comeback from the wilderness. Nixon would campaign in more states and make more stops for Goldwater than Goldwater would for himself, winning the gratitude of grassroots conservatives.

Nixon began his tack to the right in preparation for a 1968 bid for the White House. After stumping for Goldwater, the 1966 election afforded Nixon the next opportunity to position himself as a proponent of party unity and to collect IOUs from party leaders. Immediate preparations for an arduous 1966 campaign effort to resuscitate the Republican Party and position someone who could be elected in 1968. He assembled a staff of the pugnacious Patrick J. Buchanan, political savant John Sears and the ever-present Rose Mary Woods. This experience also led Nixon to see at the grass-roots level the revolution that had taken place. Nixon would launch a campaign while wealthy backers, coordinated by longtime Nixon friend and aide Peter Flanagan, funded "Victory '66," which financed the former vice president's travels on behalf of Republican candidates across the Republican spectrum, with a particular emphasis on House candidates.

Nixon would, in an endless assortment of fundraisers, cocktail parties, chicken dinners, and campaign events, bring congressional candidates needed media coverage and needed campaign contributions.

In the hinterlands, Nixon was still the man who had lost to JFK by a whisker, and most of the party knew the White House had been stolen from him by the Kennedys, the Daley machine, and the Mob. Buchanan and Sears traveled with Nixon, and Sears laid the foundation for his own network of power brokers and shrewd political operators.

Nixon noted that even in the so-called Eastern moderate states the conservative faction was competitive within the party while Goldwaterites held sway at the party level in the South, Midwest, and West. If anything, Nixon's campaign travels showed him the continued strength of the conservative wing of the GOP. Nixon would soon launch his courtship of the major figures of the Goldwater movement: Goldwater himself, the movement's intellectual guru, William F. Buckley, and, ultimately, the venerable senator from South Carolina, Strom Thurmond.

Nixon would be unhappy when Republican National Chairman Ray Bliss, a nonideological mechanic who Nixon helped install after the Goldwater debacle, refused funding for an airplane for some of Nixon's campaign trips and also declined to let Nixon give the party's formal response to one of president.

Richard Nixon understood the value of chits. Starting in 1952, he had campaigned indefatigably in an endless stream of state and big county Republican dinners, Republican fundraisers, and Republican candidate campaign outings and press conferences. With the non-partisan-appearing General Eisenhower leading the country for eight years, the partisan road fell to Nixon. Dick Nixon knew that the Ohio Republican county chairman whose dinner you spoke at recently would someday likely be a delegate to a Republican National Convention. As a Republican who had defeated an incumbent in 1946, he knew those he helped their first term in Congress would "owe him." Starting in 1952, 1954, 1956, 1960, 1964, and 1968, Nixon would pick up many IOUs on what Ronald Reagan would call the "mashed potato circuit," an endless array of hotel party receptions and dinners.

Even in 1965 Nixon would campaign for the Republican candidates in the off-year elections in New Jersey. In the Old Dominion State, Nixon would stump with A. Linwood Holton, who was challenging the political supremacy of the Byrd machine in Virginia.

Holton would run well and go on to be one of the key organizers in Nixon's campaign in the South. A moderate Republican from Big Stone Gap, Holton would come back in 1969 to be the first Republican governor elected since Reconstruction.

Nixon would campaign for winners and losers, liberal Republicans and archconservatives. He would show up at the Cuyahoga County Republican dinner in Cleveland, the Nassau County Republican dinner on Long Island, and Republican venues both bigger and smaller. "Nixon was the one guy who got along with both Rhodes and Taft," longtime Republican Chairman Robert Hughes told me. "Jim Rhodes played footsies with Rockefeller but that was only to get Rocky's money for the state party," Hughes added.

If anything, grassroots affection for Nixon only grew after he shrewdly stumped for Goldwater in 1964 while Nelson Rockefeller, George Romney, and William Scranton took a walk on the Goldwater-Miller ticket. Nixon also tacked sharply to the right on foreign policy and the Vietnam War. Out from under Eisenhower, Nixon could finally be the tough proponent of a hard military line on the Communists as he had been in the private counsels of Ike's administration. Nixon pounded LBJ and the Democrats on their handling of the war, at the same time supporting the basic policy of escalation. Nixon knew he was driving a wedge between the Democrats, a wedge that ultimately would drive LBJ from the race in 1968. Nixon's tough line in Vietnam won him Goldwaterite support in the party.

"Hell, he came to South Dakota for Goldwater when we couldn't get Barry himself to come," said Jim Stockdale, a longtime Republican who lived in South Dakota between Republican political campaigns, where he was an itinerant political operative. "Everyone here was real grateful Dick Nixon was the guy who showed up."

"Dick Nixon could always be counted on," former Governor Jim Rhodes of Ohio told me. "Hell, we'd fight with his advance men who never wanted the schedule to let him get down with the people, but he always showed up to headline our state dinner." The feisty Rhodes would serve as Ohio state auditor and then as governor from 1963–1967. He would make a miraculous comeback to serve a second term from 1968–1971. Like Nixon, Rhodes was ideologically "flexible." "I was in the state house when he was vice president and he came to Columbus," Rhodes remembered. "My job was to line up every single Republican running for the House that year. Vice President Nixon came in and methodically posed for a picture with each one to use in their campaign. Dick Nixon was a guy you could count on."[24]

Rhodes would argue so strenuously with Nixon's advance men about the schedule when Nixon visited the Buckeye State that he finally once hijacked a presidential motorcade, taking it to a state fairgrounds, which the vice president's handlers thought they had knocked off the schedule. Rhodes commandeered the motorcade because the state policeman riding the lead motorcycles worked for him, as did the cops in the rest of the caravan. Nixon was a big hit at the Ohio State Fair. "You could, of course, get Ohio by taking Rhodes for vice president, but who would want responsibility for that?" Richard Nixon said in 1968.

Nixon was brutal in his attacks on the Johnson administration. "The high cost of Johnson," he kept saying. He was relentless in his critique of Johnson's conduct of the Vietnam War. "I can get under his skin," Nixon said. Reporters and politicians were stunned when President Lyndon Johnson issued a blast at Nixon, thus elevating him in the Republican filed and making him the face soon to be resurgent Republic Party.

At a White House news conference on November 4, the Friday before the elections on Tuesday, Lyndon Johnson would issue a blistering attack on Nixon. When a reporter asked Johnson to comment on Nixon's criticism of the Manila communiqué, a "peace proposal" from the South that the North would never buy but was Johnson's first bid to end the war. Johnson would hit the roof.

Stunned reporters scribbled furiously as the president assaulted the former vice president:

> I do not want to get into a debate on a foreign policy meeting in Manila with a chronic campaigner like Mr. Nixon. It is his problem to find fault with his country and with his government during a period of October every two years. If you will look back over his record, you will find that to be true. He never did really recognize and realize what was going on when he had an official position . . . You remember what President Eisenhower said, that if you would give him a week or so he would figure out what he was doing.
>
> Since then he has made a temporary stand in California, and you saw what action the people took out there. Then he crossed the country to New York. Then he went back to San Francisco, hoping that he would be in the wings, available if Goldwater stumbled. But Goldwater didn't stumble. Now he is out talking about a conference that obviously he is not well prepared on or informed about."

Johnson's position on the war and the Manila peace feeler, claiming that it made clear that the United States and its allies would stay in South Vietnam only "so long as our presence is necessary" to protect that country's territory and put an end to the fighting. Then he turned is fire on Nixon again:

> They know that and we ought not try to confuse it here and we ought not try to get it mixed up in a political campaign here. Attempts to do that will cause people to lose votes instead of gaining them. And we ought not have men killed because we try to fuzz up something. When the aggression, infiltration, and violence cease, not a nation there wants to keep occupying troops in South Vietnam. Mr. Nixon doesn't serve his country well by trying to leave that kind of impression in the hope that he can pick up a precinct or two, or a ward or two.[25]

While flying with Buchanan from New York to a speech in Waterville, Maine, Nixon made up his mind to reply in sorrow rather than in anger—to be firm in his position but reasoned, low-keyed, even forgiving. "Jesus, how he hit us," said Patrick J. Buchanan as he boarded the small plane at LaGuardia Airport that was to ferry Nixon to Maine, where he would campaign for Republicans. Nixon couldn't believe his good fortune but elected not to return fire. Nixon praised Johnson as "hard-working" and said that the issues should be "discussed like gentlemen."

"Let the record show that all over the world I have defended the administration's announced goal of no surrender to aggression. I have defended it in the capitals of the world and here at home against members of the president's own party."

Nixon chose to respond to Johnson more in sorrow than in anger. Describing Johnson as "very tired" he correctly pointed out that he had more consistently defended the president's policy in Vietnam than many in Johnson's own party. The Republican Congressional Committee paid for a thirty-minute television slot made available to Nixon on the Sunday before the election. Nixon was also on ABC's *Issues and Answers* that day. When asked about Johnson, he said, "I think I understand how a man can be very, very tired and how his temper then can be very short. And if a vice president or a former vice president can be bone weary and tired, how much more tired would a president be after a journey like yours?"[26]

Nixon seized the moment as he had in the 1952 Checkers speech. It was not surprising then that early polls showed Nixon leading Johnson by as many as six points. Nixon thought he could beat LBJ.

Interestingly, Eisenhower issued a stanched defense of Nixon as "one of the best-informed, most capable and most industrious vice presidents in the history of the United States."[27] As he had in 1962, Ike's public announcements of Nixon were growing more positive as the old man sought to repair some of the damage that was made in his backhanded 1960 comments about Nixon, emanated from his flip comment that it would "take him a week" to assess what Nixon had accomplished as vice president. With Nixon running on "experience counts" as a theme in 1960, Ike's off-hand comment had been damaging.

On May 4, 1990, at a seminar of Johnson administration veterans, John Gardner, the former secretary of HEW, recalled that LBJ had said of the "chronic campaigner" remark: "I shouldn't have made that crack about Nixon. It was dumb."[28] Johnson had made an intemperate blunder—or had he? According to Joseph Califano, LBJ's chief White House aide on domestic affairs, Johnson's boost to Nixon was intentional, designed to elevate the one Republican LBJ thought would be easiest to beat. "When Johnson returned to his office [after the press conference] and saw the wire-service tickers lead with his characterization of Nixon as a 'a chronic campaigner,'" Califano wrote later in the *Triumph and Tragedy of Lyndon Johnson*, "he chortled, 'That ought to put him out front!'" Johnson's attack on Nixon had been purposeful.

LBJ was cagey enough to know that he didn't want to face Rockefeller with his millions or a new face like Governor George Romney. LBJ knew Nixon was the only politician in the country who was more polarizing than Johnson himself. Johnson greatly underestimated Nixon's deft use of television to reinvent himself as a more likeable, relaxed elder statesman who Americans thought had the foreign policy experience to end the war. Ironically, Johnson wanted to run against Nixon and Nixon wanted to challenge Johnson.

Nixon's arduous path of hard work paid off in spades in 1966 as the net gain of 47 house seats, 3 Senate seats and 8 governorship seats showed the Republican Party was fully resurgent and fully competitive in 1968. The party also gained 557 State Legislative seats, cancelling out their loses in the 1964 debacle. The big winners of the night were the Republican Party and Richard Nixon. In an ebullient mood he took his staff to El Morocco "for spaghetti." It was a night of celebration as they toasted the returns. After Nixon returned to his Fifth Avenue apartment, he had John Sears call him with West Coast returns. "Ron is in!" he said when learning Reagan had defeated Nixon's old nemesis, Pat Brown.

Even Nixon's wary rival, Rockefeller, asked for and got a Nixon endorsement when Nixon visited Syracuse, a conservative upstate city where Rockefeller's pollsters said he needed more conservative votes in his third term to get a come-from-behind victory over New York City Council President Frank O'Connor.[29] Rockefeller also paid Franklin Delano Roosevelt Jr., so useful to Jack and Bobby Kennedy in smearing Hubert Humphrey as a draft dodger in Wisconsin in 1960,[30] to run as the New York Liberal Party candidate for governor to siphon votes from O'Connor while Conservative Party candidate Paul Adams drained some Republicans from Rockefeller. Rocky won. Still, Nixon knew he had no standing in the politics of his new home state campaigning only when asked for congressional candidates.

The 1966 elections would also produce Nixon's most serious challenger for the 1968 Republican nomination. Former actor Ronald Reagan's victory in California made him a national figure and the darling of the Goldwater wing of the GOP. The canny Nixon knew Reagan was a far more formable challenger than New York Governor Nelson Rockefeller. This proved to be correct.

It is in this period that Nixon had a curious relationship with a beautiful Chinese woman in her early thirties who worked as a hostess at the Opium Den in the Hong Kong Hilton Hotel where Nixon stayed. Chinese-American Republican businessman Harold Lee introduced her to Nixon. On the first occasion in 1966 Liu and Nixon were photographed together by the Hilton's house photographer in 1966. Her second encounter came when Nixon and Bebe Rebozo were visiting Hong Kong and Nixon invited her and another woman to their suite at the Mandarin Hotel. The relationship would not become public until 1976, when the *New York*

Times revealed that the FBI, believing the woman, Marianna Liu, was a spy, had investigated an alleged "affair" between Nixon and Liu.

The FBI was concerned that Nixon, privy to national secrets due to eight years of top national security briefings became concerned Nixon could be blackmailed. The FBI report shows that Nixon sent Liu an expensive bottle of Channel No. 5 perfume after their first encounter. As requested by the CIA, Nixon was under twenty-four-hour surveillance in Hong Kong by the authorities there because of Liu. The royal colony intelligence agency gave the CIA infra-red photos of Nixon and Liu taken through the window of Nixon's hotel suite bedroom. Hong Kong authorities suspected Liu was a spy for the Communists. J. Edgar Hoover would later use the incident to pressure Nixon after he became president.[31]

Charles McWhorter, then handling Nixon's schedule, confirmed to me Nixon saw her often between 1964 and 1967. Liu herself would tell the *New York Times* she saw Nixon on every trip except one, a fact also confirmed by McWhorter. Liu would later move from Hong Kong to Nixon's hometown of Whittier. The sponsors on her residence application included two close associates of Nixon's. Nixon sent flowers to Liu during a 1967 hospitalization. The glamorous Chinese woman would visit Nixon in the White House three times.[32]

Liu told the *National Enquirer* she had "many dates" with Nixon in Hong Kong and said she had danced with him on a yacht. "I knew he cared for me," she said, and "despite my constant warnings he still insisted on seeing me and being alone with me." The *National Enquirer* published a detailed two-part series on the Nixon-Liu "relationship," claiming it was sexual. Liu denied this and sued the *National Enquirer*. According to veteran investigative journalist Anthony Summers, her lawsuit with the *National Enquirer* was settled out of court after Liu's attorney advised their client that the paper's reporting was "true." Nixon also denied the relationship was intimate,[33] but John Sears also thought Nixon's relationship with Liu extended into the bedroom. "He saw her every time he passed through Hong Kong, and he passed through Hong Kong every time he passed through Asia," Sears later chuckled.[34]

Liu has consistently denied that it was a love affair. She would visit Nixon's gravesite after his passing.[35]

NOTES

1. The Global Jewish News Source, October 2, 1968.
2. Jules Witcover, America: The Year the Dream Died, p. 79.
3. Tony Zoppi, "Dallas After Dark," Dallas Morning News, Nov. 22, 1963.
4. Russ Baker, Family of Secrets, p. 185.
5. Ibid., p. 186.
6. Ibid.
7. "Politics and Presidential Protection: Staff Report," HSCA, Second session, 1979, p. 508.
8. Phillip F. Nelson, LBJ: The Mastermind of the JFK Assassination, p. 374.
9. David Pietrusza, 1960: LBJ vs. JFK vs. Nixon, p. 387.
10. Don Fulsom, "Richard Nixon's Greatest Cover-up: His Ties to the Assassination of President Kennedy."
11. Anthony Summers, The Arrogance of Power, p. 262.
12. Alan Peppard, "Kennedy rival Nixon left Dallas as JFK arrived in November 1963," Dallasnews, Nov. 2013.
13. http://blog.nixonfoundation.org/2013/11/richard-nixons-letter-jackie-kennedy/.
14. Leonard Garment, Crazy Rhythm, p. 71.
15. Church Committee deposition of Frank Sturgis, April 4, 1975.
16 Lamar Waldron, Watergate: The Hidden History, p. 295.
17. Anthony Summers, The Arrogance of Power, p. 263.
18. Robert Novak, The Agony of the G.O.P., 1964, p. 367–368.
19. Cabell Phillips, "Goldwater Likens Nixon to Stassen," New York Times, June 11, 1964.
20. Ibid.

21. Stephen E. Ambrose, Nixon: The Triumph of a Politician, 1962–1972, p. 51.
22. Charles Mohr, "Scranton Attack Like a Slap by Friend, Goldwater Feels," *Pittsburg Post-Gazette*, June 13, 1964.
23. Stephen E. Ambrose, Nixon: The Triumph of a Politician, 1962–1972, pp. 50–54.
24. Conversation with author, 1984.
25. Tom Wicker, One of Us: Richard Nixon and the American Dream, pp. 284–285.
26. Tom Wicker, One of Us: Richard Nixon and the American Dream, p. 286.
27. Tom Wicker, One of Us: Richard Nixon and the American Dream, p. 285.
28. Ibid.
29. William Safire, *Before the Fall*, p. 28–33.
30. Carl Solberg, Hubert Humphrey: A Biography, p. 209.
31. Summers, Anthony Summers, Official and Confidential, pp. 371–376, noting document, Director to SAC San Francisco, Aug. 18, 1976, FBI 105-40947-8.
32. Anthony Summers, The Arrogance of Power, pp. 269–270.
33. *San Francisco Examiner, San Francisco Chronicle*, Feb. 8, 1981.
34. Conversation with John Sears.
35. Anthony Summers, The Arrogance of Power, pp. 269–270.

CHAPTER NINE

THE BRIGHT YOUNG MEN

"The first impression that one gets of a ruler and of his brains is from seeing the men that he has about him."

—Niccolo Machiavelli[1]

Richard Nixon, in his long political career, was deeply affected by the men around him. As the 1968 presidential election approached, his original mentor, Murray Chotiner, was to remain in the shadows but was always one boozy phone call away. The *political advisors* who worked for Nixon in his vice presidential days and through the 1960 campaign were still on the scene, but largely powerless. At first, an extraordinary talented and balanced team of writers, researchers, political operatives, and cutting-edge TV producers and men from Nixon's New York law firm replaced them. This team was then replaced by nonideological advance men and marketing executives who would play a significant role in Nixon's ultimate downfall.

Because Chotiner had gotten jammed up for influence peddling when Nixon was vice president, Nixon's mentor was forced to recede into the shadows. Chotiner avoided prosecution under Eisenhower's Justice Department and was compelled to lay low. It is a mistake not to recognize that he was *always there.* Chotiner knew how to keep his distance, but the evidence shows he was ever present in Nixon's 1960 face off with Kennedy, the 1962 California governor's race, during Nixon's maneuverings to first stop Goldwater then support Goldwater in 1964, during Nixon's 1966 campaign for Republican candidates, and throughout the 1968 comeback bid. Indeed, Chotiner was still on board in 1972 playing a key role in Watergate, the pardon of Teamster leader Jimmy Hoffa, and throughout the fall of Nixon's presidency.

Nixon aide Raymond K. Price, an erudite, moderate Republican and former editorial writer for the New York *Herald-Tribune* who crafted some of Nixon's finer speeches, argues eloquently in his book *With Nixon* that the president had both good and bad sides, indeed, good and bad personas. While some of his advisors from the '50s and '60s were often able to appeal to his better angles, other advisors angled for his dark side. They engaged in tactics and strategies that ultimately backfired.

By 1960, press secretary Herb Klein and Robert Finch, a handsome and moderate man who served as Nixon's personal assistant as vice president and headed Nixon's operations, were the closest men to the former vice president. They were highly capable and well liked in the press corps, even if the reporters disliked their employer. Both had a tendency to appeal to Nixon's good side and talk him out of more extreme orders.

Nixon met and was impressed by Finch when the latter ran for Congress in California in 1958 and Nixon, as vice president, was called on to campaign for the challenger. Finch joined the vice presidential staff and was the campaign director for Nixon's 1960 bid. He also worked for Nixon's star-crossed 1962 governor's race and then managed veteran Hollywood hoofer George Murphy's 1964 election to the US Senate from California, an impressive feat since Lyndon Johnson beat Barry Goldwater in California by 18 percent in the same cycle.

Finch was like "Nixon's son," according to vice presidential assistant Charles McWhorter.[2] Finch ran for lieutenant governor of

California in 1966 and won running slightly ahead of Governor Ronald Reagan. Reagan's circle never trusted Finch, viewing him as Nixon's plant within the Reagan administration. Finch later tried an unsuccessful US Senate race, and in 1968 Nixon actually offered the Republican vice presidential nomination to Finch, ultimately passing over Congressman George H. W. Bush and Massachusetts Governor John Volpe to settle on Spiro Agnew.

Finch played a role in Nixon's 1968 bid but was mostly a spokesman for the campaign, managed by Nixon's law partner John Mitchell. Nixon offered Finch his choice of cabinet jobs and wanted his fellow Californian to take Housing and Urban Development while also serving with the title of senior advisor to the president. Finch instead chose Heath, Education, and Welfare (HEW), where he advocated aggressive desegregation of the public schools. This brought him into conflict with Mitchell, who believed in a "go slow" approach he believed was less likely to result in violence. Finch also selected HEW liberals out of step with the Nixon administration as his top appointees. This further inflamed Mitchell and Nixon supporters on the right. Lyndon Johnson's longtime right-hand man, Bobby Baker, recognized the Nixon blunder. "The biggest, dumbest mistake Richard Nixon ever made was not making Bob Finch his chief of staff in the White House," said Baker. "The Washington media didn't like Nixon, but they liked Finch; he would have kept Nixon from those silly, dictatorial things. It just seemed natural to me—and to other politicians—for Nixon, who was an introvert, to have a warm, friendly guy named Bob Finch. But he put him in the worst department in town—HEW."[3]

Finch suffered a nervous breakdown while at HEW, largely because of the turbulent political cross currents and attacks from the Republican right. Finch was then moved to the White House as a "counselor to the president" and recovered sufficiently to make his own bid for the US Senate for California in 1976.

Klein, a veteran California newsman, had long been Nixon's spokesman. In 1946, Klein signed on as a press agent for

Nixon's campaign for California's twelfth congressional district seat and in 1950 handled press for Nixon's California US Senate campaign. Klein was easygoing and well-liked among the press corps, even those with a low opinion of Nixon.

Klein was ultimately warehoused with the undefined title of communications director and replaced with the more malleable Ron Ziegler, a former Disney World tour guide. Ziegler had worked as Klein's deputy in the 1962 campaign, recruited by Nixon's ultimate White House chief of staff, the brush-cut and briskly efficient H. R. "Bob" Haldeman. Haldeman had managed the disastrous 1962 California run and returned to run the show only after Nixon had locked up the 1968 nomination.

Klein was also a pivotal figure in the career of former San Diego Charger quarterback Jack Kemp. He arranged an off-season internship for Kemp in the office of California Governor Ronald Reagan. Kemp, a conservative, moved to the Buffalo Bills, ran for and won election to Congress in the Buffalo suburbs in 1970, and provided crucial intellectual support for Reagan's 1980 campaign for president. Kemp ran for president himself in 1988, served as Secretary of Housing and Urban Development, and was selected as the vice presidential nominee by Senator Bob Dole in 1996. Klein was a behind-the-scenes adviser to Kemp until the latter's death in 2009.

Pulitzer Prize–winning journalist and White House speechwriter William Safire remembered Klein's "routine refusal to carry out these ukases [Nixon's more strident orders to freeze out reporters critical of Nixon] are why Old Hand Klein was not in close, and why he emerged from the ruins [of Watergate] with his reputation intact."[4] Indeed, in his post–White House years, Klein returned to professional journalism as respected editor-in-chief of the *San Diego Union*, where he retired in 2003.[5]

Before the arrival of the Pretorian guard derided in the media as the "Berlin Wall"—Haldeman and Assistant to the President for Domestic Affairs John Ehrichman—Nixon had jettisoned his 1960 advisors like Klein and Finch in favor of a new team known as "the Bright Young Men."

"The Bright Young Men" were largely recruited by Nixon's New York law partner Leonard Garment. Nixon carefully assembled this extraordinarily balanced team of young men, with an average age of thirty-eight, who helped him engineer the greatest comeback in American political history. Garment was Nixon's unlikely choice to help him assemble the new team to navigate the waters of a changing Republican Party. With their help, Nixon reinvented himself, paced himself carefully, and assembled a new voter coalition built on traditional Republicans and former Democrats no longer comfortable in their party. In the process, they rethought the entire process of marketing and advertising to affect public opinion. They were the first to use television in a way that still dominates presidential politics today.

A litigator at the Nixon, Mudge, Rose, Guthrie, and Alexander Law Firm at 20 Broad Street, Garment was a liberal Jewish Democrat who voted for John Kennedy in 1960. Garment had the soul of an artist, and, while he quickly advanced to the head of his class at Brooklyn Law School, he played part-time clarinet and tenor sax with the Woody Herman and Henry Jerome orchestras.[6] His views were diametrically opposed to those of Nixon, although he wasn't terribly political. Garment was, however, intrigued at the idea of putting a two-time loser in the White House. He had a flair for showbiz, the dramatic, and the law. Richard Nixon speechwriter Richard Whalen remembered him as clever and quick-witted, saying, "The game was the thing," for Garment.[7]

"He wore a slightly perplexed and harried expression," Whalen wrote. "Restless, quick-moving, and faster-talking, he did not look like a veteran of Wall Street litigation . . . An aura of show biz still clung to him and crept into his conversation, along with the jargon of his new concerns—polling, media and advertising. The outgoing Garment was the organization's chief talent scout, recruiter, and promoter, as well as self-appointed liaison man between Nixon and alien worlds. It was Garment who sat up all night in his kitchen rapping with people like Dick Gregory."[8]

Despite their personality and cultural differences, the former jazz musician and the son of a grocer from Yorba Linda, Nixon and Garment became close. On one particular trip to Miami in 1965, Nixon and Garment were scheduled to spend the night in a newly finished home. Nixon suspected the developers of the real estate project had booked him there as a publicity stunt, so he quickly ordered the driver to turn back forty miles in the opposite direction to the home of Nixon's friend, businessman Elmer Bobst. The gates were locked at the Bobst home. Still, Nixon instructed his driver to return in the morning, and he turned to Garment and said, "Come on, Garment. It's over the wall we go."[9]

"So over we went, two New York lawyers, briefcases and all," Garment recalled. "We were able to get into the pool house, which had twin beds."[10]

"There Nixon was, with his big head sticking over the covers," Garment continued. "The lights were off, but he couldn't sleep—he never could—and he just kept talking. He talked for what must have been an hour, sounding sad and determined, about the things that meant a lot to him. If he couldn't live in politics, he said, how was he to live? We had been talking about him running for president. And he said if he couldn't play a real role, on that front or otherwise, he'd be dead very soon."[11]

When Nixon hit the road in 1966, fighting his chronic insomnia, he would phone Garment late at night after a combination of sleeping pills and a couple of cocktails. Nixon shared his ambitions with Garment, even his dreams and his worries. "I was the disembodied presence to whom Nixon could unload his daily deposit of anxieties until he was carried away by alcohol, sedation, and exhaustion into the Land of Nod," recalled Garment. ". . . cries and whispers . . . I worried over these calls."[12]

Among his most important finds, Garment recruited John Sears, a twenty-six-year-old lawyer from Upstate New York and a shrewd, wisecracking attorney at the Nixon law firm Mudge, Rose, Guthrie, and Alexander.

Len Garment later recalled his fortunate acquisition of Sears:

"I recruited nuts-and-bolts political operators. In this endeavor, one of my greatest small claims to fame was bringing Nixon the young John Sears. Actually, Sears just turned up at my office one day in 1964. He had attended Notre Dame University and Georgetown Law School. His early ambition had been to become a psychiatrist; but during his college years he entered politics, as a partisan of John F. Kennedy. When I met Sears, he was clerking for Judge Adrian Burke of the New York court of Appeals, the state's highest court, and making the rounds of Manhattan law firms looking for a post-clerkship job. He clearly wanted a place where he could not just practice law but engage in politics as well.

Then barely twenty-five, Sears was very good looking— tanned, brown-haired, hazel-eyed, glistening like a baby seal. He was also poised and strikingly articulate, one of those young men who seem to know too much for their age. He was impressive enough in that first meeting so that even before it was over, the next step seemed obvious. "Let me introduce you to Mr. Nixon, John." They talked. When Sears and I left Nixon's office, Sears worried about whether he had made a god impression. But shortly afterwards, the candidate phoned me to say, "Get me Sears."[13]

Sears became a Nixon favorite and disciple. At the same time, he recognized Nixon's occasional excesses and misjudgments and worked to minimize them. Sears called Nixon "Milhous" behind his back. He often quoted him to illustrate a point he agreed with or to underscore some of Nixon's more amusing miscalculations. "Milhous" gave him a series of political assignments.

Sears was also a favorite of Rose Mary Woods and close to Pat Buchanan, having ridden shotgun with him in Nixon's 1966 campaigning. He remained close to both of them long after the 1968 campaign and through Rose, Sears also became a friend of former New York City policeman Jack Caulfield. Approached by the Nixon

White House, Caulfield was hired as an investigator for White House counsel John Ehrlichman. When Caulfield was called before the Senate Watergate Committee as a witness, who should appear with him as an attorney but John P. Sears! By that time he'd been purged from the Nixon White House by a jealous John Mitchell in an alliance with Bob Haldeman.

Nixon was clearly a father figure to Sears, who studied Nixon's every move and his long political pronouncements in the same way I did twenty years later. Sears grew to be like a son to Nixon, but it wasn't about small-bore politics, delegates, and county chairman and such. Nixon taught Sears how to handle *men*. It is not coincidental that Sears thought of becoming a psychiatrist before switching to a future as an attorney and political strategist.

Nixon also taught Sears the game, when to act, when to do nothing, when to make decisions. While Nixon gave lip service to big ideas, he executed on them only in governing, not in the 1968 campaign.

Sears recruited me as the director of Youth for Reagan. Four years later, he hired me to handle New York, New Jersey, and Connecticut as a regional political director for Reagan's 1980 campaign. His detailed instructions to me about how exactly to handle specific Italian-American party leaders, in manner and tone, I could see, were the lessons he learned from Nixon. Sears taught me that politics was about ideas and taking risks. Those who are given to bold plays and high risk in the advancement of new ideas are those who win. Those who aren't, don't.

"Politics is motion," Sears convinced me. "The key to moving is to be interesting to the voters," the introverted Irishman taught me. "A politician has to have something interesting to say or he will bore the voters, who will look elsewhere." Sears had a cool and aloof manner when he tossed off these maxims learned at the knee of Tricky Dick.

"Politics is about being interesting, and not boring the voters. It's about making news. Being bold. Being interesting. The worst thing you can do in politics is trying to sit on a lead or freeze the ball," Sears said. "If you are not gaining votes, you are losing votes. Sitting on a lead ultimately bores the voters and they begin to look elsewhere." Nixon himself would tell me, "The only thing worse than being wrong in politics is being boring." Sears was enough of a realist to point out that Nixon violated his own dictum in 1968 and came perilously close to losing as late momentum and interest shifted to his opponent Hubert Humphrey. By late in the 1968 campaign, Nixon aide Patrick J. Buchanan said, "Nixon was just giving the same speech day in and day out. He kept up with the same game plan and sort of froze the ball and coasted."[14]

In Ronald Reagan's 1976 and 1980 campaigns, Sears was resolute not to repeat Nixon's "near mistake." Sears believed it was essential that a campaign create the *perception* of motion and momentum. He understood the vital role that good relationships with reporters could play in creating this perception. Sears also understood why it was essential both to hold and maximize your base while maintaining the flexibility to win Independents and particularly Democrats in view of the overwhelming Democratic Party registration edge in the 1960s, '70s and '80s.

"If your base isn't slightly pissed off, you're doing something wrong," Nixon later told me. "You can't win without your base, and you can't win with just your base."

It was also Sears who taught me to think outside the box. When it came to politics, as Aristotle Onassis said of business, "The only rule is, there are no rules." Sears historic setup of George Bush in Nashua New Hampshire in 1980 stands out as the best tale of Sears, cunning. "I know Bush is an asshole," Sears told me, "and now we just have to show people." As we shall see, Sears engineered Bush's petulant meltdown on the eve of the New Hampshire primary.

In 1976, Sears's selection of Pennsylvania Senator Richard Schweicker, a moderate Republican, as Reagan's vice presidential running mate were examples of bold and brilliant moves that kept Reagan's candidacy alive until the showdown at the Republican National Convention in Kansas City.

"Milhous" schooled the cocky Sears on how to handle seasoned party powerbrokers and nail down the men Nixon needed across the country. Through Nixon, Sears met Tom Dewey, Herb Brownell, Barry Goldwater, Ronald Reagan, John Lodge, and the lesser party mahatmas of the late 1960s. Later, Sears and Nixon spent endless hours talking about a potential vice presidential choice, but only after the compartmentally minded Nixon had the nomination sewn up.

Sears shared Nixon's cynicism about the vice presidential nomination. "All our polling showed Nixon ran best alone," said Sears. This was ironic in view of Nixon's status as a loner. Even President Dwight Eisenhower said, "I don't understand how a man could have no friends." In both 1960 and 1968, Nixon went through the motions of a completely contrived "consultation" with party leaders after he had decided in seclusion who he wanted as his running mate. In both 1960 and 1968, one could argue that Nixon fumbled his choice; Cabot Lodge proved an ineffective campaigner who brought little to the 1960 ticket, and Spiro Agnew's shaky performance on the stump made him a punch line for Democrats who made TV ads that said, "One heartbeat away from the presidency. Think about it." Sears tried to affect Nixon's thinking, but his choices were made in solitude and with little input from the outside.

The former vice president also taught Sears about the electorate and how to pursue them, with a special focus on Southern whites, Northern Catholics, and blue-collar Democrats. "Go after the Italians," Sears heard Nixon barking on the phone to actor Ronald Reagan when he was running for governor. "See if you can get Joe Dimaggio to campaign with you," the Old Man counseled the former B-movie actor.

Sears also bridged the gap between many of the old pols who had been with Nixon from the beginning and the new group of "bright young men" who flanked Nixon after he joined the New York law firm.

Nixon began the quiet planning of a presidential comeback that started with valuable campaigning for Republican candidates in 1966 and advanced to a 1967 candidacy. Nixon swept the 1968 Republican presidential primaries and piled up impressive over-all vote totals despite Nelson Rockefeller's and Ronald Reagan's efforts to block his path. Interestingly, Republican turnout was as high as in the hotly contested Democratic presidential primaries where Robert Kennedy, Eugene McCarthy, and Hubert Humphrey were contending. This is particularly impressive in view of the fact that Nixon was essentially shadow boxing—neither Reagan nor Rocky ever stepped into the ring.

While the subject at hand is Richard Nixon, one must look at Sears's role in the 1980 nomination of Ronald Reagan to see the full capability of the man trained by Nixon. Bush won an upset victory in the 1980 Iowa caucuses after a Herculean physical effort. Meanwhile, Sears tried to minimize Reagan's time on the ground in Iowa to preserve the aura of Reagan as the frontrunner. It was a miscalculation Sears had to fix.

Bush soared in the polls as he basked in the media attention in the days after his Iowa upset. "Is Bush Ready?" blared a *Newsweek* headline in their cover story of the man who had lost two US Senate races and served but two years in Congress. Sears knew Bush was headed to the Granite State with a head of steam.

As Reagan's campaign manager, Sears walked Bush into a trap in the New Hampshire primary. His tactic: to agree to a two-man debate, then call for all GOP candidates to be included the day of the debate. Bush was petulant and froze when the high drama came; Reagan delivered one of the greatest lines of his career: "Mr. Green, I'm paying for this microphone!"

Bush was outmaneuvered and caught completely off guard. Proud of the successful debacle, John Sears was "Smiling like the Cheshire cat," according to Reagan speechwriter Peter Hannaford.

The news stations drilled the image of a stammering Bush and confident Reagan into the heads of the voters. The New

Hampshire primary was not even close. Reagan won in a lop-sided upset, 50 to 23 percent.

In his early service to Nixon, Sears skillfully cultivated good relations with a number of key reporters. Nixon had no press secretary traveling with him in 1966 and 1967, so media liaison fell to Sears. The major reporters of the day, like Robert Novak and the *Baltimore Sun*'s Jack Germond, were drinkers, and Sears was a man who liked his alcohol. These ties served Nixon well in his comeback bid, but ultimately caused Sears to run afoul of Henry Kissinger, John Mitchell, and Bob Haldeman. They believed any man who had cordial relations with reporters could not be trusted.

Unlike Nixon, Sears didn't consider the press the enemy. Instead, he saw them as targets to be manipulated and persuaded. He was particularly close to Novak, *Baltimore Sun* columnist Jules Witcover, Knoxville *News-Sentinel* reporter Loye Miller, and others. While Sears advanced the Nixon line, he was known as much for talking on background and never lying to reports. Sears was also a brooder who drank heavily through his brilliant career, and nothing lubricates the ears of reporters like a cocktail. It was ironic that John Mitchell, a man who also liked to get in his cups, used Sears's "heavy drinking" against Nixon's young deputy counsel in the drive to remove him from Nixon's political operation and the White House.

Journalists were to be "schmoozed, used, but not abused," said Sears, who had many close friendships with reporters from most of the major media outlets of the day. I agreed with Sears then and remain in his camp on the question of reporters. Some are honorable and can be trusted; others are not "reporters" at all but new media wannabes, where anyone with a keyboard is a journalist.

In his epic book on the 1976 election, *Marathon*, reporter Jules Witcover described Sears as a man "with a deceptively shy outer crust that camouflaged a biting humor and political toughness and skepticism. Also his appreciation of and affinity with members of the Washington press corps set him apart from most of the political operatives around Nixon and Reagan. Where many of the paranoid Nixon types looked upon reporters as the enemy, to be warded off at every turn, Sears saw them as an essential and unavoidable element in the drama of electing a president."[16]

"While I know that you have to disagree," Nixon wrote to me, "I still believe that the best way for a conservative to handle the media is to treat them with courteous contempt. As you may recall, I made this point in one of my press conferences. One of the reporters asked if I hated the press. I answered, No. Love and hate have one thing in common. You must respect the individual involved. I regret that there are very few members of the fourth estate who deserve respect as objective fair reporters."[17]

Interestingly, Sears, scouting a 1976 presidential contender while the Nixon White House roiled, told Ronald and Nancy Reagan in their Pacific Palisades, California, home that Agnew and Nixon were toast. The Reagans were stunned and impressed with the accuracy of his prediction. How could he know? Reagan aide Mike Deaver said Sears cinched the captaincy of Reagan's 1976 presidential bid when he appeared to be prescient.[18]

After Nixon's surprise running mate, Spiro T. Agnew, proved to be an inept performer on his vice presidential tour, Sears was detailed to the Agnew plane to bring order and an end to self-inflicted wounds. He managed to coexist with the Haldeman and Ehrlichman axis in this period, but his closeness to Nixon and his deep political relationships at the party's grassroots level across nation, as well as his precocious and wise-guy nature, irked John Mitchell. It was a godsend: by driving Sears out of the White House and Nixon's entourage, Mitchell saved Sears the taint of Watergate and probably his career.

Mitchell ultimately replaced Sears with Harry Dent, a former aide to South Carolina Senator Strom Thurman, who had convinced old Strom to leave the Democratic Party and switch to the GOP (and Barry Goldwater) in 1964. Dent was an affable evangelical minister who understood the transition going on in the South in which white Democrats were fleeing the party of Jefferson and Jackson for the new, more conservative Republican Party. While Dent was a capable operative, he did not have the world view of Sears, who understood that the coalition Nixon was trying to cobble together for the future included *both* Southern conservative and Northern and Midwestern moderates. Goldwater had swept the Deep South, which informed Dent's view, whereas Sears was more skillful in positioning Nixon in the center where he could win votes both to his left and to his right. Dent went on to work with Republican National Committee Chairman George H . W. Bush and in 1980 fronted a South Carolina primary campaign for Bush. He lost miserably.

* * *

According to speechwriter Richard Whalen, Nixon had a clear vision of the team he wanted around him for his second run for the White House:

> Nixon wanted a small research and writing staff—"no more than six"—*young* men who were skilled "generalists." (I noticed that he had picked up some of the jargon of business.) Romney had a staff of twenty. "I'll take my two researchers any time." Nixon, who had been over the road before, didn't need as large a staff as a new-comer. But, regardless of the number of men around him, would he delegate responsibilities? He hadn't in 1960. This time, he assured me, he would let his staff run him. "That's why I want to pick it so carefully."
>
> People with ideas, Nixon noted, were able to publicize them by assisting a political figure like him—a plain invitation. "Of course, you can have your say in magazines, and reach a national audience. But, when you're with a man going for the presidency, you have a chance not only to get your ideas across, but maybe to see them put into practice. That's a big difference."[19]

Among the team putting ideas into practice was twenty-eight-year-old Patrick J. Buchanan, a hard-hitting conservative editorialist for the St. Louis *Globe-Democrat*. Buchanan was a Scotch-Irish Catholic educated at Georgetown University and the Columbia School of Journalism. Buchanan admired Nixon's role in the Hiss case and the hard line he had taken against Communism. He revered Nixon and referred to him as "the Boss." Buchanan screened and underlined reading material for Nixon, maintaining black loose-leaf briefing books on scores of issues. He also collated the flow of opinion polls and political intelligence. Buchanan was a prolific memo writer with a sense of history despite his young age. He was part theoretician, part cheerleader, and part verbal pugilist. He, too, was devoted to "the old man" and saw Nixon as a "man of destiny."

Buchanan traveled extensively with Nixon and Sears in 1966. Like Sears, Buchanan understood Nixon's desire to forge a new governing coalition of Republicans, Orthodox Jews, blue-collar Catholic Democrats in the Northeast and Midwest. Buchanan and Nixon also nurtured the idea of going after a slice of the emerging black middle class. Buchanan and Sears understood that Nixon didn't just want to win an election, he wanted to win reelection and set the stage for Republican successors, men like George H. W. Bush, Senator Howard Baker, Senator Bill Brock, Congressman Don Rumsfeld, Mayor Richard Lugar, Massachusetts Attorney General Eliott Richardson, Congressman Don Riegel (who later became a Democrat), US Senator Ed Brooke, and others.

Former Kansas Congressman Robert F. Ellsworth, a lanky and bearded Kansan who tired of the slow pace of the House, worked with Sears on mapping out a delegate and planning Nixon's effort in the 1968 primaries. Ellsworth's politics were of the liberal Republican variety, although he was on good terms with the rising star of the other Kansas congressman, the more conservative Bob Dole. Somewhat haughty and dismissive, Ellsworth still played the perfect political balance to Sears as the Irish-Catholic conservative. Ellsworth worked at Nixon's direction with Sears to plot Nixon's 1968 rise from the ashes, which began in 1966.

Ellsworth was elected to Congress from Kansas in 1960 as Nixon was sweeping the state. He was reelected twice, and then in 1966 he lost a US Senate primary to James Pearson, a moderate Republican with whom Ellsworth had few issue differences. That same year Ellsworth met Nixon on a flight from Washington to Chicago, and, impressed with Nixon's intellect, Ellsworth became the national political director of Nixon's 1968 campaign.

Curt and somewhat officious, Ellsworth was nonetheless effective. "We don't have anybody with the political savvy of Bob Finch, but Bob Ellsworth is coming along," Nixon told Richard Whalen.[20]

Occasially glimpses of the "old Nixon" were seen. Sears and Ellsworth were stunned when the *New York Times* ran this story:

Du Bois 'Duplicity' Decried By Nixon

By DOUGLAS ROBINSON

Richard M. Nixon decried yesterday the similarity in the pronunciation of the Du Bois Club and the Boys Club of America, saying it misled people into confusing one organization with the other.

The former Vice President, who is national board chairman of the Boys Club of America, said in a statement that the confusion was "an almost classic example of Communist deception and duplicity."

The Du Bois Clubs, which claim 2,500 members across the country, was described as a Communist-front group last Friday by Attorney General Nicholas B. Katzenbach. The Boys Club, which has a nation-wide membership of 750,000 boys 7 to 17, provides recreation, guidance and handicraft instruction.

Since the labeling of the Du Bois Clubs by Mr. Katzenbach there have been several acts of violence against members. In Brooklyn, several club members were beaten by a crowd last Saturday and, in San Francisco, the club headquarters was destroyed by an explosion.

In his statement, which was issued by the Boys Club, Mr. Nixon said the Du Bois Clubs "are not unaware of the confusion they are causing among our supporters and among many other good citizens."

He described the Du Bois Clubs as a "totalitarian organization" that did "not dare risk full, frank and honest disclosure of their true aims and purposes." He appealed to the news media to "continue to focus the revealing light of truth on this Communist youth organization."

At the heart of the matter was the pronunciation of his name by W. E. B. Du Bois, a prominent Negro historian and sociologist, who became a member of the Communist party at the age of 93 in 1961, and died two years later as an expatriate in Ghana. Dr. Du Bois pronounced his name DooBOYS, rather than DooBWA, in the French manner.

Radio and television announcers and reporters in reading the new during the past several days have tended to say DooBOYS. Many listeners have apparently misunderstood this as "the Boys," rather than Du Bois.

Edward J. Stapleton, public information director for the Boys Club, said that, as a result, poison-pen letters and threatening phone calls had been received by many of the 680 individual clubs.

Nixon knew immediately it was a mistake and would revive images of him as the old 1950s "red-baiter." He told Sears and Ellsworth who expressed alarm that the matter would pass. It did.[21]

Just as he targeted Sears for extinction, Mitchell wanted to drive Ellsworth from the inner circle. He did so by constantly second-guessing the laconic Kansan. Ellsworth sought not to engage Mitchell, but ultimately lost the power struggle when Mitchell ordered him to move from New York, where campaign decisions were actually being made, to the campaign's office in Washington, which was actually a political backwater.

While Sears was purged, Ellsworth narrowly survived, albeit not in a political role. Henry Kissinger, who knew of Ellsworth's interest in foreign affairs, came up with the idea of appointing Ellsworth as ambassador to NATO, with the job of assuring European allies that their views would not be ignored as the United States discussed arms levels with the Soviet Union. "The men on Nixon's dark side were about to run out of the government one of the president's most able supporters after only a few months in 1969," syndicated columnist Robert Novak remembered. "Kissinger came to the rescue. He arranged for Nixon, who never liked to fire anyone, to send Ellsworth to Brussels as the US ambassador to NATO in April—removing him from this den of vipers for one of the best jobs in government."[22]

The job saved Ellsworth from being forced out completely. In 1974, Nixon appointed him assistant secretary of defense for international affairs. As a former House member himself, Nixon had an affinity for congressmen. As president, Nixon initially appointed Ellsworth as one of five men with the title assistant to the president, despite his opposition to Nixon's policies on the Vietnam War. His long sideburns were an anomaly in the buttoned-down Nixon White House.

Nixon staffer Jeff Bell remembered Ellsworth as an adept political infighter who often removed the names of the real authors of staff memos to Nixon and pass them to Nixon under his name as if he was the author.

Another of "the bright young men" who joined the Nixon entourage was Thomas W. Evans, often confused with Thomas B. Evans Jr., the former Republican National Committee co-chair, Nixon fundraiser, and later Delaware congressman. I recruited both Evanses to help me nominate Ronald Reagan in 1980.

Also on the new team was Dr. Martin Anderson. Impossibly young-looking with enormous glasses, he was dubbed "the Baby Doctor" by the wisecracking Sears. Anderson was a staunch conservative, an issues man who bolstered Nixon's basic conservative economic philosophy, even if it was of the chamber of commerce variety.

Richard Whalen remembered Anderson" "A brilliant, thirty-one-year-old assistant professor of economics at Columbia, Anderson had turned his doctoral dissertation on urban renewal into a devastating book, *The Federal Bulldozer*. While we talked, Anderson joined us for a few minutes. With his owlish horn-rimmed glasses and unruly forelock, he looked improbably youthful and strictly professorial. During the campaign and afterward, he proved himself a remarkably effective political operator, whose ideas somehow got through the maze. 'You have to understand, Dick,' he remarked to me one day some months later. 'Academics are born connivers.'[23]

I became friends with Anderson in the 1976 and 1980 Reagan campaigns, when Sears recruited him to the Reagan team. Even today, Anderson has the greatest instinctual feel for Ronald Reagan and his beliefs. In this, Anderson certainly surpasses Peggy Noonan, who was a nice lady but *nowhere* when Reagan won in 1980. Anderson's role as a synthesizer of ideas and effective service to Nixon and Reagan is underrated.

Key in the new Nixon entourage was speechwriter Raymond K. Price, a slight and mild-mannered man who had been an editorial writer for the *New York Herald-Tribune*. A liberal Republican, Price understood the balance and cadence Nixon wanted and was in many ways the left side of Nixon's brain. Price provided important balance to the bombastic and conservative Buchanan. Nixon relied on Price for sweeping prose while he assigned Buchanan speeches that required red meat.

Price encouraged Nixon on civil rights and toned down Nixon's racially based appeals to be subtle and symbolic, rather than the shrill and ugly entreaties of George Wallace. Price understood Nixon's obsession with words, structure, and tone in his comeback bid. In 1960, it had been slapdash. Serving as his own campaign manager, strategist, and candidate, and trying to catch up with JFK after the disastrous first televised debate, Nixon spoke mostly extemporaneously on the stump, and formal statements were put out quickly and lacked polish and thought. Nixon drove himself to exhaustion serving both as candidate and chief speechwriter. The "wordsmiths" Nixon surrounded himself with still worked off drafts the old man had written himself on full-length yellow legal pads.

Another of "the bright, young men" was the aforementioned pugnacious *Fortune* magazine writer Richard Whalen, who had written a Pulitzer Prize–winning biography of Joseph P. Kennedy.

Nixon utilized "the bright young men" around him and their credentials to show that he was a "new Nixon" listening to "new men" with "new ideas." Nixon told interviewers that he had hand-picked his new "first-rate" staff, in contrast to the inherited "hacks" around him in 1960.

Whalen discussed in his own biography the purpose of the "bright, young men":

> By directing the spotlight toward the fresh supporting cast, the star of the longest-running road show in American politics not only spruced up the latest production, but also assembled several credible character witnesses. We were at once ignorant and unscathed, innocent and enthusiastic. What most of us knew of Nixon's earlier campaigns was only what we had read in Theodore H. White's chronicle of the 1960 disaster; we could testify only in the present and future tenses. By certifying our supposed intimacy and influence, Nixon gave our testimonials impressive weight. Faced with questions from reporters, some of them friends and former colleagues, I could say honestly that I had never met the brooding loner described by White and other Nixon-watchers. The Nixon I knew—I did not dwell on our slight acquaintance—was open, attentive, and evidently willing to accept ideas.

Whalen believed that Nixon was best equipped to end the war and ultimately became disillusioned over Nixon's unwillingness to offer a concrete proposal to end the war while essentially putting his faith in the escalation tactics that had failed Lyndon Johnson.

Whalen quit the campaign after Nixon's nomination, after Nixon law partner John Mitchell and veteran Nixon aides H. R. Haldeman and John Ehrlichman seized control of the campaign, limiting both Whalen's access and influence with Nixon. To his credit, Whalen was early to recognize the price Nixon would pay for the isolation enforced by the "Berlin Wall" of ad men and advance operatives who tightly controlled access to Nixon.

In the end, Whalen was of course right. Nixon could have ended the war earlier and become a hero to the left. Instead, he limped through a campaign, never saying that he had a "secret plan" to end the war but implying it by sometime patting his chest as if a "secret plan" existed in the inside breast pocket of his somber business suit. Nixon believed in this period that he could leverage the Soviets and the Chinese to hasten the war, a good idea probably unexplored by LBJ but one that failed to work.

Nixon's break with his earliest advisors proved costly. To replace them, he constructed a staff of yes-men. All were reluctant to reign in his excesses and instead sought to show Nixon and Haldeman how relentless they could be, how "tough they were," following questionable orders. I have no doubt that had Nixon been elected in 1960, he would have served eight years as president without the tarnish of Watergate. Undisturbed by what he regarded as the theft of the 1960 election, and with a broader range of advisors who overlapped the Eisenhower administration, he would have governed without paranoid conspiracy.

Under Garment, Sears, Ellsworth, and Buchanan, backed by the redoubtable Rose Mary Woods, Nixon launched "Operation Candor." And always in the background was veteran Nixon advance man Nicholas L. Ruwe, who later served as deputy director of protocol and then Ronald Reagan's ambassador to Iceland, an appointment Nixon secured for Reagan. The scion of a wealthy and socially prominent Grosse Pointe, Michigan, family, Ruwe was a hunter, fisherman, superb billiards player, and skeet shooter. His invariable daily garb was a solid gray suit, a Brooks Brothers blue button-down shirt, and a solid grenadine tie that was always black, blue, or maroon. Ruwe was an advance man for Nixon in 1960 and 1962 and followed Nixon into his wilderness years in New York. An iconic news photograph showed Nixon, the private citizen, crossing the street in Manhattan with Ruwe furtively glancing around over Nixon's right shoulder. Around Nixon, Ruwe was unobtrusive, taciturn, efficient, prompt, and organized. With the boys he was garrulous, profane, a chain smoker of unfiltered Camels, and lover of "silver bullets," as he and Nixon called vodka martinis.

Less featured in the media but providing his conservative candlepower as an economic adviser to Nixon was Alan Greenspan, the future chairman of the Federal Reserve, who was a bandmate of Len Garment in the Woody Herman orchestra in the '40s. Garment fondly remembered "the saxophonist-flautist Alan Greenspan, who helped with the band's payroll (yes, the books balanced) and spent intermissions reading Ayn Rand and general economics. Twenty years later Greenspan and I, not having seen each other since band days, bumped into each other on Broad Street in downtown Manhattan and I ended up introducing him to my law partner, the presidential aspirant Richard Nixon."[24] Greenspan later joined the campaign as coordinator on domestic policy.

Also in the background as a writer for Nixon was public relations man William Safire. Safire and Nixon struck up a friendship when the PR agent helpfully steered the vice president into his client Pepsi-Cola's exhibition at a trade fair. There, Nixon staged his famous Kitchen Debate with Soviet Premier Nikita Khrushchev, while sipping from paper cups with the Pepsi-Cola logo on them. Safire joined Buchanan, Price, and Whalen as a writer and thinker for the "new Nixon." It is interesting to note that both Safire and Buchanan later emerged as prominent journalists, both being able to step away from the wreckage of Watergate.

The speechwriters Nixon assembled were incredibly talented. Nixon was obsessed with words. He famously drafted his own material and labored over changes and suggestions from his writers. He was aware and enthralled with nuance, impact and messaging. He often pondered the use of one word. Unlike John F. Kennedy, who largely read the work of Ted Sorenson or Arthur Schlesinger, Nixon was his own "wordsmith." He called his writers "the Scribes." He told Whalen that he would "take his six" over the huge, paid staffs of Rockefeller and Kennedy. Nixon's writing staff had *balance*. Buchanan wrote from the right. Price wrote from the left. Whalen, although an open opponent of the Vietnam War, was fundamentally a conservative. Safire could write to the right or the left as he later demonstrated as a celebrated *New York Times* columnist.

Nixon's early campaign vehicle, the Nixon for President Committee, was chaired by Dr. Gaylord Parkinson, who had helmed the California Republican Party during the 1966 campaign of Ronald Reagan for governor. "Parky" coined the famous eleventh commandment: "Thou shall not speak ill of thy brother Republican," which had been the watchword of Reagan's success in the Golden State. It is important to note that party moderates who supported former San Francisco Mayor George Christopher in the Republican primary, were immediately recruited the Reagan entourage in the wake of the former actor's victory.

Nixon's comeback bid was almost derailed by leaks in his initial campaign apparatus. Nixon would learn that a deputy to Parkinson, Robert Walker was leaking political intelligence on Nixon's effort to both Reagan and Rockefeller.[25] Walker, it seems, felt he could have a larger role in a Rockefeller-Reagan Campaign. Walker's betrayal would be learned through a private investigator put on the Californian. Nixon would order Robert Ellsworth to fire Parkinson, Walker and four staffers he hired. "Ellsworth had purged the Washington office, down to the secretaries and switchboard operators," speechwriter Richard Whalen would recall.[26] Nixon admired Ellsworth's butchery. "Boy, can he get tough! Almost *too* tough the way he fired those Parkinson people," Nixon said.[27] This would exacerbate the tension between Nixon and Reagan, who now controlled Nixon's old California base. Nixon well understood that in the post-1964 Republican Party, it was Reagan, not Rockefeller, who posed the largest potential obstacle to his 1968 comeback.

The leaks to the ex-actor's camp would have been harmful.

Walker resurfaced as an aide to Reagan, proving the intelligence he had collected from Nixon did not damage his standing with the California governor. Walker was a primary force in convincing Reagan to hire John Sears as his campaign manager in 1976. Walker would also later emerge as a vice president of the Coors Brewing Company and recruit others to Reagan's team.

Oklahoma Governor Harry Bellmon replaced Parkinson. A story that may not be apocryphal claimed Bellmon was so dumb that once, traversing a hotel lobby in Oklahoma City, the desk clerk yelled "Bell man!" and the governor asked him what he wanted. The point remains moot: Parkinson, and later Bellmon, were front men, while Ellsworth and Sears served as Nixon's chief political operatives in the early days. Mitchell rose to take the helm from Bellmon, who went on the win Oklahoma's US Senate seat in 1968, serving as the head of Nixon's campaign.

The old Nixon warhorses came to the fore with 1960 supporters like New Hampshire Governor Lane Dwinell, former Connecticut Governor and Congressman John Davis Lodge, former Eisenhower Commerce Secretary Fred Seaton, ambassador Robert C. Hill of New Hampshire, and Walter W. Williams of Seattle, Washington, Chairman of Citizens for Eisenhower/Nixon in 1952 and later Under-Secretary of Commerce would comprise the "Nixon for President Committee."[28] Money was supplied by Nixon's friends. Aerosol valve king Robert Alplanalp, Dewitt and Lila Acheson Wallace, owners of Reader's Digest, Delaware trucking executive John Rollins, Southern California car dealer, Robert Nesen, who later served as US Assistant Secretary of the Navy, eccentric Chicago insurance magnate W. Clement Stone, and coal heiress Helen Clay Frick, put up the early money for Nixon's carefully timed White House bid. Former Eisenhower OMB Director Maurice Stans collected the money with an assist from Walter Williams. Stans had played this role in 1960 and 1962. A measure of Nixon's political rehabilitation is the fact that money was plentiful for his '68 comeback bid, while he had struggled to raise money for his 1962 governors' race only a year after losing the presidency to JFK by a whisker.

Until 1968, *every* presidential campaign was headquartered in Washington, DC. While Nixon's campaign had a storefront there for appearances, his operation worked out of his law firm in the beginning and expanded to discreet rental space in New York City, only blocks from Nixon's post Fifth Avenue apartment that he rented from Nelson Rockefeller, who was his neighbor in the building and landlord. Ellsworth commented on the "kabuki theater" of the Washington headquarters; nothing happened there, the action was in New York.

Of the bright young men who surrounded Nixon early in his comeback bid, the men recruited by Garment most definitely leaned to the right. More importantly, Nixon made much of his commitment to "new ideas." Although, most new ideas were jettisoned in the fall campaign as Nixon hedged his bets on the Vietnam War. Instead he stuck to relatively broad platitudes, including law and order, black capitalism, and the rebuilding of American prestige abroad.

Indeed, these men of ideas who inspired Nixon to climb out of his image as a two-time loser were pushed aside later by marketing and public relations men who favored style and appearance over substance.

NOTES

1. Richard Whalen, Catch the Falling Flag, p. 52.
2. Conversation with author.
3. Deborah Hart Strober and Gerald S. Strober, The Nixon Presidency: An Oral History of the Era, p. 55.
4. Robert D. Novak, The Prince of Darkness: 50 Years Reporting in Washington (Kindle Locations 3907-3908).
5. Ibid
6. Richard Whalen, Catch the Falling Flag, p. 23.
7. Richard Whalen, Catch the Falling Flag, p. 59.

8. Richard Whalen, Catch the Falling Flag, p. 22.
9. Leonard Garment, Crazy Rhythm, p. 85.
10. Ibid.
11. Anthony Summers, The Arrogance of Power, p. 264.
12. Anthony Summers, The Arrogance of Power, p. 316.
13. Leonard Garment, In Search of Deep Throat, pp. 34–35.
14. Jules Witcover, Very Strange Bedfellows, p. 45.
15. Craig Shirley, Rendevous with Destiny, p. XXX.
16. Jules Witcover, Marathon, p. 73.
17. Letter to author, June 8, 1987.
18. Lou Cannon, Reagan, p. 192.
19. Richard Whalen, Catch the Falling Flag, p. 13.
20. Richard Whalen, Catch the Falling Flag, p. 24.
21. Douglas Robinson, "Du Bois Duplicity Decried by Nixon, *New York Times,* March 9, 1966.
22. Robert D. Novak, The Prince of Darkness: 50 Years Reporting in Washington (Kindle Locations 3918-3921).
23. Richard Whalen, Catch the Falling Flag, p. 24.
24. Leonard Garment, Crazy Rhythm, p. 37–38.
25. Allen, Robert S. Scott, Paul. "Leaks Plague Nixon Backers," *Rome News-Tribune,* Sept. 1, 1967.
26. Richard Whalen, Catch the Falling Flag, p. 19.
27. Ibid. p. 24.
28. Lewis Chester, Godfrey Hodgson, and Bruce Page, An American Melodrama: The Presidential Campaign of 1968, p. 255.

CHAPTER TEN

THE BIG ENCHILADA AND THE RISE OF THE MERCHANDISERS

"We joined up with the Old Man to do something for the future, something that would continue. This won't."

—John Sears[1]

Nixon had made the tragic mistake of managing his own campaign for president in 1960. Party leaders like his "campaign manager" Len Hall and vice presidential aide Robert Finch were powerless; Nixon made all crucial decisions, from the campaign schedule right down to the color of the bumper stickers. At the same time he worked himself into an exhausted frenzy. Nixon understood he needed a campaign manager this time around, someone to whom he could delegate real responsibility. He was under pressure to find a world-class manager in whom he could invest all his confidence. Many old-line Nixonites who had not yet rejoined the entourage were concerned about Nixon's track record of grabbing the wheel at crucial times. The man who emerged was Nixon's law partner: John Newton Mitchell.

Because Nixon had an inferiority complex and a chip on his shoulder, he tended to gravitate to self-made men who exuded a sense of confidence and even bravado. This explains Nixon's camaraderie with Philadelphia Mayor Frank L. Rizzo and big John Connally. This explains Nixon's attraction to Mitchell. Mitchell had a serene confident manner and unpreturbable nature that Nixon admired. "I've found the heavyweight!" Nixon exclaimed to William Safire in early 1967.[2]

John Mitchell had merged his firm with Mudge, Rose, Guthrie, and Alexander shortly before Nixon joined the firm. As a bond lawyer and expert on the bond market, Mitchell had designed complex bond issues for states and municipalities including putting together complex and enormous state borrowings by Nelson Rockefeller's New York State. As a result of this specialty, Mitchell knew a vast amount of detail concerning state and local politics and had a good network of financial and legal movers and shakers in the various states.

John Mitchell also had "fuck you" money and lived in an opulent home on a golf course in Westchester. Mitchell was a calm and judicious man, slow to anger and serenely confident in his judgment and demeanor. Len Garment, who also recruited Mitchell in his talent search, saw the lawyer as confident, but limited in his political ability:

> Mitchell was certainly not a bad man, as the cliché machine painted him during and after Watergate. But Mitchell, in contrast to Sears, knew less about politics than he was thought to know and, more important, considerably less than he should have known. Mitchell was the master of a narrow piece of the political world, municipal financing. From this fact he made the faulty generalization that he was similarly the master of all politics.
>
> Intimations of Mitchell's future troubles appeared in the 1968 campaign, where the most pervasive internal battle was between those who believed in political technique above all and those who insisted on the value, intrinsic and instrumental, of ideas in

politics. Mitchell's laconic tough-guy stance put him habitually in the camp of the former. More, underneath Mitchell's confident exterior lay a deep unsureness about himself. Therefore he would not brook disagreement. If I had not enjoyed such senior status in the campaign, he would have treated me as a major antagonist. As it was, Mitchell's insecurity led to flare-ups between him and what must have seemed to the older man like an impossibly self-assured Sears.[3]

Mitchell's outward serenity was deceptive. In fact, he was deeply unsure of himself given his lack of political experience. The stocky man had put himself through school playing professional hockey until sidelined from hip injuries. He could be jaunty, upbeat, and jocular. Although he and his second wife Martha were known in New York society, he only rarely socialized with New York's financial elite. Like Nixon, he came up the hard way and wasn't impressed with the Ivy League degrees and social airs of the New York establishment.

I first met Mitchell in 1968 when I hitched a ride to the Republican National Convention in Miami, booking a room at the shabby Wofford Beach Hotel. I was sharing my hotel with an overflow of Reagan delegates from California who couldn't get into the Deauville Hotel, the official residence of the California Delegation. I came equipped with a letter of introduction from Governor Lodge and was assigned to be a gofer for John Mitchell. In all my years in politics I have never met a more decent or kinder man than John Mitchell; far different than the gruff caricature of him created by the national press. I later learned what a calming and moderating influence Mitchell could be on Nixon.

Mitchell gave me an envelope that carried a letter, or in some cases I suspected cash, and pulled a $10 bill from his own money clip to give me give me cab fare to whichever hotel and politician expecting an envelope. One night around dinner time, Mr. Mitchell came by the messenger pool, handed me a $10 bill and told me to go across the street to LUMS, a popular beer joint, and buy two hotdogs steamed in beer and covered with sauerkraut. He told me to slather both with mustard and "eat them both," he said with a wink.

On another occasion Mr. Mitchell instructed me to deliver a heavy envelope to Congressman Bradford Morse of Massachusetts, a Brahmin and very liberal Republican. My instructions were to call the congressman's hotel room from the lobby and he would tell me what room to bring the package to.

I called his room but there was no answer. I called again and this time someone knocked the phone onto the floor, finally, a woman gave me the room number and quickly hung up. I jumped the elevator only to find the hotel room door ajar. I could hear heavy breathing. I slowly pushed the door open only to see two enormous white buttocks splayed with pimples pounding away on top of a prostitute. The congressman, covered in sweat, reached out for the envelope and grunted, "Get the fuck out." I ran like hell.

Mitchell initially agreed only to organize Wisconsin for that state's pivotal primary. Using a network of bond lawyers in the state and their own rolodexes of high-profile contacts, Mitchell organized Wisconsin down to the precinct level, tying down the most influential movers and shakers in the state.

Mitchell's future problems were intimated in the 1968 effort, where the campaign had a deep divide and internal fight between those who believed in political technique above all (Haldeman, Ehrlichman et al.) and those who believed in the value and power of ideas in politics. Mitchell's stoic tough-guy stance put him habitually in the camp of the former. More importantly, underneath Mitchell's confident demeanor lay a deep sureness about himself. Therefore, once he took power in the campaign, he brooked no disagreement.

Mitchell, in turn, recruited Mississippi Goldwater backer and oilman Fred Larue, Arizona attorney Robert Mardian, Kentucky Governor Louie Nunn, and former Arizona Republican Chairman and Goldwater confidant Richard Kleindienst as his political deputies. By the time the Southern State Republican chairmen met in Atlanta in May 1968, Mitchell had emerged as "El Supremo," later referred to in the Watergate tapes as "The Big Enchilada." Mitchell was known to his deputies for his imperturbable manner as "Old Stone Face."

As accomplished and tough as he was, Mitchell had a growing "Martha problem." The gruff New York attorney's Southern belle wife, Martha, resented the time "her John" spent "electing Mr. Nixon." Desperate for attention and increasingly given to rages and indiscrete late-night phone calls, the "Martha problem" festered. On one occasion, in Mitchell's absence, bodyguard Steve King held Mrs. Mitchell down—in her words, "against my will"[4] —while a doctor injected sedatives to calm her uncontrollable anger.

In fact, Martha raged often. She threw things, including lamps, ashtrays, and just about anything she could get her hands on. Incredibly, she blurted out claims about Nixon's Mob ties and financial dealings. Martha also wanted to "travel with the president" on Air Force One, but Nixon gave Haldeman explicit instructions to "keep that woman away from me."

"He [Mitchell] was proud of her; she had that manic zest," said Len Garment, his former law partner and longtime friend, who recommended Mitchell to Nixon."He didn't know what she would do next—go over the edge, or the parapet. At the end, he was very much distracted and not thinking clearly—which is an explanation, not an excuse."[5]

Ironically, Los Angeles advertising executive H. R. "Bob" Haldeman and Seattle zoning lawyer John Ehrlichman were the two most nonideological members of the 1968 Nixon entourage and controlled access to Nixon after the Miami convention until the time Nixon fired both men from his White House.

Haldeman and Ehrlichman joined the Nixon entourage only after Sears, Ellsworth, and John Mitchell wrapped up the nomination. Ehrlichman even declined a request from deputy campaign director Richard Kleindienst to help recruit a Nixon chairman for Washington State. "I'm not getting involved in politics," Ehrlichman told a stunned Kleindienst. Although the two Christian Scientists had been advance men in Nixon's 1960 effort and were heavily involved in the disastrous 1962 gubernatorial bid, Haldeman and Ehrlichman held back, skeptical that the scarred and damaged Nixon was still politically viable.

The two veteran Nixon aides watched apprehensively as Nixon and the new team around him reinvented the former vice president. They watched him roll through the primaries and were able to join the campaign on their own terms. They always intended to run things if the bid became viable and with a division of John Mitchell, serving as campaign manager, they did.

Haldeman, who was a senior executive at the J. Walter Thompson Agency in Los Angeles, had served as an advance man in Nixon's 1960 campaign. He recruited Ehrlichman to do advance and political work. Ehrlichman actually spied on Nelson Rockefeller disguised as a driver in Rockefeller's motorcade across North Dakota while the New York governor contemplated a challenge to Nixon for the 1960 nomination. "During the three days I was there I managed to pick up some good political information from friendly local people in Fargo and Bismarck," said Ehrlichman. "The candidate for Lieutenant Governor, himself a delegate, told me everything he knew. Three days after Rocky left North Dakota and I returned to Seattle, Nixon's regional campaign staff came to North Dakota to undo whatever Rockefellers visit might have gained him."[6]

Haldeman managed Nixon's 1962 gubernatorial campaign and Ehrlichman again did advance work. After the bitter experience of 1962, both Haldeman and Ehrlichman wondered whether Nixon was through as a political force. Ehrlichman thought Nixon's change in demeanor after a few cocktails was damaging and would affect his campaign:

I told Nixon that it seemed obvious that he would be running again in 1968 and that I would be asked again to help him. He responded that he had not yet decided what to do. I said that, all things being equal, he would have my support, but that I was very much troubled by his drinking. I was in no position to ask him to stop, nor would I even intrude that way into anyone's personal life. But, I continued, I didn't want to invest my time in a difficult presidential campaign that might well be lost because the candidate was not fully in control of himself. Nixon asked if I thought that was why he lost in 1960 or 1962; I said I didn't think so, although his impulsive press conference after the election in California in 1962 was one episode of the kind I feared should he run again.

Nixon didn't try to brush me off or change the subject, as I had anticipated he might. He said that if he decided to run he wanted my help. He felt it was not unreasonable of me to expect that he would keep himself in the best condition in the campaign. Everyone had the right to expect that at him. He thanked me for coming to talk to him about it. I understand his reply to an undertaking, quid pro quo. If he wanted me to work, then he would lay off the booze.

As far as I'm concerned, he kept that bargain during the 1968 campaign.[7]

Haldeman and Ehrlichman, having been badly burned in the 1962 effort, held back from rejoining the Nixon entourage, concerned about Nixon's track record of self-management and hoarding decisions free of advice or input. They did not surface in Nixon's 1968 campaign until the Republican National Convention in Miami Beach.

The Nixon Nominator, a campaign newsletter dated June 1968, noted, "H.R. Bob Haldeman, Los Angeles advertising executive, civic and educational leader, is joining the Nixon campaign as Richard Nixon's personal chief-of-staff. The announcement was made today by Nixon campaign manager, John N. Mitchell. A long-time political associate and friend of the former Vice President, Haldeman was his campaign tour manager in the presidential election of 1960."

Haldeman arrived with his fellow Christian Scientist side-kick Ehrlichman, ending any sense of "openness" or "candor" in the Nixon entourage. "The bright young men" lost their access to the candidate as the campaign ended. "The Germans," as Haldeman and Ehrlichman became known within the White House, and their scurrying squads of close-cropped, buttoned-up ex-advance men took over with Teutonic thoroughness."[8]

Haldeman's contemporaries remember him as cold, efficient, extremely organized, but fundamentally a gentleman. Ehrlichman did not fare as well in the estimation of his colleagues: "A sneaky son of a bitch," Murray Chotiner later told me.

Abrasive, curt, highly organized, and extremely effective, Ehrlichman served as Tour Director for Nixon's post-convention bid and then emerged as Nixon's White House counsel. Later, he moved over to run the domestic policy as assistant to the president. In this job, Ehrlichman dominated domestic policy much in the way Henry Kissinger dominated foreign affairs, although Nixon also relied on Secretary of Labor George Schultz on domestic affairs. Every major domestic program was under the stiff, humorless, but ambitious Ehrlichman. Ideologically, Ehrlichman was a moderate who molded Nixon's environmental policies as well as his restoration of the rights of Native Americans, not to mention federal revenue sharing, anti-drug programs, and welfare reform.

Attorney General Richard Kliendienst, who had served as Barry Goldwater's Senate campaign manager and joined Nixon's effort in 1968 as a deputy to John Mitchell, said Ehrlichman resented the swift rise of Mitchell.

Kleindienst recalled another confrontation with the terse and somewhat pompous Ehrlichman:

The best—or worst, as you will—example of our differences occurred during the week before the convention opened in Miami

Beach. The Nixon hotel headquarters was the Doral. The top floors were set aside for the staff. The very top floor was reserved for the some sixty people in the delegate operation. Everybody who had business on the top floors was given a baldheaded eagle pin to wear for identification. Without a pin, no one was allowed on the top floors—no matter what.

To show off the proficiency of the Nixon organization, I invited Ray Bliss, the national Republican party chairman, and Senator Bellmon of Oklahoma, both longtime friends of mine, to come over for a tour. Bliss would be talking to everybody in town and I wanted to impress him.

They showed up at the receptionist's desk in the hotel lobby at the appointed hour and asked to be escorted to my office, a room on the top floor.

'I'm so sorry, gentlemen, but no one is allowed up there,' the little girl with the pretty little Nixon hat sweetly informed them.

Bliss and Bellmon asked her to call me. I came down immediately.

'Don't worry, sweetie-pie, I'll take them up myself.'

Things ceased being sweet when she announced to me, in the presence of my two distinguished guests, 'Mr. Ehrlichman's orders are that no one, *absolutely* no one, is permitted up there who doesn't have the pin.'

'Gentlemen, please wait here a minute. I'll be right back!'

I entered Ehrlichman's office with a little frustration, but nevertheless confident that the problem would be solved quickly. Not so. My nonpolitical associate firmly informed me there would be no exceptions.

'John, old boy,' I responded with some acerbity, 'I'm going downstairs and I'm going to bring Bliss and Bellmon up to my floor. If you try to stop me, one or the other is going to be on the plane for either Arizona or Washington this afternoon.' They came up with me. Perhaps, for the country's sake, one of us should have gone home that day.[9]

The depth of Ehrlichman's ambition and resentment of Mitchell, who he saw as a "newcomer" in Nixon's entourage was demonstrated when Kleindienst's nomination to succeed Mitchell as attorney general was pending Senate confirmation and the Arizonan's prospects appeared bleak:

> Not only did Ehrlichman not particularly care for John Mitchell or me (I remember now some cruel and demeaning statements Ehrlichman made to the president about Mitchell in the days immediately after John left the Committee to Reelect the President), but Ehrlichman, so I was informed, decided, as the Nixon presidency went on, that he wanted most of all to be attorney general. During my confirmation hearings for attorney general in 1972, when prospects were not too sanguine, my old friend Bob Mardian, then head of the Internal Security Division of the Department of Justice, was asked one day to step out of my office to take a call from the White House. The caller was Ehrlichman, who asked Bob if he would consent to be deputy when Ehrlichman was nominated as attorney general![10]

Incredibly, Ehrlichman turned bitter, claiming, "Nixon lied to me about Watergate." He later dumped his wife, took up with a younger Native American woman, and grew a beard. He never spoke to Nixon from the day he was fired. But don't feel sorry for Ehrlichman: he ran the illegal break-in at the Los Angeles office of Dr. Fielding, the psychiatrist for Daniel Ellsberg, leaker of the Pentagon Papers.

Former New York City cop John Caulfield recalled that Ehrlichman, a lawyer, approved the break-in at the psychiatrist's office with the un-lawyerly admonishment, "Don't get caught." The group known as "the Plumbers" illegally broke into the doctor's office with Ehrlichman's approval.

On Caulfield's recommendation, it was also Ehrlichman who recruited tough-talking, New York cop Anthony Ulasewicz. Ulasewicz performed more than ninety-three "investigations" at White House direction, first under Ehrlichman and later under White House counsel John W. Dean. It is significant that, while Lyndon Johnson generally left his snooping to the FBI and went to great lengths to establish some legal cover for the actions, the

Nixon group established their own extra-legal intelligence gathering operations to operate outside government channels. The two gumshoes reported to Ehrlichman.

Caulfield and Ehrilichman vetted Ulasewicz in May 1969 at LaGuardia Airport. He was told he would receive his orders from Caulfield with the understanding that they came from Ehrlichman and, initially, President Nixon. "You'll be allowed no mistakes," Ehrlichman told Ulasewicz. "There will be no support for you whatsoever from the White House if you're exposed."[11] John Mitchell put a finer point on it, calling Ehrlichman "a conniving little SOB."[12]

Veteran reporter Robert Novak recalled an eerie premonition from Patrick J. Hillings. "Hillings at age twenty-seven had won the congressional seat vacated by Nixon when he ran for the Senate. For the next eight years, Hillings was Nixon's man in the House of Representatives. He ran for attorney general of California in 1958 but was defeated in the Republican primary by Caspar Weinberger. I took it for granted that Nixon's election meant that Hillings, only forty-five in 1969, would be a top White House aide. Consequently, over dinner that Saturday night, I was surprised when Hillings informed me he would not be joining the Nixon administration.[13]

"Not a chance!" Pat told me. "Those teetotaling Christian Scientists don't want any part of me, and I don't want any part of them."

"What Christian Scientists?" I asked.

"Haldeman and Ehrlichman," he said, referring to two Nixon aides who had eclipsed him. I wasn't aware of Bob Haldeman's religion. I was barely aware of John Ehrlichman's existence. Hillings's subsequent remarks are emblazoned in memory. "I don't trust a man who never takes a drink. It's worse than that. I know Dick Nixon about as well as anybody in politics, and I know his weaknesses. The Christian Scientists will bring out the worst in him."[14]

The arrival of Haldeman and Ehrlichman and their army of crew-cutted advertising men changed the atmosphere and tone of

Nixon's campaign. Gone was the access the bright, young men had to "the old man." Now, all paper and appointments with Nixon flowed through Bob Haldeman. A Berlin Wall came down around Nixon and old advisors, new advisors, and political staff members were required to put everything in writing, routing all paper through Haldeman. John Mitchell could see and talk to Nixon any time he wanted, but for those on the writing and research, issues and political staff access became extremely limited. According to former Ohio State Attorney General and US Senator William Saxbe, who Nixon later named attorney general, "One of Nixon's problems were that he surrounded himself with guys that had no involvement in a political campaign. I referred to Haldeman and Ehrlichman as Nazis when I was in the Senate; that is the way they operated."[15] What Saxby meant was not that Haldeman and Ehrlichman had never been in campaigns, but that they had not handled political roles, they had only handled logistics. They were campaign mechanics.

In the words of Richard Whalen, the staffers had been reduced to "automatons in a cause completely without substance."[16] Whalen showed up at the Republican National Convention and was told he had been demoted. He was denied entry to the eighteenth floor where Nixon stayed, and he could no longer discuss issues with the candidate face-to-face. "Go see John Ehrlichman," Whalen was told.[17]

Ehrlichman was unknown to Whalen and upon introduction the stocky lawyer told him that he would look into the dilemma and to return the next day. The following day, Ehrlichman told Whalen there had been no mistake, he would not be granted admittance to the eighteenth floor, and if he were needed, he would be summoned. Whalen did not take the news lightly:

> "Just who the hell are you?" I asked. "I've never laid eyes on you or heard your name mentioned. And I'll be damned if I'm going to take orders from you." "Look," he said, his own temper rising, "I've

been with Nixon a long time, and I've seen writer and researcher types like you come and go. You'll go where I say you go."

"Fuck you," I said, walking out.

The wounding reference to "writer and researcher types" hurt precisely because I knew it was true. The issues men who had put their brains and pens at Nixon's disposal in former years had indeed come and gone without a trace. I decided to stand my ground.[18]

The Berlin Wall descended around Nixon. The candidate, who had been so accessible to the press through the primaries and convention, no longer submitted to interviews and would campaign with the revolutionary but repetitive use of television advertising. The emphasis of the campaign was no longer on the working press or making news. Nixon staged a masterful campaign but won in a three-way race with the same 46 percent of the vote he had in the polls from the very beginning.

Sadly, Nixon not only acquiesced in this isolation, he required it. He was an introvert in an extrovert's business, lacking in physical grace or the ability to make small talk, he was socially awkward, nondexterous, and reserved. "I'm just not a back-slapping kind of guy," Nixon would say. "I just can't let my hair down around people." Extraordinarily effective as a speaker in stadiums filled with thousands, a charismatic speaker in large groups and small, Nixon was terrible in one-on-one interaction. His smiled was forced and his jokes threadbare. He didn't seem to know where to place his hands and was utterly lacking in physical grace. Nixon liked to be alone—to think, to brood, to read books and classified cables translated from Russian and Chinese. Many said this explained Nixon's strange friendship with Charles G. "Bebe" Rebozo. "Nixon likes to be alone," Chotiner would tell me, "and when he's with Bebe he is." The two of them were known to sit for hours without saying a word, while Rebozo sunned himself in the Miami sunshine, and Nixon, who never felt comfortable in a sportshirt, brooded and made notes on a long, yellow pad.

At the same time, presidential aide John Ehrlichman described a surreal scene where he and Nixon on vacation in Miami were up to their necks in azure, blue water and perfect Florida sunshine, when Nixon launched a conversation on arcane domestic policy issue.

Nixon was a loner who didn't see the damage his isolation caused. Besides being socially awkward, he was mechanically inept and incredibly reserved, attributes that reinforced his loner tendencies. Unlike LBJ, he enjoyed none of the camaraderie and backslapping that characterized every level of politics in the 1960s. Even his Chief of Staff Bob Haldeman said Nixon was "stiff and artificial."[19]

Above all, it is important to understand that Nixon hated confrontation. "This would be a great job if you didn't have to deal with people" he said as president. As he rose in power his tendency for total isolation would grow. He would send orders to his cabinet through subordinates. He rarely saw members of the White House staff. Haldeman and Ehrlichman would say later it was Nixon, not they, who blocked access to Nixon's door—but neither did they argue they he should see anybody.

Under the "New Germans" rule, Mitchell was forced to get along with the new Haldeman, Ehrlichman combine. "You handle the body, I'll handle the politics," the pipe-puffing, campaign manager would say.

"Mitchell usually acted in the campaign in alliance with Haldeman and Ehrlichman," said Len Garment. "It was not that the three men were fond of one another; instead, they were in competition with each other to see who the toughest, most effective manager was."[20]

Mitchell systematically eliminated Ellsworth and Sears. Sears knew the fix was in when the super-efficient and meticulous Haldeman left his name off the printed White House staff list. Haldeman's supercilious assistant Larry Higby told Sears it was an oversight. Sears was gone soon after.

Mitchell's purge of Sears was a fork in Nixon's road; the chosen path led him to Watergate. Sears' sources in the White House remained impeccable after his departure from the Old Executive Office building. Sears remained close to ex-cop Jack Caulfield, who was working for White House counsel John Dean, who was a prime mover pushing the approval of the Watergate break-in plan. Sears also remained close to Rose Mary Woods, who the super-efficient Haldeman had tried to get moved from her office outside the Oval Office to the Old Executive Office building. Haldeman sent Woods a dozen long-stem roses the morning he asked her to move her office. "Fuck you," was the churchgoing Woods's reply. Starting with Nixon as a stenographer in his congressional office, Woods remained in a position to see and hear and would later famously take the rap when she claimed she had inadvertently caused the 18 ½-minute gap in his White House tapes.

The elimination of professional politicians and elevation of technocratic ad men around Nixon was a huge factor in the evolution of Watergate. Practical politicians were locked out as White House staffers jockeying for power climbed the ladder by showing how ruthless and dedicated to Nixon they could be.

Nixon's lack of a true ideology, his aversion to risk taking on the Vietnam War issue, and the rise of the ad men around him, combined with his increased isolation, would alienate speechwriter Richard J. Whalen. "I was ashamed of what I was doing," Whalen later wrote. "I was ashamed of being in the company of mediocre merchandisers behind a façade of concealing a sad mixture of cynicism, apprehension, suspicion, and fear—especially fear. Fear of the next man higher up, fear of being found out by the encircling press. Ambition kept worried and discouraged staff members in line."[21] Whalen resigned from the Nixon entourage after the Miami Beach convention.

Interestingly, Dr. Henry Kissinger, who later emerged as Nixon's chief foreign policy operative, as national security advisor, and later secretary of state, was Rockefeller's highly paid national security advisor in '68 and was secretly sending memos to Democratic nominee Hubert Humphrey suggesting how to deflate Nixon on foreign policy issues. Dr. Kissinger liked us to believe he figured out how to play the Chinese and the Russians against each other to put the Cold War on the path to oblivion, making the fall of the Iron Curtain inevitable. It would take President Ronald Reagan to finish the job. Kissinger was a courtier and an extraordinary brown-noser and flatterer. His ass kissing reflected in the White House tapes is enough to make you puke. In his dealings with anyone other than Nixon, he was power mad, conniving, mercurial, temperamental, and given to fits of rage that led to threats of resignation whenever he didn't get his way.

Kissinger was an unlikely man to helm the Nixon foreign policy initiatives. Kissinger was a vitriolic critic of Nixon while working for Rockefeller. More importantly, Kissinger was a protégé of rabid anti-Communist and foreign policy hard-liner Dr. Fritz Kraemer. Early in Nixon's term, when the president suggested that he might visit China, Kissinger told him "fat chance." However, in his pursuit of both power and international prominence, Kissinger abandoned the hard-line teachings of Kraemer and his backers at the JCS and Pentagon to embrace Nixon's policy of accommodation with the Soviets and Chinese.

Dr. Kissinger is in many ways responsible for what was to become a key act in the Watergate drama. Nixon and those around him feared little from the government study that analyzed Americans stepping in shit in Vietnam. A shocked LBJ discovered that the left wing of the Democratic Party, for whom he had delivered *sweeping* civil rights and social welfare legislation, had turned on him with a vengeance. Nixon figured the so-called Pentagon Papers would only make LBJ and JFK look bad. A seething Henry Kissinger convinced him otherwise.

"He is a sexual deviant," the rotund professor from Harvard bellowed. "The man's a pervert! This action undermines our capability to conduct foreign policy in a confidential manner. It is essential that this man [Ellsburg] be discredited." Kissinger's rage of course fueled the break-in of "the Plumbers" at the Los Angeles office of Dr. Lewis J. Fielding, Ellsburg's psychiatrist. The actual break-in was directed by Ehrlichman and was among the counts that sent the haughty White House domestic policy advisor to prison. Dr. Kissinger walked away from this seamy low point in the Watergate history.

Kissinger, an egomaniac and courtier of Nixon, was as paranoid as his boss; he just hid it better. He would demand wiretaps on perceived enemies such as NSA staffers and reporters long before the Watergate break-in. Kissinger would also drive the break-in at the office of Daniel Ellsberg's psychiatrist supervised by White House counsel John Ehrlichman long before Watergate. The imbalance in Kissinger's temperament is largely ignored because of his longevity. Deeply paranoid, obsessively secret, extraordinarily prideful, and incredibly duplicitous, Kissinger was working as a "consultant" for the State Department under Lyndon Johnson and was involved in the plans for the surprise bombing halt that Johnson would call in the days before the 1968 election. Kissinger would tip Nixon, thus guaranteeing himself a place in Nixon's foreign policy machinery as the new president chose his team. Because Kissinger was unsure of Nixon's receptivity based on Kissinger's long anaganism of the former vice president, the Harvard doctor passed the information through mutual friend William F. Buckley Jr. Kissinger's temper was volcanic and his abuse of subordinates legendary. Nixon once told me he lost count of how many times Henry threatened to resign. It was Kissinger's reaction to the leak of the Pentagon Papers that drove the Nixon administration to wiretap both White House and NSC personnel as well as several newspaper reporters and columnists. Note the backlash that occurred in 2014 when the Obama administration was revealed to be monitoring the telephones of reporters. The wiretaps Kissinger demanded were administered by his then Deputy General Alexander Haig and FBI Deputy Director William Sullivan. These wiretaps, conducted between 1969 and 1971, became one of the deepest secrets of the Nixon administration, and both Kissinger and Haig acted repeatedly to conceal their existence from the public.

Sears's access to Nixon, cocksure manner, and sarcastic wit drove campaign manager John Mitchell crazy. Sears's broad network of Republican relationships built up during his campaign travels with Nixon in 1966 were superior to Mitchell's own—largely bond lawyers or investment bankers. Nixon had promised Sears he would control GOP patronage after the election; Mitchell had cronies of his own to hire. Sears *threatened* John Mitchell.

First, Mitchell relocated Sears from New York to the DC headquarters, where nothing happened. He then put him on the road to help the hapless Spiro Agnew, who was having trouble getting his sea legs as a national candidate. After Sears became deputy counsel to the president, Kissinger, Mitchell, and Haldeman wiretapped him.

Len Garment recalled the Sears purge by the Haldeman-Ehrlichman-Mitchell combine:

> That Nixon was not, needless to say, the Nixon that Sears encountered via the persons of John Mitchell, Bob Haldeman, and John Ehrlichman. Sears was no less a political calculator than they. Anyone who could conceive of pairing Ronald Reagan with Richard Schweiker, as Sears did in 1976, has earned a permanent place in the political calculators' Hall of Fame. Sears was a skilled political operator who also stirred something in Nixon's larger, more poetic nature. This was precisely the part of Nixon's nature that Mitchell, Haldeman, and Ehrlichman took to be their job, to emotionally suppress, encouraging instead Nixon's implacable toughness. They succeeded.[22]

Sears's downfall at the White House came by way of a phone tap on journalist Henry Brandon. Brandon, in one phone conversation, quoted an unnamed White House official as having said, "The president is weak. He has difficulty saying no. He wants to please all and he dislikes having to make a choice . . . With a man like this, Henry Kissinger, of course, has great influence."[23]

Haldeman made sure the quote got back to Nixon. Soon after, Sears was gone.

"Perhaps because it was so trenchant, Nixon suspected Sears," said Garment. "Perhaps because he had felt such affection for Sears, Nixon turned on him with fury. Mitchell ordered the FBI to undertake the round-the-clock surveillance of Sears. He said it was at the express direction of the president."[24]

Columnist Robert Novak would remember the departure of Sears and what it revealed of Nixon. The men on Nixon's dark side were about to run out of the government one of the president's most able supporters after only a few months in 1969:

> John Sears stayed on at the White House six months longer than Ellsworth, but was not so fortunate. Mitchell was determined to be done with his brilliant young former law partner, complaining that Sears drank too much and talked too much to the press. What I think really bothered him was that Sears was not afraid of John Mitchell.
>
> By the early summer of 1969, Sears later informed me, "I felt I didn't have any effectiveness. I had outlived my usefulness." He was never fired but in October left voluntarily—not dreaming at age twenty-nine that a man of his intelligence, charm, and ambition never again would be on a government payroll. I asked whether he saw the president before he left. "No, he was embarrassed. I did ask to see him once when I had decided to go. I was refused the opportunity. I am sure he was embarrassed."

Could Richard Nixon not bear to face a valuable young lieutenant who had resigned? Sears later sat in the small conference room in our expanded little suite of offices on Pennsylvania Avenue, eating a sandwich lunch with me, and talking about Nixon:

> He can be a very tough guy as long as he doesn't have to see the other guy. In personal relationships, he has a good bit of coward-ice because he can't do things they can do. He can't make small talk. He can't talk and derive a result that's satisfactory. He doesn't want to get involved in confrontations with people.
>
> He's supposed to be [a] hard, tough politician, and he can't take what another politician is saying about him. He'll sit there and act really strong, hard, tough. He's not. He's saying all those things to convince himself, also to convince the people [in the room], because that's part of convincing himself. That's part of the reason he doesn't like to see a whole lot of people.

These words, never published until now, are a corrective to the White House tapes and the Haldeman diaries, pored over by historians who conclude that Nixon was a tyrant in embryo. Based on Sears's assessment, Nixon was a fraud—a make-believe tough guy.[25]

Sears was a more determined and formidable foe than Mitchell and Haldeman imagined, but even he was driven out. While Garment's contention that Sears was Deep Throat was wrong, Sears himself has admitted to being a source for Carl Bernstein. I believe Sears also orchestrated the public exposure of the clandestine Nixon "Townhouse Operation" in 1970 in which favored US Senate candidates were showered in secret corporate cash.

Nixon's entourage contained characters far more odious than the self-aggrandizing Kissinger. Before John Mitchell was scheduled to resign as attorney general and move to the Committee to Reelect the President, H. R. Haldeman recruited thirty-four-year-old Jeb Stuart Magruder to set up the committee as acting chairman until Mitchell arrived. A cosmetics marketing guy from Southern California, Magruder was impossibly handsome and clean cut, resembling a Ken doll.

The old Nixon hands like Nick Ruwe, Charlie McWhorter, and Ron Walker called Jeb Stuart Magruder "Steve Stunning" for his model looks. Everything about Jeb Magruder was too perfect. He had perfect hair, perfect teeth, a perfect wife, perfect kids, a perfect golf swing, a perfect tennis arm, a perfect tan, and perfectly polished shoes. Magruder and his family had all-American good looks, and Magruder also took brown-nosing and social climbing to a whole new level. He could be obsequious if you were on the political and social scale above him and an utter dick if you were on the political or social scale below him.

Late one night during Nixon's 1972 reelection campaign, I was leaving the CRP headquarters when the elevator stopped on the floor occupied by the senior staff of the 1700 Pennsylvania Avenue building, and Jeb Stuart Magruder got on. We both said hello but then rode to the basement garage in silence. Magruder and I walked toward our cars. I was driving a red Volkswagen Bug that had a "Reelect the President" bumper sticker as well as one for the reelection of Congressman Joel T. Broyhill of Virginia. "Is this your car?" Magruder asked. I nodded. "What is this?" he asked, pointing to the Broyhill sticker with his highly polished wingtip. "Get it the fuck off of there." He turned and proceeded to his car without further comment.

Magruder would regret this incident later. My boss at CREEP, scheduling director J. Curtis Herge, conspired with Nixon communication guy Bill Ratigan and concocted a practical joke to persuade Magruder that I was the nephew of quirky Chicago insurance millionaire and Nixon confidant W. Clement Stone. Stone was the largest single donor to Nixon, giving over a million dollars in 1972 campaign money. He gave millions more to the Republican National Committee and had been a secret funder of the "townhouse fund," a covert 1970 campaign effort that was a precursor to Watergate and more about which we shall cover later.

Herge figured out that to convince Magruder, we had to convince Magruder's right-hand man, Bart Porter, who was Herge's boss and indirectly mine. Herge told Porter that John Mitchell, who knew Herge from the Mudge Rose law firm, called him to ask how Clem Stone's nephew was working out on the campaign. Porter was in Magruder's office spilling the beans before Herge could hang up the phone. The next day I received a lunch invitation from Magruder, who had not acknowledged me in the elevators since he told me to remove my bumper sticker. We ate at San Souci, which in those days was where the power elite ate lunch. I saw Robert Novak huddled in a corner dining with an admiral. I saw Joseph Califano, LBJ's Mr. Fix-it, with Katherine Graham, publisher of the Washington Post. Magruder turned on the charm. He told me he was looking at a political career in his now home state of California after serving a "suitable number of years in a cabinet post." He'd be looking for a young team of guys down the road, suggesting there might be a job for me, W. Clement Stone's nephew. He had eyes on Uncle Clem's wallet. Indeed, Magruder announced a candidacy for secretary of state in California, which, needless to say, collapsed in the tempest of Watergate. "Bart [my boss] says you're a man who can keep his mouth shut, and that you're totally loyal to the president. I will need men like you," Magruder said pompously.

This ruse of me being Clement Stone's nephew was worth milking for all it was worth until a chilling day in which it was announced that at the request of the president, W. Clement Stone, the largest single donor to the Committee for the Re-election of the President, would visit the office for a briefing by campaign officials. I imagined being fired by a red-faced Magruder when Stone would tell him that he didn't have a nephew working for the campaign. Porter would be furious, too, and he knew a hundred other guys who would want my job.

Somehow, Ratigan managed to escort Mr. Stone from the White House to the Reelection Committee offices, where he hastily explained the practical joke and the gyrations we had put Magruder through. "Pompous ass," spat the old man, who gamely agreed to play along. I later learned that Magruder groveled to the insurance executive telling him what good care he had taken of Mr. Stone's nephew.

Also appealing to Nixon's dark side was gung ho marine Charles "Chuck" Colson. Colson was one of the few who could evade Haldeman's careful system and get Nixon's approval or direction for politically risky hardball tactics that often yielded little. Haldeman ordered Colson to check with him, even on direct orders the president issued. Colson came from Capitol Hill, where he was an aide to US Senator Leverett Saltonstall of Massachusetts. He was gung ho for Nixon's new majority coalition and maneuvered to bring Catholics and union members into the fold using the Vietnam War as a wedge issue whose opponents enraged the "silent majority."

Colson, for example, seriously entertained firebombing the Brookings Institute to obtain a copy of an FBI report that allegedly would have proved that LBJ used the FBI to wiretap Nixon's hotel rooms and campaign plane during the 1968 campaign when Nixon was having back-channel talks with the South Vietnamese to kill LBJ's October Surprise. Colson actually planned to send in burglars disguised as firemen to rifle Brookings files for the document Nixon wanted. Vice presidential aide David Keene told me Colson's greatest talent was in writing memos, taking credit for planted news stories and manufacturing telegrams and messages to the White House backing Nixon on major speeches and his Vietnam policy. "Colson was essentially full of shit," Keene told me. Colson would feed Nixon's dark side and contribute to the mania for "intelligence" and "dirty tricks."

He was effective in his outreach to unions that would become an important part of Nixon's second term blowout in 1972. While it is generally thought that it was Colson who arranged for Nixon to issue a pardon to convicted Teamster boss Jimmy Hoffa, in fact the codicle that barred Hoffa from union activities or serving in the union office was drafted and inserted by White House Counsel

John Dean. Attorney General John Mitchell wanted no part of the pardon deal knowing that Colson and Nixon wanted a quid pro quo in both cash and endorsements to spring the imprisoned union leader. While Colson transmitted interim Teamster President Frank Fitzsimmon's desire for a prohibition of Hoffa's future involvement in union politics to the president, the Mob boys would go to the back door; Murray Chotiner told me he and "Dean got it done."

Journalist Don Folsum covered the deal in *Nixon's Darkest Secrets:*

> Breaking from clemency custom, Nixon did not consult the judge who had sentenced Hoffa. Nor did he pay any mind to the US Parole Board, which had unanimously voted three times in two years to reject Hoffa's appeals for release. The board had been warned by the Justice Department that Hoffa was Mob-connected. Long-time Nixon operative Chotiner eventually admitted interceding to get Hoffa paroled. "I did it," he told columnist Jack Anderson in 1973. "I make no apologies for it. And frankly I'm proud of it."
>
> Hoffa evidently bought his way out funneling as much as $800,000 to Nixon. Teamsters expert William Bastone said in 1966 that James P. ("Junior") Hoffa and racketeer Allen Dorfman "delivered $300,000 in a black valise" to a Washington hotel to help secure the release of Hoffa "Senior" from the prison. The name of the bagman on the receiving end of the transaction is redacted from legal documents filed in a court case. Bastone said the claim is based on "FBI reports reflecting contacts with (former Teamster boss Jackie) Presser in 1971." In a recently released FBI memo confirming this, an informant details a $300,000 Mob payoff to the Nixon White House "to guarantee the release of Jimmy Hoffa from the Federal penitentiary."[26]

But there was more: a $500,000 contribution to the Nixon campaign by New Jersey Teamster leader Anthony Provenzano "Tony Pro." the head of the notorious Provenzano family, which, a House panel found in 1999, had for years dominated Teamsters New Jersey Local 560. The Provenzanos, were linked to the Genovese crime family and controlled Local 560. They were deeply involved in criminal activities, including murder, extortion, loan sharking, kickbacks, hijacking, and gambling. The contribution was delivered and President Nixon played golf with "Tony Pro."

Lyn Nofziger, the bombastic press secretary and later White House political assistant for Governor and President Ronald Reagan, was one of the toughest pols I knew. He had a sweet, sentimental side, a great sense of humor, and tremendous loyalty to those who had toiled in the vineyards of Ronald Reagan. Nofziger was no slouch when it came to tactics and was deeply respected among reporters as a straight shooter. According to White House gumshoe John Caulfield, who performed intelligence investigations for White House counsels John Ehrlichman and John Dean, Nofziger went to White House Chief of Staff H. R. "Bob" Haldeman to tell him that "Colson will get the president into trouble some day." Nofziger's warning was met with a steely response. "He gets the job done."[27]

Mitchell sent his deputy Robert Mardian to keep an eye on Haldeman's man Magruder, a climber who ass-kissed those above him and treated everyone under him like shit. Magruder pushed the intelligence plan that included the Watergate break-in put together by former FBI agent and New York Assistant District Attorney G. Gordon Liddy.

Liddy was the very crew-cutted model of a former FBI agent. At the time of his arrest he had sprouted a mustache and would jauntily be smoking a cigar when approached by reporters outside the courthouse. Liddy was open in his views about his love of German martial music and his gene pool. He was a tough law-and-order prosecutor and gun enthusiast. After the final break-in Liddy would famously offer to stand on a street corner where those higher up in the conspiracy could have him shot. "I don't think that is necessary," mumbled a stunned Jeb Magruder. Nixon himself would call Liddy "an asshole."[28]

Ironically, Liddy, who would play a pivotal role in Watergate, came to Washington and began his climb in the administration through the good graces of Congressman Gerald Ford, who would ironically later benefit from Liddy's botched break-in by replacing Nixon as president.

In 1968, Liddy ran in the Republican primary for Congress against mid-Hudson Valley Republican scion Hamilton Fish Jr., whose father held the congressional seat and whose great-grandfather was US secretary of state to Ulysses S. Grant. While Liddy would lose the Republican primary, he retained the nomination of the New York Conservative Party, and it was feared that he would drain enough votes from the moderate Republican Fish to let Democrat John S. Dyson win the seat. Liddy would first meet Ford when he chauffeured him around Dutchess County when the minority leader visited the district for a Republican Party event. Republican County Chairman George Reid would promise Liddy a job in Washington if he would back off in his Conservative Party bid for Congress (it was too late to have Liddy's name on the ballot). Harvey Dann, a prominent local insurance man, recruited Liddy to run the Nixon/Agnew campaign, burnishing his résumé for a Washington appointment. Fish, through his father, former Congressman Hamilton Fish Sr., appealed to Ford, who arranged for Liddy to be hired at the Treasury Department in return for a pledge that he would drop his congressional candidacy on the Conservative line and focus on the Nixon campaign in his home county of Dutchess.

"They interviewed Gordon at Treasury," John Barry, administrative assistant to Congressman Hamilton Fish told me. "The White House was pushing it, but this Greek [Rossides] had met Gordon and was resisting. Hammy had to put the arm lock on Ford to make it happen. Ford made it happen." This one act by Ford would bring down Nixon and made Ford president. So you can blame Ham Fish," said Barry. Indeed, Liddy's brief tenure at the Treasury Department would be turmultuous: he made a pro gun speech to the NRA, criticizing his own department. Shortly thereafter John Dean would recruit Liddy to be legal counsel to the reelection campaign on the recommendation of Egil "Bud" Krough.

I first met Liddy when he served as counsel to the Finance Committee to Reelect the President. Early one morning when arriving for work, I felt him eyeing me on the elevator. He said nothing. By the time I had poured a cup of coffee and gotten to my desk, my secretary handed me a message that Mr. Liddy wanted to see me in his office. I took the elevator to a different floor where the Finance Committee was housed. Sally Harmony, Liddy's secretary, a pleasant and efficient woman, motioned me to go right in. Liddy was reading a stack of papers. "Close the door," he said, without looking up. He looked up from his work to stare at me with intensity. "Get a fucking haircut; you represent the president of the United States. Now get the fuck out of here."

Although he was eccentric and colorful, Liddy emerged from the Watergate drama as the only man with any sense of honor. When caught, Liddy admitted his guilt and took his punishment. He refused to rat out those above him and was rewarded with maximum time. He would ultimately prevail in a litigation inspired by John Dean and filed by Dean's lawyer for Ida "Maxie" Wells, who disputed Liddy's truth telling about the break-ins, as we shall see. Liddy did what he did for ideological reasons and in my view was used by both John Dean, Jeb Magruder, and the Central Intelligence Agency.

Liddy was not experienced intelligence operative, and he was mislead by both McCord and Hunt about who both of their real loyalty was to—the agency. Liddy was a true believer, and he saw the campus radicals and groups like the Black Panther's as lawless and dangerous subversives.

The explosive Liddy would become frustrated when Mitchell rejected his proposed broad intelligence-gathering program code-named "Gemstone." When Magruder put his hand on Liddy's shoulder to console him and told him to come back with a scaled-down plan, Liddy famously shouted, "Get your hand off me or I'll kill you!"[29]

As a veteran of eight national Republican presidential campaigns, starting with Nixon and ending with George W. Bush's recount effort in Florida, with service in Ronald Reagan's three presidential campaigns, I have seen political operators come and go. When it comes to manipulating the government, the media, and the people around him, I have seen few equal John Wesley Dean. Dean has successfully woven a narrative of Watergate that is largely untrue, at the same time skillfully distancing himself from his own egregious crimes and manipulations. As we shall see, his finessing of facts, coupled with outright fabrications, is extraordinary.

Just the speed in which Dean rose in the Nixon entourage is extraordinary. Because he worked at the Justice Department prior to becoming a White House counsel, which previous White House counsel John Ehrlichman viewed as a largely ministerial job, the Haldeman-Ehrlichman axis assumed that "Dean was a Mitchell man." Dean skillfully played the Haldeman, Ehrlichman, and Mitchell camps around Nixon against each other to enhance his own power and access. Indeed, it was Dean who relentlessly pushed the political intelligence plan that included the Watergate break-in. When he seized on intelligence gathering as his ticket to the inner circle, Dean went from a small-time bureaucrat to a key White House insider with fast access to the president and his highest aides.

Incredibly, Dean admitted this in a draft of his bestseller *Blind Ambition*. "Haldeman's interested in campaign intelligence for 1972," Dean wrote. "I reflect on how I might take advantage of Haldeman's preoccupation. I was still building my law firm seeking new business and I knew the campaign would be a stepping stone to those who distinguished themselves. But as I looked ahead, I saw the Counsels' own office performing rather menial campaign tasks. [They did] legal chores hardly important enough to be admitted to the inner circle. If the Counsels' office could play the same role at the Republican Convention we played on May Day, special White

House tie lines, half hourly reports, I knew we'd be in the thicket . . . We had a jump on other White Houses offices in demonstration intelligence. Why not expand our role to all intelligence? That would be of interest to the President and the campaign."[30]

The ascendancy of John Wesley Dean in Nixon's entourage was deadly. Dean was an ambitious and ruthless operator. He roomed with Barry Goldwater Jr. at Staunton Military Academy in Virginia and was close to Senator Goldwater and his family. Dean later married the stepdaughter of Senator Thomas C. Hennings, whom he later divorced. Senator Hennings secured Dean's employment at Washington law firm Welch and Morgan in 1965.

Dean's employment at the firm ended when it was learned that, while on assignment to prepare a television license for the Continental Summit Television Corporation, he secretly filed "a rival application for himself and some friends," according to veteran Washington reporter Jack Anderson.[31] The application was for the Greater St. Louis Television Corporation, and it was discovered that Dean was a secretary for the company and a shareholder. When Dean was confronted with his double-dealing, he responded, "You don't have the right to ask me about that!"[32]

"One attorney described his exit as a 'Forced departure,'" wrote Anderson. "Another reported more explicitly that Dean wasn't even allowed to pick up his belongings, which were returned to him by mail."[33]

Following his disgraceful exodus at Welch and Morgan in February 1966, Dean was employed as the chief minority counsel to the Republican members of the United States House Committee on the Judiciary Committee from 1966–1967. Dean got the job only because Senator Goldwater himself called the minority staff director and the ranking minority committee member in the House. Dean then spent two years as associate director of the National Commission on Reform of Federal Criminal Laws.

On July 9, 1970, after Ehrlichman left the position to become Nixon's chief domestic adviser, Dean was made counsel to President

Richard Nixon. John Mitchell had attempted to discourage Dean from the post.

"I hate to see you go to the White House, because that's an awful place," Dean was told by Mitchell. "[Y]ou're going to go on up in the Department of Justice—you'll have a better job there."[34]

Dean accepted the counsel job and his modus operandi to work himself into a key position in the White House was intelligence gathering. Dean was later determined to be the "master manipulator of the cover-up" by the FBI.[35]

Reappearing in Nixon's orbit was E. Howard Hunt. Hunt was a member of Operation 40, a secret Vice President Nixon—directed CIA operation to topple Fidel Castro and reappeared in Dallas on November 22, 1963.

Interestingly, Nixon was aware of Hunt's work on clandestine operations with the White House prior to him becoming a formal consultant with his White House. When ruminating with Colson about how to break into the Brookings Institute, Nixon can be heard on the tape to say **"Get Hunt."** He would say it three months before Hunt joined the White House staff as a consultant.

Hunt would know, and indeed, be a big part of, Nixon's deepest secrets.

NOTES

1. Richard Whalen, Catch the Falling Flag, p. 272.
2. James Rosen, The Strong Man: John Mitchell and the Secrets of Watergate (Kindle Locations 802-803).
3. Leonard Garment, In Search of Deep Throat, pp. 34–35.
4. "Martha Mitchell Speaks Out," Ellensburg Daily Record, Sept. 13, 1972.
5. http://nixonfoundation.org/2013/07/len-garment-longtime-nixon-aide-and-advisor-dies-at-89/.
6. John Ehrlichman, Witness to Power: The Nixon Years, p. 22.
7. John Ehrlichman, Witness to Power: The Nixon Years, p. 35.
8. Richard Whalen, Catch the Falling Flag, p. 256.
9. Richard Kleindienst, Justice, p. 50.

10. Ibid, p. 51.
11. Len Colodny and Robert Gettlin, Silent Coup, p. 95.
12. James Rosen, The Strong Man: John Mitchell and the Secrets of Watergate (Kindle Location 947).
13. Robert D. Novak, The Prince of Darkness: 50 Years Reporting in Washington, p. 180.
14. Robert D. Novak, The Prince of Darkness: 50 Years Reporting in Washington, p. 180
15. Deborah Hart Strober and Gerald S. Strober, The Nixon Presidency: An Oral History of the Era, p. 55.
16. Richard Whalen, Catch the Falling Flag, p. 216
17. Ibid. p. 196.
18. Ibid.
19. Edmund Kallina, Kennedy v. Nixon, p. 39.
20. Leonard Garment, In Search of Deep Throat, pp. 39–40.
21. Richard Whalen, Catch the Falling Flag, p. 210.
22. Leonard Garment, In Search of Deep Throat, p. 257.
23. Ibid.
24. Ibid.
25. Robert D. Novak, The Prince of Darkness: 50 Years Reporting in Washington (Kindle Locations 3937-3938).
26. Don Fulsom, Nixon's Darkest Secrets, p. 24.
27. John Caulfield, Shield #9-11-NYPD, p. 98.
28. Vivienne Sanders, Access to History, p. IV.
29. Jeb Magruder, An American Life, p. 191.
30. Colodny interview with John Dean, Jan. 5, 1989.
31. Jack Anderson, "John Dean Once Fired For 'Unethical Conduct,'" The Tuscaloosa News, April 5, 1973.
32. Richard Kleindienst, Justice, p. 143.
33. Jack Anderson, "John Dean Once Fired For 'Unethical Conduct,'" The Tuscaloosa News, April 5, 1973.
34. Len Colodny and Robert Gettlin, Silent Coup, p. 97.
35. FBI Watergate Investigation, OPE Analysis.

CHAPTER ELEVEN

THE COMEBACK

"This time vote like your whole world depended on it—
This time Nixon."

—slogan

On a typically warm spring morning in Atlanta, Richard Nixon
would be sweating through his suit. April 9, 1968, would be no
exception. The world was watching Martin Luther King Jr.'s funeral,
and the former vice president was in town to pay his respects.

After King's assassination, Nixon's close aide John Mitchell
opposed his attendance. Nixon, who had enjoyed a good relation-
ship with King, decided he would go to the service but not join the
King family on their three-and-a-half-mile march from Ebenezer
Baptist Church, where the reverend had preached to Morehouse
College.

The conservative South was important to his presidential campaign, and Nixon knew he must attend. Still, he had to keep a low
profile to appease his white Southern supporters. His advisors
feared some far-right Southerners might bolt to George Wallace,
who was running on a segregationist line.

Travel aide Nick Ruwe accompanied Nixon to King's funeral.
Ruwe told me the former vice president decided he would arrive
late and take a back-row seat in the church's VIP section. To keep it

short and sweet, he also would not march behind King's caisson to Morehouse with Bobby, Ethel, and Jackie Kennedy, Jesse Jackson, Hosea Williams, Dr. Ralph Abernathy, Daddy King, and the others. Instead, Nixon told Ruwe to pick him up at a side door of the church as the dignitaries queued up to march.

As Rev. Abernathy finished his sermon, calling King's assassination "one of the darkest hours of mankind," Nixon turned to slip out. He stopped short with a huge hand on his shoulder.

"Mr. Nixon, you gonna march?" It was Los Angeles Laker Wilt Chamberlain, whom Nixon had met at a previous event.

All eyes were surely on the seven-foot-one black Los Angeles Laker's center as he towered over the five-foot-eleven Republican candidate for president. Nixon wisely obliged. Ruwe was confused to see his boss lining up behind the funeral procession, led by two local mules pulling a simple wooden wagon bearing the murdered Martin Luther King Jr.'s coffin.

Ruwe waved frantically to Nixon as he maneuvered the car down an adjacent street at the same slow speed of the procession. "Nixon seemed to look right through me," he later told me.

Three blocks into the march, Nixon told Chamberlin he had to get to the airport. The NBA star was in a hurry too, and asked for a lift. Wilt "The Stilt" would go to work as a paid Nixon surrogate thereafter, and 1968 presidential campaign unfolded.

* * *

Nixon began plotting his second presidential run the moment he was defeated in his first. He used the years 1960 through 1968 to analyze every aspect of his narrow loss, determined to apply all the lessons learned to his 1968 run for the White House.

In 1960, he was frustrated carrying the baggage of the Eisenhower administration, in power for eight long years. Kennedy was relentless in his criticism of what he viewed as the stand-patism of the Republicans without directly accusing the popular Eisenhower. Nixon, in many cases, was forced to defend policies with which he disagreed. Kennedy's admonition that America "had to get moving again" was easily more compelling than Nixon's theme of "experience."

Nixon's greatest single advantage in 1968 was that his party was "out." It is always easier in politics to be the "out" party; you can attack without having to defend. Nixon also benefited mightily from a deep split in the Democratic Party. High inflation and the Vietnam War made Lyndon Johnson vulnerable, and Nixon thought he could beat him. In fact, a July 1967 Harris poll proved LBJ only five points ahead of Nixon, 46-41.

Another important dynamic of the 1968 race was the independent candidacy of Alabama Governor George Wallace. The segregationist managed to get on the ballot in all fifty states through a hodge-podge of small independent parties coupled with his own American Independent Party. Nixon realized Wallace's appeal went beyond Southern conservative voters, who were likely to vote for Nixon if Wallace was not in the race; he also appealed to Northern and Midwestern blue-collar union voters who were Democrats and would have difficulty ever pulling the Republican lever.

Nixon clearly understood that, unlike the 1960 race where he needed to get 50 percent plus one, the new dynamic could allow him to become president with the Republican base and a healthy swath of conservative Democrats and suburban moderates concerned about inflation, the war, and rising crime. He knew he would likely become president with less than 50 percent of the vote—but only after skillful management of the Wallace issue.

In 1960, Nixon's pace had been frantic and the campaign had been focused on the working print press. He paced himself more carefully in the 1968 effort, with a campaign geared to the dynamics of television.

In 1968, Nixon also had the advantage of a resurgent GOP with Republican governors seizing or holding governorships in New York, Pennsylvania, Ohio, Florida, Michigan, and California. Republicans had also added forty-seven House members and three

Senators in the 1966 election. The party had been decimated in 1958, leaving a weak base for Vice President Nixon's attempt to win. The 1968 Republican Party was much stronger and hungrier for victory after the 1964 Goldwater blowout.

Nixon also had the advantage of a united Republican Party. His vanquished primary challengers—Michigan Governor George Romney, California Governor Ronald Reagan, and New York Governor Nelson Rockefeller—all offered unambiguous support.

In Rockefeller's case, although Nixon did not carry New York State, there was no evidence of the governor dragging his feet like he did in 1960. This was where Nixon's status as "the most broadly accepted man" paid off. While the liberal and conservative factions of the party could not live with leadership by each other, "Nixon was acceptable to both sides." While he may not be their first choice, he was the most broadly accepted second choice. His record as an anti-Communist and the man who "nailed" Alger Hiss combined with his slashing attacks on the Democratic left satisfied the Sunbelt conservative while his civil rights record and stout internationalism pleased Eastern liberals.

Recognizing his liabilities and his reputation as a "loser," Nixon later said he entered the Republican primaries intent to win them resolutely to dispel the stink clinging to him since his back-to-back defeats for president and governor of California. To recast himself, he worked with some of the most talented public relations experts in history.

* * *

Nixon's famous animosity towards reporters is perplexing: the press made Richard Nixon. Favorable newspaper coverage of his role nailing Alger Hiss as a Communist spy made him a national figure. He generally enjoyed favorable newspaper coverage in his eight years as vice president, where he used his adept knowledge of the workings of the Eisenhower administration to leak stories selectively and curry favor with the big newspapers.

Nixon remembered well how quickly the press had turned on him in the 1952 secret fund scandal. There, he salvaged his vice presidential candidacy by going on national TV in the celebrated Checkers speech—contrary to the orders of Eisenhower's advisors that he quit the ticket. Nixon distrusted the press from that day forward. It got worse in 1960, when reporters heaped praise on the handsome and cultured John F. Kennedy and painted him as a frumpy relic of the 1950s.

The press corps bought heavily into the myth of Camelot, even before Jackie Kennedy gave it that name. They regarded Nixon as hopelessly square, solidly middle-class as well as devious, deceptive, and ambitious. Still, more national newspapers would endorse Nixon than Kennedy in the 1960 contest.

According to biographer Stephen Ambrose, "The way the press had fawned on Kennedy had made Nixon furious and jealous; all that money and the things Kennedy had gotten away with had made Nixon resentful." From then on, Nixon would blame the media for many of his professional difficulties and his eventual resignation.

Nixon also blamed the press for his 1962 loss to Pat Brown in the California gubernatorial race. "Most of the media are out of step politically with the rest of the country,"[1] Nixon would later write. "[The] media consider themselves outside of and above the society at large, looking down haughtily as they fire thunderbolts at us."[2]

Some reporters, like Richard Bergholz of the *Los Angeles Times*, were just outright hostile. Still, Nixon earned more than his share of newspaper endorsements in his race against Brown too.[3] "Why did the media hate him so much? I have always thought it was because he was vulnerable and showed it when attacked," assessed Nixon speech writer Ben Stein. "He did not have the tough hide of a Reagan or an Obama. Like the schoolyard bullies they are, the media went after him for his vulnerability" (Ben Stein, "The Truth about Nixon," CNN.com, June 4, 2014).

Nixon's response to the broad perception that he was tricky, devious, duplicitous, and manipulative with the press was to launch "Operation Candor." Biographer Anthony Summers would incorrectly report that "Operation Candor" was launched in the days of Watergate. In fact, it was the title of an earlier Nixon strategy to soften press suspicion and belligerence. He made himself accessible to the working press on the record and was willing to answer any question on any subject. He used these opportunities to demonstrate a more relaxed and easy-going demeanor; he used self-deprecating humor to soften his image.

Although Nixon attempted to renegotiate his relationship with the press, there were certain drawbacks in "Operation Candor." For some reason, Nixon could not resist the impulse to point out to reporters exactly where he was being political. In 1967, Stephen Hess and David Broder, the essentially cautious and sympathetic (to Nixon) coauthors of *The Republican Establishment*, noted that the man always "compounded his own problem," by letting reporters see "Nixon the Manipulator," "the man of technique, not of substance . . . Nixon is not content to be admired. Rather than let the reporters discover for themselves how he adapts his basic speech to the situation, he goes on to say, 'Now, this is a pretty conservative district, so you'll notice I don't bear down as heavily on . . .' or 'The Democratic incumbent here has been a very good Congressman, so I'm going to have to stay away from personalities and concentrate on . . .'"

For some odd reason, he insisted on pointing out to reporters the artifice of his performance as if he was proud of the stagecraft. He explained, in detail, some of his various political devices and his motives for using them. For example, he told reporter Jules Witcover that the occasional favorable comment about the opposition was "a device, of course, to show I'm fair-minded."[4]

It was on the stump, even more than to reporters, that Nixon worked Operation Candor. Of course, he made sure people knew how candid he was being, by constantly drawing their attention to it. Some of his oft-used phrases preceding a statement included: "to be perfectly candid," "speaking quite frankly," "putting it bluntly," "let me be quite precise," and "let me make it perfectly clear."[5] If

Nixon was being accused of being tricky and secretive he went to great lengths to appear frank and candid. While the media heard Nixon brag about his techniques, the voters only saw the new "candid" Nixon.

In fact, "Operation Candor" served its purposes through 1967 and the string of Republican primary victories through early 1968 and would still be operational going into the Republican National Convention in Miami.

After Nixon's convention coronation, he entered a whole new world of television in the general election. His team had already tested the medium on a regional and state basis in Nixon's $10 million nomination drive. During the primaries, Nixon spoke to voters through earned media coverage of his campaign and cutting-edge television commercials. The ads reintroduced Nixon to voters under tightly controlled conditions that were artfully made to look spontaneous.

In the 1960 general election, Nixon's disastrous performance in the first debate with John F. Kennedy nearly ended his career. The contest gave the American public the visual of a sweaty, pasty, uncomfortable, shuffling Nixon. In contrast, Kennedy was tanned, calm, and presidential. It revived the picture of Nixon as untrustworthy, as "Tricky Dick." Media theorist Marshall Mcluhan said Nixon resembled "the railway lawyer who signs leases that are not in the best interests of the folks in the little town." The much-ballyhooed "last press conference" set Nixon back even further.

Nixon's relationship with television scalded him in 1960. It was a far cry from his September 1952 Checkers speech, when he used the medium skillfully to save himself. And experts were poised to use television to land him in the White House.

In November 1967, White House speechwriter Ray Price wrote one of the best campaign strategy memos in history; it rates a full read by anyone with an interest in politics. In his early-stage strategy discussion, the aide framed Nixon as a tentative frontrunner with uncertain support and a robust challenger in Romney. He called Reagan the charismatic candidate, and Rockefeller the not-Nixon.

According to Price, Nixon's greatest challenge was overcoming the conventional wisdom that he couldn't win—and it had to be accomplished by early April. Price described a soiled candidate who just "feels" like a loser. And his advice: understand the depth of the sour sentiment and simply start over with Nixon.

"…[W]e should be concentrating on building a received image of RN as the kind of man proud parents would ideally want their sons to grow up to be: a man who embodies the national ideal, its aspirations, its dreams, a man whose image the people want in their homes as a source of inspiration, and whose voice they want as the representative of their nation in the councils of the world, and of their generation in the pages of history.[6]

"That's what being a 'winner' means, in Presidential terms.

"What, then, does this mean in terms of our uses of time and of media between now and April 2?

"For one thing, it means investing whatever time RN needs in order to work out firmly in his own mind that vision of the nation's future that he wants to be identified with. This is crucial. It goes beyond the choice of a slogan, beyond the choice of a few key 'issues'; it's essential to the projection of RN as the man for the '70s.

"Secondly, it suggests that we take the time and the money to experiment, in a controlled manner, with film and television techniques, with particular emphasis on pinpointing those controlled uses of the television medium that can best convey the image we want to get across.

"I know the whole business of contrived image-mongering is repugnant to RN, with its implication of slick gimmicks and phony merchandising. But it's simply not true that honesty is its own salesman; for example, it takes makeup to make a man look natural on TV. Similarly, it takes art to convey the truth from us to the viewer. And we have to bear constantly in mind that it's not what we say that counts, but what the listener hears; not what we project, but how the viewer receives the impression . . . One of our great assets for 1968 is the sense that RN comes to the fray freshened by an experience rare among men in public life, and unique among those of his generation: after a meteoric rise, followed by eight years at the center of power and the grinding experience of a Presidential campaign, time as a private citizen to reflect on the lessons of public service, on the uses of power, on the directions of change— and in so doing to develop a perspective on the Presidency that no serious candidate in this century has had the chance to achieve. It's a perspective that an incumbent cannot have, because one has to get away from the office to see it whole; and that an outsider cannot have, because one has to have been there to know its nature.

"Another thing we've got to get across is a sense of human warmth. This is vital to the Presidential mystique, and has largely been the 'hidden side' of RN, as far as the public is concerned. And it can be gotten across without loss of either dignity or privacy. It shines through in a lot of those spontaneous moments that have been caught on film."

Price's strategy memo describes the power of television in ways that stand true a half-century later. In his view, Nixon needed to be cut loose on television in safe but inspiring circumstances, in "cool" uses of TV leaving "cool" impressions. "In this third dimension," he wrote, "style and substance are inseparable." He proposed first dispatching the stink of two failed campaigns, then selling the new, improved Nixon as a unique specimen.

Veteran advertising man H. R. "Bob" Haldeman also understood how television would revolutionize the daily campaign. Instead of running Nixon ragged through grueling days of campaigning with multiple events, Nixon would pace himself by seeking one major media event timed for maximum evening television coverage per day. The Nixon shown to voters through the television news was tanned and relaxed, and he played to maximum-capacity rallies put together by his able advance man "Rally John" Nidecker. One- on- one interviews with the candidate were rare, and Nixon ducked the big weekend talk shows like *Meet the Press* and *Face the Nation*, relenting to do them only in the closing weeks, when the race with Humphrey appeared close. Nixon would talk to voters on the evening news and through the relentless shower of thirty- and 60-second TV ads.

Seeking to make Ray Price's memo a reality, Leonard Garment put together and led a media team comprised of himself, former CBS executive Frank Shakespeare, and J. Walter Thompson ad man Harry Treleaven. Together they would make Nixon more accessible to voters by making the candidate less accessible to the press. While Shakespeare and Treleaven certainly understood the medium, it was twenty-eight-year-old Roger Ailes who transformed Nixon's public image through remarkable use of television.

Prior to working for Nixon, Ailes was the boy wonder executive producer of *The Mike Douglas Show*. Ailes, who had worked himself up from prop boy three years prior, was responsible for turning Douglas's career around and transforming his show into a ratings bonanza.

Ailes knew television. On January 9, 1968, he met Nixon backstage, who was scheduled for an interview on set with Douglas.

"It's a shame a man has to use gimmicks like this to get elected," Nixon said, flippantly.

"Television is not a gimmick," Ailes said.[7] "Mr. Nixon, you need a media advisor."

"What's a media advisor?" Nixon asked.

"I am," the twenty-seven-year-old responded.[8] Len Garment hired Ailes soon after as a part-time media consultant. The Nixon of 1968, instead of regarding television again with hangdog indifference, hired staffers who could quote media theorists like McLuhan like scripture, men in touch with the new age of electronic media. These men knew what was said on the box was not nearly as important as what was seen on it.

As media critic Neil Postman noted: "[T]hink of Richard Nixon, or Jimmy Carter or Billy Graham, or even Albert Einstein, what will come to your mind is an image, a picture of a face, most likely a face on a television screen (in Einstein's case, of photograph of a face). Of words, almost nothing will come to mind. This is the difference between thinking in a word-centered culture and thinking in an image-centered culture."

To Marshall McLuhan, it didn't matter that Nixon was intellectually superior or more able to explain policy; his style was not suited to the medium of TV. Kennedy, more poised, quippier, and cool, came across to television viewers as the more agreeable candidate. Style was the substance of television. As McLuhan famously said, "The medium is the message."

Or as Joe McGinniss, who penned the advertisement-angled 1968 campaign book *The Selling of the President*, wrote, "The medium is the massage and the masseur gets the votes."[9]

Ailes was less poetic when describing communication in the new age of media. "I wasn't worried about the message; I was worried about the backlighting," he said.[10]

Jules Witcover summed up the revolutionary multitrack media strategy of the new Nixon after the Nixon traveling entourage in New Hampshire went to a secret TV taping the morning after a party the Nixon staff had for the press. No presidential campaign would ever be the same. It set the template for how presidential campaigns would be run. Ailes would recrest the magic for George Bush in "Ask George Bush," and Mitt Romney would utilize the staged "exposure" to real voters:

> For many of the political reported at the party, there had been too many New Nixons for them to accept easily this latest version of a friendly and candid one. Yet Nixon at the press party had made a specific point of assuring his assembled guests that this time around he would be making himself available frequently for briefings and interviews, and that reporters would not be kept in the dark about anything he was going as a campaigner.
>
> Early the very next morning, however, as the press corps slept, Nixon, Buchanan and a few other aides slipped out of the hotel.

They drove over deserted roads to the near town of Hillsborough, where a small group of townspeople, farmers and college students handpicked by the local Nixon committee had gathered for an "entirely unrehearsed" discussion with the candidate at the Hillsborough Community Hall. A paid television crew recorded the scene for use in later television commercials. When word leaked out, Buchanan defended the slippery caper on grounds that the presence of reporters might "inhibit those people."

The goodwill generated by the press party didn't last very long in light of that episode. Nor was it restored the next day when the traveling press corps was taken by bus to another "entirely unrehearsed" meeting of preselected locals—but obliged to remain outside the hall as uniformed guards admitted the citizen props for another taping session.

What the press corps was seeing—or, rather, not seeing—was the second segment of a basic two-tracked campaign for the presidency that had been carefully thought out by Nixon and aides during the long night of his private citizenship after 1962.

The first track was the obvious and unavoidable public campaigning in the primaries—the speeches, the rallies, the handshaking walks through small towns—that was traditional in the presidential politics of the era . . .

It could, however, be carefully controlled in what the candidate said and did and when he said and did it. Nixon in 1960 had campaigned nonstop, with events from morning to night daily that wore him into the ground in the process. In 1968 he would severely limit his appearances on the first, public, track. With television becoming increasingly dominant in presidential politics, Nixon would hold relatively few public appearance each day, almost always well scripted, and timed early enough in the day and located conveniently enough to major airports for television crews to ship their film of the events by air to the network shows in New York.

Meanwhile, on the second track, Nixon would be presented to the voters in the most positive light, in television commercials prepared by Madison Avenue wizards, fashioned sometimes from the closed-door meetings with preselected voters and sometimes carefully created in television studios. This second track, unlike the first, could be pursued out of easy scrutiny by the press, and in time it began to crowd out the first track as the view of the candidate actually seen by the voters. It was expensive, to be sure, but at the time there was no federal limitation on how much money could be contributed to or spent on a presidential campaign. And Nixon had a powerful fund-raising operation going that generated all the funds needed for the second track.[11]

Roger Ailes recognized that instead of changing Nixon, it would be easier to control the medium. He knew if the campaign was putting out the product, every detail was under their direction. "Those stupid bastards on the set designing crew put turquoise curtains in the background," Ailes said as they designed a set in Chicago prior to the fall campaign. "Nixon wouldn't look right unless he was carrying a pocketbook."[12]

Ailes worked to erase Nixon's image as a partisan slasher by making him look calmer, more mature, more balanced, and more measured. He made Nixon look like a statesman who was knowledgeable, firm, and experienced. Just as important, Ailes schooled Nixon on how to work with the camera to avoid looking shifty and, above all, to seem like he had the gravitas to be president. Ailes also struggled with Nixon's propensity to sweat under the klieg lights, a quality when combined with his shifty eyes, made Nixon look nervous and even duplicitous.

More importantly, Ailes created a format that made it appear Nixon was being spontaneously questioned and was risking all. In fact, the atmospherics of the television exchange were tightly controlled and Nixon was risking absolutely nothing. In the post-convention phase of the campaign, where the national and local press had no access, the patented answers Nixon delivered in Ailes tightly controlled format were how most voters received Nixon's position on the issues. "He [Nixon] felt that if the public heard his own words directly, the chances of effective distortion by newsmen diminished," wrote Herb Klein.[13]

The "man in the arena" concept, developed by Ailes, was so effective that it would later be used by two other presidential candidates uncomfortable in their own skin: George H. W. Bush and Mitt Romney. The in-studio audience was handpicked. The questions were written beforehand. The answers were scripted, Nixon was center stage, and the furious media was locked outside the studio looking in.

In a meticulous outline of the format, Ailes detailed everything from the tanning of the candidate and Nixon's posture, to the desired gender and race demographic of the audience.

Ailes used the "man in the arena" tapings to humanize Nixon, who, standing without a podium and surrounded by people, appeared spontaneous, warm, slightly humorous, self-deprecating, more mature and seasoned, and, above all less tricky. The partisan slasher of the 1950s was gone. Here was a man of vast experience, who had used his time out of office to reflect on the great challenges of our times and was ready to provide a war-divided America with "new ideas and new leadership."

Ailes' deft camera work as Nixon responded to questions from "typical Americans" sold people the new Nixon. In fact, the canny media consultant had extenders fitted to all TV camera zoom lenses, and had Nixon's eyes specially lit so as not to appear dark or shifty. The close camera work created an intimacy that, for the first time ever, made people comfortable with Richard Nixon.

Aware hot television lights made Nixon sweat, Ailes mandated the studio air conditioner be turned up at least a full four hours prior to the broadcast and limited camera rehearsal as much as possible to keep the lights off and the heat down. All studio doors were ordered sealed. Ailes had Nixon dab himself with a chemically treated towel between takes to avoid the beads of sweat that would form on his upper lip.

Ailes also controlled Nixon's major speeches and an effective, but staged telethon in the closing days of the campaign. Nixon drafted most of his own major speeches on yellow legal pads, longhand. He strained through several arduous drafts, only stringing together 2,500 to 3,000 words a week.[14]. Nixon "didn't recite the speech, but 'saw' the text unreeling before his mind's eye," he would tell speechwriter Richard Whalen.[15]

Ailes displayed the new Nixon in the former vice president's acceptance speech at the 1968 Republican Convention in Miami Beach. These were the days of gavel-to-gavel network coverage, with all three networks broadcasting the speech to millions.

Many years later, Nixon told me over dinner in his Saddle River, New Jersey, home that it was Ailes who taught him how to drop his voice for emphasis as opposed to picking up the volume. Nixon used the technique with great effect in his "I see a small boy who hears far off train whistles in the night" speech where he described how he lived the American dream.

The speech was so effective at displaying the new Nixon—and burying the old one—that Ailes cut it into thirty- and sixty-second TV spots, which ran through September. Ailes took his final shot at the electorate in a two hour election eve telethon broadcast live nationwide.

Ailes' freewheeling style did not mesh well with Nixon's Teutonic high command. The media advisor had a blunt and direct style; he would tell you exactly what he thought. Although Ailes thought Nixon had the capability to be president, he wasn't a sycophant, like most of the men Nixon gathered around himself. The television genius ran afoul of Haldeman when he was quoted as saying:

"Let's face it, a lot of people think Nixon is dull. Think he's a bore, a pain in the ass. They look at him as the kind of kid who always carried a bookbag. Who was forty-two years old the day he was born. They figure other kids got footballs for Christmas, Nixon got a briefcase and he loved it. He'd always have his homework done and he'd never let you copy. Now you put him on television, you've got a problem right away. He's a funny-looking guy. He looks like somebody just hung him in a closet overnight and he jumps out in the morning with his suit all bunched up and starts running around saying, "I want to be President." I mean this is how he strikes some people. That's why these shows are important. To make them forget all that.[16]

Nixon would find more innovative ways to utilize the medium of television and soften his public image. In the midst of the 1968 campaign, Nixon agreed to help out a friend, NBC writer Paul Keyes, in providing a cameo for the show Paul worked as head writer on *Roland and Martin's Laugh-In*. The cameo was brief, only five seconds and four words long, but its influence was out of proportion to its size. *Laugh-In* producer George Schlatter would later apologize for what he believed was his role in helping to elect President Nixon.[17]

While most readers today will be unfamiliar with *Laugh-In*, during its five-year run from 1968 to 1973 it sought to represent the alternative culture of the late sixties for a mass audience. That is, it appealed to young members of the hippie movement for its appearance and somewhat manic style, while still being able to be enjoyed by the individuals who made up what Nixon would popularize as "the silent majority," *Laugh-In* felt new enough to woo America's youth, while being old enough in content to protect the sensibilities of an older generation of viewers as well.[18] As a result of this duality it was tailor made for Nixon's campaign in 1960, in which the old anti-Communist who cut his bones in exposing Alger Hiss, mellowed his image to avoid turning off voters.

In the years after his 1962 electoral defeat in the California governors race, Paul Keyes had become a fixture in Nixonland. He was placed on the payroll intermittently between then in the campaign, largely used to write jokes for Nixon's speeches, and generally make Dick Nixon appear more likeable.[19] *Laugh-In* cohost Dan Rowan recalled that during the 1968 campaign, Keyes would receive calls from Nixon "four or five times a week," and it was this closeness that enabled him to talk Nixon into appearing on the show.[20]

However, Nixon's decision to participate in the show met with concern among many of his senior staff, to whom the idea of a potential president taking part in a cheap and somewhat vulgar gag (earlier in the bit one of the show's female characters suffered a number of unfortunate accidents, including having her dress ripped off and her underwear soaked in water) appeared inappropriate. After some negotiation regarding what exactly Nixon would say on the show between Keyes, Schlatter, and the Nixon team the participation in the "sock-it-to-me" gag was decided upon. Schlatter recalls that Nixon required around "six takes" because in his early shots Nixon appeared angry or irritated.[21]

Ultimately, the end result of the *Laugh-In* gag was worth it for the Nixon camp. The candidate comes off even today as, if not a natural comedian, an earnest and enthusiastic participant. Some have pointed out that the genius of Nixon's performance lies not in the quality of Nixon's acting, but rather in the unique manner in which he addressed the performance.[22] If you watch the clips available online today of the entire gag, one is struck by the way in which the other actors speak the line not as a question (that is, they do not appear to be asking, "[are you going to] sock it to me?"), but rather as a statement, or declaration (i.e., "here we go again"). Nixon stood that on its head, and presented the line as a surprised question, exactly as one would expect any normal individual to do so when confronted with the potential to endure one of the show's torments for those being "socked."

It is strange to consider and perhaps objectively a little silly; however, this simple distinction is enough to help make Nixon appear more normal. After the appearance, and in realizing the potential effect the show had, apparently unintentionally, had on a close race, they reached out to the campaign of Vice President Humphrey and offered to let him make a similar cameo. Humphrey's camp passed on the opportunity, fearing that the show creators would manufacture a way of making the candidate look silly; in point of fact, Schlatter has claimed that all they wanted Humphrey to say was, "I'll sock it to you, Dick!"[23] In the end, *Laugh-In* was but one part of the effort to "reinvent" Nixon during the 1968 campaign, but it must be viewed as one of the most successful parts in which Nixon managed to find some common cause with the countercultural movement sweeping across Americas youth.

Many amusing anecodotes came from the '68 campaign. Nixon often golfed with show business legend Jackie Gleason. Gleason's appetite for alcohol, food, and beautiful women was legendary. Gleason was a good golfer, and he and Nixon would hit the links in Miami Beach when Nixon was president. Nixon needed only two drinks to be as inebriated as Gleason. They would have many rounds in the clubhouse after playing a Miami Beach course. A particular drunken night of revelry between the chief executive and "The Great One" would become Internet legend. Gleason's last wife, Beverly, had revealed that the president and the actor became engaged in a vigorous drunken conversation about UFO's and that Nixon had taken Gleason to a secret military installation when he showed the comedian proof of alien beings. "He [Jackie] and Nixon were in contact quite a bit and I'm not sure how that was arranged, but it seems that their meetings were set up by an associate of Nixon's," said Mrs. Gleason. "After he got back, he was very pleased he had an opportunity to see the dead little men in cases, he · explained to me what they looked like and was still talking about it the next day."[24] The last Mrs. Gleason offered no documentation, but her story is widely believed in the new media. Gleason would tape an effective television appeal for Nixon in the former vice president's 1968 comeback bid. Wearing a $1,500 three-piece suit, natty tie, and red carnation, Gleason stared into the camera and said, "I don't usually get involved in politics, but we need Dick Nixon," in a devastatingly effective television spot engineered by television genius Roger Ailes.[25]

* * *

Despite his years of preparation, Nixon's renomination at the 1968 Republican National Convention in Miami Beach was, as the Duke of Wellington said at Waterloo, "a close-run thing."

Nixon correctly foresaw the collapse of George Romney's campaign and was always apprehensive about the maneuvers of Nelson Rockefeller, the one man with the money to deny him the presidency. Still, Rockefeller was indecisive in times requiring bold moves, and Nixon always knew Reagan was the most likely competitor to stop his bid for another shot at the ultimate prize.

Thanks to the best campaign team in contemporary US politics, the Nixon who approached the 1968 Republican nomination was very differently positioned than he was in 1960. But the GOP was not the party he led to defeat in 1960, either.

Until 1964, Nixon did not grasp the extent power in the Republican Party had shifted from the Eastern/Wall Street wing of the party to the Sunbelt conservatives. It was a hard-learned lesson: in 1960 he tried to tailor his national candidacy to the establishment by letting Rockefeller dictate the party platform and taking Brahmin Henry Cabot Lodge as his running mate. Even with Goldwater's name being put forward for president prematurely at the 1960 convention, Nixon didn't yet recognize the conservative tidal wave to come. In 1962, he offended California's right wing by denouncing the notorious John Birch Society. While he still won the Republican primary for governor, a right-wing oilman, Assemblyman Joe Shell, ran well against him. Nixon knew right-wingers sat on their hands and watched him lose to Pat Brown by almost three hundred thousand votes.

Nixon's maneuvering in late 1963 and early 1964, when he tried and failed to urge party moderates into blocking Goldwater without leaving his own fingerprints, also carried with it the false assumption that party moderates could actually stop the Arizona senator. It was a fool's errand. Standing at that convention podium, Nixon finally saw the fervor of the delegates who nominated Goldwater and their loud remonstrations against Nelson Rockefeller, the preeminent symbol of the party's Eastern establishment. At that moment, watching the boisterous delegates, he realized the Republican base had shifted from beneath party moderates.

John Mitchell and Richard Kleindienst would build a formidable national organization that would sweep the primaries, clinch the nominations, and defeat the Democrats in the fall.

Kleindienst would note in his memoirs that "[i]n putting together the delegate field force I turned to my former coworkers in the 1964 Goldwater delegate campaign. I chose those I thought most effective. First on board were Dick Herman from Omaha and Bob Mardian from Pasadena. In addition to taking over the Midwest and the western regions for us, they were responsible for recruiting other regional directors and state chairman. It wasn't long before the whole field organization was in place. For some strange reason *The New York Times* and the Washington Post—not exactly Nixon or Goldwater supporters—never picked up the fact that the Nixon delegate operation was composed mainly of persons who were part of the Goldwater field operation."[26]

An interesting book on Nixon's impact on the modern-day political culture, Rick Perlstein's *Nixonland*, claims Nixon's 1968 campaign was rocked by Ronald Reagan's late entry into the race and a Reagan-Rockefeller alliance to deny him victory on the first Miami Beach ballot. This is wrong: Rockefeller was never a threat from the left; Nixon feared Reagan from the right. Still, he eyed the Manhattan millionaire warily.

In fact, the Nixon team's meticulous preparation would ensure that Reagan, despite his formidable talents at persuasion and the growing affection for him on the Republican right, could not pry the nomination loose from the former vice president.

Just as he had in 1960, Nixon regarded New York Governor Nelson Rockefeller as a potential rival for the 1968 nomination. Rockefeller counted on Romney to block Nixon's early ascent, but harbored ambitions to enter the race himself. Shockingly, Rockefeller prepared to enter the race after the early collapse of

Romney, who stumbled badly after claiming that US military figures had "brainwashed" him over the war in Vietnam. The comment killed his campaign.[27]

Romney campaigned aggressively in New Hampshire while the supremely organized Nixon paced himself, visiting the Granite State only three times. Polls indicated Romney faced certain and decisive defeat, so he withdrew. Since it was too late to remove his name from the primary ballot, Nixon swamped the governor badly.

A hastily organized Rockefeller write-in for New Hampshire failed miserably, too, but afterward the millionaire appeared to step into Romney's role as the foil to Richard Nixon. His campaign moved forward under the appearance of a national draft effort directed by Maryland Governor Spiro T. Agnew. The draft failed to gain steam, but that didn't dampen Agnew's enthusiastic support. The national press corps was certain that Rockefeller was preparing to join the fray and openly challenge Nixon. Rockefeller did nothing to dispel this perception when he scheduled a televised press conference. The reporters were stunned at Rockefeller's surprise announcement that "a majority of Republicans favor the candidacy of former Vice President Richard Nixon" and that he would not run. Rockefeller's announcement would hit like a bomb. Journalist Dennis Wainstock would describe the scene:

"Rockefeller had failed to give Spiro Agnew, head of the national draft Rockefeller headquarters in Annapolis, advance notice. 'Rockefeller had a list of people he was to call before making his announcement,' recalled [Rockefeller aide Emmett John] Huges. But Rockefeller's public relations adviser, Ted Braun, insisted that 'it would just upset you to have these conversations before you go into your press conference.' Agnew had invited the press to his office to watch what he expected to be Rockefeller's announcement of candidacy. After hearing Rockefeller's withdrawal, observers noted, Agnew 'just sat there frozen… saw his jaw open slightly for a second,' and 'a kind of barely perceptible sick grin came over his face for an instant.' 'it made Agnew look like a total fool,' recalled Huges. 'He never forgave 'Rocky' for it.'" [28]

According to author Jules Whitcover, Rockefeller's grave error threw a window of opportunity wide open for Nixon:

"Agnew's disappointment and humiliation were not lost on the Nixon camp. John Sears, the young lawyer in Nixon's law firm who was serving as a principal delegate-hunter, was in Alaska at the time, courting Governor Walter Hickel. As Sears recalled the situation later:

"Nixon was going crazy thinking Rockefeller was getting into the race, so I told him I'd go up to Alaska and get Hickel to come out for him. He'd been for Romney, and Nixon had been mad at him over that.

"So I called up Milhous and said, 'One thing you've got to do, is call up this guy Agnew.' He thought Agnew was a Rockefeller guy so he was fighting me over it, which made you feel pretty good, because if he was fighting over it, it meant he was probably going to do it. But he didn't like the idea. I told him, 'Look, if you're even seen with the guy in the next week, it'll do a lot.'" [29]

The relationship between Nixon and his vice president, Spiro T. Agnew, is a curious one that bears analysis. Agnew was considered a "moderate Republican" largely because his opponent in the 1966 governor's race had been segregationist George Mahoney. Mahoney's campaign slogan was "a man's home is his castle." Mahoney won the Democratic primary in a multi-candidate field. Agnew, the Baltimore County executive, was able to cobble together a coalition of blacks, Republicans, Jews, and liberal Democrats to beat Mahoney. When Baltimore's city erupted with racial violence, Agnew took a surprisingly hard line, which was noted among party conservatives including Nixon.

Despite the elaborate deception of Nixon "consulting" party leaders, John Sears told columnist Jules Witcover that Agnew had been selected several weeks before the convention. Agnew solved a problem for Nixon. Nixon needed a united party to have any kind of shot in 1968. Agnew was acceptable to party liberals like Rockefeller, Javits, Scranton, Congressman John Lindsay, and George Romney. Agnew was also acceptable to Strom Thurman and Barry Goldwater. Nixon's circle of advisors, including Sears and Buchanan, all favored Reagan. Nixon had no intention of being overshadowed by his running mate. Speechwriter Richard Whalen pushed Oregon Senator Mark Hatfield, who was becoming a vocal opponent of the Vietnam War. This was a nonstarter because of Nixon's cultivated strength in the South.

Then Nixon focused on Massachusetts Governor John Volpe. Volpe would have been a naked grab with the Catholic vote, and Volpe would have been the first Italian-American nominee for the national ticket. Instead, Nixon split the difference and took Agnew. It was to be a blunder almost as great as his bum selection of Henry Cabot Lodge in 1960. It is important to note that Agnew was a handsome man, always elegantly tailored and carefully groomed. He made a good first impression, but he was a political amateur who found it hard to adjust to the pressure cooker of a national campaign.

Nixon's initially misread Agnew. "There can be a mystique about the man," Nixon assured reporters. "You can look him in the eyes and know he's got it."[30] Nixon's assessment of Agnew would later change. He told me Agnew was "well meaning" but a "dope." Nixon had no qualms, though, about selecting Agnew because he had no intention of committing himself to the proposition that Agnew would be his successor as president or even the presidential nominee of the Republican Party.

Agnew stumbled through a series of gaffes early in his campaigning, but Nixon, ever mindful of the way Eisenhower undercut him as presidential candidate, remained supportive. Agnew's appearances were focused on Southern and border states, where he proved to be somewhat effective, limiting the defection of white conservatives to Wallace.

Nixon, later froze Agnew out of any other policy or political role other than that of attack dog in the new administration. He did, however, assemble a talented staff that included longtime Bush associate Roy Goodearle, press secretary Vick Gold, special assistant David A. Keene, who had been national chairman of Young Americans for Freedom, and scheduler John Damgard. Sears would have charted Agnew's grab for the 1976 nomination if Agnew had survived.

Nixon used Agnew as much as Eisenhower had used him to attack the president's critics on the left. Due to this, Agnew gained a substantial following of the right wing of the party. He decorated the media, the academics, and the hippies. In 1970 he took the lead in attacking the Senate Democrats as "radic-libs" or "radical liberals." Agnew did agitate against some of the more progressive policies of the Nixon administration, such as the Family Assistance Plan. After 1964, though, Nixon was always cognizant of his right flank. He was glad when the FAP—a proposal of Daniel Patrick Moynihan—went down in the Senate, but unlike Agnew, Nixon understood optics. At the same time Nixon was furious when Agnew spoke up at an NSC meeting about his opposition to the president's proposed opening to China.

* * *

Nixon and Agnew met soon in New York City, and both men walked away impressed. While he didn't leave the Rockefeller camp immediately, the Maryland governor made clear signals he was looking favorably upon Nixon. Nixon would ask Agnew to give his nominating speech, and to the surprise of virtually everyone Spiro T. "Ted" Agnew would end up as Nixon's vice presidential running mate and the vice president of the United States. He would resign after pleading *nolo contendere* to charges of accepting bribes and cheating on his taxes in 1974. Agnew would tell me he was set up to be moved out of the line of presidental sucession and would make this compelling case in his own book

Rockefeller and Nixon were cordial rivals since Rocky was elected governor of the Empire State in 1958. When Rockefeller was assistant secretary of state for Latin American affairs under President Dwight Eisenhower, he shared Nixon's conviction that Castro was a Communist and had to go. Rockefeller was probably even more deeply concerned than Nixon because of his family's vast Latin American holdings in countries where Castro was seeking to export Marxism and nationalize industries and land holdings.

The Dartmouth-educated Rockefeller had deep ties to the Eastern establishment and was close to the the pillars of that community, the Dulles brothers, John Hay "Jock" Whitney, John McCloy, Walter Thayer, Henry Luce, the Cowles brothers, and Tom Dewey. He also had close ties to the CIA; he made his Latin American business available to the agency as a front. Nixon and Rockefeller were friendly prior to Rocky's big governor win in 1958. Rockefeller weighed a challenge to the two-term sitting vice president in 1960, but former Republican National Chairman Len Hall and the cagy, dapper Tom Dewey convinced him not to run.

"I would have put Dewey on the Supreme Court. Hell, I would have made him Chief Justice if he'd have taken it. An enormously able man," Nixon told me over dinner in his Saddle River home after we split a bottle of Chateaubriand. "Hell, he got Rocky out, but by the time I offered Dewey the slot after '68, he thought he was too old."

Rocky made a half-hearted effort on Nixon's behalf in New York State in 1960. Nixon refused to concede the state to Kennedy, and baseball great Jackie Robinson campaigned with Nixon in New York City, while running mate Henry Cabot Lodge did a late tour of upstate hitting Syracuse, Rochester, and Buffalo. Rocky later earned the enmity and hatred of the party's right wing when he openly sought to block Goldwater's nomination in '64 and linked the Arizona Senator with "extremists" like the John Birch Society and the Ku Klux Klan.

Nixon was leery of Rockefeller throughout his career. He knew the governor, like the Kennedys, paid large salaries to extraordinarily talented and capable staffers and that he had access to the highest reaches of the New York *Herald-Tribune*, the voice of liberal Republicanism of the time.

Watching the New York governor flirt with the primaries, then back away, Nixon knew Rockefeller wasn't going away. Nixon also knew he had the resources and the access to launch a formidable drive for the 1968 nomination. But he also knew the party had shifted beneath Rockefeller's feet—and Dick Nixon had shifted with it.

* * *

Nixon and Campaign Manager John Mitchell understood his weakness on the right in a second ballot and always knew it was Reagan, not Rockefeller, who might pose problems the second time around and win the nomination on the third. That's why Nixon had worked so hard to recruit key party conservatives. This was made particularly difficult by Reagan himself, who wouldn't let on he was running at all.

It is important to examine the seriousness of Ronald Reagan's first, furtive, and well-funded attempt to snatch the Republic presidential nomination from Richard Nixon. Reagan would go to great lengths to later deny his all-out quest for nomination in 1968. In fact, the first meeting Ronald Reagan held to discuss his 1968 bid for president was held at Reagan's home in Pacific Palisades the day after he was elected governor in 1966.[31]

Nationally known newspaper columnist Robert Novak told me of interviewing Reagan after the 1980 election but before the inaugural and said, "Well, Governor, the third time is the charm." Reagan looked at Novak quizzically until he said, "You know, '68, '76, and now this time."[32]

Reagan said, "Well, Bob, you know I never really did run in 1968. Some people tried to get me into the campaign, but I never endorsed it or participated."[33] If you consider the delegates from outside California he hot-boxed in a small trailer just outside the Miami Beach Convention center, then Reagan told a white lie.

Reagan traveled thousands of miles, gave dozens of speeches, and even reached out to arch-foe Liberal Republican Governor Nelson Rockefeller in a bid to stop Nixon and turn the 1968 convention in his favor.

Reagan gave an Academy Award performance with his denials, but Reagan and his aides ran a furtive bid for the 1968 Republican presidential nomination presaging his challenge to Ford in 1976 and his triumph over Carter in 1980.

Ronald Reagan's official biography says he ran for president in 1976, 1980, and 1984. Later in his a career, Reagan would cling to the fiction that he was only a favorite son for California at the 1968 convention and didn't run for president in 1968. His friend William F. Buckley who was both an opponent and sympathizer in Reagan's furtive '68 bid covered for the Gipper in his own book of remembrances. Yet Buckley was well aware that *National Review* publisher Bill Rusher was a key player in Reagan's bid.

In fact, less than two years after being elected governor, Reagan launched a stealth, well-funded, tenacious, and hard-fought bid to snatch the Presidential nomination from former Vice President Richard Nixon. He used Governor Nelson Rockefeller as a pawn to try to deadlock the convention so delegates would turn to Ronnie Reagan.

Meeting at the Bohemian Grove in California, Nixon had actually tried to trick Reagan into make a pledge during the actor's 1966 governor's race that he would not run for president in 1968 to remove an issue that had hurt Nixon in his own governor's race in 1962. Indeed, voters thought Nixon was using the governor's office as a stepping stone to another White House bid. But Reagan saw Nixon's ploy and declined.[34]

Reagan, funded by a cabal of millionaire backers, led by two wealthy oilmen, the architect of the 1964 Goldwater nomination and anxious aides, maneuvered energetically for the 1968 Republican nomination. In fact, Reagan's manager would coordinate closely but secretly with Rockefeller's campaign manager, Len Hall, while the two governors schemed to block Nixon.

Not all those around Reagan were for this early presidential bid. Reagan Press Secretary Lyn Nofziger and political aide Tom Reed were chief among the "presidentialists," while Reagan Chief of Staff William P. Clark and Reagan legal counsel Ed Meese opposed a campaign for the presidency after less than two years in the governor's office.[35] Casper Weinberger, who would serve Nixon as OMB Director and serve Reagan as secretary of defense, had been a latecomer to the Reagan team. Weinberger had been a liberal Republican assemblyman from Northern California who would serve as California Republican State Party chairman when Nixon ran for governor in 1962. Weinberger would initially support former San Francisco Mayor George Christopher against Reagan in the California primary for governor. In his own memoir *In The Arena*, Weinberger remembered the situation around Reagan:

By 1968, a group of Reagan loyalists was pushing the governor hard to run for president. I was not in favor because I thought he should finish his gubernatorial term. I'm not sure that the governor himself ever really authorized a campaign. It was only at the Republican convention that year that he reluctantly allowed his name to be presented as a candidate. But he was a realist, and though he received quite a few votes, he quickly told backers to support Richard Nixon, which they did—though the Nixon people continued to harbor a distrust of the Reagan people.[36]

Reagan Kitchen Cabinet members Henry Salvatori, a millionaire oil man, and fellow millionaire, auto dealer Holmes Tuttle wanted Reagan to be president as early as 1968 and generated the money for Reagan's surreptitious bid for the nomination. J. D. "Stets" Coleman of Virginia was a funder, as was theme park owner Walter Knott of Knott's Berry Farm. (Salvatori would actually abandon Reagan in 1976 when the governor challenged President Gerald Ford.)

Legendary political strategist F. Clifton White, who I worked for in New York in the 1970's, was paid handsomely by the Reagan Kitchen Cabinet to engineer a Reagan nomination. White had run the draft-Goldwater campaign that earned the senator the party nomination in 1964, so his conservative connections were unsurpassed.

White engineered the Reagan effort with a small band of draft-Goldwater veterans, including Rusher, Montana publisher Frank Whetstone, Kansas State Senator Tom Van Sickle, and New Mexico rancher Andy Carter, who had run a strong race for the US Senate against veteran Senator Joseph Montoya (D-NM).

The money underwrote the cost of Reagan's travel to thirteen states in search of delegates, fees for White, TV and radio for a write-in campaign in Nebraska, and a draft campaign for Oregon. There, Reagan took a stunning 23 percent of the vote without being a candidate.

Many conservatives distrusted Nixon and thought his 1960 campaign hadn't really drawn the differences with liberal John F. Kennedy required to defeat him. "Nixon ran a 'me too' campaign," *National Review* publisher William Rusher said. Yet conservatives generally found him acceptable and preferable to the hated Rockefeller, whose big-government, big-spending, Eastern liberalism and failure to endorse the Goldwater ticket made him a "party wrecker" in the eyes of the conservatives who had swept to power at the 1964 convention.

Nixon skillfully exploited the fact that Rockefeller was anathema to the right. To do it, he had to earn the right's respect. According to Nicole Hemmer of the Associated Press, some modern-day Republicans could learn a thing or two from the old man:

"Like Romney, Nixon faced a skeptical right-wing media that lambasted him as a 'political weathervane' and a 'dedicated phony.'" Tough words, but Nixon couldn't simply write off the conservative broadcasters who said them. As his speechwriter Pat

Buchanan explained, Nixon understood that to win in 1968 "he had to make his peace with the Goldwater wing of the party."

Many from the Goldwater drive were co-opted by White and campaign chairman John Mitchell. Goldwater's chief lieutenant Richard Kleindienst, Mississippian Fred LaRue, Alabama's John Greneir, Texas Senator John Tower, and Texas GOP Chair Peter O'Donnell had all joined the Nixon comeback crew.

Nixon methodically picked off the Goldwaterites one by one. Through conservative stalwart Pat Buchanan, he skillfully recruited the support of conservative writer William F. Buckley Jr., who Reagan, pondering his own late bid, had been sweet-talking. But Buckley was a Nixon doubter since his first run for president.

"[I]n 1960, the once-popular Nixon found right-wing media particularly hostile territory. At *National Review*, William F. Buckley Jr. was persuaded Nixon would prove 'an unreliable auxiliary of the right.' Clarence Manion, host of the 'The Manion Forum' radio program, agreed. 'Like you,' he wrote Buckley, 'my first 1960 objective is to beat Nixon. He is an unpredictable, supremely self-interested trimmer and has never been anything else.'"

Buchanan reported that Rusher, Buckley's *National Review* colleague, was among those finagling for a late Reagan candidacy. Nixon started wooing Buckley by having Buchanan send speech drafts to Buckley for comment. Nixon had Buchanan call the young editor frequently for advice and spoke to him occasionally himself in the courtship. Nixon even dropped by Buckley's maissonette in Midtown Manhattan "for a drink." Nixon knew Rusher was among those privately pushing Reagan to launch a formal 1968 presidential bid. Buckley polished off an entire bottle of red wine in the hour they were together. Nixon had a gin martini made by the statuesque Pat Buckley, who later told friends he was "odd."

Aides knew one martini was Nixon's limit. After two, Nixon got loquacious; after three he got loud and mean. Regardless, Nixon left with Buckley's support. According to Nicole Hemmer, Buckley may have been in his corner earlier:

In January 1967 [Nixon] invited Buckley, Bill Rusher (publisher of *National Review*), and other members of the conservative media to his sprawling Fifth Avenue apartment. There he exhibited his virtuosic command of foreign and domestic policy. Rusher remained unmoved—Rusher would always remain unmoved when it came to Nixon—but Buckley? There was no surer way to Buckley's heart than a vigorous display of intellect and insight. As Neal Freeman, Buckley's personal aide, recalled: 'I knew when we went down the elevator, early in the evening, that Bill Buckley was going to find some reason to support Richard Nixon.' True, Nixon was no conservative, but the heart wants what it wants. And a smart, experienced, electable Republican was exactly what Buckley wanted in a 1968 candidate. More than a year before the election, he was recommending Nixon as the "wisest Republican choice."[37]

National Review would follow suit with a weak but crucial endorsement. Buckley would end up powerless to help his friend Ronald Reagan when, to his surprise, Reagan dropped the façade of being "favorite son" candidate and announced a formal bid for the nomination. Still, Reagan faced an uphill battle in the South, where Nixon had recruited a powerful ally.

Eyeing the ideological shift of the party, Nixon was able to secure vitally important Southern conservative support thanks to an influential Southern politician who, like George Wallace, had run a pro-segregation campaign for president in 1948. South Carolina Senator Strom Thurmond had served as both governor and US senator as a Democrat but had bolted to the GOP when Barry Goldwater challenged Lyndon Johnson. Thurmond was a leading anti-Communist in the US Senate and was quite well known across the South as an early segregationist. Importantly, he was also every bit as well-known and revered in the South as Wallace.

The esteemed senator first came around to Nixon in May 1968, during Nixon's sessions with Southern Republican Party chairmen in Atlanta.[38] Texas GOP Chairman Peter O'Donnell presided over the Atlanta meetings, and Senator Thurmond was one of the most important participants. He flew into Atlanta for the second and last day's sessions, and after attending said, "I've been highly pleased with the statements the former Vice-President made today. I think he's a great man, a great American, and I think he would be a great president." [39]

Nixon always said that the main issues he discussed in those meetings were national defense, protections against textile imports (the textile industry was very important in South Carolina), and civil rights. He pointed out that Thurmond knew he supported the 1964 Civil Rights Act and would not compromise this position. His only promise on desegregation was not to make the South "a whipping boy." [40]

Nixon told me he later sat in a private meeting with "Ole Strom" where the blunt senator, who spoke with a thick Carolina low country accent in a loud staccato, barked questions at the former vice president about the Supreme Court, segregation, states rights, defense policy, and law and order. The exchange satisfied Thurmond that Nixon would be a friend to the South, meaning the South would be treated like every other state. Nixon said he wouldn't pursue policies that were punitive to the South. Thurmond never asked directly about the desegregation of the schools, because by that time the senator concluded that the Supreme Court ruling requiring desegregation would be ultimately carried out. By 1968, Thurmond was resigned to a "go slow policy."

Nixon left that meeting with an historic commitment from Thurmond. The senator's top aide, Harry Dent, drove Nixon to the airport with Pat Buchanan. Dent outlined for Nixon how Thurmond could be the answer to the "Wallace problem": the fear that Wallace would drain conservative general election votes from Nixon in the South, allowing Humphrey to win with votes of blacks and poor whites, the remnants of the once solid Democratic South. (Indeed, the Nixon campaign would later deploy the senator and his aide as their Southern front in the general election.)

On June 22, Strom Thurmond endorsed Nixon and announced that all of South Carolina's twenty-two delegate votes would be cast for him. He said he stood with Nixon on issues including domestic lawlessness, Vietnam, the rise in the cost of living, Supreme Court overreach, and the need for the nation to maintain its military strength. Thurmond said "he did not agree with Nixon on every single issue," but added, "[h]e is the most acceptable and electable candidate."[41] Thurmond said he had "no harsh words" for Wallace, but he knew the Alabama governor had little chance of being elected president.[42]

Nixon also recruited former Arizona Republican State Chairman Richard Kleindienst. He had campaigned for Kleindienst when he ran a hopeless campaign for governor in the days before the Republican Party became a force in mostly Democratic Arizona. Kliendienst was personally close to Goldwater and had been inserted by the senator into his own 1964 general election campaign as "field director." (White, who had engineered Goldwater's nomination, was nearly frozen out of the Goldwater general election. Instead, Kliendienst wisely pulled him in as a de facto "codirector.")

Kleindienst reprised his 1964 role in the Nixon campaign, running field operations and reporting to campaign manager John Mitchell. Together, Mitchell and Kliendienst built the most sophisticated delegate tracking and handholding operation Republicans had ever seen. If you were a national party convention delegate, the Nixon men knew where you were in 1964, what brand of Scotch you drank, and what bank held your mortgages. Occasionally, a delegate would get a call from his banker telling him, "Nixon's the one."

Mitchell recognized Reagan as the biggest problem, but he was slow to recognize the true force of Reagan's late grab for the nomination. Instead, fulfilling Nixon's wish to win big, he focused on guiding Nixon through a series of overwhelming primary victories.

In fact, the lack of formal opposition after Romney dropped out in late February reduced Nixon to shadow boxing Rockefeller and Reagan.

After Reaganites attempted a Nebraska write-in, Reagan allowed his name to stay on the Oregon primary ballot.[43] Still, turnout in the Republican primaries was high because President Johnson and the Vietnam War, coupled with inflation and a decline in the buying power of the dollar, made Republicans eager for change. Nixon swept them all, winning an average of 67 percent of the vote and racking up dozens of delegates bound by law to vote for him on the crucial first ballot.

Nixon called Mitchell in Miami Beach from a hotel in Montauk, Long Island, where he had gone to polish his nomination acceptance speech and relax, to the extent that Richard Nixon could relax at all.

"Is there anything I should know before I head there? Anything you want to tell me?" he asked.

"No," said the taciturn and confident Mitchell, who then hung up. By the time Nixon landed in Miami Beach, Reagan's dash for the nomination was in full bloom. Thurmond and Dent asked for a meeting with Mitchell and Nixon as the clamor for Reagan surfaced in Nixon's Southern strongholds.[44]

* * *

Reagan had already dazzled a routine and sleepy platform committee hearing. "We must reject the idea that every time the law is broken, society is guilty rather than the lawbreaker," he said. As for campus radicals, the California governor said, "It is time to move against these destructive dissidents, it's time to say, 'Obey the rules or get out.'" Reagan brought the committee to a standing ovation when he said, "It is time to tell friend and foe alike that we are in Vietnam because it is in our national interest to be there."

Looking tanned and fit and wearing an off-white linen sports jacket, Reagan turned on the Hollywood charm to chip away

Nixon's support, seeking that elusive delegate who would tip the majority of a Southern state, bound by the unit rule, to the California governor. The unit rule required that a state's entire delegate vote be awarded to the candidate who had a majority of the delegation. At the same time, White and his agents reminded conservatives of Nixon's 1960 selection of Lodge and his acquiesce to Rockefeller's demands for revisions in the 1960 Republican platform. Fatefully, Nixon had flown to New York in the middle of the night—without the knowledge of his campaign manager Len Hall, his top aide Robert Finch, or his press secretary Herb Klein—to meet Rockefeller at his Manhattan manse and hammer out a revised platform. Conservatives called it "the sell out on Fifth Avenue," while Goldwater denounced it as the "Munich of the Republican Party."

"Tricky Dick?" White's men whispered. "He's a loser."

M. Stanton Evans, boy-wonder editor of the *Indianapolis News*, produced a polemic, "The Reason for Reagan," which was published and mailed to all Southern and Western delegates. The booklet made a case for Reagan's record and his suitability for 1968. It bore no disclaimer, save the author's name and title. White called on *National Review* publisher Bill Rusher, an ally since Young Republican days, to get the pro-Reagan treatise out to activists.

"A Proven Winner," said the Reagan posters with the actor's broad-shouldered Hollywood-style photo, subtly echoing Rockefeller's "Rocky has never lost an election." Rockefeller unveiled the support of six former Republican National chairman, including Len Hall, once Nixon's campaign manager and now running Rockefeller's convention operation; Meade Alcorn, who had been GOP chairman under Eisenhower; and Arthur Summerfield, who had also chaired the committee under Ike. It was difficult for Rocky to gain a foothold despite the fact that his grip on the mighty New York delegation was complete. Senator Clifford Case was holding the New Jersey delegation, where Rockefeller thought he had strength. He was also denied a sweep in neighboring Connecticut, where Nixon snatched three delegates from the wealthy Fairfield County suburbs.

Ultimately, Nixon and Mitchell would have to undertake a risky gambit to insure their success on the first ballot. Both men knew that a surging Reagan would erode their support on a second ballot. Nixon's reputation as a loser would resurface as his candidacy faded on subsequent ballots, while a Reagan vs. Rockefeller battle ensued. Bergen County New Jersey Republican Chairman Nelson Gross and Atlantic City state senator and political boss Frank S. "Hap" Farley quietly had commitments for Nixon from a third of the delegates pledged to liberal Senator Clifford Case, as a favorite son, on the first ballot. Mitchell convinced Gross and Farley to have a delegate call for a roll-call vote in which each delegate would step to the microphone to record their vote on national television. What came next shocked the hall.

Case fumed as New Jersey delegate after New Jersey delegate trooped to the microphone to vote for Richard Nixon. Nixon had challenged no other favorite son, despite a raft of supporters in Ohio where Governor Jim Rhodes held the delegation as a favorite son in a maneuver to help Rockefeller. Nixon had support in the delegation including that of former Senator John Bricker and Congressman Robert Taft Jr., but made a decision not to mount an insurgency. (A US attorney appointed by Case would later indict Bergen County Chairman Nelson Gross on corruption charges, even though Gross was briefly appointed assistant secretary of state.)

The spadework in the South was important to Nixon's convention strategy. He actually toured all eleven states of the Confederacy between 1967 and 1968 and had carefully targeted the South in his campaign trips for congressional and Senate candidates in 1966. Nixon was still a celebrity as a former vice president and presidential contender, and his appearance allowed congressional candidates to both raise money and publicity they could not otherwise earn. Everywhere he went, Nixon buttoned down commitments from the Goldwater men, who universally saw Nixon as the candidate to stop the deep-pocketed and despised Rockefeller. He recruited Mississippi GOP Chairman T. Clarke Reed, and Goldwater firebrand John Grenier.

In Georgia, Congressman Howard "Bo Callaway" signed on. Callaway had run first in the Georgia governor's race when Democrats nominated arch-segregationist Lester Maddox and a progressive former Governor Ellis Arnall ran as an independent. The Georgia Constitution requires a candidate of the governor to get a majority of the vote so when that did not occur, it was thrown to the Democratic legislature. They awarded the governorship to Maddox.

South Carolina textile magnate Roger Milliken committed to the former vice president after a discussion on textile trade policies. Milliken and his brother Gerrish, who lived in Connecticut, had been substantial fundraisers for Goldwater.

Even as Nixon toured the South, he was careful to pledge his support for civil rights and to reject segregation. Nixon said he would support an anti-segregationist plank in the national Republican platform but would not denounce state Republican platforms, saying any attempt to dictate to them would be unrealistic "and unwise." Nixon knew that Goldwater's opposition to the 1964 Civil Rights Act had made him popular in the South but eliminated him as a national candidate in the rest of the country. He would not set foot in the same trap; he had a strong record on civil rights as a US senator and vice president. After all, as vice president, Nixon had defended Eisenhower's decision to send the National Guard to Little Rock, Arkansas, to quell violence and ensure safe desegregation of the schools.

The week before the Miami Beach convention kicked off, *Time* magazine published a cover of a dream Republican ticket: Nelson Rockefeller for president and Ronald Reagan for vice president. Rockefeller had commissioned a series of polls that allegedly showed that he ran stronger than Nixon against Humphrey in the industrial states of the Midwest and the northeast. He spent lavishly on newspaper ads touting his poll numbers, with the headline "Rocky has never lost an election." Never really a convention threat, Rockefeller's strategy was undone when a Gallup poll was published just days before the convention showing Nixon leading the wealthy New York governor by sixteen points.[45]

While Reagan and White and their ragtag band of operatives tried to pry delegates off of Dick Nixon, Dent arranged to send a telegram from "Ole Strom" to every Southern delegate:

> Richard Nixon's position is sound on law and order, Vietnam, the Supreme Court, military superiority, fiscal sanity, and decentralization of power. He is best for unity and victory in 1968. Our country needs him, and he needs our support in Miami. See you at the convention.
>
> —Strom Thurmond US Senator

Thurmond worked the phones relentlessly, calling state chairman and delegation leaders at their Miami Beach hotels. Thurmond was blunt: He told sympathetic chairman that he "loved Ronnie Reagan" and that "he would support him next time" but it was crucial to nominate Nixon, who could be competitive in every region in the country, while Goldwater had only scored in the South and the West.

Still, Reagan maneuvered. While posing as a "favorite son" candidate for California, Reagan traveled widely in his secret attempt to stalemate a Nixon first-ballot victory, in hopes the convention would turn to the former movie star. Nixon told me himself that "the convention's heart belonged Reagan" and the California governor would have been nominated if he had stumbled.

The actions of Nelson Rockefeller in late 1967 and early 1968 are perplexing. As noted, Rockefeller had supplied Michigan Governor George Romney with money and staff early in the race, only to see him self-destruct. Then Rocky jumped in as an announced candidate with the best pollsters and advertising men Madison Avenue could buy. He paid millions for a nationwide media blitz to convince Republicans Nixon was a loser and that only Nelson Rockefeller could win for the GOP. It was a flawed strategy.

The irony, of course, is that both Reagan and Rockefeller believed that had Nixon stumbled, the nomination would fall into their hands. Because Rockefeller spent millions of dollars in massive but ineffectual national advertising just before the convention, he is remembered today as the principal challenger to Richard Nixon in 1968. Rockefeller breezed into Miami Beach, where his top political aides George Hinman, Jack Welles, Bill Ronan, William Pfeiffer, and George Humphries set up shop at the Americana Hotel.

Rockefeller bought the support of six former Republic national chairmen to back his last-minute bid, holding a rally on a windy Miami Beach to announce their support. Present were former Republican national chairmen Bill Miller (who had been Goldwater's running mate in 1964), Meade, Alcorn, and Hall, who had borne the title of campaign manager in Nixon's 1960 campaign. "Six Former Republic National Chairman Can't Be Wrong," a painted banner declared from above the podium. But they were.

Aides who opposed Reagan's 1968 national effort told me that a fretful and angry Nancy Reagan was worried that her husband was running too early and might "look foolish." She was privately furious at Reagan's aides Lyn Nofziger and Tom Reed, who were among the "presidentialists" who were pushing Reagan to make an all-out bid for the office after barely two years in the governor's office.[46]

Reagan's effort was hampered severely by his lack of a formal declaration of candidacy. At every stop in his well-received pre-convention tour of the South, the former actor was told that his candidacy was desired but that delegate votes could not be committed without a full-bore declared candidacy. The Nixon men continued to exploit the fears of many would-be Reagan backers that Nelson

Rockefeller could exploit a split on the right that would leave the reviled New York governor as the party nominee.

Reagan insisted he wasn't an avowed candidate. When California put his name in nomination, he also insisted he would "be a candidate at that time" who delegates could vote for. This was an uncomfortable role for Reagan, who preferred to be honest with the press and in his political dealings. Reagan chafed at not competing as an open candidate.

In a moment of high drama, Reagan formally announced he was a candidate at the Miami Beach Convention. The announcement stunned and angered Nancy Reagan, who first heard about it on the radio. She blamed Nofziger and former Senator Willam F. Knowland, whose bad political judgment in 1958 had cost him both his Senate seat and the California governorship. (Interestingly, many believed Knowland ran for governor instead of for re-election to the US Senate in a foolish gambit to control the California Republican delegation in 1960, try to deny Nixon the presidential nomination and take it himself.)[47]

Nofziger had allowed Knowland an audience with Reagan, without senior staff approval, where Knowland persuaded Reagan to drop the ruse and become an announced candidate. The idea appealed to Reagan for its honesty and raised his competitive instincts: Reagan wanted be president in 1968.

Nancy Reagan was furious and thought they had stampeded Reagan into a rash announcement that would embarrass her husband. Nancy Reagan held a grudge against Nofziger for years. His slovenly appearance—Nofziger looked like a wax pear that sat on the radiator too long—didn't endear him to stylish First Lady, either.

In his official autobiography, Reagan claimed he hadn't been a candidate in 1968. He maintained that he made no effort for the nomination and he never maneuvered for the nomination. In fact, Reagan visited thirteen states to woo party sachems and potential delegates, concentrating on the South with trips to Texas, Louisiana,

Georgia, Mississippi, South Carolina, and Florida. Reagan addressed a caucus of every Southern delegation and specifically urged the Mississippi and Florida delegations to break their "unit rule" to pry loose votes for the Gipper. In the end, it would be too late.

Nixon's 1960 choice of Ambassador Henry Cabot Lodge for vice president still rankled party conservatives. Reagan's pitch for the nomination stoked widespread conservative concern that Nixon would choose another liberal Republican, like New York City Mayor John Lindsay or Illinois Senator Charles "Chuck" Percy, for Vice President. Reagan and his band of operatives did everything they could to exploit this fear.

Reagan's first opening in Miami came when the *New York Times* ran a story speculating that, if nominated, Nixon would choose one of three men as his running mate: New York's Rockefeller, Mayor Lindsay, or Sen. Percy. All represented the party's liberal wing. This story caused a near revolt in the Southern delegations pledged to Nixon.[48]

The slogan of Reagan supporters was "The double cross is on." James Gardner, the ultraconservative and ambitious chairman of the North Carolina delegation, began spreading the word that he was supporting Reagan. On the convention floor, the Nixon forces could feel slippage. Columnist Rowland Evans reported that Ohio's Gov. Rhodes said, "It's a new ball game," after Reagan's announcement, and that Rhodes planned to throw Ohio's support to Reagan with Rhodes to become his running mate.

Reagan worked to raid the Southern delegations only to find the venerable Strom Thurmond working as a "fire brigade" to extinguish any insurgency Reagan got going. Thurmond insisted again and again that Nixon would select no running mate who would "split this party." A struggle for the Florida, Mississippi, Georgia, and South Carolina delegates ensued.

Thurmond later claimed he had no "veto power" over Nixon's choice for vice president. As "First Bid" reveals, Thurmond actually slipped Nixon a note that said, "Acceptable—Agnew, Volpe;

unacceptable—Lindsay, Percy, Hatfield." With that note, Strom Thurmond laid the groundwork for a vice presidential resignation, two un-elected vice presidents (Ford and Rockefeller), an unelected president (Ford), and the election of a peanut farmer.

When Reagan inroads were reported in Georgia, Congressman Bo Calloway introduced Thurmond to their caucus. He told them, "We have no choice, if we want to win, except to vote for Nixon. We must quit using our hearts and start using our heads. I love Reagan, but Nixon's the one." Thurmond showed up after Reagan addressed each delegation to argue why staying with Dick Nixon was the right thing to do.

Later that Tuesday, before meeting with the South Carolina delegation, Reagan met privately with Thurmond in the senator's hotel room. Reagan asked a Thurmond aide to leave so the two men could be alone. Asked a few minutes after the meeting what he told the California governor, Thurmond said, "I told him I would support him next time." Reagan could not move "Ol' Strom."

When slippage from Nixon was reported in the Florida delegation, Thurmond rushed to meet with them at the Doral County Club, holding a majority for Nixon in a delegation that voted by unit rule. Elsewhere, he worked to shore up weak spots and to recruit uncommitted delegates.[49]

Thurmond's role in stopping Reagan wasn't unassisted. Although he visited the Mississippi delegation, so did Barry Goldwater. Mississippi Republican Chairman Clarke Reed said that Goldwater (who won 87 percent of the Mississippi vote in 1964) meant more than in holding that state's delegates for Nixon over Reagan.

Reagan's second convention opportunity came when delegates streaming into the Miami Beach Convention Center saw newsboys hawking a "bulldog" edition of the next morning's *Miami Herald* with a banner headline that Oregon Sen. Mark Hatfield would be the vice presidential nominee: "HATFIELD VEEP PICK."[50]

The story sparked pandemonium again among the Southern delegations. Harry Dent, Thurmond's aide, raced from delegation to delegation, insisting the story was false. At one point he spotted Don Oberdorfer, who wrote the *Herald* story, as the reporter was walking in front of the Louisiana and Georgia delegations.[51] Dent cornered him and offered him a $300 bet that his story was wrong. Oberdorfer saw Dent jumping up and down and heard something about $300 that he didn't understand. "I thought it was a joke," Oberdorfer said. "I wouldn't bet $300 on anything."[52]

Dent yelled through a megaphone to the delegates that Oberdorfer wouldn't bet on Hatfield. He played on their suspicion of Yankee journalists to calm the delegates. Nixon's floor leader at the convention, Maryland Congressman Rogers Morton, stayed busy that evening scurrying with Thurmond from one Southern delegation to another.

Thurmond was not alone in fighting this final Reagan surge, either. Bill Buckley's role as a Nixon supporter and key support from Barry Goldwater, Senator John Tower, and Congressman Bill Brock also helped Thurmond repulse Reagan's attempts to stampede the Southern delegates committed to Nixon or held in place by the unit rule.

Even more crucial than Senator Strom Thurman to Nixon's renomination was 1964 standard-bearer Barry Goldwater. As a party man, Goldwater's relationship with the vice president was good, although he and party conservatives were outraged in the run-up of the 1960 convention, when Nixon hopped a secret late-night flight to New York and met with Governor Nelson Rockefeller, ceding changes in the 1960 Republican national platform. Ironically, Rockefeller was demanding planks supporting increases in defense spending, as well as a more pro-civil rights plank. The media called the "Treaty of Fifth Avenue," although Goldwater called it the "Munich of the Republican Party," a reference to Neville Chamberlin's concessions to Hitler in 1938.

Conservative anger with Nixon, would translate itself into a last-minute plan by delegates from South Carolina, Arizona, Louisiana, and Texas to put Goldwater's name before the 1960 convention as a rival to Nixon.

In the act that made Goldwater a national public figure, the Arizona senator would allow them to go forward only to ask for the floor so that he might withdraw his name and ask his delegates to vote for Nixon. It was a seminal moment in the founding of the conservative movement that would ultimately triumph in the election of Ronald Reagan.

Goldwater thundered to a packed house in Chicago's International Amphitheatre. "We are conservatives," he continued. "This great Republican Party is our historical house. This is our home." Goldwater also preached reasonable pragmatism saying, "Now some of us don't agree with every statement in the official platform of our party, but I might remind you that this is always true in every platform of an American political party." Goldwater slashed the Democrats. "We can be absolutely sure of one thing. In spite of the individual points of difference, the Republican platform deserves the support of every American over the blueprint for socialism presented by the Democrats!"

"Let's grow up, conservatives. If we want to take this party back, and I think some day we can. Let's get to work."[53] "I believe, for this task, Richard M. Nixon is the most intelligent, dedicated, and experienced leader in the Nation. He is our candidate—he is the only man who can lead us to a November victory."

Goldwater would be critical of Nixon's 1960 campaign, as will be revealed later. Goldwater would become peeved in 1964 when Nixon got frustrated trying to secretly engineer a "Stop Goldwater" drive without his fingerprints in the hopes that once stalled, the Goldwater and Rockefeller forces struggling over control of the party would turn to Nixon as a compromise. Nixon

would blow his cover at the June Republican governor's conference where Nixon would issue a broadside against the frontrunner from Arizona.

Goldwater himself remembered:

Despite the tribulations on the road to San Francisco the convention, we still hoped, would be a happy triumph. Instead, it
was a bloody Republican civil war. Nixon, Rocky, Scranton, and
Romney united in a Stop Goldwater movement. They launched
the most savage attack that I had witnessed in my political career.

Reversing the conservative image he had projected in the
two previous months, Nixon attacked just about everything I had
said and done since announcing my candidacy. He concluded,
"Looking to the future of the party, it would be a tragedy if
Senator Goldwater's views, as previously stated, were not challenged—and repudiated."[54]

Nixon spun on a dime to back Goldwater. Nixon's hard stumping for Goldwater in 1964 melted whatever reservations the Arizonan
had about Nixon and seemed to bury the memories of Nixon's late
efforts to block Goldwater's nomination.

From this point on Goldwater would function as Nixon's agent
to repeatedly push Ronald Reagan not to launch a premature bid
for the 1968 nomination. With Goldwater, Buckley, Thurmond,
Tower, Carl Curtis, Everett Dirksen, and the key Goldwater legions
locked up, Reagan would have nowhere to go in 1968.

Goldwater would be largely a critic of the progressive drift of
Nixon's first term but would break with Nixon only after release of
the so-called Smoking Gun tape. "He's a two fisted liar," Goldwater
would bellow. Goldwater would lead a delegation of US senators
calling on Nixon to resign in August 1974.

Sure enough, with the support of all the GOP's separate factions in place, Nixon won the GOP nomination on the first ballot.
In his speech to the convention, polished up since arriving from

Montauk, he appealed to the "silent majority" of Americans. It was a theme he revisited throughout the general election.

Nineteen sixty-eight began a bitter rift between Barry Goldwater and Ronald Reagan that festered when Barry backed Nixon, grew worse when Goldwater supported Ford over Reagan in 1976, and become so bad Goldwater said Reagan was "just an actor" in 1987, long after Reagan's eight years in the governor's office. Goldwater later loudly told columnist James Jackson Kilpatrick that Reagan's record is "a lot of shit" when President George H. W. Bush bestowed a Medal of Freedom on Reagan in 1993.

Even with Nixon's consolidation of the party's right wing, his renomination margin was, in fact, quite narrow. But for a swing of eight delegate votes, America would have endured no Watergate, neither would Spiro Agnew, Nelson Rockefeller nor Gerald Ford have been vice president. Ford would not have been president and neither would Jimmy Carter. George H. W. Bush would likely never have been president, either, and therefore neither would his son, George W. Bush. The Vietnam War might have had a different outcome. Cuba might be free.

A swing of just eight votes at the 1968 Republican Convention would have nominated Ronald Reagan for president, ended the comeback bid of Richard Nixon, and the trajectory of history would have been changed.

Had Nixon been denied the Republican presidential nomination, there would be no vice president Agnew, thus no Agnew resignation and no elevation to the vice presidency for Gerald Ford. No Nixon resignation, so no President Ford and thus no Vice President Rockefeller, who was appointed by Ford to fill the vacancy caused by his own promotion. Jimmy Carter's election was based almost completely on the country's reaction to Watergate, which would not have happened.

Nixon's spade work on the right paid off but Reagan's late drive for the nomination after eighteen months of playing coy came closer to snatching the presidential nomination from the former vice president than had been recognized. It came very close to happening, although nearly everyone involved would later re-write history regarding Governor Ronald W. Reagan's intense, well-funded, carefully orchestrated effort to seize the 1968 Republican nomination. Reagan would not win the presidency for another twelve years.

Of course, Reagan would have had a hard slog against Hubert Humphrey in the general election. Reagan was inexperienced, just two years into his governorship. And while Nixon had positioned himself to sound as if he had a plan to end the war to attract dovish general election votes, Reagan's hard line support for the war in Vietnam would have cost him dearly—just like the anti-war fervor had driven LBJ from the race.

At about the time Nixon was gearing up in New Hampshire, things continued to get worse for President Johnson. Throughout February 1968, the news from Vietnam would grow increasingly gruesome. A new Gallup Poll showed only 50 percent of the American public approved of Johnson's handling of the war and by the end of the month, Walter Cronkite had also questioned the Vietnam War. The respected television newsman asked in a special CBS report whether or not the war was winnable. Johnson, after watching Cronkite's editorial, reportedly said to an aide that if he had lost Cronkite, then he had "lost Middle America."[55]

The open warfare and deep division in the Democratic Party also played to Nixon's advantage. Although President Lyndon Johnson had abandoned his previous status as a segregationist who blocked every civil rights bill from 1937 to 1957, his escalation of Vietnam and the threat of the military draft created deep division among the party rank and file. While Johnson held tight the Democratic Party reins and knew how to manipulate federal patronage to keep the state and big city Democratic organizations on board, party liberals urged Senator Robert F. Kennedy, General James Gavin and Minnesota Senator Eugene McCarthy to challenge Johnson.

"A party that cannot unite itself, cannot unite America," Nixon would say at a hundred campaign rallies.

The counterculture, Kennedy-loving Democrat idealists who despised Johnson and his war got their candidate on November 30, 1967, with Minnesota Senator Eugene McCarthy. He vowed to run his campaign solely against Johnson's Vietnam policies and built up a campaign largely made up of anti-war youths. Two months later, as the North Vietnamese Tet Offensive rocked Vietnam and dealt the Americans a severe blow, McCarthy's anti-war position grew into a credible threat.

Sure enough, when McCarthy poured most of his resources into the first Democrat primary on March 12 in New Hampshire and nearly beat Johnson with 42 percent of the vote, it became quite obvious that the incumbent president was beatable. This attracted former Attorney General and now-Senator of New York, Robert F. Kennedy, who had been reportedly mulling a presidential run for months. He wanted to challenge Johnson, but did not wish to disunite the Democrats, especially since his brother had so carefully pieced the party together only eight years earlier. But McCarthy's near victory convinced Kennedy that LBJ could and should be defeated.

While many hailed RFK's entrance into the race at first, others saw him as being ruthless and opportunistic—only using McCarthy's win to build his own support. The anti-war left was bitterly divided.

Meanwhile, as anti-war fervor continued to grow, everything changed on March 31, 1968. Johnson appeared on live television to address the nation about halting the bombing in North Vietnam in favor of peace talks. LBJ then shocked the nation by announcing that "with America's sons in the fields far away, with America's future under challenge right here at home, with our hopes and the world's hopes for peace in the balance every day, I do not believe that I should devote an hour or a day of my time to any personal partisan causes or to any duties other than the awesome duties of this office—the presidency of your country. Accordingly, I shall not seek, and I will not accept, the nomination of my party for another term as your president."

In 1967, counterculture organizations began focusing their plans on protesting the war during the 1968 Democratic Convention. Countless anti-Vietnam War protests had already broken out across the country.

In 1968, President Lyndon Johnson's favorability ratings were only around 30 percent and polls showed a meager 23 percent favorability for his policies on the Vietnam War. In the months preceding the convention, more than a hundred cities were ravaged by riots; and political turbulence erupted on college and university campuses. Martin Luther King Jr. was assassinated on April 4, after which riots broke out across the country, including Chicago, where Mayor Richard Daley reportedly issued a "shoot to kill" arsonists order to the police. On June 5, Senator Robert Kennedy was assassinated after he won the California primary.

On March 23, 1968, the National Mobilization Committee to End the War in Vietnam (MOBE), an umbrella organization for anti-war groups, met at a camp at Lake Villa, Illinois, to plan a youth festival that would coincide with the Democratic National Convention. Their common cause was to end the Vietnam War and to challenge the Democratic Party leadership. The Youth International Party (Yippies) and Students for a Democratic Society (SDS) joined in the planning. The city of Chicago denied them a permit to converge in the city. The Yippies came to the convention anyway.

Senators Eugene McCarthy and Robert F. Kennedy both entered the campaign in March to challenge Johnson for the party's presidential nomination. Party dissension caused Johnson to drop out of the race. On March 31, 1968, President Lyndon Johnson addressed the nation calling for a halt of the bombing in North Vietnam. In the same televised speech, he made the surprising announcement that he would not run for reelection.

After Johnson's announcement, the purpose of the convention became the selection of a new presidential nominee to run as the Democratic Party's candidate for the president. Organizers of protests were thrown off by Johnson's announcement; it created uncertainty among the anti-war organizers' convention plans. Humphrey officially entered the race on April 27. Because Humphrey was closely identified with Johnson's policies on the Vietnam War, the activists chose to go through with their plans to demonstrate at the convention.

A number of anti-war activists had joined the presidential campaigns of anti-war candidates Kennedy and Senator Eugene McCarthy of Minnesota. Kennedy and McCarthy had been running against Vice President Hubert Humphrey. Senator McCarthy was seen as the peace candidate because of his markedly anti-war stance. Humphrey represented Johnson's stand on the war. Even though 80 percent of the primary voters were for anti-war candidates, the delegates defeated the peace plank 1,567 ¾ to 1,041 ¼.

Humphrey compiled his delegates in caucus sates that were controlled by the Democratic Party establishment. At the time of Robert Kennedy's assassination on June 5, the delegate count was: Humphrey 561.5, Kennedy 393.5, and McCarthy 258. After his death, Kennedy's delegates remained uncommitted. Although Humphrey had not entered a single primary, he won the Democratic nomination. It is speculated that Chicago Mayor Daley and President Johnson pulled strings behind the scenes.[56] The anti-war delegates felt betrayed.

The heat and humidity in Chicago portended the violence that was to erupt. Mayor Daley repeatedly boasted to reporters, "Now thousands will come to our city and take over our streets, our city, our convention." Added to that, the city taxi drivers had called a strike prior to the start of the convention.

The 1968 Democratic National Convention was held at the International Amphitheatre in Chicago from August 26 to August 29, 1968. Inside the Ampitheatre the elevators were working erratically, and the phone service wasn't reliable. The air conditioning failed to cool the hot air on the convention floor. The internal fighting among the delegates was telecast nationwide. The frustration over anti-war resolutions erupted in bitter floor fights. Daily shouting matches between frustrated delegates and party bosses lasted until early morning hours. The internal fighting among the delegates was televised across the nation. With the nomination of Hubert Humphrey, the delegates who opposed the war felt betrayed. The party bosses, not the people, 80 percent of whom voted for anti-war candidates in the primaries, had won.

The only common interest shared among the party regulars, anti-war delegates, and pro-Humphrey delegates was their doubt about winning an election over the Republican Party that had a unified front behind the nomination of Richard M. Nixon. The opposition groups, a mixed bag of hippies, Yippies, radicals, and moderates, that gathered to protest the convention represented a wide range of philosophies. But they were unified in the cause of ending the Vietnam war and challenging the Democratic Party to adopt a platform that would ensure that result.

The street violence began Sunday August 25. Anti-war leaders had tried to get permits from the city to sleep in Lincoln Park and to demonstrate outside of the convention site. Those permit requests were denied, although the city did offer them permits to protest in Grant Park. But in Lincoln Park, the protesters refused to leave when the park was officially closed. Chicago police bombarded them with tear gas and moved in, beating the protesters with billy clubs to force them out of the park. Seventeen reporters were attacked along with the demonstrators. Throughout the convention, police targeted reporters along with the protesters in Lincoln Park and Grant Park.

On August 27, from the convention floor, CBS's Dan Rather, wearing a headset, attempted to get a statement from a Georgia delegate who was leaving the convention hall. Security shoved Rather and then allegedly punched him in the abdomen and knocked down. Rather said the guards told him to "get the hell out."[57]

August 28, 1968, is known today for a "police riot." According to eyewitness accounts of the event, at approximately 3:30 p.m., a young boy lowered the American flag at Grant Park, a site which had been approved by a city permit. Ten thousand demonstrators gathered there were were met by twenty-three thousand police and National Guardsmen. The police broke into the crowd and assaulted the boy, while the crowd threw food, rocks, and chunks of concrete at the police.

Tom Hayden, one of the leaders of Students for a Democratic Society, encouraged protesters to move the demonstrations into the streets so that if they were to be teargassed, the entire city would be teargassed; and if blood were spilled, it would happen throughout the city. It is said that there was so much tear gas used on the protesters that it made its way to the Hilton Hotel, where it affected Hubert Humphrey while in his shower. [58]

Live under TV lights, the police were taunted with chants of "kill, kill, kill." The police were indiscriminate in spraying demonstrators and bystanders alike with Mace. The coverage of the police assault in front of the Hilton Hotel on the evening of August 28 is the most famous image of the 1968 Chicago demonstrations.

In the convention hall, Connecticut Senator Abraham Ribicoff used his nominating speech for George McGovern to criticize the violence going on outside the convention hall. Upon hearing Ribicoff's remark, "with George McGovern we wouldn't have Gestapo tactics on the streets of Chicago,"[59] Mayor Daley responded with a remark that wasn't picked up by the microphones but was later revealed by lip-readers: "Fuck you, you Jew son of a bitch! You lousy motherfucker! Go home!"[60]

That night, NBC televised both the demonstrators being beaten by the police and the festivities over Humphrey's victory in the convention hall. America clearly saw that the Democratic Party was bitterly divided.

After the calamity of the Democratic National Convention in Chicago, Nixon gained a broad lead over hapless Hubert Humphrey, who struggled mightily to forge his own identity. He was also vexed by a conundrum: he had cast off the image of his subservience to Lyndon Johnson, while at the same time keeping Johnson's support. Only a break with Johnson's Vietnam policy would make that possible. Humphrey struggled to put distance between himself and LBJ to bring party doves back into the fold without alienating the still powerful sitting president.

Nixon's final lead in the polls dwindled as the vote share for independent candidate George Wallace slipped and Wallace's Democratic supporters shifted back to the party of their ancestors. A Humphrey surge began, aided by the scrappy underdog nature of his campaign in the closing weeks, while Nixon's carefully staged effort seemed canned and boring. It was: the Republican candidate stuck to his broad campaign themes and scrupulously avoided making any actual news at all.

Humphrey made substantial gains in September by distancing himself from Johnson. He was now identified in ads as "Democratic candidate Hubert Humphrey," and he focused on Southern voters who found Wallace too radical. He gained back the labor vote with major help from union leaders, and he was further aided by the fact that Wallace—who peaked in polling at 21 percent in September—selected infamous general Curtis LeMay as his running mate. After LeMay suggested that tactical nuclear weapons be used in Vietnam, the anti-war conservative vote that supported Goldwater in 1964 was promptly back in play.

By October, Humphrey grew increasingly anti-Vietnam and called for an all-out halt to bombing. Johnson's infamous "October Surprise" occurred the weekend before the election: Johnson announced a bombing halt, and even a possible peace deal. The "Halloween Peace" gave Humphrey a boost. Coupled with the late endorsement of the anti-war Senator McCarthy, Nixon and Humphrey were in a dead heat.[61]

Apparently, Nixon and his team were expecting the October Surprise. Nixon saw it as a political maneuver that Johnson would try to use to box him in on his "peace talks" proposal. To counter, Nixon and campaign manager John Mitchell had opened back channels of communication with the president of South Vietnam, Nguyen Van Thieu. They worked through Anna Chennault, the notorious dragon lady whose husband, Claire Chennault, had founded the Flying Tigers airline. Chennault was in touch with the South Vietnamese ambassador and passed a discreet message to President Thieu that the South should refuse the three-party talks and hold out for a better deal after Nixon won reelection.

Thieu, sensing a double-cross from LBJ, was happy to comply. His announcement deflated the last-minute swing to Humphrey, and Nixon had the final successful chess move in his rivalry with Johnson.

Unfortunately, J. Edgar Hoover learned of Chennault's back channel, then wiretapped him through the FBI, and advised Johnson, who was furious. He said on White House tapes that Nixon had "blood on his hands" and labeled the action "treason." An angry Johnson called Nixon to confront him, but Nixon denied any knowledge of the maneuver. Nixon aide Haldeman later remembered that Nixon, he, and traveling aide Dwight Chapin dissolved in hilarious laughter after Nixon hung up.

As I outlined in my book *The Man Who Killed Kennedy*, the fact that Johnson even dragged out his "October Surprise" in hopes of securing Humphrey the election was questionable and pure power politics cloaked as foreign policy. LBJ had no consessions from the North Vietnamese and no breakthough in the Paris peacetalks. .When the move failed, Johnson ordered the NSA to maintain surveillance and even wiretap certain members of the South Vietnamese embassy and Nixon campaign. He never revealed what Nixon's team had done. Neither did Humphrey, who was convinced of his own victory. As the ultimate joke, Humphrey said that they didn't make Nixon's campaign's actions public as an "uncommon act of political decency."[62]

Mentor Murray Chotiner taught young Dick Nixon the dark arts.

John Sears was like a son to Nixon.

Nixon traveling aide Nick Ruwe saw it all.

When Nixon moved to New York he lived in Rockefeller's apartment house.

Nixon liked to be alone. When he was with Rebozo, he was.

Barry Goldwater made Nixon's comeback possible.

H. R. "Bob" Haldeman was known for his brisk efficiency.

Mitchell said Ehrlichman was "a sneaky SOB."

The improbable meeting. Nixon and Presley compare cuff links.

Martha Mitchell was the attorney general's greatest problem.

Gerald Ford got G. Gordon Liddy his position in the Nixon administration.

White House counsel John Dean spilled the beans.

Nixon wanted CIA director Helms' file on the JFK hit.

CIA operative E. Howard Hunt knew Nixon's deepest secrets.

"These establishment types like Richardson cannot be counted on when the chips are down," said Nixon.

Nixon wanted Connally to succeed him.

Nixon drops Haig's fourth star at the ceremony. Haig took him down.

Ford was a man on whom Nixon had leverage.

Nixon emerged as a foreign policy advisor for Clinton.

The youngest member of the CREEP staff meets the candidate.

Advising Nixon in the 1980s.

Quiet manipulations were commonplace in the 1968 race. Texas Governor John Connally played a central role in another backroom drama, according to author Jules Whitcover:

"One of the pieces not being picked up by Humphrey, incidentally, was John Connally, courted ardently by Nixon agents in Texas upon his return from the Democratic convention. Connally, disgruntled, agreed privately to help Nixon win support from conservative Texas oilmen and politicians, with an unspoken prospect that he would be taken into the Nixon cabinet—if Nixon carried Texas."[63]

Connally, under pressure from LBJ, later double-crossed Nixon, appearing with Johnson and Humphrey at a huge Houston rally on the eve of the election. Fifty-eight thousand people filled the Astrodome; Frank Sinatra served as the master of ceremonies. Between the bombing halt and Humphrey's movement in the polls, Connally had switched sides. To the surprise of the Nixon men, Texas went narrowly for Humphrey.[64] The double-cross, as we shall see, would not slacken Nixon's ardor for John Connally.

In the end, none of it mattered. Nixon was an old dog whose team knew all the new tricks, and he was prepared for any attempted backstabbing by Johnson, Humphrey, or anyone else. With the "October Surprise" out of the way, and a closing Gallup poll had Nixon up 44–36 percent on Humphrey with Wallace at 15 percent.

NOTES

1. Richard Nixon, *In the Arena*, p. 255.
2. Ibid.
3. Stephen Ambrose, *Nixon: The Education of a Politician*, p. 650
4. Jules Witcover, *Resurrection of Richard Nixon*, p. 211–212.
5. Stephen E. Ambrose, *Nixon: The Triumph of a Politician*, 1962–1972, pp. 121–122.
6. Michael Novac, *Choosing Presidents*, p. 47.
7. Joe McGinniss, *The Selling of the President*, p. 63.
8. Gabriel Sherman, *The Loudest Voice in the Room*, p. 33.
9. Joe McGinniss, *The Selling of the President*, p. 30.

10. Tom Junod. "Why Does Roger Ailes Hate America?" *Esquire*. Jan. 2011.
11. Jules Witcover, *The Year the Dream Died*, pp. 69–70.
12. Joe McGinniss, *The Selling of the President*, p. 64.
13. Herbert Klein, *Making It Perfectly Clear*, p. 61.
14. Richard Whalen, *Catch the Falling Flag*, pp. 10–11.
15. Ibid.
16. Joe McGinniss, *The Selling of the President*, p. 103.
17. "Nixon gets socked in Laugh-In's most famous, and influential, five seconds," Noel Murray, A.V. Club. Sept. 13, 2012, http://www.avclub.com/article/nixon-gets-socked-in-ilaugh-inis-most-famous-and-i-84881.
18. "The Comedy Writer That Helped Elected Richard M. Nixon," Kliph Nesteroff, http://blog.wfmu.org/freeform/2010/09/richard-nixons-laugh-in.html
19. "Sock it to me: behind the scenes of Richard Nixon's 'Laugh-In' cameo," Brian Abrams, http://www.deathandtaxesmag.com/190513/sock-it-to-me-nixons-laugh-in-cameo-that-won-the-1968-election.
20. Ibid.
21. "The Unthinking Man's Nixon's Four Second Moment," The New Nixon, http://blog.nixonfoundation.org/2008/09/forty-years-one-day-on.
22. Ibid.
23. "Sock it to me: behind the scenes of Richard Nixon's 'Laugh-In' cameo, Brian Abrams.
24. Kenny Young, *UFO Frontier*, p 25.
25. Joe McGinniss, *The Selling of the President*.
26. Richard Kleindienst, *Justice*, pp. 47–48.
27. Lewis Chester, Godfrey Hodgson, and Bruce Page, *An American Melodrama: The Presidential Campaign of 1968*, p. 101.
28. Dennis D. Wainstock, *Election Year 1968: The Turning Point*, p. 51.
29. Jules Witcover, *Very Strange Bedfellows*, p. 9.
30. https://www.senate.gov/artandhistory/history/common/generic/VP_Spiro_Agnew.htm.
31. Lou Cannon, *Governor Reagan: His Rise to Power*, pp. 266–270.
32. Conversation with Robert Novak.
33. Ibid.
34. James Mann, *The Rebellion of Ronald Reagan: A History of the End of the Cold War*, p. 234.
35. Lou Cannon, *Reagan*, p. 158.
36. Casper Weinberger, *In the Arena*, p. 164.

37. Nicole Hemmer. "Richard Nixon's Model Campaign," *The New York Times*, May 10, 2012.
38. Nadine Cohodas, *Strom Thurmond & The Politics of Southern Change*, p. 396.
39. "Thurmond Praises Nixon," p. D5.
40. Richard Nixon, *RN: The Memoirs of Richard Nixon*, pp. 304–305.
41. "Thurmond Throws Support to Nixon, Says He Offers America's Best Hope," *Charlotte Observer*, June 23, 1968, p. A10.
42. "Thurmond Urges Johnson Not to Fill Court Vacancy," Charleston News and Courier, June 22, 1968, p. A6.
43. Lou Cannon, *Governor Reagan: His Rise to Power*, p. 258.
44. James Rosen, *The Strong Man: John Mitchell and the Secrets of Watergate*, p. 50.
45. James Rosen, *The Strong Man: John Mitchell and the Secrets of Watergate*, p. 52
46. Lou Cannon, Reagan, p. 163.
47. Ibid, p. 164.
48. Garry Wills, *Nixon Agonistes*, p. 273.
49. Jack Bass and Marilyn Thompson, Ol' Strom, p. 230.
50. Ibid.
51. Ibid.
52. Ibid.
53. George Will. "The Cheerful Malcontent," *Washington Post*, May 31, 1998.
54. Barry Goldwater, *Goldwater*, p. 174.
55. Frazier Moore, (July 18, 2009). "Legendary CBS anchor Walter Cronkite dies at 92". GMA News, Associated Press, Retrieved June 22, 2013.
56. Todd Gitlin, *The Sixties: Years of Hope, Days of Rage*, p. 332.
57. http://www.corbisimages.com/stock-photo/rights-managed/ BE062374/dan-rather-at-the-1968-democratic-national.
58. Todd Gitlin, *The Sixties: Years of Hope, Days of Rage*, p. 331.
59. David Farber, *Chicago `68*, p. 201.
60. David Farber, *Chicago `68*, p. 201.
61. Theodore H. White, The Making of the President, 1968 (1970).
62. Robert Dallek, *Nixon and Kissinger: Partners in Power*, pp. 73–74.
63. Jules Witcover, *The Year the Dream Died*, p. 351.
64. Jules Witcover, The Year the Dream Died, p. 427.

CHAPTER TWELVE

PLASTIC AND STEEL

"Yes, you can."
—Pat Nixon to her husband seconds before the Checker's
Speech, a time when he was mired in doubt

An analysis of the great setbacks and triumphs of Nixon's career would be incomplete without a better understanding of the role of Patricia Ryan Nixon. Until now, historians have largely misunderstood the significance and actions of Pat. Pat Nixon was completely unlike her public image as forged in the 1950s and 1960s. She was a warm, engaging, and confident woman who had proved a great political asset in Nixon's political career. She was the first wife of a candidate for a major office to strike out and campaign for her husband alone; she attended campaign events without him by her side. She was enormously well liked for her middlebrow tastes, her warmth, and her openness. She consistently topped the lists when Americans were polled about the most admired women in America. But she was, in truth, far more than the tight-lipped supportive "campaign wife" that was her public persona.

When polls showed in 1960 that Pat Nixon was more popular than her husband, a *faux* "Pat Nixon for First Lady" campaign sprung up. I am convinced that if Thelma Catherine Ryan had agreed to the young California attorney's request for a date on their first meeting, there might never have been a First Lady, Pat Nixon. The young Whittier High School business teacher was not at all attracted to Dick Nixon when they met during tryouts for a local amateur drama production despite his relative good looks, eloquent manner of speech, and obvious intelligence. She was determined to chart her own course and be free to do whatever she wanted to, which included traveling; a serious relationship was not something she wanted or needed at that moment. If those who in later years labeled her "plastic Pat" had known of her iron constitution and steely determination—attributes she exhibited throughout her public life—they never would have branded her with such a demeaning epithet. Least likely of all to do so would be Nixon himself, who was dogmatic in his pursuit and determined to win her over, even to the point of learning where she lived and sending her roses on her twenty-sixth birthday. Her numerous attempts to cool his ardor only fueled his attraction to the young woman whose father had nicknamed her Pat because she was born on St. Patrick's Day eve.

Pat was not ready for a serious relationship when she met Nixon in the winter of 1938. Perhaps driven by her father's years as a seaman and gold miner, she wanted to travel, and as a school-teacher, she had the summers off to do so. With that in mind she had saved money from her teaching jobs, which included also working as a night-school instructor, to pay for experiences that were a world away from her difficult and dreary childhood in Ely, Nevada. During the week she devoted all her efforts to her students, but on the weekends she fled small-town Whittier for short trips elsewhere. "I never spent a weekend in Whittier the entire time I taught there," she proudly admitted years later.[1] Even those weekend jaunts away did not deter Nixon, who had met her during tryouts at a local theater production. He even resorted to penning romantic letters to her, not something that came naturally to a man born into the Quaker faith and its avoidance of shows of emotion. As their friendship (and her attraction to him) grew, he took every opportunity to put the relationship on a more permanent basis, promising her adventure and a better life than she had had in Ely or Whittier. After they had appeared together in a local play attended by Nixon's parents Frank and Hannah, he invited Pat to their home. The gathering had to be awkward because Hannah Nixon, a rather cold and stoic individual, did not embrace her prospective daughter-in-law and never could warm to her.

I know it's difficult for most people who never met Nixon and knew him only in the harsh light of the adversarial press that constantly hounded him to believe that he could court any woman with flowers, poems, and heartfelt letters in which he expressed his devotion to her. But, in fact, that is precisely what the young Nixon did unabashedly. Slowly, this most independent of women—who was not content to simply settle into domesticity with a husband and children and become the dutiful, loving wife that was expected of women in those years between the World Wars—was won over by his dogged determination, an attribute he later relied upon as he climbed to the pinnacle of political power, the White House. On a long motor trip with a friend from Southern California to Vancouver, British Columbia, in 1939, Pat realized that she missed Nixon. With his promising law practice, Nixon began to take an interest in local politics with a thought to perhaps run for office himself. (And when he did, he lost in his first attempt.) Much as she tried to hide it even to herself, she had to admit she was in love with Richard Nixon. Nevertheless, she established a three-month hiatus on his proposals, a last attempt to truly understand her feelings for him. As their very sympathetic biographer Will Swift put it, "Beneath her glamour and verve, Pat was surprisingly similar to Dick's standoffish, pious, and unglamorous Quaker mother, Hannah, whom he professed to revere."[2] And on a drive to Dana Point in March 1940, Nixon proposed and Pat accepted. The woman who had put travel and adventure ahead of marriage and a family would soon have a lifetime of both in abundance, and in ways that she could not have imagined.

They were married in a Quaker ceremony in Riverside, California, on June 21, 1940, and spent a good part of the next year traveling around the United States, Canada, even to Cuba, the Panama Canal, and neighboring Costa Rica. The strong-minded, independent woman whom the press would quite erroneously dub "plastic Pat" would be tested by the US entry into World War II. Soon after Pearl Harbor, the Nixons moved to Washington, DC, where Nixon went to work at the Office of Price Administration in the tire-rationing division, a vital wartime defense measure to conserve rubber, most of which came from areas in the South Pacific that were being overrun by the Japanese. Pat also got a job at OPA as an assistant business analyst. Restless after less than a year on the job, Nixon realized that if he was to have any success in politics he couldn't stay stuck behind a desk in Washington. He enlisted in the navy and left Pat in August 1942 for Rhode Island and Officers Training School. When he was stationed Ottumwa, Iowa, Pat joined him there, and together they watched corn grow at the end of an unfinished runway. Knowing that stateside duty would not be an asset in a political career, Nixon applied for sea duty as soon as openings were posted, and he was transferred to the South Pacific for fourteen months. Pat stayed behind in San Francisco where, with her degree in marketing, she landed a new job at the OPA West Coast offices as a price economist. Will Swift, a psychologist as well as their biographer, asserts that Nixon's "frustrating and ultimately undistinguished role on the outskirts of the real war, brought up old feelings of inadequacy, heightening his attachment to Pat."[3] In her letters she tried to assuage Nixon's regrets for leaving her by reminding him of her independence and willingness to accept challenges.

Within her small circle of friends in San Francisco, Pat Nixon was the embodiment of the strong, dutiful wartime wife, staying home mostly after work, eschewing large social gatherings, and saving as much of her OPA salary as she could to build a nest egg for when he returned. Lieutenant Nixon came home in August 1944.

When Nixon decided to run for Congress against Jerry Voohis in the autumn of 1945, he had some doubts; he'd lost a run for a state assembly seat in 1940 partially due to a lack of funds, and he didn't want to have a similar experience five years later. Despite the risks involved, and having to spend a good deal of their own money, Pat knew it was what he wanted, and she encouraged Nixon to go for the GOP nomination although she disliked politics and always would. Biographer Anthony Summers quotes Nixon family friend Earl Mazo as saying, "She didn't want politics, ever. Her friends were never political friends."[4]

The couple returned to Whittier briefly to try to begin a new phase in their life together. The first step was to convince the local Republican leaders that he was the best candidate. Together Nixon and Pat spoke to hundreds of businessmen, civil leaders, and ranchers. Nixon impressed them by his convictions and determination; Pat, however, realized that she was not as much of an effective speaker, so she elicited a promise from Nixon that she would not have to give any political speeches. Nevertheless, the nomination was his, and Nixon immediately threw himself into planning strategy to win the 1946 midterm election and represent California's twelfth district in the US Congress. Despite her innate aversion to politics, and being pregnant with their first child, Pat, a great marketer, enthusiastically threw herself into the campaign by selling her share of a parcel of land she and her brother owned and using the $3,000 to print campaign brochures. She also campaigned tirelessly right up to a couple days before Tricia Nixon was born on February 21. The new mother went back to campaigning three weeks later while Hannah Nixon's mother took care of Tricia. But the stress of a new baby combined with that of the campaign began to take its toll on both Nixons.

One incident was indicative of that stress. While Nixon was studiously prepping for and totally focused on an important radio address, Pat suddenly walked into the studio, interrupting his concentration. He became irate and "ordered her out with as little ceremony as he would have a dog."[5] It taught Pat an important lesson in her public behavior that she applied throughout the rest of Nixon's political career and which no doubt contributed to the perception that she was his plastic partner.

The former schoolteacher thus learned to tread carefully and stay silent whenever Nixon was engrossed in work. In public together, her role was just to smile, but behind the scenes Pat became an astute and formidable campaign partner who believed in her husband's political beliefs, and when things got tough on Nixon, she was the one who stiffened his resolve to fight on. Pat sat with Nixon all throughout election night, buoying his spirits when it appeared that Voorhis was leading. It was a great victory for the young politician, and as Nixon said years later after two presidential victories, he and Pat were never happier than on that evening. The Nixons had fought bravely "and at times ingloriously," biographer Swift judged, and "for the most part they would not shrink from the pattern for the rest of their lives." [6]

Back again in Washington, Pat threw herself into working in Nixon's office on Capitol Hill while he spent his days and many, many evenings immersed in legislative and committee affairs. During those eight years Pat was often alone, especially when Nixon was traveling, and work she did in his office wasn't enough to compensate for his absence. But she played the good soldier and kept her grievances and, at times, her anger to herself. Pat began to exhibit a new maturity and demanded that he devote more time to her and Tricia, and in the process he gave her more support and respect. Although he could express his love for Pat, he was incapable of explaining many of his other traits to her, including his obsessive drive for a career during which being a member of the House of Representatives was only a way station. Politics, the "Red Scare," and Nixon's pursuit of Alger Hiss while a member of the House Un-American Activities Committee (HUAC) quickly came to dominate his life. According to one source, Nixon did seek psychological help after about ten years of marriage to gain a better understanding of his relationship with Pat, but he was "so very inhibited." "Nixon depended on Pat because he trusted her, and she stayed with him. But that was for politics. The truth is, his only passion was politics."[7]

The Hiss case made Richard Nixon a rising star. It also made him anathema to Democrats and many independents who saw him as having spearheaded a witch hunt. Pat, who had seen the seamier side of politics in the Voorhis campaign, now saw her husband as something of a hero, and the attacks on him in the press angered her. Although she publicly defended him to the hilt and would continue to stand by him, insisting that what Nixon had done was right, the attacks on her husband further soured her on politics and public service. The Hiss episode widened "still further the growing gulf in their marriage."[8] According to biographer Swift, "Pat was so wounded by the Hiss episode that she could barely speak about it to her daughter some thirty years later."[9] Julie Nixon Eisenhower wrote later that, "Vindictiveness of some of the Hiss supporters caused an irreparable crack in her idealistic view of politics." And in defense of Nixon, Pat told her daughter, "The reason people have gone after Daddy is that no one could control him—not the press, not the lobbyists, not the politicians. He did what he felt was right, and from the time this became apparent in the Hiss case, he was a target."[10]

The Nixon's next battleground was the 1950 senatorial campaign in which Nixon was pitted against the popular Democrat Helen Gahagan Douglas, the wealthy and glamorous wife of actor Melvyn Douglas who had ties to many Hollywood and Broadway leftists. In addition to branding her as a communist sympathizer who would promote state socialism if she were elected, Nixon—with his wife's willing participation—used Pat as an avatar of traditional family values to contrast the Nixon's middle-class foundation. Pat became the poster child for the ideal mother, homemaker, and wife. Beneath the surface, however, she did lots of the spadework, researching material Nixon could use in his speeches blasting Douglas. It was her way to respond to the candidate's attacks on her husband, which upset her more than she ever let on. Will Swift perhaps summarized Pat best when he wrote, "No one crossed Pat Nixon . . . lightly nor did she forget a slight to her husband—in her mind an attack on him was an attack upon her."[11] As one Nixon aide recalled, Pat "could be waspy" when scolding Nixon in private, "but when the opposition did that, she lit into Nixon, demanding 'How could you let them do that?'"[12] Publicly, however, Pat attended thousands of women's teas and shook hundreds of thousands of ladies' hands in her energetic campaigning for her husband. The many miles Nixon and Pat logged in their station wagon campaigning up and down California paid off. Nixon garnered more than two million votes and beat Douglas by some 680,000, the largest margin of victory in the senatorial races that year.

It wasn't long before the Nixons confronted new and more critical challenges. Shortly before the 1952 Republican National Convention Nixon's name began circulating as a potential vice presidential candidate to run with Dwight Eisenhower. In those days presidential tickets were decided by several "balancing" factors. Nixon's age (he was just thirty-nine) contrasted well with Ike's grandfatherly image; Nixon was a lifelong outspoken Republican, while Ike had been courted also by the Democrats. Eisenhower, although born in Texas and raised in Abilene, Kansas, was considered "East Coast," while Nixon was a native Californian. Nixon would secretly be promised the vice presidential nomination by Governor Tom Dewey if he aided the nomination of Eisenhower while publicly supporting California favorite son Earl Warren. The Nixon's argued over whether he should accept, Pat decidedly against it because of the many more official duties that would be thrust on Nixon's shoulders, leaving even less time for him to be a father to their growing daughters. She also did not want them to be exposed to more press attacks that she knew would come with such high public exposure.

However, in the end she again deferred to his career goals conceding that she could "make it through another campaign."[13]

As we shall see, two months into that campaign, the Eisenhower-Nixon ticket was rocked by allegations against Nixon that sorely tested whether Pat could indeed "make it through." The *New York Post* then a liberal-left daily, claimed that while in the Senate Nixon had received about $18,000 (then a significant sum) from wealthy Californians to supplement his Capitol Hill salary. The newspaper said the slush fund was deposited in a California bank and used by Nixon for hotels, airfares, gambling in Cuba, and for printed materials and postage for thousands of Christmas cards. Nixon insisted there was no impropriety, that the bank account had been created by unknown supporters of his and used for legitimate expenses. He promptly called the story a communist smear. But the sparks of scandal had been lit and, like a California fire stoked by Santa Ana winds, it quickly became a full-blown inferno that could not be ignored.

Calls for Nixon to resign from the ticket became commonplace, and Pat's greatest fear became a reality. The *New York Times* published a list of the fund's contributors, calling them a "Who's Who" of wealth and influence. Many of the so-called Eastern establishment such as Bernard Baruch, Henry Cabot Lodge, and Harold Stassen, turned on Nixon demanding that he withdraw and that Eisenhower select a new running mate. Oscar Solbert, of the Eisenhower Research Service, said Nixon should withdraw, noting a cable that if he did, "he will go down in history as great hero who sacrificed himself for his own high principles and Ikes [sic] great crusade . . ." and he urged Nixon "to withdraw personally, unequivocally, irrevocably, and immediately."[14] The men around Eisenhower were almost unanimously a hanging jury when it came to the fund, and "there seemed to be a consensus among the advisers that the senator [should] discretely offer his resignation from the ticket," wrote biographer Roger Morris.[15] Throughout the maelstrom Ike, a political neophyte in his first campaign, irked Nixon by saying little to encourage him to stay on; instead, the general told his running mate to go on television to explain himself and let the American public decide his fate. It was Dewey who first proposed that Nixon go on television to explain the fund and how he used it all, although in Nixon's own memoir he credits the idea of taking his case to the American people on television over the heads of print journalists to his early political mentor Murray Chotiner, of whom we will learn much more. When the Nixons arrived in Portland, Oregon, several of their friends from Whittier, including Nixon's former law partner Tom Bewley, flew up to prop up his faltering morale and urge him to stay the course. As soon as they left, a despairing Nixon called in Pat, and together they went to a nearby morning service at a Quaker meetinghouse. Between the service and Pat's company, Nixon returned to his hotel suite renewed and refreshed, although the battle was far from over.

Nixon warily booked prime time on NBC television on September 23 (to follow Milton Berle's top-rated comedy show) to state his case. But even before his live address to some sixty million people, the ordeal had further strained their marriage and altered their partnership. "Pat became more estranged from the tumultuous world of politics, while Nixon grew to be even more the righteous, resentful gladiator, with the wounds of combat a price he was willing to pay. The contrast between their overachieving public personas and their complicated private feelings would become ever more dissonant over time," Swift said."[16] Nevertheless, just before airtime, Nixon—never comfortable discussing his personal life, especially in public—wavered. "I don't think I can do it," he told Pat. She took him by the hand, led him onto the set that had been designed to look like a typical American living room, and said, simply, "Yes, you can."

Throughout Nixon's dramatic and defiant public defense of his actions and his explanation of how the fund had been set up and used, Pat sat stoically beside him, no more mobile than the furniture on the set. Some viewers might have assumed she had stage fright, but that certainly was not the case. She knew his political future was on the line. After all, before her marriage she had had some small parts in movies and did some stage acting as well. In this performance she knew her role was to remain silent, her eyes riveted on Nixon, and to do nothing to upstage him. After all, Nixon's entire political future (as well as hers) was on the line. If he failed and was removed from the ticket, he would finish his one term as senator and it was highly unlikely he would be reelected.

Looking directly into the camera, Nixon spoke of their modest home and middle-class upbringing. He extolled Pat's frugality, noting that she didn't have a mink coat, "she has a respectable Republican cloth coat and I always tell her she looks good in anything." In the parlance of the sport he loved best, Nixon then tossed the winning touchdown when he admitted to having accepted one gift—a black and white cocker spaniel sent to his daughters that Tricia named Checkers. "And you know, like all kids, they loved the dog. And I just want to say this, right now, that regardless of what they say about it, we are going to keep it." The so-called Checkers speech (a title Nixon came to dislike greatly) has gone down in history as not only having saved Nixon's political career but also as one of his finest moments in public life. Even Mamie Eisenhower, watching the speech on TV with Ike, choked up with emotion.

Nixon first thought the speech was a failure. Pat reassured him that he was wrong, the speech was by no means a failure, and taking the unfamiliar role of political analyst, she even praised him for attacking the finances of the Democratic presidential nominee, Adlai Stevenson. Practically overnight public opinion shifted from the decidedly negative to overwhelmingly positive. Nixon had adroitly removed the decision from Ike's hands by urging viewers to contact the Republican National Committee who had the technical legal authority to replace him as the party's vice presidential nominee. The El Capitan television studio that Nixon was broadcast from, the Eisenhower campaign offices, and the Republican

National Committee were inundated with a deluge of letters and telephone calls backing Dick.

Whatever misgivings Pat may have had about the course Nixon and she had embarked upon, she kept them to herself. But one incident clearly reveals how she felt about the affair and her ever-growing dislike of politics. Eisenhower would finally embrace Nixon as his running mate in Wheeling, West Virginia. On the trip back to the airport afterward, the two candidates rode in one limousine and their wives in a trailing vehicle. According to Roger Morris, Ike didn't acknowledge the ordeal Nixon had just been through and talked mostly about campaign tactics. "The conversation in the trailing limousine was more candid. Mrs. Eisenhower had been silent most of the way but nervously began to speak when they became separated in the gloom from the rest of the motorcade. The Nixon story had only hurt the campaign, she was saying. 'I don't know why all this happened when we were getting along so well.' Pat Nixon replied in controlled fury, 'But you just don't realize what *we've* [italics as printed] been through.' Her icy tone, she told her daughter a quarter century later, 'ended the conversation.'"[17]

Besides pulling Nixon's political career out of the dustbin of history, the Checkers speech served as a template for how Pat would deal with Richard Nixon's future campaigns that led him into and then out of the White House. She would handle their life together with two personas. One, as the smiling supportive wife in public who could connect especially with women voters and said all the right things when interviewed (she won over so many voters that many "We Like Nixon" banners were altered to "We Like Nixons"). Then there was the private Pat who spoke her mind to Nixon, telling him off when she thought it necessary even if it provoked her to tears and him to a furious outburst. As Anthony Summers writes: "The crisis [over the secret fund] had only multiplied Pat's previous doubts. 'Why?' she had sobbed. 'Why should we keep taking this?' . . . Three decades later, when Pat's daughter Julie asked her to discuss the fund, she turned her face to the wall for long minutes before replaying [sic]. 'There was so much pain in her eyes,' Julie recalled, 'that I could not bear to look at her.'"[18] Looking back on that period in his life, Nixon himself later acknowledged the pain the episode had caused her. "I knew how much it had hurt her, how deeply it had wounded her sense of pride and privacy. I knew that from that time on, although she would do everything she could to help me and help my career, she would hate politics and dream of the day when I would leave it behind . . . ."[19]

Pat did her "second lady" chores dutifully throughout the eight years of Nixon's vice presidency. She went along with Nixon when Eisenhower sent him on a seventy-day goodwill visit to nineteen Asian countries in the fall of 1953, prior to which Pat had pored over State Department documents to learn as much as she could about the places they would visit, in effect becoming Nixon's living *Michelin Guide*. Although she hated the thought of leaving the girls behind, she accepted her role as a high-level distaff envoy and even rankled the men at Foggy Bottom when she added to her "woman's role" of visiting schools, hospitals, shopping, and social teas speaking out for women's rights in a bold attempt to break down some of the traditional Asian barriers that prevented women from social and professional advancement. In Australia, New Zealand, and Malaya, her appearances forced previously all-male bastions to admit women to their private sanctuaries. To many she was the first woman of her generation to balance being a dutiful wife with advocating for the public prominence and the worth of women. In following the path of Eleanor Roosevelt, Pat Nixon demonstrated "through her attentions to others the values that Mrs. Roosevelt spoke about explicitly."[20] A profile of Pat Nixon's public life published in the Sunday magazine *Parade* noted that she "invited foreign women to events they had never been allowed to participate in and encouraged them to build their self-confidence during her trips throughout the Far East, Africa and the Soviet Union during the 1950s and the 1970s."[21] She also won praise from the local press when in 1955 she and Nixon made a month-long trip to Central America that included Pat's visit to a leprosarium in Panama. There she shook hands with patients; something many people would have declined due to the mistakened belief that the disease was contagious and incurable.

When Nixon's 1958 trip to Latin America turned violent, Pat showed her inner strength. The tour of Latin America in 1958 provoked anti-American demonstrations. Those demonstrations turned violent when protestors turned into an unruly mob wielding pipes. Upon their arrival, Communist-inspired crowds in Caracas chanting "death to Nixon," spit at them, and threw rocks. During the playing of the Venezuelan national anthem on the tarmac, Pat stood stoically beside Nixon, no doubt frightened, as tobacco juice rained down on her red suit from the mob above. Riding in separate limos from the airport into Caracas, the Nixons again encountered a threatening situation when the anger spilled into the streets and the mobs tried to overturn their limos. Pat was the picture of clench-jawed poise as glass shards from the limo window flew into her lap. Nixon himself was the picture of steely calm when one of his Secret Service agents unholstered his weapon with the belief that the mob would soon turn Nixon's limousine over and set it ablaze or lynch the visiting dignitaries. The local police vanished as the engulfing mob blocked the exit of the vice presidential limousine. Then, as if by magic, the mob would briefly part and the traveling American dignitaries would escape the howling rock throwing throng.

Intelligence reports said agitators planned to bomb them when Nixon was to lay a wreath at the tomb of Simon Bolivar, so that event was cancelled. But the violence there and elsewhere rattled the couple to their core. They realized that their lives were truly in danger. And while most press accounts singled out Nixon for praise for the courage to stand up to the angry demonstrators— even goading them by standing fast when someone spit directly in his face—Pat too showed equal courage by continuing the tour as planned. The popularity of both Nixons soared in the United

States, as they had showed personal courage in the face of dangerous adversity while representing their country.

Upon their return Pat gave numerous interviews to women's
magazines in which she again promoted the important role that
women could play in all walks of life. At the same time she continued to embody the American Housewife, so much so that she was
named Outstanding Homemaker of the Year in 1953, Mother of the
Year in 1955, and the nation's Ideal Wife in 1957 by the Homemaker's
Forum. "Every bit as much as her husband, Pat sought to control
and promulgate her image" as the paragon of perfection, Pat Nixon
biographer Will Swift said. "She allowed photographers to snap
pictures of her vacuuming or pressing her husband's pants, but
she made sure that there were no photos of her staff."[22] (Any such
staged photos of recent first ladies would be deemed incredulous
and a source of mockery and humor especially by the late night TV
wits. It's hard to imagine Nancy Reagan or Hillary Clinton at an
ironing board.) At the same time Pat impressed Eisenhower with
her intelligence and political savvy as a capable emissary of the
United States who studiously pored over dossiers prior to meeting foreign officials. Perhaps her only public faux pas during those
years came when she stretched that public image of the perfect wife
in a perfect marriage a bit too far. She insisted to a reporter that
she and Nixon never quarreled because their opinions were always
alike, clearly a lie, as any married couple would know. And when
the reporter wrote that they were slow to anger and always even-
tempered, that only underscored the fable.

Eisenhower's heart attack in 1955, which pushed Nixon to
within a heartbeat of the presidency, gave Pat reason not to want
Nixon to serve a second term on the ticket. She saw how much of
a physical toll the job had taken on him—and her—thus far. When
Ike recovered, he left Nixon in the lurch once again, failing to publicly endorse him on the ticket again as his second in command,
saying it wasn't up to him to tell his vice president what to do (a
strange statement from the man who previously had commanded

the world's greatest military force involving thousands upon thousands of soldiers, airmen, and sailors from several nations). This vacuum would create the opportunity for a "Dump Nixon" movement spearheaded by former governor Harold Stassen. Nixon had the strong and broad support of party regulars for another term and Eisenhower's letting the question of Nixon's candidacy linger was yet another humiliation Dick suffered at the hands of Ike. Nixon again fell into a depression over the perceived slight and, according to Swift, visited several physicians, some of whom prescribed barbiturates for him.[23] When Nixon's mood revived after a Miami vacation with his pal Bebe Rebozo, Pat changed her mind about a second term and told a close friend that no one–meaning Eisenhower–would "push us" off the ticket. Ike's refusal to act gave Nixon the green light, and the couple campaigned aggressively and successfully.

While Nixon and Ike worked independently for the most part, their spouses had a different relationship. Mamie came to rely increasingly on Pat, often tasking her with chores at short notice such as filling in for her at White House occasions. Whether this was due to Mamie's many years as a military wife used to the common practice in the service of assigning tasks to the wives of subordinates or of her sincere friendship for Pat Nixon, the chronic stress on Pat led to severe back strain and a hospital stay early into Ike's second term.

That assessment proved true also on their two subsequent trips abroad. The Nixons went to London in November 1958 to honor the GIs who died there in the war. During the four-day visit Nixon's clear, concise speeches won over a normally skeptical British press (always eager to knock down an American envoy a peg or two) as well as the English Speaking Union. Pat matched her husband by eliciting rare positive reviews from the women of Fleet Street, who praised her for her manners and wardrobe (this was the 1950s after all). By this time, of course, Pat had learned how to handle the press and to avoid saying anything that could damage the Nixon's carefully cultivated image of partnership and domestic bliss. So when she was asked at a press conference for women reporters at the American ambassador's residence to describe her marriage, she replied, "This might sound exaggerated, but I am just as much in love with my husband as I was on the first day."[24] It was as ambiguous a statement as ever uttered by the most expert of politicians, and it satisfied the ladies of the British press who of course were unfamiliar with her early ambivalence toward the young Nixon.

In July 1959, the Nixons went to Moscow, where Nixon famously engaged Soviet Premier Nikita Khrushchev in the so-called "kitchen debate," at an American model home exhibition. While dutifully attending to her scheduled visits to kindergartens, pioneer camps, farmers markets, and the GUM department store, Pat also engaged the Soviet leader, questioning him as to why his wife and those of other Soviet officials were not included on a welcoming banquet guest list, a common practice of communist leaders everywhere who preferred not to bring their wives into the public. Khrushchev, however, gave in to her request. And when she met with some of the women she urged them to play a more active role in their country. Her frankness and candor impressed Khrushchev so much so that at a luncheon at his dacha, the Soviet leader intervened when his deputy Anastas Mikoyan tried to engage her in a conversation, saying, "Mrs. Nixon belongs to me. You stay on your side of the table."[25] And when Nixon raised the issue of missile fuels and Khrushchev had no reply, Pat said to him half-jokingly, "I'm surprised that there is a subject you're not prepared to discuss, Mr. Chairman. I thought that with your one-man government you had everything firmly in your own hands."[26] Her performances in Moscow and also in Poland afterward earned Pat rave reviews at home. The *New York Times* labeled her a diplomat in high heels.

Despite their diplomatic triumphs abroad in the late 1950s, the Nixons in the early 1960s "lived through two enormously painful electoral defeats, both of them rife with bad luck, poor judgment, and self-doubt. Pat bore the hardship of two political campaigns she definitely did not relish, and Nixon submitted to a restless interim year out of the political arena."[27] The 1960 presidential campaign was a study in contrasts; Vice President Nixon was only forty-seven years old, but he had already been in the public eye for about a dozen years, and with his five-o'clock shadow and studious expressions, he came across as much older than his youthful Democratic opponent Senator John F. Kennedy, who was actually only four years Nixon's junior. And Pat, the stay-at-home, cloth-coat-clad mother, had the insurmountable task of competing for America's affections against the designer-clad, bilingual, former photographer and career woman Jackie Kennedy. The 1960 campaign introduced the American people to televised presidential debates, so it was only natural for reporters to suggest that the two women debate a topic they believed was of interest to all American women—fashion trends. Pat said she was willing, but only if the topic was "something of value," and in her mind fashion definitely was not. There was no distaff debate (and never has been).

While some viewers and reporters saw Jackie as a bit too perfect, labeling her a phony, Pat came across all too often as stiff and programmed, an unemotional smile pasted on her face. To her credit she agreed with some of the criticism, telling one reporter, "I may be dying, but I certainly wouldn't say anything about it."[28] And she "spoke only occasionally about her fear of making a mistake that would hurt her husband—a fear that left her tense, curtailed her spontaneity in public, and allowed her detractors to caricature her."[29]

However, when Nixon promised to campaign in all fifty states, while his advisers told him not to, Pat stood by his side. And as the pace of the campaign grew more frantic and the days before the election dwindled down to a precious few, Pat's calm, steady hand on the tiller was in great contrast to Nixon's increasingly angry outbursts and frustrations. She did get angry at him, however, when he used an aide as a go-between to cancel their private dinners together because of another campaign chore he chose over her company, she made sure to tell him so. As the *Parade* article reported, both Pat and Nixon agreed that she was emotionally and physically stronger than he was. During their international trips and political campaigns, she could easily work for fifty hours non-stop with little to eat.[30]

In the final month of the campaign, Nixon's advisers realized Pat's value and her popularity with American women. They dubbed the week of October 3, "Pat Week," and sent out colorfully decorated vehicles to canvass key districts under the slogan, "Pat for First Lady." And in the final sprint to Election Day she campaigned with Nixon on a barnstorming tour of several states, during which the couple managed only a few hours of sleep each night. But if the 1952 "secret fund" controversy didn't cause Pat to hate politics completely, the fraud in the 1960 election surely did.

In the end, Kennedy won by a hair's breadth. Prior to the official final tally, Nixon went on TV from his bedroom suite at the Ambassador Hotel in Los Angeles and acknowledged his loss. If you look at the 1960 video, you see Nixon smiling broadly, which must have taken a superhuman effort, when he says, "If the current trend continues, Senator Kennedy will be the next president of the United States." The video also shows Pat clearly on the verge of tears. According to one published story, she then quickly took refuge in her separate hotel bedroom, where she could escape the frenetic campaign. When a friend passed by her door later, Pat beckoned her to come in. "Now I'll never get to be First Lady," she reportedly said.[31] She was not initially in favor of Nixon running for president, however as she had done so many times when she was confronted with challenges—many not of her own doing— she had thrown herself wholeheartedly into the campaign and did whatever she could to win. The loss stayed with her for the rest of her life, and she always believed that Nixon should have insisted on a recount.

Pat Nixon was well aware of John Kennedy's "womanizing" and deeply resented the efforts by the Democratic Madison Avenue ad men, efforts funded by JFK's wealthy father, to depict the naval veteran as a "family man." Pat Nixon told friends she looked forward to moving back to California and a more normal life.

The Nixons went first to Florida to decompress and then to New York for Christmas. They returned to Washington, where they sat through the Kennedy inauguration on January 20, and then promptly left for the Bahamas. They planned to stay for a month, but like many vacationers who soon grew bored with the soporific pace of their holiday hideaway, the Nixons returned to the states after only two weeks. Nixon himself was incapable of relaxation.

The former vice president moved to Los Angeles in February to rekindle his career as an attorney while Pat stayed in DC so their daughters could finish school there. It was their longest separation since the war. Pat and the girls returned to California in June, and the Nixons moved into a new home in the Beverly Hills area. The Nixons had shopped for a new home, but ultimately decided on a home in the Trousdale Lake area of Bel Air and were inordinately proud of the home. The following year it would be learned that Nixon had been sold the lot for a bargain-basement price by developer Clint Murchison Jr., who financed the development with millions from the mobbed-up Teamsters pension fund. Murchison would host Nixon in Dallas on November 21, 1963, the day before John Kennedy was murdered in that city.

Time healed many of her wounds as Pat renewed old friendships and together they began to entertain friends and other visitors. There, Nixon penned *Six Crises*, which hit the bookshelves in 1962. His dedication to Pat, "who also ran," was viewed as cold and perfunctory, but Pat took it lightly, knowing of her husband's aversion to any public displays of affection, even in print.

Nixon's decision to seek the governorship of California in 1962 once again sorely tested their marriage because Pat had had enough of campaigns, even one confined to her home state. She wanted none of it, preferring to stay home as a family and to travel a bit. She even warned Nixon that if he chose to run, she would not campaign with him, so turned off politics as she was. Nevertheless, despite all her doubts about the wisdom of another grueling political campaign, she acknowledged his need to run. "I'm trapped," she told a friend. "Which way can I go? He can't help it. He must always have a crusade."[32] So when Nixon threw his hat in the ring, so did Pat. While Pat would not take to the hustings till the final weeks of the 1962 campaign, she would attend dozens of events and shake thousands of hands in Nixon's ill-fated California drive. She must have been told with maddening frequency what a great First Lady she would have made.

Nixon's bitter California loss, his first in his home state, validated Pat's earlier fears and she retreated to suffer again in silence while he uttered his famous "You won't have Nixon to kick around anymore because, gentlemen, this is my last press conference." It was perhaps the only statement that Nixon made during the entire campaign that she cheered, yelling "Bravo!" while she and the girls watched his press conference at home on TV. Yet, when the defeated man came through the door later, she rushed to hug him as he bolted past her and into the backyard to mourn alone. The loss caused the terms of their marriage to shift again. Pat was no longer as willing to cater to Nixon.

After Nixon's defeat the family flew to Europe and then to Egypt with their close friends Jack and Helene Drown, before relocating to New York. People who knew Pat then said they "never saw her happier" than when her husband was "retired" from politics. Daughter Julie wrote, "As far as my mother was concerned, the '62 campaign was best forgotten,"[33] and she enjoyed the anonymity that New York City afforded its residents and visitors. But in 1967 as Nixon edged toward a second Republican presidential nomination, "Mother was unmistakably troubled as she faced the prospect of another political race," Julie wrote.[34] Even as late as that Christmas, Pat was not on board. But "she told him she would help if he felt he had to make the race"[35] because deep down she believed in Nixon's talent and ability to solve many of the problems created by the ongoing Vietnam War.

When the "new nixon," sewed up the Republican Party's presidential nomination in that turmoil-filled summer of 1968, Pat too was seen as a new woman, more outgoing and less reserved than anyone could remember. I think it was those years in the wilderness that had had a calming and restorative effect on her. Pat affected an easier and more modern "look." While never a purchaser of couture like Jackie Kennedy, she still dressed in a simple and flattering style. She loved to shop at Bloomingdale's in New York, knowing full well that the days of privacy would soon be over. As for the inevitable criticisms, she said, "I am who I am and I will continue to be."[36] As she told Gloria Steinem in a 1968 interview, "Now, I have friends in all the countries of the world. I haven't just sat back and thought of myself or my ideas or what I wanted to do. Oh no, I've stayed interested in people. I've kept working. Right here in the plane I keep this case with me, and the minute I sit down, I write my thank you notes. Nobody gets by without a personal note. I don't have time to worry about who I admire or who I identify with. I've never had it easy. I'm not like all you . . . all those people who had it easy."[37]

Pat rallied to support Nixon's comeback campaign with a makeover. She abandoned her Mamie Eisenhower–style bangs for the popular bouffant hairdo of the day in a lighter blond color. Still a handsome woman at fifty-five, she was again an asset on the campaign trail. As Julie Nixon Eisenhower wrote, "It took courage to re-enter public life as spiritedly as she did. She had no illusions about campaigns or Washington; no confidence that success lay at the end of the rainbow. She knew that her husband was bucking history by running. If he won, he would be the only presidential candidate to have been defeated, denied re-nomination four years later, and then succeeded in recovering sufficient political strength to win on the second bid,"[38] And she broke new ground when she became the first presidential candidate's wife to go on her own campaign tour instead of just appearing with her husband at selected events. She even was able to put up with Nixon's autocratic campaign manager and later White House Chief of Staff Haldeman (known as the "Iron Chancellor"), who snidely called her "Thelma" behind her back.

In the closing hours of the 1968 race and with the evaporation of Nixon's earlier lead over LBJ's vice president Hubert Humphrey, the polls were showing a much closer race than expected. The Democratic-leaning Harris poll even had Humphrey leading Nixon by 3 percent. Nixon prepared his wife and daughters for the possibility that they might once again experience defeat. At 6 a.m. with the election still in doubt and TV commentators reporting that Chicago Mayor Richard J. Daley was holding back (largely Republican) precinct votes from Cook County, Pat experienced a wave of nausea recalling the voter fraud of the 1960 campaign. She ran into the bathroom, where she was sick to her stomach. After Daley was forced into releasing the votes, Illinois went to Nixon, giving him a stunning, come-from-behind victory by some half million votes over Humphrey. Pat had been spared a replay of that terrible night in 1960.

The White House had changed greatly since the Eisenhower administration, and so had coverage of the First Lady, which had been perfunctory as far as Mamie Eisenhower was concerned. Now substance replaced the superficiality of the First Lady reportage, and Pat saw the press on a regular basis. And by the end of the Nixon presidency Pat had visited seventy-eight countries, the most ever by a First Lady.[39] Her daughter Julie said Nixon's first campaign manager in Whittier in 1946, Roy Day, made perhaps the best assessment of how Pat would play the role of First Lady. In an interview the day after Nixon's election, Day said, "Well, she'll never be traipsing along behind the president, she'll never be in front of him, but she'll always be at his side."[40] In fact, during the Nixons' historic trip to China in 1972, Pat enchanted Chinese Foreign Minister Zhou En-lai so much that he gave two rare pandas to the United States as a gift to her from China.

Although most everyone who remembers the JFK White House credits Jacqueline Kennedy for the major makeover of the mansion, it was Pat who quietly and without fanfare transformed the mansion's rather pedestrian art collection into a preeminent national treasure. And just as she had been an excellent hostess in her own home, she was equally attentive to all guests at the White House, hoping to make everyone, from foreign heads of state to Appalachian quilt makers, feel at ease in the historic building. When I attended a Christmas party at the Nixons' home in Saddle River, New Jersey, I found her to be friendly and deeply devoted to her husband. She was charming and gracious to everyone, a sharp contrast to Nancy Reagan, who had her intense likes and dislikes and never bothered to hide them.

When the end of the Nixon presidency loomed in August 1974 and the family gathered in the Lincoln Sitting Room to discuss whether he should resign or fight charges of an impeachable offense, it was Pat who first said, "But, why?" She did not even deign to look at the transcripts of the incriminating phone call tapes that the rest of the family read during the meeting. As Nixon wrote in his *Memoirs*, "Pat, who had let the others do most of the talking in our meeting, told me that now, as always before, she was for fighting to the finish."[41] I met Mrs. Nixon as a sixteen-year-old at the Women's National Republican Club in Manhattan in late 1967. I was wearing an enormous "Nixon for President" button and approached the low dais where she was seated. "I like your button," she said. I was beaming.

In the holiday season of 1979 I would spend two hours with Pat Nixon at a Christmas party for staff, family, and the inner circle where both she and the former president socialized. Nixon gave a brief speech about Christmas and the state of the country and toasted the new year by a enumerating the challenges of the forces of freedom around the world. "Always remember those in uniform, the men and women serving this country," Nixon said. "I was one of them. They risk their lives and give their all every day, while others sit on their butts and complain about everything." Pat Nixon stared adoringly at her husband through his entire remarks just as she had on thousands of platforms across the country in 1952, 1956, 1960, 1962, 1968, and 1972. It was a gaze the media would use to mock her, but it was undiminished. She had an amazing ability to put people at ease and seemed to have an amazing repoire with children.

Pat Nixon's cousin, Ned Sullivan, lived in Westchester and had served as an advance man to Nixon on occassion. Sullivan was friendly with Nixon crony Robert Abplanalp and his Republican consigliere Bill Griffin, a burly Irishman. Ned and I chatted with Mrs. Nixon about the looming 1980 presidential contest. Mrs. Nixon's cousin Ned was a Connally man. I argued for Reagan. Mrs. Nixon heard both arguments, whereupon she winked and said "I like Reagan." She then turned on her heel to join another group of Nixonites imbibing in the holiday cheer.

The media caricature of Pat Nixon as passive or without recognition that she was the source of Nixon's strength misunderstands this determined and resilient woman who achieved so many firsts as the second lady and on the campaign trail.

When *Time* magazine asked the ex-president about that press sobriquet "Plastic Pat," Nixon replied, "[H]er plastic was tougher than the finest steel."[42]

NOTES

1. Will Swift, *Pat and Dick*, p. 21.
2. Ibid., 30.
3. Ibid., 51.
4. Anthony Summers, *The Arrogance of Power*, p. 36.
5. Will Swift, *Pat and Dick*, p. 66.
6. Ibid.
7. Anthony Summers, *The Arrogance of Power*, p. 40.
8. Roger Morris, *Richard Milhous Nixon: The Rise of an American Politician*, p. 506.
9. Will Swift, *Pat and Dick*, p. 97.
10. Roger Morris, *Richard Milhous Nixon: The Rise of an American Politician*, p. 506.
11. Ibid., 106.
12. Ibid., 103.

13. Anthony Summers, *The Arrogance of Power*, p. 118.
14. Roger Morris, *Richard Milhous Nixon: The Rise of an American Politician*, p. 796.
15. Ibid., 803.
16. Anthony Summers, *The Arrogance of Power*, p. 117.
17. Roger Morris, *Richard Milhous Nixon: The Rise of an American Politician*, p. 848.
18. Anthony Summers, *The Arrogance of Power*, p. 139.
19. Ibid.
20. Will Swift, *Pat and Dick*, p. 126.
21. "Richard and Pat Nixon: 10 Things You Didn't Know About Their Marriage," *Parade*, Jan. 7, 2014, online: http://parade.conde-nast.com/249558/parade/richard-and-pat-nixon-10-things-you-didnt-know-about-their-marriage/.
22. Will Swift, *Pat and Dick*, p. 132.
23. Ibid., 136.
24. Ibid., 147.
25. Ibid., 150.
26. Ibid.
27. Ibid., 153.
28. Ibid., 156.
29. Ibid.
30. "Richard and Pat Nixon: "10 Things," *Parade*, Jan. 7, 2014.
31. Anthony Summers, *The Arrogance of Power*, p. 216.
32. Ibid., 176.
33. Julie Nixon Eisenhower, *Pat Nixon: The Untold Story*, p. 215.
34. Ibid., 231.
35. Ibid., 234.
36. Judith Viorst, "Pat Nixon is the Ultimate Good Sport," *Sunday Magazine, New York Times*, Sep. 13, 1970, 13.
37. Gloria Steinem, "In Your Heart You Know He's Nixon," *New York* magazine, Oct. 28, 1968, http://nymag.com/news/politics/45934/index11.html.
38. Ibid., 235.
39. Ibid., 254.
40. Ibid., 255.
41. Ibid., 420.
42. "Richard and Pat Nixon, Ten Things," *Parade*, Jan. 7, 2014.

CHAPTER THIRTEEN

A NEW BEGINNING

"The greatest title history can bestow is that of peacemaker."
—Richard Nixon

lvis "The King" Presley showing up one day in late 1970 outside the gates of the White House is one of the truly bizarre intersections of politics and pop culture of the twentieth century. Two years prior Nixon had orchestrated one of the greatest political comebacks of all time. Elvis had also staged a career-reviving comeback of his own two years earlier. After the British invasion, the Beatles and other bands of "the swinging sixties" had taken all the gas out of Graceland. Amid declining record sales, and dwindling attendance for his films, built around half-baked song offerings such as "Do the Clam," and "Petunia, the Gardener's Daughter," the King needed a spark. In 1968, Elvis appeared on NBC and, much like Nixon had, used a team of media gurus to redefine his image and turn the schlocky irrelevance of the previous years on its head. The comeback special pulled in the highest ratings for NBC that year.

Only two years later, Elvis was bloated and often tranquilized by massive amounts of prescription drugs. Often in the company of the gun-totting, pill-popping, raucous yes-men playfully dubbed the "Memphis Mafia," Elvis sought license for he and his hillbilly army to legally carry firearms and pharmaceuticals. Elvis thought a badge from the Federal Bureau of Narcotics and Dangerous Drugs might do the trick. Enter Nixon.

"The narc badge represented some kind of ultimate power to him," Priscilla Presley later wrote. "With the federal narcotics badge, he [believed he] could legally enter any country both wearing guns and carrying any drugs he wished."[1]

To this end, Elvis vowed to help the president by becoming an undercover federal agent who would fight the drug element, hippie culture, and Black Panthers. The King promised this and more in a handwritten letter scribbled illegibly on American Airlines stationary en route to DC.[2] "I can and will do more good if I were made a Federal Agent at Large and I will help out by doing it my way through my communications with people of all ages," Presley continued. "First and foremost, I am an entertainer, but all I need is the Federal credentials. I have done an in-depth study of drug abuse and Communist brainwashing techniques and I am right in the middle of the whole thing, where I can and will do the most good.'[3]

Nixon aide Egil "Bud" Krough bought the Presley ruse. Krough even thought that the King could put out an anti-drug album titled *High on Life* that could be cut at a rehabilitation clinic, a Nixon administration spin on Johnny Cash's *At Folsom Prison* for the recovering addict set.

Elvis showed up to the White House in an ensemble that included tight purple velvet pants, a matching velvet cape, an oversized lion's head pendant, and one of his signature ham-sized belt buckles. Nixon aide Dwight Chapin insisted that Elvis meet Nixon—that this could be an opportunity for the perennially square Nixon to connect with the youth element. "You must be kidding," H. R. Haldeman replied.[5]

Nixon, who so often greeted guests to the Oval Office with trinkets from his desk, was brought a souvenir from Presley—a World War II Colt .45 pistol that was quickly confiscated by the Secret Service. "You dress kind of wild, don't you, son?" Nixon asked on greeting the bedazzled pop star. "Mr President, you've got your show to run and I've got mine," Presley answered.[6]

The Richard Nixon Show at the White House began almost two years earlier. Election Day proved to be extremely close—it wasn't until the next day that the television networks and newspapers finally called Nixon the winner. The key results came down to California, Ohio, and Illinois, all of which Nixon carried by only three percentage points or less. If Humphrey had carried all three of these states, he would have won the election. If he had won just two of them—or even just California—Wallace would have succeeded in his quest to prevent an electoral majority. The race would have gone to the Democrat-controlled House of Representatives, dashing Nixon's hopes again.

While Nixon's Electoral College vote count with thirty-two states was certainly larger than Humphrey's thirteen states, the popular vote margin was a mere 500,000 votes, or about 1 percent. Nixon said Humphrey left a gracious message congratulating him, noting, "I knew exactly how he felt."[7]

The fact is, in 1968 there were so many factors in play no one can claim Nixon won because he pandered to the darker side of Southerners. Several of his actions and speeches during the campaign prove this false, as do election season polling numbers. When the 1968 campaign began, Nixon was at 42 percent, Humphrey at 29 percent, and Wallace at 22 percent. When the campaign ended, 43.4 percent of Americans voted for Nixon, Humphrey came in at 42.7 percent, with Wallace at 13.7 percent. Nearly 9 percent of the national vote that had deserted Wallace were Democrats who originally deserted Humphrey.

Wallace's final vote totals further support the idea that the South had a limited role in the general election: he won only 13 percent of the popular vote and 46 electoral votes with five states.

Critics of the "Southern Strategy" failed to realize that Nixon had to win in other regions to earn the 270 electoral votes he needed.

If Nixon would have made his pandering for Southern votes more obvious, he risked losing support in Northern industrial states, which would be political suicide. Nixon commented, "There were going to be seven key states in the 1968 presidential campaign: New York, California, Illinois, Ohio, Pennsylvania, Texas, and Michigan. Of these I had won only California and Ohio in 1960."[8]

Furthermore, the South was not and could not be central to Nixon's campaign, as Nixon himself later said. "The Deep South had to be virtually conceded to George Wallace. I could not match him there without compromising on the civil rights issue, which I would not do."[9]

This "Southern Strategy" was much more complex than most people understood. It was more of an "Outer" Southern Strategy. Previous battles with Reagan and Rockefeller never forced Nixon to focus on strategies to win over the Southern delegates, but now it was critical.

During his meetings with Thurmond, the Atlanta state Republican chairman, Florida delegates and other important Southern political leaders, Nixon never made any unreasonable promises. Although he emphasized issues that were popular to Southern voters, the transcripts of these private meetings show that the message was consistent throughout his many encounters with Southern politicians.

Some people have claimed that Nixon told Thurmond that he would slow down desegregation if elected.[10]

Exactly the opposite happened, as Nixon described later in his memoirs:

"Schools in the South and all across the country opened in the fall of 1970 without violence and in compliance with the Supreme Court's order. The dramatic success of our Southern desegregation program is eloquently told by the statistics. By 1974 only 8 percent of black children in the South were attending all-black schools, down from 68 percent in the fall of 1968."[11]

Although unintentionally, Nixon probably helped spread desegregation through his Southern campaign strategy, which was originally conceived to bring more Southerners into the electoral process, which it did, but it also had other consequences. Patrick Moynihan saw the impact Nixon had with his Southern Strategy. In 1970 he said, "There has been more change in the structure of American public school education in the past month than in the past 100 years." And in 1970, there was no violence, as when John F. Kennedy was president, for example, and over 375 people were injured and 2 persons were killed at the University of Mississippi when it integrated. Nixon's desegregation followed his general policy of dealing with the South, which Ehrlichman said was done "his way, with conciliation and understanding and not in a fashion that would abrade the political sensibilities of Southerners and conservatives."[12]

Quite contrary to the negative press the 1968 campaign received for the Southern Strategy initiative, it was actually a great success, both in terms of the impact it made in the campaign and also for the effect it had on school integration in the South. President Nixon broadened his appeal to Southern voters during this time, which allowed him to carry the region for the 1972 presidential election, in which he acquired an astounding 70.5 percent of the votes. It was a remarkable feat, and on that led to the Republicans dominance in the South for the next forty years.

Nixon's 1968 campaign is an interesting case too because of its unusual nature in American political history. Since the Republican Party first ran a candidate for president in 1856, only twice has an individual who previously lost a general election campaign won the presidency—Nixon in '68, and Democrat Grover Cleveland in 1892. The only other cases of an individual who ran in a general election as a major party candidate (at least) twice unsuccessfully, were the populist Democratic crusader William Jennings Bryan (who ran three times, in 1896, 1900, and 1908), Republican Governor of New York Thomas Dewey (he of the infamous, "Dewey Defeats

Truman" mistaken *Chicago Tribune* headline) in 1944 and '48, and Democrat Adlai Stevenson, who fell to the Eisenhower-Nixon team twice in 1952 and '56.

Many having been nominated previously would mount a second bid for the presidency, including Herbert Hoover and Hubert Humphrey, only to fail in their attempt to be renominated. Nixon and Cleveland were the only two men to be nominated, lose, and be renominated *eight* years later and win.

What distinguishes the cases of Cleveland and Nixon is that their losses were sufficiently close as to keep alive their chances in the eyes of party members. Cleveland, in fact, having first been elected to the presidency in 1884, won the popular vote despite losing the Electoral College to Benjamin Harrison, in 1888 and won reelection in 1892 becoming the first (and to date only) president to serve two nonconsecutive terms. Nixon, as we have noted, lost an exceptionally close vote in 1960 that was riddled with fraud in key states, against the supremely charismatic Jack Kennedy. If Bill Clinton was the comeback kid, Dick Nixon was the original comeback kid.

We cannot examine the life of Richard Nixon without also discussing his many successes during his time in the presidency. While he is perhaps best remembered for the twin pillars of post-Nixon media coverage, China and Watergate, the Nixon presidency was one of the most prolific in terms of crafting lasting reform to government and its operation. Indeed, in many ways we forget the myriad ways in which Nixon, the old cold warrior and Republican, oversaw one of the most moderate-to-progressive administrations of the later twentieth century.

Those who thought Nixon was a fiscal conservative who planned to repeal the New Deal and Great Society were shocked. The Nixon administration saw a period of high inflation and unemployment—"stagflation." When Nixon took office in January 1969, unemployment was at a low 3.3 percent, but inflation was rising. In order to cool what Nixon's in-house economic advisor Dr. Arthur Burns saw as an overheating economy, Nixon elected on a policy of monetary restraint. Though the policy showed gradual positive results, the quick, larger increments of economic success eluded the early administration and the country lulled in a fiscal depression.

Concerns about reelection would be *the* primary consideration in the economic decisions of Nixon's first term. Unemployment rose to 6 percent by the end of 1970, a politically damaging high. In that year, Nixon appointed Arthur Burns, chairman of the Federal Reserve. Burns, who would come to be known as the "Pope of Economics" told the president that he must hold federal spending under $200 billion or Burns would continue to keep a firm grip on the money supply in order to fight inflation.

With unemployment ballooning over 6 percent in 1971, Treasury Secretary John Connally predicted Nixon's course: "Number one, he is not going to initiate a wage-price board. Number two, he is not going to impose mandatory price and wage controls. Number three, he is not going to ask Congress for any tax relief. And number four, he is not going to increase federal spending."

Virtually overnight the president reversed course. In August 1971 Nixon announced a New Economic Policy that shocked his supporters. The NEP violated most of Nixon's economic principles. Nixon stunned his own party by instituting wage and price controls, a 10 percent import tax, and a closure of the "gold window," preventing other nations from demanding American gold in exchange for American dollars. I believe Richard Nixon's biggest mistake as president was his decision to discontinue the dollar's link to gold on August 15, 1971. Accompanied by wage and price controls, it brought to a climax the notion, personified by LBJ in the Great Society of the 1960s, that economic policy could be conducted in a top-down fashion from Washington, DC, with little or no input from the free market or the American people.

Though Federal Reserve chairman Arthur Burns resisted the move at a secret weekend Camp David conference that consisted of

Nixon's top advisers, it put unprecedented power in the hands of an increasingly unaccountable Fed, which eventually in December 2008 began a five-year-plus experiment in price controls. The zero interest rate policy would freeze the American economy in a low-growth mode during the Obama years.

Nixon's move was popular at first. It enabled Burns and the Fed to gun the money supply in advance of the 1972 election, leaving the Democrats with no rebuttal. Nixon famously remarked, "We are all Keynesians now." But inflation exploded to double-digit levels in the first year of Nixon's second term. At the time many attributed the inflation crisis to an Arab oil embargo in response to Nixon's pro-Israel stance during the 1973 Sinai war, the simultaneous spike in food prices refutes that explanation. The 1973–75 inflationary recession was the worst since the 1930s and undoubtedly was a key factor in the toxic political climate that led to Nixon's impeachment and resignation in August 1974, just three years after his decision to end the gold standard. When Nixon left office, the economy was cratering, with rising unemployment and inflation, gas lines, and a weak stock market. "Probably more new regulation was imposed on the economy," wrote Herb Stein, the chairman of Nixon's Council of Economic Advisers, "than in any other presidency since the New Deal."

There are, however, other ways in which Nixon the president proved himself to be an unrepentant pragmatist. His domestic achievements are surprising to those who think of today's Republican Party. Nixon bona fides on Civil Rights are not well known. Vice President Nixon cast the tie-breaking vote against amending what became the Civil Rights Act of 1957 to give violators of the voting rights provisions and the right to a trial by state jury (thus guaranteeing that violators would not be punished by all-white juries in the Southern states). Senator Kennedy supported the amendment.[13] Dr. Martin Luther King praised Nixon for rounding up virtually every Senate for the bill. As US senator, Nixon had supported every major piece of civil rights or anti-lynching legislation—all of it killed by Senate Majority Leader Lyndon Johnson, then the leader of the Southern bloc in the Senate.

From 1969 to 1972, President Nixon increased the budget for civil rights programs from $75 million to more than $600 million. Perhaps the president's crowning achievement on civil rights, however, was the request for and implementation of the Emergency School Aid Act, for the purpose of ending forced busing and finally bringing about the end of school segregation as originally called for by the Supreme Court in 1954. For this purpose Nixon requested, and in 1971 would receive, $1.5 billion in appropriated funds from Congress over the course of 1971 and 1972.[14] The results were undeniable, between 1968 and 1974 the percentage of Southern schools that were desegregated skyrocketed from 10 percent to 70 percent. The US Commission on Civil Rights wrote in 1975 that "it has only been since 1968 that substantial reduction of racial segregation has taken place in the South."[15]

During his presidency, Nixon pioneered the affirmative action program—leading to an increase in federal purchases from black businesses to increase from $13 million to $142 million—and created an Office of Minority Business Enterprise under the auspices of the Department of Commerce.[16]

Indeed, Nixon had long felt that blacks had been treated unfairly in America and worked energetically during his presidency to do what he could to rectify that mistake. Between 1969 and when he left office in 1974, Nixon was able to raise the civil rights enforcement by 800 percent, double the budget for black colleges and universities, appoint more blacks to federal posts than any other president, including Lyndon Johnson, and adopted the Philadelphia Plan mandating quotas for blacks in unions and for black scholars in university faculties.

Nixon also created the Environmental Protection Agency (EPA), halted dumping in the Great Lakes, passed the Clean Air Act, and opposed an amendment to protect school prayer.

In addition, during Nixon's presidency a number of other major environmental and health safety bills into law. Among these were the Noise Control Act (1972), the Marine Mammal Protection Act (1972), the Endangered Species Act (1973), and the Safe Drinking Water Act (1974).[17]

Nixon proposed more ambitious programs than he enacted, including the National Health Insurance Partnership Program, which promoted health maintenance organizations (HMOs). He overhauled federal welfare programs. Nixon's welfare reform was the replacement of much of the welfare system with a negative income tax, a proposal by conservative economist Milton Friedman. The purpose of the negative income tax was to provide both a safety net for the poor and a financial incentive for welfare recipients to work.

Nixon's Family Assistance Program was the brainchild of Pat Moynihan, the former Kennedy aide who Garment recruited to work on domestic issues such as poverty and urban policy. Harvard Professor Daniel Patrick Moynihan was a New York Democrat who held positions in the Kennedy and Johnson administrations. Moynihan would later secretly conduct an investigation of the JFK assassination at the behest of a bereaved and bewildered Attorney General Robert F. Kennedy. Moynihan lost a bid for New York City Council president. The Moynihan that Nixon hired was described as "good Pat" by former Moynihan staffer and later supply-side guru Larry Kudlow, as opposed to "bad Pat" who would move left and downplay his ties to the Nixon administration before snatching a US Senate seat in New York.

Moynihan was a thinker, a staunch anti-Communist, and a solid liberal. He helped Nixon think outside the box on urban policy, the problems of the black community, and welfare. Moynihan would craft the controversial Family Assisstance Plan, which would have provided more payments to poor people and which drove the Republican right crazy. Moynihan appealed to Nixon's more prgressive instincts and convinced him that Disraeli had been successful in convincing the UK to adopt some liberal reforms because his ties on the right were so strong. It was *because* Disraeli was a Tory that he could get these things done, Moynihan would tell Nixon. Moynihan's memos were famously pungent. His writing was prolific and to the point. An Irishman, but an Anglophile, Moynihan would ultimately be appointed ambassador to India by President Ford, where he would review Indian troops while wearing a bowler and carrying a furled umbrella in a sharply cut Savile Row suit.

Moynihan would often sport a jaunty bowtie, seersucker suits in summer, and herringbone tweeds in the winter. He popularized the Irish walking hat. Moynihan was one of the bright lights of Nixon's presidency.

Nixon's support for the Family Assistance Plan was bold and, apparently, insincere. While Nixon won kudos from the left for proposing FAP, H. R. "Bob" Haldeman noted in his diary that Nixon secretly hoped the Senate would reject the program because "we can't afford it." Conservatives were up in arms over the FAP proposal. Conservative members of Congress attacked it. All the while, Nixon milked the credit for proposing it from the left and being glad of its demise.

One part of Nixon's welfare reform proposal did pass and become a lasting part of the system: Supplemental Security Income (SSI) provides a guaranteed income for elderly and disabled citizens. Nixon also pushed large increases in Social Security, Medicare, and Medicaid benefits. During his presidency, Nixon also proposed an expansion of the food stamp program.

Perhaps his least talked about progressive proposal, however, is one that would shock many today. Nixon was the first American president to propose a universal insurance mandate, the same mandate that now forms the backbone of President Obama's Affordable Care Act (aka, "Obamacare"). Nixon's plan was called a Comprehensive Health Insurance Plan (CHIP). CHIP required, among other things, that employers provide comprehensive health coverage for all employees, a substantial number of mandated benefits, and a government insurance program to cover individuals who could not afford health insurance.[18] Nixon maintained that this program "let us keep . . . as the guiding principle of our health programs [that] government has a great role to play—but we must always make sure that our doctors will be working for their patients and not for the Federal Government."[19] In short, Nixon saw CHIP as the best way to avoid a slide into socialized medicine; interestingly, the plan was killed by Senator Ted Kennedy for not being liberal enough.[20]

Nixon also had a legacy that lasted beyond his term in office in the personages of his four appointed Supreme Court justices: Chief Justice Warren Burger, and Associate Justices Harry Blackmun, Lewis Powell, and (future Chief Justice) William Rehnquist. The Burger appointment was the first by President Nixon, as he was to succeed retiring former Chief Justice Earl Warren, a man hated by conservatives around the country. While Warren retired during the final months of the Johnson administration, a Senate filibuster of the Johnson nominee, sitting Justice Abe Fortas, allowed Nixon to make the appointment and steer the court in a direction he felt more appropriate. Burger had made a name for himself in opposing the direction of the Warren Court and was known as a believer in a strict read of the Constitution—a so-called "strict constructionist."[21] It is worth noting that during his tenure as chief justice, no major decision from the Warren era was overturned. In this, his appointment must be considered a disappointment for Nixon. Burger, would also author the opinion that forced Nixon to turn over the White House tapes ultimately leading to Nixon's resignation.

H. R. "Bob" Haldeman, President Nixon's chief of staff, wrote in his diary on September 17, 1971, that the president was considering Philadelphia District Attorney Arlen Specter for an appointment to the US Supreme Court. "The attorney general wants guidance from the President on what he wants to do on a replacement [Supreme Court] appointment. Feels that we've got to really think it through carefully and establish our position on it. The President said to consider Arlen Specter as a Jewish seat."[1] Nixon and Haldeman had discussed Specter several months earlier, in June 1971, according to the Oval Office tapes:[2]

> **RN:** Mr. Specter, he's a very impressive fellow, Jewish . . . liberal . . . hard-line.
> **HRH:** Hard-line lawyer.
> **RN:** With good credentials.
> **HRN:** Which is unusual for a Jew.
> **RN:** Yeah. Good credentials and he's got very good communication with the young people and the Blacks and the rest because he's got imaginative procedures like, for example, in the field of drugs, he's got this program that he's against legalizing marijuana which is a position that's exactly right, because the evidence points to that . . . That's the kind of guy, you know, I've been thinking of.
> **HRH:** He could run your thing, couldn't he?
> **RN:** In Pennsylvania.
> **HRH:** No, here—your dope thing if you don't get what's-his-name?
> **RN:** Hmm, yeah, I don't think he'd do that . . . His future is there . . . We do have some appointments to the Supreme Court. If you go the Jewish route . . . I'm glad we've seen him . . . He's got a great future . . . I will never see him acting an asshole like this [Pennsylvania US Senator Richard] Schweiker . . . Man, he's tougher. He's a Jew that's come up like Henry Kissinger.

Mitchell summonsed Specter to Washington. By the time Specter arrived at the Justice Department Nixon had changed his mind. Specter remembered, "I was escorted to Mitchell's inner office and shook the attorney general's hand. We sat for twenty to twenty-five minutes. Mitchell talked about the weather. Whatever he'd wanted to discuss with me when he phoned urgently on Friday, he'd changed his mind by Monday."[22]

When Abe Fortas resigned from the court in 1969 the Nixon administration would then endure the embarrassment of nominating first Clement Haynsworth, and then G. Harold Carswell to fill the seat, and having neither confirmed by the Senate. No president since Hoover had endured a single outright defeat on nominations for the court, and Nixon endured two in short order. Haynsworth, then the chief judge of the Fourth Circuit Court of Appeals, was accused of having issued decisions favoring segregation as well as decisions that brought him financial benefit.[23] Ultimately the nomination would be opposed by a coalition including liberal Republicans and Northern democrats; and Haynsworth was defeated by a vote of 55 to 45. Similarly, Carswell was criticized for having an unusually high reversal rate (the rate at which higher courts reversed his decisions) and made an enemy of civil rights activists for his vocal support of white supremacy while running for office in Georgia.[24] Carswell particularly was an abject failure by members of the Nixon staff (specifically, John Mitchell) to adequately vet potential nominees. The defeats of Haynsworth and Carswell were attributed to the poor political judgment of Attorney General John Mitchell and provide early evidence that Mitchell, who would ultimately lose his balance in Watergate was beginning to teeter.

After the series of setbacks the administration went for a home run nomination in Minnesotan Harry Blackmun, who passed the Senate by a vote of 94-0 (with the six absent senators having expressed their support for Blackmun's nomination). Blackmun was a lifelong Republican and had been recommended to Nixon by Chief Justice Burger, who had served as Blackmun's best man, and as such Blackmun was expected to join a conservative resurgence on the court. For those expecting such, however, Blackmun would ultimately prove a disappointment, as he would become gradually more liberal at the same time as the court itself moved to the right. Blackmun would author the *Roe vs. Wade* decision establishing a constitutionally protected right for a woman to have an abortion, and in one of his last acts on the bench famously concluded that he no longer believed capital punishment to be constitutionally permissible.[25]

Following the Blackmun nomination, Justice Hugo Black retired from the court in September 1971 along with Justice Harlan, both for reasons relating to ill health. Nixon announced his intention to nominate Arkansas attorney Hershel Friday and California appeals court judge Mildred Lillie—Lillie would have been the first woman to be appointed to the Supreme Court.[26] However, shortly after the announcement the American Bar Association rated both nominees unqualified. This has been viewed by many as a convenient excuse allowing the ABA to obscure their own discomfort with the idea of a woman on the court—again we see Nixon ahead of his time on women's rights.[27]

Following this latest setback with judicial nominations, Nixon would proceed to nominate Lewis F. Powell, who had turned down the nomination to succeed Abe Fortas, and William Rehnquist to the court. Powell was confirmed relatively easily, by a vote of 89-1, however the Rehnquist nomination was more contentious. Rehnquist's nomination was opposed by the AFL-CIO, the United Auto Workers, and the NAACP, however, Rehnquist too was eventually confirmed by a voted of 68-26, with all but three liberal Republicans voting in support of the nomination.[28]

*   *   *

In addition to his substantial achievements in domestic policy, it is President Nixon's foreign policy achievements that are the aspects of his presidency most often lauded across the political spectrum. From ending the war in Vietnam, to opening up China and signing the first arms control agreement with the Soviet Union, Nixon proved one of the most successful foreign policy presidents of the twentieth century. There seem to have been two primary driving forces behind the administration's foreign policy, these motivations fall under the general headings of the so-called "Nixon Doctrine" and détente with the Soviet Union.

Like his predecessor LBJ, Nixon would be bedeviled by the Vietnam War. Johnson's detractors in the counterculture would now refocus their ire at "Tricky Dick." Nixon would drain some of this antagonism by ending the Selective Service System and moving the United States to an all-volunteer army. It is important, however, to note that Nixon *reversed* the policies of the Johnson administration, which had been relentless in its escalation of the war. Richard Nixon would begin withdrawing American troops originally committed to Vietnam from JFK and then greatly increased by LBJ. Resisting the impulse to "cut and run," Nixon would direct Defense Secretary Melvin Laird to conduct orderly troop withdrawals from Vietnam, at the same time stepping up aerial bombardment of the North Vietnamese in a bid to both cover the American withdrawals and to drive the North Vietnamese to the bargaining table.

President Nixon announced what has come to be known as the Nixon Doctrine in a press conference in Guam on July 25, 1969. Nixon further outlined three principles that would drive American foreign policy in an address to the American people on the Vietnam War from November 3, 1969. These were:

1. The United States will keep all of its treaty commitments.
2. [The United States] shall provide a shield if a nuclear power threatens the freedom of a nation allied with us or of a nation whose survival we consider vital to our security.
3. In cases involving other types of aggression, we shall furnish military and economic assistance when requested in accordance with our treaty commitments. But we shall look to the nation directly threatened to assume the primary responsibility of providing the manpower for its defense.[29]

The purpose of this speech is multifaceted. Domestically, it served as a commitment from President Nixon to the American

390

people that he remained committed to bringing the war to a successful conclusion. Internationally, it served to make clear to US allies that we would not abandon them in an hour of need, but that going forward the initial responsibility for their defense must lay with their own military forces—this speech presaged the process of "Vietnamization" in which South Vietnamese forces assumed ever greater proportions of the fighting.[30]

In the years following his election, the Nixon administration sought to bring the North Vietnamese back to the table, without much success. The North Vietnamese had little incentive to negotiate in good faith, as they held out for a better hand on the backs of military successes, the ongoing drawdown of American troops, and continuing domestic opposition to the war in the United States. However, following the mining of Haiphong Harbor, North Vietnamese forces were halted, and Nixon resumed the large-scale bombing of North Vietnamese targets north of the Demilitarized Zone. Coupled with the suspension of military aid to North Vietnam by the Soviet Union and China was enough to bring the Vietnamese to the table in advance of Nixon's reelection in 1972.[31] On January 9, 1973, following Nixon's decision to subject North Vietnam to twelve days of bombardment by American aircraft, the Vietnamese returned to the negotiating table and reached a settlement with the president based on terms Nixon had proposed in November. On January 21, Nixon secured the acquiescence of South Vietnamese President Thieu, and on January 27 the peace treaty was signed in Paris.[32] After Nixon's fall, the US Congress would refuse Nixon's successor Gerald Ford's request for continued military aid to South Vietnam, and the country would ultimately fall to the North.

The Nixon Doctrine would not just inform the evolving face of the Vietnam War, but extend throughout the president's foreign policy. In the Middle East the doctrine resulted in a decrease in active US military presence, supplemented by a dramatic increase in the sale of arms to US allies in the region. For example, arms transfers from the United States to the Shah in Iran increased from

$103.6 million in 1970 to $552.7 million in 1972; in the case of the Saudis the amount of arms transfers exploded from $15.8 million in 1970 to $312.4 million in 1972.[33]

* * *

The pinnacles of Nixon's foreign policy achievement, opening up China and détente (détente is a French term, which literally means "relaxation") with the Soviet Union, should be seen as twin sides of the same coin. Successful détente with the Soviet Union was dependent on bringing the Soviet leadership to the table. In 1968, with the United States embroiled in the war in Vietnam, there was no obvious rationale for the Soviets to ease pressure on the United States. This was a fact that Nixon recognized, and as such reconciliation with China became the method to exercise pressure on the Soviets and bring Soviet General Secretary Brezhnev to the negotiating table.

The story begins not in Washington, but on the Soviet-Chinese border in 1969. In March 1969, Chinese forces of the People's Liberation Army (PLA—not to be confused with the group of the same name in the Palestinian Territories) attacked Soviet border guards on Zhenbao Island, instigating a series of clashes between the two sides throughout spring and fall 1969. The significance of these clashes is often understated, if mentioned at all, in the story of rapprochement between the United States and the People's Republic of China. On December 10, 1969, National Security Advisor Henry Kissinger "burst into [the office of President Nixon's Chief of Staff, H. R. Haldeman] in a great state of excitement to report that we had just received word that the Chinese in Warsaw had come to our embassy indicating that they wanted to meet with us, and, more significantly, that they wanted to use the *front door*," Haldeman recorded in a journal he kept at the time (italics from the original text).[34] The importance of Chinese willingness to be openly seen in discussions with the United States was a momentous break from prior practice, in which all discussions between the two countries had occurred in secret. According to Haldeman, Kissinger then went on to inform him that in light of the previous border clashes Kissinger felt that the rift between the Soviets and Chinese was "very serious," and that "[Kissinger] expected that there was a very strong probability that the Russians would attack China by April 15th."[35]

Kissinger felt confident in his assertion that a Soviet assault was imminent against the Chinese as a result of US aerial reconnaissance photographs that showed the Soviets had moved "nuclear-armed" divisions within two miles of the Chinese border. Specifically, these photographs showed that hundreds of Soviet nuclear warheads had been stacked in piles, and eighteen thousand tents had been erected by the Soviets "overnight in nine feet of snow."[36]

According to Haldeman, over the course of 1969 there had been a series of overtures from the Soviets attempting to orchestrate a "surgical strike" (inasmuch as a strike utilizing nuclear weapons could be called "surgical") against the PLA's nuclear capacity. President Nixon, conscious of the extraordinary death toll such a strike would involve, turned the Soviets down. Incredibly, the Soviets were not dissuaded by their rejection by the United States and made it known to President Nixon that the Soviets intended to go it alone.[37]

While it was not widely known during the campaign, there were clear indications that President Nixon had concluded the time had come to open relations with so-called "Red China." In a Foreign Affairs article from October 1967 titled, "Asia After Viet Nam," Nixon wrote, "Any American policy toward Asia must come urgently to grips with the reality of China . . . we simply cannot afford to leave China forever outside the family of nations, there to nurture its fantasies cherish its hates and threaten its neighbors."[38] The border crisis between the Chinese and Soviets created an opportunity to open the door to cooperation between the United States and China while simultaneously weakening the Soviets enough to help keep them at the table. In this way, the response to the Sino-Soviet crisis of 1969–1970 should be viewed as the beginning of "triangularization."

After receiving word from the Soviets that they were planning on moving with or without US support, Nixon and Kissinger arrived at the plan that would culminate in the December 10 meeting in which Kissinger informed Haldeman that the Chinese wanted to talk. Kissinger contacted the US ambassador to Poland (earlier secret talks had been held between the two sides in Warsaw), Walter Stoessel, and instructed him to find the highest-ranking Chinese envoy to Poland he could at a social function and inform him that the United States was looking to resume talks.[39]

The initial approach went farcically, with the Chargè d'Affaires at the Chinese embassy, whom Stoessel attempted to engage in conversation during a reception hosted by the Yugoslav delegation, turning and walking out of the room. Stoessel was forced to run after him to deliver his message—Chinese Premier Chou En-lai would later make light of this in a meeting with Kissinger in China, saying, "If you want our diplomats to have heart attacks, approach them at parties and propose serious talks."[40]

The Soviets received the message. Several days after reports of impending talks between the United States and China began to surface in diplomatic and intelligence circles, the Soviets withdrew their nuclear forces from the border with China.[41] A global catastrophe had been avoided, and in January 1970 the ambassador met with Chinese representatives in Warsaw.[42] During this meeting the US ambassador was instructed to inform the Chinese that President Nixon would be interested in sending a representative to Beijing, or receive one in Washington, for further discussions. This proposal was neither agreed to, nor rejected by the Chinese—in this case, silence was golden.

From the conclusion of that first meeting, events began to unfold quickly. Nixon began deliberately slipping remarks into his discussions with those heads of state, specifically Mr. Charles deGaulle in France, Nicolae Ceauşescu of Romania, and Yahya Khan of Pakistan. This was a deliberate strategy, intended to produce a sense that there was "a new attitude in Washington," a message that would make its way back to Beijing.[43]

In April 1970, Nixon allowed the export of goods to China that had been manufactured elsewhere with American components. This measure was followed in July by the release of Bishop Walsh, a Catholic priest they had imprisoned. Later in July, Nixon went further and permitted US oil companies to refuel cargo ships bound for China. In August Nixon went a step further, inserting a line into a speech he gave to the editors of midwestern newspapers, arguing that "the deepest rivalry which may exist in the world today . . . is that between the Soviet Union and China."[44]

In spring 1971 Nixon lifted all restriction on the use of US passports for travel to China. This led to the much-publicized invitation by the Chinese of the United States ping-pong team to play in China (an invitation that was reciprocated by the US team after their arrival in Beijing). Chou En-Lai personally received the US team in the Great Hall of the People, an honor that few diplomats could claim.[45]

Shortly after the "ping-pong diplomacy," during a state visit to Pakistan, then a close ally of China, Nixon indicated to Yahya Khan that he was willing to send a secret high-level envoy to China. Khan passed along the message, and then in December the Pakistani ambassador to the United States hand delivered a message from Chou en-Lai indicating China's willingness to accept such an envoy.[46]

It should be noted before advancing to the sequence surrounding Kissinger's secret meetings in China just how much this was Nixon's brainchild, not Kissinger. In fact, Haldeman recounts that when told early on in the presidency that "[Nixon] seriously intends to visit China before the end of his second term," Kissinger, ever the Europeanist, responded with an amused smile and "fat chance."[47] Kissinger has received the accolades (including a Nobel Peace Prize), but in truth he was a beneficiary of Nixon's ambitious policy—not the mastermind of it.

However, Kissinger's initial opposition to the policy would transform into his ownership of it. After several months of back-and-forth diplomacy regarding the timing, Kissinger pulled Nixon aside during a state dinner for the president of Nicaragua, the Chinese had presented a window between June 15 and 20 for the meeting with Kissinger.[48] Due to travel constraints revised dates of July 9 arrival and July 11 departure were suggested and accepted by the Chinese. Kissinger would fly from a military airport in Islamabad, Pakistan, to a private airport outside Beijing.[49]

The meeting between Kissinger and En-Lai on July 10 concluded with an invitation for President Nixon to visit China in 1972. It was a coup when it was announced on July 15 that Nixon would visit China in February 1972; the global balance of power had been completely overturned. Upon hearing the news, former British Prime Minister Harold MacMillan said, "[Nixon has] brought the oldest civilization in the world back into the game to redress the new Russian empire."[50]

In fact, MacMillan may have been better informed than he realized. One of the primary motivating factors for Nixon in reaching out to China was in pursuit of a rebalancing of US-Soviet relations. Nixon also fundamentally rethought the basis of US-Soviet relations; during previous administrations relations had been "compartmentalized" with the specific issues being addressed individually and not on the whole.[51] However, Nixon saw this as a failing in US diplomacy, Nixon demanded "linkage," whereby US-Soviet relations would be viewed through the paradigm of the totality of variables, from Vietnam to Egypt to trade.

Before Nixon could achieve détente with the Soviet, however, he had one more goal to strengthen his hand beyond China—an anti-ballistic missile system. The debate in Congress and US foreign policy circles was impassioned. In both circles the thought of an ABM system, which could neuter or significantly weaken the Soviet nuclear deterrent, was seen as an inherently destabilizing act. Nixon would only win approval of the measure in the Senate by a single vote, but the Soviets got the message—Nixon meant business, and it was better to work with him than work against him.[52]

In 1972, Nixon's efforts in China and at home with the ABM Treaty bore fruit. Nixon and Secretary Brezhnev signed an anti-ballistic missile treaty (a concession to the Soviets), a preliminary agreement to limit Soviet arms (a measure that would evolve into SALT 1), and a basic outline for US-Soviet relations.[53]

* * *

At 6 a.m. on Saturday October 6, 1973, White House Chief of Staff Alexander Haig woke up President Nixon at his home in California with news that Egypt and Syria had attacked Israel.[54] The news of the war shocked the American foreign policy and intelligence communities to such an extent that a study prepared by the CIA Center for the Study of Intelligence in conjunction with the Nixon Presidential Library concludes, "To intelligence historians, the October 1973 war is almost synonymous with 'intelligence failure.'"[55]

It became clear in the hours after the attack that the Arab forces had surprised Israeli forces and the Israeli state faced the greatest threat to its survival since the original war of independence. Along the border with Syria, along the so-called Golan Heights 180 Israeli tanks faced 1,400 Syrian tanks supplied by the Soviet Union; likewise Egypt crossed the Suez with 80,000 soldiers facing little Israeli opposition.[56]

In the days following the Yom Kippur attacks Israel suffered a number of setbacks, and Washington became increasingly concerned. Nixon alone concluded that the United States must step in to back Israel against Arab forces whose primary military supplier was the Soviet Union—the 1963 war became more than just necessary to save the Jewish state, it became a struggle between the world's preeminent superpowers.[57] Kissinger opposed the US action.

It is one of history's great ironies that it was Nixon whose airlift would play an integral role in the salvation of the Jewish state, as in the years since the release of the Watergate tapes it has become one of the established facts of the Nixon mythos that the president was a raving anti-Semite. The tapes that have been released since

Watergate continue to damn the president, who seemingly maintained a sort of cognitive dissonance when it came to several prominent Jewish members of his senior staff, Kissinger, White House counsel Leonard Garment, and speechwriter William Safire, as well as economist Herb Stein. In one rant from 1971, Nixon rails against the Jews, who, in his estimation, were both "all over the government" and disloyal; he told Haldeman that the Jews needed to be controlled by emplacing someone at the top "who is not Jewish."[58] Incredible, given the position in which he would find himself in two short years, Nixon would argue to Haldeman that, "most Jews are disloyal," and "generally speaking, you can't trust the bastards. They turn on you."[59] In another exchange, just months before the 1973 war, Nixon rants to Kissinger about American Jews and what he saw as their selfish view of foreign policy. On a call on April 19, 1973, Nixon reveals a concern that American Jews would "torpedo" a US-Soviet summit vowing that, "If they torpedo this summit . . . I'm gonna put the blame on them, and I'm going to do it publicly at nine o'clock at night before eighty million people."[60] Then, most damning, Nixon would go on to argue, "I won't mind one goddamn bit to have a little anti-Semitism if it's on that issue . . . they put the Jewish interest above America's interest and it's about goddamn time that the Jew in America realizes he's an American first and a Jew second."[61]

Yet, despite all of this, Nixon would play a pivotal role in protecting the Jewish state, as Nixon recognized that the defeat of Israel was unthinkable for US interests. Nixon went to Congress to request authorization for emergency aide for Israel despite the Gulf States announcing a price increase of 70 percent in the wake of the Arab assault. After Nixon went to Congress for authorization, the Gulf States responded vigorously, announcing a total boycott of the United States, causing the oil shock of 1973.[62]

The Gulf States' retaliation simply served to further entrench the opposition of many who had fought to slow or halt the shipment of weapons to the Israelis (the former being represented by Secretary of State and National Security Advisor Kissinger, the latter being represented by Secretary of Defense Schlesinger).[63] Nixon hit the roof when he leaned that Kissinger was delaying the airlift because of his concern that it would offend the Russians. Despite the opposition of his national security and foreign policy brain trust, Nixon ordered the airlift, saying, "We are going to get blamed just as much for three planes as for three hundred," and later in exasperation at the slow start of US support, said, "Use every [plane] we have—everything that will fly."[64]

Finally, after several days of internal politicking amongst the upper echelons of the administration, Nixon got his airlift Operation Nickel Grass. Over the course of the airlift 567 missions were flown, delivering over 22,000 tons of supplies, and an additional 90,000 tons were delivered to Israel by sea.[65] Later in her life, Israeli Prime Minister Golda Meir would admit that upon hearing of the airlift, she began crying during a cabinet meeting.[66]

Nixon's loyalty drove him to save a US ally from the threat of utter destruction despite the real risk of economic crisis and political cost to himself. To borrow the phrase from the Kennedy clan, in Nixon's decision to aide Israel we see a true "profile in courage."

In a January 1973, *U.S. News & World Report* article titled, "Behind Nixon's Reorganization," the country and the political-industrial complex were made aware of an administration plan that would shake DC to its core. If Nixon had thought that the fight to win confirmation for his early judicial nominees was difficult, his fight to reorganize the government would help contribute to his downfall.

On September 15, 1972, Nixon met with John Dean and Haldeman to discuss Nixon's frustration with the working of the federal bureaucracy. During this meeting, Nixon decided that after the election, "we're going to have a house cleaning."[67] This desire was brought about by a frustration with his ability to run the extensive federal bureaucracy; in particular, Nixon had grown frustrated with the senior administrative bureaucracy across the government.

Many members of the senior administrative bureaucracy had been appointed under Democratic administrations, and Nixon viewed it as impeding his ability to get government to respond to him. Haldeman has recounted one particular aspect of the conversation regarding the Defense Department bureaucracy: "Mel Laird, he didn't change anybody . . . the people who ran the Pentagon before [the 1968 election] are still running the goddamn Pentagon."[68]

Nixon and his men vowed to change the power balance in government or fail in the attempt. In the days following the election, a group of five individuals headed to Camp David by helicopter to set about Nixon's reorganization: President Nixon, John Ehrlichman, Haldeman, Todd Hullen, and Larry Higby. To quote Haldeman, "for the next two months we would reside at Camp David, trying to take the Executive Branch of the government apart and put it back together in a model that would work."[69]

The eventual model would radically redesign the government and effectively replace the cabinet. In its place there would be four "super-cabinet" officers, whose offices would be in the White House and would report directly to the president. These offices would be divided up to govern the following areas of responsibility: Economic Affairs (overseeing, for example, Commerce), Human Resources (e.g., the Office of Personnel Management), Natural Resources (e.g., Interior), and Community Development (e.g., Transportation).[70] In addition to these "super-cabinet" officials, four of the traditional cabinet posts would retain their position within the diminished cabinet: State, Defense, Justice, and Treasury.[71]

This reorganization would have radically changed the manner in which the federal bureaucracy, by instituting a more hierarchical system to the madness that is the federal bureaucracy where each cabinet-level position holds theoretically equal standing. In practice, no one would argue, there is an effective hierarchy in the federal government; for instance, the primacy of the secretary of education is over the secretary of defense. However, in the Byzantine world of the federal bureaucracy there were, in Nixon's estimation, too many cooks in the kitchen—far too many for him, or any president for that matter, to effectively oversee.

At the time that the proposed reorganization became public knowledge, Nixon's popularity had soared to its highest ever level—a fact that would soon change. Nixon had made enemies of every major power group in government, from the media to the intelligence community. However, that is for a later chapter. What is important for now is that Nixon had engineered an alliance of all the major power centers, and the target of that alliance was Nixon. The institutions of government unanimously opposed Nixon's plans to reorganize the government as a "power grab." Coupled with his threats to the CIA and his continued discussion of eliminating the Oil Depletion Allowance, the proposed reorganization would threaten the political establishment and be a major factor in Nixon's downfall.

It is one of history's great ironies that Richard Nixon, the student of humanity, deftly navigated negotiations with Chairman Mao and Leonid Brezhnev, but would ultimately fail to accurately predict the response of his opponents at home.

During his first term Nixon also maneuvered to dump Vice President Agnew in 1972. The man Nixon wanted to succeed him was none other than the man who had orchestrated the Texas voter theft that cost Nixon the White House in 1960—John Bowden Connally, LBJ's right-hand man and governor of Texas. Connally's connection to the public was that he was in the car when JFK got shot. This gave him a key Camelot connection and great value to Nixon. The 1960 race was so close that Nixon had benefited just from being in the race with Kennedy, a factor that would improve when JFK was martyred. Nixon succeeded in getting Connally to join his cabinet in 1971. Nixon was enamored with the handsome, silver-haired Connally, who moved with a swagger and Texas-sized confidence. Connally stepped down as treasury secretary in 1972 to head "Democrats for Nixon." Nixon planned to dump Agnew for the self-assured Connally. However, Vice President Spiro Agnew, a favorite of the right for his bellicosity and militarist tendencies, gathered an unprecedented 45,000 write-in votes for vice president in the New Hampshire primary, while Nixon was drubbling anti-war Congressman Paul N. "Pete" McCloskey and conservative challenger John Ashbrook. So Nixon abandoned his goal of making Connally vice president.

Nixon seriously considered appointing Connally his chief of staff after the firing of Bob Haldeman. Connally had no connection to Watergate. Connally was a strong proponent of burning the White House tapes. It is worth considering what would have happened if Nixon had selected Connally rather than Haig to helm his team for the Watergate fight for survival. Nixon might have survived, if it weren't for the coarse revelations on the tapes.

For all Nixon's accomplishments during his first term in office, they were marred by four secrets that would pave the way to Watergate. The first was the formation of an extra-legal Secret Invesigative Unit under the direction of John Ehrlichman and David Young, dubbed "the Plumbers," because their aim was to plug leaks from the Nixon foreign policy apparatus. They broke into the office of Dr. Lewis Fielding, the psychiastrist for Daniel Ellsburg, self-admitted leaker of the Pentagon papers. The second was the 1969–1971 wiretaps placed on NSC staffers, White House aides, and selected reporters. The third was a military spy ring operating inside the White House that was purloining and copying sensitive NSC documents and spiriting them off to the Pentagon, and the last was the Huston Plan named for White House aide Tom Charles Huston, which sought to bypass the FBI and CIA in a new effort to surveil anti-war protestors and leaders in violation of their civil rights. Attorney General John Mitchell called these all "the White House horrors." Of these we shall hear more.

NOTES

1. Peter Carlson. "When Elvis Met Nixon," *Smithsonian Magazine*, Dec. 2010.
2. Letter from Elvis Presley to Richard Nixon, Dec. 1970.
3. Ibid.
4. Tom Leonard, "Day Elvis begged Nixon to let him be a secret FBI agent," *MailOnline*, Aug. 14, 2013.
5. December 21, 1970. Nixon Meets Elvis, History.com.
6. Tom Leonard, "Day Elvis begged Nixon to let him be a secret FBI agent," *MailOnline*, Aug. 14, 2013.
7. "1968 Year in Review," UPI, retrieved June 17, 2010.
8. Richard Nixon, *RN: The Memoirs of Richard Nixon*, p. 316. Semple, "Nixon Preparing to Court 7 or 8 Industrial States," p. A20.
9. Richard Nixon, *RN: The Memoirs of Richard Nixon*, p. 316.
10. Reg Murphy and Hal Gulliver, *The Southern Strategy*, p. 2.
11. Richard Nixon, *RN: The Memoirs of Richard Nixon*, p. 443.
12. John Ehrlichman, *Witness to Power: The Nixon Years*, p. 198.
13. Emmett Rensin, "Richard Nixon, Hero of the American Left," *Salon*, May 5, 2013.
14. Richard Nixon, "Special Message to the Congress Proposing the Emergency School Aid Act of 1970," May 21, 1970, http://www.presidency.ucsb.edu/ws/?pid=2509.
15. Patrick J. Buchanan, "The Neocons and the Southern Strategy," December 30, 2002. http://buchanan.org/blog/pjb-the-neocons-and-nixons-southern-strategy-512.
16. Robert Brown, "President Nixon Strong on Civil Rights," The Richard Nixon Foundation, http://nixonfoundation.org/2013/02/robert-brown-president-nixon-strong-on-civil-rights/.
17. "American President: A Reference Resource," Miller Center at the University of Virginia: Richard Milhous Nixon, http://millercenter.org/president/nixon/essays/biography/4.
18. Peter Ubel, "Another Early Obamacare Supporter: Richard Nixon," *Forbes*, Feb. 2, 2014.
19. Ibid.
20. Emmett Rensin, "Richard Nixon, Hero of the American Left," *Salon*, May 5, 2013.
21. Linda Greenhouse, "Warren E. Burger is Dead at 87; Was Chief Justice for 17 Years," *The New York Times*, June 26, 1995.

22. Arlen Specter and Charles Robbins, *Passion for Truth*, pp. 231–233.

23. Tanya Ballard, "Supreme Court Nominees Who Were Not Confirmed," *The Washington Post*, Oct. 27, 2005.

24. Ibid.

25. "Callins v. Collins," Justice Blackmun, dissenting, No. 93-7054, February 22, 1994. Stating, "From this day forward, I no longer shall tinker with the machinery of death. For more than 20 years I have endeavored—indeed, I have struggled—along with a majority of this Court, to develop procedural and substantive rules that would lend more than the mere appearance of fairness to the death penalty endeavor. Rather than continue to coddle the Court's delusion that the desired level of fairness has been achieved and the need for regulation eviscerated, I feel morally and intellectually obligated simply to concede that the death penalty experiment has failed."

26. "Justice Lillie Remembered for Hard Work, Long Years of Service," Metropolitan News Service, Oct. 31, 2002.

27. Ibid.

28. Congressional Record, Senate #46197, Dec. 10, 1971, http://www.senate.gov/reference/resources/pdf/450_1971.pdf.

29. Richard M. Nixon, "Address to the Nation on the War in Vietnam," Provided Courtesy of the Nixon Library. November 3, 1969. http://www.nixonlibrary.gov/forkids/speechesforkids/silentmajority/silentmajority_transcript.pdf.

30. James C. Humes, *Nixon's Ten Commandments of Leadership and Negotiation*, p. 107.

31. James C. Humes, *Nixon's Ten Commandments of Leadership and Negotiation*, p. 108.

32. James C. Humes, *Nixon's Ten Commandments of Leadership and Negotiation*, p. 112.

33. F. Gregory Gause, *The International Relations of the Persian Gulf*, p. 22.

34. H. R. Haldeman, *The Ends of Power*, p. 89.

35. Ibid.

36. H. R. Haldeman, *The Ends of Power*, p. 90.

37. Ibid.

38. Richard M. Nixon, "Asia After Viet Nam," *Foreign Affairs*, Oct. 1967.

39. H. R. Haldeman, *The Ends of Power*, p. 92.

40. Ibid.

41. H. R. Haldeman, *The Ends of Power*, p. 93.

42. James C. Humes, *Nixon's Ten Commandments of Leadership and Negotiation*, p. 60.
43. James C. Humes, *Nixon's Ten Commandments of Leadership and Negotiation*, p. 61.
44. Ibid.
45. James C. Humes, *Nixon's Ten Commandments of Leadership and Negotiation*, p. 62.
46. Ibid.
47. H. R. Haldeman, *The Ends of Power*, p. 91.
48. James C. Humes, *Nixon's Ten Commandments of Leadership and Negotiation*, p. 63.
49. Ibid.
50. Ibid., p. 64.
51. Ibid., p. 37.
52. Ibid., p. 38.
53. Ibid.
54. "6 October 1973: The Yom Kippur War Begins," *The New Nixon*. http://blog.nixonfoundation.org/2011/10/6-october-1973-the-yom-kippur-war-begins/.
55. Matthew T. Penney, "Intelligence and the 1973 Arab-Israeli War," *CIA Center for the Study of Intelligence*, p. 7, https://www.cia.gov/library/publications/historical-collection-publications/arab-israeli-war/nixon-arab-isaeli-war.pdf.
56. "How Richard Nixon Saved Israel." *The New Nixon*, http://blog.nixonfoundation.org/2010/10/how-richard-nixon-saved-israel/.
57. Ibid.
58. George Lardner Jr. and Michael Dobbs, "New Tapes Reveal Depth of Nixon's Anti-Semitism," *Washington Post*, Oct. 6, 1999, http://www.washingtonpost.com/wp-srv/politics/daily/oct99/nixon6.htm.
59. Ibid.
60. "Newly uncovered Nixon tapes reveal anti-Semitic stance," *The Jerusalem Post*, Aug. 22, 2013, http://www.jpost.com/International/Newly-uncovered-Nixon-tapes-reveal-anti-Semitic-stance-323953.
61. Ibid.
62. "Richard Milhous Nixon," *University of Virginia: Miller Center*. http://millercenter.org/president/nixon/essays/biography/5.
63. James C. Humes, *Nixon's Ten Commandments of Leadership and Negotiation*, p. 153

64. Ibid.
65. "How Richard Nixon Saved Israel," *The New Nixon*, http://blog.nixonfoundation.org/2010/10/how-richard-nixon-saved-israel/.
66. James C. Humes, *Nixon's Ten Commandments of Leadership and Negotiation*, p. 153.
67. H. R. Haldeman, *The Ends of Power*, p. 172.
68. H. R. Haldeman, *The Ends of Power*, p. 171.
69 H. R. Haldeman, *The Ends of Power*, p. 173.
70 H. R. Haldeman, *The Ends of Power*, p. 168.
71. Ibid.

CHAPTER FOURTEEN

THE BREAK-INS

"It is in the political agent's interest to betray all the parties who use him and to work for them all at the same time, so that he may move freely and penetrate everywhere."
—E. Howard Hunt[1]

The June 1972 weekend of the Watergate break-in, I had just settled in with a takeout pizza and a six-pack of beer when the phone rang.

"Porter residence," I said. I was house-sitting for my boss at the Committee to Re-elect the President, Herbert L. "Bart" Porter. Porter was a plucky ex-marine USC graduate recruited for the White House staff Chief Robert Haldeman. He was on the West Coast attending the senior staff meetings.

"Is Bart there?" said a gruff voice I recognized as James McCord. I had seen McCord around the CRP office at 1700 Pennsylvania Avenue. Stout and balding, with the fading remains of what must have been a military-style haircut, McCord had dark circles under his eyes and a tendency to mumble.

"No, he and Mrs. Porter are out of town," I said. "I'm just house-sitting. This is Roger Stone. I work at the committee." I was a surrogate scheduler, handling the campaign schedules of the Nixon daughters and cabinet members, as well as members of Congress campaigning for Nixon's reelection.

"OK, tell him Jim McCord called. Tell him I'm in the lockup, and tell him the jig is up."[2] He hung up, and I remember thinking, *this doesn't sound good at all.*

The Nixon men were security obsessed. I carried an official ID, which I had to show a security guard in order to get to my office, but not before using a passcard to go through two electronically sealed doors. Our wastebaskets were collected and shredded each evening, even if they only contained innocuous trash. Leaving the office and your desk and cabinets unlocked would get you fired. The place had the corporate hush of a Fortune 500 company headquarters, with burnt-orange carpets. The phone had bell tones rather than rings. On the walls were blowups of official photos of the president and Mrs. Nixon in their travels. There was no bunting, banners, posters, or campaign paraphernalia. It felt more like IBM than a presidential campaign headquarters, and security was tight. They needed a man like McCord, who became the security director for CRP.

Less than a year after that phone call, three days before the Watergate burglars were to be sentenced, McCord handed a letter to Chief Judge for the US District Court for the District of Columbia John Sirica. The explosive document would bring the whole house of cards collapsing on the Nixon White House. It would also bring down a president.

*   *   *

While history has preferred the narrative spun by the *Washington Post* and government agencies charged with investigating or prosecuting the Watergate crimes, the scholarship and persistence of authors Leonard Colodny and Robert Getlin, as well as author James Hougan and journalists Russ Baker and Phil Stanford, has called for a reassessment of what Watergate was really about and who the real villains were.

As we shall see, forces in the national security apparatus who opposed Nixon's détente policy worked with senior officials in the CIA who feared Nixon's efforts to obtain the full records of the CIA's involvement in the Bay of Pigs and the JFK assassination. Big Texas oil interests, furious with Nixon's lack of reliability on the oil depletion allowance (the sweetheart tax breaks for the oilmen), also undermined Nixon, making him vulnerable to his howling critics on the left who controlled both houses of Congress. Their allies were a hostile national press. These forces drove President Nixon from office and into political exile. He escaped prison for Watergate crimes only through skillful use of the remaining cards he held.

As with the JFK assassination and the Warren Commission, the official version of Watergate—as supplied by the mass media, the Watergate special prosecutor, and the Senate Watergate Committee—is far from the complete story.

Watergate is far more than a "second-rate burglary." While our analysis generally will focus on two entries into the DNC on May 28 and June 17, 1972, Watergate has come to represent a broader series of abuses that, when uncovered, drove Nixon from office. Instead of using the FBI or the CIA to do their sleuthing, as both John Kennedy and Lyndon Johnson did, the Nixon White House utilized private investigators and freelance burglars in illegal intelligence gathering long before the Watergate break-ins. You don't need to be a lawyer to understand that law enforcement officers have criminal immunity while private gumshoes are operating without such shield.

John Ehrlichman supervised a break-in at the office of Daniel Ellsburg's Los Angeles–based psychiatrist in a search for files damaging to Ellsburg—an example of how Nixon's men operated outside the law. LBJ invented a "national security cover" when he wanted the FBI to wiretap or burglarize a target. Nixon's men stood on no such formality. It reveals a mindset and arrogance of those Nixon men who believed they were invulnerable and their deeds would never be scrutinized. A practical pol would reject such tactics, but not the coterie of ad men and marketing types who filled the Nixon White House.

At the same time, the Nixon men believed the Kennedy campaign used extra legal means to wiretap Nixon during the 1960 campaign. LBJ had used the technology too. It's easy to see how the Nixon men rationalized the break-ins, and even the president himself. "When the President does it, that means it is not illegal," Nixon later told television journalist David Frost.[3]

*   *   *

Any review of Watergate must begin with two vital questions. Nixon was leading McGovern by nineteen points in the Gallup polls at the time of the first break-in. He needed no new political ammunition to win his impending landslide. So why break in? McGovern was "by far the weakest national candidate that the Democrats could nominate," Bob Haldeman later wrote. "So Nixon didn't need political information to defeat him."[4]

And why the Democratic National Committee? Any seasoned political veteran knows that during a presidential campaign the action is at the nominee's campaign headquarters. The national party committees are sleepy backwaters controlled at arm's-length by the nominees. "Why would anyone break into a National Committee Headquarters?" Nixon asked Haldeman after the break-ins. "Nothing but crap in there. The real stuff is in the candidate's headquarters, not the Committee's."[5]

Author Lamar Waldron has argued compellingly that the burglars were seeking a record of the CIA-Mafia plot to assassinate Castro, approved by Nixon as vice president and cemented by ex-FBI man Robert Maheu, later a major domo to Howard Hughes. There is also compelling evidence that Nixon was after records he believed were in Democrat headquarters that further exposed the Hughes loan to his black sheep brother.

Moreover, some of the burglars were looking for photographs of call girls and related documents potentially damaging to the White House.

To understand Watergate, and the various political interests behind it, we must first look at the complicated relationship between CIA Director Richard Helms and Nixon. The CIA and President Nixon shared dark secrets. Until 1959, Vice President Nixon headed a task force within the Eisenhower administration to assassinate Cuban leader Fidel Castro. Nixon also approved the CIA outreach to the Mafia, authorizing ex-FBI man Robert Maheu to reach out to dapper mob fixer Johnny Rosselli and involve the Mafia in anti-Castro efforts. The operation culminated in the failed 1961 Bay of Pigs invasion sanctioned by President Kennedy.

Several of the CIA operatives and assassins involved in Nixon's plans to overthrow and kill Castro, including E. Howard Hunt and Frank Sturgis, were subsequently involved. Nixon understood that the backlash from the failed Bay of Pigs invasion inspired his allies in the CIA to join the 1963 plot to murder John F. Kennedy. Hunt, Sturgis, and fellow Bay of Pigs operative Bernard Barker all resurfaced on the ground in Dallas that day. These same men turned up in the 1972 Watergate burglaries. This is not a coincidence.

Nixon was well aware that former CIA Director Allen Dulles had buttoned up the Warren Commission investigation and suppressed the agency's role in Kennedy's death. He clearly understood LBJ's central role in the assassination. Nixon was correct when he called the Warren Commission "The greatest hoax ever perpetuated."[6] When he became president, he tried to seize proof of what really happened.

"Who shot John?" Nixon asked Helms. "Is Eisenhower to blame? Is Johnson to blame? Is Kennedy to blame? Is Nixon to blame?"[7]

According to Haldeman, Nixon's frequent references to the Bay of Pigs were code. "It seems that in all of those Nixon references to the Bay of Pigs, he was actually referring to the Kennedy assassination," he wrote. So when Nixon warned of the "incident" being exposed, he was referring to the truth behind JFK's murder. Despite Haldeman's later attempts to recant this theory, his cowriter on the book, Joseph DiMona, insists the passage is authentic. "It is preposterous to think that Bob Haldeman, of all people, would allow any writer to 'invent' information or erroneous theories to be published in a book under his name. The 'theory' survived five drafts of the most meticulous editing known to man."[8]

Clearly, Nixon badly wanted to get his hands on the CIA records of the Bay of Pig veterans. If the covert assemblage of CIA assassins with underworld bosses was a frightening secret held by the commander in chief, the idea that the Nixon-arranged Operation 40 was somehow involved in the Dallas coup d'etat was terrifying. Although Haldeman said that Nixon had turned him down when he suggested reopening and gathering the facts surrounding the JFK assassination, White House domestic policy advisor John Ehrlichman said Nixon requested all of the CIA records on the Kennedy assassination and was rebuffed by the agency. It is logical that Nixon, a lawyer, asked Ehrlichman, a fellow lawyer, to obtain the records rather than Haldeman, an ad man.

The CIA resisted. "Those bastards in Langley are holding back something," a frustrated Ehrlichman told Haldeman. "They just dig their heels in and say the President can't have it. Period. Imagine that. The Commander-in-Chief wants to see a document and the spooks say he can't have it . . . From the way they're protecting it, it must be pure dynamite."[9]

At the same time, Nixon understood that his approval of the CIA-Mafia plots against Castro, if exposed, could sink his reelection. Presidents aren't supposed to have open dealings with the Mafia. Nixon knew that Helms had intimate knowledge of Operation 40, and therefore his efforts to obtain proof of the CIA's involvement in Kennedy's murder was a desperate bid to acquire the documentation to check Helms's possession of Nixon's anti-Castro role. "Nixon and Helms have so much on each other, neither of them can breathe," said Senator Howard Baker.[10]

Nixon's battle to obtain the JFK assassination records was also an attempt to gain leverage over the rogue agency. This was to be Nixon's "insurance policy" against the CIA. If threatened, Nixon would expose the agency's involvement in Kennedy's death, which took place at the time that he, Nixon, was in political exile without formal governmental influence of any kind.

Haldeman held these very same suspicions and shared them in his 1978 book about Watergate, *The Ends of Power:*

> And here's what I find most interesting: Bill Sullivan, the FBI man that the CIA called at the time, was Nixon's highest-ranking loyal friend at the FBI. (In the Watergate crisis, he would risk J. Edgar Hoover's anger by taking the 1969 FBI wiretap transcripts ordered by Nixon and delivering them to Robert Mardian, a Mitchell crony, for safekeeping.)
>
> It's possible that Nixon learned from Sullivan something about the earlier CIA cover-up by Helms. And when Nixon said, "It's likely to blow the whole Bay of Pigs" he might have been reminding Helms, not so gently, of the cover-up of the CIA assassination attempts on the hero of the Bay of Pigs, Fidel Castro—a CIA operation that may have triggered the Kennedy tragedy and which Helms desperately wanted to hide.[11]

It *was* clear Helms wanted to closet the Mafia-CIA compact, even after it was eventually revealed to the public. He never gave the lethal partnership a mention in his nearly five-hundred-page, whitewashed biography *A Look Over My Shoulder: A Life in the Central Intelligence Agency,* published in 2003.

"I was never sure why President Nixon distrusted me, aside from associating me with Allen Dulles and other East Coast, Ivy League, establishment figures whom he loathed and thought of as dominating the upper brackets of OSS and subsequently CIA," Helms wrote. "In contrast, I always had an excellent relationship with Lyndon Johnson, who had at least as much claim as Nixon to have been born in a log cabin, and whose views of Ivy Leaguers were, at the best, reserved."[12]

A scene in Oliver Stone's *Nixon* further explored the dichotomy between Nixon and Helms. "I'm honored, Dick, that you'd come all the way out to Virginia to visit us at last," said Helms (played by Sam Waterson). "My friends call me Mr. President," replied Nixon (played by Anthony Hopkins).[13]

Nixon and Johnson had contrasting relationships with Helms because they both had two important, yet different, roles in his career. Helms oversaw the Cuba fiasco, which Nixon had spurred forward. He was the deputy director for plans of the CIA at the time of the Kennedy assassination and had intimate working knowledge of Operation 40, their use of Mafioso, and was in deep with many of the main players. In 1966, to ensure the secrets of the assassination were kept safe, President Lyndon Johnson promoted Richard Helms to director of the agency.

Richard Helms was also a harsh opponent of Nixon's policy of Vietnamization, the drawdown of American troops that would turn responsibilities of the war over to the South Vietnamese forces. The CIA was heavily invested in Vietnam and thought that the election of Nixon would remove the restraints they felt under LBJ to conduct a more aggressive effort of sabotage and terrorism. The agency was also deeply involved in the drug trade, and an American pullout would have severely hampered their operations; thus, the CIA's motives for the removal of a crippled Richard Nixon as well as those of the JCS and the Pentagon.

Former Director of the CIA and Warren Commission member Allen Dulles described Helms as "useful," a man who "knew how to keep his mouth shut."[14] Richard Helms was a CIA man to the marrow; his loyalty was to the agency alone, and he became bitterly obstinate whenever asked to divulge CIA secrets. Richard Helms's arrogant disdain for questioning surfaced during a recess of the House Select Committee on Assassinations hearings. The *Washington Post's* George Lardner reported the following exchange:

"Helms told reporters during a break that no one would ever know who or what Lee Harvey Oswald represented. Asked whether the CIA knew of any ties Oswald had with either the KGB or the CIA, Helms paused with a laugh and said, 'I don't remember.' Pressed on the point, he told a reporter, 'Your questions are almost as dumb as the Committee's.'"

Helms maintained close ties with his Operation 40 associates following the assassination. He disclaimed any close relationship post-Watergate, but he considered CIA agent and author E. Howard Hunt a protégé. Helms not only lent Hunt money when the veteran spook was in financial difficulties, but he also urged several television and movie producers to adapt Hunt's spy novels for the screen.[15] As a security measure and to further collect information on executive activity, Helms made moves to place Hunt in the White House.

In *Watergate: The Hidden History*, Lamar Waldron explained the advantages of Hunt's "reassignment":

> Getting Hunt into the Nixon White House was the perfect solution to several problems, but the approach would have to be made carefully, to avoid arousing the suspicions of Nixon or his aides that CIA veteran Hunt was some type of CIA "plant." In hindsight, it's obvious to many that's exactly what Hunt was. Pulitzer Prize–winning *New York Times* journalist J. Anthony Lukas wrote that "there are those who believe that Hunt had never really resigned from the CIA and was still acting more or less on behalf of the Agency" when he went to work for the Nixon White House. Included among those with that opinion would be Charles Colson, who—after Watergate—realized that "all the time Hunt was on the White House payroll . . . Hunt's secretary was on the CIA payroll." That led Colson to ask, "Was Hunt, supposedly a retired CIA agent, actually an active agent while in the White House?"[16]

Hunt "retired" from the agency for the third time in his storied career on April 30, 1970. He had done so previously in 1960 and 1965 to advance counterintelligence projects.[17] Clearly, Hunt worked simultaneously for the White House and the CIA.

Helms placed Hunt in the Robert R. Mullen Company, a public relations firm representing a Howard Hughes tool company strategically located at 1701 Pennsylvania Avenue, across the street from the building that in 1971 would headquarter the Committee to Reelect the President (CRP).[18] Senate Republican minority leader Howard Baker later filled in Special Counsel to the President Chuck Colson on the particulars of Hunt's arrangement. "Baker said that the Mullen Company was a CIA front, that [Hunt's] job with the Mullen Company was arranged by [CIA director] Helms personally." While Hunt worked at the Mullen Company, Baker added, his pay had been adjusted to equal his CIA salary.[19]

The Mullen Co. *was*, in fact, a CIA front. The company was run by Robert Bennett, the son of Senator Wallace Bennett of Utah, a longtime friend and supporter of Richard Nixon and an elder in the Mormon Church. After the *Washington Post* broke the Watergate story, Bennett boasted to his CIA handlers about providing information to *Post* reporters Woodward and Bernstein that led the aggressive reporters away from the CIA's role in the Watergate operation.

It was confirmed in a June 1972 FBI memorandum that Hunt continued to work for the agency on an "ad hoc basis."[20]

Retired Air Force colonel L. Fletcher Prouty, who had approached the Mullen Co. to find a White House contact, knew that Hunt's job at the PR firm was a cover. "The date was in either February or March of 1971," stated Prouty in sworn testimony to the Church Committee. "It was in the offices of the Mullen Company. The man I went to see was Bob Bennett. After a brief talk, primarily with what I wanted done, he said, well, I have a man that can help you with that. And he called in an office and said, Howard. And Howard came out and it was Howard Hunt."

"I knew Howard Hunt," Prouty continued. "I had known him since at least the Bay of Pigs program. But I knew in CIA practice you don't recognize people. So, I never said a word, I never batted an eye to him. But I knew he was CIA, and I knew in my mind he was on duty."[21]

Hunt referred Prouty to Alexander Butterfield, a CIA opera-tive who had already secured employment in the White House. Butterfield was a retired US Army Air Force pilot who in 1969 resigned to become the deputy assistant to President Nixon. Just prior to his Pennsylvania Avenue appointment, Butterfield was "the senior American military officer in Australia," and was the military's "CIA liaison there."[22]

By the 1970s, the agency had "positioned CIA personnel and agency-oriented disciples inconspicuously throughout the White House," according to Prouty.[23] "There were contact people from the CIA in various parts of government," Prouty explained to Church Committee Counsel Michael Madigan. "And that used to be my job. I used to be the contact man in the Pentagon. And I knew that when I called Treasury or the Customs Bureau I would call a certain person. And when I would call even different departments in the Pentagon I would call contact people, people who were cleared, they had Agency clearances. And they had sometimes specific project clearances, and it is a procedure, it is a network, it is designed for that . . . and the only way I heard about the contact was, not that I was able to say that Butterfield was the contact, but that they brought up the name of Butterfield, and they said, we will get this business done."[24]

"The [1975 House of Representatives Inspector General] Report revealed there were CIA agents in "intimate components of the Office of the President," Haldeman later wrote. "I was 'intimate,' Ehrlichman was. Kissinger was. Who else was intimate in an official sense? Alex Butterfield, who sat right outside the President's office?"[25]

At the height of the Watergate scandal, Butterfield exposed Nixon by revealing the existence of the secret White House taping system to the Senate Watergate Committee. He was not asked about the taping system while under oath. Instead, he simply dropped a bombshell.

Rose Mary Woods, Nixon's personal secretary, always con-sidered Butterfield a CIA plant in Nixon's midst.[26] That Hunt, a CIA operative, would refer Prouty to Butterfield, bolstered the suspicion that Butterfield was a CIA plant in the Nixon White House. Butterfield also had ties to General Alexander Haig; both Haig and Butterfield worked for Joseph Califano, who was special assistant to Army Secretary Cyrus Vance. Ironically, it was Haig who wrote and coordinated many of the drafts for the plan for a coup in Cuba in the summer and fall of 1963.[27]

Haig proved to be the pivotal figure in Nixon's downfall. Haig was closely affiliated with a core of senior military officers who revered geopolitical and military strategist Fritz Kraemer. Kraemer, a hard-liner, was adamantly opposed to Nixon and Kissinger's détente with the Chinese. In fact, many military officers feared they were merely instruments of Nixon and Kissinger's dictator-like control, and felt an information gap widening between themselves and the White House.

In his 1976 memoir, *On Watch*, Naval Operations Admiral Elmo R. Zumwalt Jr. expressed his concern about "the deliberate systematic and, unfortunately, extremely successful efforts, of the President, Henry Kissinger, and a few subordinate members of the inner circle to conceal, sometimes by simple silence, more often by articulate deceit, their real policies about the most critical matters of national security: the strategic arms limitation talks (SALT) and various other of the aspects of 'détente,' the relations between the United States and its allies in Europe, the resolution of war in Southeast Asia, the facts about America's military strength and readiness. Their concealment and deceit was practiced against the public, the press, the Congress, the allies, and even most of the officials within the executive branch who had a statutory responsibility to provide advice about matters of national security."[28]

Nixon and Kissinger were conducting foreign policy outside the normal channels. "Nixon's style of governance was highly secretive, and his presidency hung precariously on the constantly shifting lines of 'back-channel' communication that he encouraged among Kissinger, Haig, the Joint Chiefs, Defense Secretary Melvin Laird, and Secretary of State William Rogers," wrote James Rosen in *The Atlantic.*[29] The Joint Chiefs, deeply suspicious of détente, were desperate to know what Nixon and Kissinger were up to.

This breach of information between the White House and the military led to further infiltration of outside agents at 1600 Pennsylvania Avenue carried out by a naval spy ring. The spy ring was a precursor to Watergate, involved Alexander Haig, and was detected and disclosed to Nixon. In December 1971, Charles E. Radford, a twenty-seven-year-old navy stenographer assigned to the National Security Council, working closely with both Kissinger and Haig, confessed to sifting through burn bags of top-secret White House documents and delivering these documents to the chairman of the Joint Chiefs, Admiral Thomas H. Moorer. The back channel later became known as the "Moorer-Radford affair."

"Yeoman Radford collected literally thousands of documents from the White House and, while on foreign trips, documents that ranged from private messages between Kissinger and Nixon that involved their secret China gambit, to negotiating stances over sensitive European military bases, to closely guarded policy papers put together by Kissinger's staff, to Nixon's strategy and timetables for withdrawing troops from Southeast Asia," wrote Len Colodny and Robert Gettlin in the meticulously researched *Silent Coup.*[30]

When first questioned by White House aides John Ehrlichman and David Young, Weilander confessed his role in the spy ring and confirmed that Radford had passed on copies of purloined documents, which in turn were sent to JCS Chairman, Admiral Thomas Moorer. More importantly, Weilander implicated Haig in the operation. To cover Haig's tracks, Department of Defense General Counsel Fred Buzhardt reinterviewed Weilander and this time the admiral omitted Haig's involvement.

On December 21, 1971, Nixon, Mitchell, Haldeman, and Ehrlichman met in the Oval Office to discuss what to do about the spy ring.

"The important thing is to handle [Radford's superiors] in a way that they do not talk," Nixon said.[31]

It is important to note that Nixon's first reaction was not to conduct an intense examination of the spy ring and purge the government of the malcontent conspirators. In a move that characterized Nixon, he buried the espionage. In doing so, he left those involved in power, able to "bury" him given the chance. This decision was made in spite of Nixon's suspicions of Haig.

"I'm afraid that Haig must have known about this operation," Nixon said. "It seems unlikely he wouldn't have known."[32]

In fact, at the same time Haig was working closely with another young naval officer who served as a liaison between the upper echelons of the White House and the Pentagon. His name was Bob Woodward. Three years later, supplied with a steady diet of information from Haig and other malcontents in the military and intelligence community, the *Washington Post* reporter kept the Watergate story alive and pinned it directly on the president and his top staff.

"How does a guy that is nine months at the *Washington Post* City section have a source at the highest level of our government, who trusts him with damaging information about the President of the United States?" asked Len Colodny.[33] It is a question we will return to.

E. Howard Hunt petitioned Charles Colson for work at the White House during his entire year of employment at the Mullen Co. A fellow Brown University graduate, Colson, like Dean, knew intelligence was the key to gain favor with the president. Colson, who once said he would run over his grandmother for Nixon,[34] was tangled in Nixon's dark side. He was eager to feed the malignant inclinations of the president. At the time he was being courted by Hunt, Colson, at the direction of John Dean, was compiling Nixon's "enemies list," which catalogued politicians, journalists, and activists the administration perceived as threats.

To Attorney General John Mitchell, Colson was bolstering "[t]he president's worst instincts."[35] "That fucking Colson is going to kill us all," Mitchell told Len Garment.[36]

Hunt's White House employment was approved on July 7, 1971. Nixon needed someone skilled in the clandestine arts to compile unfavorable information on military analyst Daniel Ellsburg, who leaked the Pentagon Papers to the *New York Times*. Nixon also needed someone to ransack the Brookings Institute, a nonprofit liberal think tank in Washington, and obtain information to shed negative light on the Vietnam bombing halt devised by LBJ in 1968.[37] The president hoped the pilfered reports from Brookings would help counteract negative attacks on the White House. Clearly, Nixon knew about Hunt prior to his employment at the White House. A week before Hunt's hiring, Nixon's demand for the spy was clear:

> President Nixon: Brookings, I want them just to break in and take it out. Do you understand?
> Haldeman: Yeah, but you have to have somebody to do it.
> President Nixon: That's what I'm talking about. Don't discuss it here. You talk to [E. Howard] Hunt. I want the break-in. Hell, they do that. You're to break into the place, rifle the files, and bring them in . . . just go in and take it . . . I mean clean it up![38]

Richard Helms was an opportunist who had maneuvered to get Hunt into the White House, offered a prompt recommendation to Haldeman. "[Richard] Helms describes this guy [Hunt] as ruthless, quiet and careful, low profile," Haldeman told President Nixon. "He gets things done. He will work well with all of us."[39]

Helms later denied not only his recommendation, but any knowledge of Hunt's initial employment at the White House.[40]

Some of Hunt's work for Nixon was linked with an event the seasoned agent was well acquainted with: the JFK assassination. All of Hunt's work for the White House was communicated back to the CIA.

Washington attorney Doug Caddy, who later served as the criminal lawyer for the burglars in the Watergate break-in, is another notable who confirmed Hunt's continued employ with the CIA. Caddy said that in April 1972, Hunt and CIA General Counsel

Lawrence Houston tried to recruit him for work with the Agency. Caddy worked at the Mullen Agency, but did non-CIA work for the General Mills account.

On one occasion, Hunt traveled to Miami to meet with two Cuban exiles with whom he had worked during the Bay of Pigs invasion. These men, Bernard Barker and Eugenio Martinez, who we will find later were part of "The Plumbers" outfit, accompanied Hunt to a meeting with a woman who claimed to have information about Castro's reaction to the Kennedy assassination. White House counsel Charles Colson told Washington lawyer Henry Cashen, a veteran Nixon advance man and lawyer at the Shapiro Law Firm that Colson would join after leaving the White House that Hunt's trek to Miami was at his direction and in response to a letter the woman had written to the president.

Colson told Cashen, a dapper man who wore a fresh bouton-niere and jauntily tied bow tie every day, "I brought the letter to the president's attention. He sat bolt upright and said 'Send someone down!' Nixon had a voracious appetite for information about the Kennedy assassination."[42]

The woman said Castro had been morose. Hunt reported this back to both the White House and the CIA. The fact that the Cuban leader was not jubilant over the death of his rival would, of course, confirm Nixon's suspicion that Kennedy was not murdered by a "communist," as J. Edgar Hoover had insisted to him. Nor had it been a plot by the Cubans, as LBJ had told many in the aftermath. Johnson repeated this fiction to journalist Leo Janos, Chief Justice Earl Warren, Warren Commission member Richard Russell, and TV journalist Mike Wallace.

Hunt's role dramatically increased alongside Nixon's concern about the Pentagon Papers, which was intensified by Henry Kissinger. National Security Advisor and later Secretary of State, Kissinger left Watergate relatively unscathed, but was instrumental in playing to the insecurities that drove Nixon to order the illegal activities of "The Plumbers." Kissinger, who similarly concealed his role in the cover-up of military atrocities in Vietnam and Cambodia, buried his part in encouraging break-ins and wiretaps.

Nixon was initially unconcerned with the leak of the Pentagon Papers, a secret Department of Defense study about the origins of the Vietnam War. He thought it would reflect badly on Kennedy and Johnson, who had escalated the war, but not on himself: he had been away from politics for most of the period. Kissinger convinced him otherwise. "It shows you're a weakling, Mr. President," Haldeman overheard Kissinger arguing. "The fact that some idiot can publish all of the diplomatic secrets of this country on his own is damaging to your image, as far as the Soviets are concerned, and it could destroy our ability to conduct foreign policy."[43]

* * *

The Special Investigations Unit, tasked with collecting intelligence and plugging leaks, later known as simply "The Plumbers," was created on July 24, 1971. The unit included Howard Hunt, G. Gordon Liddy, David Young, and Egil "Bud" Krough. The "plumbers" recruited Frank Sturgis, Bernard "Macho" Barker, and Eugenio Martinez for the break-in of Dr. Fieldings office and their penetration of the Watergate. Liddy recruited James McCord.

Oddly, a month before the Pentagon Papers were published and two months before his employment at the White House, Hunt began to rally Bernard Barker and other members of his old Operation 40 outfit. "Hunt's visit to Barker [in April 1971] was, pure and simple, a get-ready-for-action call. You'd have to be an idiot to think otherwise," Charles Colson later said. "But there wasn't any action anticipated. Not then. The Pentagon Papers hadn't been published. The Plumbers were months away. So you tell me: How did Hunt know [in April] that he'd need the Cubans?"[44]

One of the Bay of Pigs veterans who broke into the Watergate, Eugenio Martinez, was still on the CIA payroll while working with "The Plumbers." Like Hunt, Martinez had "retired" yet was still reporting to his case officer and collecting his CIA compensation.

Hunt was known to Martinez by his Bay of Pigs pseudonym "Eduardo."

"We went to a Cuban restaurant for lunch and right away Eduardo told us that he had retired from the CIA in 1971 and was working for Mullen and Company," wrote Martinez years later. "I knew just what he was saying. I was also officially retired from the Company. Two years before, my case officer had gathered all the men in my Company unit and handed us envelopes with retirement announcements inside. But mine was a blank paper. Afterward he explained to me that I would stop making my boat missions to Cuba but I would continue my work with the Company. He said I should become an American citizen and soon I would be given a new assignment. Not even Barker knew that I was still working with the Company. But I was quite certain that day that Eduardo knew."[45]

Nixon had come to believe that a Cuban Dossier that outlined the CIA-Mafia compact and the attempted assassination of Fidel Castro was in the possession of the Democrats and, in particular, in the office of Democratic National Committee chairman Larry O'Brien. This was the information some of "The Plumbers" were looking for at the Democratic National Committee's Watergate Hotel headquarters. "I believe Nixon told Colson to get the goods on O'Brien's connection with Hughes," wrote Haldeman. "I believe Colson then passed the word to Hunt who conferred with Liddy who decided the taps on O'Brien and Oliver, the other 'Hughes phone,' would be their starting point."[46] This was confirmed by Mafioso Johnny Rosselli, who participated in the CIA plots to kill Castro, and by "Plumber" Frank Fiorini.

"We knew that this secret memorandum existed—knew it for a fact—because the CIA and the FBI had found excerpts and references to it in some confidential investigations," said Fiorini. "But we wanted the entire document [which was] a long, detailed listing [of the] various attempts made to assassinate the Castro brothers."[47]

Hunt and the Cubans were the most capable and appropriate candidates for the mission. They had training and experience with an intelligence agency that excelled in covert operations; they would be able to aptly identify the document as they had been on the ground in the Bay of Pigs and in Dallas. They also had as much reason as Nixon to keep quiet about the contents.

Lamar Waldron, in his exhaustive, investigative recap of the Watergate break-ins, does an exceptional job of providing the motives of Nixon, Helms, and Hunt in getting their hands on the Cuban Dossier:

> The Cuban Dossier lists familiar names and shows why Nixon, Helms, and Hunt—as well as godfather Santo Trafficante—would have been worried in 1972 about the report becoming public: Those named include these CIA assets, all linked to Trafficante: Tony Varona (named three times, the first during the CIA-Mafia plots), Hunt's best friend Manuel Artime (and several of his associates), Rolando Cubela as well as his CIA contact Carlos Tepedino, and Trafficante henchman Herminio Diaz. The Dossier begins with a mid-1960 attempt (involving "a gangster . . . equipped by the CIA"), at the time when Vice President Nixon and Hunt were involved with the CIA's anti-Castro operations. The Dossier lists twenty-eight attempts in all, ending with the December 1971 attempt to assassinate Fidel in Chile. It included two attempts that Rosselli had hinted at in his disclosures to Jack Anderson: Helms's unauthorized plots to kill Fidel on March 13, 1963 (at the University of Havana), and on April 7, 1963 (at the Latin American Stadium). Johnny Rosselli's name is in the few pages added to the 1975 version of the Cuban Dossier, but there is no way to know if he was named in the original 1972 version.[48]

While there is no solid evidence of Nixon ordering the break-ins at the DNC, it can be assumed that the president wanted this dossier found and destroyed *by any means necessary*. O'Brien was a likely candidate to be in possession of such a document. Early in the Nixon administration, O'Brien had been a consultant to the

Howard Hughes organization and had contact with the eccentric business magnate's closest aide, ex-FBI agent Robert Maheu. Maheu, whose services were occasionally tapped by the CIA, was directed by then-Vice President Nixon to reach out and make contact with mobster Johnny Rosselli.

The paranoid Nixon believed that his old Operation 40 associates were likely involved in the '63 Dallas coup. He would have been tearing his hair out over the possibility that O'Brien, once a part of JFK's intimate nucleus of aides dubbed the "Irish Mafia," knew about Nixon's role in the CIA-Mafia plots. Nixon had already been burned twice by loans from O'Brien's employer, Howard Hughes. To say that Nixon was obsessed with Hughes, and thus with O'Brien, would be an understatement.

Like a bad penny, Nixon's hapless brother Donald resurfaced. According to a 1976 *Playboy* article, John Meier, a former Hughes associate, worked with former Vice President Hubert Humphrey and others to feed misinformation to Donald that they hoped he would tell the president. Their plan worked; Donald told his brother that the Democrats had a lot of previously unreleased information on his illicit dealings with Hughes and that Democratic National Committee chairman Larry O'Brien had the documents.[49] If the Democrats hoped the Nixon campaign would do something foolish with the information even though Nixon was far out in front in the polls, they were right. Nixon bought it and Watergate unfolded.

CIA Director Helms monitored the Watergate break-in after James McCord or Hunt assuredly made him aware as a security measure for the agency. In the summer of 1973, Helms testified at the Erwin Committee investigation that the CIA had no involvement in the Watergate affair. However, he was forced to testify that Eugenio Martinez was still active on the CIA roster.[50] In May 1973, McCord had written in a memorandum to the Senate Watergate Investigating Committee that the CIA feared the Nixon White

House would gain "complete political control over . . . CIA" to make the agency conform to White House policy.[51]

In hindsight, it is evident that some of "The Plumbers," and those they recruited, remained employed by the CIA, each working with different levels of actionable information. Hunt was on the mission to find out if there was a Cuban Dossier and follow subsequent CIA orders. The Cubans were to follow the orders of Hunt. McCord, hired by Liddy, was chosen by the CIA to monitor and, if necessary, sabotage the mission.

H. R. Haldeman, Nixon's chief of staff, who was heavily involved in the Watergate cover-up, correctly surmised that the CIA monitored the break-ins with "plants" and had at least one agent, McCord, sabotage the operation.[52]

A year after the break-ins, in an article for *National Review*, former CIA station chief and Glenn Miller Orchestra trumpeter Miles Copeland[53] also concluded that Watergate turned into a CIA trap led by McCord.[54]

Who was James McCord? According to Richard Helms, McCord was a "serious, straitlaced staff security and counter-audio specialist. He had retired with a good record."[55] McCord spent a good portion of the '50s and '60s working for the CIA's Office of Security.[56] In the words of *Secret Agenda* author Jim Hougan, the Office of Security "is an action component of the CIA, with hands-on responsibility for some of the agency's most sensitive matters. Accordingly, and unlike most other sections of the CIA, the Office of Security reports directly to the Director of Central Intelligence. In effect, the OS is an extension of the director's office in a way that other CIA components are not . . ."[57]

There was a photograph on the wall of McCord's office at CRP, where he worked as security director. The photograph was inscribed by CIA Director Richard Helms: "To Jim / With *deep* appreciation."[58] James McCord's "retirement" from the CIA on August 30, 1970, was similar to Hunt's. He was going into *deep* cover.

McCord, like Hunt, was likely a double agent, who intentionally botched the surreptitious entry into the Watergate. The many errors and strange movements of McCord during both the unsuccessful and successful break-ins at the DNC are indicative of an ulterior plan. Recently released 1973 Bureau of Prisons evaluations of the burglars state, "James McCord is said to have taken his orders directly from Gordon Liddy and while he too was a technician, he operated somewhat independently from the others." While it is true McCord took his orders from Liddy, he did not follow them. McCord, it was later revealed, also had two ex-FBI men working for him, Alfred Baldwin and Lou Russell. Both were virtually unknown to the other burglars, both played featured roles in the break-ins.

* * *

The break-in team was experienced, but the operation was amateurish—a strange paradox. The errors made by the Watergate burglars are so manifest that it is clear that the burglars purposely botched the job with one more target in their sights. Consider how the conspirators expertly left a trail of mistakes as evidence for law enforcement:

- The team had a meeting the night before the break-in in a Howard Johnson room booked on the stationery of a Miami firm, which employed Watergate burglar and Operation 40 member Bernard Barker. When Barker was later arrested, he had his hotel room key in his pocket. There, investigators found materials that further incriminated the group.
- James McCord booked his room opposite the Watergate Hotel, at the Howard Johnson, in the name of his company.
- Neither Hunt or Liddy made any effort through their many contacts to spring McCord from prison before it was revealed that he was linked with the CIA.
- Before the break-in, each of the burglars were given $100 bills, equaling between $200 and $800. All the bills had serial

numbers that were close in sequence. When Hunt and Liddy found out that the burglars had been caught, they cleared their hotel room of evidence, but left a briefcase holding $4,600, which by serial number, directly linked it to the money given to the burglars.

- Address books taken from Bernard Barker and Eugenio Martinez linked them directly to E. Howard Hunt.
- After the burglary, Hunt locked a wealth of incriminating evidence in his White House safe, including electronic gear from the burglary, address books, and notebooks with information tying the men involved directly to the break-in.
- Break-in surveillance man Alfred Baldwin subsequently leaked the story of the burglary, with names, to a lawyer named John Cassidento, a supporter of the Democratic Party.
- On May 22, 1972, McCord and former FBI agent Alfred Baldwin booked Room 419 at the Howard Johnson Motor Inn using the name of McCord's company. The Howard Johnson was opposite the Watergate Hotel. McCord hired Baldwin to monitor electronic bugs McCord had planted in the DNC headquarters.

McCord very clearly had his own agenda. "We never knew where he was going," Martinez would remember.[59]

The double agents involved in the Watergate break-in were not lazy criminals. They were seasoned professionals, skilled in covert operations. The Watergate break-in was simultaneously a botched job and a successful cover-up.

There were two important pieces of information Baldwin let slip in the aftermath of Watergate to slightly tip McCord's hand. Baldwin maintained to the FBI, Congress, and the *Los Angeles Times* that he began monitoring calls from the DNC as early as Friday, May 26—two days before the first successful break-in and the alleged planting of a listening device.[60]

The night of May 26 was the first of two unsuccessful attempts to get into the DNC offices, but Baldwin, in another absent-minded confession, offered up a revelation to the *Los Angeles Times*—McCord was in the DNC. McCord was the executive director of the Association of State Democratic Chairmen in Spencer Oliver's office.

According to Baldwin, McCord "turned on a light in [Oliver's] office, came over to the window, pulled the drapery and shut the light off . . . I saw McCord. I can specifically say I saw McCord. His features are distinguishable, and he came right over to the window and pulled the drapery. He had the light on."[61]

What was McCord doing alone in Spencer's office? One can assume that McCord was bugging a specific phone in the DNC for Baldwin to begin monitoring.

McCord's suspicious behavior continued during the second unsuccessful break-in attempt at the Watergate on May 27, when the burglars went into the Watergate through the front door of the office building, all wearing suits, and all checked in with the security guard.

The situation was strange to Eugenio Martinez. Like the break-in at Dr. Fielding's office, "There wasn't a written plan, not even any mention of what to do if something went wrong."[62] Martinez, regardless of his misgivings, went along with the slipshod mission.

"Anyway, all seven of us in McCord's army walked up to the Watergate complex at midnight," wrote Martinez. "McCord rang the bell, and a policeman came and let us in. We all signed the book, and McCord told the man we were going to the Federal Reserve office on the eighth floor. It all seemed funny to me. Eight men going to work at midnight. Imagine, we sat there talking to the police. Then we went up to the eighth floor, walked down to the sixth—and do you believe it, we couldn't open that door, and we had to cancel the operation."[63]

It is strange that expert clandestine operators, equipped with rubber gloves, the electronic surveillance equipment to bug the DNC, cameras to snap pictures of the important documents, and falsified identification to get them by the security guard had brought the wrong tools to jimmy the same door that McCord had presumably entered through two nights prior. Even more unusual, while the burglars were attempting to bust into the DNC offices on the sixth floor, McCord disappeared once again. Martinez, concerned about McCord's whereabouts, located him two floors above:

> McCord would be going to the eighth floor. It is still a mystery to me what he was doing there. At 2:00 a.m. I went up to tell him about our problems, and there I saw him talking to two guards. What happened? I thought. Have we been caught? No, he knew the guards. So I did not ask questions, but I thought maybe McCord was working there.[64]

In fact, McCord *had* worked at the Watergate building earlier that year to check Attorney General John Mitchell's apartment for security breaches. John Mitchell's wife, Martha, believed McCord actually used these opportunities to bug the attorney general's apartment. This made sense for the purpose of information gathering.[65]

Vigilio Gonzalez, tasked with picking the locks, was sent to Miami for the correct tools. Upon his return on the evening of May 28, the first of two successful entries into the Watergate offices commenced. While in the DNC offices, pictures of documents were allegedly taken and a bug was allegedly planted, but according to Watergate burglars Rolando Martinez and Frank Sturgis, O'Brien's office was never a target. Sturgis said he had not "been in or near O'Brien's office" and was given no directive to do so.[66] A source within the DNC close to investigators Len Colodny and Robert Gettlin revealed that "the actual bugging target was a phone in the office of the chairman of the Democratic State Governors association, noting that Spencer Oliver, among others, sometimes used a phone in that nearly always vacant office."[67] E. Howard Hunt also confirmed that a target of the break-in was the phone used by Oliver and his secretary, Ida "Maxie" Wells.[68]

G. Gordon Liddy, who ordered the burglars to raid O'Brien's office, supplied the same account of the caper. "The FBI never found a listening device near the office of Larry O' Brien," said Liddy. "The burglars didn't go near there, although those were the orders I gave. When they went in, they put a device on the telephone in the office right outside the office of R. Spencer Oliver."[69] Liddy maintained though, consistent with the hypothesis that Larry O'Brien was the concern of the Nixon White House, that he *had* received orders that the DNC chairman was their target. "The orders I received were to break into the office of Larry O'Brien . . . and to put in two bugs," said Liddy. "One [bug was put on] his telephone to monitor those conversations and the other, a room bug to monitor any conversations in the room. And photograph anything lying about. Those are the instructions I gave to Mr. Hunt. Those instructions were not carried out. Someone countermanded them. They didn't go anywhere near Mr. O'Brien's office. In fact, they went to the four-button telephone that was in the office of Ida 'Maxine' Wells."[70]

It was an office that O'Brien never made calls from. What could a bug on a phone used by Spencer Oliver reveal? A theory supported by considerable evidence, broke first by Anthony Summers in *The Arrogance of Power*, is that the information collected by Baldwin from the phone Oliver and Wells used was from a different operation; a CIA safe house set up as a brothel in a Columbia Plaza apartment where many high-profile pols, both Republican and Democrat, were being serviced. This theory was further substantiated books by Len Colodny and Robert Gettlin in *Silent Coup*, Phil Stanford in *White House Call Girl*, J.Anthony Lukas in *Nightmare: The Underside of the Nixon Years*, and Anthony Summers in *The Arrogance of Power*.

While being deposed, Baldwin admitted that most of the phone calls he was tapped into concerned a dining arrangement with "sex to follow" and that "eight out of ten" people would have surmised that the calls regarded the scheduling of an escort for the evening.[71] The calls made on this particular phone "apparently in the belief it was one of the more private lines," Baldwin said, "were explicitly intimate."[72] Strangely, although two tape recorders were available for Baldwin's use, and were more suitable for surveillance work, he chose to transcribe the phone conversations by hand, making them all but illegible to anyone but him.[73] "Whoever McCord's assistant was, he was no typist," said Liddy. "The logs revealed that the interception was from a telephone rather than a microphone that relayed all conversation in the room, and that the telephone being tapped was being used by a number of different people, none of whom appeared to be Larry O'Brien."[74]

Ehrlichman later said the transcripts from all the monitoring resulted in three "rather obscure synopses."[75] What was the point of monitoring a Columbia Plaza call-girl service being scheduled from the offices of the DNC? It is a theory we will return to.

"The Plumbers" took photographs of DNC office documents in this particular break-in. It was a job assigned to Bernard Barker, who shot two rolls of film and gave them to Howard Hunt, who said McCord "had been given the films . . . to develop. After a few days, Liddy asked him . . . where the developed prints were," continued Hunt. "McCord apparently reported to Liddy [that] the photographer he knew was not in the vicinity, he was on vacation or something, and Mr. McCord could not get the films developed. Therefore, Mr. Liddy asked Mr. McCord to turn the films over to me . . . At about the same time Mr. McCord turned the films over to me, I was going down to Miami . . . I had called Barker to ask him if he had or knew what we call a 'person of confidence' to print the film. He said certainly. He met me at the airport within a day or so, I delivered the film cassettes to him . . . [and] within an hour or so . . . he came back to me and said the films were all set."[76]

When developed, the photographs showed hands covered in surgical gloves holding DNC documents against a shag rug. There was no rug of that kind in either the DNC offices or in the hotel rooms where the burglars were holed up in. *These were not the same photographs that were taken inside the DNC.*[77]

The White House men, Magruder and Dean in particular, unhappy with the take from the first break-in and the useless phone transcripts, ordered another.

The burglars returned to the DNC on June 17 for their second and final break-in. Days before, on June 9, a frantic Jeb Magruder had called Liddy into his office. Liddy provided the account of the meeting in his autobiography, *Will*:

> He swung his left arm back behind him and brought it forward forcefully as he said, "I want to know what O'Brien's got right here!" At the word *here* he slapped the lower left part of his desk with his left palm, hard. "Take all the men, all the cameras you need. *That's* what I want to know!"
>
> There was a world of significance in Magruder's gesture. When he said "here!" and slapped that particular portion of his desk, he was referring to the place he kept his derogatory information on the Democrats. Whenever in the past he had called me in to attempt to verify some rumor about, for example, Jack Anderson, it was from there that he withdrew whatever he already had on the matter. *The purpose of the second Watergate break-in was to find out what O'Brien had of derogatory nature about us, not for us to get something on him or the Democrats.*[78]

The final break-in was legendarily bush league. McCord and Baldwin, while attempting to fuse a pair of batteries together for a microphone transmitter that was to be concealed in a smoke alarm, melted them. In another suspicious move, McCord had *forgotten* the correct batteries.[79] McCord signed into the Watergate building at 10:50 p.m. and, proceeding to the eighth floor, began to backtrack down the stairwell to the garage, stuffing latches with paper and covered them vertically with tape. Even in the estimation of Liddy (who was not a CIA man) this technique was amateurish. "Burglars don't tape the locks," Liddy wrote. "They wedge a matchstick in between the bolt and opening, then snap it off in a flush. I would not have approved that method; if discovered by a guard, it's a dead giveaway; he knows immediately he has a burglary on his hands."[80]

It *was* a dead giveaway. McCord finished taping the doors at 11 p.m. returned to Baldwin's lookout at the Howard Johnson's, and noticed that the DNC was still occupied. Security guard Frank Wills discovered the doors taped at midnight. Wills removed the paper and the tape, made note of the door tampering in his security log, and telephoned his superiors.

At 12:05 a.m. the last straggling worker, Bruce Givner, made his way out of the DNC, yet McCord told his coconspirators that the target was still occupied. After waiting forty minutes, McCord phoned Hunt at the Howard Johnson's at 12:45 a.m. He told Hunt the headquarters were clear and that he was making his way over to Hunt's room at the Watergate Hotel. To go from one hotel room to another took McCord fifteen minutes, arriving at 1:05 a.m. McCord said that in the interim time he had gone back across the street to verify that the locks were still jammed and the doors were still propped open. In McCord's recollection *"the tape was still there."*[81]

Today, we know this is false. The tape had been removed an hour prior to the time McCord left the lookout. When McCord later returned to the doors with the burglars, he feigned disbelief that the tape had been removed. "They returned with a stunned look on their face," McCord said. "The door was locked and the tape had been removed!"[82]

So where did McCord disappear for fifteen minutes, and more importantly, why did he delay the operation and lie about his whereabouts?

In the unaccounted for fifteen minutes, McCord rendezvoused with Lou Russell, a hard-drinking ex-FBI agent-turned-private-eye who became known as the sixth man of the Watergate break-in. Russell, a close associate of Carmine Bellino, the Kennedy operative who bugged Nixon's hotel room before the 1960 debates, was employed by McCord's security consulting firm, McCord

Associates, while also working for Washington lawyer Bud Fensterwald. The loquacious Russell had revealed to Fensterwald and two of the lawyer's associates that he had been making time with call girls at the Columbia Plaza apartments near the Watergate and was tape recording conversations between the call girls and their johns at the DNC offices.[83] Prior to documenting the sexual liaisons of the call girls, Russell had acquired $3,000 worth of surveillance equipment from private detective John Leon, who surmised that the gear was for McCord.[84]

"I had three or four meetings with Russell," said Robert Smith, a Russell associate, "and among other things he claimed—and I have no reason to doubt it—that there was a tape recorder operating against a couple of prominent Democratic leaders. They were picking up these conversations in which they were making dates with women over the phone . . . for sexual liaison purposes."[85]

McCord testified that Russell "was not there the night of the break-in at the Howard Johnson Motel or anywhere in the vicinity."[86] This was yet another McCord lie. Russell and his daughter supplied a different story of his whereabouts. Russell, who had gone to visit with his daughter in Benedict, Maryland, on the night of the June 17 break-in, admitted to leaving her house when he found she was not there and drove to the Watergate Hotel to dine at the Howard Johnson's restaurant. Russell told the FBI that he was eating at the HoJo restaurant as "a trip down memory lane" from 8:30–10:30 p.m. and drove back to Benedict to see his daughter upon finishing.[87] Russell's daughter recalled that at just past midnight Russell said he needed to return to Washington to do "some work for McCord."[88] This placed Russell's arrival time at the Watergate in line with McCord's disappearing act.

Why would McCord want to meet with Russell?

John Leon, who had helped the Kennedy operative Carmine Bellino bug Nixon, believed McCord told Russell to contact the authorities and the Democrats. Jim Hougan fleshed this theory out in his masterful history of the break-ins, *Secret Agenda*: "[John] Leon was convinced that Watergate was a set-up, that prostitution was at the heart of the affair, and that the Watergate arrests had taken place following a tip-off to the police; in other words, the June 17 burglary had been sabotaged from within, Leon believed, and he intended to prove it . . . In an investigative memorandum submitted to GOP lawyer Jerris Leonard, Leon described what he hoped to prove: that Russell, reporting to Bellino, had been a spy for the Democrats within the CRP, and that Russell had tipped off Bellino (and the police) to the June 17 break-in."[89]

This claim has some merit. Following the arrest of the Watergate burglars, Russell was taken care of by Carmine Bellino through his friend William Birely, who supplied Russell with a new car, spending money, and a rent-free furnished apartment in Silver Spring, Maryland.[90] Russell's new life would not last long. On May 9, the Watergate Committee subpoenaed Russell. On May 18, 1973, hours before his employer Jim McCord was to begin his testimony before the Watergate Committee, Russell suffered a heart attack. On the day of his release one month later, Russell confided to his daughter that he had been poisoned, that someone had entered the residence Bellino had secured for him, and "switched pills on me."[91]

Only two weeks after his release from the hospital, Russell suffered his second major heart attack, this one fatal. His body was buried quickly the next day; an autopsy was never performed.[92]

John Leon was angered by the death of his friend. He believed Russell held many of the secrets of Watergate. Leon was prepared to reveal not just the secrets of Watergate, but also the pre-debate bugging of Nixon's hotel room. On July 13, 1973, before a press conference exposed the 1960 wiretapping could be held—and only weeks after Russell died—Leon died of a similar, mysterious heart attack.[93]

Bob Woodward later claimed there was "nothing to the story" of Russell and his connections to Watergate, brushing Russell off as an "old drunk."[94]

If Russell *did* tip off the authorities, it is likely the man he reached out to was Carl Shoffler, one of the arresting officers. Shoffler and two other *off-duty* officers had completed their shifts at midnight. Post shift, they imbibed at an after-hours spot and were parked close to the DNC offices, dressed in casual clothes when they received the call of an incident at the Watergate.[95]

At 1:10 a.m., when McCord and the burglars found that the tape had been removed which indicated that the unlatched door had been discovered, it was McCord, against the advice of Hunt and Liddy, who decided to press on. The burglars once again jimmied the doors and re-taped the latches. They made their way up to the sixth floor without McCord, who had once again disappeared. "McCord did not come in [to the office building] with us," recalled Eugenio Martinez. "He said he had to go someplace. We never knew where he was going [when we left the command post]."[96]

At approximately 1:30 a.m. Frank Wills again discovered that the doors had been tampered with, again removed the tape, and this time called the authorities. Shoffler and crew, waiting less than two blocks away, went into action. At 1:40 a.m. McCord returned to the Watergate and made his way up to the sixth floor (Wills had not removed the tape this time). When McCord arrived on the sixth floor he assured Martinez that he had removed the tape on the way up, so they could not be detected. McCord, in reality, had not removed the tape.

Shortly after 2 a.m., Shoffler and the two other off-duty, plain-clothes officer caught the burglars in the DNC offices on the sixth floor near the desk of Maxie Wells. When the officers had the burglars against the wall, Shoffler could see Martinez fumbling for something.

"He made a motion with his hand toward the chest area," Shoffler said. "I glanced at him, noticed it, put his hand back on the wall in a forceful way and told him to keep his hands on the wall . . . Martinez was not complying with the directive he had been given and again was going into that chest area and in a very forceful way was put back against the wall. There was a brief struggle with him over him trying to do something in that chest area. Keep in mind we had already patted him for weapons. It was at that particular time, the second time, when I thought *maybe somehow we missed something*. So, I reached into the area he was going to and pulled out a notebook with a key on it."[97]

The key was later determined by the FBI to fit the desk of Maxie Wells.

"I really do believe, as simple as this may sound, we wouldn't be sitting around with all the puzzles and all the mysteries, had we taken the time to find out exactly what that key would lead us to," Shoffler said later. "Obviously it was overlooked."[98]

When Nixon heard about the break-in and the subsequent arrests while on vacation in Key Biscayne, he was dumbfounded:

"It sounded preposterous. Cubans in surgical gloves bugging the DNC! I dismissed it as some sort of prank," Nixon said. "The whole thing made so little sense. Why, I wondered. Why then? Why in such a blundering way . . . Anyone who knew anything about politics would know that a national committee headquarters was a useless place to go for inside information on a presidential campaign. The whole thing was so senseless and bungled that it almost looked like some kind of a setup."[99]

Years later, Haldeman echoed that suspicion:

I believe that in years to come historians will find themselves actually laughing at the DNC Headquarters break-in when they study the facts. *Never before has a crime been so well advertised and widely known ahead of time.* The CIA knew about it because Eugenio Martinez, one of their agents, was on the Watergate team and was reporting regularly to his CIA case officer. That wasn't bad enough. Larry O'Brien, the actual target, was specifically told that the break-in at his DNC Headquarters was going to occur.[100]

Haldeman said, "This series of clear, unmistakable errors appears to be deliberate sabotage and if so the CIA, or a CIA agent acting alone, may have interfered in an historic way which was eventually to bring down the government."[101]

The White House tapes demonstrate that Nixon knew the Watergate break-in was a CIA setup. Nixon opponents cited the June 23, 1972 "smoking gun tape" and a specific exchange between Haldeman and Nixon:

Bob Haldeman On the investigation, you know, the Democratic break-in thing, we're back in the problem area because the FBI is not under control because [L. Patrick] Gray doesn't exactly know how to control them. And they have—their investigation is now leading into some productive areas because they've been able to trace the money, not through the money itself, but through the bank, you know, sources—the banker himself. And it goes in some directions we don't want it to go. Also, there have been some things, like an informant came in off the street to the FBI in Miami with— who is a photographer or has a friend who's a photographer, who developed some films through this guy [Bernard] Barker and the films had pictures of Democratic National Committee letterhead documents and things. So he's got . . . there's things like that that are going to, that are filtering in. [John] Mitchell came up with yesterday, and John Dean analyzed very carefully last night and concludes—concurs now with Mitchell's recommendation that the only way to solve this—and we're set up beautifully to do it, in that the only network that paid any attention to it last night was NBC, who did a massive story on the Cuban—

President Nixon: —that's right.

Haldeman: . . . thing. But the way to handle this now is for us to have [Vernon] Walters call Pat Gray and just say, "Stay the hell out of this. There's some business here we don't want you going any further on." That's not an unusual development.

President Nixon: Mm-hmm.

Haldeman: And that would take care of it.

President Nixon: What's the matter with Pat Gray? You mean he doesn't want to?
Haldeman: Pat does want to. He doesn't know how to, and he doesn't have any basis for doing it. Given this, he will then have the basis. He'll call Mark Felt in and the two of them want to cooperate because he's ambitious.
President Nixon: Yeah. Yeah.
Haldeman: He'll call them in and say, "We've gotten a signal from across the river to put the hold on this." And that'll fit rather well because the FBI agents who are working the case, at this point, feel that's what it is: [that] this is CIA.[102]

This exchange has been taken out of context. On an earlier tape, Haldeman said, "the FBI agents who are working this case, at this point, feel that's what this is. This is CIA . . ."[103] Haldeman also told Nixon that Pat Gray, the acting FBI director, would call Richard Helms and tell him." I think we've run right in the middle of a CIA covert operation."[104] Interestingly, Dean told Haldeman that using the CIA to limit the FBI investigation into the Watergate break-in was John Mitchell's idea. It wasn't.

"Of course, this is a Hunt [operation, and exposure of it] will uncover a lot of things," Nixon replied. "You open that scab there's a hell of a lot of things and that we just feel that it would be very detrimental to have this thing go any further. This involves these Cubans, Hunt, and a lot of hanky-panky that we have nothing to do with ourselves . . . This will open the whole Bay of Pigs thing . . ."[105]

Andrew St. George, a reporter with multiple ties to the intelligence community, alleged in *Harper's Magazine* that he visited CIA headquarters after the break-ins and received confidential information that Watergate burglar Eugenio Martinez for one had been informing the agency about the break-ins before they occurred.

Helms's response to the Andrew St. George article is a classic example of CIA spin. "That fellow is a discredited individual. The

Senate Armed Services Committee went into his background and so forth, and if you take Andrew St. George as a witness, you can believe anything."[106]

Tennessee Senator Howard Baker, Vice Chair of the Senate Watergate Committee, said the CIA, and the agency's function in Watergate, was like "animals crashing around in the forest—you can hear them but you can't see them."[107]

Following public testimony, Baker requested that a summary of the CIA's role in Watergate be drafted for the perusal of the Committee. What Baker's report revealed was incredible:

- The Mullen Company maintained a relationship with the CIA since the company's incorporation in 1959. Hunt had gotten the Mullen Company job with Richard Helms' blessing and "Hunt's covert security clearance was extended by the CIA; he was witting of the Mullen cover; and, on occasion he undertook negotiations with the Agency with respect to that cover—*even after becoming employed at the White House.*"[108] It was also revealed that Mullen Company President Robert Bennett became the liaison between Liddy and Hunt in the weeks following the Watergate arrests and that R. Spencer Oliver, whose office was bugged, was the son of Hughes's personal Mullen account executive, Robert Oliver. The Mullen Company / CIA relationship was so complex that the Agency paid half of Bennett's attorney fee for his Grand Jury appearance.
- A CIA memorandum dated March 1, 1973, noted that "Bennett felt he could handle the Ervin Committee if the Agency could handle Hunt." The memorandum also suggested, in the words of the report, that "Bennett took relish in implicating Colson in Hunt's activities in the press while protecting the Agency at the same time."[109] Bennett was feeding stories to *Washington Post* reporter Bob Woodward, in

exchange Woodward would not reveal Bennett as his source and "was protecting Bennett and Mullen and Company."[110]

- CIA operative Lee R. Pennington Jr. helped Jim McCord destroy documents following the Watergate break-in. When the FBI, in their investigation, asked for information about Pennington, they were purposely misled, furnished with files pertaining to a former employee with a similar name. The director of security of the CIA ordered the removal of information pertaining to the real Pennington from the CIA Watergate files and this information was not made available to the committee until February 1974.

- An in-house investigation of the Watergate break-in started almost "immediately" after the arrests and at the time the CIA was in a state of "panic." The "very secretive investigation" was assigned to Executive Director of the CIA William Colby and was "instructed to keep no copies of his findings and to make no records."

- Senator Majority Leader Mike Mansfield sent out a letter to every federal agency asking to retain materials evidentiary to the Watergate scandal. One week later, CIA Director Richard Helms destroyed tape-recorded telephone conversations between himself and Haldeman, Ehrilchman, and President Nixon, as well as room tapes that recorded conversations (at Helms's desk) concerning Watergate. Logs of the room conversations were made available to the Senate Watergate Committee, but contained "gaps."[111]

- Throughout Howard Hunt's employment at the White House, he was given use of CIA materials and the assistance of CIA personnel. CIA testimony that the agency "had no contact whatsoever with Mr. Hunt subsequent to 31 August, 1971," was erroneous.

- Eugenio Martinez, still working with the CIA throughout his involvement with the White House operation, kept his CIA case officer in the know. The agency subsequently withheld the case officer's contact information, and when the officer was requested by the committee for inquiry, they were told by the agency, he was "on an African safari." In testimony, a second CIA case officer, contradictory to the CIA statement, said the former was in Miami at the time he was requested. The first case officer was subsequently transferred to Indochina and not made available to the Senate committee.

Howard Baker believed the CIA had a large influence on the break-ins, the arrests, and the cover-up of Watergate. He was not a man who could be easily discredited. Baker would run for president in 1980 and emerge as President Ronald Reagan's chief of staff in the Gipper's second term. Then Director of the CIA William Colby, possibly fearing the report would leak or reopen inquiries concerning Watergate, quickly sent a letter to Baker. Colby requested that certain material in the report be deleted "on security grounds," and stated that the report was faulty. "It appears we have come to differing views on this subject," Colby wrote. "If the report is made available to the public in the form proposed, I am concerned that the Agency can be the subject of what I deem to be unjustifiable conclusions that Agency officers or employees were knowingly involved in the break-ins in the Watergate or Dr. Fielding's office or subsequent cover-ups."[112]

"I mean, it doesn't take a genius to figure out that Watergate was a CIA setup," said Frank Sturgis. "We were just pawns."[113]

The Watergate break-ins did not begin as a CIA operation, but men still employed by and more loyal to the agency than the president carried them out. Intelligence men had been placed in key positions throughout the White House, and the Watergate break-ins, as we shall see, became a threat to an ongoing CIA operation. The break-ins were sabotaged. Nixon's suspicions led to the axing of Director Helms, who was reassigned as US ambassador to Iran. Helms did not take the dismissal lightly, and it was later speculated that Helms blackmailed Nixon into the post, lest he release more knowledge about Watergate.

"Of all the accusations made about me and about my leadership of the agency itself, I have resented none more than the charge I blackmailed President Nixon," Helms told British television host David Frost. "It is nonsense. I did not blackmail him; I threatened him with nothing."

Yet, a threat *was* issued. On November 20, 1972, Helms was summoned to Camp David and told that his time as director of the CIA was coming to a close. Jim McCord sent the following letter to Jack Caulfield on December 21: "Sorry to have to write you this letter but felt you had to know. If Helms goes and the WG [Watergate] operation is laid at the CIA's feet, where it does not belong, every tree in the forest will fall. It will be a scorched desert. The whole matter is at a precipice right now. Just pass the message that if they want it to blow, they are on exactly the right course. I'm sorry that you will get hurt in the fallout."[114]

* * *

This was not the first time the CIA attempted to destroy Nixon. In fact, according to CIA assassin Edward Kaiser, the CIA had attempted to assassinate the president on two separate occasions in early 1972. Although Watergate burglar Frank Sturgis recruited Kaiser for the Nixon job, Kaiser backed out when he learned Nixon was the intended target.

Howard Liebengood, the chief of staff for two senators and prominent Washington lobbyist, told Kaiser that "[t]he president was supposed to be assassinated." The first place he was supposed to be assassinated at was in Key Biscayne, the second place was when he was supposed to give a speech at the time of the Vietnam Veterans Against the War convention in Miami Beach 1972. Veteran CIA assassin Edwin Kaiser was to supply the weapons to assassinate Nixon with. Kaiser was recruited by Sturgis for the plot, but Kaiser didn't want any part of domestic assassination. Kaiser told

Liebengood, "I don't get myself involved in politics." Liebengood was a longtime aide to Howard Baker, one of the first Republicans elected to Congress in Tennessee who moved onto the US Senate. An amiable moderate, Baker began his service on the Watergate Committee as a partisan of Nixon. Baker and his Republican counsel Fred Thompson picked up the CIA thread in the Watergate story but its revelations were essentially stalled by the committee Democrats that Republican Senator Lowell Weiker habitually joined on procedural votes. A further investigation of the CIA role was denied. Baker's incredible report was in the back of a six-hundred-page book gathering dust at the Library of Congress, missed by the media but largely unknown until today. Liebengood assisted Thompson in the Baker-authorized investigation of the CIA connection to Watergate.

Liebengood and I were friends because he worked for Baker while I was working for Reagan. In 1989, Liebengood's highly successful lobbying firm, Gold and Liebengood, was acquired by Young and Rubicam, as was my own lobbying firm, Black, Manafort, Stone, and Kelly. We became collegues. "Kaiser and Sturgis were both CIA assassins," Liebengood told me. They both insisted that they had not been informed that Richard Nixon was the target until after the intended weapon was obtained and Kaiser recruited for the hit. Both Sturgis and Kaiser insisted they had been led to believe that they were to execute a "Communist," said Baker's longtime confidant. "Kaiser balked when he realized it was a domestic political hit," Liebengood continued.

Scott Kaiser, the son of Ed Kaiser, learned much from his father about the assassination attempts on Nixon:

> The 1972 Republican Convention was coming to Miami Beach, Florida. Nixon frequently spent weekends on Key Biscayne with his crony Charles G. "Bebe" Rebozo. In a "Secret, Eyes Only" memorandum prepared for USDC Judge William M. Hoeveler, CIA operative Gerald Patrick Hemming Jr. claimed that: "During January 1972 I was contacted by FBI Agent Robert Dwyer in

reference to assisting a Miami FBI project involving Ed Kaiser and Frank Sturgis that motivated a 1972 meeting with Alcohol, Tobacco and Firearms Miami Supervisor Hale for backstop briefing. Sturgis was at the time a White House/Special Operations Group operative, and was later arrested at Watergate during June 1972."

In April 1976, my father told Author Dick Russell: "There were some plans for the convention. I talked to some of the people participating in it, who later participated in the Watergate thing. Create a shoot-out using the Yippies and the Zippies and the other 'hard core commies' they were so worried about. The people I spoke to were going to put some of this equipment in their hands, and some in law enforcement hands, and use some of the local vigilantes to start a shoot out. This would finally straighten out Washington as to where the priorities were on overcoming the 'domestic communist menace.'" Hemming stated to this researcher in 1993: "I get a phone call from (CIA operative) Bob Dwyer. I hadn't talked to him in months, since the Nixon compound thing (Nixon had complained about protestors outside his compound in Key Biscayne, and Sturgis and Kaiser had been ordered to rough up some demonstrators). Some of Veciana's boys had a scheme to have a Cuban Comar fire a STIX missile at the compound. There was a similar plan to attack Guantanamo during the Bay of Pigs. They were gonna take out Nixon and put Agnew in power. I told Dwyer that to me it was all a provocation, and would end up in arrests, and I'm the fucking guy standing in the middle."

Ed Kaiser was involved in both plots to assassinate Nixon, but after he found out that it was a "political assassination" he didn't want any part of it, when Nixon was giving a speech in Miami Beach at the VVAW Convention there was suppose to be a shoot hit, my father was suppose to have supplied the silencers, others were suppose to shoot into the crowd of demonstrators while Frank Sturgis was suppose to take out Nixon, but none of this happened because my father went to the FBI. AJ Weberman who was there said Kaiser saved his life that day. Those against detente with Russia or China, later to be called neocons wanted Nixon out. The right wing Big Oil Barons close to furious about Nixon's hedging on the Oil depletion allowance and his outreach to the Reds wanted him gone. When the Assassination plots failed the Dean driven, Liddy and Hunt executed break-in at the DNC, infiltrated and thus monitored by the CIA provided the "boys" at the Pentagon and Langley the chance they needed for a coup de etat.[115]

Gerald Patrick Hemming was no stranger to conspiracy. As an ex-CIA man, he served as Lee Harvey Oswald's case officer at Atsugi Naval Air Station in Japan, a point of origin for top-secret U-2 flights. Hemming was later part of an American effort aiding Fidel Castro to overthrow Cuban dictator Fulgencio Batista. A CIA memo later stated that Hemming, along with E. Howard Hunt and Frank Sturgis, were involved in the assassination of John Kennedy, according to former special assistant to the Deputy Director of the Central Intelligence Agency Victor Marchetti. The memo was invoked in the 1983 libel suit *Hunt v. Liberty Lobby*, which Hunt brought against Marchetti and his publisher over a Marchetti article linking Hunt to the JFK assassination.[116] In 1976, under arrest for gun smuggling, Hemming began to divulge facts about his CIA past.

Helms wanted to ride out his post as director until his sixtieth birthday on March 30, 1973. This allowed Helms to go out on his own terms, voluntarily leaving his post at the minimum age of retirement. His wish was not granted. A new director was named on February 2, and Helms was effectively ousted.

McCord followed through on his threat. On March 23, 1973, Judge Sirica read a letter from McCord aloud to the Senate Committee. The letter detailed political pressure from the White House and the perjury of defendants as a result, as well as his claim that the Watergate break-ins were not a CIA operation (with the caveat that the Cubans might have been misled to believe that it was). The letter was the biggest sham in the Watergate hearing, until the masterful performance of John Dean.

Dean came to represent what went wrong with the Nixon presidency. Upon becoming president, Nixon separated himself from his coterie of trusted advisors and confidants, the men who appealed to the Nixon's better decisions and actions. With the exception of Attorney General John Mitchell, the men who occupied the White House were not Nixon men and he did not have control of them, having handed authority over to Haldeman and Ehrlichman.

"Haldeman and Ehrlichman shield the President by monopolizing him," an assistant to the president noted. "One of them is present at every meeting in the Oval Office—Nixon sees no one alone. Every meeting follows precisely, down to the second, the 'talking paper' prepared in advance. Haldeman sees everything—even the daily news summary is reviewed before it goes in to the Old Man. Nixon's made himself their captive. How can he find out whether his orders are carried out? All the channels flow back to Haldeman?"[117]

Nixon, of course, demanded the isolation that the "Berlin Wall" would impose. After resigning and departing for his exile in San Clemente, Nixon would be visited by a lawyer from President Ford's staff to discuss the disposition of his papers and records. "You know," Nixon said. "I'm really sorry I didn't spend more time in the White House talking to people like you. Bob, of course, always prevented it. But I've been thinking over the last few days. If I had it to do all over again, that's one of the things I would do differently. Talk to people like you, I mean."[118]

Richard Whalen, the Pulitzer Prize–winning writer who had helped Nixon reinvent himself in '68, had, like so many of the other "bright young men," slipped away from Nixon. Whalen experienced Nixon's withdrawal firsthand and had the foresight to predict the damage it would cause. "No potential danger is more ominous in a free society than the secret leaching away of presidential authority from the man the people choose to the men he chooses," Whalen wrote the year of the break-in. "To whom are they responsible? To him and their own consciences, of course, which is the essence of the danger when a President is protected even from the knowledge of what is said and done in his name."[119]

"The way you, you've handled it, it seems to me, has been very skillful," Nixon told Dean on September 15, 1972, "because you—putting your fingers in the dikes every time that leaks have sprung here and sprung there."[120]

A year later, in testimony before the Senate Watergate Committee, Dean implicated President Nixon and Attorney General Mitchell in the break-ins and the cover-up, exposed the distribution of "hush money from the White House to keep a lid on the scandal, set the Watergate investigators on the trail of the secret White House recording system and revealed the creation of a Nixon's enemies list. Jeb Magruder, who reprehensibly heaped the blame for the break-ins at the Attorney General's door, would also smear Mitchell in slanderous testimony.

In fact, Mitchell and Nixon did not order or have extensive knowledge of the break-ins. In the end, Nixon's paranoia and solitary nature left him without loyal and able men to turn to.

In the end, Nixon was alone in the White House.

NOTES

1. Tad Szulc, *Compulsive Spy*, p. 180.
2. Author's conversation with Jim McCord.
3. George Will, "If the President does it, it's legal?" *New York Post*, Aug. 17, 2013.
4. H. R. Haldeman, *The Ends of Power*, p. 5.
5. Ibid., p. 8.
6. Kevin Anderson, "Revelations and gaps on Nixon tapes," BBC News. March 1, 2002.
7. Larry Sabato, *The Kennedy Half-Century: The Presidency, Assassination, and Lasting Legacy of John F. Kennedy*, p. 313.
8. Anthony Summers, *The Arrogance of Power*, p. 198.
9. Russ Baker, *Family of Secrets*, p. 181.
10. Lamar Waldron, *Watergate: The Hidden History*, p. 436.
11. H. R. Haldeman, *The Ends of Power*, p. 40.
12. Richard Helms, *A Look Over My Shoulder*, p. 27.

13 Oliver Stone, *Nixon*, Hollywood Pictures, 1995.
14. Thomas Powers, *The Man Who Kept the Secrets*, p. 38.
15. Lamar Waldron, *Watergate: The Hidden History*, p. 42.
16. Lamar Waldron, *Watergate: The Hidden History*, pp. 848–849.
17. Jim Hougan, *Secret Agenda*, p. 6.
18. Tad Szulc, *Compulsive Spy*, p. 106.
19. Russ Baker, *Family of Secrets*, p. 200.
20. Jim Hougan, *Secret Agenda*, p. 9.
21. Church Committee Testimony of L. Fletcher Prouty, July 16, 1975.
22. Lamar Waldron, *Watergate: The Hidden History*, p. 779.
23. Kathryn S. Olmsted, *Challenging the Secret Government*, p. 77.
24 Church Committee Testimony of L. Fletcher Prouty, July 16, 1975.
25. H. R. Haldeman, *The Ends of Power*, p. 109.
26. H. R. Haldeman, *The Ends of Power*, p. 203.
27. Lamar Waldron, *Watergate: The Hidden History*, p. 242.
28. Len Colodny and Robert Gettlin, *Silent Coup*, p. 10.
29. James Rosen, "Nixon and the Chiefs," The Atlantic, April 2002.
30. Len Colodny and Robert Gettlin, *Silent Coup*, pp. 13–14.
31. James Rosen, "Nixon and the Chiefs," The Atlantic, April 2002.
32. James Rosen, "Nixon and the Chiefs," The Atlantic, April 2002.
33. "Book Discussion on Silent Coup: The Removal of a President," Booknotes C-SPAN, Jan. 25, 1991.
34. Howard Chua-Eoan, "The Watergate Dirty Trickster Who Found God" *Time*, April 21, 2012
35. James Rosen, *The Strong Man: John Mitchell and the Secrets of Watergate* (Kindle Locations 461-4694).
36. Ibid.
37. Lamar Waldron, *Watergate: The Hidden History*, p. 863.
38. Ibid., p. 864.
39. Ibid., p. 867.
40. Richard Helms, *A Look Over My Shoulder*, p. 30.
41. Interview with Charles Colson.
42. James Rosen, *The Strong Man: John Mitchell and the Secrets of Watergate*, p. 156.
43. Jim Hougan, *Secret Agenda*, p. 29.
44. Eugenio Martinez, "Mission Impossible," http://watergate.info/burglary/eugenio-martinez-account-of-watergate-burglary.
45. H. R. Haldeman, *The Ends of Power*, p. 159.

46. Lamar Waldron, *Watergate: The Hidden History*, pp. 1030–1031.
47. Lamar Waldron, *Watergate: The Hidden History*, pp. 1032–1033.
48. "Hughes Nixon and the C.I.A.", Playboy magazine, September 1976
49. H. R. Haldeman, *The Ends of Power*, p. 133.
50. H. R. Haldeman, *The Ends of Power*, pp. 145–146.
51. Ibid., p. 145.
52. With two top aides to Richard Nixon, Leonard Garment and later Chairman of the Federal Reserve Bank Alan Greenspan playing with the Woody Herman Orchestra, the number of jazz musician tangentially involved in Watergate is interesting.
53. Miles Copeland, "The Unmentionable Uses of a CIA," *National Review*, Sept. 14, 1972.
54. Richard Helms, *A Look Over My Shoulder*, p. 27.
55. Jim Hougan, *Secret Agenda*, p. 9.
56. Jim Hougan, *Secret Agenda*, p. 11.
57. Ibid., p. 22.
58. Eugenio Martinez, "Mission Impossible," http://watergate.info/burglary/eugenio-martinez-account-of-watergate-burglary.
59. Jim Hougan, Secret Agenda, pp. 153–154.
60. Ibid., p. 153.
61. Eugenio Martinez, "Mission Impossible," http://watergate.info/burglary/eugenio-martinez-account-of-watergate-burglary.
62. Eugenio Martinez, "Mission Impossible," http://watergate.info/burglary/eugenio-martinez-account-of-watergate-burglary.
63. Ibid.
64. Jim Hougan, *Secret Agenda*, p. 150.
65. Len Colodny and Robert Gettlin, *Silent Coup*, p. 140.
66. Ibid., p. 138.
67. Len Colodny and Robert Gettlin, *Silent Coup*, p. 156.
68. Deborah Hart Strober and Gerald S. Strober, *The Nixon Presidency: An Oral History of the Era*, p. 347.
69. Investigative Reports, "The Key to Watergate," A&E, Sept. 18, 1992.
70. Jim Hougan, "Hougan, Liddy, the Post and Watergate," www.jimhougan.com.
71. Anthony Summers, *The Arrogance of Power*, p. 417.
72. Jim Hougan, *Secret Agenda*, pp. 162-163.
73. G. Gordon Liddy, *Will*, p. 322.

74. J. Anthony Lukas, *Nightmare: The Underside of the Nixon Years*, pp. 201–202.
75. Jim Hougan, *Secret Agenda*, p. 156.
76. Ibid., pp. 156–157.
77. G. Gordon Liddy, *Will*, pp. 236-237.
78. Jim Hougan, Secret Agenda, p. 181.
79. G. Gordon Liddy, Will, p. 232.
80. Jim Hougan, "The McCord File," *Harper's*. Jan. 1980.
81. Ibid.
82. Russ Kick, Abuse Your Illusions: The Disinformation Guide to Media Mirages and Establishment Lies, p. 20.
83. Jim Hougan, Secret Agenda, pp. 117–118.
84. Anthony Summers, The Arrogance of Power, p. 419.
85. Jim Hougan, "The McCord File," *Harper's*, Jan. 1980
86. Jim Hougan, *Secret Agenda*, p. 183.
87. Ibid., p. 192.
88. Ibid., p. 310.
89. Webster Griffin Tarpley and Anton Chaitkin, *George Bush: The Unauthorized Biography*, p 253.
90. Ibid.
91. Jim Hougan, *Secret Agenda*, p. 306.
92. Ibid., p. 311.
93. Webster Griffin Tarpley and Anton Chaitkin, *George Bush: The Unauthorized Biography*, p. 253.
94. J. Anthony Lukas, *Nightmare: The Underside of the Nixon Years*, p. 206
95. Jim Hougan, Secret Agenda, p. 198.
96. Investigative Reports, "The Key to Watergate," A&E, Sept. 18, 1992
97. Ibid.
98. Richard Nixon, *RN: The Memoirs of Richard Nixon*, p. 626.
99. H. R. Haldeman, *The Ends of Power*, p. 128.
100. H. R. Haldeman, *The Ends of Power*, p. 146.
101. Conversation between Richard Nixon and H. R. Haldeman, June 23, 1972.
102. Russ Baker, *Family of Secrets*, p. 176.
103. Ibid., p. 178.
104. Ibid.
105. https://www.cia.gov/library/center-for-the-study-of-intelligence/kent-csi/vol44no4/html/v44i4a07p_0013.htm.

106. Jefferson Morley, "Watergate's Final Mystery," *Salon,* May 5, 2012.
107. Summary of Highlights of CIA Activity in Watergate Incident, Final Report of the Senate Select Committee on Presidential Campaign Activities.
108. Ibid.
109. Ibid.
110. Ibid.
111. Letter from William Colby to Howard Baker, June 28, 1974.
112. Jim Hougan, *Secret Agenda,* p. 183.
113. Fred Emery, *Watergate: The Corruption of American Politics and the Fall of Richard Nixon,* p. 235.
114. E-mail from Scott Kaiser.
115. Hunt v. Liberty Lobby, http://www.leagle.com/decision/198313517 20F2d631_11255.xml/HUNT%20v.%20LIBERTY%20LOBBY.
116. Richard Whalen, *Catch the Falling Flag,* p. 255.
117. Barry Werth, *31 Days,* p. 242.
118. Richard Whalen, *Catch the Falling Flag,* p. 225.
119. "Watergate Retrospective: The Decline and Fall," *Time,* Aug. 19, 1974.

CHAPTER FIFTEEN

GEMSTONE

"The more I got into this, the more I see how these sons of bitches have not only done Nixon in but they've done me in."

—John Mitchell[1]

John Dean was well aware that President Nixon and the men around him had a thirst for intelligence. He used this White House fixation to propel himself into the president's inner circle. Although he has labored mightily to bury the public record, John Dean wanted the franchise on political intelligence and keenly understood the dynamics and tensions between the Haldeman-Ehrlichman axis and Attorney General John Mitchell. He adroitly exploited this tension to push successive campaign intelligence proposals and enlisted Gordon Liddy, Jeb Magruder, and Chuch Colson to help him move the ball.

In his retelling of the facts in both his Senate testimony and his book *Blind Ambition*, Dean labors mightily to distance himself from these plans and their fumbled execution. Interestingly, in a book proposal, but not in his book *Blind Ambition*, Dean detailed his plan. Dean wrote in a draft for his book *Blind Ambition*, "I reflected on how I might take advantage of Haldeman's preoccupation. I was still building my law firm seeking new business and I knew the campaign would be a stepping-stone to those who distinguished themselves. But as I looked ahead, I saw the Counsels' own office performing rather menial campaign tasks. [They did] legal chores hardly important enough to be admitted to the inner circle. If the Counsels' office could play the same role at the Republican Convention we played on May Day, special White House tie lines, half hourly reports, I knew we'd be in the thicket . . . We had a jump on other White Houses offices in demonstration intelligence. Why not expand our role to all intelligence? That would be of interest to the President and the campaign."[2]

Dean made a play to be intelligence czar and had great assets for such an undertaking in detectives Jack Caulfield and Tony Ulasewicz. Post-Watergate, Dean disavowed knowledge of Caulfield's intelligence work in the White House, much of which was performed for Dean. Dean would say he had never met Ulasewicz. This is false. Although Ulasewicz took his orders directly from Caulfield, Dean and Ulasewicz had several distasteful encounters. "Every crease in his suit was perfectly ironed, every hair on his head in place, and he had a smooth, almost hairless face," Ulasewicz later wrote. "Everything about him appeared too delicate and too neat for me. I took an instant dislike to him and dismissed him as a smooth operator."[3]

In *Blind Ambition*, Dean wrote that Caulfield had been assigned to him by Bob Haldeman, and "I don't know why." This is also false. As Caulfield lays out in detail in his own memoir he, and later Tony Ulasewicz, were first recruited to work for the White House Counsel's office for John Ehrlichman, and Dean inherited both when he took the post. Both Ehrilchman and Dean used the detectives for many investigations. Amazingly, Dean later claimed he didn't know what Caulfield actually did.

"I saw a desire [by Dean] to take greater chances as [Dean] saw the potential rewards," said White House detective Jack Caulfield. "And the key to the ball game was intelligence—who was going to get it and who was going to provide it. Dean saw that and played the game heartily . . . I was getting my instructions from Dean . . ."[4]

Dean was not satisfied with having the two veteran gumshoes working for him on a limited assignment basis. He knew only something bigger would be his ticket to real power in the Nixon entourage. This required a more sophisticated, better-funded design, and Dean asked Caulfield to develop an intelligence plan. Caulfield, hardboiled and a cop's cop, was a cautious investigator who knew legal limits. Gregarious, hard drinking, and honest, Caulfield knew the dangers of breaking the law for a political campaign set to face to voters. In his very readable biography *Shield #911-NYPD*, the decorated cop, Caulfield, who had worked on intelligence operations for the New York City Police Department, made the case that his proposal was aggressive, but *legal*.

Over lunch, Caulfield told Magruder and Dean his idea to set up a private security firm to carry out the secret affairs. Through the firm, Caulfield believed, he could carry out assignments for CRP, the Republican National Committee, as well as corporate clients. The plan would not only provide valuable intelligence, but if uncovered it also provided separation from the White House. Named Operation Sandwedge, the plan was drafted by Caulfield and handed over to Dean for consideration. Budgeted at a half million dollars, Sandwedge was an "offensive intelligence-defensive security" operation that resembled an early version of the Watergate break-ins and proposed to:

> Supervise penetration of the Democratic presidential nominee's entourage and headquarters with undercover personnel;
> Conduct surveillance of Democratic primaries, convention, and meetings;
> Develop a derogatory information investigative capability worldwide; and
> Meet "any other offensive requirement deemed advisable."[5]

Sandwedge's implementation was contingent on the approval of Attorney General John Mitchell. When Dean presented the idea, the sensible Mitchell did not commit to any "hard decisions."[6]

Dean subsequently told Caulfield he didn't think the proposal was "going anywhere."[7] A disappointed Caulfield abandoned the project and, eventually, the Nixon White House for a position at the US Department of Treasury.

Later, Caulfield believed that if Sandwedge had been approved, the errors of Watergate could have been avoided. To him, it was aggressive but legal in its proposed methods for intelligence collection. There is reason to believe John Dean felt similarly: he later said to Nixon ". . . uh, in retrospect—that might have been a bad call-'cause he (Caulfield) is an incredibly cautious person and—and, would not have put the situation to where it is today."[8]

Caulfield said, "I go a lot further and say that error was, in fact, the most monumental of the Nixon Presidency in that it rapidly created the catastrophic path leading directly to the Watergate complex—and the President's eventual resignation."[9]

On the contrary, in a taped interview with Watergate historian Len Colodny, Dean said, "I was never in the loop on any of that and, and Caulfield, ya know, was assigned to my staff, much to my mystery as to what the hell he was gonna do and why he was there, I mean, I scratched my head for a long time before I, and, it just kind of came out in dribs and drabs as to what he was doin'."[10]

But according to authors Phil Stanford and Len Colodny, Dean was directly involved in Sandwedge—he was actually a coauthor of the plan.[11]

Mitchell refused to approve Sandwedge. Campaign Manager Jeb Magruder would have us believe Mitchell later approved a more grandiose plan that included highly illegal surreptitious break-ins. Mitchell deputy Fred LaRue, the only other person in the room, vigorously disputed Magruder's account, as does Mitchell himself.

Dean, of course, did not stop at Sandwedge. It was this lust for influence that made John Dean the real power behind the notorious Gemstone plan.

Next, Dean handed the baton off to colorful ex-FBI man G. Gordon Liddy. According to Dean's own book *Blind Ambition*, he pushed to have Liddy hired as the legal counsel to the Finance Committee for the reelection of the President. Dean incorrectly said that he promoted Liddy for the job of general counsel to the Committee to Reelect the President, a different entity. Technically, Liddy worked for Finance Chairman Maurice Stans, not deputy director Jeb Magruder.

"Dean realized that the way to increase his influence was through political intelligence, so when Caulfield—to Dean's dismay—decided to resign to set up his own detective agency, Dean—to his horror—realized he was going to lose his operative, so I was recruited," said Liddy.[12] Liddy, like Caulfield, was someone who could perform tasks in the interest of Dean.

Dean had knowledge of Liddy's break-in at Dr. Fielding's office. He encouraged Liddy to develop a "first-class intelligence operation."[13]

"You mean Sandwedge?" asked Liddy.[14]

"No. We're going to need something much better, much more complete and sophisticated than that," replied Dean. "How's a half a million for openers?"[15]

Well," Liddy said, "You're talking the right numbers, anyway. Half a million is just about right for openers, and it'd probably take another half before we're finished. That doesn't bother you?"[16]

"No, problem," Dean answered.[17]

Liddy was also provided with the twelve-page analysis and proposal for Sandwedge with a comment added from Dean that it had been "inadequate."[18]

"Liddy was told to put together this plan, you know, how he would run an intelligence operation," Dean said later, without stating that it was he who gave the order. Dean told Nixon it was Colson who most likely pushed Liddy to develop the proposal. "I think he (Colson) helped to get the push, get the thing off dime," Dean told the president.[19]

The operation, urged on by Dean and drafted by Liddy, was named Gemstone, a series of clandestine and illegal exploits, each named after a precious stone, which landed at $1 million. The massive undertaking included chase planes, prostitutes, and the beating, drugging, and kidnapping of anti-war demonstration leaders who would be stowed in Mexico and held there until after the Republican National Convention.

On January 22, 1972, accompanied by Dean and Magruder, Liddy presented his plan to John Mitchell in the attorney general's office. As Liddy ran through his checklist of bribery, kidnapping, and prostitution to the attorney general, the two men who had encouraged the operative, Dean and Magruder, sat there "like two rabbits in front of a cobra."

When Liddy concluded his far-fetched proposal, the straight-faced attorney general removed the pipe that had been clenched between his teeth, took time to repack, relight, and paused to puff and collect his thoughts.

"Gordon, that's not quite what I had in mind," Mitchell said, adding that Liddy should come up with something a bit more realistic, effectively nixing the proposal and ending the meeting. Liddy was miffed at Mitchell's brusque response to the plan; he had supplied what he thought the attorney general had requested, but it was clear that Mitchell had not been filled in beforehand on the figures or design. In fact, Mitchell saw Liddy's proposal as ludicrous. "I think it can best be described as a complete horror story that involved a mish-mash of code names and lines of authority, electronic surveillance, the ability to intercept aircraft communications, the call girl bit and all the rest of it," Mitchell later told the Senate. "The matter was of such striking content and concept that it was just beyond the pale. As I recall, I told him to go burn the charts and that this was not what we were interested in. What we were interested in was a matter of information gathering and protection against demonstrators."

". . . In hindsight, I not only should have thrown him out of the office, I should have thrown him out of the window."[20]

While Liddy felt put off by Mitchell, he felt betrayed by Magruder and Dean. These were the men who pushed the proposal, encouraged Liddy to think big, and remained silent when his submission was rejected. Liddy recalled the moment in his autobiography, *Will*:

> I walked out of Mitchell's office with fire in my eyes. Before we even reached the car, in which John Dean was to join us for a ride back to the White House, I unloaded on both of them. "Thanks for all the help. What the hell does he mean, 'realistic'? You're the one, John, who said there'd be 'half a million for openers.' I've got top people committed and standing by on the basis of a budget of a million, in good faith. What's going on?"
>
> Magruder was solicitous. "Mr. Mitchell," he said, "sees more of the picture than any of us. It may be that contributions aren't up to what they were expected to be by now and there just isn't the money for intelligence and dirty tricks they thought would be available. These things happen in campaigns. You've got to be flexible. You're going to have to cut out the most expensive stuff."
>
> "It's clear," chimed in Dean, "that he wants a less broad-gauged program. Jeb's right, you're going to have to cut it back."[21]

Following the first Gemstone meeting, Liddy went back to the drawing board, halved the budget and eliminated the more extreme measures of the plan, cutting it down to $500,000. The updated plan was "less spectacular and therefore more acceptable," Magruder said.[22]

Another meeting was arranged for February 4, 1972, and again attended by the attorney general, Liddy, Magruder, and Dean. Mitchell was again dissatisfied at what was being proposed, so much so that Dean saw him "wince" during the presentation,[23] and he decided to call the meeting to a close.

Perhaps with the fear that if the meeting ended at that moment the project would be scrapped completely, Dean intervened. "Sir, I don't think a decision of this kind should come from the attorney general's office. I think he should get it from somewhere else—completely unofficial channels."[24]

Dean's later version to Nixon was outlandish, given that it was Dean who desired the intelligence plan and its approval. I said, "You all pack that stuff up and get it the hell out of here 'cause we just, you just can't talk this way in this office and you should re-examine your whole thinking."[25]

Outside of the office, Liddy was once again seething. "Now, I want a fucking decision and I want it fast!" Liddy yelled at Magruder. "What John said was unfortunate, but he has a point," Magruder answered. "Don't worry; I'll follow through on it and get you a decision."[26]

The February 4 meeting was significant not only because it was the second time Mitchell rejected a Dean-sponsored intelligence plan (third if Sandwedge is included), but also because the stories of Dean and Magruder began to diverge from those of Liddy, Mitchell, and others. This was when, Dean and Magruder argued, particulars of what became the Watergate break-ins were considered.

Dean and Magruder contended that this was the first time a surveillance operation, with the specific target of Democratic National Chairman Larry O'Brien, was discussed. Magruder said O'Brien was the first name mentioned in a meeting about a surveil-lance operation. In Magruder's story, O'Brien was bugged at both the Fontainebleau hotel in Miami, where the convention was to be held, and in his DNC office at the Watergate.[27]

Dean, who claimed he was late to the meeting, had three ver-sions of what was mentioned in the meeting regarding the surveil-lance of O'Brien. In private testimony, Dean claimed the meeting touched on O'Brien and the Fountainbleau. Only days later, in a television interview, Dean claimed that he could not recall if these items were discussed. In this version, Dean wavered, saying there "may have been something as to potential targets, and later that "none were named." In the later part of 1974, taking the stand in *US v. Mitchell*, Dean was asked once again about the second meet-ing, stating that when he entered, the three men were "talking about targets, possible targets of electronic surveillance."[28]

Both Liddy and John Mitchell maintained that neither Larry O' Brien or the DNC were mentioned as potential targets during the February 4 meeting. Mitchell added that the DNC was "basically ceremonial" and not an interest to him. Liddy said the DNC was not a target for break-in until March, and at that time it was an order from Magruder.[29] Magruder once again told Liddy that the proposal at $500,000, which Dean had assured Liddy was an approved start-up figure, was "too expensive."[30] Liddy once again halved and redrafted his proposal.

The third and final meeting where Gemstone was discussed took place on March 30, 1972, in Key Biscayne, Florida. Mitchell was vacationing with his wife, Martha, and daughter at the Florida House, owned by Nixon pal Bebe Rebozo.

Present at the meeting in Key Biscayne were Mitchell, Magruder and high-ranking Nixon White House aide Fred LaRue. Magruder was presenting Mitchell with a series of papers with items to make decisions on. The intelligence plan, which included bugging the DNC office of Larry O'Brien, was at the bottom of the pile. Again, later recollections contradicted when the discussion turned to the intelligence proposal. Magruder recalled that approval of the operation was "a reluctant decision," but was given the go-ahead by Mitchell. Mitchell's version is consistent with his apparent distaste of the previous two meetings. "We don't need this," Mitchell said he responded. "I am tired of hearing it. Out—let's not discuss it any further."[31]

LaRue's account lends support to the argument that Mitchell did not approve the proposal. "Mr. Magruder, as in the previous proposals, handed this paper to Mr. Mitchell," said LaRue. "Mr. Mitchell read it, he asked me if I had read it and I told him I had. He asked me what I thought of it and I told him I did not think it was worth the risk."[32]

LaRue said that Mitchell then replied, "Well, this is not something that will have to be decided at this meeting." [33] The meeting, and his lack of assertiveness in rejecting the idea of the break-in, haunted Mitchell for years.

"Under the setting and the circumstances, what was said was vehement enough to [convey] 'Get the hell out of here and don't bring any of that nonsense around me,'" Mitchell recalled. " . . .The conclusion I've come to in my own mind [is] that these things were under way and they were going to go ahead regardless."[34]

The many accounts of the meeting in Key Biscayne make it probable that no matter what Mitchell said in the meeting, Magruder had to leave with the plan approved.

G. Gordon Liddy, not present at the Key Biscayne meeting, knew where the idea and the approval of the Watergate break-ins derived. "Dean was the highest-level person to sign off on Watergate," said Liddy.[35]

Despite LaRue and Mitchell's accounts to the contrary, Watergate prosecutors accepted Magruder's testimony. Magruder went a step further with his account of the Key Biscayne meeting three decades later, adding the claim of an overheard phone call between the president and the attorney general.

According to Magruder, Mitchell called Haldeman and Ehrlichman to discuss the DNC/wiretapping enterprise further. Magruder said that sometime during the call he heard the familiar voice of Nixon on the other end personally giving the order for the break-ins.

"John . . . we need need to get the information on Larry O'Brien, and the only way we can do that is through Liddy's plans," Nixon allegedly told Mitchell.[36]

"And I could hear his voice distinctly indicating that he wanted the Liddy plan to go ahead," Magruder added. "And Mitchell got off the phone and said to me: 'Jeb, tell Maurice Stans to give $250,000 to Gordon Liddy and let's see what happens.'"[37]

According to John Taylor, executive director of the Richard Nixon Library and Birthplace in Yorba Linda until 2009, Magruder's claim is undoubtedly false. "The White House Daily Diary, which details all the president's meetings and telephone calls, shows that

Mr. Ehrlichman did not meet or talk with President Nixon at any time on March 30, 1972," Taylor said.[38]

Even John Dean would contradict Magruder's late claim, telling the Associated Press, "I have no reaon to doubt that it happened as he describes it, but I have never seen a scintilla of evidence that Nixon knew about the plans for the Watergate break-in or that the likes of Gordon Loddy were operating at the reelection committee."

Dean historian Stanley Kutler, an expert on Nixon's White House tapes, called Magruder's allegation "the dubious word of a dubious character."

Magruder and Dean had good reason to issue different recollections than the others in the Gemstone meetings. By passing the buck to Mitchell, Dean and Magruder assumed the role of two lower-level White House functionaries who "were just following orders." Dean looked the part at the Watergate hearings, as well. Gone was the long-haired, modish, Porshe-driving White House operative everybody knew; the John Dean who showed up to the Watergate hearings looked nebbish, with a short haircut in a conservative suit. Even his contacts were gone. Instead, he wore horn-rimmed glasses.

Dean was crafty and adept at taking ideas and credit from others and pinning blame to another when he was cornered. Although there is substantial evidence to show that Dean originated the Watergate break-in plots, it was Liddy who presented the plots, Mitchell who was approved them, and Magruder who provided oversight. When the Watergate break-ins went awry and the subsequent cover-up fell apart, it was Dean who approached the prosecutors, offering testimony against both Mitchell and Magruder in exchange for his own immunity.

"We have a cancer—within, close to the Presidency, that's growing," Dean told Nixon in March 1973. "It's growing daily. It's compounding, it grows geometrically now because it compounds itself."[39]

Nixon could not see the cancer. It was standing right in front of him.

"He is an amazing character; I don't think there is an ounce of morality in him," said Richard Kleindienst. "To have pulled off what he did—and in the manner in which he did it—is one of the most amazing stories. I think John Dean thought he could pull off almost anything—and he almost did."[40]

In the end, Mitchell stumbled. The attention he paid to his mentally fragile wife, coupled with his bold self-assurance in a post he was not well accustomed with, buried him. As Garment said, Mitchell "strode with his overconfidence into his post as attorney general—and into a jungle." The office that Mitchell walked into was far away from the world of municipal financing from which he had come.

"Mitchell did not pay attention to the dangers and risks of the small stuff—like Liddy's activities; the campaign chicken-shit stuff," said former Justice Department official Donald Santarelli. "He should have recognized that the small items are the ones that bring big men down. He didn't appreciate the degree of long knives, and how fatally they can cut."[41]

Only weeks before the first Watergate break-in attempt, Dean instructed Ulasewicz to case the DNC offices. Ulasewicz later claimed this request only went as high as Dean.

"Dean wants you to check out the offices of the DNC," Caulfield told Ulasewicz.[42]

Ulasewicz "complied and simply walked through the offices as a visitor, casing out the location of desks, who sat where, and any other useful information."[43]

"I can absolutely flat out tell you that isn't true," said Dean, rejecting the theory that he had anything to do with the reconnaissance. But he then added a caveat: "You know, I don't have any knowledge of ever sending Tony Ulasewicz in. Whether somebody came in to my of—if Caulfield ever came into my office and said, 'John, I think Tony should go into the office' and I'm in the middle of somethin' else and don't even reflect on it and I say, 'Whatever you think, Jack,' uh, you know, which I did a lot. Uh, you know, I just, 'Go on and do it,' or . . ."[44]

It's a mystery why Dean laid the blame on Caulfield. This bizarre reimagining begs belief that Caufied devised a plan to scope the layout of a target about which he knew nothing. Ulasewicz was certain Dean was behind the order to conduct a walkthrough of the Watergate. Consider the following exchange between Len Colodny and Ulaswicz:

> **COLODNY:** Where he's asking you to do the Watergate thing, do you think it's the President that wants that?
> **ULASEWIZ:** Nope
> **COLODNY:** You know it's Dean.
> **ULASEWICZ:** I know it's Dean.[45]

In other words, Dean had Ulasewicz stake out the DNC and look for *particular* locations in the offices. Knowing these locations came in handy for Dean when the actual break-ins transpired.

Years later, after he was blamed for authorizing the Watergate break-in, an operation he expressed time and again was not right for the Nixon White House, Mitchell learned of Dean's order to Ulasewicz to inspect the offices. In the words of Len Colodny, Mitchell "went bananas."[46]

* * *

History has decided that John Dean is the hero of Watergate: the reluctant and courageous young whistleblower who mesmerized the nation; "the human typewriter,"[47] as some writers called him, whose incredible recall and recitation of events that transpired within the White House helped bring down a president. As with the Kennedy assassination however, the version of events accepted by the mainstream media is not the complete truth.

Incredibly, Dean has sought to control the historic narrative of Watergate established by Woodward and Bernstein after his careful orchestration of events in the Senate Watergate Hearings. In fact, John Dean's testimony directly contradicts his own book, *Blind Ambition*. His version of events is self-serving, evasive, deceptive, and is designed to deflect his own responsibility for the Watergate break-in and cover-up.

On April 17, 1973, Nixon summoned the White House press corps. One of his announcements on that day was that no one in his administration would receive immunity from prosecution. Two days later, Dean, who had to that point been in his own words to the president, "all over this thing (the cover-up) like a blanket,"[48] immediately released a statement. "Some may hope or think that I will become a scapegoat," the statement read. "Anyone who believes this does not know me, know the true facts, nor understand our system of justice."[49]

Dean bartered for immunity, and it fast became apparent he would sacrifice anyone for it. "Having struck out when he used Haldeman and Ehrlichman as bait, Dean now began to dangle a larger prize—the president," wrote the Senate Watergate Committee's Chief Minority Counsel, Tennessee attorney Fred Thompson. "News stories indicating that Dean would implicate Nixon began to trickle out."[50] In a tactical maneuver to whet the appetite of the public, it was Dean's team that leaked the stories to newspapers and magazines.[51] As the chief witness for the Watergate Senate Committee, Dean turned state's evidence in return for a minimal sentence. Despite coauthoring Gemstone with G. Gordon Liddy, despite playing *the* key role in the cover-up, Dean served only four months in prison. The less culpable John Mitchell served nineteen months, Haldeman and Ehrlichman both served eighteen months, Magruder did seven months, and G. Gordon Liddy, who was sentenced to *twenty years*, was imprisoned for nearly fifty-two months.

Interestingly, Watergate saboteur Jim McCord also served only four months in prison, substantially less than his counterparts.

"Let me tell you," said Dean. "All those guys are pissed off that I stood up and blew the whistle . . . I fucked up their lives . . . which was good."[52]

The move was classic Dean, using others to his own benefit. "John doesn't have a circle of friends," a Dean associate told the

New York Times. "He never has and he never was liked. He doesn't have the bonhomie or camaraderie. Everything he does is done with a point or a purpose with his peers and it shows. He tends to use them for an advantage."[53]

Dean was lauded for his testimony, yet it was filled with inaccuracies. It didn't matter: Dean was the lone witness to connect the crimes of Watergate to the highest offices of the White House. "It seemed obvious that the committee members considered Dean such an important witness that it was unwise to risk his displeasure," wrote Fred Thompson. "And that was not the only advantage Dean obtained in his dealings with the committee: not until the morning of his public testimony did we receive his 245-page statement and the fifty documents he submitted with it. As a result, we found ourselves racing through the material he offered at almost the same time that he was reading it to the nation. There was no chance to analyze it, or to prepare questions based on it."[54]

* * *

In the years following Watergate, new details have emerged adding context to the break-ins, and specifically Dean's role in them. In 1976, when John Dean released his blockbuster tell-all book covering his years in the Nixon White House, the Watergate break-ins and the aftermath, it was greeted as a brave and authentic retelling of the times. *Blind Ambition* was a work of "unsparing honesty,"[55] in the words of former Clinton aide and journalist Sydney Blumenthal.

Dean trumpeted his own veracity in the opening pages. "This book is a portrait—not a black-and-white photograph—of five years of my life. It represents my best effort to paint what I saw and reproduce what I heard. I have included detail, texture, tone, to make this history more vivid—though, I trust, no prettier. I prepared for the writing of *Blind Ambition* the same way I prepared to testify before the Ervin Committee, before the special prosecutors, and in the cover-up trial."[56]

"To reconstruct what occurred, I reviewed an enormous number of documents as well as my own testimony," Dean continued. "To borrow my lawyer's phrase: *'I'm ready to get on the box—take a lie-detector test."* [57] (emphasis added)

For a decade, this was an accepted truth. Then it started to unravel.

In the eighties, when historians Len Colodny and Robert Gettlin began work on the book that would become *Silent Coup*, an unparalleled investigative analysis of the Watergate scandal, their research did not begin in the Nixon White House. In fact, the book the two men originally intended to write was a look at *Washington Post* reporter Bob Woodward in the years following Watergate. Colodny and Gettlin tracked Woodward's career back to his job working in naval intelligence as a briefer for Alexander Haig. Woodward by way of his work for Haig led Colodny and Gettlin back to the White House, to Watergate, and eventually, to John Dean.

According to Colodny, Dean was initially ecstatic about a couple of writers coloring in his years at the Nixon White House, even suggesting that he would be a prime candidate to pen the foreword to the book.[58] Colodny and Gettlin then focused their research on Watergate, interviewing top men in the White House during that much-maligned period. Dean quickly became skittish. "Len, it's too painful," Colodny recalled of Dean's reply. "I've been through this, I don't want to talk about it any more, it's over. Read everything that I said in the courts, in the Senate Committee, what I wrote in *Blind Ambition,* and the White House tapes."[59]

"For the next year, that's all I did," Colodny continued, "was sit there and read everything he said. Not verbatim, but by subject matter. And low and behold, in four different venues, sometimes five different venues, he never told the same story twice and by the time he got to his book *Blind Ambition,* he would actually drop the lies."[60]

Colodny found many contradictions between Dean's testimony and his book, between things Dean told Colodny and others and what actually transpired: the pressing of Caulfield for an intelligence plan and the perpetuation of Sandwedge after it was snuffed by Mitchell; pushing Liddy to create Gemstone, ordering Ulasewicz to case the Watergate; initiating the cover-up; handing the FBI files to Gray, some of which had to do with Watergate, and urging the bureau to destroy them.

Interviews with Ehrlichman, Magruder, Caulfield, Ulasewicz, and Mitchell painted a much different picture. Caulfield told a particularly interesting story about Dean's duplicity. In January of 1973, Dean contacted Caulfield with a very important three-pronged message to be delivered to Jim McCord:

"A year is a long time;"
"your wife and family will be taken care of;"
"You will be rehabilitated with employment when this is all over."[61]

Dean's message to McCord was simple: plead guilty, save the president, and you will be granted executive clemency and taken care of when the Senate Committee is adjourned. On March 13, 1973, Dean blatantly lied to President Nixon about initiating the offer of clemency to McCord. Caulfield covered this in his remembrance of the Watergate scandal in *Shield #911-NYPD:*

"Dean deceived the president when he reported that McCord initiated the so-called commutation subject: "Uh, McCord did ask to meet with somebody and it was Jack Caulfield" . . . (It was Dean who) initiated that specific commutation subject with McCord via a telephone call to me . . .

So, that was the type of sophisticated evasion of the facts in which Dean was engaged at that moment, further, what is now retrospectively clear is that both Dean and McCord were, in fact, the historical catalysts that initiated a rapidly descending "funnel cloud" (a.k.a. Watergate) and sent it heading directly for the White House."[62]

If these Nixon White House men are taken at their word, John Dean had been the prime mover behind both the Watergate break-in and the cover-up. Colodny felt compelled to ask Dean about his own blatant conflicts of memory. Dean's response was incredible, to say the least.

"I'm gonna be very honest with you," Dean told Colodny in a 1989 telephone interview. "I didn't even reread my testimony when I wrote my book."[63] This astonishing assertion by Dean directly contradicts his foreword to his own book.

Colodny then presented Dean a specific example. In Dean's Senate testimony, the young counsel stated that the White House "didn't have much to do with DNC Chairman Larry O'Brien"; while in *Blind Ambition*, Dean wrote, "The O' Brien inquiry lay dormant, but it was not lost from his [Haldeman'] memory, or from mine. The president began planning for his reelection campaign and reached out in a new direction—one that later merged with a new O'Brien investigation."[64] If this lone example amongst many was correct in the book and erroneous in testimony, Dean had perjured himself. As we have shown, the White House *did* have a fixation with O'Brien.

The telephone conversation is full of similar contradictions. Those with any doubts should go online at Colodny's website Watergate.com to hear the entire tape of Dean confronted with the discrepancies. One can see why Dean has fought so hard to suppress this tape; it cuts directly to the core of his credibility.

Dean blamed his book publishing company Simon and Schuster and claimed he was pressured into the O'Brien angle and other details that conflicted with his testimony by editors looking for a more salacious, marketable angle.

"I'll tell, let me tell what the st—, I can go through that process for you," Dean explained to Colodny. "What happened is, the editors got real excited, interesting wanted to make it more intriguing. That's why all that shit got in there. My testimony is what I'm going to stand on."

When contacted, Simon and Schuster's powerhouse editor Alice Mahew, a partisan Democrat who has worked with writers such as Stephen Ambrose and David Brooks, said Dean's allegation was completely fabricated. "I never told John Dean what to put in his book, and, ah, that's a lie, L-I-E—that is spelled, L-I-E," Mahew emphatically asserted.[65]

Years later, in a civil suit against Watergate burglar G. Gordon Liddy, Dean, on the stand and under oath, attempted to cover his trail of contradiction by admitting that large portions of *Blind Ambition* were not actually written by him, but instead by a ghostwriter, Pulitzer Prize winner Taylor Branch.[66]

Dean repeated the charge against Branch again during his early 1990's lawsuit against author Len Colodny. In a deposition under oath, Dean said:

Q: You state as follows: "I turned away from Liddy for a moment to absorb Strachan's name. This was the worst blow since Magruder's call. I felt queasy. I really didn't want to know more because I had to assume that if Strachan knew, Haldeman knew, and if Haldeman knew, the President knew. It made sickening sense. Now I understand why Strachan had called earlier." Do you see that?
A: I do.
Q: Is that an accurate description of your reaction upon absorbing Strachan's name?
A: No. Pure Taylor Branch.
Q: He just made that up?
A: Absolutely made it up out of whole cloth.

Mahew, intimately involved in the book's production, vehemently denied that Branch invented facts. "And Taylor Branch who wrote the book . . . would never have been party to . . . such dishonest behavior," said Mahew.[67] Branch also denied concocting any facts in the book.[68]

Dean not only denied writing portions of the book, but also denied reading through the parts he *had not* written before it was published. Dean testified that he was bedridden with a fever at the time the proofs for the book arrived, and his wife did not want him to get ink on the sheets attempting to make corrections in his condition.[69]

The civil suit also forced Dean to once again confront his Watergate testimony, and some gems came out of the grilling:

"It could be that I misspoke myself";
"It's either a misstatement or an incorrect transcription";
"Highly possible—I just misspoke myself";
"We were trying to 'paint with the broadest brush we could'";
"I was maybe not artfully stating here";
"Maybe it was imposing hindsight on events";
"That is a less than accurate description";
"Obviously it was a self serving answer";
"I think everything I have said there is accurate to the degree I have said it."[70]

According to Liddy, he chided Dean into litigation so "the country will have the chance to find out whether, as the defendants believe, *Silent Coup* is an important work of history, or, as the Deans told the judge, a 'tissue of lies.' In the process, this lawsuit should provide the country with the opportunity to learn the real history of the Watergate break-in. Why were we ordered to go into the DNC in the first place?"[71]

That question has perplexed historians for decades. There was particular interest in information pertaining to the CIA-Mafia connection in the Bay of Pigs and beyond, purportedly stored in a file called the "Cuban Dossier." There was also the Hughes Loan information, which posed a potential danger to Nixon's reelection.

The Hughes Loan dirt, it was believed, may have been in the possession of Larry O'Brien, who had done lobbying work for the reclusive billionaire.

The burglars, though, did not seem to have a particular interest in the office of Larry O'Brien. Indeed, the lookout room (Room 723 of the Howard Johnson's Motor Inn) where McCord hire Alfred Baldwin was conducting his surveillance work, gave a line of sight directly into the office of Spencer Oliver, where the phone bug was planted during the first break-in. O'Brien's DNC office of was not visible from Baldwin's vantage point. When Carl Shoffler and two other police officers caught the men, one of the burglars, Eugenio Martinez, kept reaching for a key that was on his person. The key, which was not seen by the Watergate Committee or federal prosecutors, was determined by the FBI to "fit the desk of MAXIE WELLS," the secretary of Oliver.[72]

It later became clear to G. Gordon Liddy, that although he had been persuaded to organize and direct the Watergate break-ins, he had been used. Although there were men in the White House interested in what Larry O'Brien knew, what O'Brien knew was of no particular interest to John Dean.

"The orders I received were to break into the office of Larry O'Brien . . . and to put in two bugs," recalled Liddy. "One on his telephone to monitor those conversations and the other, a room bug to monitor any conversations in the room and photograph anything laying about. Those are the instructions I gave to Mr. Hunt. Those instructions were not carried out. Someone countermanded them. They didn't go anywhere near Mr. O'Brien's office. In fact, they went to the four-button telephone that was in the office of Ida 'Maxine' Wells. It was clear that I served as what we call in the intelligence a cut out, a circuit breaker between John Dean and John Dean's baby, which was Watergate."[73]

What in particular was John Dean looking for?

It is the contention of many (including Colodny, Gettlin, author Phil Stanford, Liddy, Special Counsel to the President Charles

Colson, and others) that, in the first break-in, Dean was looking to get his hands on sexual dirt that could be used against the Democrats. The phone bugged in the first break-in, it is postulated, had been used to arrange meetings between politicians and prostitutes.

Indeed, even left-wing Pulitzer Prize–winning *New York Times* journalist J. Anthony Lukas had to admit, "So spicy were some of the conversations on this phone that they have given rise to unconfirmed reports that the telephone was being used for some sort of call girl service catering to congressmen and other prominent Washingtonians."[74] Some of the phone calls on this particular line dealt with "political issues," most dealt with "personal matters."[75] Many of the calls were made with the confirmation, "We can talk; I'm on Spencer Oliver's phone."[76] While being deposed, Baldwin admitted that most of the phone calls he was tapped into concerned a dining arrangement with "sex to follow" and that "eight out of ten" people would have surmised that the calls regarded the scheduling of an escort for the evening.[77]

In 1991, Len Colodny and Robert Gettlin released *Silent Coup*. Colodny and Gettlin asserted that the second and final break-in was enacted by Dean to protect his future wife, Maureen "Mo" Binder, who was involved in a call girl ring that supplied courtesans to the DNC and White House politicians. According to Phil Stanford:

> [Dean] is, in fact, Watergate's arch villain. Not only did he order the fateful break-in at the DNC offices, but once the burglars were arrested, he directed the White House cover-up. And then, when it became obvious that the cover-up was going to crumble, Dean switched sides in exchange for a deal and became the star witness for the prosecution. Precisely what Dean expected to accomplish by sending burglars into the DNC—whether to gather information on some of the call girl ring's clients, who were being referred from the DNC, or to save himself from a possible political sex scandal remains unclear . . . if he did in fact order the break-in, it undoubtedly had something to do with the fact that Dean's live-in

girlfriend at the time, Maureen, was a close friend and former roommate of [Heidi Rikan].[78]

Dean has labeled many of those who have advanced this theory as "revisionists" and "Nixon loyalists." In fact, it was Lukas who first wrote about the connection between the Columbia Plaza prostitution ring and the Democratic National Committee. Investigative journalist Anthony Summers also raised questions about the call-girl ring, citing a *Washington Evening Star* story that exposed the operation, which was run by a Washington attorney and staffed by part-time secretaries and office workers. Summers noted that among the clients was "a lawyer at the White House." The *Evening Star* reported that White House aide Peter Flanigan had called the US attorney to determine if there was potential damage to the Nixon administration.[79] Neither Lukas nor Summers can be considered "revisionists" or "Nixon loyalists"; both are respected liberal journalists.

Before she was Mrs. Maureen Dean, Mo Biner was a roommate of Erika "Heidi" Rikan, aka Cathy Dieter, an ex-stripper described by Mo as a girl who was "single, well-to-do, and had plenty of time to spare."[80] Rikan's younger sister Kathie called Heidi a "high class prostitute" and Rikan had also once told her maid that she was "a call girl at the White House."[81] Mo Dean herself wrote, "I 'moved in' with Heidi . . . My mail came to Heidi's apartment, most of my clothes were deposited there."[82] Dentist Jack Garfield, who once dated Biner, said Mo described Riken as "my wild friend" and a "courtesan."[83] Indeed, Rikan and Biner were so close that a photograph of Rikan appears in Maureen Dean's book on Watergate, *"Mo": A Woman's View of Watergate*. It's a snapshot of her posing with Mo and John Dean at their wedding, hastily arranged as the Watergate scandal took down the White House.

Riken was also a girlfriend of Joe "Possum" Nesline, the crime boss of DC who ran illegal gambling halls and call girl operations. The Nesline/Rikan relationship was confirmed to Colodny and Gettlin by a Washington police detective who had investigated

Nesline,[84] and also by a 1965 FBI report on Nesline.[85] Rikan even joined a threesome with Nesline and her girlfriend Josephine Alvarez while touring in Rome.[86]

"No question, Heidi is the mob's girl," Stanford wrote in *White House Call Girl*.[87] "Before the year is out, the mob will even be using Heidi to lobby Dean over Hoffa's release from prison."[88]

Rikan's connection to Nesline also provided her a valuable network of customers and illegitimate businessmen to frequent a cathouse in the Columbia Plaza Apartments.

Phillip Mackin Bailley, a young Washington lawyer, helped Rikan expand her business into the Watergate offices and the DNC. Bailley met Rikan at an orgy she hosted in the Adams Morgan neighborhood of DC "Don't be afraid," Rikan told Bailley. "My name is Erika. Take off your clothes. We're going to have some fun."[89] As Bailley was leaving, he handed Rikan his business card, and later tipped Rikan off to a sting on the whorehouse.[90]

Bailley later helped Riken set up a base of clients in the DNC. Bailley had bragged to Rikan that he had a close relationship with R. Spencer Oliver, and Rikan sent him to establish contact. On the day Bailley went to see Oliver, according to Colodny and Gettlin, he was out of the office and Maxie Wells gave the lawyer a tour of their Watergate offices. A deal was eventually struck, and one client per day was referred to Rikan from DNC headquarters.

According to Stanford, Bailley showed up at the Columbia Plaza apartment in late September 1971 and was greeted at the door by none other than Lou Russell,[91] the hard-living ex-FBI man who worked for CIA man Jim McCord and later admitted to a conspicuous schedule on the night of the Watergate break-in. It was on this early autumn day that Bailley also stumbled into the room with recording equipment.

"What Bailley has stumbled into appears to be nothing less than a CIA sexual blackmail operation," wrote Stanford. "Certainly, it has all the earmarks. We may never know for sure, if only because at the height of the Watergate scandal despite a specific request from a Senate committee attempting to pursue the CIA's role in Watergate—the CIA simply destroyed all its records of its internal taping system."[92] It is evident that Russell had, in fact, purchased $3,000 worth of surveillance equipment around this time.[93]

Although Colodny and Gettlin did not have actual records of the call girl ring, author Phil Stamford obtained Heidi Rikan's "little black book" from her daughter, found amongst her mother's possessions. Rikan had listed former Commerce Secretary Maurice Stans, who was the finance chairman of the Committee to Reelect the President, Deputy Directory of Protocol and former Nixon traveling aide Nick Ruwe, Deputy Director of CRP Jeb Stuart Magruder, Senate Watergate Committee Counsel Sam Dash, and Connecticut Senator Lowell P. Weicker Jr. Along with their names were their unlisted phone numbers.

How did these men come to arrive on Rikan's list? How many were introduced to her by John Dean?

Nick Ruwe talked about the high-end call-girl operation over drinks at the Pisces Club in Georgetown, a private watering hole opened by Frank Sinatra intimate, restaurateur, and Spiro Agnew aide, Peter Malatesta. "We sent all the diplomats and visiting foreign dignitaries there," Ruwe said as he dragged deeply on an unfiltered Camel. "We knew the agency boys were filming them." The unmarried Ruwe was known for his hard drinking and easy access to female companionship when he was not serving as a traveling aide or advance man for Richard Nixon. "Nick Ruwe was himself the biggest cocksman this town ever saw," said a longtime Nixon aide. "Honey Trap," he said, referring to the Columbia Plaza brothel. When California Republican William Bagley asked him what the chief of protocol did, Ruwe said, "We have ten Arabs coming to town, and they've ordered twenty prostitutes—none of them Jewish."[94]

Ruwe eventually married First Lady Bette Ford's social secretary and bought a palatial home in the pricey Kalorama section of Washington, DC.

Another regular was Texas/New York socialite millionaire Emil "Bus" Mosbacher. Mosbacher's deputy was his running buddy, Nick Ruwe. Both socially prominent Ruwe and Mosbacher bonded in 1961 when Nixon dispatched Ruwe to Texas to work on the successful election of Professor John Tower, a Republican, to the seat vacated by Lyndon Johnson's elevation to the vice presidency. Tower was the first elected from Texas since the Reconstruction era.

Mosbacher frequented the high-end call girl ring that operated out of the Columbia Plaza Apartments. According to an FBI document I obtained, Mosbacher was also a regular at the New York whorehouse of Xaviera Hollander, known as the so-called Happy Hooker. When Hollander was busted, New York tabloids reported that among her customers were movie stars, athletes, titans of industry, and a White House lawyer. These reports rang alarm bells in the White House, and John Dean was assigned to find out who was in Hollander's little black book and whether "the Nixon administration had any vulnerability," as presidential aide Peter Flanigan asked the FBI. Dean sent New York gumshoe Tony Ulaseicz to try to secure the client list and any political dirt on Democrats or Republicans it might contain. Interestingly Mosbacher, a dashing two-time America's Cup winning yachtman, would resign the very prestigious position of US State Department Director of Protocol only two weeks after the Watergate break-in.

"Sometime after Nixon's resignation, in a report suppressed officially but leaked to the press, the House Intelligence Committee revealed that the CIA had provided foreign heads of state with 'female companion,' wrote Anthony Summers. "Several leaders including King Hussein of Jordan had so benefited."[95]

During a meeting on June 3, 1991, Bailley told Liddy that tasteful photographs of the Columbia Plaza call girls were kept in Well's desk. According to Bailley, various personnel were involved and were rewarded for wrangling appointments and new clients.

"Some members of the DNC were using the call girl ring as an asset to entertain visiting firemen," Liddy said to a student audience at James Madison University. "And to that end they had a manila envelope that you could open or close by wrapping a string around a wafer. And in that envelope were twelve photographs of an assortment of these girls and then one group photograph of them. And what you see is what you get." It was kept, he said, in that desk of Ida Maxine Wells. "Thus, the camera [and] all the rest of it. And what they were doing is as these people would be looking at the brochure, if you want to call it that, and making the telephone call to arrange the assignation that was being wiretapped, recorded and photographed."[96]

Bailley's exciting and lucrative referral service did not last long.

On June 9, 1972, the *Washington Star* ran a story headlined "Capitol Hill Call-Girl Ring." The article was salacious:

> The FBI here has uncovered a high-priced call girl ring allegedly headed by a Washington attorney and staffed by secretaries and office workers from Capitol Hill and involving at least one White House secretary, sources said today.
>
> A 22-count indictment returned today by a special federal grand jury names Phillip M. Bailley, 30, as head of the operation. Sources close to the investigation said that among the clients of the call girl operation were a number of local attorneys holding high positions in the Washington legal community and one lawyer at the White House.[97]

There is little doubt John Dean saw this article and panicked. Dean called John Rudy, the prosecutor in the Bailley case, within an hour of the paper hitting the newsstands. "He told me he was the President's counsel, and that he wanted me to come over to the White House," Rudy recalled. "He wanted me to bring 'all' the evidence but, mostly, what I brought were Bailley's address books. Dean said he wanted to check the names of the people involved, to see if any of them worked for the President."[98]

Benton Becker, an attorney and aide of President Ford, who, along with Alexander Haig negotiated the Nixon pardon, remembered the story Rudy, and Rudy's boss Don Smith, told him of their trip to Dean's office. When Rudy and Smith arrived with the two address books, Dean had his secretary Xerox copies of both. When she returned, Dean went through the copies meticulously, circling specific names with a pen. Becker said that one name in particular piqued Rudy's interest.

"He [Rudy] had close contact with that book not only on that occasion but subsequently throughout the Bailey prosecution that he recollected and remembered that a notation in Phil Bailley's book was the notation 'Mo Biner.'[99]

Eight days after Rudy was summoned to Dean's office, Magruder summoned Dean to his office. As detailed prior, an impatient Magruder ordered Liddy and the burglars back into the DNC. Liddy was correct in his revelation that "[t]he purpose of the second Watergate break-in was to find out what O'Brien had of derogatory nature about us, not for us to get something on him or the Democrats."[100] Ida "Maxie" Wells was a liaison between the pols working at the DNC and prostitutes working at the Columbia Plaza apartments. The three plainclothes officers caught Eugenio Martinez with the key to her desk in his possession, which he tried mightily to hide until he was restrained. One of the burglars had also placed a camera on her desk, which was there when the Schoffler and the other cops arrived.[101]

Schoffler said that Wells was shocked to learn there was a camera on her desk and exclaimed, "My God, they haven't gone in there."[102]

One question that needs to be raised . . . If the pamphlet was indeed in Well's desk, was Mo "Clout" Biner featured amongst the pictures?[103]

Shortly after the break-ins, in late June 1972, Dean and Biner went through a "break-up" and Biner moved back to her home state of California for the summer. This is, not coincidentally, at a time when subpoenas were being issued in the call-girl case.[104] In the fall of '72, Biner moved back to DC and Dean insisted on marrying her despite working amidst the busy reelection campaign. When Haldeman was sent a memo from Dean on October 5, his one-word response was: "Reconsider."[105] Dean could not wait and married Biner on October 13. The rush to elope was calculated; if Mo was Dean's wife, it would be tougher for her to testify against him if the Watergate investigation went to trial.[106]

* * *

Dean has been zealous in his attempt to control *his* history of Watergate. Aided by his move to the left, which provides him shelter from the conservative mainstream media, he strives to put the black hat on Richard Nixon and John Mitchell. He strains to mislead and deflect attention away from his own actions in planning, pushing, and then covering up the break-in, before cutting a lenient deal with prosecutors. Dean is certainly entitled to make his case, but he is not entitled to control evidence that proves he may be guilty of an enormous fraud.

Aiding in this fraud is liberal college professor and "Nixon hater" Professor Stanley Kutler. Kutler has altered transcripts of Nixon White House tapes to make Dean come off more favorably in more that one instance. Anyone who reads the March 13 transcript in his book *Abuse of Power: The New Nixon Tapes* and then listens to the actual tape online will hear that "Professor Kutler" is perpetuating a fraud. Today, Kutler admits to being a "close friend" of Dean's.

"I am responsible for whatever was transcribed," said Kutler, "Did I make any mistakes? Of course. Did I ever make a deliberate mistake, did I ever deliberately transform a negative into a positive? Please, I'm a trained historian. I don't work that way."[107] Ah, but he does work exactly that way.

In the March 13, 1973, conversation *not included* in *Abuse of Power*, Dean told Nixon that White House aide Gordon Strachan had knowledge of the Watergate break-ins before the burglaries. When compared to Dean's testimony, where Dean professed no prior knowledge in the White House, it is another clear case of perjury.[108]

It is important to recognize that Dean's admission that a White House staffer knew about the break-in and received transcipts of the wiretap prior to Dean's so-called "cancer on the preisiency" conversation with Nixon on March 21, 1973, contradicts his claim that he did not know of White House involvement until then. Frederick J. Graboske, who, as the supervising archivist in charge of processing the Nixon tapes at the National Archives, worked with Kutler, said that what the "historian" did was "deliberate." "In the history profession, you never change the original evidence; Dr. Kutler has changed the original evidence," said Graboske. "I'm sorry that it has come to this."[109]

The *New York Times* reported Kutler's treachery in a piece by Patricia Cohen. Historian Joan Hoff was also critical of Kutler's actions. "What this dispute over the Nixon tapes really demonstrates is the need for an authoritative set of transcriptions which the government should have undertaken years ago," Hoff wrote. "By authoritative I mean transcriptions that include every word, pause, grunt, stutter, expletives, and uhs, etc. to prevent more misuse and/or distortion of the Nixon tapes."[110]

This is not the only instance of "historian" Kutler altering evidence to depict Nixon negatively. Former Nixon Chief of Staff Reverend John Taylor, an exacting man and a friend of mine, called Kutler's work "sleight of hand" in a damning analysis:

> In the wake of Sunday's *New York Times* article, critics and defenders of historian Stanley Kutler have focused on his transcripts of Watergate conversations from March 1973. His 1997 book, Abuse of Power, also included an apparent attempt to edit a transcript to make it appear that by June 1972, the month of the Watergate break-in, President Nixon had become aware of the White House Plumbers' September 1971 break-in at the Los Angeles office of Daniel Ellsberg's psychiatrist, Lewis Fielding.
>
> Mr. Nixon always maintained that he didn't learn about the Ellsberg caper until the spring of 1973. If he'd known about it during the first days and weeks of the Watergate coverup, it would put his statements and actions in a much darker light.

Nixon critics have been understandably eager to find evidence that he knew in advance about either break-in as well as that he was mindful of the Plumbers' illegal activity as the Watergate coverup got underway in June 1972. Rick Perlstein joined the counterfeit smoking gun club with 2008's Nixonland when he misconstrued the meaning of a secondary source to make the President look guilty of foreknowledge of an illegal burglary.

Kutler's sleight of hand occurs in his transcript of a July 19, 1972 conversation between the President and political aide Chuck Colson. In an editor's setup, Kutler wrote:

Colson is full of praise for his friend [E. Howard Hunt, arrested at the Watergate], knowing that he had broken into Ellsberg's psychiatrist's office. "They weren't stealing anything,' Colson rationalized. 'They had broken and entered with an intent not to steal, [only] with an intent to obtain information."

Having gotten the reader thinking about the Ellsberg break-in, Kutler alters the rest of the conversation to remove any explicit reference to its real subject, the June 1972 break-in. His transcript begins with the President and Colson discussing Hunt's background and effort to compile a reliable psychological profile of Ellsberg. They ponder whether this entirely legal work might be drawn into the Watergate investigation. According to Kutler, the conversation proceeds as follows:

President Nixon: You've got to say that's irrelevant in a criminal case.
Colson: It clearly will be irrelevant in the civil case, because it had nothing to do with the invasion of privacy. I'm not sure in a criminal case whether it is a sign that will be relevant or not. Of course, before a grand jury there's no relevance . . .

They weren't stealing anything. Really, they trespassed. They had broken and entered with an intent not to steal, with an intent to obtain information.

The conversation has just jumped from Ellsberg to the Watergate break-in. Bet you didn't notice. Kutler has invited those who question his transcripts to go to the National Archives and listen themselves. Back in 1998, we did. Here's what the tape really says. Pay special attention to what Colson and the President say after Kutler's ellipses:

President Nixon: You've got to say that it's irrelevant in a criminal [unintelligible].

Colson: Clearly—the civil case has to do with the invasion of privacy, for information. I'm not sure in the criminal case whether these assignments [for the Plumbers] will be criminal [Kutler has "relevant"; tape is unclear] or not. Of course, before a grand jury, those would be irrelevant. I wouldn't worry about it.

President Nixon: It's none of his [the prosecutor's] damn business.

Colson: He knows it has nothing to do with Watergate. [Pause] Magruder obviously would—[12-second deletion for personal privacy]. They weren't stealing. Really, they trespassed.

This transcript of a small portion of a conversation reveals three things about Abuse of Power.

First, Kutler's transcripts are sloppy—"it is a sign" instead of "these assignments," for instance. In the settlement we negotiated of his successful lawsuit against the National Archives to free up this cache of tapes, he won a few months of exclusive access to them. He brought in court reporters and rushed his book out, but he didn't have to do it that way. If he had taken his time and published accurate, complete transcripts, he might not be under fire today.

Second, it does appear that Kutler wanted his readers to conclude that when President Nixon was talking to Colson, he already knew about the illegal Fielding break-in in September 1971. One indication is his deletion of the reference to Jeb Magruder, who was centrally involved with the June 1972 break-in but had nothing to do with the Fielding adventure. Also questionable is Kutler's decision to skip a response by the President in order to combine two of Colson's comments.

Kutler himself lent credence to the appearance that he manipulated the record. When I first wrote about Abuse of Power in the March 1998 issue of the "American Spectator," a reporter from the Orange County Register, a seasoned pro named Ann Pepper, called Kutler and asked him what he thought about my charge that he was misleading readers about the timing of RN's knowledge of the Fielding job. Kutler couldn't have been more definitive in his own defense:

Richard Nixon knew, and the tapes I discuss in my book prove it. If (Taylor) wants to say Richard Nixon never said (expletive) or called the Jews (derogatory names), he's a liar. There is always a possibility for error, but I never changed the transcripts intentionally and I didn't do it at all as far as I know. At this point, to say that Richard Nixon didn't do these things is ludicrous.

Still, when the paperback edition of Abuse of Power came out, Kutler made a telling change in his setup of the July 19 conversation. It now reads,

"They weren't stealing anything," Colson rationalized the Watergate break-in [emphasis added by me; phrase added by Kutler].

If I had a hand in that, I didn't get a footnote—just an e-knuckle sandwich from our brawler of a scholar Stanley, who said on an historians' blog in 2005:

[I]n a scarcely-noted review of my book in an obscure right-wing magazine, Taylor accused me of distorting and inventing tapes. For himself, he managed to find things in the tapes that just were not there, anxious as he was to fulfill Nixon's constant refrain that the tapes would exonerate him.

The third and perhaps biggest problem with Kutler's amended account of this moment in history is that it obscures the conversation's essentially exculpatory nature. Remember that the conventional wisdom is that President Nixon acquiesced in the John Dean-approved plan for limiting the Watergate investigation to keep the FBI and prosecutors from learning about the Plumbers' other illegal activity. And yet here are two lawyers talking desultorily about Hunt's situation. Is this what they'd say if they were afraid the public was about to learn about the White House horrors? There's no talk of covering up, no reference to hush money, and no suggestion of guilt—just Messrs. Nixon and Colson agreeing that Hunt's prior work had nothing to do with Watergate.

All along, President Nixon's Watergate defense was based on national security, specifically his rock-ribbed belief that the Plumbers' legitimate work investigating Pentagon Papers leaker Daniel Ellsberg during wartime shouldn't be drawn into the investigation of the purely political Watergate break-in. Though he doesn't call special attention to them, Kutler's book contains many conversations from the second half of 1972 in which the President makes the national security vs. Watergate distinction and urges aides to own up about involvement in illegal political activity.

Fred Graboske and his team of tape reviewers at the Nixon Project at the National Archives deserve great credit for identifying tape segments that would help as well as hurt RN. Kutler deserves credit for including some of the helpful conversations in his book. Of course in another of Kutler's spin-zone editor's notes about another exculpatory conversation in which RN says, on October 16, 1972, that he doesn't want Dwight Chapin and others to lie about Watergate, Kutler just accuses President Nixon of speaking for the tape recorder to make himself look good later.[111]

Perhaps John Dean's greatest misdirection is his consistent effort to distract from, ignore, and obfuscate the White House tape of March 13, 1973, in which he clearly tells Nixon that White House aide Gordon Strachan had been receiving transcripts of the wiretaps that were the fruit of the Watergate break-in. Instead, Dean directs our attention to the March 21 tape, which he alleges is the first time he told Nixon that the Watergate conspiracy touched the White House.

Dean duplicity and mastery of spin are reflective in Dean's book *The Nixon Defense* the publication of which is simultaneous with this book. The inconsistencies and fabrications in Dean's previous book as well as his testimony under oath before various government agencies already bring his actions into question. Incredibly, in his new book, Dean doesn't mention the White House tapes between March 13 and March 20 at all! These key tapes show Dean's manipulation of the evidentiary record. The book is badly mistitled. Rather than *The Nixon Defense*, it should be called *Dean's Defense*, and the lack of documentation or authentication of the former White House counsel's assertions undermines his book.

I have bootleg galleys and rely on the scholarship of noted lawyer, author, and lecturer Geoff Shepard, who eviscerates Dean and his selective use of the tapes to hide and distract from his true role in events. Read Appendix 5 for a detailed outline of Dean's slick duplicity. Don't put this book down until you read this monograph.

One thing is for certain: John Dean should not decide the narrative of history. In fact, his lifelong mission of keeping his version of events agreed upon is coming apart at the seams.

NOTES

1. Rosen, James, The Strong Man: John Mitchell and the Secrets of Watergate, Kindle Locations 5108-5110
2. Len Colodny Tapped Interview with John Dean January 5, 1989
3. Stanford, Phil. White House Call Girl, p. 89
4. Baker, Russ. Family of Secrets, p. 226
5. Emery, Fred. Watergate: The Corruption of American Politics And the Fall of Richard Nixon, p. 75
6. Hyde, Henry. Committee on the Judiciary House of Representative. Impeachment, p. 57
7. Caulfield, John. Shield # 9-11 NYPD, p. 86
8. Caulfield, John Shield #9-11 NYPD, p. 130
9. Ibid, p. 132
10. Dean/Colodny Interview Transcript and Tape— January 5, 1989. http://www.watergate.com/John-Dean/Blind-Ambition-Redux-Blind-Aversion.aspx
11. White House Call Girl p62
12. Strober, Deborah H., Strober, Gerald S. The Nixon Presidency: an Oral History of the Era, p. 248
13. Liddy, Gordon G. Will, p. 252
14. Ibid
15. Ibid
16. Ibid
17. Ibid
18. Caulfield, John Shield #9-11 NYPD, p. 138

19. http://www.nixonlibrary.gov/forresearchers/find/tapes/water-gate/wspf/886-008.pdf
20. Hougan, Jim. Secret Agenda, pp. 98-100
21. Liddy, Gordon G.. Will, pp. 276-277
22. Rosen, James. The Strong Man, p. 265
23. Hougan, Jim. Secret Agenda, p. 101
24. Rosen, James. The Strong Man, p. 267
25. White House Transcript. March 21, 1973. http://www.nixonlibrary.gov/forresearchers/find/tapes/watergate/trial/exhibit_12.pdf
26. Liddy, Gordon G. Will, p. 281
27. Rosen, James. The Strong Man, p. 267
28. Rosen, James. The Strong Man, p. 267
29. Hougan, Jim. Secret Agenda, p. 103
30. Hougan, Jim. Secret Agenda, p. 104
31. Hougan, Jim. Secret Agenda, p. 105
32. Hougan, Jim. Secret Agenda, p. 105
33. Ibid
34. Rosen, James. The Strong Man, p. 274
35. Strober, Deborah H., Strober, Gerald S. The Nixon Presidency: an Oral History of the Era, p. 323
36. Kerr, Jennifer. "Ex-aide contends President Nixon gave order for Watergate Break-in." The Day. July 24, 2003
37. Schodolski, Vincent J. "Watergate Claim by Magruder Contested." Chicago Tribune. July 31, 2003
38. Ibid
39. White House Transcript. March 21, 1973. http://www.nixonlibrary.gov/forresearchers/find/tapes/watergate/trial/exhibit_12.pdf
40. Strober, Deborah H., Strober, Gerald S. The Nixon Presidency: an Oral History of the Era, pp. 280-281
41. Strober, Deborah Hart. Strober, Gerald S. Nixon: An Oral History of his Presidency, p. 292
42. Baker, Russ. Family of Secrets, p. 227
43. Baker, Russ. Family of Secrets, p. 227
44. Dean/Colodny Interview Transcript, Jan, 5 1989
45. Ibid
46. Ulasewicz/Colodny interview. 5/21/88
47. Neisser, Ulric. "John Dean's Memory: A Case Study," Cognition, vol. 9
48. Cohen, Patricia. "John Dean's Role at Issue in Nixon Tapes Feud," New York Times. January 31, 2009

49. Kalb, Barry. "John Dean Steps into the Spotlight." The Evening Star and Daily News. June 25, 1975

50. Thompson, Fred. At That Point in Time, p. 60

51. Ibid

52. John Dean/Len Colodny interview, January 5, 1989

53 Kalb, Barry. "John Dean Steps into the Spotlight." The Evening Star and Daily News. June 25, 1975

54. Thompson, Fred. At That Point in Time, p 65

55. Blumenthal, Sydney. Editorial Review for Blind Ambition. Amazon. com http://www.amazon.com/Blind-Ambition-The-End-Story/dp/0976861755

56. Dean, John. Blind Ambition, p. 5

57. Ibid

58. "Book discussion on Silent Coup: The Removal of a President." Booknotes C-SPAN. January 25, 1991

59. Ibid

60. "Book discussion on Silent Coup: The Removal of a President." Booknotes C-SPAN. January 25, 1991

61. Caulfield, John. Shield #9-11 NYPD, p. 89

62 Ibid, p. 128

63. John Dean/Len Colodny interview, January 5, 1989

64. Dean, John. Blind Ambition, p. 155

65. Alice Mahew/Len Colodny interview. http://www.watergate.com/John-Dean/Alice-Mayhew.aspx

66. Liddy, G. Gordon. When I Was a Kid, This Was a Free Country, p. 171

67. Alice Mahew/Len Colodny interview. http://www.watergate.com/John-Dean/Alice-Mayhew.aspx

68. Liddy, G. Gordon, Will, p. 502

69. Liddy, G. Gordon. Will, p. 501

70. Investigative Reports. "The Key to Watergate." A&E, September 18, 1992

71. Ibid

72. Lukas, J. Anthony. Nightmare: The Underside of the Nixon Presidency, p. 201

73. Ibid

74. Ibid

75. Hougan, Jim. "Hougan, Liddy, the Post and Watergate." www.jim-hougan.com

76. Stamford, Phil, White House Call Girl, p. 17

77. Summers, Anthony. Arrogance of Power, p. 422
78. Dean, Mo. "MO": A Woman's View of Watergate, p. 40
79. Stanford, Phil. White House Call Girl, p. 28
80. Colodny, Len. Silent Co up, p 130
81. Ibid, p. 52
82. Colodny, Len. Gettlin, Robert. Silent Coup, p 130
83. FBI investigative report of Joseph Francis Nesline, February 2, 1965
84. Stamford, Phil. White House Call Girl, p. 41
85. Ibid, p. 60
86. Ibid
87. Stamford, Phil. White House Call Girl, p. 66
88. Ibid
89. Ibid, p. 77
90. Ibid, p. 83
91. Hougan, Jim. Secret Agenda, p. 117
92. Summers, Anthony, Arrogance of Power, pp. 421-422
93. Summers, Anthony. Arrogance of Power, p. 421
94. Liddy speech at James Madison University, April 2, 1996
95. Hougan, Jim. Secret Agenda, p. 172
96. Ibid
97. Investigative Reports. "The Key to Watergate." A&E, September 18, 1992
98. Liddy G. Gordon, Will, pp. 236-237
99. United State Court of Appeals for the Fourth Circuit. Wells v. Liddy.
100. Ibid
101. Burris, Charles. "It's the 40th Anniversary of the Watergate Conspiracy," LewRockwell.com. September 12, 2013
102. Colodny, Len. Gettlin, Robert. Silent Coup, p. 153
103. Colodny, Len. Gettlin, Robert. Silent Coup. P. 232
104. Ibid
105. Cohen, Patricia. "John Dean's Role at Issue in Nixon Tapes Feud" New York Times. January 31, 2009
106. Ibid
107. Ibid
108. Hoff, Joan. "HNN hot topics: The Watergate Transcript Controversy http://hnn.us/article/61197
109. Taylor, John. "Kutler, Nixon, And The Ellsberg Break-In" February 5, 2009 http://episconixonian.blogspot.com/2009/02/kutlering-nixon-tapes.html

CHAPTER SIXTEEN

NIXON AND THE BUSHES

"Clean, Clean, Clean."
—George Bush, when asked about
illegal funds provided to his 1970 Senate race.

Any examination of Nixon and Watergate is incomplete without a review of the role of future President George H. W. Bush and his long and beneficial relationship with Nixon. Bush's direct connection to Watergate is key. The money used to finance the White House Special Investigations Unit (or Plumbers) in 1971–72 was provided by George Bush's business partner and lifelong intimate friend, Bill Liedtke, the president of Pennzoil. Bill Liedtke was a regional finance chairman for the Nixon campaigns of 1968 and 1972. Liedtke reportedly exceeded his quota by the largest margin among all his fellow regional chairmen. Liedtke says that he accepted this post as a personal favor to George Bush.

In 1972, Bill Liedtke raised $700,000 in anonymous contributions, including a single contribution of $100,000 that was laundered through a bank account in Mexico. Part of this money came from Bush's crony Robert Mosbacher, later Bush's secretary of commerce. Two days before a new law was scheduled to begin making anonymous donations illegal, the $700,000 in cash, checks, and securities were loaded into a briefcase at Pennzoil headquarters and picked up by a company vice president, who boarded a Washington-bound Pennzoil jet and delivered the funds to the Committee to Re-elect the President at ten o'clock that night.

These Mexican checks were given to Maurice Stans of CREEP, who transferred them to Watergate burglar Gordon Liddy. Liddy passed them on to Bernard Barker, one of the Miami Cubans arrested on the night of the final Watergate break-in. Barker was actually carrying some of the cash left over from these checks when he was apprehended. When Barker was arrested, his bank records were subpoenaed by the Dade County, Florida district attorney Richard E. Gerstein, and were obtained by Gerstein's chief investigator Martin Dardis.

Dardis told Carl Bernstein of the Washington Post that the $100,000 in four cashier's checks had been issued in Mexico City by Manuel Ogarrio Daguerre, a prominent lawyer who handled Stans's money-laundering operation there. Liedtke eventually appeared before three grand juries investigating the different aspects of the Watergate affair, but neither he nor Pennzoil were ever brought to trial for the CREEP contributions—money for the break-in administered from one of Bush's intimates and at the request of Bush, a member of the Nixon cabinet from February, 1971 onward.

On June 23, 1972, in the famous "smoking gun" tape, Nixon and Haldman can be heard discussing the money Bush's financial circle routed through Mexican banks and how to hide it from the FBI.

President Nixon: Well, maybe he's a . . . He didn't—I mean, this isn't from the Committee, though; this is from [Maurice] Stans$^\nabla$.Committee to Re-elect the President, or CREEP. Maurice Stans was the finance chairman of CREEP.

Haldeman: Yeah. It is. It was . . . It's directly traceable and there's some more through; some Texas people in—went to the Mexican bank which they can also trace through the Mexican bank. They'll get their names today. And—

President Nixon: Well, I mean, there's no way that—I'm just thinking if they don't cooperate, what do they say? That they were approached by the Cubans? That's what Dahlberg has to say, and the Texans too.

Haldeman: Well, if they will. But then we're relying on more and more people all the time. That's the problem. And it does stop if we could, if we take this other step [directing the CIA to tell the FBI to limit the Watergate investigation].

President Nixon: All right. Fine.

This is, of course, the taped conversation that sealed Nixon's fate.

* * *

Richard Nixon made George Bush's career. George Bush's father was the upright and tough Prescott Bush, a banker, internationalist, and golfing buddy of Dwight Eisenhower. "A fine golfer," Ike said. Prescott was a key advocate of Nixon for 1952 because he had first brought Nixon's attention his friend Tom Dewey, the "Dean" of the Eastern Establishment. Prescott had raised money on Wall Street for Nixon's 1946 campaign. Nixon's opponent Jerry Voorhis was a critic of big business and big banks. Voorhis wanted to close the Federal Reserve. "Prescott Bush is one of the men who made Dick Nixon," Chotiner told me. Dewey looked at Nixon because of Bush's suggestion and after Nixon got on the short list of "acceptable" candidates for Ike's running mate. Prescott urged Ike to take Nixon on the ticket on a golf course in Greenwich, Connecticut. Nixon owed Bush. Nixon campaigned for Bush in his 1964 and 1966 races. The Bushes snubbed their noses at their social friends the Rockefellers when they supported Nixon early in 1960 and again in 1968.

Prescott Bush's rich friends tried get young George H. W. Bush on the 1968 ticket. Nixon went all-out for Bush in 1970 in the Seante race only to be out manueverd by LBJ and John Connally, who inserted an ex-congressman into the race. After that it was the appointive track where Bush nutured his ambitions. Nixon made George H. W. Bush UN Ambassador with cabinet rank out of respect for Prescott Bush. "Keep George Bush, he'll do anything for us," Nixon tells Haldeman while shuffling his cabinet in the White House tapes.

When I told Nixon I had seen an elderly Senator Prescott Bush address the 1966 Republican State Convention, Nixon said, "He was a good man. Tough as nails. Made millions as an investment banker. A real blue nose. Rocky's divorce drove him crazy. Played golf with Ike a lot and was one of those who backed Tom Dewey's play to put me on the '52 ticket."

At the height of Nixon's Watergate problems, Nixon begrudgingly took one of his last calls of the day. Nixon had just made a TV address on Watergate. Republican National Committee Chairman George H. W. Bush, a constant nuisance for Nixon, had been trying to get through to the president all night. When Nixon finally took Bush's call, Bush noted that he had been trying to get through earlier, Nixon responded, with annoyance in his voice that he had "been on the phone, George, all night."[1]

Bush was a suck-up and brown-noser with Nixon. Bush made sure to let Nixon know that Barbara had "just attended a Republican leadership conference" and wanted to talk to Nixon before he "went to sleep." In the conversation, Bush reviewed the press reaction to the address and surmised that it was not positive. Bush told Nixon to call him for any support that the Republican National Committee could provide, calling the commentators "arrogant bastards." "The thing that burns me up is the feeling that you had and it came through and there's so little credit," Bush told Nixon, who replied he thought "the people may understand it" and "to hell with the commentators."[2]

Nixon made a point to assure Bush that "the main thing is, you had nothing to do with this goddamn thing. We're gonna go on." Bush assured Nixon "this is going to come out good." Nixon closed the conversation by thanking Bush, belittling in jest calling him "boy."[3]

What made Nixon at the end of a difficult and long day make a point to assure Bush that he had nothing to do with Watergate? Further, why did Nixon take Bush's call, who at that time was serving as Chair of the Republican National Committee? The answers come in the close relationship Nixon had with H. W. Bush, his father Senator Prescott, and the strong ties the Bushes carried with Texas oilmen.

Bush only held the position of RNC Chair as a consolatory prize for once again being passed over for vice president in 1972. Nixon showed slight deference to the Bush clan, and his irreverence would later came back to haunt Nixon during his downfall.

George Bush's first of three unsuccessful attempts to become vice president would come in 1968. Few reporters have delved deeply into the symbiotic relationship with the blue-blooded Bush family, pillars of the Eastern Establishment, and Richard Nixon, the grocer's son from Yorba Linda. Yet it is indisputable that if Nixon had never become president, neither would George H. W. Bush, nor his son George W. Bush. Without the Nixon presidency, there would not have been a Bush dynasty.

Ground-breaking and renowned journalist Russ Baker, whose masterful *Family of Secrets* has done more to illuminate the long and complicated relationship between the Bush family and Richard Nixon, delved deeply into Nixon's odd relationship and resentment of the Eastern Establishment. "Generally, Richard Nixon was known to be a wary and suspicious man," wrote Baker. "It is commonly assumed that he was paranoid, but Nixon had good reasons to feel apprehensive. One was probably the worry that someone would unearth the extent to which this self-styled outsider from Whittier, California, had sold his soul to the same Eastern Establishment that he publicly (and even privately) reviled. At the same time, he knew that those elites felt the same about him. They tolerated him as long as he was useful . . ."[4]

George H. W. Bush's long ambition to become president of the United States is traced to his early life. His move from Connecticut to Texas, his quick rise to leadership in the Texan Republican Party, and his two unsuccessful races for the US Senate were all milestones in his effort to get to the White House.

Like Richard Nixon, Bush was a man without ideology. Like Nixon, Bush knew how to sound conservative. Like Nixon, Bush enjoyed substantial funding from Eastern and Wall Street sources. However unlike Nixon, Bush could move easily in Eastern elite circles. Both men would endanger deep suspicion on the far right.

That Bush would ever become president is unlikely based on his series of failed electoral attempts. Indeed, Bob Woodward and Walter Pincus would note, "His loss to Lloyd Bentsen in the 1970 Senate race had taken him out of Texas elective politics for the immediate future. A two term congressman, he was 46, married with five children, and wanted to remain in public life. But if he was not to win elections, then his next steps up the political ladder would depend on his ability to ingratiate himself with more successful politician—Nixon, Gerald R. Ford and Ronald Reagan."[5]

It would be a mistake to assume Bush's affable, friendly, unfailingly polite and sometimes goofy style as benign. His vapidity and obfuscation was a mirage. Underneath it lie consuming political ambition, steely determination, boundless energy, and remarkable physical discipline for a relentless travel to pursue his political goals. Barbara Bush brought a vindictive streak; she remembered everyone who was *not* for her husband. Despite his "nice guy" image, George Bush was high-handed, secretive, and fueled by an incredible sense of entitlement. One of the purposes of this chapter is to help the reader understand Bush's complex relationship with Nixon and to shed light on Bush's early and longtime service to the CIA.

Incredibly, both Nixon and Bush would find themselves in Dallas on November, 22, 1963. Nixon would acknowledge his visit; indeed, he held a well-covered press conference on November 21. We have explored the circumstances that brought Nixon to Dallas on that fateful day. Bush, on the other hand, would dissemble on the subject of his whereabouts and, for some reason, would go to great lengths to mislead the FBI about his movements on November 22. We shall reexamine this.

Like Nixon, Bush was also disciplined and extremely well organized. He was a model candidate, traveling relentlessly, shaking hands, writing notes, and building his friends list. He was always collecting: people, addresses, supporters, and money. Like Nixon, Bush's long toiling in the party vineyards would ultimately pay dividends. Only Richard Nixon was a more indefatigable campaigner. Bush would exhibit much of the same resilience that Nixon displayed in his drive for the presidency. Nixon, however, had won two national elections as vice president as well as his party's nomination for the presidency prior to his ultimate election in 1968.

Bush's path was more difficult. He was defeated in two US Senate races, passed up for the vice presidency four times by two presidents and ultimately trounced in his own presidential bid of 1980 by Ronald Reagan. Ultimately, through hard work, persistence and luck Bush, like Nixon, would succeed in his ultimate goal of winning the presidency.

Prescott Bush was among the Eastern clique that would foist Richard Nixon on Dwight Eisenhower. This would come to haunt Nixon. As Russ Baker observed, "[T]he further Nixon rose, the more he resented the arrogance of his Eastern elite handlers. Though he would continue to serve them diligently throughout his career, his anger festered—perhaps in part over frustration with the extent to which he was beholden."[6]

Bush's drive for the vice presidency would begin when he was a mere congressman from a suburban Houston district. Bush and his father were major backers of Richard Nixon in his 1968 comeback bid. Together with Texas business associates Hugh Liedke and Robert Mosbacher, the Bush's raised big money for Nixon's bid. Once Nixon was nominated, Bush would mount the first of his drives to be selected for vice president.

Although only in Congress four short years, George and Prescott Bush orchestrated an effort to get major party figures to urge Nixon to place George as his running mate. Prescott Bush would get Tom Dewey, instrumental in Nixon's own selection as vice president, to urge Nixon to take the young Texan on the ticket. Texas Senator John Tower, elected in a special election to fill Johnson's senate seat in 1961, pushed Bush with Nixon. CEOs of Chase Manhattan, J. P. Stevens, and Pennzoil also pressured Nixon. Of course, Brown Brother Harriman weighed in.

The Bush family–Nixon relationship would be rife with brown-nosing, cultivation, political support, financial support, appointments, treachery, and betrayal. The extraordinarily intense political and corporate pressure put on Nixon to select a mere congressman George H. W. Bush as his running mate was rejected by Nixon. Senator Prescott Bush would write Governor Tom Dewey (who had strongly urged Nixon to select young Bush) that Nixon had made a "serious error."[7]

William Middendorf, II, a longtime GOP fundraiser for Barry Goldwater, Nixon, Gerald Ford, and Ronald Reagan who later served as Secretary of the Navy, describes the major effort in the 1968 GOP convention to bring Bush on the ticket in his memoir *Potomac Fever: A Memoir of Politics and Public Service*. On the day after Nixon was nominated, Middendorf and his associate, New York financier Jerry Milbank, went to Nixon's hotel room to talk about the vice presidential choices. "It was pretty early, I think it was about 7:30, I think it was his bedroom, actually, reading the paper. I said we've got delegates pretty much lined up for George, and it looks like he'd be a very popular choice among the delegates," Middendorf recalled. "That's when he told me that, 'Oh, gee, fellas, I'm going with my man Spiro T. Agnew,'" the little-known governor of Maryland who would later resign in a scandal.[8]

Prescott Bush was furious with Nixon's passing over Bush for the little-known Agnew; he would share his anger in a letter to Tom Dewey, the Eastern kingmaker who had "made" Eisenhower.

After being rejected by Nixon for the 1968 ticket, George Bush moved his trajectory to the White House into 1976. Bush would serve four years as vice president in Nixon's second term and then become the presumptive Republican nominee. In order to put this plan in motion, Bush would first need to win the Texas US Senate seat in 1970, which would force Nixon to dump Agnew and replace him with the son of Senator Prescott Bush. Bush's brother Jon would confirm the 1970 race was to position Bush as a vice presidential contender and presidential candidate. *Washington Post* reporter, Bob Woodward would write that "Bush led the short list for the '72 nomination," while his colleague David Broder reported that Bush's selection was assured. A funny thing happen on the way to the 1972 Republican nominating convention, Bush would be derailed in his 1970 race would have to delay his presidential ambitions for a full ten years—despite mounting two more intense secret campaigns to be picked for vice presidential nominations. [9]

Washington Post syndicated columnist Robert Novak was convinced that Nixon had promised Bush the vice presidency in 1972 as an inducement for Bush to leave a safe House seat and make his second unsuccessful bid for the US Senate in 1970. Despite Bush's longtime cultivation of Lyndon Johnson, LBJ and his Bourbon Democrat ally John Connally had killed Bush's Senate aspirations by defeating vulnerable liberal Ralph Yarborough in the Democratic primary and replacing him with conservative Democrat Lloyd Bentsen. Bentsen held on to conservative Democrats but ran up Democrat-like majorities in the black and Hispanic communities to trounce Bush. [10]

Encouraged to run for the US Senate in 1970, Nixon promised Bush he would be on the short list for vice president in 1972. Indeed, Lee Atwater would tell me Harry Dent told him Nixon told Prescott Bush that George would replace Agnew in '72. Lyndon Johnson and Texas Governor John Connally would block that ascendancy, ironically when Bush was defeated in the Texas Senate race. Yet Nixon would loyally provide appointed jobs as UN ambassador and Republican National chairman that would, in the end, allow Bush to revive his presidential ambitions.

George Bush inherited his desire to be president from his father. Investment banker Prescott Bush would often times tell his wife that he regretted never establishing a political career early in life to eventually mount a presidential bid. The family patriarch, Prescott was a tall, ramrod straight, and imposing man. As an investment banker with Brown Brothers-Harriman, a bipartisan powerhouse, Prescott worked with his partners to manipulate the levers of power in order reap financial gain from national and international policy. In this vain, Russ Baker has speculated that Prescott Bush was the Eastern banker who visited Southern California in 1946 to bring big eastern money to rookie congressional candidate Richard Nixon.[11] Nixon's opponent incumbent Jerry Voorhis had offended the eastern financial elite with a proposal to eliminate the Federal Reserve.[12]

Prescott Bush indeed decided to enter politics late in life. He narrowly lost the US Senate seat in 1950 when it was revealed in the heavily Catholic state of Connecticut that he and his wife has contributed to Planned Parenthood. Bush, a friend and golfing partner of Dwight Eisenhower, was among those who urged Ike to take Nixon on the 1952 ticket. That same year, Prescott would win a special election to fill the seat of US Senator Brien McMahon, who died unexpectedly.

* * *

The "TownHouse Operation" was an early campaign finance scheme devised by John M. King that eventually evolved into Watergate. The general outline of the operation, as suggested by King, was a system whereby large donors were able to directly contribute to Senate and House candidates, rather than using the traditional method of donating money to the National Party Committee and allowing the party elites to determine where to distribute it. President Nixon directly approved of the scheme in late 1969 after Chief of Staff H. R. Haldeman presented it to him in the Oval Office.[13]

No one would benefit from this secret fund more than US Senate candidate George Bush. The Nixon White House's sensitivity regarding the Townhouse Operation would surface during the so-called ITT scandal in which it was alleged that the communications giant contributed $400,000 to the Republican National Convention effort in San Diego in return for a favorable antitrust ruling from John Mitchell's Justice Department. Jack Gleason, who had run the day-to-day operations of the TownHouse Operation, had gone to work as a consultant for ITT in the run-up to the 1972 convention. White House Chief of Staff Bob Haldeman and Domestic Advisor John Erlichman would instruct White House counsel John Dean to contact Gleason's lawyer when Gleason was subpoenaed. The Teutonic Christian Scientist duo wanted Gleason to assert his Fifth Amendment rights if questioned by the committee regarding the White House fundraising operation. Dean warily convinced the two that a Fifth Amendment declination to answer questions would bring greater scrutiny and cause a minor furor expanding the ITT investigation into troublesome areas for the White House.

Following the receipt of approval from Nixon, Haldeman and Commerce Secretary Maurice Stans set up the "Townhouse Operation—so-called because it was run out of a townhouse in northwest DC—to ensure that the Republican Party fielded candidates whose primary loyalty was to Nixon, not the Eastern Establishment of the party.[14] Nixon had never trusted the Eastern Establishment of the GOP and saw the opportunity to establish an independent location for party supporters to donate as, "one of our most important projects for 1970."[15] While Bush was a scion of an old Establishment Republican family through his father, former Connecticut Senator Prescott Bush, Nixon was confident that Bush, "[would] do anything for the cause."[16] Indeed, Bush's 1970 Texas Senate campaign was a primary beneficiary of the Townhouse

Operation, with Bush receiving $106,000, of which the Bush campaign failed to report $55,000.[17]

Pulitzer prize–winning author J. Anthony Lukas would report: "In March 1970 Haldeman; Harry Dent, a White House political adviser; and Dent's assistant, Jack A. Gleason, decided that a special fund was needed for that fall's Senate and House races. Haldeman asked Kalmbach to do the bulk of the fund-raising, urging him to 'get cash whenever you can get it.' And 'old reliable' Herb did raise some $2.8 million of the $3.9 eventually garnered for the fund. According to a confidential memo from Kalmbach to Haldeman, two of the President's friends—W. Clement Stone, a Chicago insurance executive, and Donald Kendall, board chairman of PepsiCo, Inc.—each pledged $250,000. H. Ross Perot, a Texas millionaire, also came in with $250,000. Claude C. Wild, Jr., Gulf Oil's Washington vice president, was listed for $25,000. Edward J. Gerrity, Jr., International Telephone and Telegraph's vice president for public relations, was listed for $50,000 (although Gerrity says he never paid it).

"The money was collected and the funds disbursed by Jack Gleason out of a back-room office in the basement of a townhouse at 1310 19th Street, N.W., and thus the operation known as the Townhouse Project. The contributions were siphoned into congressional campaigns in at least nineteen states, including crucial contest in Maryland, Tennessee, Florida, Indiana, and North Dakota. The whole project was illegal because Dent, Gleason et al. were functioning as a political committee and such committees could not support candidates in two or more states without having a treasurer who filed public reports to Congress."

Kalmbach, Gleason, and Dent were all convicted for their activities in the project. Kalmbach served six months of a six-to-ten-month sentence and was fined $10,000. Dent was sentenced to one month of unsupervised probation. Gleason received a suspended sentence.[18]

There is also evidence that an integral part of the rationale for the Townhouse Operation was not simply an opportunity to win seats for loyal Nixonites, but also to provide leverage over those very same elected officials. In short, the Townhouse funds were used up front as a "carrot," but the Nixon White House was not above using it as a "stick" after the fact.[19] Referred to as the "six project," Haldeman ordered that $6,000 in cash be delivered to approximately fifteen Republican candidates. Among the fifteen candidates listed was Mr. Bush, with Nixon White House records indicating that either Bush or his campaign manager accepted the funds from a Townhouse operative named Jack Gleason.[20] Bush would claim, I believe correctly, that state campaign regulation did not require the filing in Texas of the Townhouse contributions in 1970 and that his campaign treasurer had adhered to all relevant campaign laws at the time. Nonetheless, the Townhouse "scandal" would be a meme for the duration of Bush's political career. It would be surfaced his intra-party rivals in 1976 when he ran a boiler room operation to urge Gerald Ford to select him as vice president as well as being raised again when Ford again passed over Bush for VP when he dumped Nelson Rockefeller. It would surface yet again after Bush won the Iowa caucuses when old Nixon hand John Sears, then managing the campaign of Ronald Reagan, fed the information to vitriolic *Manchester Union Leader* publisher William Loeb. While it is true that Bush received more from the secret fund than any other candidate, it is important to note that most of the Townhouse cash was generated by Bush money men Bill Liedtke and Robert Mosbacher, who later served as Bush's secretary of commerce. As we shall see, it also the Bush money apparatus that financed the actual Watergate break-in; the bills found on the Watergate burglars by police came from a Mexican bank where the Bush money had been laundered.

While Poppy was never charged with campaign finance violations in connection with the Townhouse Operation, President Nixon's personal attorney Herbert Kalbach, Nixon political strategist Harry S. Dent Jr., and former White House aide Jack Gleason—the operation's chief fundraiser—and the later two administrators of the fund, all pled guilty to violations of federal election law in 1974.

When former Congressman Donald J. Irwin, who sought the Democratic nomination to challenge Weicker in 1976, pointed out that Weicker had never reported the great bulk of the Townhouse moneys, the Connecticut press ignored him. After all, Nixon had no greater critic than Lowell Weicker.

Weicker would later claim that as Republic National Chairman Bush would call him and say, "I have the Townhouse records right here, what do you think I should do with them? Burn them?" Bush for his part admits speaking to Weicker but denies any suggestion that he would burn the Townhouse records as ridiculous as the originals of the files had already been sent to the Senate Watergate Committee and the Watergate Special Prosecutor. Bush insisted that he sent copies of the records that pertained specifically to Weicker's received contributions to the Senator which Weicker would subsequently deny ever receiving. A more likely interpretation to the bombastic Connecticut senator is that Bush was letting Weicker know that the White House was well aware of Weicker's hypocrisy.

*　*　*

From the very beginning Weicker made no secret of his intention of "getting" Richard Nixon. Author Victor Lasky would offer a hard-boiled analysis of Weicker's actions: "Probably the biggest leaker was Weicker. For a Republican, the senator was an oddity. He had actually fought for his job on the committee while most Republicans were running the other way. From the very beginning Weicker operated on his own with a team of five investigators who became known as the Third Front.

Ironically Weicker had been elected to the Senate with Nixon's support. At the behest of the president's chief political adviser, Murray Chotiner, money from a secret White House fund collected for the 1970 congressional campaign was siphoned off to aid a duly appreciate Weicker. As a result Weicker held Chotiner in high esteem. When Chotiner died in 1974, one of those prominent in attendance at the Washington Hebrew Congregation services was Weicker. (Also there was President Nixon, bidding farewell to an old comrade; such are the vagaries of politics.)

Weicker made his way into the Senate through a fluke. He ran against two opponents. The endorsed Democrat was a freelance clergyman and ADA pooh-bah named Joseph Duffey; but a great may unreconstructed Democrats preferred the incumbent Tom Dodd, who had been censured by his peers on charges most people by now have forgotten. "It was a delightful campaign," wrote C. H. Simonds in *The Alternative*. "While Weicker went about portraying him as a one-man Weatherman bomb-and-orgy squad, poor Duffey devoted his scanty energies to refereeing staff disputes over whether or not to bill himself as *The Reverend*; Dodd, meanwhile, bumbled along with chin up and smile bright and every hair in place . . . and so Weicker went to Washington, giving the last laugh to Dodd, who must be laughing still as he beholds the pompous clowns who censured him, yawning and squirming through his successor's weepy tirades."

In one programmed outburst during the Watergate hearings, Weicker—making sure the cameras were focused on him—had cried out, "Republicans do not cover up, Republicans do not go ahead and commit illegal acts, and God knows Republicans don't view their fellow Americans as enemies to be harassed; but rather I can assure you that Republicans . . . look upon every American as a human being to be loved and won." At the same time he denounced the White House for allegedly seeking to smear him, claiming that Charles Colson had been leaking nasty things about him to the press. Naturally Weicker was opposed to leaking. Except of course when he did the leaking. For, as it turned out, Weicker and his staff were feeding out confidential materials to press people on an almost daily basis. Weicker's arrogant disregard of the rules shocked most of his colleagues. As columnist Nick Thimmesch observed, the senator "acted every bit as high-handed as anyone in Nixon's White

House ever did and could have well been a Watergate himself if he had the opportunity.""

As I had detailed previously despite the fact that Weicker insists in his memoir *Maveric:* A Life in Politics, he had cautioned Nixon advisor Murray Chotiner not to provide covert aid to Tom Dodd, the now disgraced Democrat US senator who was running as an Independent. Chotiner and White House fundraiser Herbert Kalmbach would dispatch former New Jersey State Senator Harry Sears, a friend of John Mitchell's to Hartford with two suitcases of cash to fuel Dodd's effort. Dodd, the very model of an august Roman senator, finished with twenty-five, pulling Catholic Democrats off of the Democratic nominee Rev. Joe Duffey, thus electing Weicker with 41 percent of the vote. Between the Townhouse cash and the secret subsidies to Dodd, Murray Chotiner elected Lowell Weicker. Let no good deed go unpunished.

Senate Watergate Committee Majority Counsel Sam Dash would admit that Weicker would vote with the panel Democrats for any broader subpoena power or area of investigation, saying in essence that Weicker was in the bag and the committee Republican were powerless to stop the one-sided investigation of Nixon in the Watergate matter.

Additionally, while Bush was never charged in connection with the operation, it was not for lack of trying. Nixon White House documents from July 1973, shortly after Mr. Bush became chairman of the Republican National Committee, indicate a willingness by Mr. Bush to burn party records related to Townhouse. Prosecutors' notes from an interview with Mr. Gleason include the following quote, "Bush called Weicker, asked whether he should burn [records of payments from the Townhouse Operation to the RNC]." That is to say, Bush indicated a willingness to obstruct an investigation into the Townhouse Operation, actively conspired to obstruct justice, and presumably was willing to lie under oath should investigators come looking for RNC records relating to the operation.

The Bush-Weicker-Gleason relationship bears further discussion. While Senator Weicker was one of the beneficiaries of the Townhouse funds during the 1970, to the tune of $71,000,[21] he has only admitted to reporting the $6,000 in cash, while ignoring the other $65,000 we now know him to have received.[22] Additionally, Weicker, who served as an enemy to the administration during the Watergate proceedings, eventually hired Jack Gleason as a legislative aide.[23] It seems bizarre that an individual who made his reputation by turning on the administration in the name of good governance would hire the man responsible for gross campaign finance violations, targeting Weicker's own campaign.

While Bush's involvement with the Townhouse Operation was well documented from the moment the story broke, the events surrounding Townhouse were damaging to Bush multiple times over the duration of his political career. After Nixon's resignation and Ford's ascension to the presidency, one of the most burning political questions in the country was whom Ford would choose as his vice president. Many viewed Bush, who at this point had served in many high-profile positions, as one of the front-runners, along with New York Governor Nelson Rockefeller. While Ford had already selected Rockefeller for the position over the course of August 16/17, 1974, *Newsweek* ran a piece on August 18 speculating that Bush's ambitions for the office have been badly damaged "because of alleged irregularities in the financing of his 1970 Senate race."[24] While it remains unclear who leaked the information to the press (Bush has always believed it to be Ford political adviser Melvin Laird; Ford biographer James Cannon has reported that Ford's senior aide Donald Rumsfeld, considered by some a dark horse for the position, leaked it to further his chances), it is quite certain that Bush's chances were essentially nonexistent as a result of his involvement in the Townhouse Operation.[25]

Nineteen seventy-four was not the end of the grief that Bush would endure as a result of his involvement with Nixon's Townhouse operation. At the end of 1975 Bush, at that point serving as head of the US Liaison Office in Beijing, was angling for an appointment by President Ford to head the Commerce Department.[26] Bush felt that Commerce would position him for a chance to be named to the Ford ticket in 1976, as Rockefeller had announced his intention to step away from the vice presidency at the end of the term. However, Ford decided to appoint Bush Director of the Central Intelligence Agency. The agency was at that time battling two congressional hearings, and Bush, given his legacy as RNC chair during Watergate and as a recipient of Townhouse funds, was highly controversial.[27] Bush, to his disappointment, was made to agree to Ford's decision to remove him from contention for the vice presidency as a condition of his appointment to the CIA.[28] Again, Bush's political ambitions were thwarted as a result of his Townhouse involvement. Interestingly, while the majority of the Senate was placated by this compromise position, and Bush was confirmed 64-27, two of the 41 GOP Senators did not support Bush's confirmation—including the abstaining Lowell Weicker.[29]

Again, and again, Townhouse and the Nixon connection rose to challenge Bush in his ambitions. During his 1980 campaign, on the heels of his success in the Iowa Caucuses, Townhouse would again plague Bush. The *Manchester Union-Leader*, an unabashedly conservative paper, very much pro-Reagan in his campaign against Bush, would again revive the charges against Bush regarding Townhouse.[30] So concerned was the Bush camp about the possibility that the allegations would again surface, that the Watergate special prosecutor, Leon Jaworski, who had cleared Bush of wrong doing, was given a place on Bush's presidential steering committee; this despite Mr. Jaworski's professed Democratic allegiance.[31]

The Townhouse Operation would further hinder Bush's political ambitions during his run for reelection as president in 1992, the twentieth anniversary of the Watergate break-in. An in-depth *New York Times* article published in June 1992 revived the debate of Bush's involvement with Townhouse and presented much of the evidence discussed above. The allegations of Bush's willingness to destroy evidence, while denounced by the Bush camp, was particularly damaging to his campaign.[32] The details of Bush's involvement with Townhouse struck many as illustrative of his political careerism at best, and evidence of the type of cynical calculation and aloofness through which prism many voters had come to view Bush. It was perhaps not as fatal in '92 as it had been in 1974, however, his involvement with Townhouse still cost Bush dearly at a time when he was attempting to recover from a surprisingly difficult, for an incumbent, primary campaign.

Bush's brother Jonathan Bush said that George was "getting in position to run for president." Peter Roussel, Bush's highly regarded press aide from 1970 to 1974, said, "There were high hopes for him in that race. It was one of the premier races of that year, and a lot of people thought, well, Bush is going to win this Senate race, and there's probably a good chance that'll be the stepping stone for him ultimately going to run for president." Bush lost, however.

As a victim of two unsuccessful Senate campaigns, Bush's political future was in doubt. For the next eighteen years, he was not in control of his political career. He was well suited to advance his career by serving others in administrative posts, but it seemed a dead end. When Nixon offered him an insignificant job as assistant to the president, Bush made his case for more.

*　*　*

When Bush heard that Nixon Treasury Secretary David Kennedy was leaving, he inquired of the president for the job. He was shocked to learn that his nemesis John Connally would be taking that job. "Bush hated Connally," David Keene, Bush's 1980 political honcho, told me at the time. Bush sold Nixon on going to the UN as ambassador. Bush got to brush up his foreign policy credentials and attend endless cocktail parties. He wrote notes, kept in touch with his friends, and bided his time.

Kissinger and Nixon both considered Bush a lightweight. He was never told of the back-channel communiqués with the Communist Chinese. He staked himself out at the UN as a hard-liner for Nationalist China and against the Reds. Bush was kept in the dark about Nixon's visit to China. George and Barbara Bush lived blissfully ignorant in a sumptuous double apartment at the Waldorf Towers, where Herbert Hoover had lived and Mrs. Douglas MacArthur was still a neighbor.

Nixon would then appoint Bush chairman of the Republican National Committee.

Senator Bob Dole served Nixon well as chairman of the Republican National Committee. Day-to-day operations were run by cochair Thomas B. Evans, Jr., later a Delaware congressman and an important early supporter of Ronald Reagan in 1980. Nixon decided to sack Dole for no other good reason other than he had gotten beaten up for attacking Democrats on behalf of Nixon. The president asked Bush to take Dole's place. "Dole is still pissed about it," Scott Reed, the Kansas senator's 1996 campaign manager, told me in 2013. Bush would use the party post to cultivate organizational Republicans making alliances with Goldwaterites like Arizona's Dean Burch and Nebraska's Dick Herman. Bush would defend Nixon as the Watergate scandal gained steam but would, after the release of the so-called Smoking Gun tape tell Nixon it was time to throw in the towel.

John Sears made short work of Bush presidential aspirations in 1980.

Nixon was stunned when Reagan selected Bush to be vice president. "Nancy thinks he's a jerk," the former president confided in me. "And Ron doesn't like him. After that Nashua thing [the Nashua, New Hampshire, Republican debate] Ron never got over his dislike for the guy." Nixon had been in touch with Kissinger during the Republican National Convention as the former secretary of state labored mightily to convince Reagan to take former President Gerald Ford for vice president and divide the country's top job into a copresidency. "Henry is getting grabby," Nixon told me. "It'll never work." A week after the Republican National Convention, Nixon would tell me, "even Bush is better than that crazy Ford idea."

"Bush was dead as Kelsey's nuts," Nixon confided. "Two losing races for the US Senate and then he fumbles the nomination after winning Iowa. Ron blew political life into a loser." Sometimes Bush's presidency would enrage the thirty-seventh president. "Why the hell can't he speak English?" Nixon would ask me. "He acts like one of those goddamn country clubbers."

NOTES

1. Walshe, Shushannah. "Bush 41, Reagan consoled Nixon During Watergate. ABC News. August 21, 2013.
2. Ibid.
3. Guariglia, Matthew. "New Nixon Tapes: Prez Tells George H.W. Bush He Had 'Nothing to Do With Those Goddamn Things' [AUDIO]" The Heavy http://www.heavy.com/news/2013/08/new-richard-nixon-tapes-george-bush-kennedy-assassination/
4. Baker, Russ. Family of Secrets: The Bush Dynasty, the Powerful Forces That Put It in the White House, and What Their Influence Means for America,160.
5. Pincus, Walter. Woodward, Bob. "George Bush: Man and Politician." The Washington Post. August 9,1988
6. Baker, Family of Secrets, 164.
7. Baker, Family of Secrets, 161.
8. Bedard, Paul. "Nixon Nearly Picked Bush as VP: Instead, Spiro T. Agnew got the nod in 1968, says book." US News & World Report, 10 Aug. 2011.
9. Pincus & Woodward, "George Bush: Man and Politician."
10. Novak, Robert. The Prince of Darkness: 50 Years Reporting in Washington, p. 144.
11. Baker, Family of Secrets, 164.
12. Allen, Gary. The Man Behind the Mask, p. 131
13. Dean, John. Blind Ambition, 59-62.

14. Werth, Barry, 31 Days, pp. 115-116
15. Ibid
16. Ibid
17. Esper, George. "Bush Says No Wrong Involved in Acceptance of Funds," Associated Press. February 7, 1980
18. Lukas, J. Anthony, Nightmare: The Underside of the Nixon Years, p. 111.
19. Gerth, Jeff. Pear, Robert. "Files Detail Aid to Bush by Nixon White House, New York Times June 11, 1992
20. Ibid
21. Armstrong, Scott, "Weicker Raises Funds Question Involving Bush," The Washington Post, February 29, 1980
22. "Campaign Gift Cleared: Weicker" The Meriden Record. July 1, 1976
23. Armstrong, Scott, "Weicker Raises Funds Question Involving Bush," The Washington Post, February 29, 1980
24. Werth, 2006 pp. 114-116
25. Ibid
26. Pincus, Walter. Woodward, Bob. "Presidential Posts and Dashing Hopes; Appointive Jobs Were Turning Points" The Washington Post, August 9, 1988
27. Ibid
28. Ibid
29. Tarpley, Webster Griffin. Chaitkin, Anton. George Bush: The Unauthorized Biography, Chapter 15
30. Parmet, Herbert. George Bush: The Life of a Lone Star Yankee, p. 226
31. Esper, George. "Bush Says No Wrong Involved in Acceptance of Funds," Associated Press. February 7, 1980
32. Gerth, Jeff. Pear, Robert. "Files Detail Aid to Bush by Nixon White House, New York Times June 11, 1992

CHAPTER SEVENTEEN

WOODSTEIN

"Obviously, Haig was hiding things from the president, including his Woodward connection. Later, when Woodward was causing so much grief and Haig was not leveling with us about the connection, we wondered why not."

—Nixon speechwriter Ray Price.[1]

John Dean pulled off an incredible hoax. He pulled it off on the Watergate Committee, he pulled it off on the American people, and he profited wildly off it. But while Dean played a big part in Watergate and the subsequent cover-up, his actions paled in comparison to the duplicitous, premeditated power grab of General Alexander M. Haig. Using journalist Bob Woodward, Haig manipulated the Nixon presidency and drove Nixon from office.

Although I don't believe there was a "Deep throat," the alleged source of the *Washington Post's* Woodward and Carl Bernstein, I am certain Al Haig was one of the key confidential sources who made up a composite for Deep Throat.

I never believed that Deep Throat, the enigmatic figure who, concealed by smoke and shadows, guided cub reporters Woodward and Bernstein to the truths behind Watergate, was number-three FBI man Mark Felt.

I have never believed the claim by Woodward and Bernstein or the claim by Felt himself. Felt himself did not reveal to his family that he was the fabled Deep Throat until 2002. At the time Felt came out as Deep Throat he was enfeebled, had suffered a stroke, and was "in and out of lucidity," in the words of his daughter Joan.[2] Indeed, Felt's daughter also admitted that money was a factor in the decision to go public with the identity of Deep Throat.[3]

Even after the Felt's declaration in 2005, the jury is still out on Deep Throat. David Obst, the literary agent for Woodward and Bernstein, responsible for marketing *All the President's Men*, admitted that Deep Throat was, indeed, a "literary device." Obst discussed this in an interview with television journalist Brit Hume:

> *Obst*: I was their literary agent, and I sold the book to Simon & Schuster at the beginning of October of 1972, and the boys kind of got stuck on how to write it. In fact, they turned in a draft, and the publisher kind of hinted that they'd like their money back. And they were really kind of stuck.
>
> And then Bob had dinner one evening with Robert Redford and William Goldman, a screenwriter, and shortly thereafter, he came up with this brilliant idea of doing the book as his own personal story. And suddenly . . .
>
> *Hume*: His and Carl's, right?
>
> *Obst*: Yes, his and Carl's, of course. And suddenly, this character of "Deep Throat" showed up, and . . .
>
> *Hume*: Had you ever heard of this "Deep Throat" figure before that time?
>
> *Obst*: No. There was no "Deep Throat" character.[4]

White House insider Len Garment would write a book that incorrectly concluded that John Sears was Deep Throat. Garment is wrong, but the point is immaterial. Sears admitted to being a high-level source for Carl Bernstein, described in their book *All the President's Men* as a former, high-level Nixon aide. Sears's revelations to Bernstein were in fact more important than the information that came from the composite of Deep Throat.

Barry Sussman, the editor who supervised Woodward and Bernstein, said that there was a Deep Throat, but he was for the most part worthless. "The reason Deep Throat remained anonymous, so that even *Post* editors didn't know who he was, is that his contribution was unimportant," wrote Sussman.[5]

An interview with *Washington Post* editor Ben Bradlee by reporter Jeff Himmelman, revealed Bradlee had candidly admitted to Barbara Feinman, who had aided Bradlee with his memoirs, that he had his doubts about the existence of Deep Throat. "You know I have a little problem with Deep Throat," Bradlee had told Feinman. "Did that potted [plant] incident ever happen? . . . and meeting in some garage. One meeting in the garage? Fifty meetings in the garage? I don't know how many meetings in the garage . . . There's a residual fear in my soul that that isn't quite straight."[6] Bradlee would add that he believed Watergate was blown out of proportion. "Watergate . . . (has) achieved a place in history . . . that it really doesn't deserve . . . The crime itself was really not a great deal."[7]

Himmelman had for years worked as Woodward's research assistant. In April 2010, Himmelman was helping Bradlee research a book and stumbled upon the 1990 Feinman interview in a box at the *Washington Post* storage facility.[8] Himmelman's reveal of Bradlee's doubts about Deep Throat were not out of malice. Woodward was a friend. It was Woodward who had praised Woodward in the dedication to his 2000 book, *Maestro*.[9] Himmelman's "standards of accuracy and fairness . . . are the absolute highest," wrote Woodward.

It was simply a reporter doing the job of a reporter. Surely, Woodward, who had revealed so many of other people's secrets would understand, even respect Himmelman's reporting.

Woodward instead went on the attack. Himmelman was labeled by Woodward as "dishonest" and the information that was published about the reporter was called a "betrayal."[10] It seemed that

Woodward did not enjoy Himmelman's "accuracy and fairness" when turned against him. "Those standards have not changed; it's just that I uncovered some information that Bob Woodward happens not to like, and he is doing everything he can to distract attention from it," Himmelman wrote. "If there is any lesson that Ben Bradlee taught me in the four years I spent working with and studying him, it is that powerful people rarely welcome the truth and will often go to great lengths to keep it from coming out. Ben dealt with that throughout his career, and I am seeing it firsthand right now."[11] In 2011, Bradlee would reaffirm to Himmelman his doubts about Deep Throat.[12]

When Mark Felt finally emerged from the shadows of Watergate, the reception was underwhelming. Perhaps because many correctly believe that the outing of Felt still did not answer the questions of Watergate. Felt probably was *one* of the reporters' sources, but his access was limited. As the son of former director of the FBI Pat Gray pointed out, when Woodward handed over his "Deep Throat" interview notes in 2007, something was amiss. "The first thing that struck me was that some of the information passed to Woodward in these meetings could not have come from Mark Felt," said Ed Gray.[13] Gray compared the reporter's notes to the text of *All the President's Men* and found several significant tells. One particular segment of the notes dealt with John Mitchell's orchestration of an internal CRP investigation. A quote from Deep Throat that concerned the investigation read, "*We* had assigned guys to him to help." This sentence was omitted from the final manuscript.[14] Why? Because *we* would have meant the source was someone who had access not only to the President's inner circle, but was involved in the internal investigation of the White House staff. Felt could claim neither. Gray confirmed that the source for another interview note that concerned wiretaps was also not Felt, it was Mitchell associate Donald Santarelli. Santarelli himself confirmed this. "That was definitely me," he said. Subsequently, Bob Woodward was asked if the source was Santarelli and replied, "[A]bsolutely not."[15] Ed

Gray, and his father before him, correctly came to the conclusion that Deep Throat was "the composite fiction that knowledgeable people like my father always insisted he had to be. 'X,' whoever he was, was just a part of the fable."[16]

It stands to reason that Deep Throat did exist, but was a composite, an amalgamation of figures that served as informants to the two reporters. Deep Throat *did not* exist in the original *Washington Post* stories. Melding the many sources of the reporters into one certainly added more dramatic effect to the novel. Investigative journalist Edward Jay Epstein also holds this theory. Epstein attributes it to the fact that the information from Deep Throat could not come from one part of the government, but had to derive from "multiple sources who worked in different parts of the government."[17] It would not be the first time Woodward would invent a story to fit a narrative. In 1987, Woodward claimed to speak to former director of the CIA William Casey before his death for his book *Veil: The Secret Wars of the CIA.* "Indeed, Woodward did try to enter the hospital room, but was interdicted by the agent in the hot seat [outside Casey's door] and gracefully shown to the exit," said Kevin Shipp, a former CIA agent on security detail outside of Casey's hospital room. "'We, myself included, were there 24 hours a day, seven days a week," Shipp wrote. "All of us were under orders to let no one into the room."[18] Shipp added that had Woodward impossibly made his way into the hospital room, he could not have gotten an interview. The brain tumor Casey was suffering from had rendered him incapable of speech.[19] Casey's widow, Sophia, backed Shipp's claim and added she had seen CIA records and that "Bob Woodward got in and was caught by security and thrown out," before entering Casey's room.[20] Yet, Woodward said he *had* gained access to the room and he *had* spoken to Casey. Woodward also claimed that, incredibly, Casey chose Woodward as the recipient of a deathbed confession. Casey reportedly acknowledged to the reporter that he knew about an illegal diversion of funds by the Reagan administration from Iranian arms sales to Contra rebels attempting to overthrow the Nicaraguan government. When my boss and friend President Ronald Reagan saw the fabrication in Woodward's book and a *60 Minutes* interview coupled with Woodward's assertion that Casey believed the president was a "strange" man, who was "lazy and distracted,"[21] he was appropriately angry. "He's a liar & he lied about what Casey is supposed to have thought of me," Reagan wrote in his diary.[22] William Casey's widow said that it was all a Woodward-created untruth. "Bill would never say that about the President," Sophia Casey said. "Bill loved Reagan and they were very close. It's been very hurtful. It is terrible for the family. You can imagine how Reagan feels."[23]

If Woodward had no problem with inventing the words of a dying man, he surely had no problem inventing Deep Throat. An additional purpose of having a single essential informant, code-named Deep Throat, was to better dissemble the many informants of Woodward, especially Al Haig and Robert Bennett.

Woodward did not want it known to the public that during his own military service in the navy, while assigned to work for the National Security staff at the White House, Woodward often briefed General Alexander M. Haig, who later became a major source for Woodward. In fact, Woodward told bold lies to conceal this background to anyone who looked into it. "I never met or talked to Haig until sometime in the Spring of '73," Woodward said. "I defy you to produce somebody who says I did the briefing, it's just—it's not true."[24] In fact, it was true and individual's in Woodward's past would prove it. Among those who remembered Woodward's past as Haig's protégé was chairman of the Joint Chiefs of Staff, Admiral Thomas H. Moorer, who, as part of a national security leak, was receiving NSC documents pilfered by Navy Yeoman Charles Radford, who was aided by Haig. "Of course," Moorer replied when asked if he remember that Woodward was the briefer for Haig."[25] Defense Secretary Melvin Laird would also concede, "I was aware that Haig was being briefed by Woodward, yeah."[26] Laird served sixteen years in Congress before serving as Nixon's defense secretary. He was a

shrewd, cagey, and often self-serving leaker. He had deep press contacts and relationships and was particularly close to *Washington Post*
columnist Robert Novak. It was Laird who orchestrated the systematic withdrawal of troops from Vietnam. Laird was a valid source to
confirm that Woodward worked for Haig.

Pentagon spokesperson Jerry Friedheim would also confirm
Woodward's position. "He was moving with those guys, Moorer,
Haig, the NSC staff, and other military types," Friedheim said.[27]
It was only after Woodward learned there were taped interviews
with these men of rank who acknowledged Woodward's role with
Haig, the reporter would say that the theory had "surface plausibil-
ity to it."[28]

Why would Woodward want to conceal his military intelligence
background? There are a few reasons. The Moorer, Haig, NSC staff
circle was the very same that young Navy Yeoman Charles Radford
worked for when lifting top-secret documents and running a back
channel of White House secrets back to the Pentagon. The revelation
of Woodward in a similar role around that same time period might
warrant extensive questioning. The revelation of Woodward's
assignment as Haig's briefer would also reveal where the reporter
was getting a large portion of his information. Haig would not
want it known to Nixon that he was leaking stories that would
eventually topple the floundering president. Nixon already had his
suspicions of the general, and if Haig were revealed as a source, in
the words of Colodny, "even the fourth star would not be enough
to protect the general from the president's well-known wrath."[29] In
essence, the two men were helping each other. Woodward by way
of the leaks from Haig was to become, in the words of the *Weekly
Standard* editor Fred Barnes, "the best reporter of his generation,"[30]
while Haig would maneuver into a position as White House chief
of staff.

"The fortunes of Deep Throat, of Alexander Haig, and of Bob
Woodward had been intertwined since hours after the break-in of
June 17, 1972," wrote Colodny and Gettlin.[31] Although Colodny

and Gettlin would conclude that Deep Throat was Haig, I believe they were only partially correct.

Robert Bennett, head of the Mullen Company, was another one of the sources that comprised the mysterious Deep Throat. As we covered with the Baker investigation of the CIA, Bennett fed stories to a grateful Woodward while the reporter helped deflect the role of the CIA in Watergate. Also, Baker's report revealed that Bennett's attorney fees for his Senate Watergate Committee appearances were partially paid for by the agency. Bennett wove a White House–centric narrative for Watergate that was fit to print for Woodward. Woodward was the king of access journalism, "an author whose books are written by his sources," in the words of the late British/American journalist Christopher Hitchens.[32] Only three weeks after his first talk with Woodward, Bennett would brag to his CIA case officer Martin Lukoskie "that he had dissuaded reporters from the *Post* and *Star* from pursuing [stories] implicating the CIA in a Watergate Conspiracy."[33]

Charles Colson became certain of the CIA's culpability in Watergate when he got a look at an internal agency file on Watergate in the spring of 1974. The file further detailed the role of Bennett in the manipulation of Woodward. "Then there's [the] memo of March 1, 1973, which, to me, was the most critical document of all," Colson said. "It was from the chief of the Central Cover Staff, Eric W. Eisenstadt, to the deputy director for plans. In it, there were specific references to various articles published by Woodward, which had been fed to Woodward by Bennett. And the articles were attached. It was comical, actually. I opened the file, the first time, and here was a story from the Washington Post (February 10, 1973): "Hunt Tried to Recruit Agents to Probe Senator Kennedy's Life." And here was Eisenstadt, taking credit for the article, along with the "Whispers about Colson" story from the March fifth edition of *Newsweek*.

It was all very self-congratulatory, about "what a good job the CIA is doing," and how Schlesinger had commended them "for diverting attention away from the agency."[34]

While the elite media would call the dynamic *Washington Post* writing duo "Woodstein," they were in fact two different and distinct reporters who I believe had two different objectives in their coverage of the Watergate case. It is important to understand that Woodward and Bernstein worked independently and did not share their notes, files, or sources. I first met Bernstein when he knocked on my apartment door in a one-bedroom apartment I was sharing with my then-girlfriend off of Dupont Circle. In his shoe leather approach to his Watergate investigation, Bernstein had obtained a CRP staff list and was working his way through it. Because of McCord's phone call to the Porter household on the weekend of the break-ins, I knew that CRP was dissembling when they claimed no connection to the late-night entry into the DNC. I found Bernstein straight forward, trustworthy, and willing to follow the Watergate story wherever it went. I would later learn that one of Bernstein's most important sources was John P. Sears.

Alan Pakula, who worked with both reporters in the making of the movie version of *All the President's Men*, wrote, "Underneath all the arguments and fights—way down, they hated each other."[35] Woodward went on to write a number of controversial and profitable books, whereas Bernstein would lose a fortune in his high-profile divorce and dissipate the rest on wine, women, and song. A wealthy friend of mine in New York told me he met Bernstein at a cocktail party and extended the veteran reporter his business card. The next day, Bernstein called him seeking a $10,000 loan.[36] Woodward's embrace of Mark Felt as Deep Throat was, in my opinion, a tactical decision that did not comport with the truth. Too many seasoned critics were on to the fact that Deep Throat was most likely a literary device and that the source did not exist. In that sense, Felt's public announcement was useful to Woodward. Only Carl Bernstein could queer this deal.

I firmly believe Bernstein's seminal article for *Rolling Stone* outlining the intelligence community's infiltration of the media is a shot across his partner Woodward's bow. Bernstein's ground-breaking book on CIA infiltration of the media bore a message to Woodward that his old partner understood Woodward's deep connections to the intelligence community and that Bernstein would not be left behind in the saga of Watergate.

Bernstein had his own strange connection to the Columbia Plaza call girl ring. Bernstein was an acquaintance of porn shop owner and pimp Buster Riggin. Riggin had helped organize the working hours of the Columbia Plaza madams[37] and, according to confidential FBI and DC Police informant Robert Merritt, was an associate of DC crime boss Joseph Nesline and White House call girl Heidi Rikan.[38] Bernstein was an irregular patron of Riggin's DC smut shop.

That Bernstein would seek out erotica at Riggan's store is not odd; the journalist was a porn enthusiast and his sexual pursuits have become a thing of legend. Screenwriter/ author Nora Ephron, who was married to Bernstein for four years in the late seventies, said that the reporter was "capable of having sex with a venetian blind."[39] Indeed, while his wife, in the late stages of pregnancy, awaited the couple's second child, Bernstein began an affair with Margaret Jay, wife to the British ambassador to Washington.[40] The affair was only the tip of the iceberg, as Bernstein had been a philanderer for majority of his marriage to Ephron. The womanizing Bernstein was later the subject of Epron's bestselling book later turned movie *Heartburn*.

Bernstein was so sexual that he became a regular at underground swinger parties held in the Northern Virginia suburbs of Arlington and Fairfax. These private parties were attended by a number of CIA personnel including John Arthur Paisley,[41] an electronics expert who was connected to the Nixon "Plumbers." In 1979, the bloated corpse of Paisley was found in Chesapeake Bay, a bullet wound was found behind his ear, and two thirty-eight-pound diving belts had weighted down his body.[42] I myself, dabbling in the swinger lifestyle in Washington in the seventies, would see Bernstein at the parties where threesomes with two women seemed to be his favorite. Clearly, Bernstein was using his celebrity to fuel his carnal desires, leading Woodward to order a post-investigation to see if Bernstein had been compromised in his sexual CIA contacts.

Haig and his Pentagon patrons knew that it was only a matter of time before Nixon would be forced from office, and it was Haig who would walk Nixon inexorably toward the exit, while at the same time brokering control of Nixon's papers and tapes, as well as the pardon of the thirty-seventh president. Haig's leaks to Woodward would also explain some of the more bizarre stories regarding Nixon's deterioration in *The Final Days*, where Woodward was clearly being briefed by one of the few men who still had access to Nixon. *The Final Days* would recount Nixon's growing isolation, his heavy drinking, and his conversations with portraits of dead presidents on his nocturnal wanderings through a darkened White House.

NOTES

1.   Strober, Deborah Hart. Strober, Gerald. *The Nixon Presidency: An Oral History of the Era*, p. 285
2.   Campbell, W. Joseph. "Did Watergate's 'Deep Throat' know he was 'Deep Throat' April 15, 2012 http://mediamythalert.word-press.com/2012/04/15/did-watergates-deep-throat-know-he-was-deep-throat/
3.   Arak, Joel. "'Deep Throat' Daughter: $ a Factor. CBSNEWS. June 5, 2005.
4.   Noah, Timothy. "Yes, Virginia, there is a Deep Throat." Slate.com. May 8, 2012
5.   Sussman, Barry. "Why Deep Throat was an Unimportant Source and Other Reflections on Watergate." July 24, 2005. http://www.rjionline.org/ccj/commentary/why-deep-throat-was-unimportant-source-and-other-reflections-watergate
6.   Himmelman, Jeff. "The Red Flag in the Flowerpot" New York Magazine. April 29, 2012

7. Buchanan, Pat. J. "The unraveling Myth of Watergate." Human Events. May 25, 2012
9. Hunter, Derek. "Bob Woodward, Liar." The Daily Caller. May 16, 2012
10. Ibid
11. Byers, Dylan. "Jeff Himmelman calls out Bob Woodward. Politico. April 30, 2012
12. Gray, L. Patrick. In Nixon's Web. p. 479
13. Ibid, p. 480
14. Ibid, pp. 488-489
15. Ibid, p. 491
16. Noah, Timothy. "Yes, Virginia, there is a Deep Throat." Slate.com. May 8, 2012
17. Stein, Jeff. "Woodward dismisses CIA guard's dispute of Casey death-bed visit." Washington Post. September 21, 2010
18. Ibid
19. Neumeister, Lawrence. "William Casey's Widow Refutes Contents of Woodward's Book." Kentucky New Era. September 28, 1987
20. Ibid
21. Reagan, Ronald.The Reagan Diaries (Kindle Locations 11473-11475).
22. Neumeister, Lawrence. "William Casey's Widow Refutes Contents of Woodward's Book." Kentucky New Era. September 28, 1987
23. Woodward/Colodny and Gettlin interview. March 6, 1989
24. Moorer/Gettlin interview.
25. Laird/Colodny and Gettlin interview. March 6, 1989
26. Friedheim/Gettlin interview. September 25, 1990
27. Benatar, Giselle. "Endless Conspiracies," Entertainment Weekly. November 1, 1991
28. Colodny, Len. Gettlin, Robert. Silent Coup, p. 288
29. Barnes, Fred. "The White House at War, The Weekly Standard. December 2, 2002
30. Colodny, Len. Gettlin, Robert. Silent Coup, p. 283
31. Hitchens, Christopher. "Bob Woodward: Stenographer to the Stars," Salon.com. July 1, 1996
32. Waldron, Lamar. Watergate: The Hidden History, p. 621
33. Hougan, Jim. Secret Agenda, p. 273
34. Shepard, Alicia C. "After 30 Years, The Scoop on Woodward and Bernstein." November 26, 2006

35. Interview with Joseph J. Jingoli - August 26, 2011
36. Merritt, Robert. *Watergate Exposed*, p. 4
37. Merritt, Robert. http://www.watergateexposed.com/watergateexposed-blog.html
38. The Reliable Source. "Carl Bernstein recalls post-divorce relationship with Nora Ephron. *The Washington Post*. June 27, 2012
39. "Unfaithfully Yours: Adultery in America. *People*. August 18, 1986.
40. Havill, Adrian. *Deep Truth*, p.105
41. "Nation: The Puzzling Paisley Case," *Time*. June 22, 1979

CHAPTER EIGHTEEN

"PARDON ME"

"I'll stay long enough to get Nixon the pardon"
—Alexander M. Haig[1]

Joachim Bertran was rail thin, with a black pencil mustache. His appointment as the military attaché in the Washington, DC, Cuban Consulate was considered a plum posting. Back in Cuba, Bertran had taught military strategy at the academy, which is somewhat of a joke since Joachim, in the vein of Cuban revolutionary José Martí, was more of a poet than he was a soldier.

I met Bertran in rabidly anti-Communist right-wing circles where he and Barker were both active through the seventies. Bertran and his wife, Olgaita, were close friends of Bernard "Macho" Barker and his third wife.

Second Lieutenant Bertran was not particularly political, and his wife and two children lived a comfortable existence in the Maryland suburbs of DC. They read in the newspapers about the fall of Batista. Bertran received orders to return to Havana for "debriefing." The night before he was to leave a CIA man knocked on his door and told him he was on a list to be "liquidated" by the Castro regime and that return to his homeland was unwise. He never returned to Cuba. His savings and what meager assets he had were lost. Because his command of English was not strong, he would struggle as a Fuller Brush man, printer, and shoe sales-man. He would retire in Miami, spending nights playing domi-nos in the meeting hall of the 2506 Brigade veterans, which also housed a musty Bay of Pigs museum. It was there that Joachim would become intimate with Barker. "He was a bulldog of a man, but quiet," Joachim would tell me. "He looked like just another business man until you looked in his eyes," he said. "He had the eyes of a killer."

Joachim continued. "Macho knew Haig from the planning of the Bay of Pigs. He said they saw him strutting around the JMWAVE headquarters [a CIA planning station and Cuban exile training facil-ity south of Miami]. They called him 'El Pollo' because he strutted like a rooster. Macho said even the military guys laughed because Haig habitually wore every medal and ribbon he had," he told me over mojitos in a rundown bar on Calle Ocho in the Little Havana section of Miami.

"Hunt, Eugenio [Martinez], Sturgis, hell, we all knew Haig," Bertran told me. Haig not only worked to serve his masters at the JCS and the CIA in muting the détente policies of Nixon and Kissinger in favor of a harder-line military stance, but also had a direct connection to at least four of the Watergate burglars through his Bay of Pigs experience.

To understand both the fallout from the Watergate break-ins and President's Gerald Ford's ultimate pardon of his predecessor Richard Nixon, one needs to understand General Alexander M. Haig. Al Haig was a tough, brilliant military man with a reputa-tion for handling difficult problems. Haig was a renowned bureau-cratic infighter and strategic leaker who understood Washington, the Pentagon, the Central Intelligence Agency, and the media of his day.

Immaculately groomed and spectacular tailored, whether in his uniform or in a suit, the chain-smoking Haig had served as a "clean-up man" for both Democratic and Republican presidents. When President John F. Kennedy wanted to invade Cuba at the Bay of Pigs, the man who drafted the plan was Al Haig. When Lyndon Johnson and Army Secretary Joseph Califano needed something done, the man charged with responsibility was Al Haig. When Nixon and Kissinger wanted to have someone wiretapped, they called Al Haig. When Kissinger needed someone to negotiate the fine details of the cease-fire in South Vietnam, he sent Al Haig. When Richard Nixon wanted to remake geopolitics by reaching out to the Chinese and then playing them off against the Soviets in order to slow the arms race and disengage from costly American entanglements abroad, the man he and advisor Henry Kissinger turned to was Al Haig.

Haig was a soldier's soldier but was also a master political operator, administrator, and power politician. He served on the staff of General Douglas MacArthur in Japan as a young officer. During the Korean War, Haig was responsible for maintaining MacArthur's intelligence and maps and briefing the general daily on both. Haig was later awarded two Silver Stars and a Bronze Star as an aide to General Edward Almond, MacArthur's chief of staff.

Haig's military résumé is impressive. His days in the Pentagon began in 1962, when he served a two-year post as a staff officer in the Office of the Deputy Chief of Staff for Operations. Haig served as deputy special assistant to Secretary of Defense Robert McNamara until the conclusion of 1965. While working for McNamara, Haig reported to Joseph Califano, who at that time was McNamara's chief special assistant. The Haig-Califano relationship would survive after Haig's service in a Republican White House and staunch Democrat Califano would remain a close advisor to Haig throughout his career, including his stormy tenure as Ronald Reagan's secretary of state.

It is important to note that Haig was not only a desk warrior; he sought out and excelled in the theater of combat. Haig led a battalion of the First Infantry Division in Vietnam and saw plenty of action. During the Battle of Ap Gu in March 1967, Haig's battalion was pinned down by the Viet Cong. Haig flew to the scene in a helicopter, which was shot down and quickly enmeshed—Haig in the heart of the battle. For the next three days, Haig and his troops fought off waves of Viet Cong as a force three times the size of his own bore down upon his men. Haig troops, inspired by his powerful example, managed not only to hold the vicious horde off, but also to kill 592 enemy soldiers. For his command and valor, Haig was awarded the Distinguished Service Cross, the country's second-highest honor for heroism, by General William Westmoreland. It was no surprise that Haig revered swashbuckling General Douglas MacArthur.

Promoted to colonel for his heroics, Haig became a brigade commander of the First Infantry Division in Vietnam. Haig's knack for strategy on and off the battlefield made his eventual transition to geopolitics seamless. "Politics and soldiering are very, very close," Haig would say. "[They're both] fields where a man lays everything on the line to win or lose. They're tested by the vote or they're tested in battle. When one doesn't win, the results are fatal; and in the case of the military, quite fatal. So I have a great respect for politicians."[2] In 1969, he was appointed military assistant to Dr. Henry Kissinger, who served as presidential assistant for National Security Affairs. Haig attained the appointment at the recommendation of military geopolitical strategist Fritz Kraemer, who was the primary mentor for both Haig and Kissinger. Kraemer would say, "Above all he is a man of strong character besides being intelligent and gifted with an innate understanding of political and psychological issues."

Often donning a monocle, carrying with him a riding crop, and wearing riding jodphurs and immaculately polished knee boots, Kraemer may have looked flaky, but he was a brilliant tactician who, with Haig and Kissinger, also counted amongst his disciples General Creighton Abrams, Lieutenant General Vernon Walters, who served as Deputy Director of Central Intelligence and Ambassador to the United Nations, Major General Edward Lansdale, and former Secretary of Defense Donald Rumsfeld.[3]

In his twenty-seven-year career in the Pentagon as a senior civilian counselor to defense secretaries and top military commanders, Kraemer would mentor generations of military minds and work under ten US presidents.[4] Eulogizing the powerful strategist in 2003, Kissinger would say that Kraemer "was the greatest single influence of my formative years, and his inspiration remained with me even during the last thirty years when he would not speak to me."[5]

Kraemer's military philosophy was built around the concept of "provocative weakness," which can be best summed up by Donald Rumsfeld in his farewell speech after his resignation in 2006. "It should be clear that not only is weakness provocative, but the perception of weakness on our part can be provocative as well," Rumsfeld said. "A conclusion by our enemies that the United States lacks the will or the resolve to carry out missions that demand sacrifice and demand patience is every bit as dangerous as an imbalance of conventional military power."[6] Kraemer himself continued to broadcast his message until his death. "We will absolutely have to have so visibly, so obviously, the wherewithal to cope with aggressors, that every, even the most determined troublemakers can calculate for themselves that we indeed have all the things to cope with aggression," Kraemer said in 1990 at a conservative leadership conference that explored the role of nuclear weapons in the post–Cold War world.[7]

The fact that Al Haig survived as the assistant to Henry Kissinger is testimony to both his temperament and resilience. The notoriously temperamental and mercurial Nixon foreign policy advisor was known for the abuse and destruction of his own staff. Haig himself, though, was also known to belittle and intimidate like a "schoolyard bully" over Kissinger, according to a source close to both men.[8] Former NSC colleagues suggest that Haig endured Kissinger's verbal abuse in group meetings but was capable of intimidating him physically one on one. Several NSC members said that Kissinger feared Haig might attack him physically if they got into a heated argument.

Both Haig and Kissinger came to represent two camps in the Nixon administration. Kissinger began to work with Nixon and sought an accord with America's adversaries. Kissinger believed that this was his path to power and largely abandoned Kraemer's bedrock principle of "provocative weakness." At the apex of the Vietnam War, Nixon began an attempt to hand the war over to the forces of South Vietnam whilst withdrawing American forces. Even if the Vietnamese reached a peace accord, it was now Kissinger's philosophy that the United States would allow the country to take their own "purely Vietnamese" course and thereafter develop "in keeping with the historical traditions and experience of the Vietnamese people."[9]

Haig was aghast at kowtowing to the enemy and believed any such actions were anathema to the fight against Communism and a betrayel of America's responsibility. Haig saw Nixon and Kissinger move toward détente as treasonous. Kraemer, according to Haig was a "spellbinder" who combined "logic, factual knowledge and conceptual depth with a spirited and inspirational personal demeanor,"[10] Although, he sometimes humored Nixon's ideas in order to play the role of loyal soldier, Haig had other plans.

Haig would simultaneously work over Nixon and Kissinger. "Haig moved in on Henry and he moved in from the very beginning," wrote Seymour Hersh in *The Atlantic Montly.* "First of all, he was Henry's butler and his chauffeur. Henry never knew the kind of perks that could be arranged—private planes for trips to New York for dinner, limousines—and he loved it. Haig also was very shrewd politically where Henry was naive. He was advising Henry at first on how to handle Haldeman and Ehrlichman. When Henry had to wear a white tie and tails for his first White House dinner, it was Haig who went to Henry's house and helped him dress for the first time."[11] At the same time, Haig was double-dealing on Kissinger. One way was through Nixon's insatiable love of gossip. Another was through his hard-line approach to politics, which bolstered Nixon's confidence. A third way was by spying on Kissinger. As we covered previously, Haig was a key figure in a military spy ring in which a Yeoman courier had rifled desks, burn bags, and even the briefcase of Secretary of State Henry Kissinger to copy documents and forward them to the chairman of the Joint Chiefs of Staff. Haig also had a penchant for listening in on Kissinger's private phone calls. In his NSC office, Kissinger had installed a private phone line in which a third party could privately listen in. Haig used this privledge liberally. On one such occasion, Haig, tapped in, whispered to Chuck Colson, who was standing nearby, "He's selling us out on Vietnam!" and later told Colson "I['ve] got to get ahold of Kraemer."[12] Kraemer would come to the White House weeks later in an attempt to reinvigorate Kissinger's warrior spirit.

Haig was a born schemer, a self-serving egomaniac. "Al Haig was a neurotic narcissist with an unquenchable craving for power," wrote political journalist Christopher Hitchens.[13] With the power of hindsight, one thing is perfectly clear: Haig was ultimately out for himself, and in his quest to slow détente he went so far as to review the notes of private meetings between Kissinger, Nixon, and Chinese leaders. Nixon and Kissinger "are selling us out to the Communists!" Haig told Haldeman aide Dwight Chapin.[14]

In the early years of the Nixon White House, Haig was somewhat loyal to both Nixon and Kissinger. Haig knew, in the words of Seymour Hersh, "that future promotions lay with Kissinger as much as with the President."[15] Haig also shared dark secrets with both men.

A continuing vulnerablilty for *both* Kissinger and Haig was their in involvement in the 1969–'71 wiretaps place on NSC staffers, White House aides, and prominent journalists. Haig and Kissinger had a mutual interest in keeping the entire sordid affair from becoming public, and worked in concert to bar public exposure of the wiretaps. When word of the wiretaps ultimately leaked to Woodward, his source Deep Throat tried to deflect blame away from the FBI and the administration, claiming the taps were placed by the same rouge elements of the CIA and the FBI who broke into the Watergame (Hunt, McCord, and Liddy). Once again General Haig left his prints on a lie, this one designed to bury the role of he and Kissinger in the taps. Interestingly, when the wiretaps finally became public and posed an issue in Kissinger's confirmation to be secretary of state, Haig and Kissinger would both deflect total blame for the wiretaps onto Nixon and Kissinger. They would deny "initiating" the taps, even though it was he who agitated for them and made up the list of the those to be seruptitiously eaves-dropped upon.

By the fall of 1972, Haig had begun to circumvent Kissinger to meet directly with the president. "Henry would be an absolute wreck, he'd be close to a nervous breakdown because the president was meeting with Haig," recalled an NSC aide.[16] Despite believing that Haig had been involved in the naval spy ring, Nixon was impressed by Haig's confidence and swagger. Getting close to the president had its perks. Incredibly, with Nixon's help, Haig went from colonel to four-star general in a matter of four years, skipping the rank of general entirely. Nixon awarded Haig two more stars, expediously jumping over 240 ranking officers to become eligible for his next post: vice chief of staff of the US Army, to which[17] the US Senate confirmed him in October 1972. Haig's new post put him directly in line for his next promotion.

Following the resignation of White House Chief of Staff Bob Haldeman on April 30, 1973, Haig made his move. Departed Nixon aides Haldeman and White House Counsel Charles "Chuck" Colson, both pushed Haig for the vacant Chief of Staff slot in their own self-interest; both hoped for executive clemency from Nixon before he left office. Haig double-crossed Haldeman on this score too, presenting Nixon with the option of pardoning Haldeman and his collegues for their Watergate crimes at the same time pardoning those who had illegally avoided service in the Vietnam war, a surefire nonstarter for Nixon. The president said no.

Nixon was considering the appointment of John Connally as his chief of staff, with whom the president was enamored, but Nixon staffers hardly knew. In lieu of Connally, Nixon decided on Haig, who served as White House chief of staff, while still retaining his army commission, during the height of the Watergate affair from May 1973 until Nixon resigned on August 9, 1974.

Nixon loved Haig's military bearing and use of military language, which Haig used to buck up Nixon's toughness. "We're at the point that we can see the barbed wire at the end of the street. What we have to do is mobilize everything to cut through it," Haig would bark at Nixon during the Watergate debacle.[18] Haig was the ultimate courtier with a false bonhomie. "He was not a nice guy trying to play a nice guy, it was totally phony," said Jeff Bell, who met with Haig as one of the Manhattan Twelve, conservatives, including William Buckley, who suspended their support of the Nixon administration after Nixon's tilt to the left on both foreign policy and domestic issues.[19] Many in the "New Majority" were shocked to learn that Nixon never intended to repeal the New Deal of the Great Society and that the growth of government and spending would continue to grow. Many on the right hung with Nixon for sentimental reasons, he was, after all, the man who nailed Alger Hiss, but his support on the right began to wane. Haig had been assigned by the president to meet with the disgruntled conservatives.

Nixon had no way of knowing that Haig often mocked him behind his back, often mincing in a limp wristed manner to imply that Nixon and his best friend Charles "Bebe" Rebozo had a homosexual relationship.[20] This is, to say the least, doubtful.

In addition to the tasks ordered by an increasingly distracted Nixon, Haig had his own agenda as chief of staff. "Nothing is possible without power,"[21] Fritz Kraemer had told him time and again. As White House chief of staff, Haig would use his considerable power to conceal three things: his role in the wiretaps, his facilitation of the naval spy ring, and his connection to the White House

"Plumbers." This third cover-up is important, because it lends credence to the theory that Haig knew about the break-in at the office of Daniel Ellsberg's psychiatrist as well as the Watergate break-ins well in advance. The possession of this knowledge allowed the tactful Haig to plot his maneuvers well in advance. As we have stated, Haig had a connection to Barker, Hunt, and the Bay of Pigs veterans. Phllip Gailey in the *New York Times* reported that Haig held regular progress meetings with the codirectors of the "Plumbers," Egil "Bud" Krogh Jr. and David R. Young Jr., and worked as a liaison between the "Plumbers" and the National Security. When he obtained ultimate power in the White House, Haig would do everyting in *his* best interest to bury these nefarious actions and bury the president alongside them.

Upon becoming chief of staff, Haig would slow walk Nixon to resignation, and then would skillfully broker the deal for Nixon's pardon from Ford. Haig used his new position to wield control at a greater level than the departed Haldeman. "The changes were fundamentally that Al controlled everything—everybody and everything," said Haldeman's former aide Larry Higby.[22] In order to radiate his increased clout, Haig would return to wearing his four-star uniform, even though he had largely worn the less-formal suit and tie during his days as Kissinger's chief deputy.

Haig has been largely credited with keeping the government running while President Nixon was preoccupied with Watergate and was essentially seen as the "acting president" during Nixon's last few months in office, and the power-mad general was not afraid to show it. At one point in his reign, when the new chief of staff found out about a staff meeting decision made without him he "began pounding the table with his fist . . . and said two or three times, 'I am the chief of staff. I make all the decisions in the White House,'" said Nixon's staff assistant Steve Bull. "We all thought he was crazy."[23]

As Haig wielded his new power with shocking force, the reclusive Nixon backed into the shadows of the White House, increasingly sedated by drinks the general plied him with. "He's just unwinding," Haig told Kissinger at one point in March 1974, when an especially lubricated Nixon threatened to drop a nuke on Capitol Hill. "Don't take him too seriously."[24]

A series of significant events, manipulated by Haig, frame the general's special interest in sinking the Nixon presidency. The first was Haig's handling of the admission by Alexander Butterfield that made Watergate investigators aware of a taping system in the White House. On July 13, 1973, Butterfield had sat down with the investigators and admitted the president's conversations in the Oval Office had been recorded. Butterfield was scheduled to divulge his secret in public testimony to the committee on Monday, July 16. Nixon was unaware of the admission or the impending testimony.

Haig had been definitely told of the taping system by his old comrade Butterfield in May 1973. Shortly after this conversation, Deep Throat began pushing Bob Woodward to look into Butterfield, and Woodward in turn pushed the committee. Haig had additionally learned of Butterfield's admission to investigators and pending testimony, at the very latest, by Sunday, July 15.[25] This is important because had Haig told the president that weekend about the impending testimony, Nixon *could have* invoked executive privilege and blocked Butterfield's appearance before the committee. Laid up in Bethesda Naval Hospital with viral pneumonia, Nixon remained unaware about Butterfield's admission or impending testimony. White House logs prove that Haig met with Nixon in the hospital on three separate occasions over the weekend—once on Saturday and twice on Sunday. In Nixon's memoirs, he recalled that he "continued to take calls and see Ziegler and Haig," while he was sick.[26] Yet Haig neglected to inform Nixon that Butterfield was to testify until *Monday morning*. Woodward had also learned from a source about Butterfield's admission that weekend. In an odd move, the *Washington Post* also decided to hold the story past Sunday, the day of the paper's highest readership. No one wanted to tip the president off, and by the time Nixon found out, it was obviously too late. "I can't conceive of that information being withheld from the president for an entire weekend," said Press Secretary Ron Ziegler.[27] When Nixon found out, he was, in his own words, "shocked."[28]

The decision by Haig to withhold this information ensured that Butterfield would testify to the existence of the tapes and got the legal ball rolling for subpeonas to release them. Following Butterfield's testimony, Haig developed an incredible lie, which he repeated many times: that he did not know about Butterfield's testimony beforehand. "As I heard his (Butterfield's) testimony, I thought, *oh my God.* And I ordered the whole taping be ripped out immediately," Haig recalled on one occasion. "When Nixon says, in his memoirs, that I called him that Monday morning to tell him that Butterfield was going to testify, he is wrong. I didn't know about it until I saw him on television."[29] One thing was true about Haig's assertion—following Butterfield's testimony, he controlled the fate of the tapes.

On July 19, Nixon noted in his bedside pad that he "should have destroyed the tapes after April 30, 1973."[30] In fact, Nixon still had the chance to destroy them. It is obvious that the White House tapes were central to Haig's plan. Haig warned against Nixon's better interest that destroying the tapes would "forever seal an impression of guilt in the public mind."[31] Haig would later proclaim that the president's decision *not* to destroy the tapes was his "big mistake."[32]

After Haig willed the revelation of the White House tapes, the general maneuvered for their release to the Watergate Committee. This was tricky and exemplified Haig's deft double-dealing. Watergate Special Prosecutor Archibald Cox was looking into the Watergate scandal but also had begun sniffing into the Moorer-Radford naval spy ring.[33] To continue effectively down the road to Nixon's resignation while remaining relatively unscathed, Haig needed Cox gone. Deputy Attorney General William Ruckelshaus admitted he would receive complaints "from Haig about Cox's people—or about Cox himself—moving against some aspect of the charges against the White House that were unrelated to Watergate."[34] Cox, who Nixon referred to as "that fucking Harvard professor," was looking into the White House "Plumbers," which would lead to more of Haig's unsavory actions.[35]

Attorney General Elliot Richardson had assured Haig that if Cox had asked for any more tapes, he *could not* support Nixon and *would not* agree to fire Cox. Yet, Haig convinced Nixon that Richardson *would* support Nixon's withholding of any more materials and "support me in the controversy that was bound to ensue," according to Nixon. This was patently untrue, but it convinced Nixon that Richardson was on their side. "Richardson's resignation was something we wanted to avoid at all costs," Nixon said later.[36] If Nixon had known that Richardson supported Cox and would also not weigh in on requests for more tapes, he might have been less induced to fire Cox, and this of course was a tremendous threat to Haig.

In Haig's retelling, Richardson had promised him that he would resolve the situation by offering an acceptable compromise to Cox, but later when Haig reached him and asked if Richardson was on board, the attorney general replied, "No, Al. I'm sorry, I'm not."[37] Haig added that Richardson's voice was "very slurred."[38]

The result of Haig's deception was the Saturday Night Massacre on October 20, 1973, where to the utter shock of Nixon, Richardson and William Ruckleshaus promptly resigned and Cox had to be fired by Solicitor General Robert Bork. "While I fully respect the reasons that have led you to conclude that the special prosecutor must be discharged, I trust that you understand that I could not in the light of these firm and repeated commitments carry out your direction that this be done," Richardson said.[39] The move, orchestrated by Haig, greatly turned the public against Nixon.

Nixon's own notes, recounted in his memoir, are instructive:

(1) Cox had to go. Richardson would inevitably go with him. Otherwise, if we had waited for Cox making a major mistake which in the public mind would give us what appeared to be good cause for him to go would mean that we had waited until Cox had moved against us.

(2) We must learn from the Richardson incident what people we can depend on. Establishment types like Richardson simply won't stand with us when chips are down and they have to choose between their political ambitions and standing by the President who made it possible for them to hold the high positions from which they were now resigning.

(3) As far as the tapes were concerned we need to put the final documents in the best possible PR perspective. We must get out the word with regard to no "doctoring" of the tapes.

(4) We must compare our situation now with what it was on April 30. Then the action with regard to Haldeman and Ehrlichman, Gray, Dean, and Kleindienst did not remove the cloud on the President as far as an impression of guilt on his part was concerned. In fact it increased doubt and rather than satisfying our critics once they had tasted a little blood, they liked it so much they wanted far more. Since April 30 we have slipped a great deal. We had 60 percent approval rating in the polls on that date and now we stand at 30 percent at best.

(5) Now the question is whether our action on turning over the tapes or the transcripts thereof helps remove the cloud of doubt. Also on the plus side, the Mideast crisis, probably if the polls are anywhere near correct, helped some what because it shows the need for RN's leadership in foreign policy.

(6) Our opponents will now make an all-out push. The critical question is whether or not the case for impeachment or resignation is strong enough in view of the plus factors I noted in previous paragraph.[40]

The final move by Haig, which proved to be the deathblow to Nixon's presidency, was the 18 ½-minute gap found on the Watergate tapes. Historians and archivists have now argued for forty years over the 18 ½-minute gap in the tapes and what was erased. Various scientific methods have been used in an attempt to recall the words, all to no avail. The contemporaneous notes of Bob Haldeman are also missing, so determining what Nixon and Haldeman were talking about remains a mystery. I submit, however, that it is not the content of the gap but the act of erasure *itself* that was the motive of the person who erased the tape. I submit that there was *nothing* of note in the 18 ½-minute gap. In the end, it was not what was on the tapes that provided the final push to get Nixon out of office, but what *was not* on them. Nixon said that when he learned about the gap, "I practically blew my stack."[41]

Nixon secretary Rose Mary Woods admitted to and immediately reported an inadvertent five- minute gap while she was transcribing tapes at Camp David. Nixon, Haig, and White House Counsel Fred J. Buzhardt were apprised of this accident erasure but Buzhardt strangely counseled that the erasure was not problematic because the conversation was not among those subpoenaed by the court. Buzhardt should have looked again. Was Buzhardt's mistake an act of sabotage?

When the tape was ultimately turned over to the Special Prosecution Force, listeners were stunned to find the full 18 ½-minute gap, which was in fact six multiple erasures. The tapes were in the custody and control of Secret Service liaison on the White House staff Alexander M. Butterfield and were available to White House Counsel Buzhardt. At that juncture, Deep Throat specifically tipped Woodward and Bernstein about "deliberate erasures," even though multiple other White House sources told the *Washington Post* that they didn't think the tapes had been doctored or played with. Haig, one of the composite of sources that were dubbed Deep Throat by Woodward, set Nixon up with an erasure that was most probably hiding nothing of significance but still had the effect of bringing Nixon down. In December 1973, Haig testified that "perhaps some sinister force had come in and applied the other energy source and taken care of the information on that tape." Judge Sirica then asked Haig if anyone had suggested to him who the sinister force might have been. "No, your honor," Haig replied.[42]

After his effectual sabatoge of the Nixon administration, Haig played an instrumental role in finally persuading Nixon to resign and negotiating his pardon. The pardon was as important to Haig as it was to Nixon. The Watergate scandal had gone far enough. A prolonged, extensive investigation of Nixon's role in the matter would eventually turn up the unsavory revelation that many roads of inquiry led to Haig. It is vital to understand that Nixon did not particularly want the pardon. He communicated repeatedly that any pardon for his actions in Watergate or otherwise could not be rendered with a statement of admission by him. Although exhausted, deeply demoralized, and drinking, Nixon was prepared to go to trial if he was charged in the Watergate matter. "Haig described Nixon as a man dancing on the point of a pin," Barry Goldwater said. "He was someone who could be set off in any one of several directions. It would be best not to demand or even suggest that he resign. Every time that thing had happened in the past, Nixon had reacted defiantly. The best thing to do would be to show him there was no way out except to quit or lose a long battle. Haig summed everything up succinctly: The President needs to know there are no more alternatives, no more options."[43]

Nixon knew he held many cards. Nixon knew that Operation 40, the CIA-Mafia plot to kill Castro had become the Bay of Pigs fiasco, which in turn had morphed into the murder of John F. Kennedy. Nixon knew what the American people would not learn for twenty-three years, that Warren Commission member Gerald Ford, then a congressman, purposely altered the Kennedy autopsy records. At the behest of FBI Director Hoover, Ford changed the description of the location of the wound in Kennedy's upper back to the base of his neck to accommodate the government's now largely discredited "single-bullet theory," holding that JFK had been shot soley from the rear and that one of only three bullets fired hit both Kennedy and Govenor John Connally.

William C. Sullivan, the FBI's number-two man, recounted in his book *The Bureau: My Thirty Years in Hoover's FBI* that "Hoover was delighted when Gerald Ford was named to the Warren Commission. The director wrote in one of his internal memos that the Bureau could expect Ford to 'look after FBI interests,' and he did, keeping us fully advised of what was going on behind closed doors. He was our man, our informant, on the Warren Commission."

Sullivan said that Hoover had been watching Ford from the beginning. "Our agents out in the field kept a watchful eye on local congressional races and advised Hoover whether the winners were friends or enemies. Hoover had a complete file developed on each incoming congressman. He knew their family backgrounds, where they had gone to school, whether or not they played football [Ford played football at Michigan], and any other tidbits he could weave into a subsequent conversation," Sullivan said. "Gerald Ford was a friend of Hoover's, and he first proved it when he made a speech not long after he came to Congress, recommending a pay raise for him. He tried to impeach Supreme Court Justice William O. Douglas, a Hoover enemy."

Strangely enough, Sullivan himself would be killed in a "hunting accident" only days before he was to testify before the House Select Committee on Assassinations. He was shot dead near his home in Sugar Hill, New Hampshire, on November 9, 1977. Courts ruled that he had been shot accidentally by fellow hunter Robert Daniels, who was later fined $500 and stripped of his hunting license for ten years.

Conservative pundit and reporter Robert Novak said in August 2007, "[William Sullivan] told me the last time I saw him—he had lunch at my house—he had been fired by Hoover and he was going into retirement—he said that 'Someday, you will read that I have been killed in an accident, but don't believe it, I've been murdered,' which was a shocking thing to say."[44]

Sullivan was one of six top FBI officials who died in the six months before they were to testify before the House Select Committee in 1977. Others included Alan H. Belmont, special assistant to Hoover; Louis Nicholas, another special assistant and Hoover's liaison with the Warren Commission; James Cadigan, a document expert who handled papers related to the murder of John F. Kennedy; J. M. English, former head of the FBI forensic sciences laboratory where Oswald's rifle and pistol were both tested; and Donald Kaylor, an FBI fingerprint chemist who examined prints from the JFK case.

FBI documents declassified in 2006 detail even more about Ford's role as the FBI informant and agent and the crucial role Ford played in doctoring the autopsy to accommodate the cover-up. Assistant FBI Director Cartha "Deke" DeLoach regularly met secretly with Ford to inform the FBI on the status of the Warren Commission investigation. "Ford indicated he would keep me thoroughly advised as to the activities of the Commission," DeLoach wrote in a memo. "He stated this would have to be done on a confidential basis, however, he thought it should be done."

The Associated Press reported that DeLoach wrote a memo on December 17, 1963, about a meeting with Ford in which the deputy director laid out a problem. "Two members of the Commission brought up the fact that they still were not convinced that the president had been shot from the sixth floor window of the Texas Book Depository," DeLoach wrote. "These members failed to understand the trajectory of the slugs that had killed the president. He [Ford] stated he felt this point would be discussed further but, of course, would represent no problem." Indeed, we shall see what Ford meant by "no problem."

Here, more specifically, is the problem DeLoach described. The initial draft of the Warren Commission report stated, "A bullet had entered his back at a point slightly above the shoulder to the right of the spine." This description matches that of JFK's personal physician, Admiral Burkley, who attended the autopsy at Bethesda Naval Medical Center, and noted that the wound was "in the upper posterior about even with the third thoracic vertebra."

In fact, autopsy photographs of JFK's back, show the wound in his back, two to three inches below the base of the neck. A diagram by Burkley included in the Warren Commission's owns report confirms this location. The actual physical evidence demonstrates that the first draft of the Warren Commission report was indeed accurate. Photographs of bullet holes in Kennedy's shirt and suit jacket, almost six inches below the top of the collar, place the wound in the upper right back.

As American history professor Michael L. Kurtz pointed out in *The JFK Assassination Debates*, "If a bullet fired from the sixth-floor window of the Depository building nearly sixty feet higher than the limousine entered the president's back, with the president sitting in an upright position, it could hardly have exited from his throat at a point just above the Adam's apple, then abruptly change course and drive downward into Governor Connally's back."

Ford did Hoover's bidding. His handwritten edit on the classified document said, "A bullet had entered the base of the back of his neck slightly to the right of his spine." This change was later revealed in declassified papers kept by the Warren Commission's general counsel and accepted in the final report. "A small change," Ford told the Associated Press when it surfaced decades later in 1997.

Ford, a public supporter of the single-assassin theory, insisted that his edit had intended to clarify meaning, not change history. However, the effect of his alteration is clear. With this "small change," he bolstered the commission's false conclusion that a single bullet had passed through Kennedy and hit Governor Connally—thus solidifying what is now known as "The Magic Bullet Theory." Indeed, the Associated Press stated that Ford's "small change" became "the crucial element" to determine that Lee Harvey Oswald had been the lone assassin.

All of this was unknown to the public at the time of Ford's appointment to the vice presidency in 1973. The American public first learned of Ford's alteration in 1997, over three decades after Kennedy's assassination, and this information was only released as a result of the Assassination Records Review Board (ARRB). Interestingly enough, the ARRB was formed as a response to Oliver Stone's film *JFK*. For the first time in generations, the public demanded an in-depth examination to determine what was fact and what was covered up. In 1992, Congress passed the JFK Assassination Records Collection Act to empower the ARRB to declassify JFK assassination records.

Richard Nixon did know of Ford's role in the cover-up of the true details of Kennedy's death, having learned about it from the number-three man at the FBI, William J. Sullivan, according the White House Chief of Staff Bob Haldeman. Nixon also knew the CIA's true role in Kennedy's murder and how the Bay of Pigs fiasco and his conduct of the Cuban Missile Crisis had marked Kennedy for removal from office, an act facilitated by Lyndon Johnson for his own reasons. LBJ was facing criminal indictment, political ruin, and jail at the hands of Attorney General Robert Kennedy and knew that JFK intended to dump him from the 1964 ticket.

Nixon had used this knowledge successfully prior to leveraging it for a pardon as well as control of the papers and tapes from his presidential years. Indeed, when Nixon instructed Haldeman to tell Richard Helms of the CIA to order the FBI to desist in their pursuit of the Watergate break-in lest they inadvertently lay bare the whole "Bay of Pigs thing," the response from Helms was violent but effective.

A CIA memo made clear that the agency would adhere to its request and "desist from expanding the investigation into other areas which may well, eventually, run afoul of our operations."[45]

Nixon also knew by the time of his resignation that the Watergate break-in had involved a number of individuals with CIA connections, and many of them had been on the ground in Dallas on November 22, 1963. In his directions to Haldeman, he said, "Hunt . . . will uncover a lot of things. You open that scab there's a hell of a lot of things . . . tell them we just feel that it would be very detrimental to have this thing go any further. This involves these Cubans, Hunt, and a lot of hanky-panky that we have nothing to do with ourselves."[46]

As White House Chief of Staff Bob Haldeman said, Nixon clearly understood the connection between the Cuban invasion and the JFK assassination. Although Nixon would struggle to obtain proof of the CIA's involvement, Nixon knew that he could make the charge under oath with millions of American's watching.

Years later, Haig would retire to Palm Beach, where he continued to drink and resumed his three-pack-a-day cigarette habit despite his history of heart problems. In 2013, I was contacted by Richard H. Greene, a retired sewing machine company executive who had also retired to Palm Beach. Green claimed he had been drinking with the chainsmoking retired general at the Bath and Tennis Club when the subject of the pardon came up. Haig recalled Nixon's instructions to him. "Tell them if Dick Nixon's going down I'm taking everyone down with me, that prick [CIA Director Richard] Helms, Lyndon, and Jerry Ford are going down with me" was the way Haig phrased it. "The Old Man knew what Ford had done for Hoover in the JFK matter," Greene told me Haig said." He had them by the balls.[47]

Nixon's longtime advance man Nick Ruwe told me, "Nixon knew the Dallas setup. He had Ford by the balls," using eerily similar language to that attributed by Greene to Haig.

Using General Al Haig as his agent, Nixon let Ford know that he would expose the CIA's involvement in the JFK assassination and Ford's role in altering the autopsy records if he went to trial in the Watergate scandal. Thus, Nixon would use this information to avoid prosecution and jail to blackmail Gerald Ford for a full, free, and unconditional pardon. Nixon's secret would not only destroy his presidency—it would save him from prison.

Haig presented several pardon options to Ford on August 1, 1974, a few days before Nixon eventually resigned. Woodward, in a 1998 interview with Ford, reported: "Ford said about his August 1 meeting with Haig that 'yes, on paper, without action it was a deal, but it never became a deal because I never accepted."[49] This was Ford's cover story. In fact, Haig was so confident of a Nixon pardon that he brought with him to the meeting two sheets of yellow legal paper. Once again, Woodward would be the first to learn a key element of a private meeting that involved Haig. "The first sheet contained a handwritten summary of a president's legal authority to pardon," wrote Woodward. "The second sheet was a draft pardon form that only needed Ford's signature and Nixon's name to make it legal."[50]

Haig saw Ford twice on August 1. His first meeting with Ford was not sufficient because presidential assistant Robert Hartmann had inserted himself into the proceedings. "I had the impression that [Haig] didn't feel he could be as forthright as he normally might have been," said Hartmann. "[I]t was equally obvious that [Haig] wished I would go away."[51] Haig left and returned later, ensuring that no one witnessed the meeting.

Hartmann, Ford's counselor, was furious when he learned that Haig had returned to the White House to discuss a pardon with Ford and immediately demanded that Ford create a "record" that no agreement on a pardon existed. Haig thought Hartmann was out of his depth. Hartmann said the pompous and imperious Haig was "an asshole." Yet Haig secured what he went back to the White House to get—a deal that would remain secret until now.

Haig told Ford point-blank that Nixon *knew* that Ford had doctored the JFK autopsy report at the behest of Hoover and that the thirty-seventh president was prepared to lay this fact out for the American people if he went to trial over the charges against him. This would explain Ford's resolve to deliver the pardon despite the almost unanimous opposition of his hand chosen circle of advisors.

Nixon had a one-two punch in store for Ford. Nixon told me, "We had pictures with Ford in bed with a broad," which FBI executive Sullivan had covertly snapped for the FBI at a hotel suite in the Sheraton Carlton Hotel, where Capitol Hill wheeler-dealer Bobby Baker regularly entertained congressmen and senators with prostitutes. Hoover was among those who had copies of the photos exposing Ford in flagrante delicto. It is unlikely that Hoover needed this blackmail evidence in the Warren Commission matter, as Hoover was a patron of Ford's who had supported his early election to congress financially and for whom Ford pushed enormous budget increases for the FBI in the Congress. Ford was also an appropriations water carrier for the CIA. Ford was inclined to do Hoover's bidding in covering up what transpired on November 22, 1963. Nixon, Haig assured Ford, would "take everyone down with him," presumably revealing not only Ford's actions on the Warren Commission but the CIA's own dark secrets regarding the Bay of Pigs and the agency's dark ties to the plot in Dallas that included Johnson, the agency, elements of organized crime, and big Texas oil men like Clint Murchison. In fact, the *Washington Post*'s Bob Woodward would report on December 18, 1975, quoting unnamed sources, that Haig had secured a commitment from Ford that Nixon would be pardoned after Ford took office.[52]

In his important book *31 Days*, author Barry Werth notes that Ford seemed intent on pardoning Nixon from August 1 forward, despite vociferous opposition from his own staff, including Hartmann, lawyers Phillip Buchen, and Benton Becker, and the young Donald Rumsfeld. With Ford beginning to think about reelection, his aides told him that pardoning Nixon would bring his post-resignation popularity down and pose problems in winning a new term. Although Ford always prefaced every discussion about the pardon with the caveat "I haven't decided yet," it was clear that the die had been cast in the seminal Haig-Ford meeting of August 1.

Haig had also received assurances that Nixon's tapes and papers, which contained significant evidence of Haig's role in the Moorer-Radford military spy ring as well as the 1969–71 wiretaps on government officials and reporters, would go with the ex-president to San Clemente post-resignation. Haig would also broker an agreement from Watergate prosecutor Leon Jaworski that allowed Nixon to take the materials to California with the condition that certain documents and tapes would be made available to the special prosecutors.

Haig knew that Ford's pardon of Nixon had been coerced with blackmail and that Nixon needed not to seek control of his tapes and records or offer a statement of contrition in order to land the pardon. When Ford lawyer Benton Becker ventured to San Clemente to discuss both the tapes, records, and pardon issue, he was intercepted by acting Chief of Staff Ron Ziegler, who told him Nixon would not budge on a statement of guilt or give up control of his presidential records. It was clear to Benton that Haig had tipped Ziegler and Nixon that neither would be required in the deal with Ford.[53]

Nixon's knowledge of the dark deeds of Dallas in late 1963 would afford him the leverage to pressure Ford for a full, free, and unconditional pardon. Nixon would begin immediately a protracted legal fight to control his tapes and records, a fight he would ultimately lose. It is important to note that prior to Nixon, all federal rulings held that a president's presidential records were his personal property. It was only for Nixon that the courts said this was untrue.

Haig would briefly remain as President Ford's chief of staff, essentially using the position to spirit some of Nixon's papers and records out to California.

Ford was able to grant the Nixon pardon because Spiro Agnew had been shunted out of the way.

Although Agnew had little impact on the policies of the Nixon administration, he did enjoy the perks of office. The handsome vice president was a ladies man whose dowdy Baltimore wife, Judy, was oblivious to Agnew's short- and long-term affairs. After Agnew publicly befriended and embraced singer Frank Sinatra, a lifelong Democrat who had been instrumental in the Mob's support of Kennedy in 1960, and had campaigned for Hubert Humphrey in 1968, Agnew would spend weeks partying with the slender Hoboken crooner while Sinatra retainer Peter Malatesta supplied an endless stream of high-end call girls for Agnew in Palm Springs and Beverly Hills. Agnew would pull Old Blue Eyes into the GOP camp with Sinatra's endorsement of Ronald Reagan's reelection in 1970. Shunned by the Democrats, Sinatra backed Nixon in 1972 and delivered Sammy Davis Jr., who backed Nixon in an awkward moment at the Miami Beach Convention when Sammy referred to Nixon as "one groovy cat," which he clearly wasn't.

In 1973 Attorney General Elliot Richardson informed Nixon that Agnew was under investigation for corruption and had been accused of taking bribes. The Justice Department would make a case against Agnew, and Deputy Attorney General Henry Peterson reviewed the case. A group of Baltimore developers claimed they had made cash payments to Agnew while he was county executive, governor, and vice president. The government made a tax evasion case as well, but the cash itself was hard to trace, if it existed at all. Agnew had not been bribed by check.

Nixon, ever wary of confrontation, would dispatch Haig to tell Agnew he must resign. Agnew said Haig told him to "[g]o quietly or else." Agnew would write that Haig's clear message was that his life was being threatened and that the CIA would kill him if he resisted. Agnew knew Nixon was slipping and that Haig was the "de facto President." The first reports of the CIA secret efforts to kill Castro had just broken, and Agnew feared he would be killed in a staged car accident or faked suicide. Agnew recorded the moment in his own book *Go Quietly, or Else*:

"Since the revelations have come out about the C.I.A.'s failed attempts to assassinate Fidel Castro and other foreign leaders I realize even more that before that I might have been in great danger. Haig's words to Dunn that after indictment 'anything may be in the offing' could only be construed as an open-ended threat. I did not know what might happen to me. But I don't mind admitting I was frightened. This directive was aimed at me like a gun at my head.

"I feared for my life. If a decision had been made to eliminate me—through an automobile accident, a fake suicide, or whatever—the order would not have been traced back to the White House any more than the 'get Castro' orders were ever traced to their source. Perhaps I overreacted, but my mental state after months of constant pressure was hardly conducive to calm and dispassionate evaluation. The American people should know that in the last hectic year or more of his residence in the White House, Richard Nixon did not actually administer all the powers of the presidency. As I have stated earlier it was General Haig who was the de facto President. Haig had the power of the bureaucracy at his command, and the Washington insiders knew he was standing there behind Nixon, pulling the strings. Haig had direct connections with the CIA and the FBI and every other agency. For four years, he had been Henry Kissinger's chief deputy with clear access to all the government; his power extended into any agency he chose. The very survival of the Nixon presidency was threatened."[54]

Nixon dispatched Haig to tell Vice President Agnew that he must resign. Agnew said that Haig threatened him and said they could "play it nice or play it dirty." Agnew, who with millions of Americans had just learned about the CIA's involvement in political assassinations through the Church Committee in the US Senate probing CIA abuses, said in his own book that he believed his life was threatened by Haig.

Agnew himself told me that the case against him in which he ultimately plead nolo contenedre (no contest) was fabricated by the

Justice Department under pressure from the CIA anxious to remove him from the line of presidential succession when they saw Nixon teetering. I met Agnew at a seafood restaurant on the Eastern shore in a lunch arranged by former National Chairman of Young Americans for Freedom David A. Keene, who was later an Agnew aide. Keene joined us.

Agnew monopolized the conversation, insisting he was innocent and that the Justice Department had "put pressure on a bunch of Jews" to lie about cash payments allegedly made to him while he was vice president. "I was railroaded," Agnew told me. At the time, both Keene and I saw Agnew comments as self-serving and essentially disregarded them. Agnew would become deeply anti-Semitic, which would aid him in some post-vice-presidential business deals in the Middle East. He was, after all, still a former vice president of the United States. In light of the CIA's now exposed role and the desire to move Nixon out of power and install the more pliable and stable Ford, Agnew's claims need to be reviewed anew.

Agnew ultimately concluded Nixon wanted him gone. "I regret that I never confronted Mr. Nixon about the threatening message from Haig. I guess it was partly out of fear and partly knowing from experience he wouldn't give me a straight answer that I never asked Nixon if he personally authorized the threat to drive me from office. I suppose he would have denied it. At the time, I could not bring myself to believe that the President was not reluctantly being forced into this position by his advisers. I did not have the advantage of hindsight, of knowing for sure how I was being railroaded, until long after I was out."[55]

Agnew ultimately pleaded not guilty to tax evasion charges. As Agnew put it "[T]hese gifts were not taxable income and I had no obligation to report them. My actual net worth was less than two hundred thousand dollars. I had what was left of my small inheritance from my father, the cash value of my life insurance—bought many years before, and the comparatively small equity in my mortgaged home. Part of the threat to me was the reminder that my wife could be implicated in the tax charge; they could prosecute her too because we filed joint returns.

"The prosecutors insisted I had to plead guilty to some felony charge. I told my lawyers, as I had told them before, 'I'm not going to plead guilty to bribery or extortion. If I've got to do something to settle this, I'll plead nolo contendere to a tax charge.' They asked, 'What tax charge?' I said, 'Well, say that in late 1967 I collected some contributions for the 1968 campaign, and maybe held the money past the end of the year and didn't use it until the next year so that it was technically "income" for me.' It was simply a rationalization so that I could tell the judge I had received the money technically as unreported 'income.' The tax collectors at the I.R.S. later took every bit of testimony of my accusers as being true and billed me for taxes on my fictitious income. When I protested, the IRS official said, 'You want to contest it? Take us into court.' That would have meant trying the same issues in a civil hearing and a further circus for the news media as well as heavy legal fees and a tremendous sacrifice of my precious time needed to start making a living again. Moreover, I wanted to try my hand at international business because I knew it would be impossible for any US company to hire me without being pestered to death by my enemies. The I.R.S. said they would have to have my passport lifted as I might become an 'absconding debtor.' That would have made it impossible for me to do business overseas. They billed me for $150,000 in back federal income taxes, including interest and penalties. The irony is that I never got that money; I had to borrow money to pay the taxes on income I never received. As a condition of the settlement, I had to say in court the tax evasion charge was true. In effect, I had to twist the truth to make it possible for the judge to accept the settlement."[56]

Agnew would say the same thing in his book that he told me at lunch over crab cakes. [57]

The fall of Agnew would provide Nixon with an opportunity. In his selection of Ford to replace Agnew, Nixon passed over long-time intraparty rival and former Kissinger boss Nelson Rockefeller. Nixon had feared Rockefeller early in his career, but by the time he was president, he was no longer wary of Rocky. In the White House tapes, Nixon can be heard inquiring of Haldeman if any cabinet member or dignitaries have called the White House prais-ing one of his televised speeches to the nation. "Rockefeller called," Haldeman said. "Yeah, well screw him," Nixon replied.

"Nixon thought Ford was his insurance policy," John Sears told me. "He thought Jerry was so dumb that they'd never impeach Nixon." Nixon by-passed Nelson Rockefeller and Barry Goldwater and chose Gerry Ford for vice president because Ford, well-liked on Capitol Hill, was no political or intellectual heavy-weight and was a man on whom Nixon had *leverage*.

"The shock following the Nixon pardon caused members of Congress and the press to reflect back on the Nixon-Ford relation-ship throughout the entire Watergate affair in search for further clues to why Ford felt compelled to take such an extreme political risk for his political mentor," wrote former Nixon aide Clark Mollenhoff. "It had not put Watergate behind the nation but had brought it back into the full spotlight. It seemed unlikely that President Ford's compassion for Nixon was the only factor involved."[58]

Ford had already assisted the Watergate cover-up. The US House of Representatives Banking and Currency Committee, chaired by Texas Democrat Wright Patman, had begun a vigorous investiga-tion of the money trail that financed the break-in, large amounts of which were found as cash on the burglars at the time of their arrest. Patman was the first to confirm that the largest amount going into Miami bank account of Watergate burglar Bernard Barker, a CIA operative since the Bay of Pigs invasion, was the $100,000 sent in by Texas CRP chairman William Liedtke, longtime business part-ner of George Bush. The money was sent from Houston to Mexico, where it was "laundered" to eliminate its accounting trail. It then was sent to Barker's account as four checks totaling $89,000 and $11,000 in cash.

Patman was prepared to relentlessly pursue the true sources of this money as the best route to the truth about who ran the break-in and why. This meant Watergate would have unraveled before the 1972 elections. House Republican leader Gerald Ford led the attack on Patman from within the Congress. On October 3, 1972, the House Banking and Currency Committee voted 20–15 against continuing chairman Wright Patman's investigation. The vote prevented the issuance of twenty-three subpoenas for Nixon reelection officials to testify before the committee. Ford, New York Governor Nelson Ford, and Rockefeller were targeted committee members. Six Democratic members of the committee voted with the Republicans against chairman Patman.

Lyndon Johnson had also realized Ford's utility when he appointed Congressman Gerald Ford to his highly sensitive position on the Warren Commission investigating, and obscuring the truth of, John Kennedy's murder.

Ford's cooperation may have been motivated by other factors. Bobby Baker, secretary of the US senator, wrote that Washington lobbyist Fred Black, a crony and secret business partner of Baker and LBJ, had a suite at Washington's Sheraton Carlton Hotel. There, he often arranged for call girls to entertain congressmen and senators. The FBI surreptitiously filmed the action. According to Baker, Ford was a frequent visitor. In other words, much like Nixon, Lyndon Johnson had the goods on Jerry Ford.[59] "Jerry Ford was always up Lyndon's ass," Nixon told me.

Haig would stay on as Ford's chief of staff essentially to button up the details of Nixon's pardons and to spirit away numerous of Nixon's documents and records to the exiled president in his compound in San Clemente, California. Ford, forced into a pardon he didn't want to issue, would tell confidants, "I know I will go hell because I pardoned Richard Nixon."[60]

Ford had retained Nixon's cabinet and most of his staff, including Haig. At the same time Ford brought Robert Hartmann, Benton Becker, Phillip Buchen, Melvin Laird, and ultimately Donald Rumsfeld into his circle. They were no match for skilled bureaucratic infighter Al Haig. All opposed a pardon for Nixon, recognizing the political cost to Ford. None of them would understand the special leverage Haig had on Ford and why, from the beginning, Ford was headed toward issuing the pardon even when he was saying publicly and privately that he "hadn't made up his mind." The Ford men demanded a statement of guilt and contrition from Nixon. Haig also knew Nixon would stand in the dock rather than issue such a proclamation. "Nixon had Ford totally under his thumb," said Alexander Butterfield. "He was a tool of the Nixon administration—like a puppy dog. They used him when they had to wind him up and he'd go 'Arf, Arf.'"[61] Ford *was* Nixon's insurance policy.

Roger Morris, a former colleague of Haig's on the National Security Council early in Nixon's first term, wrote that when Ford pardoned Nixon, he effectively pardoned Haig as well.[62] Haig remained White House chief of staff during these early days of the Ford administration, for just over about one month, and was replaced by Donald Rumsfeld in September 1974.

Because a confirmation hearing in the senate would subject Haig to questions about Watergate as well as the 1969–71 wiretaps on White House officials and newspaper reporters, Ford appointed Haig to a job that required no Senate approval. Ford appointed Haig to a NATO post being vacated by General Andrew Goodpaster, a longtime associate of General Dwight D. Eisenhower.

Haig served as the Supreme Allied Commander Europe (SACEUR), the Commander of NATO forces in Europe, and Commander-in-Chief of United States European Command (CinCUSEUR). With Reagan's election in 1980 Nixon would reward Haig by convincing the new president to appointed Haig secretary of state. Finally Haig would eclipse his old boss and later rival

Henry Kissinger. In 1980, Haig had a double heart bypass operation. As is often the case with such surgeries, Haig would undergo a substantial personality change and would "lose a step" during this period. Perhaps this would explain the gaffe for which Haig was best known.

* * *

Haig's appointment was actively opposed by Vice President George Bush, White House Chief of Staff James A. Baker III, Baker aide Richard Darman, and Reagan aide Michael K. Deaver. Haig did not help himself by declaring that he would be the "vicar" of foreign policy under Reagan. The White House troika of Baker, Deaver, and Darman would aid mightily in Haig's ultimate downfall.

Interestingly, Haig's confirmation in the US Senate would be endangered when Senator Paul Tsongas demanded access to the Nixon-Haig tapes. Who should come to the rescue, but *Washington Post* reporter Bob Woodward who said that Haig should be confirmed without access to the tapes, denigrating the tapes reliability because, he wrote, "the audio quality is terrible, and making the transcriptions as maddening as the man (Nixon) himself." Woodward openly praised Haig for easing Nixon out of office. This again shows that the three-pack-a-day Haig was the model for the fictitious heavy-smoking Deep Throat in both the *All the Presidents Men* book and movie. As we have shown, Deep Throat did not exist as one source, but was a composite that included Haig, William Sullivan, and Mitchell aide Donald Santarelli. It is important again to note that Deep Throat was Woodward's source. At the same time, former White House aide and political strategist John Sears was talking to Carl Bernstein. Sears maintained impeccable midlevel relationships in both the White House and the Committee to Reelect the President after his own departure from the White House. He admitted to White House Counsel Len Garment that he was the "former Nixon administration official," identified as a source in *All the President's Men*.

More importantly, Haig clashed immediately and publicly with Vice President George H. W. Bush over amendments that would clarify the presidential line of succession in the event that President Reagan was incapacitated. Bush was actively planning Reagan's ouster, where I believe he set Reagan up in the Iran-Contra Scandal, which briefly threatened Reagan's presidency. "I was out of the loop," Bush famously said when questioned about his role in the administration's backdoor efforts to trade arms for hostages. Haig would lose this clash, and Reagan would approve the clarification Bush sought that would allow him to assume power if John Hinkley had succeeded in murdering Reagan or Reagan had been impeached or resigned in the Iran-Contra matter. Bush would quietly push for both of these as vice president, leveraging his network of CIA connections in Central America and the Middle East. Bob Woodward would pen a story quoting unnamed sources saying Haig had been "set up"[63] and naming Bush, Baker, Deaver, and Darman as those who had engineered Haig's ouster. The source said that Haig was displaced over "policy differences," an oblique reference to Haig's desire to pull the Reagan foreign policy to an early "neocon" position. Haig would remain a protégé of Dr. Kraemer. Yet again, Woodward's source is quite obviously Haig.

Haig then made a tactical blunder that Bush and his allies would jump on. On March 30, 1981, in the wake of the assassination attempt on President Ronald Reagan, Haig addressed reporters. "I am in control here." Although Haig was in fact directing White House crisis management until Vice President Bush arrived in Washington to assume that role, reporters and Washington power brokers saw Haig's comments as a clumsy overreach.

In defense of Haig, it is important to see his entire statement, which was, "Constitutionally, gentlemen, you have the president, the vice president, and the secretary of state in that order, and should the president decide he wants to transfer the helm to the vice president, he will do so. He has not done that. As of now, I am in control here, in the White House, pending return of the vice president and in close touch with him. If something came up, I would check with him, of course."[64]

The US Constitution, including both the presidential line of succession and the Twenty-fifth Amendment, dictates what happens when a president is incapacitated. However, the holders of the two offices between the vice president and the secretary of state, the Speaker of the House (at the time, Tip O'Neill) and the president pro tempore of the Senate (at the time, Strom Thurmond), would be required under US law (3 U.S.C. § 19) to resign their positions in order for either of them to become acting president. Considering that Vice President Bush was not immediately available, Haig's statement reflected political reality, if not necessarily legal reality. Haig later said, "I wasn't talking about transition. I was talking about the executive branch, who is running the government. That was the question asked. It was not, 'Who is in line should the President die?'"[65] The national press would pounce on Haig's remark to depict him as both power hungry and mad. They were egged on by Bush and his White House allies until Haig became a distraction. They would succeed in driving "the Vicar" out.

Haig, addicted to the taste of power and with a military record as impressive as Eisenhower's, would launch a quixotic campaign for the Republican presidential nomination in 1988. Although he enjoyed relatively high name recognition, Haig never registered more than of single digits in national public opinion polls. He was a fierce critic of then Vice President George H. W. Bush, questioning Bush's leadership abilities, questioning his role in the Iran-Contra scandal, and calling Bush a "wimp" in an October 1987 debate in Texas. Despite extensive personal campaigning and TV advertising in New Hampshire, Haig remained stuck in last place in the polls. Days before the February 1988 New Hampshire primary election, Haig withdrew his candidacy and endorsed Senator Bob Dole. Dole ended up losing to Bush in the New Hampshire primary by ten percentage points. In the end, I am persuaded that but for the White House stewardship of General Alexander M. Haig, the Nixon presidency might have survived. If the Watergate debate had remained between Nixon and chief critic John Dean, the political will probably did not exist for Nixon's removal. It was only the tapes, controlled by General Haig, and his longtime military associate Butterfield, that brought Nixon down.

* * *

Nixon watchers have been endlessly fascinated by the 37th president's televised remarks to the White House staff in the hours before his exile to San Clemente. Pat Nixon, so mindful of her tears during the televised agony of Nixon's 1960 de facto concession remarks, was furious when she learned that the president's remarks would be carried live. "We owe it to our supporters," Nixon told her. "We owe it to the people."

The first family entered the crowded East Room of the White House with its gold curtains and grand chandeliers. The room was packed with cabinet and sub-cabinet members, Republican lawmakers, White House staff and their spouses. Ed and Tricia Cox, as well as David and Julie Eisenhower accompanied the Nixons.

Nixon's red-rimmed eyes fought back tears and his face was drenched with sweat as he began to speak. Nixon's remarks were a surreal and rambling soliloquy that still achieved his aims—to put his spin on his years in the arena. "Greatness comes not when things go always good for you," Nixon said, "but the greatness comes and you are really tested when you take some knocks, some disappointments, when sadness comes, because only if you have been in the deepest valley can you ever know how magnificent it is to be on the highest mountain." Then, in a stunning piece of self-appraisal he added, "Always remember, others may hate you. But those who hate you don't win, unless you hate them, and then you destroy yourself."

The legal proceedings and civil lawsuits against Nixon at the end of his presidency allegedly destroyed him financially. At one point, his bank account was reportedly down to a balance of $500.

He left office broke, as well as physically, mentally, and emotionly exhausted. His greatest comeback was still ahead.

NOTES

1. Werth, Barry, 31 Days, p. 83
2. Lukas, J. Anthony. *Nightmare: The Underside of the Nixon Years*, p. 438
3. Hodgson, Godfrey. "Fritz Kraemer: Briliant Geopolitical Strategist Who Launched Henry Kissinger's Rise to Power." *The Guardian.* November 11, 2003
4. Ibid
5. Kissinger, Henry. "Remembraces—Fritz Kraemer." http://www.henryakissinger.com/eulogies/100803.html
6. Rutenberg, Jim. "Rumsfeld: No 'graceful exits' from Iraq." *Pittsburg Post-Gazette.* December 16, 2006
7. "Strategic Weapons in the Changing World." *CSPAN.* November 9, 1990
8. Colodny, Len. Gettlin, Robert. *Silent Coup*, p. 54
9. Colodny, Len. Shachtman, Tom. *The Forty Years War*, pp. 36-37
10. Colodny, Len. Shachtman, Tom. *The Forty Years War*, p. 30
11. Hersh, Seymour. "Kissinger and Nixon in the White House." *The Atlantic Monthly.* May, 1982
12. Colodny, Len. Shachtman, Tom. *The Forty Years War*, p. 58
13. Hitchens, Christopher. "Death of a Banana Republic," *Slate*, Feb. 22, 2010
14. Colodny, Len. Shachtman, Tom. *The Forty Years War*, p. 134
15. Hersh, Seymour. "Kissinger and Nixon in the White House." *The Atlantic Monthly.* May, 1982
16. Colodny, Len. Gettlin, Robert. *Silent Coup*, p. 53
17. Colodny, Len. Shachtman, Tom. *The Forty Years War*, p. 146
18. Colodny, Len. Gettlin, Robert. *Silent Coup*, p. 407
19. Phone interview with Jeff Bell. February 2014
20. Colodny, Len. Gettlin, Robert. *Silent Coup*, pp. 294-295
21. Colodny, Len. Shachtman, Tom. *The Forty Years War*, p. 29
22. Colodny, Len. Gettlin, Robert. *Silent Coup*, pp. 292-293
23. Ibid, p. 293

24. Dobbs, Michael. "Haig said Nixon Joked of Nuking Hill." *The Washington Post.* May 27, 2004
25. Colodny, Len. Gettlin, Robert. *Silent Coup,* p.331
26. Nixon, Richard. *RN: The Memoirs of Richard Nixon,* p. 898
27. Colodny, Len. Gettlin, Robert. *Silent Coup,* p. 335
28. Ibid, p. 334
29. Strober, Deborah Hart. Strober, Gerald. *The Nixon Presidency: An Oral History of the Era,* p. 393
30. Nixon, Richard. *RN: The Memoirs of Richard Nixon,* p. 901
31. Colodny, Len. Shachtman, Tom. *The Forty Years War,* p. 191
32. Ibid
33. Wicker, Tom. "Case of Navy yeoman curiouser, curiouser." *Eugene Register-Guard.* February 17, 1974
34. Strober, Deborah Hart. Strober, Gerald. *The Nixon Presidency: An Oral History of the Era,* p. 373
35. Colodny, Len. Gettlin, Robert. *Silent Coup,* p. 342
36. Ibid, 347
37. Strober, Deborah Hart. Strober, Gerald. *The Nixon Presidency: An Oral History of the Era,* p. 441
38. Ibid
39. Kilpatrick, Carroll. "**Nixon Forces Firing of Cox; Richardson, Ruckelshaus Quit. The Washington Post, October 21, 1973**
40. Nixon, Richard. *The Memoirs of Richard Nixon,* p. 969
41. Woodward, Calvin. Benac, Nancy. "Nixon's gap "an accident." *Philly. com,* November 11, 2011
42. Associated Press. "Haig says 'sinister force' theory raised in discussing tape gap.' *Eugene Register-Guard.* December 6, 1973
43. Goldwater, Barry. *Goldwater,* p. 277
44. Novak, Robert. The Prince of Darkness, pp. 210-211
45. Haldeman, H.R. *The Ends of Power,* p. 33
46. Ibid
47. Correspondence with Richard H. Greene. October 13, 2013
48. Ibid
49. Werth, Barry. 31 Days, p. 344
50. Fulsom, Don. *Nixon's Darkest Secrets,* p. 233
51. Colodny, Len. Gettlin, Robert. *Silent Coup,* p. 419
52 Woodward, Bob. Bernstein,Carl. "Ford Disputed on Events Preceding Nixon Pardon," *The Washington Post,* December 18, 1975,

53. Anderson, Jack. "The was no advance deal in Ford's pardon of Nixon." *The Prescott Courier.* July 1, 1976
54. Agnew, Spiro. *Go Quietly, or Else,* p. 192
55. Ibid, p. 193
56. Ibid, p. 193-194
57. Ibid, p. 192
58. Fulsom, Don. *Nixon's Darkest Secrets, p. 234*
59. Baker, Bobby, Wheeling and Dealing: Confessions of a Capitol Hill Operator, p. 209
60. Thompson, Hunter. "He was a Crook." *Rolling Stone.* July 16, 1994
61. Fulsom, Don. *Nixon's Darkest Secrets,* p. 235
62. Morris Roger, Haig: The General's Progress, pp. 320-325
63. Havill, Adrian. *Deep Truth,* p. 183
64. "Alexander Haig," TIME Magazine, April 2, 1984
65. Alexander Haig interview. 60 Minutes II, April 23, 2001

CHAPTER NINETEEN

FIGHTING FOR HIS LEGACY

"Nixon was a fighter. From the minute he resigned he fought for his legacy."
—Carl Bernstein speaking at Florida Atlantic University,
February 19, 2014

Richard Milhous Nixon had served a total of 2,026 days as the thirty-seventh president of the United States before he left the White House on August 9, 1974. Nixon biographer Jonathan Aitken wrote that "during the early months after his resignation Nixon was a soul in torment. He spent days shut away behind the guarded walls of his Oceanside, CA home. He made a brave show of keeping up appearances while he deteriorated both emotionally and physically to the point where he had close calls with a nervous breakdown and with death. At the same time Nixon told Sen. Barry Goldwater that rumors that he had lost the will to live were 'bullshit.'"[1]

Aitken stated that Nixon made efforts "to remain presidential without the Presidency. Each morning he arrived in his office at 7 a.m. prompt, immaculately dressed in coat and tie despite the 100-degree heat. He was guarded by a detail of eighteen Secret Service men, given medical attention by Navy corpsmen; provided with transport by the marines and supplied with secure communications by the Army. He was attended upon by a retinue of some twenty assistants, aides and secretaries who had volunteered to accompany him to California." But there was essentially no business to be done. Rod Ziegler, his former press secretary, sat with him alone for hours each day with nothing to do but discuss pending lawsuits and plot battle over public control of the White House tapes.

Although Nixon was originally allocated $850,000 by the House of Representatives to fund his move to California and transition to post-presidential life, Congress reduced this amount to only $200,000, which was to be used to cover the costs of office rent and salaries for his team of staff, for a period of six months.[2]

With only $200,000 given to him by the General Services Administration, he moved his small staff to California to be near his beloved La Casa Pacifica, a property he purchased in 1969 that became his presidential retreat, christened, "the Western White House." The property was found for the president in 1969 by a young White House aide instructed by Nixon to go to California and find a suitable presidential retreat. During better financial times, Richard and Pat Nixon purchased the private Spanish-styled estate as a sanctuary where they could entertain dignitaries and run the business of the United States in a secure and serene environment, and as a private place to conduct his presidential duties outside of Washington. It remained a hub for international negotiations both in his presidential and post-presidential years. Breshnev, the Soviet leader, would call on Nixon at his post-presidential retreat.

In 1974, Nixon became sick with phlebitis in his left leg, a blood-clotting disorder that causes veins to be inflamed. Doctors told him that he needed to be operated on or he could possibly die. He chose the operation. The illness just happened to be around the time that Haldeman, Dean, and Ehrlichman were on trial.

Nixon was subpoenaed to testify but, by chance, he was granted a dismissal by the presiding judge, who trusted the ailment was not just a ruse after three court-appointed lawyers examined him and said he was in no current condition to testify. Others were skeptical of the timing of his illness and accused the former president of faking the ailment so he didn't have to go to court.

After the presidential pardon, Nixon released the following statement:

> I was wrong in not acting more decisively and more forthrightly in dealing with Watergate, particularly when it reached the stage of judicial proceedings and grew from a political scandal into a national tragedy. No words can describe the depth of my regret and pain at the anguish my mistakes over Watergate have caused the nation and the presidency, a nation I so deeply love, and an institution I so greatly respect.

If anyone thought Nixon was grateful for the pardon by Ford, they were mistaken. As Ford struggled to fend off a challenge from Ronald Reagan in the snows of New Hampshire, Nixon announced he would travel to China at the invitation of Chairman Mao. Nixon's visit would only serve to remind voters of Ford's pardon of his predecessor. It was the last thing Gerald Ford wanted in the news. John Sears, who was now working for Reagan, had urged Nixon to take the trip. "He didn't need much convincing" he told me. The Chinese cooperated in order to signal their lack of happiness with Ford. It was a terrible blow to Ford.

A 1976 article in the *Washington Post* about that year's presidential campaign managers stated—probably on the basis of an interview with Sears—that Nixon continued to call Sears for advice, even during his Watergate troubles. Monica Crowley, who served as Nixon's assistant after his presidency, wrote that Nixon and Sears were still in touch, even though Sears played a key role in Nixon's downfall by shaping the Watergate narrative through Bernstein and other major reporters.

Sears's role in Watergate was based on loyalty to the Nixon he knew: the wise man, the teacher, the father figure. Sears's own father had perished in a fire when Sears was young. Sears revered Nixon as the gold standard of political calculation. The Nixon with whom Sears had signed up was a man capable of understanding and championing great policies. This was not the Nixon Sears saw in the self-imposed clutches of Haldeman, Ehrlichman, Haig, and Colson. Sears's loyalty was to Nixon's ideas and his own sense of pubic service, honed in long conversations with the Nixon he remembered. The Nixon he helped take down was not the same man.

Ford's reelection prospects also took a hit from John Dean. Dean appeared on the *Today* television show to publicize his book, aptly titled *Blind Ambition*. NBC was interested in publicizing his book too. They had just bought the television rights to it. In the course of his interview, John Dean announced a new "fact" about Watergate. House Minority Leader Gerald Ford, at President Nixon's instigation, had successfully squelched the Patman investigation of the financing of the Watergate break-in. Dean's charge was essentially true, and Ford's adamant denial did little.[3]

Nixon was plagued with lawsuits that dragged on almost throughout the rest of his life. These civil suits wore him down emotionally and drained his liquid assets. He seized the opportunity to make some quick cash by writing his memoirs. Legendary Agent Swifty Lazar negotiated a $2 million advance. Nixon would ultimately go on a prolific writing spree that included the writings of ten post-presidential books on domestic policy and international affairs and, of course, his memoirs.

Beyond writing books, Nixon also sought out other public-relations opportunities that he thought would earn him some money and allow him to spin his version of Watergate. One of those opportunities came in 1976: the Frost interview.

A few years after Nixon resigned, he was approached by British talk show host David Frost who proposed doing a paid interview show that would delve deep into the Watergate scandal, and finally ask the questions that America, and the rest of the world, wanted answered.

Frost paid him $600,000 for a taped interview. The show received fifty million viewers when it aired in 1977. It was one of the highest-rated shows of all time. The show helped Nixon out of his desperate financial situation, but, more importantly, it helped improve his image around the world, although Frost got Nixon to go further in atoning for Watergate than others had. After the Frost interview, Nixon seemed reinvigorated and wanted to jump back into international travel and foreign affairs—the two cards he would use to reinvent himself yet again as a foreign policy expert. Isolated from his daughters and their husbands as well as their grandchildren on the East Coast, he and Pat soon began looking for properties to buy that were closer to "the fast track." New York City would be their next move.

In 1980, Richard and Pat Nixon sold their beloved La Casa Pacifica property so they could move to New York City and be closer to the hub of politics and business on the East Coast. He sold the California estate to the founder of a pharmaceutical company, who also happened to be a big Republican donor who later developed the surrounding parcels of land into residential home sites to create a community now called Cotton Point Estates.[4]

When it was reported that Nixon sold his California home, the General Services Administration of the U.S Government demanded that the ex-president reimburse them in the amount of $703,367 for items that were installed on the La Casa Pacifica property for post-presidential operations and security. The GSA claimed the items were abandoned by Nixon when he moved, and the costs for those upgrades now needed to be repaid. These items that Nixon had installed were a $6,600 gazebo, a $13,500 heating system, $217,006 for lighting and electronics, $137,623 for landscaping, $2,300 for a flagpole, in addition to many other upgrades to the house that were installed by the Secret Service and other government contractors for security and to facilitate the operations and duties of an ex-president.

Nixon refused the demand by the General Services Administration and countered with a public notice for the agency to remove the unwanted items and restore the home to its original condition within sixty days. He also sent a check to the GSA for $2,300 for repayment of the flagpole fee. Nixon claimed the Secret Service insisted on the upgrades to the property. His belligerence paid off, and the GSA desisted.

Finding suitable housing accommodations in New York City for the ex-president and his wife would be a tricky task. The first co-op that the presidential couple wanted to purchase on Madison Avenue didn't want the exposure that a disgraced ex-president would bring to the building, so they were denied admittance. The couple was also denied the ability to purchase another choice New York City property after the building residents joined forces and voted to deny Richard and Pat Nixon's application for residency. George Leisure told a reporter at the time, "Everyone signed against them. Money's not enough here."

On August 10, 1979, the Nixon's found a townhouse to buy at 142 East 65th Street, on the Upper East Side, for $750,000, next door to David Rockefeller and other notable power brokers. It was a more suitable location for a man who was accustomed to socializing with world leaders.

After only eighteen months in New York City, the Nixons sold their townhouse and bought a home in Saddle River, New Jersey, where they had found a home within a peaceful community that was away from the big, loud, and crowded city and that also afforded them quick and easy access to Washington, DC and New York City. Pat and Richard Nixon entertained visiting kings, foreign ambassadors, and, most importantly, their grandchildren in their Saddle River home.[5] The GSA provided office space at 26 Federal Plaza in Manhattan. Nixon would ultimately give up his Secret Service protection saving taxpayers millions.

Given his well-known aversion to the press, it was surprising that Nixon asked me to arrange a series of small dinners with select reporters for background discussions on politics and foreign affairs. "I want guys who don't remember Hiss," Nixon said.

Nixon published his memoir, *RN: The Memoirs of Richard Nixon,* in 1978, the first of ten books he was to author after leaving the White House. This was followed by a series of foreign policy tomes that outlined Nixon's views on the future of US relations with Russia, China, and the Middle East. Nixon visited the White House in 1979, invited by President Jimmy Carter for the state dinner honoring Chinese Vice Premier Deng Xiaoping. Carter initially refused to invite Nixon, but Deng said he would visit Nixon in California if the former president was not invited. Nixon had a private meeting with Deng and visited Beijing again in mid-1979.

When the former Shah of Iran died in Egypt in July 1980, Nixon defied the State Department, which intended to send no US representative, by attending the funeral. Though Nixon had no official credentials, as a former president he was seen as the US presence at the funeral of an ally.

Throughout the 1980s, Nixon maintained an ambitious schedule of speaking, writing and foreign travel. He met with many third-world leaders. He joined Presidents Ford and Carter as US representatives at the funeral of Egyptian President Anwar Sadat. On a trip to the Middle East, Nixon made his views known regarding Saudi Arabia and Libya, which attracted significant US media attention. Nixon journeyed to the Soviet Union in 1986 and on his return sent President Reagan a lengthy memorandum containing foreign policy reommendations and his personal impressions of Soviet Leader Mikhail Gorbachev. Nixon connected with Soviet reformer Boris Yeltsin after the fall of the Iron Curtain. Yelstsin aide Michael Caputo told me, "Yeltsin was getting political advice from Nixon on what to do in the former Soviet Union and in the US." They were on the phone constantly. Yeltsin sent messages to Clinton through Nixon.

The *Washington Post* ran stories on Nixon's "rehabilitation." In 1986, Nixon was ranked in a Gallup poll as one of the ten most admired men in the world. Around this time Nixon gave a tour-de-force speech to the American Newspaper Publishers' Association. Political pundit Elizabeth Drew wrote, "Even when he was wrong, Nixon still showed that he knew a great deal and had a capacious memory, as well as the capacity to speak with apparent authority, enough to impress people who had little regard for him in earlier times." *Washington Post* publisher Katherine Graham shook Nixon's hand and ordered a three-page spread called the "Sage of Saddle River."

Although Nixon had served as a back-channel foreign policy and political advisor for Ronald Reagan, his contacts with President George H. W. Bush, who's ascendency he aided, were minor and formal. With the collapse of the Soviet Union and the emergence of China, Nixon set his sites on a dialogue with President Bill Clinton, who eventually defeated Bush in 1992.

Nixon understood the delicacy of the situation. He couldn't invite himself. He had to finagle Clinton into an invitation. He sent the message through Senator Bob Dole and Democratic strongman Robert Strauss.

These efforts were met with frustration, as Clinton was described as noncommittal when approached. That meeting was far more difficult to arrange than might be thought. At this point, I will step aside and let veteran newsman Martin Kalb, who was a good friend and solid journalist, tell the story in his book, *The Nixon Memo:*

"Ever since Clinton's election in November 1992, Nixon had been trying to see Clinton and ingratiate himself with the new administration. He realized that it would not be easy. Nixon and Clinton were poles apart in experience, in outlook, and in ideology. Nixon was a Cold War Republican, Clinton a baby-boomer Democrat. Nixon expanded the American war in Southeast Asia, Clinton marched in protest against it. Nixon personified

Watergate, Clinton's wife had worked for Nixon's impeachment on the staff of the House Judiciary Committee. Still, Nixon wrote Clinton a long, substantive, and thoughtful letter of congratulations. And in a November 19, 1992, op-ed piece in *The New York Times*, he praised Clinton for 'aggressively addressing a number of important issues during the transition period.'

"But if Nixon expected a quick response, he was to be disappointed. Shortly before Clinton's inauguration, in mid-January 1993, Nixon resumed his effort to make an impact on the president-elect. He got Roger Stone to send an 'urgent' message to Clinton— that the situation in Russia was 'very grave' and that Clinton was not getting the 'straight story' from the State Department, principally, Nixon said, because Baker was a roadblock. Again, there was no response fro Clinton or any of his aides.

"Immediately after the inauguration, Nixon, undaunted, sent another 'urgent' message to Clinton. This time Stone used Richard Morris, a pollster from Arkansas, as his intermediary. Stone told me that the Nixon message contained three points and what can only be construed as a whiff of political blackmail. First, Stone said that Clinton would find Nixon's perspective on Russia to be 'valuable.' Second, a Nixon-Clinton meeting would 'buy' the president a 'one-year moratorium' on Nixon criticism of his policy toward Bosnia and other matters. And third, a Clinton-Nixon meeting would generate Republican support for aid to Russia and possibly for a budget compromise on Capitol Hill. Stone continued, 'Morris told the Clintons that if Nixon was received at the White House, he couldn't come back and kick you in the teeth.'

"A few days later, on the eve of Nixon's February 1993 visit to Moscow, according to Stone, Morris called him and said that Clinton had agreed in principle to a meeting with Nixon, but no date had been set. Another week passed. Nixon, in Moscow, had met with Yeltsin and promised action. Stone called James Carville and Paul Begala, two of Clinton's closest political advisers, and urged that a date be fixed, especially since now Clinton could also benefit from a Nixon briefing on his meeting with Yeltsin. Begala immediately saw the political advantages of a meeting. In his mind there was no point in antagonizing Nixon, not when so much of the Clinton program rode on a degree of GOP cooperation on Capitol Hill.

"Prodded by Stone, Begala rode herd on the matter of the meeting. He told John Podesta, who managed the traffic flow into the Oval Office, to make certain that the three-point Nixon message reached the president's desk. 'You really ought to call him,' Begala advised. Yes, Clinton agreed, but again nothing happened.

"For his part, as days passed with no call from the White House, an increasingly frustrated Stone encouraged Nixon to 'bludgeon' Clinton in much the same way as he had Bush. During the Vietnam War, as president, Nixon had employed a tactic that French journalist Michel Tatu labeled 'credible irrationality,' Nixon's way of frightening the North Vietnamese into believing that he would be capable of doing anything to achieve his ends and they had better be accommodating. In this spirit he let Stone spread the work in Washington that he was losing his patience. Stone called Tony Coelho, a former Democratic congressman from California with superb contacts at the White House, and warned that Nixon was on the edge of exploding. The situation in Russia was desperate. Nixon had ideas—and a short fuse. Could Coelho help arrange a Nixon meeting with Clinton? The implication was clear: a meeting would buy time, information, and maybe cooperation; further delay would buy upheaval in Russia and political confrontation at home.

"Nixon also sniffed the political and journalistic winds and figured that, along with the private pressure, it was time for him to go public again. He decided that another 'shot across the bow,' as Stone put it, was now in order. It was to be a warning shot at the new administration that Nixon had to be recognized as a player in policy deliberations on Russia and Yeltsin. Once again, the shot was to be fired from the op-ed page of the *New York Times*. Stone later recalled warning his White House contacts that the 'piece could be gentle or not so gentle.'"[6]

When I approached both James Carville and Paul Begala, solid practitioners of the political craft and friends, they both said the president was receptive and said he would reach out to the thirty-seventh president. But the call did not come. Clinton advisor Dick Morris learned that Hillary was blocking the initiative, and it was Morris who would break the logjam by arguing that protocol would eliminate Nixon as a critic of the administration if he was received in a respectful way and that Clinton's liberal bona fides allowed him to safely reach out to the ex-president. "If only Nixon can go to China, only Clinton can invite Nixon," Morris successfully argued. Nixon was delighted when the invitation came.

After Nixon's death, here is what I wrote for *The New York Times:*

"So what did you think of him?" I asked Richard Nixon after his first meeting with Bill Clinton.

"You know," Mr. Nixon replied, "he came from dirt and I came from dirt. He lost a gubernatorial race and came back to win the Presidency, and I lost a gubernatorial race and came back to win the Presidency. He overcame a scandal in his first campaign for national office and I overcame a scandal in my first national campaign. We both just gutted it out. He was an outsider from the South and I was an outsider from the West."

Thus the 37th President revealed the special kinship he felt with the 42nd, despite their differences in party, philosophy and generation. And Mr. Nixon had a special reason to reach out: he was so deeply committed to the cause of increasing U.S. aid for the emerging republics of the former Soviet Union that he violated his own ironclad rule in dealing with successors—to give advice only when asked.

Mr. Nixon had dark suspicions that Hillary Rodham Clinton was blocking him; in 1974 she had served on the staff of the House committee that recommended impeaching him. More likely, the all-consuming confusion of a new Presidency was to blame. In any event, the call finally did come, and a few days later, on March

8, 1993, the two men met in the living room of the White House family quarters for a long private talk about aid to Russia.

It was a moment Mr. Nixon had foreseen. In 1992 he heard through the grapevine that President George Bush's strategists were weighing inviting him to the Republican National Convention. Mr. Nixon reviewed his options with me. "I could go to the convention and give a speech praising Bush," he said, "but that would be boring, and the only thing worse in politics than being wrong is being boring. I could go to the convention and deliver a rip-snorting attack on Clinton. If I do that and Clinton is elected, it would be very hard for me to reach out to him on the situation in Russia."

Although Mr. Nixon wanted badly to be accepted again at his party's convention, he issued a statement that afternoon that he would not attend and did not wish to be invited.

In the end, Mr. Nixon came to like Mr. Clinton and had enormous respect for his political talents. "You know that bit he does where he bites his lip and looks like he is pondering the question?" he asked me. "I think it's practiced, but let me tell you, it's great television."

He thought the Whitewater affair could pose serious problems. When I pointed out that the poll numbers reflected no damage to Mr. Clinton's popularity, Mr. Nixon observed that Watergate had not hurt him either, until the televised Senate hearings. "The American people don't believe anything's real until they see it on television," he said. "When Whitewater hearings are televised, it will be Clinton's turn in the bucket."

Perhaps. But if Mr. Nixon's advice to his young successor provides for a surer American foreign policy and increases the chances of peace, then we all profited more than either of them.

—*New York Times*, April 28, 1994

The two presidents forged a solid bond of respect and admiration toward each other during the time Clinton was in office. Nixon often praised him for his political talents, but he thought some of his tactics were staged. He told me, "I think it's practiced, but let me tell you, it's great television."

Nixon blamed Hillary Clinton for blocking his early attempts to meet with the president calling her a "red hot," a term used to describe extreme leftists in the 1950s. In 1974 Hillary Clinton was a staff lawyer for the House of Representatives Judicial Impeachment Inquiry Committee, which was responsible for investigating whether or not there was enough evidence to impeach or prosecute President Nixon for the Watergate affair. Hillary had been fired for her role in writing fraudulent legal briefs, lying to investigators, and confiscating public documents to hide her deception and conspiring to hinder the defense of Richard Nixon. "She was out to get me," the former president told me when he called to brief me on his White House visit. "He [Clinton] really appreciates my help and he's much smarter than Bush," Nixon said ebulliently. Clearly, Nixon thought he was in play again, despite Hillary's best efforts.

Hillary's actual role in 1974 bears examination. Hillary began her political career at Yale Law School, where she was a close confidant of her political professor, Mr. Burke Marshall, the chief political strategist for the Kennedys.

Mr. Marshall helped Hillary get her job as a congressional staff lawyer, which then allowed him to place her in the Watergate investigative committee through his close connections to the Democrat chairman of the House Judiciary Committee, Peter Rodino, a congressman from New Jersey.

Hillary's placement as a House of Representatives lawyer allowed Marshall to then inject her into the Judiciary Committee that was investigating Watergate. In addition to Hillary, there were two other close allies of Marshall that were also added to the Nixon impeachment inquiry staff to harm Nixon's defense. They were John Doar, who was Marshall's deputy when he was in the Justice Department and whom Rodino appointed as head of the impeachment inquiry staff, and the other was Bernard Nussbaum, who was assistant US attorney in New York and a close friend of Rodino's. Nussbaum was placed in charge of directing the investigation into Watergate and Nixon's potential prosecution.

It was a partisan project that Hillary Clinton, a twenty-seven year old staffer on the House Judiciary Committee, helped coordinate with senior Democratic leaders to manipulate the political process and strip President Nixon of his constitutional rights to a fair hearing.

Hillary's boss, Jerry Zeifman, the general counsel and chief of staff to the House Judiciary Investigative Committee during the Watergate hearings, fired Hillary after it was uncovered that Clinton was working to impede the investigation and undermine Nixon's defense. He told Fox News that "Hillary's lies and unethical behavior goes back farther—and goes much deeper—than anyone realizes." Zeifman maintains that he fired Hillary "for unethical behavior and that she conspired to deny Richard Nixon counsel during the hearings."

When asked why he fired Clinton, Zeifman responded, "Because she is a liar." "She was an unethical, dishonest lawyer. She conspired to violate the Constitution, the rules of the House, the rules of the committee and the rules of confidentiality."[7]

Zeifman wrote candidly about his encounter with a young Hillary Clinton when she worked for him as a staff lawyer. He mentioned a number of facts that he thought people should know about how the prospective presidential contender conducts herself. He said, "Because of a number of her unethical practices I decided that I could not recommend her for any subsequent position of public or private trust." Other Judiciary Committee staffers who worked with Clinton, such as Franklin Polk, the chief Republican counsel on the committee, have confirmed many of the details of what Zeifman has reported.

Zeifman stated, "Nixon clearly had right to counsel, but Hillary, along with Marshall, Nussbaum and Doar, was determined to gain enough votes on the Judiciary Committee to change House rules and deny counsel to Nixon. And in order to pull this off, Hillary wrote a fraudulent legal brief, and confiscated public documents to hide her deception."[8] When Nixon was leaving the Clinton White

House after a three-hour discussion with the loquacious Arkansan, Hillary greeted him as he left. "How did you find her?" I asked. "Cold, cold as ice," Nixon said.

In 2013, Hillary would show her disdain for Nixon in a discussion with an all-woman group over a glass of wine at a restaurant and tavern, La Jardin Du Roi, near her palatial home in Chappaqua. "The IRS targeting the Tea Party, the Justice Department's seizure of AP phone records and [Fox reporter] James Rosen's e-mails— all these scandals. Obama's allowed his hatred for his enemies to screw him the way Nixon did," Hillary said.

During one trip to Moscow, Nixon had a meeting and long discussions with Russian leader Mikhail Gorbachev. When he came back to the United States, Nixon reported to President Ronald Reagan in a long and detailed memorandum to explain his findings and to offer his suggestions for future diplomatic relations between America and the Soviet Union. Reagan depended on Nixon's experience and knowledge of world matters.[9]

Nixon wrote in his memoirs, "I felt that the relationship between the United States and the Soviet Union would probably be the single most important factor in determining whether the world would live at peace during and after my administration. I felt that we had allowed ourselves to get in a disadvantageous position vis-à-vis the Soviets."

* * *

The story of Richard Millhous Nixon ended where it began—in Yorba Linda, California—the city where he was born and where he was laid to rest. The thought of being buried in his birth town, near his childhood home, kept him grounded.

He often reminisced about how great it was to grow up in the small Orange, County, California town. He felt fortunate to have lived his younger years there. When he had to make the decision of where his presidential library and museum would be located, there was nothing to ponder. In his mind, it was always going to be

Yorba Linda, although some aides tried to convince him to build it closer to his La Casa Pacifica residence in San Clemente, but Nixon knew that he would not own the coastal estate forever. For him, Yorba Linda was the obvious choice for his presidential museum and library.

Between 1984 and 1990, the Nixon Foundation raised $26 million in private funds to develop the library and museum site. He wanted to build it next door to the small wooden farmhouse that his father built and where the future president had discovered his passion for politics. The Nixon Foundation is a nonprofit institution that was formed by the former president to fund the construction of his library and to educate the public about the life, legacy and times of the thirty-seventh president of the United States. The library was dedicated on July 19, 1990, with the help of three US presidents who served after Nixon, who where there to honor the ex-president.

"What you will see here, among other things, is a personal life," Nixon said at the dedication ceremony. "The influence of a strong family, of inspirational ministers, of great teachers. You will see a political life, running for Congress, running for the Senate, running for governor, running for president three times. And you will see the life of a great nation, 77 years of it—a period in which we had unprecedented progress for the United States. And you will see great leaders, leaders who changed the world, who helped make the world what we have today."

Inside the museum, the tour began with a timeline of Nixon's family history and accomplishments then proceeded to show the ex-president, as he was—a complicated, introverted, determined politician and statesman. Critics claimed the depiction of Nixon's life and legacy were one-sided and minimized the mistakes of Watergate while emphasizing Nixon's accomplishment's in the foreign and domestic realm. Each year, the library and museum feature domestic and foreign policy conferences, educational classes for schools, town meetings, editorial forums, and a full schedule of highly acclaimed authors and speakers who discuss government, media, politics, and public affairs.

The museum and library were originally designed, developed, and operated by the private Nixon Foundation, but it is now administered by the National Archives. The exhibits became much more "balanced" once the National Archives took control in 2007.

The takeover of the presidential library by the National Archives added a lot of content to the museum and library, but it also changed the tone of the exhibits. There is now much more attention to the negative side of Nixon's career than what the presidential library initially displayed when Nixon's family and friends were running it. I think the dispute over content will be a constant and ongoing battle between the Nixon family and the National Archives.

The nine-acre library and museum grounds contain the birthplace and restored childhood home of Richard Nixon, a 3-D walk-through display of twenty-two separate informational galleries, each showcasing a separate part of the president's life. There are interactive theaters, a "First Lady's" garden, a full-sized replica of the East Room of the White House and a high-tech performing arts center for stage performances and educational seminars. There is also a replica of the Lincoln sitting room and the presidential office—all of which are overlooking a large reflecting pool that is surrounded by an outdoor ceremonial pavilion.

Nixon's helicopter is also on display. Marine One (also known as Army One if Army pilots are in command of the rotorcraft) has been painstakingly restored to its original condition, as it was when it was in service as the presidential helicopter. It's the same helicopter that Nixon used on more than 180 trips while serving as president, and then used one last time when he was no longer commander in chief so he could fly home to sunny California, by way of Andrew's Air Force base, in Maryland. On departure, he boarded the helicopter on the White House south lawn then raised his arms in the victory position, waved to the crowd a fond farewell, and disappeared into the belly of the aircraft.

The sixteen-passenger "Sea King" helicopter was used in past administrations by President Kennedy, President Johnson, and President Ford, who all used this same presidential helicopter as their primary mode of airborne transport while in Washington. It's a significant piece of aviation history, appropriately placed on permanent display on the grounds of the Nixon museum.

Surprisingly not among the exhibits is the presidential limousine 100-X, which President Kennedy was shot in. Johnson had ordered the limo cleaned inside and out within hours of Kennedy's death and then had it shipped on November 25th to Detroit for "refurbishment."

Nixon himself would order the car repainted and used it extensively during his presidency.

Nixon's association with Camelot, even with the man defeated by it in 1960 would endure.

The library holds over 6 million pages of records, 19,000 still photographs, 150 reels of film, 900 audio recordings of Nixon speeches, plus 3,000 books in addition to the National Archives collection that has recently been added, to include another 42 million pages of records, 300,000 pictures, over 30,000 gifts that were given to Nixon, 4,700 hours of video recordings, and almost 4,000 hours of White House tape recordings.[10]

The presidency of Richard Nixon is probably the most documented of any other president. The movies, pictures, documents, and testimonials that have been retained of Nixon and that are on display at the presidential library and museum provide a rare perspective into the life and personality of a complicated man, who despite his many challenges, rose to the position of leader of the free world.

* * *

Resilience is the quality that best characterized Richard Nixon. Just as be began plotting his comeback bid for the American presidency the day after his razor-thin defeat by John Kennedy, I am convinced that Nixon began plotting his final campaign for elder statesman the day after he resigned the presidency in 1974.

In 1960, I scotch-taped a *Saturday Evening Post* cover portrait of Richard Nixon by Norman Rockwell to my bedroom door. I cried after staying up all night and learning that Nixon had narrowly lost the presidency the next morning. I defiantly wore Nixon-Lodge buttons to school for two weeks after the election. Although I was a gopher in his 1968 campaign and a very junior aide in his 1972 campaign, it was not until his post-presidential years that I got to know Richard Nixon and was drafted as an operative in his final campaign.

Nixon would have us believe that there was no final campaign for redemption, but in retrospect Nixon's last campaign was more measured, more painstaking, and more difficult than his comeback bid for the presidency.

I recall riding to midtown Manhattan with Nixon to attend a New York State Republican Party fundraiser at which Nixon was to be the guest of honor. It was to be his first foray in public for a political event after his resignation, and Nixon was uncertain how he would be received. Before he opened the car door, he looked me in the eye and said, "I hope this isn't too soon." The event was a triumphant success.

Nixon understood that the success of his resurrection would be contingent on his never reaching for an official role and by meting out his opinions on a judicious and measured basis. "Don't accept every speaking request and every request for an interview," he told Jeanne Kirkpatrick when she left federal service. "Speak out only when you have something to say."

When Nixon charmed Katherine Graham at the newspaper editor's association luncheon in his post-presidential years, the publisher directed *Newsweek* to secure an interview for a cover story. It was left to me to negotiate the details. Nixon agreed, and the interview was scheduled. When Chernobyl blew up, the *Newsweek* people said they would run the interview, but would put the Soviet disaster on the cover. Nixon's directions to me to be forwarded to the editors were firm and precise. No cover—no interview.

The cover ran, with the headline, "He's Back."

Nixon knew that he was relegated to a backstage role in American politics, but he played that role with enthusiasm and tenacity. When Ronald Reagan muffled his first debate with challenger Walter Mondale, Nixon calmly assured Reagan aides that the poll numbers would stabilize, the expectation for Mondale in the second debate would soar, that expectations for Reagan would drop, and that Gipper could put Mondale away with a deft one-liner. That's exactly what happened.

After months of badgering George Bush to attend a Soviet-American relations conference that Nixon put together in Washington, DC, Nixon secured Bush's acceptance and then directed me to leak a memo to the *New York Times* that outlined Nixon's belief that the Bush-Baker response to the Soviets need for aid was anemic. The *Times* ran with the story, and Bush was forced to haplessly agree with Nixon when he stood up to speak at the conference, where Nixon and deftly scheduled Bush to speak immediately after himself.

Taught by his Quaker mother not to display his emotions in pubic, Nixon was a man who kept his affection deeply in check. When I married in 1991, Nixon sent my wife and me a leather -bound edition of his book. *In the Arena* with the inscription, "To Roger and Nydia Stone—With best wishes for the year ahead," after which he wrote "Love," scratched it out, rethought it, wrote it again, and signed "Richard Nixon."

I spoke to President Nixon three times in the week before his stroke. He was intensely interested in the political repercussions of the Whitewater affair. When poll numbers seemed to indicate that the scandal was having little effect on Clinton's popularity, Nixon pointed out to me that Watergate had little impact on the voters until the televised hearings. "The American people don't believe anything until they see it on television. Eighty percent of the people receive their news from TV and when the Whitewater hearing is televised it will be Clinton's turn in the bucket."

When he died, Richard Nixon was a man content with his place in the world. Savoring his final victory and his elevation to elder statesman, his books were bestellers, he received thousands of invitations to speak, the media jockeyed to get his thoughts on the record, President Clinton consulted him on foreign policy matters, and he bathed in the love of his children and grandchildren.

Richard Nixon unexpectedly died of a stroke on April 22, 1994 at the age of eighty-one, just fourteen months after his wife, Pat, died of lung cancer.

When I first got word that Richard Nixon had passed away, I was shell-shocked. The man had so much strength left in him, I thought he would live another decade. Nonetheless, he was gone, and I needed to attend to my duties as his friend.

My phone began ringing relentlessly almost immediately after I heard of Nixon's passing. Reporters wanted quotes, TV shows wanted interviews, but all I wanted to do was be in a quiet place by myself, and grieve. It would be another month or so before I actually had an opportunity to sit down and really reflect on my career with Richard Nixon, but I felt responsible as his closest political confidant before his death, to answer all of the questions that were asked of me, although I didn't accept every interview request, purely out of deference to Nixon's old rule.

In his final "fuck you" to the Washington establishment, Nixon ordered that his body not lie in State in the Capitol Rotunda, as had the remains of Johnson, Kennedy, Eisenhower, and Truman.

Richard Nixon was buried in Yorba Linda, California, on April 27, 1994—the place of his birth, and the location where the Nixon Presidential Library and Museum is located. He was laid to rest on a plot next to his wife, Pat. He told me once that it felt fitting for him to be buried where he was born and where he grew up.

Henry Kissinger, Senator Bob Dole, former Presidents Ronald Reagan and Gerald Ford and President Bill Clinton attended the funeral to pay their respects.

The funeral service prompted some displays of emotion from men who rarely expose their softer side. Bob Dole was moved to tears during his eulogy. He said, "I believe the second half of the twenty-first century, will be known as the age of Nixon. He provided the most effective leadership. He always embodied the deepest feeling for the people he led." To tens of millions of his countrymen, Richard Nixon was an American hero—one who shared and honored their belief in working hard, worshiping God, loving their families, and saluting the flag. He called them the Silent Majority. Like them, they valued accomplishment more than ideology. They wanted their government to do the decent thing, but not to bankrupt them in the process. They wanted his protection in a dangerous world. These were the people from whom he had come, and they have come to Yorba Linda these last few days, in the tens of thousands, no longer silent in their grief. The American people like a fighter. In Richard Nixon they found a gallant one."

Dole then reminded us of a few very eloquent words Nixon once spoke: "You must never be satisfied with success. And you should never be discouraged by failure. Failure can be sad. But the greatest sadness is not to try and fail, but to fail to try. In the end, what matters is that you have always lived life to the hilt." Dole proclaimed that Nixon was strong, brave, and unafraid of controversy, unyielding in his conviction—and that he lived every day of his life to the hilt. In his closing remarks, Dole said, "The man who was born in the house his father built would become the world's greatest architect of peace, the largest figure of our time whose influence will be timeless. That was Richard Nixon. How American. May God bless Richard Nixon, and may God bless the United States."

Former Secretary of State Henry Kissinger gave some details about how Nixon shaped foreign affairs. He said, "He came into office when the forces of history were moving America from a position of dominance to one of leadership. Dominance reflects strength; leadership must be earned. And Richard Nixon earned that leadership role for his country with courage, dedications, and skill. The price for doing things halfway is no less than for doing it completely, so we might as well do them properly."

It was, however, the eulogy of President Clinton that Nixon would have enjoyed the most because it signified Nixon's success in his final rehabilitation. Clinton remembered Nixon as being a spirited politician. Clinton said, "He never gave up being part of the action. He said many times that unless a person has a goal, a new mountain to climb, his spirit will die. Well, based on our last phone conversations and the letter he wrote me just a month ago, I can say that his spirit was very much alive until the very end. On behalf of all four former presidents who are here; President Ford, President Carter, President Reagan, President Bush, and behalf of a grateful nation we bid farewell to Richard Milhous Nixon. May the day of judging President Nixon on anything but his entire life come to a close."

Henry Kissinger's biographer, Walter Isaacson, summed it up better than most. He said that his experience with Nixon impressed him as "a very complex man in everything he did, and there was a light side to him, there was a brilliance side to him, and there was a brooding side. And I think sometimes when he had the advisors appeal to his good side, he was able to do very good things."[11]

Nixons' death brought accolades from strange quarters.

Bill Clinton added, "He suffered defeats that would have ended most political careers, yet he won stunning victories that many of the worlds most popular leaders have failed to attain."[12] Rev. Billy Graham: "He was one of the most misunderstood men, and I think he was one of the greatest men of the century."[13] Boris Yelstin (Russian Leader): "One of the greatest politicians in the world."[14] John Sears: "The picture I have of him is a mosaic, an image formed from a series of vignettes often so unexpected they can never be forgotten."[15] Nixon biographer Stephen Ambrose: "Nixon was "the most successful American politician of the twentieth century."[16]

White House speech writer Ben Stein, whose father Herbert Stein was chairman of the Council of Economic Advisers under Nixon, recently said, "Let's look at him with fresh eyes. Unlike LBJ, he did not get us into a large, unnecessary war on false pretenses. Unlike JFK, he did not bring call girls and courtesans into the White House or try to kill foreign leaders. Unlike FDR, he did not lead us into a war for which we were unprepared.

He helped with a cover-up of a mysterious burglary that no one understands to this day. That was his grievous sin, and grievously did he answer for it. But to me, Richard Nixon will always be visionary, friend, and peacemaker."

Carl Bernstein: "Nixon defined the postwar era for America, and he defined the television era for America."[17] President Jimmy Carter: "His historic visits to China and the Soviet Union paved the way to the normalization of relations between our countries."[18] Former President Ronald Reagan: "There is no question that the legacy of this complicated and fascinating man will continue to guide the forces of democracy forever."[19] Even his 1972 opponent George McGovern said, "Not too many people could psychologically withstand being thrown out of the White House. It takes an enormous amount of self-discipline that I had to recognize as remarkable."[20] Not all remembrances of Nixon were favorable. Gonzo Journalist Hunter S. Thompson wrote shortly after Nixon's death: "If the right people had been in charge of Nixon's funeral, his casket would have been launched into one of those open-sewage canals that empty into the ocean just south of Los Angeles."[21] Thompson, a lifelong hater of Nixon, amid the bile, also recognized Nixon's special brand of resilience. "As long as Nixon was politically alive—and he was, all the way to the end—we could always be sure of finding the enemy on the Low Road," wrote Thompson. "There was no need to look anywhere else for the evil bastard. He had the fighting instincts of a badger trapped by hounds. The badger will roll over on its back and emit a smell of death, which confuses the dogs and lures them in for the traditional ripping and tearing action. But it is usually the badger who does the ripping and tearing. It is a beast that fights best on its back: rolling under the throat of the enemy and seizing it by the head with all four claws."[22]

I summed up my one special memory of Nixon for *Newsweek*: "Working for Richard Nixon was like working for the mafia. You never really left and you never knew when you might be called on to perform a political chore."[23] Nixon achieved his goals of a more peaceful world and a lessening of tensions with America's enemies. He built a government at once more compassionate and progressive than anyone would have imagined.

Driven from office by his terrible secrets; his approval of the CIA-Mafia plots to kill Castro, the Bay of Pigs, his reliance, along with virtually every national politician of the 1950s and 1960s, on mafia funding, the bribes he had taken from the Teamsters, his contretemps with the CIA, his knowledge of what really happened in Dallas and who was involved secured him a pardon in order to avoid prison and launch his greatest public comeback.

In 1986 the filmmaker Oliver Stone was producing his much-heralded film on Richard Nixon. After conferring with Nixon associates Garment and Ziegler, Oliver Stone made John Sears one of his chief consultants on the project; recognition that Sears's unique perspective on the Nixon psyche was vital.

Nixon friends feared the film would be a hatchet job. Instead, it is one of the most compelling films in the Stone *ouevre* presenting a surprisingly balanced portrait of the president. Actor Anthony Hopkins's portrayal of Nixon was distinctly sympathetic. Stone even had Nixon standing up to a fictional conspiracy of rich men who had helped put him in office. Sears had shaped the movie as much as he had shaped the reporting of Woodward and Bernstein.

The release of the film was accompanied by a book comprised of the screenplay and some essays, one of them by Sears. "Nixon," Sears wrote, "was the loner produced by a nation of loners. That was the reason the country could not forgive Nixon for his illegal acts, even though others had done the same. We are a land of loners and our only protection is the law. Did I want him to escape at the time?" Sears asked rhetorically. "Yes. Did I think he would? No."

But was Nixon, on balance, worth it for the country? "I would submit," Sears wrote, "that if the world survives for a million years, perhaps its finest hour may be that in the last half of the twentieth century, when the power to blow up the world rested in the hands of a few men in two very unsophisticated and suspicious countries, we didn't do it, and one American, Richard Nixon, moved the Cold War away from permanent confrontation toward victory. How can any wrong that he did compare with that?"

Richard Nixon won his final campaign.

NOTES

1. Barry Goldwater, *Goldwater*, p. 282.
2. Jonathan Aitken, *Nixon: A Life*, p. 529.
3. Malcolm MacDougall, *We Almost Made It*, p. 169.
4. Ashley Powers, "Nixon's Legacy Still Divides City," *LA Times*, http://articles.latimes.com/2007/jan/22/local/me-nixonwall22.
5. Stephen Ambrose, *Nixon: Ruin and Recovery*, pp. 527–528.
6. "CBS Evening News," April 27, 1994, interview with Rita Braver.
7. http://nation.foxnews.com/2014/02/25/hillary-fired-lies-unethical-behavior-congressional-job-former-boss.
8. Jerry Zeifman, "Crocodile Tears in Connecticut," http://www.aim.org/aim-column/hillarys-crocodile-tears-in-connecticut.
9. http://www.nixonlibrary.gov/thelife/postpresidency.php.
10. http://www.nixonlibrary.gov.
11. CNN *Crossfire* transcript #1080, April 27, 1994.
12. April 4, 1994.
13. *The Washington Post*, April 22, 1994.
14. *The New York Times*, April 23, 1994.
15. *Los Angeles Times*, April 24, 1994.
16. *CBS This Morning*, April 25, 1994.
17. *The Washington Post*, April 25, 1994.

18. *The Washington Post*, April 23, 1994.
19. *Dallas Morning News*, April 23, 1994.
20. *U.S. News*, May 2, 1994.
21. Hunter Thompson, "He Was a Crook," *Rolling Stone*, June 16, 1994.
22. Ibid.
23. Roger Stone, "Remembering Nixon," *Newsweek*, April 22, 1994.

APPENDIX 1

28 November 1967

FROM: RAY PRICE

SUBJ: RECOMMENDATIONS FOR GENERAL STRATEGY FROM NOW THROUGH WISCONSIN

We enter with these factors in the equation:

1) RN is the front-runner, maintaining or increasing strength in the polls with relatively little activity.
2) We can't be sure how solid this support is (e.g., the New Hampshire attitude that he's a good man but probably can't win, thus their votes are really being cast away—or cast for LBJ).
3) Romney is certain to conduct a high-intensity campaign, with a lot of street cornering and probably a lot of TV. This has apparently been effective in Michigan; whether it's transferable to a 1968 Presidential campaign is another question.
4) Rockefeller and Reagan continue to exercise their attractions from the sidelines. Rockefeller's strength derives principally from RN's can't-win image. He's riding high, not particularly because people like him, but because they've

been told (which is something other than thinking) that he can win and that he thus is the only realistic alternative to LBJ. At this stage of the game, poll results don't particularly show what voters think about a candidate; they reflect in large measure what they've been told. They haven't begun thinking that intensively. Reagan's strength derives from personal charisma, glamor, but primarily the ideological fervor of the Right and the emotional distress of those who fear or resent the Negro, and who expect Reagan somehow to keep him "in his place"—or at least to echo their own anger and frustration.

RN is the overwhelming favorite of the delegate types; if we can lick the can't-win thing we've got it made. This is the one possible obstacle between RN and the nomination. Thus the whole thrust of our effort should be aimed at erasing this image. How? To answer this, we have to analyze the image.

Basically, it divides into two parts:
   a) He lost his last two elections.
   b) He somehow "feels" like a loser.

We can't alter the facts of (a), and probably our capacity to get people to look at those facts realistically is limited. We can make any number of powerful arguments about the way in which those results should be interpreted: in 1960, one of the closest races in history against one of the most charismatic of American political figures, the effect of the Catholic issue, vote-stealing, defending the Eisenhower record, etc.; and in 1962, the bitter split in the California Republican party, the fact that he wasn't credible as a mere governor (too big for the job, and he showed it), etc. But politics is only minimally a rational science, and no matter how compelling these arguments—even if we can get people to sit down and listen to them—they'll only be effective if we can get the people to make the emotional leap, or what theologians call "the leap of faith." If we can make them feel that he's got the aura of a winner, they'll rationalize away the past defeats by themselves; if we can't make them feel that, no matter what the rational explanations, they'll pull down the mental blind marked with those simple words, "he lost."

The natural human use of reason is to support prejudices, not to arrive at opinions.

Then how do we attack (b)—the notion that he "feels" like a loser?

First, we bear in mind that to a lot of people he feels like a winner. It's the others we have to worry about. And we might oversimplify by dividing these into two basic groups: 1) those who themselves feel there's "something about him I don't like," or "something about him that spells loser"; and 2) those who themselves react altogether positively, but consider him a loser-type because of the way others react to him. The line between these two groups, of course, isn't sharp; and again we have to bear in mind that most people's reactions to most public figures are a mixture of positives and negatives. But for purposes of analysis, we can proceed from this division.

Polls showing RN substantially ahead can be of considerable use, particularly with those of Group (2). But there's a caveat here: poll strength is bound to fluctuate, and to the extent that our defenses against "can't-win" are built on polls, they're insecure. A slight downturn then could have a snowball effect. But if we can erase the feeling of "can't-win," then we can survive a substantial buffeting by the polls.

The hard core of the problem lies with those who themselves feel there's "loser" somehow written on him—i.e., with Group (1). If we can get these, we'll automatically get Group (2).

Again, we might divide the factors entering into the "can't-win" feeling into two broad categories: (a) historical, and (b) personal. The historical factors would, of course, include the fact of the two losses, but they run deeper. In a sense, they're all wrapped up in the fact that for years Nixon was one of those men it was fashionable to hate. It might take people a moment to remember why they were supposed to hate him, but they do remember that they were. Even in communities where he was locally popular, it was well known that he was hated elsewhere—and particularly in many of the best circles.

Generally, the sources of this hate centered around the way he practiced, or was alleged to practice, his political craft. Whatever the strange complex of passions that went into the hysterical anti-anti-communism of the postwar and McCarthy years; whatever the emotional responses of those who disliked his style, the essence of the objections lay in Nixon's cutting edge. He was viewed as a partisan figure first, a national figure second; as devious and unfair in his debating tactics—a master of unsupported innuendo, etc.

Let's leave realities aside—because what we have to deal with now is not the facts of history, but an image of history. The history we have to be concerned with is not what happened, but what's remembered, which may be quite different. Or, to put it another way, the historical untruth may be a political reality. We can't do anything about what did happen, and there's not much we can directly do about people's impressions of what happened; for better or for worse, these are part of the political folklore. Thus what we have to do is to persuade people that they're irrelevant to 1968. How? This has three prongs:

1 The passage of time; this has clearly worked in our favor. The sharp edge of memory has dulled, the image has mellowed; people don't maintain their passions forever. Also, Stewart Alsop makes an interesting point in his 1960 book, *Nixon and*

Rockefeller: that with a couple of minor exceptions, "after 1954 the anti-Nixon dossier dwindles away into almost nothing at all . . . The fact is that, since 1954, Nixon has very rarely gone too far, although the provocation has often been great." (pp. 152–53)

2 A dawning recognition on the part of some voters that they (or the chroniclers) might have been wrong, and that maybe the horror stories weren't all true after all; and

3 The natural phenomenon of growth. This is where I think there's the most gold to be mined. People understand growth, readily and instinctively; they expect people to mellow as they mature, and to learn from experience. Particularly in the case of a person with RN's recognized ability and intelligence, they'd be surprised if he didn't grow and change with the years. This doesn't mean a "new Nixon"; it simply means the natural maturation of the same Nixon, and in this context it makes the leaving behind of the old stereotypes perfectly acceptable and understandable. The great advantage of the growth idea is that it doesn't require a former Nixon-hater to admit that he was wrong in order to become a Nixon supporter now; he can still cherish his prejudices of the past, he can still maintain his own sense of infallibility, even while he shifts his position on a Nixon candidacy.

But what of the personal factors, as opposed to the historical?

These tend to be more a gut reaction, unarticulated, non-analytical, a product of the particular chemistry between the voter and the image of the candidate. We have to be very clear on this point: that the response is to the image, not to the man, since 99 percent of the voters have no contact with the man. It's not what's there that counts, it's what's projected—and, carrying it one step further, it's not what he projects but rather what the voter receives. It's not the man we have to change, but rather the received impression. And this impression often depends more on the medium and its use than it does on the candidate himself.

Politics is much more emotional than it is rational, and this is particularly true of Presidential politics. People identify with a President in a way they do with no other public figure. Potential presidents are measured against an ideal that's a combination of leading man, God, father, hero, pope, king, with maybe just a touch of the avenging Furies thrown in. They want him to be larger than life, a living legend, and yet quintessentially human; someone to be held up to their children as a model; someone to be cherished by themselves as a revered member of the family, in somewhat the same way in which peasant families pray to the icon in the corner. Reverence goes where power is; it's no coincidence that there's such persistent confusion between love and fear in the whole history of man's relationship to his gods. Awe enters into it.

And we shouldn't credit the press with a substantially greater leaven of reason than the general public brings. The press may be better at rationalizing their prejudices, but the basic response remains an emotional one.

Selection of a President has to be an act of faith. It becomes increasingly so as the business of government becomes ever more incomprehensible to the average voter. This faith isn't achieved by reason; it's achieved by charisma, by a feeling of trust that can't be argued or reasoned, but that comes across in those silences that surround the words. The words are important—but less for what they actually say than for the sense they convey, for the impression they give of the man himself, his hopes, his standards, his competence; his intelligence, his essential humanness, and the directions of history he represents.

Most countries divide the functions of head of government (prime minister) and chief of state (king or president). We don't. The traditional "issues" type debates center on the role of the head of government, but I'm convinced that people vote more for a chief of state—and this is primarily an emotional identification, embracing both a man himself and a particular vision of the nation's ideals and its destiny.

All this is a roundabout way of getting at the point that we should be concentrating on building a received image of RN as the kind of man proud parents would ideally want their sons to grow up to be: a man who embodies the national ideal, its aspirations, its dreams, a man whose image the people want in their homes as a source of inspiration, and whose voice they want as the representative of their nation in the councils of the world, and of their generation in the pages of history.

That's what being a "winner" means, in Presidential terms.

What, then, does this mean in terms of our uses of time and of media between now and April 2?

For one thing, it means investing whatever time RN needs in order to work out firmly in his own mind that vision of the nation's future that he wants to be identified with. This is crucial. It goes beyond the choice of a slogan, beyond the choice of a few key "issues"; it's essential to the projection of RN as the man for the '70s.

Secondly, it suggests that we take the time and the money to experiment, in a controlled manner, with film and television techniques, with particular emphasis on pinpointing those controlled uses of the television medium that can best convey the image we want to get across.

I know the whole business of contrived image-mongering is repugnant to RN, with its implication of slick gimmicks and phony merchandising. But it's simply not true that honesty is its own salesman;

for example, it takes makeup to make a man look natural on TV. Similarly, it takes art to convey the truth from us to the viewer. And we have to bear constantly in mind that it's not what we say that counts, but what the listener hears; not what we project, but how the viewer receives the impression. I think it was Luce and Hadden, in their original prospectus for *Time*, who laid down the rule that it's not what the editors put into a magazine that counts, but what the readers get out of it—and that rule is just as applicable to us.

The TV medium itself introduces an element of distortion; in terms both of its effect on the candidate and of the often subliminal ways in which the image is received. And it inevitably is going to convey a partial image—thus ours is the task of finding how to control its use so the part that gets across is the part we want to have gotten across.

Our concentrated viewing of clips from the CBS library left a clear impression that RN comes across decidedly unevenly—sometimes rather badly, sometimes exceedingly well, and that the greater the element of informality and spontaneity the better he comes across. This spontaneity is difficult to get in the formal setting of a standard press conference or a set speech, when he's concentrating on the arrangement of words to convey a particular thought in a particular way. Apart from all the technical gimmicks, the key difference in LBJ's TV manner at his last press conference—and what really brought it off so stunningly—was that he was no longer trying to formulate sentences, in a precise and guarded manner; he gave the impression of being no longer self-conscious about his manner of expression, but rather seemed to have his mind fixed on the thing he was talking about. It was this apparent unselfconsciousness that unleashed the power of the man; and this unselfconsciousness is the essence of spontaneity. Suddenly, LBJ was transformed from a man with a can't-win television image to a man with a can-win image, and the lesson ought not to be lost on us.

We have to capture and capsule this spontaneity—and this means shooting RN in situations in which it's likely to emerge, then having a chance to edit the film so that the parts shown are the parts we want shown. We need to build a library of such shots, which then will be available for a variety of uses—and so that, in minimum time, we can put together a variety of one- or five-minute or longer films of the man in motion, with the idea of conveying a sense of his personality—the personality that most voters have simply not had a chance to see, or, if they have, have lost in the montage of other images that form their total perceptions of the man.

The Paul Niven show came across brilliantly, and it was a fine example of an appearance in which the circumstances were right: a relaxed, informal setting: a "conversation" rather than a *Meet the Press*–type adversary proceeding; sufficient time and scope to expand on the ideas presented; a chance to bring out the qualities of the man. The people who say Nixon "can't win" tend to have a two-dimensional, black-and-white image of him; this kind of show makes it possible to bring out a third dimension, and it's in this third dimension that the keys to victory lie.

In this third dimension, style and substance are inseparable. And the substantive essence is not whatever facts may be adduced (though facts are valuable), but the sense of attitudes and approaches which have been thought through, not only in depth, but also in terms of their relationship to those other processes of government and aspects of society that they may affect.

One of our great assets for 1968 is the sense that RN comes to the fray freshened by an experience rare among men in public life, and unique among those of his generation: after a meteoric rise, followed by eight years at the center of power and the grinding experience of a Presidential campaign, time as a private citizen to reflect on the lessons of public service, on the uses of power, on the directions of change—and in so doing to develop a perspective on the Presidency that no serious candidate in this century has had the chance to achieve. It's a perspective that an incumbent cannot have, because one has to get away from the office to see it whole; and that an outsider cannot have, because one has to have been there to know its nature.

Another thing we've got to get across is a sense of human warmth. This is vital to the Presidential mystique, and has largely been the "hidden side" of RN, as far as the public is concerned. And it can be gotten across without loss of either dignity or privacy. It shines through in a lot of those spontaneous moments that have been caught on film. It would be helped by an occasional groping for an answer. Just letting the girls be seen can be a big plus. It came through at times on the Niven show, and strongly on the Carson show. One of the great plusses of the Carson show was that it hit a lot of people with the jolt of the unexpected—it showed people a side of RN that they didn't know existed, and this jarred loose a lot of the old prejudices and preconceptions.

Getting across this sense of warmth does not require being a back-slapper or a "buddy-buddy boy" or a hail-fellow-well-met. To attempt to be such would be not only transparently phony, but inappropriate; we're in a Presidential race, not at a Shriners' convention. It can and should be done subtly, naturally—and this is one of the great advantages of the TV medium (which is a close-up medium) in a relaxed setting, and also of film. Here the warmth does come across—in facial expressions, in the inflections of voice, in the thoughtful exposition of a problem in human terms and in a low-key manner.

Right now we should be concentrating as much as possible on "cool" uses of TV, and on "cool" impressions—both to establish likeability (it's in the cool use that the warmth comes through) and to fit the rhythms of a campaign that's going to hot up later. That is, we want to leave room on the upper end of the intensity scale, so that as we move toward November, we've got reaches of intensity—of "hotness"—to expand into.

So: we should use TV, but we should be selective in our uses of it. We don't need exposure for exposure's sake. We don't have to establish recognition. But we do want to close the gap between old myths and present realities: we want to remind supporters of the candidate's strengths, and demonstrate to non-supporters that the Herblock images are fiction. The way to do this is to let more people see the candidate as we see him, remembering that the important thing is not to win debates, but to win the audience; not to persuade them to RN's point of view, but to win their faith in his leadership.[1]

NOTE

1.   Joe McGinniss, *The Selling of the President* (Kindle Locations 2280-2417).

APPENDIX 2

GENERAL ELECTION

1960 Public Polling

Date of Survey	Organization	Polling	RN	JFK	
Jul-60	Gallup	Nixon vs. JFK	48	52	
7/28/60	Gallup	Nixon vs. JFK	53	47	
Sep-60	Scherwin Research Corporation	1st Television Debate	23	39	
Oct-60	Scherwin Research Corporation	2nd Television Debate	28	44	
Oct-60	Scherwin Research Corporation	3rd Television Debate	42	39	
Oct-60	Scherwin Research Corporation	Final Television Debate	27	52	
Sep-60	Gallup	1st Television Debate	23	43	*(34 even or undecided)*
Oct-60	Gallup	Final Television Debate	30	42	*(28 even or undecided)*

Date of Survey	Organization	Polling	RN	JFK	
Late 1960	CBS—Elmo Roper	Nixon vs. JFK	26	72	
10/24/60	Harris	Nixon vs. JFK	38	62	
Early Sept-60	Gallup	Nixon vs. JFK	47	46	*(7 precent undecided)*
Late Sept-60	Gallup	Nixon vs. JFK	46	49	*(5 precent undecided)*
10/24/60	Gallup	Nixon vs. JFK	45	51	*(4 precent undecided)*
11/7/60	CBS—Elmo Roper	Nixon vs. JFK	49	47	*(4 precent undecided)*
11/6/60	Gallup	Nixon vs. JFK	48	49	*(3 precent undecided)*
11/8/60	Kraft	Nixon vs. JFK	46	49	*(5 percent undecided)*
11/8/60	Princeton Research Service	Nixon vs. JFK	48	52	

APPENDIX 3

GENERAL ELECTION

1968-Public Polling

Date of Survey	Org	Polling	Nixon	Humphrey	Wallace	McCarthy	Rockefeller	Undecided	LBJ	RFK	Romney
Late 1966	Gallup	LBJ vs. Nixon	45						41		
Nov-66	Harris	Romney vs. LBJ							46		54
1/1/67	Harris	Romney vs. LBJ							47		53
3/1/67	Gallup	Romney vs. LBJ							43		52
6/1/67	Harris	Rockefeller vs. LBJ					41		59		
7/1/67	Harris	Romney vs. LBJ							56		44
7/1/67	Harris	Nixon vs. LBJ	44						56		
Oct-67	Gallup	Nixon vs. LBJ	49					6	45		
Nov-67	Harris	Rockefeller vs. LBJ					52		35		
1/6/68	Gallup	General			11	12			39		
1/6/68	Gallup	LBJ vs. Nixon	41						46		

Date of Survey	Org	Polling	Nixon	Humphrey	Wallace	McCarthy	Rockefeller	Undecided	LBJ	RFK	Romney
3/16/68	Harris	Rockefeller vs. LBJ					41		34		
May-68	Gallup	Nixon vs. Humphrey	39	36							
May-68	Gallup	Rockefeller vs. Humphrey		33			40				
5/1/68	Unknows	McCarthy vs. RFK vs. LBJ				29			27	28	
5/8/68	Gallup	Nixon vs. Humphrey vs. Wallace	39	36	14						
5/8/68	Gallup	Rockefeller vs. Humphrey vs. Wallace		33	16		40				
5/16/68	Harris	Nixon vs. Humphrey vs. Wallace	37	41	14						
5/16/68	Harris	Rockefeller vs. Humphrey vs. Wallace		40	17		37				
Jun-68	Gallup	Nixon vs. Humphrey	36	42							
Jun-68	Gallup	Rockefeller vs. Humphrey		39			36				
6/17/68	Harris	Nixon vs. Humphrey vs. Wallace	36	43	13						
6/17/68	Harris	Rockefeller vs. Humphrey vs. Wallace		40	15		36				
7/2/68	Gallup	Romney vs. LBJ							45		44

Date of Survey	Org	Polling	Nixon	Humphrey	Wallace	McCarthy	Rockefeller	Undecided	LBJ	RFK	Romney
7/3/68	Gallup	Nixon vs. Humphrey vs. Wallace	35	40	16						
7/3/68	Gallup	Rockefeller vs. Humphrey vs. Wallace		36	21		36				
7/20/68	Harris	Nixon vs. Humphrey	35	37							
7/20/68	Harris	Nixon vs. McCarthy	34			42					
7/29/68	Gallup	Nixon vs. Humphrey vs. Wallace	40	38	16			6			
7/29/68	Gallup	Nixon vs. McCarthy vs. Wallace	41		16	36					
7/29/68	Gallup	Rockefeller vs. Humphrey vs. Wallace		36	21		36	7			
7/29/68	Gallup	Rockefeller vs. McCarthy vs. Wallace			20	35	36	9			
7/29/68	Harris	Nixon vs. Humphrey vs. Wallace	36	41	16						
7/29/68	Harris	Rockefeller vs. Humphrey vs. Wallace		34	20		40				
8/1/68	Harris	Rockefeller vs. Humphrey vs. Wallace		34	20		40	6			
8/1/68	Harris	Rockefeller vs. McCarthy vs. Wallace			19	34	40	7			

Date of Survey	Org	Polling	Nixon	Humphrey	Wallace	McCarthy	Rockefeller	Undecided	LBJ	RFK	Romney
8/1/68	Harris	Nixon vs. Humphrey vs. Wallace	36	41	16			7			
8/1/68	Harris	Nixon vs. McCarthy vs. Wallace	35		16	43		7			
8/11/68	Gallup	Nixon vs. Humphrey vs. Wallace	45	29	18						
8/24/68	Harris	Nixon vs. Humphrey	50	36							
9/3/68	Gallup	Nixon vs. Humphrey vs. Wallace	43	31	19			7			
9/7/68	Gallup	Nixon vs. Humphrey vs. Wallace	43	31	19						
9/22/68	Gallup	Nixon vs. Humphrey vs. Wallace	43	28	21						
9/23/68	Harris	Nixon vs. Humphrey vs. Wallace	39	31	21						
9/25/68	Gallup	Nixon vs. Humphrey	43	31							
9/27/68	Gallup	Nixon vs. Humphrey vs. Wallace	43	28	21			8			
9/28/68	Gallup	Nixon vs. Humphrey vs. Wallace	43	28	21						
10/12/68	Gallup	Nixon vs. Humphrey	44	36							

Date of Survey	Org	Polling	Nixon	Humphrey	Wallace	McCarthy	Rockefeller	Undecided	LBJ	RFK	Romney
10/18/68	Harris	Nixon vs. Humphrey vs. Wallace	40	35	18			7			
10/21/68	Gallup	Nixon vs. Humphrey vs. Wallace	43	31	20			6			
10/21/68	NY Daily News	Nixon vs. Humphrey vs. Wallace	46	42	8						
10/21/68	Blevins Popcorn Village	Popcorn Poll	58	27	15						
10/26/68	Gallup	Nixon vs. Humphrey vs. Wallace	44	36	15						
11/2/68	Gallup	Nixon vs. Humphrey	42	40							
11/2/68	Harris	Nixon vs. Humphrey	42	40							
11/2/68	Gallup	Nixon vs. Humphrey	42	40							
11/3/68	Harris	Nixon vs. Humphrey	40	37							
11/4/68	Harris	Nixon vs. Humphrey	40	43							

APPENDIX 4

Did JFK Lose the Popular Vote?

Sean Trende
RealClear Politics

Right now the RCP averages are showing an odd situation. Mitt Romney leads nationally[1] by one point, but trails in the Electoral College by a 294–244.[2] Moreover, electoral vote number 270 (right now, Wisconsin) favors President Obama by a two-point margin.

While I believe that an electoral vote/popular vote disconnect of this magnitude is unlikely, it certainly is possible that we'll see another split between the two, especially if the popular vote is decided by less than a point. If that happens, Americans will once again receive a civics lesson in how presidents are *really* chosen.

In particular, we'll be reminded of the four canonical instances where the electoral vote and popular vote went to different candidates: 1824, 1876, 1888, and 2000. These are fairly well-known to political junkies.

Far less well-known is that we should probably include a fifth such split: 1960.

Now, just to be clear, the argument that Richard Nixon should be credited with a popular vote win in 1960 doesn't rest on theories about dead people voting in Chicago or cows voting in Texas. It does rest on a fuller understanding of Southern voting history.

Before going further, credit where credit is due. This analysis isn't something I discovered on my own. Instead, it derives from a pair of articles published in *PS: Political Science and Politics*. The first, authored by University of Illinois at Urbana-Champaign professor Brian Gaines, appeared in the March 2001 edition of that journal. The second, by George Mason University professor Gordon Tullock, appeared in the January 2004 edition. Even back in 1960, *Congressional Quarterly* concluded that it was Nixon, not Kennedy, who had won the popular vote, for the reasons that follow.

If you asked your average political aficionado when the South began to leave the Democratic Party, the answer would probably be 1964. In truth, that exit has much deeper roots. A better starting date is 1938, when FDR conducted an unsuccessful purge of conservative Southerners. The Democratic share of the vote in the South steadily declined from that date forward, as the national Democratic Party fully embraced progressivism.

Things famously came to a head in 1948, when the Democratic National Convention (to Harry Truman's private consternation) adopted a pro–civil rights plank in the party's platform. The Southern delegation walked out of the convention and formed the Dixiecrat Party.

But—and this is critical—the goal of Dixiecrats was not to win the popular vote or Electoral College outright. They recognized this as impossible at a time when Reconstruction was still a living memory for many voters (in fact, the last Civil War veteran didn't die until 1956).

Rather, the Dixiecrats hoped to deny either party a majority of the electoral vote. That would throw the election to the House of Representatives, where each state is allotted one vote. The eleven states from the Old Confederacy would surely hold the balance of power in such an election and could extract assurances on civil rights from whichever party wanted the victory the most.

It didn't come close to working (somewhat surprisingly, in retrospect), and there wouldn't be another major effort by a Southern candidate to split the Electoral College for another twenty years. But Southern states didn't give up their quest. In 1956, South Carolina, Alabama, Mississippi, and Louisiana offered up "unpledged" slates of electors who would be free to vote for whomever they wished and could make the difference in a close election.

This brings us, finally, to 1960. In that year, the canonical recitation[3] advises us that Sen. John F. Kennedy defeated Vice President Richard Nixon in an incredibly close popular vote, 34,220,984 to 34,108,157. That's a difference of only 112,827 votes.

It's also inaccurate. Three states—Louisiana, Mississippi, and Alabama—offered unpledged slates of electors. In Louisiana, the unpledged delegates came in third place to Kennedy and Nixon, receiving only 21 percent of the vote. In Mississippi, the unpledged electors won, edging out Kennedy by three percentage points; those electors eventually voted for Sen. Harry Byrd of Virginia.

But Alabama did something very, very different. At the time, voters there did not cast ballots for Democratic or Republicans tickets. Instead, they cast eleven votes, one for each elector from the state. Thus, it was possible to cast six votes for Republican electors and five votes for Democratic electors, if one so chose.

Those electors had been selected by the parties in the primary. In the 1960 Alabama Democratic primary, twenty-four electors ran as unpledged, refusing to be bound by the decision of the Democratic convention. They faced off against eleven "loyalist" candidates, who agreed to accept the national candidate. This actually gave the loyalist forces an advantage; there were eleven slots in the Democratic slate, so the odds were greater that the unpledged electors would lose out by having their votes divided too many ways.

But after an election, an extremely close runoff, and a recount, unpledged electors claimed six of the eleven slots for the Democrats, while loyal electors were awarded the remaining five slots.

In the fall, all eleven Democratic electors defeated the Republican electors. As promised, the five loyal electors eventually cast their ballots for Kennedy. As they suggested they would, the unpledged electors joined their Mississippi neighbors in voting for Byrd.

But the popular vote? It was a mess. After all, some people cast as many as eleven votes, and others case as few as one. We can only estimate that about 550,000 people voted overall. The end result is that the six unpledged Democratic electors each received between 320,957 and 324,050 votes, totaling 1,934,826. The five loyal Democratic electors each received between 316,934 and 318,303 votes, totaling 1,587,900. And the eleven Nixon electors each received between 230,951 and 237,981 votes, totaling 2,588,790 votes.

So how do you count this up? The method most frequently used is to award Kennedy 318,303 votes,[5] representing the highest number of votes cast for a Kennedy elector. Nixon is awarded 237,981 votes, representing the highest number of votes received by a Nixon elector. Others award Kennedy 324,050 votes, representing the highest number of votes cast for a Democratic elector.

This first way is certainly defensible—after all, a Kennedy elector *did* receive 318,303 votes in the state, and from a national perspective, it was an election between Kennedy and Nixon.

But was it the *best* way to do this? For starters, we end up with the rather absurd result that Harry Byrd received a majority of the electoral votes from the state, but is credited with zero popular votes.

In fact, if we are going to insist on awarding the state's popular vote to one Democrat or the other, it probably makes more sense to award it to *Byrd* and not to Kennedy. After all, his electors received the most votes.

Moreover, awarding the Democratic popular vote from Alabama entirely to Kennedy ignores the relevant electoral history: electors who were understood to support a "Dixiecratic-ish" candidate won a majority of the slots in the state's Democratic primary and probably would have swept the ticket had their votes not been split twenty-four ways to the loyal electors' eleven.

The fact that many supporters of the unpledged delegates clearly preferred Kennedy over Nixon as a second choice, when forced to make such a pick, really doesn't change another fact, which is that unpledged delegates were, overall, the most popular choice in the state that year—not once, but twice.

If you award the Democratic popular vote in the state wholly to Byrd rather than to Kennedy—again, probably more defensible than awarding the popular vote in the state wholly to JFK—Nixon wins the popular vote by 205,476 votes. (However, even with Nixon gaining Alabama's eleven electoral votes, Kennedy's election would have stood: his EV margin would have shrunk only from 303–219 to 292–230.)

But the bottom line in Alabama is that there really were Democrats who supported the national ticket, and there really were Democrats who supported the Dixiecrats. Had there been options for eleven Kennedy electors and eleven free electors, thousands of votes would have been cast for both, as was the case in Mississippi (although Nixon might well have won the state in that event). Allocating all of the popular votes to Kennedy or Byrd ignores this reality.

You could also award Byrd 324,000 votes in addition to Kennedy's 318,000 votes (and Nixon's 237,000 votes), but then you are allocating hundreds of thousands more votes than there were voters.

Probably the fairest way to allocate the votes—a method proposed by Gaines—is to add up the ballots cast for the eleven Democratic electors and then allocate six-elevenths of the total to Byrd and five-elevenths to Kennedy. This reflects the reality of the state's Democratic Party: it was split between national party loyalists and Dixiecrats.

Adopting this approach results in a Nixon victory of around 60,000 votes, which is how *Congressional Quarterly* originally calculated the results.

In the end, there are three ways to count the popular vote in Alabama: allocate all Democratic votes to Kennedy, allocate all Democratic votes to Byrd, or allocate the Democratic votes proportionally between the two candidates.

Two of those three methods result in a Nixon victory in the national popular vote. Historians choose the one that results in a Kennedy win. I don't think this is because of any conspiracy, nor is it due to bias. At the same time, though, I don't think it's because awarding Kennedy all of those votes is the best method either. Rather I think it's just due to a lazy counting of votes for Kennedy electors, combined with inertia. It's probably time for electoral historians to revisit that.

Of course, the most important thing to remember is that we don't award victories by popular vote, and that campaigns structure their strategies accordingly. Absent an Electoral College, Kennedy probably wouldn't have selected LBJ as his running mate and instead would have made a play in the vote-rich Midwest. But as a matter of historical accuracy, there are almost certainly five instances where the candidate won the popular vote, but lost the Electoral College.[5]

NOTES

1. http://www.realclearpolitics.com/epolls/2012/president/us/general_election_romney_vs_obama-1171.html.
2. http://www.realclearpolitics.com/epolls/2012/president/2012_elections_electoral_college_map_no_toss_ups.html.
3. http://uselectionatlas.org/RESULTS/national.php?year=1960&off=0&f=1.
4. http://uselectionatlas.org/RESULTS/state.php?year=1960&fips=1&f=1&off=0&elect=0.
5. Sean, Trende, Real Clear Politics, 10.19.12; http://www.realclearpolitics.com/articles/2012/10/19/did_jfk_lose_the_popular_vote_115833.html.

APPENDIX 5

John Dean's "The Nixon Defense" An Analysis by Geoff Shepard

6/27/14

John Dean appears to have collected into one place each and every admission against interest by President Nixon and his senior aides, Bob Haldeman, John Ehrlichman, and John Mitchell, from various Watergate books, the Nixon and Haldeman diaries, and the White House tapes.

Before deciding whether Dean's supposed revelations are all that is claimed, it is helpful to reread President Nixon's 1978 biography, *The Memoirs of Richard Nixon*, particularly the two sections devoted to Watergate: "The Watergate Break-in" (625–665) and "Watergate Recurs" (773–791). One might well conclude that much of what Dean claims to reveal today was already admitted by Nixon over thirty-five years ago.

But there is one overriding area of agreement between Dean and the president—and that is that Nixon did not fully appreciate the serious nature of the Watergate scandal until their meeting of March 21, 1973, when Dean first spoke of a cancer on the presidency. The ramifications will be explored in greater detail, but Dean admits, for all of the earlier bits and pieces that might be mined from earlier conversations, they were not seen as all that significant until very, very late in the day.

It also should be pointed out that the book is profoundly mistitled and that Dean's methodology is seriously flawed. The book is not Nixon's defense at all; it is an all-out attack on President Nixon. It's far more accurate to see the book as Dean's defense, his last and best effort to paint a picture of how an innocent young lawyer suddenly and unexpectedly found himself in the midst of a cabal of evil-doers—and how he alone struggled to do the right thing. (See footnote 111 at p. 488 for Dean's tortured explanation of how he ended up with immunity when only wanting to tell the truth and footnote 7 at p. 543 for his rather astounding assertion regarding finding himself in the midst of a criminal cabal.)

More suspect is Dean's methodology. By focusing only on events mentioned on the tape system and thus skipping any real discussion of what led to the break-in in the first place, of what was done by and between the president's staff outside of his hearing, and of what transpired after the taping system was removed, Dean's book presents only a very selective and partial picture of the Watergate scandal. In essence, it takes the taped conversations out of the context of the overall Watergate scandal. Finally, Dean's supposed verbatim transcriptions have neither been peer-reviewed nor made available for independent verification.

The question was, and remains, why should anyone today believe Dean's highly selective retelling? It is, in the words of Jim Croce, "like a jigsaw puzzle with a couple of pieces gone."

I. The Dean Transcriptions
In researching his book, Dean claims to have identified some thousand Watergate conversations on the White House tapes, which he and his team have transcribed, beginning in 2009 and utilizing

digitalized copies produced by the National Archives, as well as new software specifically designed for that purpose. He and his team then eliminated duplicative and irrelevant materials to condense these conversations into more readable and understandable form.

It must have been a prodigious effort. One would have had to review thousands of individual conversations just to identify those that were Watergate-related. And, then to transcribe them "from scratch," as Dean claims to have done, would be a further Herculean task.

Establishing validity: All of this effort, however, will be of little use to future scholars or to serious students of the Watergate scandal, since Dean has declined to make these claimed verbatim transcriptions available for cross-checking and verification. As he so nicely put it in his first footnote, "Anyone who wants a verbatim copy is welcome to prepare their own transcripts" (p. xviii).

It appears that Dean expects readers to take his work-product at face value, but it is difficult to see how anyone could. After all, the transcriptions have not been prepared by an independent authority or cross-checked in any manner. And Dean is hardly an objective or independent observer, with an overriding concern for any reputation for veracity. He is, perhaps, President Nixon's severest critic— and one who obviously feels a very strong need to justify his own criminal actions. Without verbatim transcripts as a reference point, it is virtually impossible to ascertain whether Dean's transcriptions are accurate and, as importantly, whether his extensive condensations are appropriate or have omitted exculpatory material.

It would be relatively easy, for example, to compare Dean's newly transcribed versions of certain key conversations with those previously prepared by others, including the White House (and released on April 30, 1974), the House Judiciary Committee (and released in June 1974), and the FBI (for use in the cover-up trial in the fall of 1974). In so doing, one could ascertain rather quickly whether Dean's transcriptions are truly "new and improved" or closely follow those done some four decades prior.

Besides, Dean has given such assurances of accuracy and completeness before, only to have to eat his own words. In the 1976 preface to *Blind Ambition*, Dean attested to its overall accuracy by asserting that he was willing to take a lie detector test regarding its truthfulness. Yet, when under oath during nine days of depositions taken in 1995–1996 in connection with his lawsuit against the publisher of *Silent Coup* (Dean v. St Martin's Press, C.A. 92-1807), time and again Dean declined to stand behind the specificity of various quotations and representations in that book. He claimed instead, that much of its dialogue had been a pure invention of his ghostwriter, Taylor Branch, and admitted that he had not even read the final version before it was published.

Selective use and quotation: Aside from threshold questions of overall accuracy, the outright misuse of tape transcripts is just what Dean's book is accusing President Nixon of having done many years before:

- He first explains why tape summaries just don't work, criticizing Nixon for reviewing Haldeman's notes about a conversation without listening to the actual tape itself:

  It is possible to get the gist of this conversation in real time, which is largely what Haldeman tried to do and indicate in his abbreviated notes. It is not possible for someone who has not listened to the recording, however, to understand it based on a few summary notes made by someone who has listened to it. For example, the tone of voice of the person speaking can be very telling. (p. 541[1])

Yet, this is precisely what Dean is asking readers to do with regard to his own summations.

- Dean later accuses the president of providing "misinformation by omitting these facts" (p. 582). Since readers have no idea what Dean may have omitted, he could well be doing precisely what he has accused Nixon of having done.

- He also asserts that Nixon:

  [W]ould use what he could of [the tapes] to his advantage. In fact, he began doing so as he listened to them, using select material he heard to reassure Haig and Ziegler of his innocence. (p. 590)

Again, there is no way a reader can tell if Dean is doing the same thing.

- He later accused Nixon of selectively choosing material to his advantage:

  [T]he president skimmed through the meetings, plucking out occasional statements by me that were consistent with his defense and dismissing matters or spinning them when they conflicted. (p. 603)

Since Dean so readily accuses others of abusive tape usage, who is to say that he hasn't done many of the same things in his own condensations? Without his verbatim transcripts, there is no way to determine what has been left out.

Honest disagreements: There also can be authentic differences over the actual wording of particular conversations. For example, Dean assures the reader that Nixon instructed Mitchell to further the cover-up in their conversation of March 22, 1973. Here is Dean's quoted version (which is virtually a word-for-word duplication of the transcript produced by the House Judiciary Committee in 1973 and introduced at the cover-up trial):

> "I don't give a shit what happens. I want you all to stonewall it, let them plead the Fifth Amendment, cover up or anything else, if it'll save it, save the plan. That's the whole point." But Nixon had to be realistic, too, so he gave the other side. "And I would particularly prefer to do it that other way, if it's going to come out that way anyway. And that's my view, that with the number of jackass people that they've got that they can call, they're going to"—The president rephrased his thought. "The story they'll get out, through leaks, charges and so forth, innuendo, will be a hell of a lot worse than the story they're going to get out by just letting it out there." (p. 341)

Here is alternative transcription of this same segment, prepared by the White House in response to the House Judiciary Committee's version, but never before released:

> I don't give a shit what happens. Go down and sto-, stonewall it; Tell 'em, "plead the Fifth Amendment, cover-up" or anything else, if it'll save 'em—save it for them. That's the whole point.

> On the other hand, I would prefer, as I said to you, that you do it the other way [to have everyone tell the truth]. And I would particularly prefer to do it that other way if it's going to come out that way anyway.

And that my view, with the number of jackass people that they've got that they can call, they're going to. The story they get out through leaks, charges, and so forth, and innuendos, will be a hell of a lot worse than the story they're going to get out by just letting it out there.

As any reader can see, there is an considerable difference of opinion over the specific words on this tape—with hugely disparate implications—but there's no way to cross-check or verify Dean's own transcription and whether it differs at all from transcriptions prepared by a number of other organizations.

II. Overview
A. Startlingly Material Omissions
Dean's methodology is deeply flawed, and, because of that, his book is glaringly incomplete as a full discussion of the Watergate scandal, particularly as to what has come to light over the past four decades. His sole focus on the tapes has enabled him to skip over hugely controversial and unsettled topics, including the following:

- Any detailed discussion of the real rationale for the break-in itself, the allegations of his own involvement, and the unresolved factual questions in those first weeks following the break-in arrests. It is interesting to note that Dean never even mentions or recognizes the issues highlighted in the whole series of books presenting differing views on Watergate, especially those by:

  ⊙ Fred Thompson, *At That Point in Time: The Inside Story of the Watergate Committee* (1975),
  ⊙ Jim Hougan, *Secret Agenda: Watergate, Deep Throat, and the CIA* (1984),
  ⊙ Len Colodny and Robert Gettlin, *Silent Coup: The Removal of a President* (1991),

⊙ James Rosen, *The Strong Man, John Mitchell and the Secrets of Watergate* (2008),

⊙ Geoff Shepard, *The Secret Plot to Make Ted Kennedy President* (2008), and

⊙ Phil Stanford, *White House Call Girl* (2014).

- In addition to starting his book in the middle of the Watergate story, Dean simply and suddenly stops his narrative on July 16, 1973, the point where the White House tape system was disclosed and removed. He thus omits any real review or discussion of the last thirteen months of the Nixon presidency.

- The questions Dean fears most: any presentation of Dean's own actions, particularly mention of the many questions that have been raised with regard to his own possibly criminal acts, has also been omitted. In the Preface, Dean asserts that he became the centerpiece of the Nixon defense (p. xxv), but then asserts that his Ervin Committee testimony and first book have already detailed his role, so he has omitted further discussion from this book (p. xxiv). But he never discussed them there either. It is as though he hopes to airbrush any record of own his criminal acts from the Watergate picture. With so many questions remaining outstanding, particularly with regard to information that has come to light since Dean's July 1973 testimony (as well as allegations in later books by Bob Haldeman, John Ehrlichman, Charles Colson, Gordon Liddy, and James McCord, and the sworn testimony given before the House Judiciary Committee and at the cover-up trial), one wonders about the real reasons for these omissions. Dean might have better explained, for example:

  ⊙ How he came to be assigned responsibility for campaign intelligence plan by Haldeman (as mentioned in opening of his March 21, 1973, meeting with President

Nixon), particularly in light of the differing description contained in Haldeman's subsequent books.

- How he recruited Liddy and introduced him to Mitchell and Magruder, particularly in light of the dramatically contrasting version in Liddy's later book.

- How he came to attend and what was said in connection with the two meetings in Mitchell's office when he was still Attorney General (on 1/27/72 and 2/4/72), again particularly in light of Liddy's book.

- His participation in the June 19, 1972, meeting in Mitchell's apartment, when most folks believe the cover-up was undertaken, particularly in light of the conflicting testimony about that meeting that was rendered by other participants during the course of the cover-up trial.

- How he rehearsed Magruder for his perjured grand jury testimony in his two appearances, after asking him to erase his name from Magruder's datebook.

- How he obtained FBI field reports, sat in on interviews, and obtained prosecutorial insights—and then improperly shared that information with Watergate defense counsel.

- How he held back and then destroyed possible personally incriminating materials from Hunt's safe—and only fessed up to having done so after having pleaded guilty to single felony.

- How he came to so mischaracterize his first meeting with President Nixon, on September 15, 1972, when he was describing it in his Ervin Committee testimony.

- How he secretly removed campaign funds for personal use on his honeymoon.

- How he acted as "chief desk officer" during the cover-up, apparently vastly exceeding the scope of his mission of behalf of his client, the president.

⊙ How he stoutly and consistently resisted any White House disclosure, saying it would harm Watergate defendants, when it appears that he was more concerned with disclosure of his own role in the criminal cover-up.

⊙ How he encouraged Egil Krogh to deny knowledge of Plumber operations in his grand jury appearance, which resulted in Krogh's being indicted for perjury.

⊙ How his own recollections, as told to prosecutors, changed so dramatically during the course of his April 1973 meetings.

⊙ How his lawyer negotiated with federal prosecutors and with Ervin Committee staff for immunity, setting one off against the other, even as Dean maintained that his only interest was in telling the truth.

⊙ How he came to spend no time whatsoever in prison, even though sentenced to a term of one to four years for his role in the Watergate scandal.

Selective usage: Dean has arranged his transcriptions into four categories, corresponding to the four parts of his book (xxiii):
I. Covering Up (35 tapes)
II. Containing (158 tapes)
III. Unraveling (110 tapes)
IV. The Nixon Defense (669 tapes)

But the book contains specific footnoted references to only 503 of these conversations. The implication is that fully half of his alleged Watergate-related tapes are missing entirely or are unworthy of any discussion. There are additional technical problems. For example, footnotes identifying at least three of the early conversations appear to be missing (see, for example, p. 32).

In addition, the extensive use of supposedly full transcriptions fades as one progresses through book. There is the appearance of great detail at the outset, but these condensations are reduced to bare allusions to embarrassing fragments as the book progresses. This is particularly true in the fourth and final section of the book.

Dean also gilds the lily. He constantly characterizes actions and statements of others in pejorative terms: "feigning surprise," "claimed," "asserted," (see, for example, pp. 312, 398, 406, and 433). It is the same with Dean's use of the introductory term "surely" (p. 596). This near-constant pejorative characterization of statements by others raises questions about the accuracy of Dean's supposed transcriptions, especially where they cannot be independently verified. In essence, Dean is spinning virtually every conversation. In contrast, his own statements are always presented as properly phrased and unquestionably true.

B. Helpful Admissions
Nonetheless, there is any number of very helpful admissions scattered throughout the 719 pages of Dean's book. For example, he asserts that:

- **No Advance Knowledge:** No one on the White House staff knew of the Watergate break-in in advance:
  - ⊙ "No doubt [Nixon] was trying to reach for doubters that he had no direct connection with the Watergate break-in, which I am confident was true." (p. 8)
  - ⊙ "I had certainly confirmed it months later [that no one on the White House staff knew of the break-in in advance] and still believed it was technically true based on all I knew. (p. 288)
  - ⊙ "Nixon noted that I had said, however, that I did not believe anyone at the White House had advance knowledge of the Watergate break-in (as I later testified, and find remains accurate to this day). (p. 591)

- **No White House Receipt of Wiretap Information:** Dean concludes that, contrary to Magruder's testimony, Strachan was never sent any wiretap information from the first break-in (May 28, 1972):

  > Whether the White House received information from the DNC before June 17, 1972, will forever remain unclear, because Haldeman instructed Strachan to clean their files. But it appears no such information, in fact, was received. Magruder later testified that he showed Strachan the fruits of Liddy's DNC wiretapping operation, but in his testimony Strachan denied he was shown such material. At the time I was reporting to Nixon, Strachan believed he had seen it because the reports he had been sent and destroyed at Haldeman's instruction, after the June 17, 1972, arrests read very much like wiretap reports; they used the language: "From a source believed to be reliable." In the weeks ahead, Strachan and Haldeman would figure out that what had been destroyed were reports from a source planted by Magruder rather than wiretap information. (Footnote 5 at p. 312).

- The **18½ minute gap** on the tape of June 20, 1972, is historically insignificant.
  - ⊙ "Haldeman's note-taking procedures have been misunderstood; he did not make a record of or even cite the highlights of what was said at any given session but instead recorded only matters that called for further attention and follow up." (p. 20)
  - ⊙ " Who was responsible for the 18 ½ minute gap—leaving behind a shrill buzz—on the tape of the June 20, 1972, conversation between President Nixon and H. R. "Bob" Haldeman, and what was erased? Two

observations should be made about these questions. First, the answers to them have virtually no historic significance whatsoever as they provide not information about or insight into Watergate that cannot already be found in abundance elsewhere." (p. 653)

- **The Smoking Gun tape** of June 23, 1972, has been totally misunderstood—and related only to an effort to keep the names of two Democrat donors confidential:

  When revealed by order of the U.S. Supreme Court in late July 1974, this became known as the "smoking gun" conversation, because it was viewed as hard evidence, demonstrating beyond question, that Nixon's final defense about the Watergate break-in in his April 30, 1973 speech, followed by his May 22nd statement, was bogus, which doomed the Nixon presidency. Ironically, this conversation has been mistakenly understood as an effort by Nixon and Haldeman to shut down the FBI's entire Watergate investigation. This appears to be the case only when viewed out of context. In August 1974, when the conversation was revealed, and Nixon and his lawyers had to focus on this conversation, he had long forgotten what was actually involved; they assumed it had the same meaning as everyone else. In reality, it was only an effort by Haldeman to stop the FBI from investigating an anonymous campaign contribution from Mexico that the Justice Department prosecutors had already agreed was outside the scope of the Watergate investigation. In approving this action, however, Nixon slightly expanded the request, saying that the FBI should also stay out of Howard Hunt's CIA-related activities. In fact, this conversation did not put the lie to Nixon's April 30 and May 22, 1973, statements, and had Nixon known that he might have survived its disclosure to fight another day." (Footnote at pp. 55–56)[2]

- There was a **clear lack of intent** on behalf of the president and his advisors to break the law.
  - ⊙ "In short, Nixon viewed Watergate in terms of 'politics pure and simple,' and he played it 'tough' because that's how the Democrats and their sympathetic news media partners played it." (p. 95)
  - ⊙ "A striking number of lawyers found themselves on the wrong side of the law during Watergate, and almost all of them did so out of ignorance of criminal law." (p. 95)
  - ⊙ "But [Nixon] was thinking politically, not legally. He understood that Magruder had largely cooked this story up by himself. There is no evidence suggesting that it ever occurred to him that this knowledge and approval of Magruder's actions effectively placed him at the top of a conspiracy to suborn perjury. (p. 119)
  - ⊙ "[I]t struck me that, with the exception of Magruder's perjuring himself . . . everyone else who had crossed the near-invisible lines onto the wrong side of the law had done so out of ignorance." (p. 421)
  - ⊙ "Nixon did acknowledge that Haldeman and Ehrlichman had 'collected money in the beginning for the defense attorney,' although their 'motives were proper, right?' When no one responded Nixon conceded: 'I think what you might say, in fairness, maybe they were trying to see that nothing blew the election. That makes sense. But I don't think it was obstruction of justice.' Surely [one of Nixon's attorneys] understood what Nixon could not grasp: Obstruction is obstruction, regardless of motive." (p. 593)[3]

- President Nixon knew relatively little about the specifics of Watergate prior to his meeting with Dean on March 21, 1973:
  - ⊙ "In fact, as his new term commenced [in January of 1973], the situation was far worse than he could begin to imagine. This was because he had remained largely uninformed of the facts, partly though his own design but also partly because of the reluctance of Haldeman, Ehrlichman and Mitchell to inform him precisely what had gone on and how matters were or were not being addressed." (p. 193)
  - ⊙ "Although Nixon interpreted the information from Colson during their January 5 conversation as more finger-pointing among his subordinates, the truth was that his staff was slowly (and finally) giving him the basic facts about what had actually occurred—while not really explaining their own roles in the affair." (p. 203)
  - ⊙ 'That applies to Mitchell, too,' I added, since the president seemed both interested and surprisingly unaware of the facts." (p. 267)
  - ⊙ Nixon said as much himself: "The reason, if I knew all the facts, then I have an idea of what could come out." (p. 282)
  - ⊙ Dean gives an excellent characterization of Nixon's situation as of April 16, 1973: "Clearly the president was starting to develop a new defense: He would say he first learned of the serious nature of the problems on March 21, which was true. (His later claim that he first learned of the cover-up on March 21, however, was not.)" (p. 421)

- The president's staff was not informing him (or themselves) of their involvement or of what had transpired.

- ◉ Nixon expressed frustration that he did not know all the facts; he had been told conflicting stories, but is clear that he was consistently and adamantly against any cover-up (pp. 232-236).
- ◉ "'I've got to know whether [Haldeman] knew about it, and I've got to know whether Colson knew about it." No one had ever laid it out for him, even when he had asked." (p. 232)
- ◉ Dean later admits that, like everyone else on the staff, he was less than candid in telling the president the full truth:

  Not knowing what else I should tell Nixon, I was as vague as Haldeman and Ehrlichman when I explained, "There is a certain domino situation here. If some things start going, a lot of other things are going to start going, and there are going to be a lot of problems if everything starts falling. So there are dangers, Mr. President. I'd be less than candid if I didn't tell you there are. There's a reason for us not, not everyone, going up and testifying." (p. 270)

- ◉ "Haldeman said he understood, yet clearly he was still not giving the president basic information that investigators would later uncover about his role leading up to the Watergate break-in. As the conversation continued, the president could merely speculate about who knew what, in order to assess his exposure." (p. 280)
- ◉ "Conversations like this were remarkably inconclusive, because Haldeman, Ehrlichman and the president were not telling one another all they knew and this lack of candor continued to the end . . ." (p. 286)
- ◉ "While Mitchell, Ehrlichman and Haldeman had once discussed the problem among themselves in the early

days, they now communicated almost exclusively through me, although Ehrlichman and Haldeman did exchange some information. No one was sharing anything with anyone else, nor with the president, who even at this late date [March 20, 1973] had no real idea of his exposure." (p. 306)

⊙ But the allegations against H and E seem almost inconsequential when they were asked to resign:

Petersen gave the president a written document summarizing the charges against the two aides as of that date [April 16, 1973] based on the information I had provided in my off-the-record conversations with the prosecutors: [Acting FBI Director] Gray's having been given material from Hunt's safe; Ehrlichman's having instructed me to "deep six" material found there; Ehrlichman's ordering Hunt out of the country; Haldeman's having been informed of my meetings with Mitchell and Liddy, during which I had rejected Liddy's plan and Haldeman had agreed. But Petersen noted, Haldeman had done nothing to "discontinue" Liddy's activities, and Magruder had told the prosecutors he had delivered to Strachan for Haldeman copies of information from "intercepted telephone conversations." (p. 425)

• The president constantly wanted to get the facts out:

"Well, God damn it, as I've often said it, John, if the facts are going to come out, let us help get them out." (p. 284)

• In this regard, Nixon constantly alluded to his experience in the Alger Hiss case as the reason for his belief as to why any cover-up would be worse than the actual facts:

"But the worst thing a guy can do, there are two things, each is bad: One is to lie, and the other is to cover up." Ehrlichman agreed, and Nixon continued, "If you cover up, you're going to get caught. And if you lie, you're going to be guilty of perjury. Now, basically, that was the whole story of the Hiss case." (pp. 105–106).

- It is important to understand that Nixon did not see the Hiss case as merely exposing a Soviet spy in the State Department. He remembered it as a devastating scandal for the Truman administration, who had made it much worse by trying to cover it up.

-

- Other of Nixon's allusions to the Hiss case are at pp. 238, 241, 243, 247, and 250, but may be two dozen actual references. The point is that the president, if asked, would clearly have responded with the advice not to lie or cover-up, because the truth would come out in any event.

- Dean denies that Watergate was part of a larger espionage/ sabotage operation, as had been so dramatically claimed by Deep Throat:

    Woodward and Bernstein had been focused on who was responsible for the break-in and on portraying it as part of a larger espionage and sabotage effort. If that operation existed in any organized fashion, I did not (and do not) know who was behind it, and even four decades later I have never found evidence for its existence; it seems, instead, to have been a fantasy scenario apparently advanced by their Deep Throat source, Mark Felt. (p. 209)

- The importance of Dean's assertion is explained in Max Holland's new article on Tim Naftali, where he describes how unprepared he was in his oral history interview with Carl Bernstein:

  > One of the critical questions that should have been put to them, as any Watergate scholar would know, has to do with the Post's centerpiece story of 10 October 1972. Occupying the prestigious upper-right quadrant of the front page, it was boldly headlined "FBI Finds Nixon Aides Sabotaged Democrats." The story was and still is regarded as the "centerpiece" of the newspaper's pre-election coverage. It seemingly tied together the scandal's disparate strands and tried to put the break-in into a context, as one element in far-flung program to subvert the Democrats if not the democratic process—which included greasing the way so that Nixon faced the one candidate he wanted to run against the most, George McGovern. (http://www.washingtondecoded.com/site/2014/06/naftali.html)

- Dean's quoted materials tend to confirm Ehrlichman's continued advocacy of getting the facts out, which was the principal defense he sought to introduce at the cover-up trial (p. 116). He was denied access to all of the other tape recordings, as well as to producing the former president as a witness, so he could not even begin to present this defense.

- In addition, the rationale for the second break-in seems to support Mitchell's legal defense that he never approved of the Liddy plan in the first place.

  - ⊙ For much of Dean's book, the discussions on the tapes place the blame for Magruder's decision to go forward

with Liddy's campaign intelligence plan on pressure
from the White House and not on any decision by
Mitchell. For example:

[On March 16, 1972] Ehrlichman provided Nixon his
well-informed "theory of the case," weaving facts with
his considered speculation, and while there were some
gaps in his knowledge, his theory was actually very
close to the truth of the matter as it was documented by
later investigations.

Ehrlichman described how the pressure built up on
Magruder, who probably called Liddy in and said,
"I'm getting unbelievable shit from the White House,
"so he needed to do something. Liddy, in turn, said he
would take care of it, but needed "a hundred grand or
whatever." Magruder sent Liddy to Sloan, who wanted
to know if the money had been approved by Mitchell.
Magruder then called Mitchell, and said, "Listen, you've
got to call Sloan and clear this." Ehrlichman reminded
the president he was speculating, and then continued:
Likely Magruder said to Mitchell, "John, you've got to
call Sloan and clear the expenditure of a hundred thousand dollars cash." And Mitchell said, "Well, what's it
for?" "Well," he said, "Gordon Liddy is going to undertake to get that information that I keep getting badgered
about from the White House." (pp. 282–283)

⊙ Several other discussions on the tapes place the blame
for Magruder going forward on Colson's call. For
example:

Reconstructing from his notes, Haldeman summarized
the report: Magruder had said, "The whole intelligence

plan was hatched here at the White House by Hunt, Liddy and Colson. And Colson called Jeb twice to tell him to get going on this thing, and he specifically referred to the Larry O'Brien information, was hard on that. And Jeb says Hunt and Liddy were in Colson's office, and LaRue was in Jeb's office on that phone call." (p. 355)

⊙ They also blame it on Strachan following up on wanting a campaign intelligence plan, due to Haldeman's tickler system:

Because McCord had claimed I was aware of the Watergate break-in, I would be called to the grand jury, and my testimony would not jibe with Magruder's. As a result, Magruder had told the CRP lawyers, aware that they would tell others, that he had a new version of "what really happened in Watergate." He was claiming that the plan had been cooked up at the White House, that it was triggered when Gordon Strachan told him, "Haldeman has said that you cannot delay getting this operation started any longer. The president had ordered you to go ahead immediately, and you are not to stall anymore. You're to get it done." (p. 346)

⊙ This is repeated again a little later, at the same time that the idea is first presented that perhaps Mitchell did approve Liddy's plan:

Haldeman now reported information I had given him from Paul O'Brien [a CRP attorney], who was "very distressed with Mitchell," because he felt Mitchell "could cut this whole thing off if he would just step forward." Haldeman explained, "As far as O'Brien can determine, Mitchell did sign off on this thing, and

Dean believes that to be the case also," although neither thought they could prove it. O'Brien was concerned because others were getting "whacked around" to protect Mitchell. Haldeman repeated for Ehrlichman's benefit Magruder's latest, that Liddy's "superintelligence operation was put together by the White House, by Haldeman, Dean and others." (p. 348)

⊙ Dean says that Petersen said during a 9 p.m. phone call to the president on April 16, 1973, that LaRue had told the prosecutors that Mitchell had approved the Liddy plan at their March 30 meeting in Miami (p. 427). (This assertion directly conflicts with LaRue's discussions with WSPF prosecutors and his testimony at the cover-up trial. It may be an error in Dean's transcription.)

⊙ Dean also says that Liddy used Mitchell's call (about inadequate intelligence) as the excuse to go back into the Watergate office building for the second break-in. Here, Dean sides with Magruder in asserting that neither Mitchell nor Magruder deliberately sent Liddy back in for the second break-in (p. 404), thus directly contradicting Liddy's own account.

• The first mention of the term "hush money" on the tapes occurs on April 14, 1973, well into the scandal's unfolding (p. 392). It does not appear anyone was informing Nixon of these payments before his March 21 meeting with Dean.

C. The Very Slippery John Dean

You wouldn't know it from reading the book, but John Dean is a convicted felon, disbarred and sentenced to a prison term of one to four years for his role in the Watergate scandal. He conveniently omits this, along with any mention of the myriad of criminal acts of which he has been accused.

Conrad Black, in his excellent Nixon biography, characterized Dean as the slipperiest of the Watergate figures. Here are some examples of how Dean appears to mischaracterize actions or to twist them to support his own point of view:

- Omits mention of his own efforts to determine if Colson was involved in approval of Liddy's plan (p. 32).
- Admits to being "desk officer" for cover-up, but represents himself as a mere transmitter of messages between the people at CRP (Mitchell, Magruder, LaRue, Mardian, etc.) and his White House superiors (Haldeman, Ehrlichman, and President Nixon) (pp. 181 and 240).
- Tells the president about the hiring of Liddy as CRP's general counsel, while omitting any mention of Liddy's all-important campaign intelligence plan (p. 269).
- Alleged comment to Haldeman following the second meeting in the attorney general's office:

  ⊙ Haldeman first repeats Dean's recollection of his comments after the second meeting on the tapes, but it appears to have been presented as a way to help Haldeman (p. 349).
  ⊙ Dean also appears to claim that Kleindienst told the president that Dean had thought he had turned the whole Liddy thing off by his comment during that second meeting ("that this should never be discussed in the AG's office") (p. 412).
  ⊙ Claims that Haldeman told him after his report of the second meeting not to do anything, just to stay away from it (p. 427). (Dean responded under oath in depositions

(when it was pointed out that it was not possible for him to have seen Haldeman after this second meeting, as claimed) that perhaps he had seen Haldeman after the first meeting. He claimed that he had a clear memory of what was said, but could not pin down the precise date. But none of his story makes sense unless it occurred after the second meeting. Haldeman ultimately concluded, as he wrote in his book, that he had Dean had been lying all along.)

- Asserted that "[n]o one on the [Ervin] committee made any suggestion whatsoever about my testimony" (p. 619), right after having admitted to having had secret meetings with Sam Dash (p. 617). This is "so Dean": could he be distinguishing Dash, a committee staffer, from actual members of the Ervin Committee? (It's a question of what the meaning of "is" is!).

- Obliquely claims he did not work with Magruder on his perjury (p. 464). This phrasing also is "so Dean." In his deposition, he appeared to deny that he suborned perjury because he was not advocating that Magruder lie; he was only helping him prepare to do so. Yet, he asserts in his book that Nixon, due to knowledge and assent to Magruder's perjury, was himself guilty of conspiracy to suborn perjury (p. 119).

- Said that he had continued to hope that his colleagues would come forward to confess their own involvement (p. 484), which (without his having admitted having done so) is presumably his explanation of why he didn't mention their involvement to prosecutors until after many meetings had occurred.

- Essentially skipped any real discussion of his March 21, 1973, evening meeting with Haldeman, Ehrlichman, and the president, as well as the subsequent meeting the next afternoon that included John Mitchell, perhaps because their content is not consistent with Dean's story line. This is where Dean confirms that he can and will prepare a Dean Report, which the president can share with the Ervin Committee—and will be used as the basis for closed hearings on testimony from current and former White House staffers. It is the president's salutary response to Dean's disclosures on the morning of March 21. Dean also asserts that he was sent to Camp David the day after the March 22 meeting and only after he had arrived was he asked to write a report (p. 340). This is directly conflicted by the tape transcript, particularly the one prepared by the House Judiciary Committee (at HJC, p. 158). There also is a wonderful quote about a Dean conversation with Haldeman's assistant, Larry Higby, where he said "I can't do a damn thing on the report, but I've got sixty pages of working out my own defense, and it's beautiful" (which certainly rings true, even though Dean denies having said it) (p. 518).

- Time and again Dean assures us that Haldeman, Ehrlichman, and Mitchell were convicted of perjury for their testimony before the Ervin Committee, without mentioning that such perjury charges were brought only against Haldeman and Mitchell and were almost all peripheral to the central Watergate story (p. 634).

- It appears that the original rationale for Dean talking with a criminal lawyer may have been explained as a way to gain specific criminal legal advice to protect everyone (p. 359).

- Dean's defense as "the fall guy" (p. 424).

- Says he only revealed the Enemies List stuff in response to a question from Senator Weicker (p. 619), without mentioning that he was Dean's neighbor, had met secretly with him in his negotiations for Senate immunity as Watergate unfolded, and that Weicker had bought Dean's townhouse in 1973, so that Dean could move to Los Angeles.

- Denied removing any documents from the White House (p. 434), but later admitted to providing Houston plan to Sirica (p. 542) and Plumbers stuff to Silbert (Footnote 24, p. 547). Query whether this also related to documents about other of the White House Horrors: the Townhouse Project, the Milk Producer's campaign donations, the president's personal taxes, and the NSC wiretaps—all of which some believe were removed by Dean over the weekend of April 21. Also, Shaffer threatens to bring RN in on "other things" (p. 520).
- Attempts to explain why he went to Ervin Committee instead of working with the prosecutors (p. 441), but the fact remains that he was offered immunity by Ervin and not by prosecutors.
- Describes his September 15, 1972, meeting with Nixon and Haldeman, without any mention that he had mischaracterized it rather dramatically in his Ervin Committee testimony (p. 155).
- While preparing his own transcripts of the White House tapes took over four years, Dean blithely accuses Nixon of not even bothering to review his own tapes in assembling the facts for his own Watergate defense. Dean then goes on to say that the president's efforts to save himself amounted to a cover-up of the cover-up (pp. 341–342).
- There is a good deal of back and forth, without any specificity, regarding Nixon's possible actions following their March 21 meeting:

  ⊙ Dean asserts that Nixon, in their conversation, instructed him to pay Hunt, which is certainly not true, since Dean did nothing following the meeting. Further, they discussed Hunt's demand as remaining unmet when Dean, Haldeman, Ehrlichman, and the president gathered at 5 p.m. that same evening (p. 498).

⊙ Yet, Dean also says that Haldeman and the president talked about Hunt's last payment, "since it involved him," without further explanation (p. 430).

⊙ Dean also asserts that Nixon had built his entire defense around not knowing anything before their March 21 meeting, but later admitted in his *Memoirs* that he knew more before that date than he had admitted (p. 540).

D. Outright Factual Errors

There are a surprising number of factual errors on items where Dean should have known better, which suggests that Dean either didn't write parts of the book or didn't read the galley proofs (as he apparently didn't do with regard to his first book, where much of the supposed dialogue turns out to have been added, allegedly without review by Dean, by his ghostwriter, Taylor Branch):

- In describing Elliott Richardson's background, the book fails to mention that he had been Secretary of HEW, which was the most long-lasting and significant of Richardson's prior cabinet-level positions (p. 530).

- Claims that Buzhardt was Haig's roommate when they were at West Point (p. 551), but Haig's book indicates Buzhardt was a year ahead of him and that Haig hardly knew him (Haig, p. 340).

- Says that Krogh pleaded guilty to two perjury counts (Footnote 9, probably at p. 319 and mistakenly omitted). While Krogh was indicted for perjury, he pleaded to a single felony count of violating Dr. Fielding's civil rights.

- Says that Colson would have been indicted for his involvement with the Plumbers (p. 592), but later indicates (correctly) that Colson really was indicted in that case (p. 642). There is a further error regarding Colson's plea, which was to having violated Ellsberg's civil rights and not to obstruction of justice, as Dean claims (p. 644).

- Says that Ehrlichman was indicted for perjury for his testimony before the Ervin Committee (p. 634), but this is not true, as later shown in indictment summary (p. 642).
- There is a significantly mixed message on the background and meaning of the Smoking Gun tape, which is dismissed as totally misunderstood in the book's beginning (pp. 55–56), yet described in great and damming detail toward the book's end (pp. 548–582 and 645). It is not just that there is no coordination between these startlingly different descriptions of the same conversation, they appear to have been drafted by different people altogether.
- There are equal conflicts and inconsistencies regarding Nixon's reactions to Dean's disclosure of Hunt's blackmail demands, which were discussed above.
- Dean claims (wrongly) to have hired Charles Shaffer, his criminal defense counsel on April 8. (p. 388). Earlier he said it was on or about March 28 (p. 359), which appears to be the better date. Regardless, Shaffer's first meeting with the prosecutors on Dean's behalf occurred on April 2.
- There is a very strange sentence about Nixon's demand that there be no cover-up as being its cause, which makes little sense:

> Had Richard Nixon not encouraged his aides to collect political intelligence by any means fair or foul, or insisted from the moment of the arrests that there must be no cover-up, neither would have taken place. (p. 619)

III. Summary Observations
- Many of Dean's disclosures are already "old news" because of Nixon's own reconstruction of this period in his *Memoirs*.

Nixon and his researchers had access to many of these same tapes, but could not quote them directly under National Archives' strictures. Regardless, the president's 1978 admissions of what he knew and when he knew it are not all that dramatically different from Dean's supposedly "new" discoveries some thirty-five years later.

- Dean's tape excerpts of what the president may have been told do not prove what he "knew":
  - ⊙ What comes through loud and clear in Dean's book is that President Nixon was assured of any number of contradictory versions of what had happened, throughout the unfolding of the Watergate scandal. As in many cases, the earliest reports were incomplete and misleading. In addition, as the scandal grew, everyone appears to have been less than forthright about their own particular actions.
  - ⊙ Busy or distracted people do not always remember what they have been told. Anyone who has been married is no doubt familiar with the accusation from one's spouse, "But I told you that last week!" when they have absolutely no memory of such a statement.
- It's only human, but what Dean suggests is that each of the president's aides consistently understated or diminished his own role as the scandal progressed. In essence, Dean's book is a continuation of this same process—of his own personal exculpation and disavowal.
- Another theme that seems consistent throughout Dean's book is the president's never-ending requests for some sort of written report. It is important to remember that the Nixon White House ran on paper, precisely because President Nixon vastly preferred to work from (and think about) written presentations. The National Security Council produced National Security Decision Memorandums (NSDMs) and National Security Study Memorandums

(NSSMs); the Domestic Council produced a myriad of papers on domestic issues, and all presidential meetings and events were the subject of extensive reports submitted in advance. Unlike casual conversation, a written report has substance; it usually reflects a great deal of thought and consideration. It was Nixon's habit to retreat to his hideaway office in the Old Executive Office Building most afternoons for study and reflection on important issues, almost always from written reports. It is no wonder that he kept asking for a written report on Watergate, but one was never produced in a timely fashion—and certainly never one produced by John Dean. It must have been exceptionally frustrating for the president.

- While not a principal focus of the book, many feel the real explanation for how the cover-up got so out of hand is what is characterized as Dean's "strategy of containment" (p. 279). Much of the enduring conflict over Watergate comes from differing testimony as to what Dean was reporting to Haldeman and Ehrlichman as the scandal unfolded. It is quite likely that they simply did not realize that Dean's efforts to "contain the problem" involved a whole series of overtly criminal acts. Dean later claimed that this was very clear from his oral reports; Haldeman and Ehrlichman claimed otherwise. Nothing in Dean's book really resolves this core issue, because there is no documentary evidence and their conversations were not recorded.

- This vast difference in recollections is highlighted by Dean's insistence that it was he who first leveled with the president, while Haldeman and Ehrlichman continued to keep the difficult facts to themselves. But Dean's great claim to having done so is specifically and solely with regard to conveying the news regarding Hunt's blackmail demands when he met with the president on March 21, 1973. Yet Dean had only learned of this demand two days before. He had been meeting or talking with the president virtually every day for almost a month. An equally valid argument on "who knew what" could be made that Haldeman and Ehrlichman did not level with the president because they, too, had been kept in the dark—by the one person working full time on containing the scandal: John Dean.

- It also is important to remember in this regard that many of the key accusations against Mitchell, Haldeman, and Ehrlichman (which figured so prominently at the cover-up trial) were not capable of objective proof and were vigorously denied by others:

  ⊙ Magruder claimed that Mitchell had approved funding for the Liddy campaign intelligence plan at their March 30, 1972, meeting in Miami. Both other attendees, Mitchell and Fred LaRue (who was also a government witness) denied this—and Mitchell produced at trial some seven examples of where Magruder said it had been approved by people other than Mitchell.

  ⊙ Dean claimed that Ehrlichman ordered Hunt out of the country on June 19, 1972. Both other attendees, Ehrlichman and Colson (who was also a government witness) denied this.

  ⊙ Dean claimed that he had told Haldeman of Liddy's plans following his February 4, 1972, meeting in Mitchell's attorney general's office. Haldeman didn't recall this, but took Dean at his word. When no such meeting could be independently verified (by Haldeman's extensive calendar or memories of his staff), Haldeman concluded the meeting had never occurred. When under oath in his law suit against St. Martin's Press and confronted with these facts, Dean dissembled and said it might have been after the earlier Mitchell meeting. In this book, Dean provides a rather different explanation (see footnote 4 at p. 311).

⊙ Dean testified that when he debriefed Liddy on June 19, 1972, right after the burglary arrests, and asked about White House knowledge, Liddy had responded that Gordon Strachan might have known. But he admitted under oath in those same depositions that he had told no one of Liddy's comment for the year and a half before his trial testimony. In this book, however, he asserts that Liddy's recollection of having said this is probably mistaken.

• The implication throughout Dean's book, however, is that the tapes that he has transcribed and excerpted prove that he had been telling the truth all along. One must continue to wonder, since it remains rather clear that President Nixon (as Dean has admitted) did not fully appreciate the magnitude of the Watergate scandal until very late in the game. Whether it was March 13 or March 17 or March 21 of 1973, is largely irrelevant in the great scheme of things. From that point on, once Dean had retained criminal defense counsel, fled to the prosecutors (and taken with him a series of devastatingly embarrassing documents on a number of unrelated issues), and perfected his side of the story, the president found himself without sufficient documentation, friends, or supporters to survive the onslaught.

• Finally, Dean's claim that any conflicts between his testimony and that of Haldeman, Ehrlichman, and Mitchell were forever fully and finally resolved when they were convicted on all counts in the Watergate cover-up trial is hardly definitive. A book due out next spring by Regnery History will show how those verdicts were a result of highly improper collusion between judges and prosecutors.

One thing is for sure: Watergate's saga will continue to unfold.

IV. The "Real" Nixon Defense

What, then, would be the "real" Nixon defense, in light of everything that we know today?

Briefly:

- Neither Nixon, Haldeman, nor Ehrlichman knew of the break-in in advance (admitted by Dean).
- But Dean did, since he had not only recruited Liddy for the position, but had attended the two meetings in Mitchell's attorney general's office where they were described.
- Contrary to Dean's assertions that he told Haldeman after the second of those meetings and told Ehrlichman of his own prior involvement right after his walk in the park with Liddy, Dean said nothing to his White House superiors. They orchestrated Mitchell's rapid resignation after the break-in arrests; they would have moved Dean out even faster had they realized he also was at risk of prosecution—and they would never have assigned him lead role in protecting White House interests in the aftermath of the break-in arrests.
- Dean sought that role and, instead of protecting the president's interests as his counsel, essentially cast his lot with those at CRP who were already effectuating a cover-up.
- Every day, all over America, lawyers defend clients accused of criminal wrongdoing without they themselves committing criminal acts. It simply never occurred to the president, Haldeman, and Ehrlichman that Dean was not acting in a perfectly legal capacity as their counsel.
- Of course they complimented Dean's work, on tape and to his face, but he never revealed the extent of his own criminal acts. He was working hard to contain the problem at CRP; they didn't inquire further as to specifics.

- As the go-between conveying information back and forth between people at CRP and the White House, Dean was in an ideal position to protect his own risk of prosecution. The one thing he could not allow was any sort of written report or disclosure of what really had happened, since it would reveal his own criminal acts, beginning with rehearsing Magruder for his perjured grand jury, but also including improperly sharing prosecutorial information with defense counsel and hiding (and then destroying) materials taken from Hunt's safe.

- When Dean informed the president of Hunt's blackmail demands, Nixon's response, announced later that same day (as well as the following day when Mitchell was present), was to inform his staff that they would have to testify without claim of executive privilege. Dean was to prepare the report that would be the basis for Nixon's public announcement to this effect.

- Instead, as the cover-up collapsed (as it should have), Dean was the first to switch sides, as well as his story, accusing his former superior of having condoned the very illegal acts that he had hidden from them. It is no wonder, when he became their principal accuser, that they felt he had been duplicitous and had to be destroyed.

- The essence of the cover-up story remains the dramatic differences in recollections between Dean on the one side and Haldeman and Ehrlichman on the other. There are no tapes of their many meetings. But one of the reasons the tapes tend to show that Nixon was kept largely in the dark about the true state of affairs may well be because so were Haldeman and Ehrlichman.

- The cover-up jury obviously believed Dean, but the question remains: did these defendants receive a fair trial—or was there judicial and prosecutorial collusion designed to improperly obtain those verdicts?

V. Remembering the Real John Dean

Dean had already encountered difficulties prior to his Watergate fame. His academic record was undistinguished, and he was fired for "unethical conduct" from his first and only stint in private practice (a boutique communications firm) after only six months.

As sometime happens in politics, he then experienced a meteoric rise in political positions, ending up as counsel to President Nixon in 1970.

It was in that position that he has stood accused of having orchestrated a criminal cover-up of those responsible for authorizing and directing the break-in into offices of the Democratic National Committee at the Watergate Office building in June 1972.

When the cover-up collapsed, as it should have, those who were the most intimately involved—and therefore at risk—were the first to run to federal prosecutors to seek immunity for their testimony against their former colleagues. Dean was the clear winner in this race, but held out for full immunity. Prosecutors concluded otherwise and insisted that his own role (as they then perceived it) was such that it required that he be punished too.

In his continuing pursuit of immunity, Dean's story began to change. Over the course of a dozen contacts with prosecutors by him or his lawyer during April 1973, Dean went from offering evidence about those responsible for the original break-in to asserting that there had been a criminal cover-up and that it had been directed by his White House superiors. The pivot point is well documented in prosecution files, as well as at page 253 in Dean's own book, *Blind Ambition*. It occurs when Charles Shaffer, his criminal defense lawyer, urges him to boost the cover-up to make himself indispensable, since the prosecutors were inclined to bring criminal charges against him for his own involvement with regard to the break-in itself:

Dean: Goddammit, Charlie. I don't want to meet with those bastards.

Shaffer: Listen, John, we don't have any choice. The cat's out of the bag. We've got to pump them full of the cover up now. I've got to up the ante with them to have a shot at immunity. That's your only chance not to be the fall guy.

Dean: I think your strategy of getting immunity is more important than ever now.

But to hear him retell it in his current book, he never wanted immunity; he only wanted to tell the truth. It was just that his lawyer was demanding immunity in exchange for his testimony. How peculiar! The fact remains that when the prosecutors took Dean at his word and scheduled his grand jury appearance for May 5, 1973, without immunity, he stiffed them and took the proposed immunity grant from the Ervin Committee instead.

There is a reason that Archibald Cox, the original Special Prosecutor, had no respect for Dean. As portrayed by Richard Ben-Veniste and George Frampton at page 107 of their book, *Stonewall, The Real Story of the Watergate Prosecution*:

> Archie Cox was particularly firm in his personal determination that Dean be prosecuted no matter what. Dean became an idée fixe for Cox. True, as a witness Dean would cement otherwise weak cases against Haldeman and Ehrlichman. But Cox preferred, if forced to choose, to take the relatively sure shot at Dean rather than the long shot against Dean's superiors. When the Saturday Night Massacre loomed close, it might have been propitious for Cox to make a deal with Dean and secure Dean's testimony against President Nixon as another weapon to hold the President off. Even then, Cox's

determination did not waiver. With all the uncertainties of Watergate that swirled around him—the weakness of evidence against Nixon's top aides without Dean's testimony, the possibility of Presidential culpability, the problems of obtaining White House evidence and of dealing with "national security"—Cox saw Dean's guilt as the one enduring constant. During a particularly difficult period Archie remarked to us, "If everything else goes down the drain the one thing I can cling to is Dean's venality."

VI. An Alternative Take

Alternatively, one could have a more nuanced view. Dean's book is going to be a fact of life and is not going to go away. Perhaps, like Peter Morgan's *Frost/Nixon* (which was equally erroneous in many respects), many will feel that Nixon comes across as a rather sympathetic figure. After all, Dean asserts:

- Nixon and his White House staff knew nothing in advance (albeit Dean skillfully excludes his own knowledge).
- Haldeman did not get any of the fruits of the one working wiretap.
- Neither Mitchell nor Magruder explicitly directed Liddy's second break-in.
- Magruder's assertion that Mitchell approved Liddy's campaign intelligence plan on March 30, 1972, surfaces very late in the game.
- Ehrlichman really did advocate full disclosure from the outset.
- The 18 ½-minute gap is "historically insignificant," and the smoking gun instruction was to protect the identities of Democrat donors and had nothing to do with Watergate.
- Nixon really didn't appreciate the extent of the cover-up until Dean laid it out for him on March 21, 1973.

Maybe we just say that it is nice to have all of the above confirmed by Dean himself—and point out that:

- His resignation was the result of a mistaken interpretation of the smoking gun.
- His alleged abuses of power seem trivial in light of Obama's.
- His accomplishments, both foreign and domestic, can stack up against any president.
- As the world burns, it might be beneficial to have Nixon's expertise in foreign affairs.
- Then quote Ben Bradlee's unpublished comment of May 16, 1990:

> I mean the crime itself was really not a great deal. Had it not been for the Nixon resignation, it would really be a blip in history. The Iran Contra hearing was a much more significant violation of the democratic ethic than anything in Watergate. Watergate was really dirty tricks and arrogance and people thinking they were all-powerful and could ride roughshod over civil liberties, but it wasn't dealing in foreign arms and buying foreign nations and shit like that.[4]

NOTES

1. All page references are to the advance uncorrected proof copy of Dean's book.
2. Dean's explanation is still incomplete. The effort was to prevent FBI interviews of apparent campaign contributions by Ken Dahlberg and Manuel Ogarrio, who were really acting as conduits for contributions from prominent Democrats, including Dwayne Andreas and a group of Texas oil and gas producers.
3. In fact, there is considerable legal conflict over the role of intent in crimes such as conspiracy and obstruction, particularly the difference between general and specific intent. This was the point that Nixon

was attempting to make in his 1977 interviews with David Frost (the actual interviews, not the later play by Peter Morgan or its subsequent movie version).

4. Jeff Himmelman. *Yours in Truth, a Personal Portrait of Ben Bradlee,* p. 212.

BIBLIOGRAPHY

Allen, Gary. *Richard Nixon: The Man Behind the Mask.* Boston: Western Islands, 1971.

Ambrose, Stephen E. *Nixon: The Education of a Politician, 1913–1962.* New York: Simon and Schuster, 1987.

Ambrose, Stephen E. *Nixon: The Triumph of a Politician, 1962–1972.* New York: Simon and Schuster, 1989.

Ambrose, Stephen E. *Nixon: Ruin and Recovery 1973–1990* New York: Simon and Schuster, 1991.

Anson, Robert Sam. *Exile: The Unquiet Oblivion of Richard M. Nixon.* New York: Simon and Schuster, 1984.

Baker, Russ. *Family of Secrets: The Bush Dynasty, America's Invisible Government, and the Hidden History of the Last Fifty Years.* New York: Bloomsbury Press, 2009.

Bass, Jack, and Marilyn W. Thompson. *Strom: The Complicated Personal and Political Life of Strom Thurmond.* New York: Public Affairs, 2005.

Bell, Jack. *Mr. Conservative: Barry Goldwater.* New York: Doubleday, 1962.

Black, Conrad. *A Life in Full: Richard M. Nixon.* New York: Public Affairs, 2007.

Brodie, Fawn E. *Richard Nixon: The Shaping of His Character.* New York: W. W. Norton, 1981.

Brownell, Herbert, with John P. Burke. *Advising Ike: The Memoirs of Attorney General Herbert Brownell.* Kansas: University Press of Kansas, 1993.

Bryant, Nick. *The Bystander: John F. Kennedy and the Struggle for Black Equality.* New York: Basic Books, 2006.

Butz, March. *Yorba Linda: Its History.* California: Taylor Publishing Company, 1970.

Cannon, Lou. *Reagan.* Toronto: General Publishing, 1982.

Cannon, Lou. *Ronnie & Jesse: A Political Odyssey.* New York: Doubleday, 1969.

Caulfield, John. *Caulfield, Shield #911-NYPD.* Indiana: iUniverse, Inc. and The Shield #911-NYPD Foundation, 2008.

Chester, Lewis, Godfrey Hodgson, and Bruce Page. *An American Melodrama: The Presidential Campaign of 1968.* New York: Viking Press, 1969.

Cohodas, Nadine. *Strom Thurmond & the Politics of Southern Change.* New York: Simon & Schuster, 1973.

Colodny, Len, and Robert Gettlin. *Silent Coup: The Removal of a President.* New York: St. Martin's Press, 1991.

Costello, William. *The Facts About Nixon: An Unauthorized Biography.* New York: Viking Press, 1960.

Crowley, Monica. *Nixon Off The Record: His Candid Commentary on People and Politics.* New York: Random House, 1996.

Daller, Robert. *Nixon and Kissinger: Partners in Power* New York: HarperCollins, 2007.

De Toledano, Ralph. *Nixon.* New York: Henry Holt, 1956.

Dean, John. *Blind Ambition: The White House Years.* New York: Simon and Schuster, 1976.

Dean, John W. *The Rehnquist Choice: The Untold Story of the Nixon Appointment that Redefined the Supreme Court.* New York: The Free Press, 2001.

Dean, Maureen, with Hays Gorey. *"MO": A Woman's View of Watergate.* New York: Simon and Schuster, 1975.

Edwards, Lee. *Goldwater: The Man Who Made a Revolution.* Regnery Publishing, 1997.

Eisenhower, Julie Nixon. *Pat Nixon: The Untold Story.* New York: Simon and Schuster, 1986.

Feldstein, Mark. *Poisoning the Press: Richard Nixon, Jack Anderson, and the Rise of Washington's Scandal Culture.* New York: Farrar, Straus and Girous, 2010.

Frank, Jeffrey. *Ike and Dick: Portrait of a Strange Political Marriage.* New York: Simon and Schuster. 2013.

Fulsom, Don. *Nixon's Darkest Secrets: The Inside Story of America's Most Troubled President.* New York: Thomas Dunne Books, 2012.

Garment, Leonard. *Crazy Rhythm.* New York: Times Books, 1997.

Garment, Leonard. *In Search of Deep Throat: The Greatest Political Mystery of Our Time.* New York: Basic Books. 2000.

Gelman, Irwin F. *The Contender Richard Nixon: The Congress Years. 1946–1952*. New York: The Free Press, 1999.

Goldwater, Barry M., with Jack Casserly. *Goldwater*. New York: Doubleday, 1988.

Goldwater, Barry M. *With No Apologies: The Personal and Political Memoirs of United States Senator Barry M. Goldwater*. New York: William Morrow, 1979.

Greenberg, David. *Nixon's Shadow: The History of an Image*. New York: W. W. Norton, 2003.

Haldeman, H. R. *The Haldeman Diaries: Inside the Nixon White House*. New York: G.P. Putnam's Sons, 1994.

Haldeman, H. R., with Joseph DiMona. *The Ends of Power*. New York: Times Books, 1978.

Harris, Mark. *Mark the Glove Boy or, The Last Days of Richard Nixon*. New York: MacMillian, 1964.

Hersh, Buton. *Bobby and J. Edgar: The Historic Face-off Between The Kennedys and J. Edgar Hoover That Transformed America*. New York: Carroll & Graf, 2007.

Hill, Gladwin. *Dancing Bear: An Inside Look at California Politics*. Ohio and New York: The World Publishing Company, 1968.

Hinckle, Warren, and William Turner. *Deadly Secrets: The CIA-MAFIA War Against Castro and the Assassination of J.F.K.* New York: Thunder's Mouth Press, 1992.

Hougan, Jim. *Secret Agenda*. New York: Random House, 1984.

Hunt, E. Howard, with Greg Aunapu. *American Spy: My Secret History in the CIA, Watergate & Beyond*. New Jersey: John Wiley & Sons, 2007.

Kabaservice, Geoffrey. *Rule and Ruin: The Downfall of Moderation and the Destruction of the Republican Party, From Eisenhower to the Tea Party*. New York: Oxford University Press, 2012.

Kalb, Marvin. *The Nixon Memo*. Chicago: University of Chicago Press, 1994.

Kallina, Edmund F. Jr. *Kennedy v. Nixon: The Presidential Election of 1960*. Gainesville: University Press of Florida, 2011.

Kelly, Kitty, *The Family: The Real Story of the Bush Dynasty*. New York: Doubleday, 2004.

Keogh, James. *This is Nixon: The Man and His Work*. New York: Van Rees Press, 1956.

Kessel, John H. *The Goldwater Coalition: Republican Strategies in 1964.* Indianapolis and New York: Bobbs-Merrill Company, 1968.

Kotlowski, Dean J. *Nixon's Civil Rights Politics, Principle and Policy.* Massachusetts: Harvard University Press, 2001.

Kurz, Kenneth Franklin. *Nixon's Enemies.* Illinois: Lowell House, 1998.

Kutler, Stanley I. *Abuse of Power: The New Nixon Tapes.* New York: Touchstone, 1997.

Lasky, Victor. *It Didn't Start With Watergate.* New York: Dial Press, 1977.

Lenzner, Terry. *The Investigator: Fifty Years of Uncovering the Truth.* New York: Penguin, 2013.

Liddy, G. Gordon. *Will: The Autobiography of G. Gordon Liddy.* St. Martin's Paperbacks, 1980.

Liebman, Marvin. *Coming Out Conservative: An Autobiography.* California: Chronicle Books, 1992.

Liebovich, Louis. W. *Richard Nixon, Watergate, and the Press.* Connecticut: Praeger Publishers, 2003.

Lukas, J. Anthony. *Nightmare: The Underside of the Nixon Years.* New York: Viking Press, 1976.

Lurie, Leonard. *The Running of Richard Nixon.* New York: Coward, McCann & Geoghegan, 1972.

Mahoney, Richard D. *The Kennedy Brothers: The Rise and Fall of Jack and Bobby.* New York: Arcade Publishing, 1999.

Magruder, Jeb Stuart. *An American Life: One Man's Road to Watergate.* New York: Athneumm, 1974.

Mankiewicz, Frank. *Perfectly Clear: Nixon From Whittier to Watergate.* New York: Quadrangle/The New York Times Book Company, 1973.

Marrs, Jim. *Crossfire: The Plot That Killed Kennedy.* New York: Basic, 1989.

Matthews, Christopher. *Kennedy & Nixon: The Rivalry That Shaped Postwar America.* New York: Simon & Schuster, 1996.

Mazo, Earl. *Richard Nixon: A Political and Personal Portrait.* New York: Harper & Brothers, 1959.

Merritt, Robert. *Watergate Exposed How the President of the United States and the Watergate Burglars Were Set Up.* Oregon: Trine Day, 2009.

Middendor II, J. William. *A Glorious Disaster: Barry Goldwater's Presidential Campaign and the Origins of the Conservative Movement.* New York: Basic, 2006.

Mitchell, Greg. *Tricky Dick and the Pink Lady: Richard Nixon vs. Helen Gahagan Douglas, Sexual Politics and the Red Scare, 1950*. New York: Random House, 1998.

Morris, Roger. *Richard Milhous Nixon: The Rise of an American Politician*. New York: Henry Hold and Company, 1990.

Nixon, Richard. *Leaders Profiles and Reminiscences of Men Who Have Shaped the Modern World*.New York: Warner Books, 1982.

Nofziger, Lyn. *Nofziger*. Washington, D.C.: Regnery Gateway, 1992.

North, Mark. *Act of Treason: The Role of J. Edgar Hoover in the Assassination of President Kennedy*. New York: Skyhorse Publishing, 2011.

Novak, Robert D. *The Agony of the G.O.P., 1964*. New York: MacMillian, 1965.

Novak, Robert D. *The Prince of Darkness 50 Years Reporting in Washington*. New York: Three Rivers Press, 2007.

Oudes, Bruce. *From: The President Richard Nixon's Secret Files*. New York: Harper & Row, 1989.

Parmet, Herbert S. *Richard Nixon and his America* Massachusetts: Little, Brown and Company, 1990.

Perlstein, Rick. *Nixonland: The Rise of a President and The Fracturing of America*. New York: Scribner, 2008.

Pietrisza. David. *1960 LBJ vs. JFK vs. Nixon: The Epic Campaign That Forged Three Presidencies*. New York: Sterling Publishing, 2008.

Powers, Thomas. *The Man Who Kept the Secrets: Richard Helms and The CIA*. New York: Alfred A. Knopf, 1979.

Price, Raymond. *With Nixon*. New York: Viking Press, 1977.

Rarick, Ethan. *California Rising: The Life and Times of Pat Brown* California: University of California Press, 2006.

Reeves, Richard. *President Nixon: Alone in the White House*. New York: Simon and Schuster, 2001.

Robb, David L. *The Gumshoe and the Shrink Guenther Reinhardt, Dr. Arnold Hutschnecker, and the Secret History of the 1960 Kennedy/Nixon Election* .California: Santa Monica Press, 2012.

Rorabaugh, W. J. *The Real Making of the President: Kennedy, Nixon, and the 1960 Election*. Kansas: University Press of Kansas, 2009.

Rosen, James. *The Strong Man: John Mitchell and the Secrets of Watergate*. New York: Doubleday, 2008.

Safire, William. *Before the Fall: An Inside View of the Pre-Watergate White House*. New York: Doubleday & Company, 1975.

Shepard, Geoff. *The Secret Plot to Make Ted Kennedy President*. New York: Sentenial HC, 2008.

Sherman, Gabriel, *The Loudest Voice in the Room*. New York: Random House, 2014.

Shesol, Jeff. *Mutual Contempt: Lyndon Johnson, Robert Kennedy, and the Feud That Defined a Decade*. New York: W.W. Norton, 1997.

Smith, Jeffrey. K. *Bab Blood: Lyndon B. Johnson, Robert F. Kennedy, and the Tumultuous 1960s*. Indiana: Author House, 2010.

Stanford, Phil. *White House Call Girl: The Real Watergate Story*. Washington: Feral House, 2013.

Stone, Roger, with Mike Colapietro. *The Man Who Killed Kennedy: The Case Against LBJ*. New York: Skyhorse Publishing, 2013.

Strober, Deborah Hart, and Gerald S. Stober. *The Nixon Presidency: An Oral History of an Era* Virginia: Brassey's, 2003.

Summers, Anthony. *The Arrogance of Power: The Secret World of Richard Nixon*. New York: Penguin Putnam, 2000.

Swift, Will. *Pat and Dick: The Nixons, an Intimate Portrait of Marriage*. New York: Threshold Editions, 2014.

Talbot, David. *Brothers: The Hidden History of the Kennedy Years*. New York: Simon and Schuster, 2007.

Tarpley, Webster G., and Anton Chaitkin. *George Bush: The Unauthorized Biography*. Washington, D.C.: Executive Intelligence Review, 1992.

Thompson, Fred H. *At That Point in Time: The Inside Story of the Senate Watergate Committee*. New York: Quadrangle/The New York Times Book Co., 1975.

Waldron, Lamar. *Watergate: The Hidden History Nixon, The Mafia, and the CIA*. California: Counterpoint, 2012.

Weicker, Lowell P. Jr., with Barry Sussman. *Maverick*. Boston: Little, Brown and Company, 1995.

Weinberger, Caspar W., with Gretchen Roberts. *In the Arena: A Memoir of the 20th Century*. Washington D.C.: Regnery Publishing, 2001.

Werth, Barry. *31 Days: Gerald Ford, The Nixon Pardo, and a Government in Crisis*. Boston: Anchor Books, 2006.

Whalen, Richard J. *Catch the Falling Flag: A Republican's Challenge to His Party*. Boston: Houghton Mifflin Company, 1972.

Wicker, Tom. *One of Us: Richard Nixon and the American Dream*. New York: Random House, 1991.

Witcover, Jules. *The Year the Dream Died*. New York: Warner Books, 1997.

Witcover, Jules. *Very Strange Bedfellows: The Short and Unhappy Marriage of Richard Nixon and Spiro Agnew.* New York: Perseus Books Group, 2007.

Zeller, F. C. Duke. *Devil's Pact: Inside the World of the Teamsters Union.* New York: Carol Publishing Group, 1996.